HANDBOOKS

919.3 MOO

31010000086662

VANCOUVER MEMORIAL LIBRARY

P9-CNI-842

WITHDRAWN

NEW ZEALAND

ANDREW HEMPSTEAD

NORTH ISLAND

SOUTH PACIFIC OCEAN

Hicks Bay

Bay of Plenty

Mount Maunganui
Matakana Island
Tauranga
Whitianga
Coromandel Range
Great Barrier Island
Mercury Islands
Coromandel
Thames
Coromandel Forest Park
Kaimai Range
Firth of Thames
Hamilton
Hauraki Gulf
Little Barrier Island
Raglan
Wellsford
Warkworth
Bream Bay
Auckland
Manukau Harbour
Russell
Kerikeri
Whangarei
Paihia
Bay of Islands
Dargaville
Kaipara Harbour
Kaitaia
Opononi
Waipoua Forest
Hokianga Harbour
Great Exhibition Bay
Ninety Mile Beach
Aupouri Peninsula
Cape Reinga

① ② ⑦ ⑩ ⑫ ⑭ ㉕ ㉖ ㉗

© AVALON TRAVEL PUBLISHING, INC.

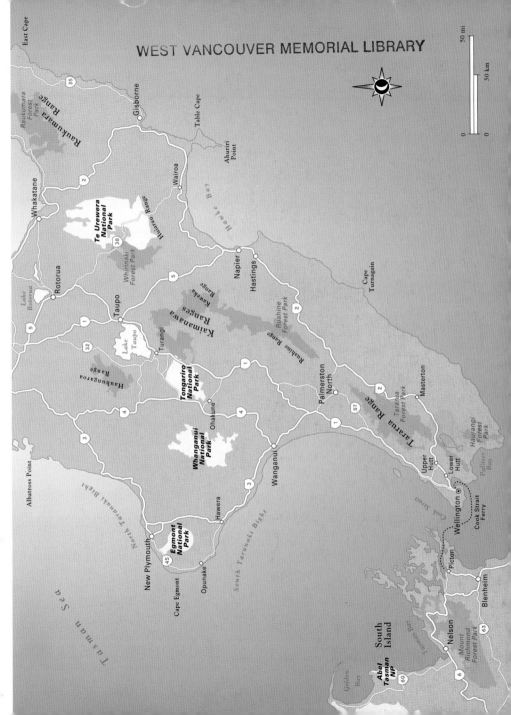

WEST VANCOUVER MEMORIAL LIBRARY

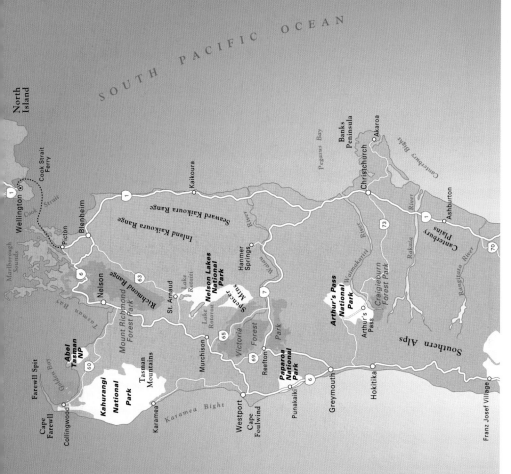

SOUTH ISLAND

© AVALON TRAVEL PUBLISHING, INC.

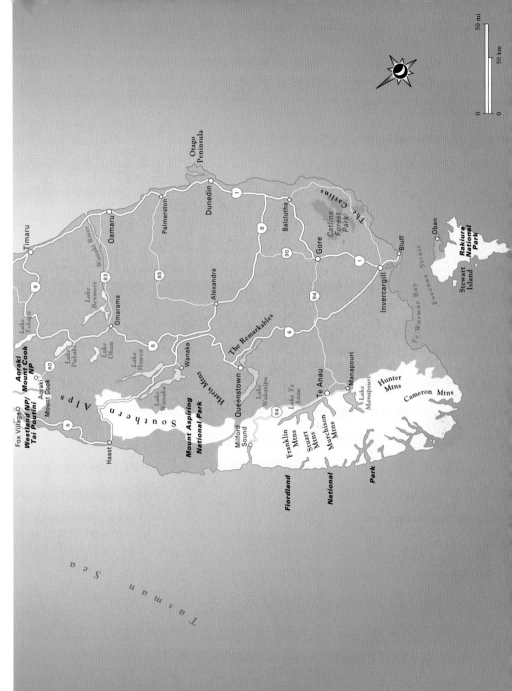

AUCKLAND

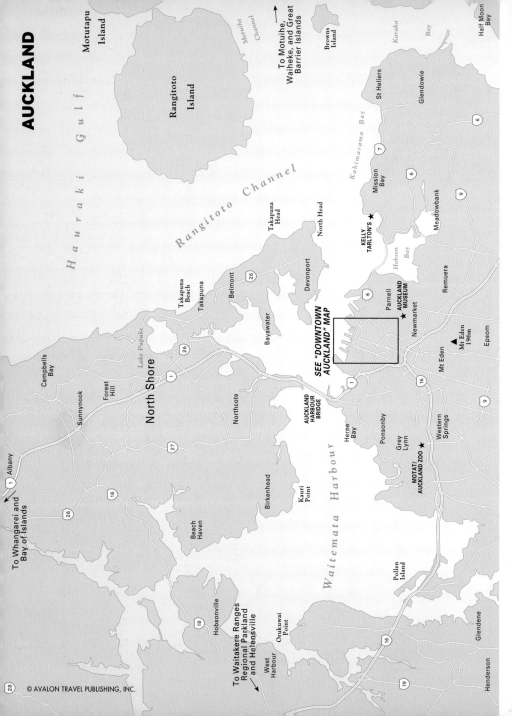

Motutapu Island

Rangitoto Island

Hauraki Gulf

Rangitoto Channel

Motuihe Channel

To Motuihe, Waiheke, and Great Barrier Islands

Browns Island

Karaka Bay

Half Moon Bay

St Heliers

Glendowie

Kahimarama Bay

Mission Bay

Meadowbank

6

7

6

9

Takapuna Head

North Head

KELLY TARLTON'S

Hobson Bay

Remuera

Devonport

Takapuna Beach

Belmont

Takapuna

26

Parnell

AUCKLAND MUSEUM

Newmarket

6

SEE "DOWNTOWN AUCKLAND" MAP

Bayswater

Epsom

Mt Eden 196m

Mt Eden

Lake Pupuke

North Shore

Campbells Bay

Forest Hill

Sunnynook

Northcote

26

1

AUCKLAND HARBOUR BRIDGE

1

16

9

Herne Bay

Ponsonby

Grey Lynn

Western Springs

27

Albany

1

To Whangarei and Bay of Islands

18

26

Birkenhead

Kauri Point

Waitemata Harbour

MOTAT/ AUCKLAND ZOO

Beach Haven

Hobsonville

18

Orukuwai Point

West Harbour

To Waitakere Ranges Regional Parkland and Helensville

Pollen Island

16

Glendene

Glenmore

Henderson

19

28   © AVALON TRAVEL PUBLISHING, INC.

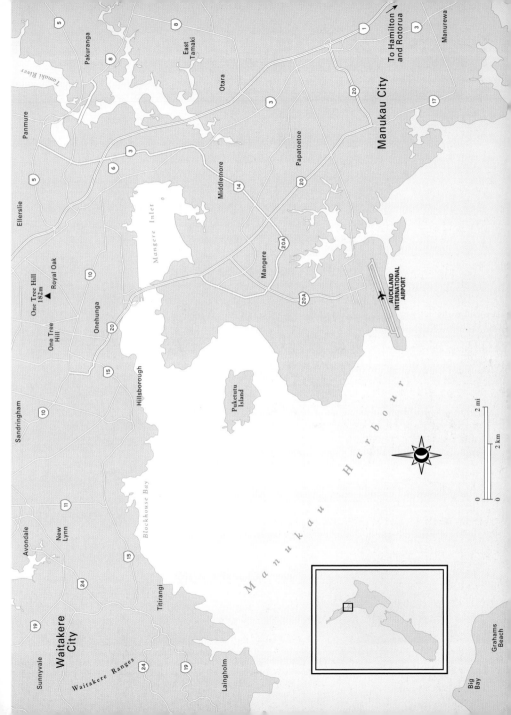

DISCOVER NEW ZEALAND

You will fall in love with New Zealand, an amazing country filled with wonderful surprises – scenery beyond belief, an energetic Maori culture, super-friendly locals, and a tourism infrastructure equal to any country in the world.

New Zealand is in the South Pacific Ocean, across the Tasman Sea from Australia and a 12-hour flight from the west coast of the United States. Lying between latitudes 34 and 47 degrees south, the country comprises two long, narrow main islands, North Island (114,500 sq km/44,209 sq mi) and South Island (150,700 sq km/58,186 sq mi). North Island, with its golden beaches, ancient kauri forests, lakes, volcanoes, thermal areas, and large cities (including Wellington, the national capital), is the more densely populated. South Island, with its snowcapped mountains, glaciers, lush native bush, and fiords, is the larger of the two, proudly called "the mainland" by residents (though North Islanders are quick to disagree). Tiny Stewart Island (1,750 sq km/676 sq mi), an unspoiled, bird-filled bush and beach

white-water rafting in the Queenstown area

paradise at the foot of the South Island, is the closest most people ever get to the Antarctic.

Surrounded by ocean, New Zealand appears to be a mere speck on the globe, and yet it's about 1,770 km (1,100 mi) from top to bottom – similar in size to the British Isles or Japan. Australia, 2,092 km (1,300 mi) northwest, is New Zealand's closest neighbor, and because of this relative proximity the two countries are often mistakenly believed to be one.

New Zealanders are addicted to the outdoors, and it shows. "Tramping," as walking or hiking is known, is by far the most popular pastime with both locals and visitors. Trails throughout the country are well marked and well maintained, and range from short paved trails to scenic overlooks to famous overnight treks such as the Milford Track. No part of the country is more than 140 km (87 mi) from the ocean, and so it's natural that water sports such as kayaking, surfing, and ocean fishing are popular, especially in the north,

grazing cattle in the shadow of Mount Cook

where the east coast is lined with beach after golden beach. Known for its excellent fishing, New Zealand also draws angling enthusiasts from around the world.

In the last decade New Zealand has gained a well-deserved reputation for adrenaline activities. The adventurous can rappel into a cave, raft through underground rivers, or go bungy jumping and jetboating. Winter brings its own enthusiasts, mostly domestic and Australian travelers drawn to the world-class skiing and snowboarding resorts known as "ski fields."

While the scenery and outdoor recreation get top billing with most visitors, the people of New Zealand will also make your trip memorable. Numbering a little over four million, New Zealanders mix mostly two cultures. The original inhabitants were Maori, descendants of Polynesians from the South Pacific. Europeans, at first from England and Scotland, came much later. While Maori culture stands strongly on its own, the country's residents come together as Kiwis.

Fantastic scenery, an appreciation of beauty, and pride in their country inspire many New Zealanders to become artists. Art comes

Kamahi Walk in Egmont National Park leads through a lush forest of *kamahi* trees.

in many forms such as painting, pottery, sculpture, glassware, spinning, weaving, and woodcarving. Maori arts and crafts are distinctive and simple yet appealing. In pockets of Maori culture, such as Rotorua, you can watch artists at work, while at Hokitika, studios are set up especially for visitors to try their hand at greenstone carving. Music, theater, ballet, modern dance, literature, filmmaking, and architecture are also well represented. New Zealand films and filmmakers continue to garnish worldwide acclaim. Wellington-born Peter Jackson filmed *The Lord of the Rings* throughout the South Island and the most recent version of *King Kong* in Wellington, but the country's diverse landscapes have also starred in hits such as *The Last Samurai* and *The Chronicles of Narnia: The Lion, the Witch, and the Wardrobe*.

If you've visited New Zealand in the past, maybe a decade or more ago, you will be pleasantly surprised with the improved quality of life and the way New Zealanders have embraced modern technology and improved their tourism infrastructure. This is particularly apparent when it comes to food and dining out. Sure you can still

Hawke's Bay

get a classic meat pie, but the corner bakery is just as likely to offer healthy variations on this classic dish, such as a gluten-free chicken, camembert, and apricot pie. This sophistication shines through especially in the larger cities and resort towns, where classic meats such as lamb, crayfish, and venison are given a modern makeover by top-notch chefs in contemporary surroundings. Adventure sports, the evolving dining scene, an amazing collection of accommodations to suit all budgets, a network of excellent visitor centers, and one of the world's best public transportation systems all reflect a makeover of the tourism industry in the last two decades.

New Zealand offers so much to see and do that fitting it all into a two-week vacation can be a challenge. You should plan on mixing city sights with off-the-beaten-path adventures. Sample local cuisine whenever possible, stay away from standard motels, mingle with the locals, and, most important of all, take the time to enjoy the unique experiences afforded simply by traveling through one of the world's most exciting tourist destinations.

Moeraki Boulders, North Otago

Contents

·MAP CONTENTS

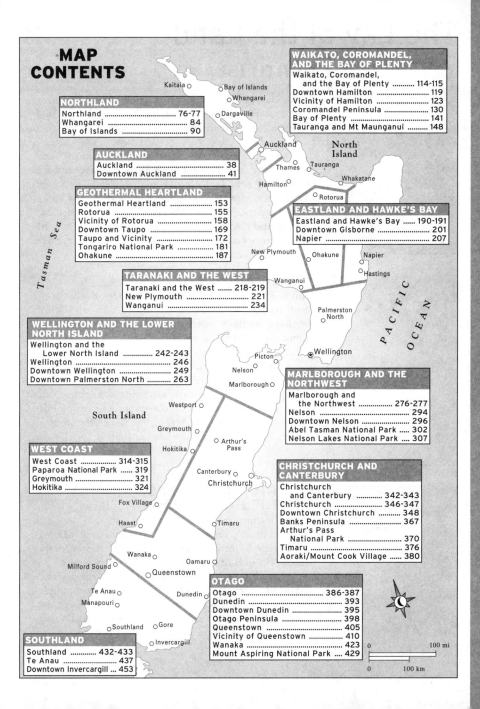

North Island

South Island

Tasman Sea

PACIFIC OCEAN

Kaitaia
Bay of Islands
Whangarei
Dargaville
Auckland
Thames Tauranga
Hamilton
Whakatane
Rotorua
New Plymouth Ohakune Napier
Wanganui Hastings
Palmerston North
Picton Wellington
Nelson
Marlborough
Westport
Greymouth
Arthur's Pass
Hokitika
Canterbury
Christchurch
Fox Village
Haast Timaru
Wanaka
Milford Sound Oamaru
Queenstown
Te Anau Dunedin
Manapouri
Southland Gore
Invercargill

0   100 mi

0   100 km

The Lay of the Land

NORTH ISLAND

AUCKLAND

If it's been a few years since you've touched down in Auckland, be prepared to be amazed. Instead of picking up a rental car and zooming off into classic New Zealand scenery, you'll want to spend some time in the country's **largest and most dynamic city.** Perched on a **magnificent harbor, museums** and **performing arts facilities** beckon the culturally minded, while **parks, islands,** and a **mass of waterways** appeal to the more energetic. Add **volcanic peaks, world-class lodging and dining,** as well as quirky attractions like a bar where the temperature never rises above freezing, and you have a destination like no other.

PACIFIC

OCEAN

NORTHLAND

Within easy reach of Auckland, the northern reaches of the North Island have an almost tropical climate, with lots of **sunshine, endless beaches,** and lots of opportunities for **swimming, boating, diving,** and **fishing.** The epicenter of the touristy action is the **Bay of Islands,** where clear, calm waters and uninhabited islands combine to create the perfect place to go cruising. Travel further north and the crowds thin out, but the beaches get better. The region also boasts an interesting natural and human history, with the chance of seeing kiwis (birds), exploring an **ancient kauri forest,** and visiting the site of the treaty signing that created the seed of a nation.

PACIFIC

OCEAN

WAIKATO, COROMANDEL, AND THE BAY OF PLENTY

Originally settled by Maori, the central section of the North Island lies directly below Auckland and within easy day-tripping distance. In the west is the Waikato, a rich farming district with the city of **Hamilton** at its heart and attractions such as New Zealand's **premier surf spot** and the underground maze of **Waitomo Caves.** East of Hamilton is the **Coromandel Peninsula,** which was once the site of a gold rush but is now sparsely settled and attractive for its forested mountain range and a seemingly endless stretch of bays and beaches.

PACIFIC

OCEAN

GEOTHERMAL HEARTLAND

As the name suggests, this is a thermally active region and one that you shouldn't miss. It is one of the most concentrated and active thermal regions in the world, with the city of **Rotorua** on top of most of the action. Here, you are invited to explore many of the most active areas, soak in hot pools, and explore the lunarlike setting of **Mount Tarawera.** South from Rotorua is Taupo, a popular vacation town for New Zealanders where the blue waters of **Lake Taupo** fill an ancient crater. Continuing south, commercialism is nonexistent in the volcanic wilderness of **Tongariro National Park,** where three volcanoes are still active, occasionally disrupting **skiers** and **snowboarders** who are drawn to the country's largest alpine resort.

EASTLAND AND HAWKE'S BAY

The eastern portion of the North Island is dominated by **unspoiled scenery** that merges native forest with a wildly beautiful coastline. It is the place where Maori first came ashore more than 1,000 years ago and where Captain Cook became the first European to lay eyes on New Zealand. Wildly popular with New Zealanders as a summer vacation getaway, the region is mostly unaffected by tourism. As a result, the drive around the **East Cape** is a great way to experience the way New Zealand was before the tourism boom. **Gisborne** is a prosperous yet laidback city, the northern extent of a region laced by **vineyards** and **sheep farms.** To the south is the **art deco hub of Napier,** sandwiched between the forested wilderness of **Te Urewera National Park** and the beautiful beaches lining the Pacific Ocean.

TARANAKI AND THE WEST

Dominated by a postcard-perfect volcano rising from a patchwork of farmland, this region stretches from **unspoiled black-sand beaches** fronting the Tasman Sea to the almost **impenetrable forests** of the North Island's west-central interior. For outdoor-lovers, the **Taranaki volcano** and surrounding **Egmont National Park** should be the focus of your time—hiking in summer and skiing or snowboarding in winter. Garden-lovers will be in their element around the port city of **New Plymouth** while history buffs will appreciate the classic colonial architecture and restored paddlesteamers in the river city of **Wanganui.**

WELLINGTON AND THE LOWER NORTH ISLAND

Through native reserves, passing vineyards, and along golden beaches, all roads lead south to Wellington, New Zealand's capital. Set around a magnificent harbor at the tip of the South Island, the city is a lot more than a stuffy hangout for politicians. Instead you find the magnificent **Museum of New Zealand,** steep streets lined with beautifully restored buildings, and a choice of accommodations to suit all budgets. But beyond the obvious, you also find a **thriving cultural scene,** an amazing array of cafés and restaurants, and **sophisticated attitude** like nowhere else in the country.

SOUTH ISLAND

MARLBOROUGH AND THE NORTHWEST

From the gateway of **Picton,** the wonders of New Zealand's South Island beckon in all directions. Like elsewhere, the region has adapted brilliantly to the needs of visitors, allowing everyone to enjoy the natural wilderness. Two hikes—the **Queen Charlotte Track** and the **Abel Tasman Coastal Track**—are perfect examples. Although it takes multiple days to walk these trails, day hikers use water taxis to zoom from one spot to another and upscale lodges along the way provide a luxurious break from the trail. And when you've finished walking, there are the wonderful wines of Marlborough, the **whales of Kaikoura,** the **wilderness lakes of Nelson Lakes National Park,** the golden **beaches of Abel Tasman National Park,** and the **birdlife of Farewell Spit.**

WEST COAST

In the West Coast, visit the coal-mining and fishing center of **Westport** in the north, wild and rugged surf beaches, a seal colony at **Tauranga Bay,** the amazing Punakaiki Pancake Rocks in **Paparoa National Park,** the West Coast commercial center of **Greymouth,** and the historic gold-mining town of **Hokitika** (a good place to browse for greenstone carvings and jewelry). Stop along the highway for a spot of trout fishing in one of several major rivers, or take a photography break at one of the many small lakes that reflect distant snowcapped peaks in their mirror-still waters, then push on south to the lush rainforests and mighty **glaciers** of rugged **Westland Tai Poutini National Park.**

CHRISTCHURCH AND CANTERBURY

The picturesque city of Christchurch, largest population center of the South Island, has a reputation for its "Englishness." Sure, it has a downtown core packed with Victorian-era buildings, a network of parkland, tree-lined streets, and the beautiful Avon River winding through town, but it also has its own distinct personality—and lots to see and do, from an ultramodern art gallery to the world's largest Antarctic museum to a nearby village whose French origins shine through. From Christchurch, a patchwork of green spreads west to the snow-capped Southern Alps. The TranzAlpine train is a good way to soak up this changing panorama in all its beauty, or drive south to Aoraki/Mount Cook National Park, where the mountains are at their most dramatic.

OTAGO

Like Canterbury to the north, Otago spreads from the Pacific Ocean west to the Southern Alps. Also like its northern neighbor, the province is anchored by Dunedin, a bustling city filled with historic attractions and modern conveniences. Beyond city limits, the landscape is a little wilder and a lot less settled than Canterbury. On Dunedin's doorstep, you can marvel at albatrosses, watch penguins, and take a rail trip though a valley uninterrupted by roads. Inland is Queenstown, one of the world's most exciting resort towns. Here, you can go bungy jumping, try jetboating, explore the historic streets of Arrowtown, and then relax at a luxurious accommodation. The pace at nearby Wanaka is a little less frantic, yet the opportunities for outdoor recreation still abound. In winter, the region comes alive with skiers and snowboarders, who have five alpine resorts to choose from.

SOUTHLAND

After leaving the commercialism of Queenstown behind you, the wilderness of Southland beckons. Much of the region is protected by Fiordland National Park, which encompasses famously scenic Doubtful and Milford Sounds and is well known for its long-distance hikes such as the Routeburn and Milford Tracks. For a day trip on a tour boat or a wilderness trek, the park is a magnet for outdoor-lovers. But Southland also has a number of lesser-known natural wonders that are well worth visiting if time allows. Stewart Island, a short ferry or flight from the mainland, is one of the best places in the country to see kiwi birds in the wild, while the Catlins has an amazing concentration of wildlife that is accessible to everyone.

Planning Your Trip

Planning a trip can be overwhelming, but it doesn't have to be. The first thing you should do is forget about any preconceived notions you have about travel to New Zealand and instead focus on the experience. Of course you'll want to take in the high-life in Auckland, experience the thermal attractions of Rotorua, and tramp through the wilderness of the South Island. But try to plan your trip around simply being in New Zealand. Think less about specific "sights" and open yourself to discovery.

Start by trying to identify the type of activities you're interested in, which regions you just can't miss, which towns sound interesting, and how much money you want to spend. Once you have put together an outline of your trip, book your accommodation choices as far in advance as possible, especially if you are traveling in summer.

Although it is not necessary to plan a complete itinerary before arriving in New Zealand, you should read up about the various transportation options and make bookings in advance. The country is blessed with a wonderful and inexpensive transportation system, and all cities and most provincial towns are linked by flights. Driving is the most practical way to travel, however, and it'll give you the flexibility to stay at lodgings located outside of the main tourist towns.

WHEN TO GO

New Zealand receives two waves of visitors—summer (Dec.–Feb.) is the busiest time of year, with the bulk of international arrivals blending with New Zealanders enjoying their summer holidays. In winter (July–Sept.), over a dozen ski fields are the focus of attention for both New Zealanders and Australians.

Climate-wise, summer is the best time to visit New Zealand. The focus at this time of year is all outdoors—camping, tramping, fishing, golfing, swimming, surfing, kayaking, and mountain climbing. The summer season is dominated by long, warm—and sometimes hot—days, everything is open, and there's plenty to do and see. Unfortunately, most visitors agree with me, and it's also very busy, especially from Christmas through the end of January, which is the summer school holiday season. Campers will need advance reservations, especially at holiday parks (the local term for campgrounds) anywhere near a lake or the ocean.

Spring (Sept.-Nov.) and fall, known locally as **autumn (Mar.-May),** are excellent times to visit New Zealand for two reasons: you'll avoid the crowds and you don't need to have a firm itinerary. In spring, New Zealand is blanketed in a rich "spring" green hue, a beautiful backdrop for mountains still covered in snow. There is also a sense of optimism for the upcoming warm months. Fall can be delightful, especially April, with lingering warm temperatures and a noticeable decrease in crowds immediately after Easter. While fall colors in general lack the intensity of those in North America, there are exceptions, such as the gold-rush town of Arrowtown, where the streets are lined with deciduous trees.

Ski fields begin opening for the **winter season (June-Aug.)** in June, although conditions are best July through early September. Winter is officially over at the end of the August calendar month, but some ski resorts stay open into October, including Whakapapa on the North Island.

It is also notable that unlike North America, but similar to Australia, New Zealand, and the United Kingdom, the seasons in New Zealand are defined meteorologically rather than astronomically. In simple terms this means that each season spans a three-month period coinciding with calendar months rather than solstices and equinoxes.

WHAT TO TAKE

Start by packing everything you think you'll need. Then put half of it back in your closet. The airlines have generous baggage limits and you can always upgrade to a larger rental car, but that's not the point—you just never need as much as you think you do.

When planning your trip to New Zealand, prepare for the outdoors. At the top of your must-bring list should be walking or hiking boots. If you buy a pair especially for the trip, make sure you wear them once or twice before leaving home—just to make sure they are comfortable. New Zealand's weather is unpredictable, especially in mountainous areas; it's best to be prepared for everything no matter which season you visit—and keep in mind that the seasons are opposite to those of the Northern Hemisphere. Even in summer, you should be geared up for a variety of weather conditions, especially if you'll be spending time in the mountainous regions of the South Island. Do this by preparing to dress in layers, including at least one pair of fleece pants and a heavy long-sleeved top. Summer travelers should also pack sunglasses and a wide-brimmed hat to provide protection from the strong sunlight. Finally, bug spray is a summer necessity in places like Abel Tasman National Park, but you can pick up the brands that are most effective once you arrive.

Wintertime temperatures vary greatly throughout New Zealand. If you're heading south to ski and snowboard, bring clothing with the same level of warmth as you would for a winter vacation in, say, Colorado or Austria. The best type of outer layer is breathable, wind-resistant pants and a jacket. Most ski fields have clothing rentals, including gloves.

A few clothing considerations apply year-round. Wet-weather clothing is a must—lightweight and breathable is best. Regardless of the time of year you plan to visit, bring a swimsuit for the many mineral pools and hot springs scattered around the country. For dining out, casual dress is accepted at all but the most upscale city restaurants or lodges, where a jacket maybe required.

Electrical appliances from North America and Europe require a current converter (transformer) to bring the voltage up. Many travel-size shavers, hair dryers, and irons have built-in converters. You will also need a socket adapter (three-pin flat); hotels and motels often provide 110-volt AC sockets for razors only.

Choosing a suitcase or backpack is also important. Think about the type of traveling you'll be doing before making a final decision. A midsize suitcase with wheels is best for carting through airports and lugging around hotels. Fold-over bags are good for keeping formal clothing wrinkle-free, but unless you're in New Zealand on business or attending a snazzy function, you probably won't require much in the way of dressy clothing. Besides, this type of suitcase is a bother to pack and unpack.

Check with your airline for baggage restrictions, as these vary from region to region. Air New Zealand, for example, allows passengers traveling from United States to check two pieces of luggage up to 23 kg (50 lbs) each. Air New Zealand flights originating in Australia, Asia, and Europe only allow one piece of checked luggage to a maximum of 20 kg (44 lbs). Bikes, surfboards, skis and snowboards, and golf clubs count as one piece, but check size restrictions at the Air New Zealand website. On domestic flights, checked baggage is restricted to one piece per passenger to a maximum of 20 kg (44 lbs). All Air New Zealand flights allow a maximum of one piece of carry-on baggage, which can weigh up to seven kg (15 lb), but more importantly its maximum dimensions (height plus length plus width) should not exceed 105 cm (41 in), or 115 cm (45 in) on international flights. Personal items such as handbags, cameras, and small laptops are not counted as cabin baggage. There are of course exceptions to these rules, so check www.airnewzealand.com for any additional information.

You should pack your carry-on with valuables, medications, smaller breakable items, a sweater, reading materials, and vital documents (driver's license, credit card, passport, a printout of your reservations, etc.). Even if you're traveling by bus, train, or your own vehicle, it's a good idea to keep all these things in an easy-to-reach carry-on-style bag. The most convenient carry-on bags are small backpacks, which can double as daypacks for sightseeing or hiking.

Deciding whether or not to bring specialty sporting equipment to New Zealand depends on the focus of your trip. If you plan to only play a round or two of golf, for example, I'd recommend renting clubs rather than bringing your own. If you're coming to New Zealand specifically to fish, it's best to take your own fly rod and waders with you (rentals are hard to come by), while flies and lures are readily available in sporting stores. Scuba diving and ski equipment are both easy to rent. If you're a mountaineer, you may want to bring your own equipment to ensure your safety, but most of it can also be rented (bring your own rope).

Explore New Zealand

THE 14-DAY BEST OF NEW ZEALAND

Tourism New Zealand says that visitors stay an average of two weeks in New Zealand. What this statistic doesn't show is that while it's possible to see all the highlights in two weeks, this leaves little time to soak up the culture, to enjoy some downtime, or to really get to know the country. Rather than try to see it all, I would suggest deciding where *not* to go first—if you're looking for warmth and the ocean, plan on giving the mountainous regions a miss; if you're from, say, Australia or California, forego the emphasis on the water and instead spend as much time as possible in the mountainous south. This itinerary assumes the former, but with an extra week, you can include a couple of days in Queenstown and then consider hiking either the Milford or Routeburn Tracks.

Day 1

Take it easy on your first day in Auckland, getting a taste for the city's nautical flavor at Viaduct Harbour and stepping back in time at the imposing Auckland Museum.

Day 2

The delightfully named Bay of Islands is your destination today. Take a tour boat through the calm waters, visit the historically important Waitangi Treaty Grounds, and then catch a ferry to Russell, where you have dinner reservations at a waterfront restaurant.

Day 3

Make your first stop Kerikeri Basin to admire New Zealand's oldest buildings. Cut across Northland and drive through the towering kauri trees protected by Waipoua Forest, then visit the Kauri Museum to learn more about these trees and their importance to the local economy. Continue south through Auckland to Hamilton.

Day 4

Waitomo is renowned for its adrenaline-filled caving adventures, but even if you're not feeling brave, it's worth venturing underground to view the amazing glowworms. Drive to Rotorua and spend the rest of the afternoon at Whakarewarewa Thermal Valley. At any

of the major hotels, enjoy a traditional Maori *hangi* (a meal cooked in the ground) for dinner and take in a Maori dance performance.

Day 5

At Whakatane, suit up to go swimming with dolphins then drive across the wilderness of the East Cape to coastal Gisborne, where the Tairawhiti Museum is filled with Maori history. Continue south to

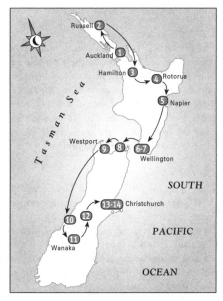

Napier for your overnight stay at a beachfront accommodation.

Day 6

Rise early for a walk along the beautiful beach fronting Napier, then join a walking tour highlighting the city's renowned **art deco architecture.** In the afternoon, join a very different tour, this one along the beach to **Cape Kidnappers,** home to a colony of gannets. Break up the drive to **Wellington** by spending the night surrounded by vineyards at **Martinborough.**

Day 7

The one sight you don't want to miss in Wellington is the **Museum of New Zealand Te Papa Tongarewa,** one of the world's most modern and dynamic national museums. Spend the rest of this day on foot, visiting the **Museum of Wellington City and Sea,** riding the **Wellington Cable Car,** and enjoying lunch at one of the restaurants scattered along **Queens Wharf.** You will have made reservations well in advance for the evening ferry departure to **Picton,** on the South Island, along with room reservations in that town.

Day 8

On an early-morning stroll along the Picton waterfront, you can admire the *Edwin Fox,* one of the world's oldest ships, before breakfast and then go for a short drive to the **Marlborough Wine Trail,** for some wine-tasting. After lunch in the wineries drive to **Nelson** and admire the many local galleries before heading out to **Abel Tasman National Park.**

Day 9

Like so many other places in New Zealand, Abel Tasman is set up for everyone to enjoy. With just one day, use the local tour company to drop you out on the **Abel Tasman Coastal Track** by boat, and then pick you up at a designated point and return to your vehicle by mid-afternoon. Drive south to **Westport** for the night.

Day 10

Head south to **Paparoa National Park** and walk the trail to **Pancake Rocks.** At nearby **Hokitika,** the many shops selling locally carved greenstone provide a choice of iconic New Zealand souvenirs. Spend the night at **Franz Josef Glacier.**

Day 11

Lake Matheson is one of New Zealand's most scenic lakes, but the main focus of the day is a **glacier tour.** These can be as simple as a self-guided walk or as adventurous as a heli-hiking trip up onto the glaciers in the heart of **Westland Tai Poutini National Park.** Drive south to Haast and then up over the spectacular **Haast Pass Highway** to **Wanaka,** where you should plan on a pre-dinner walk along the lakefront.

Day 12

Wind your way through the Otago goldfields region north to **Aoraki/Mount Cook National Park** and spend the afternoon on local walking tracks (the trail to Blue Lakes is one of the most scenic).

Day 13

With Mount Cook in your rearview mirror, it's a scenic drive out of the mountains and through farmland to the coast near Timaru. From this point, it's an easy drive north to **Christchurch.** Spend the afternoon exploring the **Canterbury Museum** and plan a walking tour through and around **Cathedral Square.**

Day 14

For your last day in New Zealand visit the **International Antarctic Centre.** It opens at 9 A.M., so any flight after noon allows time at this large museum showcasing Antarctica. If you're booked on a later flight combine a visit to the International Antarctic Centre with a morning walk through the **Botanic Garden.**

NEW ZEALAND IN ONE WEEK

A minimum of two weeks is needed to see all the best of New Zealand, but if you do have just one week's vacation (which with flying time from North America would be a 10-day excursion), the following suggested itinerary will give you a good introduction to this beautifully scenic country, but with very little downtime and some domestic flying. For this jam-packed itinerary make sure to buy your domestic flights in conjunction with your international ticket, and since you'll know when you'll be where, you can also make accommodation and rental car bookings.

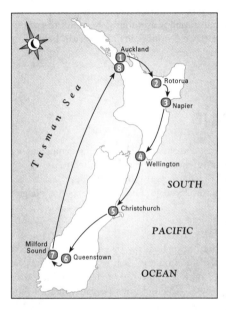

Day 1

Most international flights touch down in **Auckland** early in the morning. First up, you'll want to stretch your legs and breathe in the ocean air, and a good place to do that is **Viaduct Harbour,** where you can wander around docks filled with mega-yachts and waterfront cafés. In keeping with the nautical theme, after lunch try **sailing** and learn about the city's links to the ocean at the **New Zealand National Maritime Museum.** Choose a **Prince's Wharf** restaurant for dinner.

Day 2

Drive south, stopping at **Hamilton Gardens** en route to **Rotorua.** Dive straight into the city's geothermal attractions by visiting **Whakarewarewa Thermal Valley** and **Buried Village** before soaking up the moment at the **Polynesian Spa.**

Day 3

Continuing south, **Lake Taupo** is renowned for its trout fishing. Anglers should plan on squeezing in a quick outing onto the lake, while others should concentrate their time by exploring the volcanic wonders of **Tongariro National Park.** Drive to **Napier** and spend the evening admiring this coastal city's beachside setting and **art deco architecture.**

Day 4

One of the best places to admire New Zealand's unique plant and birdlife in a controlled environment is **Pukaha Mount Bruce,** halfway between Napier and **Wellington.** Once you've reached the capital, check into your downtown hotel and plan on spending at least an hour at **Museum of New Zealand Te Papa Tongarewa,** then walk along the waterfront to the **Museum of Wellington City and Sea.**

Day 5

Book an early flight to **Christchurch,** where the wonders of the world's most remote continent are yours to discover at the **International Antarctic Centre.** From this attraction, head downtown to bustling **Cathedral Square,** and wander through the serenity of the **Botanic Garden.**

Day 6

Take the famous **TranzAlpine train** to **Arthur's Pass National Park,** where you have a couple of hours to explore the alpine wilderness of one of New Zealand's best-loved parks. Return to Christchurch and take an evening flight to **Queenstown.**

Day 7

Book a tour to **Milford Sound,** one of New Zealand's best-known natural attractions. Busing both ways is the least expensive option, but if you choose to fly, there will be time in the afternoon for a **bungy jump.** Your second night in Queenstown is also your last night in New Zealand, so plan on a dinner splurge at Gantley's.

Day 8

Ensure your flight back to Auckland from Queenstown connects with your homebound flight. These usually depart in the evening, allowing for a lunchtime Queenstown departure, and time for a morning excursion to the historic gold-mining town of **Arrowtown.**

A WEEKEND IN AUCKLAND

While most visitors to New Zealand dedicate at least one or two weeks to seeing as much of the country as possible, there are a number of scenarios where time may be limited to only a few days—you may have some extra time at the end of a business trip or maybe New Zealand is a stopover on your way to Australia. If you do only have a few days, Auckland, the country's largest city, is a great place to spend your time.

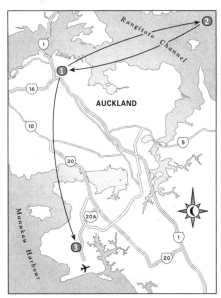

Day 1

Start your first day by enjoying breakfast at **Café Melba** and then crossing Queen Street to take the elevator to the top of the **Sky Tower**—a good way to orient yourself to the city and surrounds. Back at street level, walk down to always-busy **Viaduct Harbour.** Marvel at the large yachts and learn about Auckland's sailing prowess at the **New Zealand National Maritime Museum.** Have lunch at the **Waterfront Cafe** and then board a sailing charter boat for an exciting harbor cruise. If you're feeling fit, rent a bike for a waterfront ride or a drive to **Kelly Tarlton's,** an underground aquarium filled with local underwater species. In the eveneing, feast on a seafood dinner at **Kermadec.**

Day 2

Catch a ferry from downtown Auckland to **Waiheke Island,** which offers a delightful mix of outdoor recreation and tourist services. The trail between Oneroa and Palm Beach takes around two hours, but the end destination is one of the island's nicest beaches. Combine lunch among grape vines at the **Mudbrick Restaurant** with a tasting at the onsite winery. Spend the afternoon admiring the kinetic sculptures at **Connells Bay Sculpture Park,** or simply relax on a local beach. Before you know it, it'll be time to return to reality, and to dine alfresco at a harborfront restaurant in downtown Auckland, such as **Y-Not** at Prince's Wharf.

Day 3

After breakfast at **Strawberry Alarm Clock,** immerse yourself in Maori culture at the **Auckland Museum.** Make a visit to the trendy suburb of Parnell for some souvenir shopping and stroll through the **Parnell Rose Garden.** Plan on a lunchtime splurge at the stylish **Metropole.** On your way to the airport, take a small detour to climb volcanic **One Tree Hill** for sweeping city views.

A SOUTH ISLAND SOJOURN

Of course there's plenty of outdoor recreation on the North Island, but in this itinerary we concentrate on the South Island, where two weeks allows enough time to do an overnight hike, go sea kayaking, and explore some of the more remote regions. You could stay in hotels and motels, but in keeping with an outdoorsy theme, I suggest renting a campervan and staying in the many holiday parks and campgrounds scattered through the region. This itinerary starts and ends in Christchurch.

Day 1

Leisurely make your way out of Christchurch to **Kaikoura.** Take it easy the first afternoon with a stroll along the beach, and maybe a visit to the local seal colony. Fish-and-chips on the beach is a suitable first dinner in New Zealand.

Day 2

You're booked for an early **whale-watching** trip, with breaching sperm whales as the star of the day. Take a detour along the **Marlborough Wine Trail** before reaching **Nelson** in the late afternoon.

Day 3

Drive out to **Abel Tasman National Park,** where with advance planning you can catch a water taxi to **Awaroa Inlet** and your overnight accommodation.

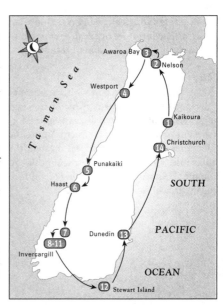

Day 4

For a wonderful day in the wilderness, start with a half-day "tramp" through native forest and along beautiful beaches via the **Abel Tasman Coastal Track** to Torrent Bay, from where the local kayak company greets you to go on a **sea kayaking** trip that ends back at Marahau. Drive to **Westport.**

Day 5

On the way down the west coast, there are dozens of places to pull off the highway and explore remote beaches and take walks through dense native forest. The busiest of these is at **Punakaiki,** where a short trail leads to the aptly named **Pancake Rocks.** Continuing south, you have made advance reservations for a guided tour to **White Heron Sanctuary,** where the magnificent namesake birds can be seen in their natural environment.

Day 6

Rise early for a walk around **Lake Matheson** and then strap on crampons for one of the many **glacier tours** offered in **Westland Tai Poutini National Park.** Push southward to one of the holiday parks around **Haast.**

Day 7

Today, your travel kicks off with a traverse of the **Haast Pass Highway,** which passes raging rivers, tumbling waterfalls, and endless forest on its route across the Southern Alps to the Otago region. Yes, you will pass through the adventure capital of Queenstown, but this trip is more about nature than jumping off bridges, so you drive through to **Te Anau.**

Days 8-11

Regardless of how quickly you could do it, New Zealand's most famous tramp, the **Milford Track,** is strictly regulated, and all hikers must spend three nights at specified huts or campgrounds before emerging at **Milford Sound.** There will be enough time after finishing the trail to drive through to **Invercargill** on your eleventh day.

Day 12

Fly or ferry to **Stewart Island.** An overnight stay allows a full day to enjoy a boat tour to the bird-filled **Ulva Island,** do a couple of short walks, and maybe rent a kayak for an evening paddle.

Day 13

On your way to the mainland, drive north to **The Catlins,** where you will be amazed at the accessibility of wildlife such as seals and sea lions. At **Dunedin** head to the **Otago Peninsula** for the unique opportunity to see albatrosses and yellow-eyed penguins in their natural habitat.

Day 14

Driving north, stop to admire the beach-strewn **Moeraki Boulders** en route to your starting point, **Christchurch.** If your return flight departs the following day, I'd recommend heading out to the **Banks Peninsula** for a final dose of New Zealand wilderness.

FAMILY-FRIENDLY NEW ZEALAND

Most children love being outdoors, which makes New Zealand an ideal destination for families. Regardless of their age, it is important not to try to squeeze too much into each day's itinerary, instead making sure each day focuses on one or two attractions and activities. New Zealand is blessed with hundreds of holiday parks that offer a range of inexpensive accommodations and facilities such as swimming pools, playgrounds, and game rooms, an ideal place to stay with kids. Two of the best are the Kennedy Park Top 10 Resort in Napier (North island) and the Pohara Beach Top 10 Holiday Park in Takaka (South Island).

North Island

Even if you don't have kids, you won't want to fit too much into your first couple of days in New Zealand, and it's best not to travel at all—instead relax in the gateway city of **Auckland**. This should include a trip to the top of **Sky Tower**, a few hours exploring the underwater world of **Kelly Tarlton's**, and maybe a day trip to **Waiheke Island**. The further north you go, the warmer it gets, which makes Northland popular with locals and travelers alike. The official attractions in this region aren't particularly kid-friendly. Instead you find lots of beautiful beaches and the opportunity to travel beyond the blacktop by **cruising through the Bay of Islands.**

South of Auckland, the **Coromandel Peninsula** beckons with more beaches, including **Hot Water Beach,** where children will delight in digging their own hot pool in the sand. If you can drag the family away from the water, plan on riding the quirky **Driving Creek Railway** to a lookout with sweeping views.

The thermal attractions of **Rotorua** are most appealing to older children, but **Wai-O-Tapu Thermal Wonderland** is less daunting (and more colorful) than the others, so it's worth visiting with all ages. Like Wanaka in the south, **Taupo** is a low-key lakeside resort town that is perfect for a break from touring. From the center of the North Island, the choices are to head east to **Napier** for more water sports or, maybe if the weather isn't as cooperative,

west to **New Plymouth,** where **Puke Ariki museum** makes learning about the region's human and natural history fun for all ages.

From New Plymouth, it's a day's trip south, with a stop to learn about the dairy industry at **Dairyland,** to **Wellington.** If you take the family to just one museum in New Zealand, make it the **Museum of New Zealand Te Papa Tongarewa,** which does an admirable job of making local history accessible to all ages.

South Island

A week is enough time for you and your family to hit most of the highlights of the South Island, but you will probably not have time to visit the west coast or Southland.

The ferries linking North and South Islands are outfitted with game rooms and play areas, but you'll want to be out on the decks, watching the birds and marveling at the remote houses scattered along the shoreline of **Queen Charlotte Sound.** To get a taste of this coastal wilderness, plan on walking a short section of the **Queen Charlotte Track.** This can be done as a day trip from Picton, or by staying overnight in one of the many wilderness lodges scattered along the trail. Also at the top of the South Island is **Abel Tasman National Park,** where all ages can enjoy a **boat cruise,** but if you have teenagers, they will probably prefer to go **sea kayaking.**

The best-known **Christchurch** sights revolve around history, but there's still plenty to keep children busy for at least a full day, including the **International Antarctic Centre,** a ride on **Christchurch Gondola,** the interactive exhibits at **Science Alive!, Willowbank Wildlife Reserve,** and **Orana Wildlife Park.** From Christchurch, plan on heading inland to **Aoraki/Mount Cook National Park,** where there are many short walks in a glaciated environment. **Wanaka** has all the scenic beauty of nearby **Queenstown,** but is much more low-key, making it one of the best places in the country to take a couple of days off from touring and concentrate on relaxation, preferably around one of the region's beautiful lakes. The town's **Puzzling World,** featuring life-sized puzzles, will keep all ages busy for at least a half-day.

THE NORTH ISLAND

© ANDREW HEMPSTEAD

The North Island lies between latitudes 34 and

42 degrees south and has a temperate climate, with rainfall levels steady throughout the year. Though more densely populated than the South Island and liberally dotted with towns and villages, it continues to boast unspoiled scenery and a diverse range of landscapes.

The far north offers kilometer after kilometer of golden sand and surf, magnificent kauri forests alive with birds and cicadas, and historic bays crowded with diving and fishing boats. Auckland, the largest city and "Gateway to New Zealand," is situated in the north. East of Auckland, on the rugged beach-fringed Coromandel Peninsula, hiking tracks wind through lush forest and logging dams that have withstood the ravages of time. In the center of the island lie the exciting city of Rotorua – home of modern Maori culture, thermal activity,

The beaches at Mount Maunganui are among the country's best.
© ANDREW HEMPSTEAD

and geysers – and crystal-clear Lake Taupo, boasting some of the country's best brown- and rainbow-trout fishing. The bush-covered ranges of Te Urewera National Park in the east have serene lakes and sparkling waterfalls, rich birdlife, and lush greenery where Maori legends seem to come alive. Tongariro and Egmont National Parks in the central and western regions claim impressive volcanoes, excellent views, hiking and climbing trails, and skiing. An abundance of rivers meanders through the island, providing fine fly-fishing, canoeing, kayaking, and white-water rafting. Wellington, the exciting and picturesque capital, lies on the windswept shores of Cook Strait at the base of the island.

Whether you're in search of sun, sand, and relaxation; exciting, active outdoor adventures; off-the-beaten-track escapades; or bustling cosmopolitan cities, the North Island has it all.

At Auckland's Viaduct Harbour, you can set sail in an America's Cup yacht.
© ANDREW HEMPSTEAD

AUCKLAND

Auckland has always had a wonderfully scenic location, but in the last decade an incredible energy has been injected into almost every corner of city, transforming this cosmopolitan center of 1.3 million into a world-class tourist destination. Most international visitors touch down in Auckland, but the city has grown into a lot more than simply a gateway to the rest of the country. It's a vibrant, exciting city, with a mix of attractions to suit both outdoor enthusiasts and those who thrive in a bustling concrete-and-glass metropolis.

Straddling a narrow piece of land between magnificent Waitemata and Manukau Harbours, Auckland is flanked by the South Pacific Ocean to the east and the Tasman Sea to the west. Downtown slopes to Waitemata Harbour, which is dotted with boats of all kinds, the water a sparkling backdrop to many colorful sails. Nicknamed the "City of Sails," Auckland has hosted the America's Cup on two occasions in the last decade. It was these races that set in motion a downtown harborfront rejuvenation that is the envy of cities the world over.

Auckland is also known for its many fine beaches, beautiful parks and gardens, and a great variety of restaurants and nightlife. The city's eastern shoreline offers calm water and protected beaches, while the western shores boast wild waves, good surfing, and desolate windswept beaches. The urban area is wrapped around a number of extinct volcanic peaks that host vantage points with great views. From these scattered lookouts, you can see how Auckland has also been developed around parks and gardens—packed on weekends with

© ANDREW HEMPSTEAD

HIGHLIGHTS

((Sky Tower: Take a ride to the top of this landmark high above the city for spectacular views of the skyline and harbor (page 40).

((New Zealand National Maritime Museum: Learn about Auckland's long association with the ocean, from the arrival of the first Maori to the America's Cup (page 42).

((Viaduct Harbour: Developed for the America's Cup, this waterfront precinct has matured into a stylish mix of restaurants and shops (page 42).

((Auckland Museum: Maori culture, natural history, and the story of Auckland are all under one roof in the imposing museum within the Auckland Domain (page 44).

((Kelly Tarlton's: Dedicated to the wonders of the ocean, this underground attraction is a good way to get a taste for the marinelife you'll experience beyond city limits (page 45).

((One Tree Hill: Walk or drive to the top of this dormant volcano, an oasis of green surrounded by suburbia (watch for grazing sheep), and immerse yourself in Maori history while enjoying sweeping city views (page 47).

((Sailing: Known as the "City of Sails," Auckland is the perfect place to try your hand at sailing, with charter yachts lining up at Viaduct Harbour for your business (page 48).

((Waiheke Island: Easily reached by ferry from downtown, this island boasts a beautiful year-round climate, secluded beaches, wineries, and many boutique accommodations (page 71).

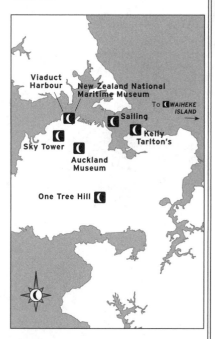

LOOK FOR **((** TO FIND RECOMMENDED SIGHTS, ACTIVITIES, DINING, AND LODGING.

walkers, joggers, cricketers, kite enthusiasts, and families enjoying the year-round pleasant climate (summer average is 23°C/73°F; winter average is a balmy 14°C/57°F).

Within sight of downtown, the 47 islands of Hauraki Gulf Maritime Park beckon. The park is accessed by ferry from downtown; a day trip will give you a taste of island life, but beautiful beaches, upscale lodgings, and world-class wineries make an overnight trip tempting.

Auckland has evolved into one of the world's most tourist-friendly cities. Budget travelers will be amazed by the high standard of inner-city backpacker lodges complete with rooftop hot tubs, while those with more money to spend can relax in one of the world's most perfectly placed Hilton hotels. The coffee in Auckland is equally impressive, with all sorts of wonderful caffeine brews equal in quality to any place I've ever been. Auckland's better

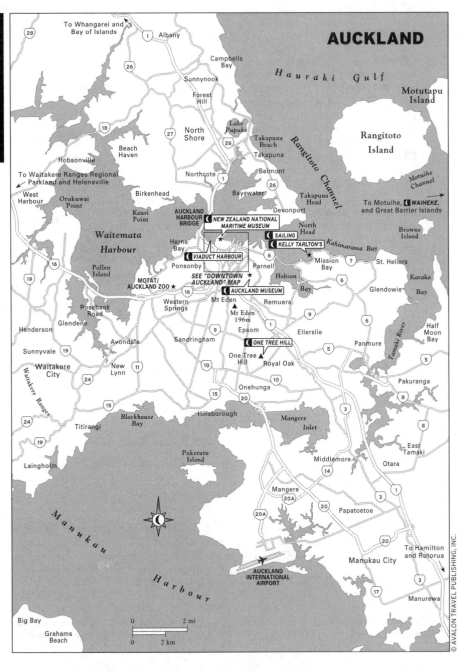

AUCKLAND

To Whangarei and Bay of Islands

Albany

Campbells Bay

H a u r a k i   G u l f

Sunnynook

Forest Hill

Motutapu Island

North Shore

Lake Pupuke

Takapuna Beach

Rangitoto Island

Beach Haven

Takapuna

Hobsonville

Northcote

Belmont

To Waitakere Ranges Regional Parkland and Helensville

West Harbour

Orukuwai Point

Birkenhead

Bayswater

Takapuna Head

Motuihe Channel

To Motuihe, WAIHEKE, and Great Barrier Islands

Kauri Point

AUCKLAND HARBOUR BRIDGE

NEW ZEALAND NATIONAL MARITIME MUSEUM

North Head

Devonport

Browns Island

Waitemata Harbour

Herne Bay

SAILING

KELLY TARLTON'S

Kahimarama Bay

Pollen Island

VIADUCT HARBOUR

Ponsonby

Parnell

Mission Bay

St. Heliers

MOTAT/ AUCKLAND ZOO

SEE "DOWNTOWN AUCKLAND" MAP

Hobson

Bay

Karaka Bay

Glendowie

AUCKLAND MUSEUM

Western Springs

Mt Eden

Remuera

Rosebank Road

Mt Eden 196m

Epsom

Ellerslie

Half Moon Bay

Henderson

Glendene

Avondale

Sandringham

ONE TREE HILL

Panmure

Tamaki River

Sunnyvale

Waitakere City

New Lynn

One Tree Hill

Royal Oak

Pakuranga

Waitakere Ranges

Onehunga

Blockhouse Bay

Hillsborough

Mangere Inlet

Titirangi

Puketutu Island

Middlemore

East Tamaki

Laingholm

Otara

Mangere

Papatoetoe

M a n u k a u

To Hamilton and Rotorua

Manukau City

H a r b o u r

AUCKLAND INTERNATIONAL AIRPORT

Manurewa

Big Bay

Grahams Beach

0   2 mi

0   2 km

© AVALON TRAVEL PUBLISHING, INC.

restaurants bring together the country's finest game and produce (and wine) for a dining experience that can run into hundreds of dollars (or under $5 for a gourmet pie from Pie Mania). To ensure your stay is as easy and worthwhile as possible, visitor centers dot the city, where staff hand out free information and make transportation and accommodation bookings at no charge.

PLANNING YOUR TIME

Most visitors to New Zealand land in Auckland at the end of a long flight. Therefore, I highly recommend you plan on spending the first night in Auckland, giving you time to acclimatize, to recover from any jet lag, and simply to spend the first day without having to "travel." Even the most free-spirited traveler will know in advance which day they will be arriving, so even if the schedule for the rest of your vacation is flexible, make accommodation reservations for the first night before leaving home. With the same thought in mind, also make reservations for the night before your departure. For those not staying in backpacker lodges, I'd recommend a downtown hotel upon arrival (close to major attractions and not a culture shock) and a characterful bed-and-breakfast to finish your New Zealand journey. This also gives you a couple of nights to savor the city's many restaurants; be sure to enjoy a waterfront dining experience.

Once the practical aspects of your stay have been organized, you can start to figure out what you want to see and what isn't so important. Obviously this has a lot to do with personal tastes, but I highly recommend everyone start from the top—literally—by riding the elevator up the **Sky Tower** to the top of New Zealand's highest building. Back at ground level, it's a short walk down to the harbor and the **New Zealand National Maritime Museum** and adjacent **Viaduct Harbour,** both of which give great insight into the city's nautical flavor (as do the restaurants around Viaduct Harbour, a great lunchtime stop if you started early). With only one full day in Auckland, you could spend the afternoon at either the **Auckland Museum** to learn about the region's natural and human history, or **Kelly Tarlton's,** to immerse yourself in the country's marinelife.

If, as I suggested earlier, you spend one night in Auckland at either end of your New Zealand trip, you could mix the above itinerary around to spend a rainy day indoors, leaving Sky Tower and the harbor for a sunny (or "fine," as they say locally) day. A fine day is also the time to travel beyond downtown to reach the low

© ANDREW HEMPSTEAD

Auckland Museum

summit of **One Tree Hill,** one of many volcanic peaks within city limits.

The ocean should be incorporated somewhere into your Auckland stay, and I don't mean simply sipping a cocktail at a harborfront bar. Jumping aboard a ferry is an easy and inexpensive way to see the city from water level, but a better way is to go **sailing** on one of the charter yachts that ties up at Viaduct Harbour.

If you have three full days in Auckland, allow yourself at least one day to visit Hauraki Gulf Maritime Park, where **Waiheke Island** and its beautiful beaches and scenic wineries are linked to downtown by ferry.

Sights

While New Zealand's largest city is filled with official attractions that you won't want to miss, there are also parks and gardens to explore, a magnificent harborfront, and many interesting suburbs. Offshore lies an archipelago of islands, easily reached as a day trip from downtown.

are within walking distance. Sky Tower is a good starting point, both for its sweeping city views and as home to the main information center. Combine the Sky Tower with harborside attractions and the art gallery, both easily reached on foot, and you will have already filled one day of sightseeing.

DOWNTOWN

Queen Street is downtown Auckland's main commercial corridor, and many attractions

(Sky Tower

For excellent views of Auckland from the Southern Hemisphere's tallest building, head

The Sky Tower rises high above the harbor.

© ANDREW HEMPSTEAD

AUCKLAND

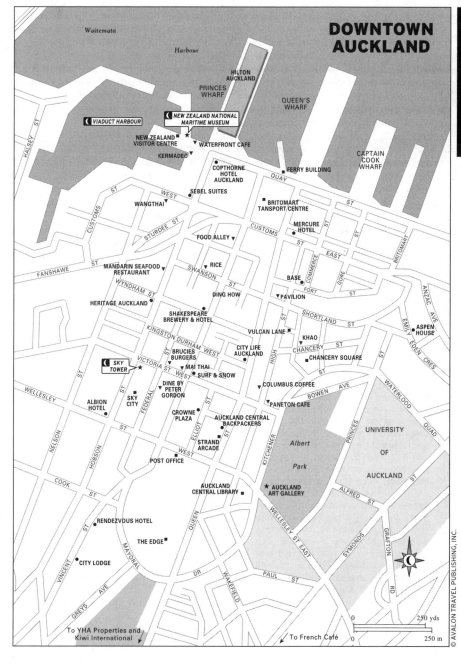

DOWNTOWN AUCKLAND

Waitemata

Harbour

HILTON AUCKLAND

PRINCES WHARF

QUEEN'S WHARF

VIADUCT HARBOUR

NEW ZEALAND NATIONAL MARITIME MUSEUM

NEW ZEALAND VISITOR CENTRE

WATERFRONT CAFE

KERMADEC

CAPTAIN COOK WHARF

COPTHORNE HOTEL AUCKLAND

FERRY BUILDING

QUAY

SEBEL SUITES

BRITOMART TRANSPORT CENTRE

WANGTHAI

WEST ST

HALSEY ST

CUSTOMS ST

STURDEE ST

MERCURE HOTEL

CUSTOMS ST EAST

FOOD ALLEY

FANSHAWE ST

MANDARIN SEAFOOD RESTAURANT

RICE

SWANSON ST

BASE

COMMERCE ST

GORE ST

ANZAC AVE

WYNDHAM ST

DING HOW

PAVILION

FORT ST

HERITAGE AUCKLAND

SHAKESPEARE BREWERY & HOTEL

KINGSTON

DURHAM WEST

SHORTLAND ST

VULCAN LANE

HIGH ST

EMILY

EDEN CRES

ASPEN HOUSE

BRUCIES BURGERS

CITY LIFE AUCKLAND

KHAO

CHANCERY ST

SKY TOWER

VICTORIA ST WEST

MAI THAI

SURF & SNOW

CHANCERY SQUARE

DINE BY PETER GORDON

COLUMBUS COFFEE

BOWEN AVE

WATERLOO QUAD

WELLESLEY ST

ALBION HOTEL

SKY CITY

FEDERAL ST

NELSON ST

HOBSON ST

PANETON CAFE

CROWNE PLAZA

AUCKLAND CENTRAL BACKPACKERS

STRAND ARCADE

ELLIOT ST

KITCHENER ST

UNIVERSITY OF AUCKLAND

PRINCES ST

Albert Park

POST OFFICE

WEST ST

COOK ST

AUCKLAND CENTRAL LIBRARY

QUEEN ST

AUCKLAND ART GALLERY

ALFRED ST

SYMONDS ST

GRAFTON RD

RENDEZVOUS HOTEL

THE EDGE

MAYORAL DR

WELLESLEY ST EAST

VINCENT ST

CITY LODGE

GREYS AVE

WAKEFIELD ST

PAUL ST

To YHA Properties and Kiwi International

To French Café

0   250 yds

0   250 m

© AVALON TRAVEL PUBLISHING, INC.

to the distinctive 328-meter (1,076-foot) Sky Tower (Victoria St., 09/363-6000; daily 8:30 A.M.–11 P.M.; adult $25, child $8). From the SkyCity casino at street level, three glass-fronted elevators whisk visitors to four observation decks in just 40 seconds. Make the Main Observation Level your first destination here; glass floor panels allow views of the city streets directly below and live weather reports flash on a screen. The highest point with public access is Skydeck, an outdoor viewing platform. Below the main deck is Sky Lounge. Before heading up Sky Tower, you can watch a documentary that takes a look at the city's history.

QUEEN STREET

Downtown's main commercial thoroughfare, Queen Street, stretches from **Waitemata Harbour** as far south as suburban Newton. This busy cosmopolitan strip bustles with businesspeople, shoppers, and tourists. On weekends it's decisively quieter, with Aucklanders preferring nearby parks and beaches.

At the harbor end, the **Ferry Building** is the departure point for ferries to the North Shore and offshore islands. Across Quay Street, the old post office has been transformed into **Britomart Transport Centre,** a transportation interchange for buses and trains. From this point, Queen Street begins its long uphill journey. Street level at the bottom end is lined with tourist-oriented businesses, such as duty-free shopping and currency exchange outlets, as well as cafés and restaurants.

A few blocks up from the harbor, **The Edge** precinct is a combination of old and modern centered around a busy square surrounded by the town hall and various entertainment venues.

Toward the upper end, Queen Street crosses Karangahape Road, nicknamed "K Road." This area has a bustling Polynesian atmosphere and a variety of foreign nationalities represented in the shops, restaurants, and takeaway food stands.

The adrenaline activities that New Zealand is so well known for start right here in Auckland. **Sky Jump** (09/368-1835 or 0800/759-586; daily 10 A.M.–6 P.M.; $195) is a bungy-type setup 192 meters (630 ft) up Sky Tower. Rather than rebounding, jumpers wrapped in a body harness come to a smooth stop a few meters above a street-side platform.

New Zealand National Maritime Museum

On Hobson Wharf at the west end of Quay Street, this museum (09/373-0800; Oct.–Apr. daily 9 A.M.–6 P.M., rest of year 9 A.M.–5 P.M.; adult $16, senior $11, child $9) showcases New Zealand's strong maritime traditions in 14 galleries—from the earliest craft used by Pacific islanders to the latest technology used in the America's Cup. The museum encompasses a floating boatshed where traditional Maori crafts are displayed and visitors can try their hand at rowing. Other galleries feature hands-on displays, local lighthouses, an audiovisual presentation in the Pacific Discovery Theatre, a collection of canoes, boatbuilding workshops, and the Hall of Yachting, which tells the story of the America's Cup. A number of historic craft are tied alongside the museum, and one of them, a small steamboat (with museum admission adult $24, senior $17, child $15), takes visitors around the dock area.

Viaduct Harbour

Immediately west of the maritime museum is Viaduct Harbour (also known as **Viaduct Basin**), developed in the 1990s for Auckland's hosting of the America's Cup. A variety of venues around Hauraki Gulf were considered for the occasion, including offshore islands, but this downtown location was the final choice for the America's Cup village, breathing new life into a rundown commercial and industrial area that was first used as a port in the 1870s. Today, the manmade harbor is filled with leisure craft and charter boats while the surrounding space holds a variety of restaurants and bars.

© ANDREW HEMPSTEAD

Viaduct Harbour

The Edge

A few blocks up from the harbor and immediately south of Wellesley Street, The Edge is a bustling precinct that centers around **Aotea Square**. The square is a popular city gathering place, filled with gardens and host to markets every Friday and Saturday. The **Civic** (corner of Queen and Wellesley Streets) opened in 1929 as a movie palace but fell into disrepair over time. After extensive renovations it reopened in 1999, restored to its former Asian-influenced art nouveau glory. In addition to showing films, the Civic hosts touring musicals and shows.

Across Aotea Square from the Civic, **Auckland Town Hall** is an Italian Renaissance–style building that dates to 1911. Like the Civic, it has undergone extensive renovations and is now home to the New Zealand Symphony Orchestra and Auckland Philharmonic Orchestra; the companies take advantage of the renowned acoustics of the Great Hall and Concert Chamber, respectively. Take

in a performance by one of these two companies to experience the town hall in its best light, or wander through the public areas daily 9 A.M.–5 P.M.

A modern addition to The Edge, the **Aotea Centre** is a multipurpose venue that includes two major theaters and the country's largest convention center.

Auckland Art Gallery

Two blocks from Queen Street is the Auckland Art Gallery (corner of Lorne and Wellesley Streets, 09/379-1349; daily 10 A.M.–5 P.M.; free), which dates to 1888 and is the oldest and largest gallery in the country. Until 2010, the original gallery will be closed for major renovations. In the meantime, the New Gallery (across Kitchener St.) displays an extensive historic and contemporary New Zealand art collection, as well as British and old master paintings, and a drawing and print collection. Free guided tours depart daily at 2 P.M. from the front desk. There's also a café open daily for breakfast and lunch, and an excellent bookstore.

Albert Park

After visiting the art gallery, take time to stroll through the Victorian-style gardens of this city park, admiring the groves of well-established oak trees, delightful fountains, and a historic rotunda. At the top end of the park is an old caretaker's cottage (daily 10 A.M.–4 P.M.), which now houses a collection of clocks from around the world.

THE DOMAIN

Auckland Domain is a large, lush, shady park within walking distance of both the city center and Parnell area. Covering more than 80 hectares, the park offers Auckland Museum, Wintergarden, Fernz Fernery, Planetarium, Herb Garden, a kiosk selling drinks and ice cream, and a restaurant that's a favorite spot for wedding receptions. On the hillsides, particularly outside the museum, kite-flying is popular—on a bright summer day the sky is alive with color and movement.

AUCKLAND

🌙 Auckland Museum

Built on the highest point of the Domain, the Auckland Museum (Domain Dr., 09/309-0443; daily 10 A.M.–5 P.M.; adult $5) boasts terrific views of Waitemata Harbour, Rangitoto Island, and the North Shore from the steps leading up to its impressive entrance. Inside is one of the best collections of Maori art and artifacts. Several floors feature a large variety of both permanent and changing exhibitions: the Hall of Pacific Art contains art and objects from islands throughout the Pacific; another exhibit explores Auckland's fascinating volcanic history, complete with sound effects and audiovisuals; other halls feature New Zealand's natural history, birdlife, ceramics, English furniture, military and maritime history, and Asian arts. You can lose complete track of time here—a good spot to keep in mind for a Sunday, when many attractions are closed, or for a rainy day. There's also a small coffee lounge and a good selection of Maori carvings, jewelry, books on New Zealand, and souvenirs available at average Auckland prices in the museum shop. For an introduction to Maori culture, attend one of the short tours of the Maori foyer with a traditional greeting, then a Maori Concert Party performance in the small auditorium at either 11:15 A.M. or 1:30 P.M. If you're driving, Maunsell Road provides access to a large parking lot ($5 per hour, or $7 per day if enter before 9 A.M.).

Other Domain Sights

The beautiful **Wintergarden** (daily 10 A.M.–4 P.M.; free) is a short stroll from the museum. Flower gardens, several greenhouses with amazing hothouse plants, a lily pond, and shady courtyards with statue-lined footpaths make this a relaxing spot to hang out. A small lake, home to a flock of greedy ducks, makes it a popular place with bread-toting children.

Fernz Fernery (daily 10 A.M.–4 P.M.; free), beside the Wintergarden, was originally a quarry. Today, more than 150 varieties of fern thrive in three distinct zones—dry, intermediate, and wet—creating a stunning collection of species found in all parts of the country.

PARNELL

Immediately east of the domain, Parnell is Auckland's oldest suburb. Today, it's a trendy little spot with chic shops, historic buildings, little cafés in shady arcades, a range of accommodations, and Italian restaurants by the handful (often residents call it "Parnelli" with a chuckle).

Parnell is a gentle uphill walk from downtown—walk along Customs Street E (at the harbor end of Queen St.), curve left onto Beach Road, pass the railway station, and make a left on Parnell Rise, which becomes Parnell Road. East of Parnell Road is **Parnell Rose Gardens** (Gladstone Rd.; free), containing more than 4,000 roses.

Historic Parnell

The city's oldest building on its original site in Auckland is 1843 **Hulme Court** (350 Parnell Rd.), but it is not open to the public. Instead, continue up Parnell Road to **St. Mary's Holy Trinity Cathedral** (420 Parnell Rd.), a wooden church dating to 1897, and then to the corner of

© ANDREW HEMPSTEAD

Parnell Rose Gardens are an enjoyable free attraction east of downtown.

© ANDREW HEMPSTEAD

Kinder House

St. Stephens Avenue, where the wooden buildings of **Bishop's Court** date to the 1860s.

Continue up Parnell Road and you soon reach **Kinder House** (2 Ayr St., 09/379-4008; Fri.–Sun. 11 A.M.–3 P.M.; adult $2). Built from Rangitoto Island volcanic stone and completed in 1857, it contains Georgian furniture, family heirlooms, and a collection of Rev. John Kinder's pioneer photographs taken between 1860 and 1888. Leave your vehicle at Kinder House and walk down the hill to **Ewelme Cottage** (14 Ayr St., 09/379-0202; daily 10:30 A.M.–noon and 1–4:30 P.M.; adult $5). Constructed of kauri, New Zealand's native timber, it is one of Parnell's many buildings preserved by the New Zealand Historic Places Trust.

EAST OF DOWNTOWN

Take Quay Street east from downtown and you quickly find yourself on a causeway across the head of Hobson Bay. From here, Tamaki Drive hugs the shoreline and passes Kelly Tarlton's before rounding Bastion Point to reach the leafy suburb of Mission Bay, where cafés and boutiques line the busy main street. It's a

pleasant drive or cycle, although it gets busy during rush hour.

◖ Kelly Tarlton's

New Zealander Kelly Tarlton, one of the world's premier underwater adventurers, spent most of his life traveling the world recovering lost treasures before developing this unique aquarium in underground storm-water holding tanks on Auckland's harbor (Tamaki Dr., 09/528-0603; daily 9 A.M.–6 P.M.; adult $28, senior $21, child $14) six km (3.7 mi) east from downtown. In 1994, eight years after Tarlton's untimely death (he died soon after the complex opened and never saw his dream fulfilled), the second stage of the project opened—a simulation of an Antarctic environment, including penguins. The journey begins by walking through a life-size replica of Captain Robert Scott's hut, complete with groaning ice and fierce winds. Then it's all aboard a Snow Cat that heads through an Antarctic whiteout, under the ice, past some penguins, and into a futuristic Scott Base. The second part of the complex is the aquarium. Travel on a moving walkway through a crystal-clear acrylic tunnel and step off at any point onto the footpath running alongside. Other than the walkway beneath your feet you're surrounded by water—all sorts of indigenous New Zealand sea creatures skim past the tunnel around you, while eels and crayfish peek out of rock crevices. The lighting, dark blue carpeting, and sound effects add to the submarine atmosphere. The tunnel darkens as you enter the deep-sea area, where sharks, stingrays, and other exotic creatures glide above and around you. In the small theater to the left of the main entrance room, an excellent audiovisual slide show features underwater photography; it's 10 minutes long and is shown every 15 minutes. Displays of shells and sea urchins and other objects of marine interest, a piranha tank (feeding time 11 A.M.) and touch tank, a souvenir shop, and lots of articles about sharks complete this Auckland attraction.

WEST OF DOWNTOWN
Ponsonby

A fashionable suburb within walking distance

from K Road, Ponsonby boasts many old homes and shops that have been beautifully restored. Entirely preserved Renall Street depicts a slice of 19th-century Auckland. Houses sit close together on the narrow and steep street, each house with a view of the harbor over the rooftops. Ponsonby is also known for its gourmet restaurants, intriguing shops, and trendy people. Buses run here from Queen Elizabeth Square past Victoria Park and College Hill. Get off at the Three Lamps stop; Renall Street is one block north.

MOTAT

In Western Springs, four km (2.5 mi) west of downtown, the **Museum of Transport and Technology** (Great North Rd., 09/815-5800 or 0800/668-286; daily 10 A.M.–5 P.M.; adult $14, senior and child $7) is commonly referred to by its acronym, MOTAT. At the site of Auckland's original water source, MOTAT gives a glimpse into New Zealand's past with exhibitions of early agricultural machinery, airplanes, vintage cars, fire and steam engines, and a pioneer village. The aviation building is a flying buff's delight, with an extensive historical display featuring Richard Pearse, a South Island farmer and inventor who it's claimed made several flights in the summer of 1902, predating the Wright Brothers 1903 exploits by over a year. Children will love the Tactile Dome, which is filled with interactive exhibits, including an earthquake simulator. Affiliated with MOTAT, nearby Sir Keith Park Memorial Airfield houses the largest vintage aircraft collection in the Southern Hemisphere.

Auckland Zoo

Also in Western Springs, the zoo (Motions Rd., 09/360-3800; daily 9:30 A.M.–5:30 P.M.; adult $18, senior $14, child $9) contains 500 exotic and indigenous animals in enclosures such as Pridelands, which is home to a variety of African species. One of the highlights is the nocturnal house, where you can see the curious kiwi (native bird and a national symbol) doing his (or her) thing during the daytime (the birds are most active in the morning—fed at 9:30 A.M.). You can also watch sea lions through an underwater viewing window. Throughout the day "Keeper Encounters" take place during animal feeding sessions. A souvenir shop and a restaurant overlook the park. The zoo is connected to MOTAT by electric tram that runs every 20 minutes along the one-km (0.6-mi) route.

Waitakere Ranges Regional Parkland

This spectacular chunk of wilderness lies on the north side of Manukau Harbour, west of Auckland (continue west along Hwy. 16 from Western Springs, then take Hwy. 19 through Titirangi). It encompasses much of the Waitakere Ranges. Formed by volcanic action about 17 million years ago, the Waitakere Ranges comprise a steep eastern face, rugged valleys, rivers, streams, and waterfalls, which cascade dramatically to the Tasman Sea. A network of nearly 150 "walks" (suitable for everyone) and "tracks" (for the more experienced hiker) covers a distance of more than 200 km/124 mi (many trails are impassable after high rainfall). The main road through the park traverses the main range and ends at **Piha,** a small seaside community at the protected south end of a beach continuously lashed by massive waves. North and south of Piha, the coastline is no less rugged, with trails leading to secluded beaches and rocky cliffs.

Start a park visit at **Arataki Visitor Centre** (09/366-2000; Sept.–Apr. daily 9 A.M.–5 P.M., May–Aug. daily 10 A.M.–4 P.M.), five km (3.11 mi) beyond Titirangi. Adorned by Maori carvings, this grand building is a lot more than a visitor center—inside, the whole natural and human history of the Waitakere Ranges is laid out, and paths lead through the surrounding forest and to raised lookout platforms. Before continuing farther into the park, pick up the excellent *Recreation and Track Guide*—it gives a good overview of the various walks.

SOUTH OF DOWNTOWN
Mount Eden

Head to the top of this extinct volcano, the highest point in Auckland at 196 meters (640 ft), for a 360-degree view of the city. Walking tracks lead around and into the large egg-shaped depression at the top where the crater used to be. It was used as an ancient Maori fortress by the Waiohua people, and their storage pits and defense terraces remain around the outside. The inner crater area shows no signs of occupation, as it was considered sacred to Matuaho, God of Volcanoes. On the lower slopes of the hill lies **Eden Garden** (daily 9 A.M.–4:40 P.M.; free), a colorful array of camellias, azaleas, and rhododendrons planted in the early 1970s. From downtown you can walk to Mount Eden in about 1.5 hours (follow the Coast to Coast Walkway signs), or catch a bus from the downtown bus terminal for Mount Eden and Khyber Pass Roads. Mountain Road takes you to the summit. You can also drive to the top.

One Tree Hill

Situated among the 60-odd volcanic cones dominating Auckland's skyline, One Tree Hill is another prominent dormant volcano (182 meters/600 ft) offering spectacular views over Auckland. It's thought to have last erupted 20,000 years ago, and in the preceding years and before European colonization up to 5,000 Maori lived on its slopes. To the Maori, it was known as Te Totara-i-ahua after the solitary *totara* tree planted on the summit in 1640. The name survived, although the original tree was cut down in the 1850s and a replacement Monterey pine succumbed to a combination of vandalism and disease in the 1990s. Surrounding the hill is **Cornwall Park,** farmland deeded to the city by John Logan Campbell in 1900. Today, sheep and cattle still graze on the grassed terraces, and you can rest in the shade of an olive grove planted by Campbell. From Greenlane West (take the Hwy. 9 exit from Hwy. 1), a road winds through the park and around the hill, eventually reaching the summit as a narrow paved thoroughfare barely wide enough for one vehicle. At the top is an obelisk.

On the southern slopes of One Tree Hill (near the Manukau Road entrance) is **Stardome Observatory** (09/624-1246; adult $12, senior $10, child $6). Displays in the foyer

A monument at the top of One Tree Hill is dedicated to Maori-European friendship.

area are open Monday–Friday 9 A.M.–5 P.M., but the real reason to visit is the multimedia presentation showcasing our solar system and beyond, which includes images of the night sky displayed on a large screen via a "sky projector." It plays Wednesday–Saturday at 8 P.M. and is followed at 9 P.M. by a space-oriented documentary. After the show, weather permitting, view the Southern Cross and other Southern Hemisphere stars from the observatory (included in the ticket price).

Auckland Botanic Gardens

This extensive 65-hectare garden lies 27 km (17 mi) south of downtown beside Highway 1. As far as botanic gardens go, they are fairly recent, having been initially developed in 1973 and opened in 1982. The former farm has been transformed, now boasting more than 10,000 plants from around the world. Within the garden is a visitor center (09/266-7158; daily 9 A.M.–4 P.M.), a small library, and a café serving light snacks during lunch hours. Admission is free.

© ANDREW HEMPSTEAD

AUCKLAND

Recreation

HARBOR CRUISES

There are so many ways to cruise Waitemata Harbour that your first stop should be the attractively renovated Ferry Building on Quay Street. You'll find **Fullers** (09/367-9111, www.fullers.co.nz) on the ground floor. Fullers runs scheduled transportation and tours to all the populated islands of Hauraki Gulf (see below) as well as to Devonport on the North Shore and around the harbor itself. One of the best ways to enjoy the harbor is to join the 90-minute **Harbour Cruise** (departs daily 10:30 A.M. and 1:30 P.M.; adult $30, senior $25, child $15).

To Devonport

While the Harbour Cruise stops only briefly at Devonport, there's so much to do in and around this North Shore suburb that it's easy to spend a day exploring the area. It's a picturesque place—from the sandy beach beside the ferry terminal, the main street leads uphill past outdoor cafés, art galleries, and trendy boutiques. From the waterfront, a one-km/0.62-mi (20-minute) walking path leads along the harbor east to **North Head,** a historic reserve once an important base for Army operations toward the end of the 19th century. Walking tracks lead to many underground tunnels and chambers, gun emplacements and batteries, and a good viewing point. Nearby **Mount Victoria,** an extinct volcanic cone rising 85 meters (280 ft), offers panoramic views of the harbor; a walking track leads to the top.

The least expensive way to cross the harbor is aboard the **Devonport Ferry,** operated by Fullers (09/367-9111; adult $9 round-trip, senior $7.60, child $4.40) from the Ferry Building. Departures are every 30 minutes 6:15 A.M.–8 P.M., then hourly (on the hour) until 10 P.M.

◖ Sailing

Pride of Auckland (09/373-4557, www.prideofauckland.com) operates a fleet of 45-foot charter yachts, easily recognized by their distinctive blue-and-white sails, from beside the maritime museum. Options include a 50-minute Sailing Experience ($48), a 90-minute lunchtime trip departing daily at 1 P.M. ($70), a 90-minute Coffee Cruise departing at 3 P.M. ($60), and a 2.5-hour dinner trip departing at 7 P.M. that includes a healthy seafood meal cooked on board ($95).

Or you can get *really* serious and step aboard yachts that competed for the America's Cup. A two-hour sailing trip costs adult $135, child $110, or pay adult $195, child $175 to participate in a three-hour race-like setting with the two yachts racing against each other. For information, contact **Sail NZ** (Viaduct Harbour, 09/359-5987 or 0800/724-569, www.sailnewzealand.co.nz).

WALKING TRACKS

The local council has done an admirable job of creating an extensive network of walking paths within city limits. The information center stocks related brochures, or head down to the experts at the **Department of Conservation** office in the Ferry Building (Quay St., 09/379-6476; Mon.–Fri. 9:30 A.M.–5 P.M., Sat. 10 A.M.–3 P.M.). The **Auckland Regional Council** website (www.arc.govt.nz) is another good source of walking trail information.

Coast to Coast Walkway

This well-marked urban walkway crosses the 16 km (10 mi) of land that separate the Pacific Ocean on the east from the Tasman Sea on the west. Take in tremendous views of the city and the main harbors; climb five volcanic peaks; saunter through parks, gardens, and woods; and listen to native birds on this remarkable track. It's a great way to appreciate the old and the new, the land and the water that make up Auckland today. The walk starts from downtown's Prince's Wharf, and at an easy pace takes about four hours to cover the 13-km (8-mi) trail through the Domain, Mount Eden, and One Tree Hill to suburban Onehunga on Manukau Harbour. A pamphlet containing a detailed map of the route, distances and average walking times, places of interest, viewing points, and parks and gardens is available from the Department of Conservation office.

Point to Point Walkway

It takes about three leisurely hours to do this 7.5-km (4.6-mi) well-marked walk, which starts on Tamaki Drive above St. Heliers Bay and meanders through parks, paddocks, and two nature reserves before ending at Point England. Catch tremendous views of the city from St. John's Ridge before finishing on St. John's Road. If you want to walk around the **Tahuna-Torea Nature Reserve** (Gathering Place of the Oyster-Catcher) along the way, add about 1.5 hours, including time-outs for bird-watching.

BEACHES
Close to Town

Beaches lie on all sides of Auckland, some surprisingly close to the city center, ranging from sheltered sandy coves on the east to pounding surf and black sand on the west. Tamaki Drive leads south out of downtown along the waterfront toward Mission Bay, Kohimaramara Beach, and St. Heliers Bay. The many sheltered beaches along the Tamaki waterfront are popular, offering good, safe swimming and calm water. The first, **Judges Bay,** is only minutes from the city center, accessible from Parnell Rose Gardens. Farther along is **Mission Bay,** known for an attractive fountain that dances at the push of a button. Here you can rent bicycles, catamarans, and windsurfers (sailboards); in summer it's usually packed. Beyond **St. Heliers Beach** is access to **Lady's** (men and women welcome) and **Gentleman's Bays** (men only), Auckland's two nude beaches. All along Tamaki Drive are boat anchorages, boat launches, changing rooms, and cafés; buses leave from the downtown bus terminal.

On the North Shore

Over Auckland Harbour Bridge to the North Shore are many more beaches to choose from. **Takapuna Beach** is one of the best known and probably most crowded, but nine others are accessible by bus from Devonport, linked to downtown by ferry.

Along the West Coast

On the west coast lie kilometers of wind- and surf-swept beaches, many quite isolated. They're beautiful but can also be dangerous; they are known for large, unpredictable swells and strong riptides. It's safest to swim at the beaches where the local surf lifesaving club is patrolling. **Piha** is a popular surf beach, patrolled in summer, as are North Piha, Karekare, and Te Henga, all within Waitakere Ranges Regional Parkland. South of Piha, the west coast meets Manukau Harbour along the sandy shores of desolate **Whatipu Beach** (accessible along Huia Rd. from Titirangi), with large sand dunes and good surfing and bird-watching.

In addition to its large surf, **Muriwai Beach,** 45 km (28 mi) from Auckland along Highway 16, is known for a long black-sand (rutile) beach, extensive sand dunes, a gannet colony, and a seaside golf course. A track leads south from the beach to **Maori Bay,** where you'll see unusual geological formations known as "pillow lavas." Behind the beach lies the small community of Muriwai, with a motor camp and fish-and-chips shop.

CYCLING

For information on cycling around the city, contact the **Auckland Cycle Touring Association** (actanz@xtra.co.nz), which organizes rides most weekends. A popular bike route around Auckland covers about 50 km (31 mi) and takes at least three hours. If you ride at a leisurely pace over a full day you'll have the opportunity to visit many city attractions along the route. A map is available from the Auckland Visitor Centre.

Rentals

Many bicycle shops rent bikes, including **Adventure Cycles** (1 Laurie Ave., Parnell, 09/309-5566 or 0800/335-566), which rents by the day or week. For those planning an extended cycling trip, rental rates are very reasonable ($90–150 per week), with panniers ($40 per week) also rented. Rentals are also available at many public places around town: Mission Bay, Okahu Bay, the waterfront, and Devonport on the North Shore. Expect to pay around $30–40 per day.

Arts and Entertainment

Current information and show times for music, opera, cabarets, theater, dance, and exhibitions are listed in weekend editions of local newspapers. For musical events the *NZ Herald* gives thorough coverage of what and where, and the Auckland Visitor Centre also has lots of information on Auckland entertainment.

Major cultural and sporting events can be booked through **Ticketek** (Level 2, Aotea Centre, Queen St., 09/307-5060, www.ticketek .co.nz).

SKYCITY

This large entertainment complex (corner of Victoria and Federal Sts. at the base of the Sky Tower, 09/363-6000) holds a wide variety of eateries and lounges, two casinos, and one of Auckland's most luxurious accommodations. The main casino room holds 100 gaming tables (blackjack, stud poker, roulette, Tai Sai, craps, and baccarat) and about 1,500 slot machines. The adjoining **New City Bar** hosts bands and karaoke nights. On Level 3, **Play** offers the same choice of gambling opportunities as the main room but on a much smaller scale and with a quieter atmosphere. The adjacent **Bar3** is a modern, upscale space, with DJ dance music later in the evening. Above the main gaming rooms, the **Atrium Bar** is a quiet, intimate lounge. **Sky Lounge,** below the main observation level of the Sky Tower, has magnificent views across Hauraki Gulf.

Sky City Theatre attracts touring acts and is home to the Auckland Theatre Company. Dinner/theater packages are available to many performances.

PERFORMING ARTS

Auckland's main music and performing arts venues are centered around **The Edge** (Queen St., 09/309-2677, www.the-edge.co.nz). On the southern corner of this precinct, the restored Italian Renaissance–style **Auckland Town Hall** comprises two chambers renowned worldwide for their acoustics, the main venues for performances by the **New Zealand Symphony Orchestra** (04/801-3890, www.nzso.co.nz) and **Auckland Philharmonic** (09/638-7073, www.aucklandphil.co.nz). Also at The Edge is the 2,380-seat Civic, a restored movie palace that reopened in 1999 with an extravagant Eastern-themed art nouveau look, complete with a simulated night sky painted on the ceiling. The Civic hosts touring musicals and shows, occasionally reverting to its original purpose and screening movies. The modern **Aotea Centre** holds two main theater venues. Other organizations performing at these venues include **Auckland Chamber Orchestra** (www .aco.co.nz), **Auckland Choral** (09/358-2892, www.aucklandchoral.co.nz), **Chamber Music New Zealand** (04/384-6133, www.chamber music.co.nz), and **Royal New Zealand Ballet** (04/381-9000, www.nzballet.org.nz). For performance details, contact the above directly; for ticketing information, contact **Ticketek** (Level 2 of the Aotea Centre, 09/307-5060, www.ticketek.co.nz).

On the University of Auckland campus, **Maidment Theatre** (8 Alfred St., 09/308-2383) hosts films, concerts, and a large variety of musical and theatrical events throughout the year, including performances produced by the **Auckland Theatre Company** (09/309-0390, www.atc.co.nz).

NIGHTLIFE
Harborside

The waterfront is an unbeatable location for an afternoon or evening drink. Most of the bars and restaurants along Prince's Wharf and around Viaduct Harbour have wonderful outdoor seating areas that take advantage of the bustling waterfront location.

Along the west side of Prince's Wharf is a strip of combination bar-restaurants, all perfectly positioned to catch the afternoon sun. Although full menus are offered at all these places, it's generally okay to just order drinks. Although drink prices at **Y-Not** (Prince's Wharf, Quay St., 09/359-9998; daily from 11 A.M.) are not as high as elsewhere along the west side of the Prince's Wharf, they are even better during Happy Hour (Mon.–Fri. 4–6 P.M.).

Facing the Ferry Building, **Provedor** (Prince's Wharf, Quay St., 09/377-1114; daily from 3 P.M.) has a few palm-fringed tables overlooking the water, but most of the action happens inside this stylish cocktail bar popular with the after-work crowd. Next door, multi-purpose **Float** (Prince's Wharf, Quay St., 09/307-1344; daily from 11:30 A.M.) has something for everyone—balcony tables with stunning water views, express weekday lunches that include a drink (from $15), happy hour (weekdays 5–7 P.M.), acoustic performances in an intimate setting (Thurs. from 9:30 P.M.), and one of the city's hippest dance clubs (1st and 3rd Friday of every month).

At the head of Prince's Wharf and accessed off the Hilton hotel lobby, **Bellini** (09/978-2000) is both one of the city's most stylish bars and its best situated. The crisp, modern decor takes nothing from the stunning water views, but you pay for the privilege—the least expensive drink is a glass of local beer for $7.50, or you can try a namesake champagne and peach cocktail for $18.

At **Minus 5°** (Prince's Wharf, Quay St., 09/377-6702; daily from 10:30 A.M.), the temperature matches the name. Customers are outfitted with winter clothing before entering a unique bar where everything is frozen, from the walls to the glasses. The cover charge is $27, which includes one vodka cocktail.

Loaded Hog (Viaduct Harbour, 204 Quay St., 09/366-6491), with its own in-house brewery, has huge glass doors that allow everyone to enjoy the sights and sounds of the harbor. While it's a good spot for a quiet drink in the afternoon and evening, a DJ spins disks until 4 A.M. Friday and Saturday. Overlooking the same harbor, **Imperial** (95–99 Customs St. W, 09/377-2720) is a little more pretentious, with a decor to match. **Trench Bar** (Viaduct Harbour, corner Quay and Lower Hobson Sts., 09/309-0412) replicates its namesake—the deepest point of the Pacific Ocean—with dim lighting and sculptures of creatures that inhabit the ocean floor. At the far end of Viaduct Harbour, **O'Hagan's Irish Pub** (101–103 Customs St. W, 09/363-2106) is set back from the water, but offers top-notch food and live Irish outdoor entertainment on Sunday afternoons from 3 P.M.

Backpacker Bars

Globe Bar (229 Queen St. at Darby St., 09/358-4877; daily from 4 P.M.) is part of the Auckland Central Backpackers complex, meaning that it fills nightly with young international travelers looking for cheap drinks and a good time. Also affiliated with backpacker lodges are **First Base** (Base Auckland, 16 Fort St., 09/300-9999) and **Fat Camel** (38 Fort St., 09/307-0181), both with cheap drinks and theme nights throughout the week. The latter hosts a variety of competitions (pool, trivia, etc.) with travel-related prizes for the winners.

Other Bars and Nightclubs

In the heart of downtown, the **Civic Tavern** (1 Wellesley St., 09/373-3684) is home to three bars, including the London Bar with an impressive variety of draft beer. A welcoming atmosphere prevails at the historic **Shakespeare Brewery & Hotel** (61 Albert St., 09/373-5396; daily from 11 A.M.), where you can sample a "platter" of traditional beers for $20.

Ensconced in one of the city's most stylish hotels, **Auckland Bar** (Rendezvous Hotel Auckland, Mayoral Dr., 09/366-5643; Mon.–Sat. from 4:30 P.M.) is a beautifully designed room with a wide-ranging drink list and daily 4:30–5:30 P.M. happy hour.

As always, the hot spots for dancing the night away to DJ music change as regularly as the patrons change their hairstyles. Downtown, the place to be for late-night drinking and dancing is **Crow Bar** (26 Wyndham St., 09/366-0398), a lounge-style cocktail bar that attracts the over-30 crowd. **Rakinos** (upstairs at 35 High St., 09/358-3535, Thurs.–Sat.) is a quieter place, often with live jazz or reggae. At the top end of Queen Street, Karangahape Road has an inner-city, bohemian feel, with a wide variety of ethnic bars and nightclubs. Upstairs on the busy corner of Queen Street, **Khuja Lounge** (536 Queen St., 09/377-3711) hosts a wide variety of musicians Tuesday–Saturday. In the vicinity, **Calibre** (downstairs at 179 Karangahape Rd., 09/303-1673; Thurs.–Sun.) offers dance and house music. Heading west along Karangahape Road from Queen Street, the scene gets sleazy, with strip clubs and sex shops dominating.

In Ponsonby, **Ponsonby Road** has a lively late-night scene, with trendy nightspots and cafés staying open until after midnight. **Lime Bar** (167 Ponsonby Rd., 09/360-7167) and the faux-tropical **Hula Hut** (212 Ponsonby Rd., 09/360-6274) are two of the more popular hangouts.

FESTIVALS AND EVENTS
Summer
The New Year is ushered in with **First Night** (www.firstnight.org.nz), which kicks off in Aotea Square at 7 P.M. Everything is free, including family entertainment and multiple music stages.

New Zealanders love their sports, so crowds are inevitable when the world's best women tennis players arrive in early January for the **ASB Classic** and the men a week later for the **Heineken Open.** Both tournaments are held at the Auckland Tennis Centre (1 Tennis Lane, Parnell, 09/373-3623, www.aucklandtennis .co.nz).

Auckland lives up to its "City of Sails" nickname over the last week of January during the **Auckland Match Racing Cup** (www .aucklandmatchracingcup.co.nz). Unlike most

other yacht races, the emphasis is on the skills of the sailors, who compete in identical yachts in a format that draws huge crowds to the area around Westhaven Marina.

The first Saturday in February, Mission Bay, east of downtown, comes alive during the **Mission Bay Jazz and Blues Streetfest** (09/575-3184, www.jazzandbluesstreetfest .com). First held in 2001, this gathering already attracts a crowd in excess of 20,000 for eating, drinking, and dancing to over 20 bands.

Devonport Food & Wine Festival (09/378-9031, www.devonportwinefestival.co.nz) takes place over the second weekend of February in Windsor Reserve on the Devonport waterfront, less than 200 meters (660 ft) from where ferries from downtown dock. Entry is $15, which includes a wine glass used to taste wines from throughout the country at booths set around the treed parkland. Many of Auckland's top restaurants and gourmet food providers are represented and entertainment is provided from two stages.

Fall
Head for Albert Park the first weekend of March for the **Auckland Lantern Festival** (09/379-2020), a colorful celebration of the Chinese New Year that begins at 5 P.M.

Pasifica (09/353-9557) celebrates the culture of the Pacific with traditional island arts, entertainment, sports, and food at Western Springs Park, off Great North Road, on the second weekend of March (Fri. night and all day Sat.). It's most popular with Islanders, but visitors are more than welcome to enjoy the festivities.

The week prior to the Easter break, the country comes to the city as ASB Showground plays host to the **Royal Easter Show** (09/638-9969, www.royaleastershow.co.nz). Expect displays of arts and crafts, livestock and equestrian events, and judging of the national wine awards.

Auckland Art Fair (www.aucklandartfair .co.nz) fills the Marine Events Centre, at Viaduct Harbour, the middle weekend of May every second (odd) year. Mirroring the wave of similar gatherings around the world, this local version showcases the contemporary work of leading artists from throughout New Zealand.

In late May, literary types congregate at Aotea Centre for the **Auckland Writers and Readers Festival** (www.writersfestival.co.nz). This biennial (odd years) gathering attracts both fiction and nonfiction writers, with a full schedule of public readings and talks.

Winter

The **Auckland International Film Festival** (www.nzff.co.nz) is a stop for the New Zealand International Film Festivals, which travels around the country showing major films from all over the world. It's held for two weeks through mid-July at venues including the Sky City Theatre and the Civic. For a schedule and ticketing details check their website.

Spring

Celebrated on November 5 each year by real kids and grown-up kids, **Guy Fawkes Night** originated in England in 1605. It commemorates the foiling of a conspiracy by Guy Fawkes and his men to blow up London's Parliament buildings and occupants, including King James I, on opening day of Parliament. Nowadays large bonfires, bonfire feasts, spectacular fireworks, and general merriment are the order of the day. Watch the Auckland sky light up; for the best viewing position head to the top of Mount Eden.

Shopping

In general, shops throughout Auckland are open weekdays 9 A.M.–5 P.M., with some downtown shops, fashionable areas of Parnell and Ponsonby, and most suburban malls also open Saturday 9 A.M.–5 P.M. and Sunday 10 A.M.–3 P.M. Late-night shopping is on Thursday or Friday until 9 P.M.

DOWNTOWN

Queen Street is lined with tourist-oriented and duty-free shops, especially the bottom end. Here you'll also find many currency exchanges. For two floors of shops, specialty stores, coffee lounges, and lunch bars in the city center, visit the Downtown Shopping Centre at Queen Elizabeth Square and Customs Street. In the attractive building that houses the **Old Customhouse Shopping Centre** (22 Customs St. W on the corner of Albert St.) you'll find shops, a restaurant and tavern, and a movie theater. Numerous other shopping arcades with regular shopping hours branch off Queen Street.

Running parallel to Queen Street, High Street and the area around nearby Chancery Street are home to many fashion boutiques, including that of **Karen Walker** (15 O'Connell St., 09/309-6299), one of the country's best-known fashion designers.

VICTORIA PARK MARKET

Markets are fun to browse at leisure—and they bring out the Aucklanders by droves on weekends, when many other places close. The biggest and most popular market (daily 9 A.M.–6 P.M.) is across from Victoria Park, within easy walking distance of downtown. Once Auckland's rubbish destructor, its 38-meter (125-ft) chimney can be seen from quite a distance. The cobbled courtyard area swarms with activity as people crowd around colorful vendor carts. The interiors of the former stable buildings have been converted into shops selling art and handcrafts, clothes and jewelry, posters, records, and all sorts of curious knickknacks. On the upper floor you can talk to local artisans and pick up bargains in woven articles, wall hangings, rugs, wool sweaters, pottery, glassware, and leatherwork. The lower floor offers a large variety of ethnic foods in the food hall; food stalls also dot the marketplace. The festive atmosphere is enhanced by daytime entertainment provided by buskers.

PARNELL VILLAGE

Parnell is a fun place to browse and buy, but don't forget your travelers checks—it ain't cheap! The village boasts a large variety of specialty shops, boutiques, and courtyard cafés. Cobblestone courtyards; wooden and wrought-iron lacework; steps up and down here, there, and everywhere; and intriguing alleyways leading to equally intriguing shops lure droves of shoppers.

MULTICULTURAL KARANGAHAPE ROAD

Locally referred to as "K Road," this is one of Auckland's oldest established shopping areas. You'll find a large variety of cosmopolitan stores and restaurants, a range of shops stocked with Polynesian and Asian foods, and many of the city's theaters in this bustling area.

OUTLET SHOPPING

Perfectly placed for last-minute shopping before reaching the airport is **Dress Smart** (115 Arthur St., 09/622-2400; daily 10 A.M.–5 P.M.), with over 100 outlet shops. In addition to international brands, you can pick up great bargains, including children's clothing from the iconic Pumpkin Patch store.

BOOKSTORES

New Zealanders are prolific readers, and this is reflected in the number of bookstores found throughout the city. Centrally located

Unity Books (19 High St., 09/307-0731) is a friendly independent with a wide selection of New Zealand titles, both fiction and nonfiction. The staff at **Time Out** (432 Mount Eden Rd., Mount Eden, 09/630-3331; daily 9 A.M.–9 P.M.) really know their books, and it shows if you go asking for advice on local literature. **Whitcoulls** (210 Queen St. at Victoria St., 09/356-5400) is the largest bookstore in New Zealand, with four floors of books and magazines, and a café. You will find outlets of this chain in most malls and suburbs. **Borders** (291–297 Queen St., 09/309-3377), one of 60 chain bookstores the company operates outside the United States, is a massive centrally located store with a café.

Auckland Map Centre (corner of Queen and Wyndham Sts., 09/309-7725) stocks all types of maps and nautical charts, as well as a selection of travel guides. Another specialty place is **Seahorse Bookshop** (22 Westhaven Dr., 09/358-5691), suitably located opposite the harbor with its huge selection of nautical reading.

One block east of Queen Street, **Anah Dunsheath Rare Books** (6 High St., 09/379-0379) is an antiquarian bookseller specializing in New Zealand history, the Pacific, and Antarctica. They also carry historical maps and postcards. **Bookmark** (46–54 Hurstmere Rd., Takapuna, 09/489-7282; Mon.–Sat. 10 A.M.–5 P.M., Sat. 9 A.M.–2 P.M.) has a serious collection of regional and maritime history.

Accommodations and Camping

Auckland offers a full range of accommodations in all price ranges. As with large cities the world over, major hotel chains have properties in the heart of downtown, but you'll be paying over $200 for a room. Less expensive rooms can be found in the motels that line all highways leading into the city, and you can generally find vacancies at these at any time of the year. A unique feature of Auckland's

accommodation scene is the large number of backpacker lodges, especially right downtown, where you can find a bed for the night for less than $25. But be warned: You get what you pay for. The better backpacker lodges can be found in outlying suburbs, such as Parnell. As throughout the country, Auckland has many bed-and-breakfasts. We've detailed our favorites below, but a more comprehensive listing can be found in the *New Zealand Bed & Breakfast Book*. Available in bookstores throughout the city, this book will prove invaluable as you travel farther afield.

DOWNTOWN
Under $50

The standard of backpacker lodging in downtown Auckland has improved greatly in the last few years, with established lodges upgrading services to compete with new places. With a location handy to both the harbor and Queen Street, **[Base** (16 Fort St., 09/300-9999, www.basebackpackers.com) is one of the best new ones. In addition to all the usual communal facilities, Base also has a popular bar and a rooftop spa and barbecue area. For women travelers, there is Sanctuary ($29 for a dorm bed), a female-only floor with upgraded bathrooms, fluffy pillows, and a feeling of camaraderie unlike other lodges. Dorm beds on the other floors are $27, rooms with two single beds rent for $68 d, and double rooms are $80–95.

Surf and Snow (corner Victoria and Albert Sts., 09/363-8889, www.surfandsnow.co.nz; dorm $23–26, $50–75 s, $65–90 d) has some of the nicest dorms in downtown, with comfortable mattresses and large lockers.

Halfway up Queen Street from the harbor, **Auckland Central Backpackers** (229 Queen St. at Darby St., 09/358-4877 or 0800/462-396, www.acb.co.nz) offers all the usual facilities expected of a large inner-city backpacker lodge—good security, 24-hour Internet access, and lots of room for cooking and relaxing. The lodge has a party bar open to the public and a quieter guest-only lounge. Dorm beds are from $25 while private rooms rent for $68 s or d ($88 with an en suite). Check the website for discounted "starter packs" that include airport transfers and city tours.

YHA New Zealand operates two backpacker lodges in Auckland, both near the top end of Queen Street. **YHA Auckland International** (5 Turner St., 09/302-8200, www.yha.co.nz; dorm $22–28, $78–102 s or d) is a relatively new hostel with its own travel agency, a book exchange, public Internet access, and all the

usual facilities such as a communal kitchen, lounge area, TV room, and bike storage. One block up the hill is **YHA Auckland City** (corner City Rd. and Liverpool St., 09/309-2802, www.yha.co.nz; dorm $24, $64 s, $74 d). This renovated hotel has 153 beds in small dormitories and a large number of basic double rooms, as well as a restaurant.

$50-100

Aspen House (62 Emily Pl., 09/379-6633, www.aspenhouse.co.nz) is a low-rise accommodation on a quieter downtown street within easy walking distance of the waterfront. The 60 rooms are mostly on the small side, and are simply but stylishly furnished. Those that share bathrooms are $49 s, $69 d, while en suite rooms with a TV go for $99 s or d. All rates include a light breakfast and self-serve tea and coffee. Out back is a garden with a barbecue area.

Many city backpacker lodges have nicer rooms than those offered at **Kiwi International Hotel** (411 Queen St., 09/379-6487 or 0800/100-411, www.kiwihotel.co.nz; $79 s, $92 d), but what this place does have are rooms with en suites and coffeemakers. Other amenities are Internet access, a laundry, a bar, and limited free parking. It's near the top end of Queen Street.

[City Lodge (150 Vincent St., 09/379-6183 or 0800/766-686, www.citylodge.co.nz; $65–75 s, $95 d) caters perfectly for travelers simply wanting to rest their head in a comfortable room. Rates are kept low by offering a minimum of services, with guests having use of a commercial-style kitchen and relaxing lounge area. Highly recommended.

One of Auckland's original hotels is the **Albion Hotel** (119 Hobson St., 09/379-4900, www.albionhotel.co.nz), dating to 1883. Four blocks west of Queen Street, its rooms are very basic but comfortable with renovated Victorian-style decor, private baths, coffee and tea supplies and fridge, TV, and telephone. Rooms immediately above the street-level bar should be avoided. Doubles and twins are $100, triples $140.

$100-200

The **Shakespeare Brewery & Hotel** (61 Albert St., 09/373-5396, www.shakespearehotel.co.nz; $100–130 s or d) took in its first overnight guests over 100 years ago. Downstairs is a popular bar with great pub food, while upstairs the guest rooms have been given a thorough revamp to offer great value in a very central location one block from SkyCity. All have en suites and some have balconies.

A decent choice for budget travelers wanting the privacy of their own room with en suite is **Auckland City Hotel** (131 Beach Rd., 09/303-2463 or 0800/569-888, www.aucklandcityhotel.co.nz; $75 s, $105 d), a few blocks east of downtown but still within walking distance (although cab travel is recommended after dark). The basic rooms have tea- and coffee-making facilities and a small fridge, and local calls are free. Downstairs is a restaurant, bar, and Internet terminal.

$200-300

A historic downtown department store has been transformed into the **⬛Heritage Auckland** (35 Hobson St., 09/379-8553, www.heritagehotels.co.nz; from $260 s or d), one the city's best-value upscale accommodations (especially if you scoop one of the Web specials, usually advertised for under $200). Public areas in the original wing have retained their 1920s art deco glory, which includes high ceilings and hardwood *jarrah* floors. In addition to well-appointed rooms (many with water views), this property features a fitness room, outdoor and indoor pools, a tennis court, and a casual dining room.

Crowne Plaza Auckland (128 Albert St., 09/302-1111, www.ichotelgroups.com; from $280 s or d) is not as fancy as other properties in this same chain, but since opening in 1991 has gained popularity with business travelers for its services and central location. Many of the rooms have great harbor views and guests enjoy use of a fitness room and the convenience of a restaurant open daily at 6:30 A.M. for breakfast, a lounge, and street-level shopping plaza. Guests in Club Rooms

($355 s or d), spread over two upper floors, enjoy upgraded everything, free breakfast, and access to a private lounge. As with all top-end Auckland accommodations, check the hotel website for rooms under $200 *with* breakfast, year-round.

CityLife Auckland (171 Queen St., 09/379-9222 or 0800/368-888; from $236 s or d) is a spacious business-class hotel with an indoor pool, a fitness room, a business center, a restaurant, and a bar. The one-bedroom suites ($270) work well for small families.

Close to the waterfront, the dull exterior of **Copthorne Hotel Auckland** (196 Quay St., 09/377-0349 or 0800/808-228, www.millenniumhotels.com; from $240 s or d) belies 187 stylish rooms with harbor views.

Over $300

SkyCity Hotel is part of the impressive SkyCity complex (corner of Victoria and Federal Sts., 09/363-6000 or 0800/759-2487, www.skycity.co.nz). The hotel itself consists of 344 luxurious rooms featuring contemporary furnishings and pleasing nautically inspired pastel color schemes. Other facilities in this full-service hostelry include 24-hour room service, a rooftop heated pool, and a large health club. Within the SkyCity complex itself are 10 eateries and lounges, a casino, and the imposing Sky Tower. Rates start at $310 s or d, but check the SkyCity website for packages that include accommodation, breakfast, and Sky Tower tickets for around $230 s or d.

At the waterfront end of Queen Street beside Queen Elizabeth II Square is **Mercure Hotel Auckland** (8 Customs St., 09/377-8920, www.accorhotels.com.au; $334 s or d), which offers standard rooms with a rack rate higher than it should be, but you should be able to score rooms for under $200 by booking online. Amenities include a fitness room, bar, and restaurant.

Overlooking Viaduct Harbour, **Sebel Suites** (85–89 Customs St., 09/978-4000 or 0800/937-373, www.mirvac.com.au; $300–550 s or d) comprises 129 units with floor-to-ceiling windows, a full kitchen, a laundry facility, and most with a private balcony.

Guests also enjoy all the services of a hotel, including room service, underground parking, and a casual Japanese restaurant.

With 455 guest rooms, **Rendezvous Hotel Auckland** (Mayoral Dr., 09/366-3000 or 0800/088-888, www.rendezvoushotels.com; $340 s or d) is New Zealand's largest hotel. Each room is spacious and elegantly decorated in earthy tones with luxurious granite-lined bathrooms. An impressive 12-story-high glass-sided atrium fills the main lobby area with natural light. Other hotel facilities include a fitness room, a business center, and a variety of eateries, including Pacific Restaurant, offering an extensive buffet breakfast. Check the hotel website for rates reduced to well under $200 year-round.

The modernistic, crisp white exterior of **◖ Hilton Auckland** (147 Quay St., 09/978-2000, www.hilton.com; from $428 s or d) has quickly become a city landmark. Located at the end of Prince's Wharf, it seems to rise from the water, with a design mimicking the sails of boats that fill the surrounding harbor. Public areas and guest rooms are well designed and slick, with sweeping water views from the in-house restaurants and bars as well as from many of the more expensive rooms. Amenities include a heated outdoor lap pool, spa services, valet parking ($30 per day), and room service.

PARNELL

A smattering of privately operated backpacker lodges are along Georges Bay Road, which runs north from Parnell Road, one of the trendiest shopping-and-dining streets in Auckland. Downtown is a 30-minute walk from the choices listed here, and airport shuttle companies will drop you at the front door.

Under $50

The pick of the budget bunch is **City Garden Lodge** (25 Georges Bay Rd., 09/302-0880, www.citygardenlodge.co.nz; dorm $22–27, $48 s, $60 d). Surrounded by extensive gardens, it's in a grand old building that was once home to the queen of Tonga. The sleeping rooms are clean and bright, with plenty of space to move. The well-manicured garden has plenty of outdoor seating and a barbecue.

The only other backpacker lodge along Georges Bay Road worthy of mention, as well as the smallest, is **Lantana Lodge** (60 Georges Bay Rd., 09/373-4546, www.lantanalodge .co.nz; dorm $22, $45 s, $56 d). It features a well-equipped kitchen, a comfortable TV room and lounge, a porch, friendly management, and plenty of good tourist information on low-budget options. (There's one noisy room, directly below the kitchen—avoid it).

$50-100

Easily recognized by its stylish blue-and-yellow exterior, the **Parnell Inn** (320 Parnell Rd., 09/358-0642, www.parnellinn.co.nz; $95–120 s or d) is a well-priced motel in the heart of one of Auckland's trendiest suburbs. The fairly standard rooms are priced right for the location, with a TV and fridge included. The more expensive rooms have basic cooking facilities.

$100-200

Parnell's Village Motor Lodge (2 St. Stephens

© ANDREW HEMPSTEAD

Hilton Auckland

Ave., 09/377-1463, www.parnellmotorlodge .co.nz; $115–190 s or d) features spacious guest rooms, each with a telephone and TV. The least expensive kitchenettes rent for $155.

Barrycourt Suites (10 Gladstone Rd., 09/303-3789 or 0800/504-466, www.barry court.co.nz) is a large motel comprising more than 100 rooms, most with private balconies and large windows that take advantage of filtered harbor views. Standard hotel rooms are $125 s or d, while the larger one- and two-bedroom units, complete with kitchens, are $160–210.

$200-300

Ascot Parnell (36 St. Stephens Ave., 09/309-9012, www.ascotparnell.com; $225–365s or d) is a charming bed-and-breakfast in a restored 1910 home on a quiet street off busy Parnell Road. It is within walking distance of downtown, and numerous restaurants and cafés are just a short stroll away. The friendly owners make you feel quite at home, and the elegantly furnished rooms are bright, spacious, and paneled in kauri, New Zealand's native timber. Breakfast is a filling affair with almost anything you want, continental or cooked.

MOUNT EDEN
Under $50

Bamber Lodge (22 View Rd. off Mount Eden Rd., 09/623-4267, www.hostelbackpacker.com; dorm $25, private rooms $53–57) offers 40 beds in a rambling 1910 homestead with spacious grounds and a small pool in a quiet residential area. Everything is spotlessly clean, the rooms are large and bright, the kitchen is fully equipped, and there's a dining area, TV room, and plenty of space for off-street parking.

Another solid choice in Mount Eden is **Oaklands Lodge** (5 Oaklands Rd., 09/638-6545, www.oaklands.co.nz; dorm $22, $42 s, $55–58 d) in a quiet residential part of this upmarket suburb. This two-story Victorian-era house features large communal areas and extensive gardens.

$100-200

A longtime favorite with readers, **((Bavaria**

B&B Hotel (83 Valley Rd., 09/638-9641, www .bavariabandbhotel.co.nz; $95 s, $139 d) is a rambling kauri villa dating to the early 1900s. It provides 11 comfortable guest rooms, each with private bath and three with balconies. In the guest TV lounge you can help yourself to tea or coffee, then enjoy the timber deck that overlooks a subtropical garden. Rates include a buffet-style breakfast.

REMUERA
Over $300

Located southeast of downtown in the leafy suburb of Remuera is **Aachen House** (39 Market Rd., 09/520-2329, www.aachen house.co.nz; $345–590 s or d), an Edwardian-era mansion converted to what many regard as Auckland's finest bed-and-breakfast. It has been totally renovated by the latest owners and now offers nine luxurious bedrooms, each with a private bathroom and decorated in period style. Breakfast is served in a large conservatory complete with a marble floor, white linen, and floor-to-ceiling windows allowing garden views. Rates also include pre-dinner drinks.

PONSONBY AND HERNE BAY

These two suburbs immediately west of downtown hold a number of backpacker lodges that are a pleasant alternative to the less-personal downtown options. You'll also find bed-and-breakfasts and a couple of solid motel choices.

Under $50

Ponsonby Backpackers (2 Franklin Rd., 09/360-1311, www.ponsonby-backpackers .co.nz; dorm $24, $42 s, $62 d) is in a historic two-story house just around the corner from lively Ponsonby Road. The facilities are all of a high standard, and the cooking and dining areas spacious. The staff will store baggage and book tours, and are keen to tell of the latest Ponsonby dining hot spots.

Just off Ponsonby Road, **Red Monkey** (49 Richmond Rd., 09/360-7977, www.thered monkey.co.nz) is a beautifully restored villa surrounded by lush gardens and a private courtyard lit with lanterns in the evening and with soothing music adding to the charm. Inside, are excellent communal facilities including an Internet terminal and TV lounge. Most guests book by the week ($175 s, $225 d) in simple single and double rooms with shared facilities, but nightly rates are possible if space is available.

$50-100
C Verandahs (6 Hopetoun St., 09/360-4180, www.verandahs.co.nz; dorm $26–28, $48 s, $66 d) is the city's finest backpacker lodge. Backing onto the green space of Western Park, this 1905 kauri-wood villa has been transformed into a home away from home for budget travelers from around the world. Facilities are of the highest standards, including immaculate bathrooms and two kitchens filled with top appliances. Verandahs is just off the top end of Ponsonby Road, a two-minute walk from the free central city bus loop (The Link).

$100-200
Sea Breeze Boutique Motel (213 Jervois Rd., 09/376-2139 or 0800/473-2273, www.seabreeze.co.nz; $115–130 s or d) features 10 inviting motel rooms, some with private balconies and harbor views. All have cooking facilities and breakfast is available.

Toward Ponsonby Road from the Sea Breeze, **Abaco on Jervois** (59 Jervois Rd., 09/360-6850 or 0800/220-066, www.abaco.co.nz; $175–269 s or d) is an old motel that has undergone some serious renovations. Each of the 14 rooms has two TVs, a kitchen outfitted with stainless steel appliances, and bathrooms with jetted tubs and in-floor heating.

NORTH SHORE
Linked to downtown by ferry, the North Shore suburb of Devonport is home to a number of upscale bed-and-breakfasts, or you can choose to stay at a smattering of motels spread through suburbs that extend north to city limits.

$100-200
A five-minute walk from Cheltenham Beach, **Villa Cambria Inn** (71 Vauxhall Rd., Devon-

port, 09/445-7899, www.villacambria.co.nz) is an early-1900s house that has been converted to a casual bed-and-breakfast. The four large rooms (each with a private bathroom), wooden floors, high ceilings, and congenial hosts add to the ambience. The rates for these rooms start at $130 s, $140 d, while in the well-tended garden the self-contained Garden Loft is $220 s or d.

Near the north end of Auckland Harbour Bridge is the **Green Glade Motel** (27 Oceanview Rd., Northcote, 09/480-7445; $115–130 s or d), one of the North Shore's least expensive motels. It's an older style, park-at-the-door place, but each of the 13 rooms has a kitchen. Take the Northcote Road exit from the Northern Motorway (Hwy. 1).

Emerald Inn (16 The Promenade, 09/488-3500, www.emerald-inn.co.nz; $165–210 s or d) is five km (three mi) north of Devonport and 50 meters (0.03 mi) from Takapuna Beach. Each brightly furnished room comes with a fully equipped kitchen and opens to a courtyard filled with greenery and a small outdoor heated pool. Amenities include a laundry, poolside dining room, and a barbecue.

Over $200
One of the best Devonport bed-and-breakfasts is the **C Peace and Plenty Inn** (6 Flagstaff Terr., 09/445-2925, www.peaceandplenty.co.nz; $295–325 s or d), overlooking the water and a one-minute walk from fine restaurants, trendy cafés, intriguing shops, and the ferry terminal. The house was built in 1888 and has been renovated and tastefully decorated. Each of the six guest rooms features individual character, a comfortable bed, and memorable touches such as fresh flowers and chocolates. The Garden Room, with a private entry and small courtyard surrounded by a scented garden, is a particular delight. In the lounge, guests can browse through the well-stocked library while enjoying complimentary tea, coffee, or port. Breakfast, in a dining area overlooking a tropical garden, is a memorable event featuring a delicious choice of fresh fruits and hot dishes such as Belgian waffles prepared by host Judy Machin.

Along with having a large number of bed-and-breakfasts, the harborside suburb of Devonport is home to the grand old **Esplanade Hotel** (1 Victoria Rd., 09/445-1291, www.esplanadehotel.co.nz; from $310 s or d), built in 1903 and last renovated in 2002. It stands opposite the ferry terminal, separated only by landscaped gardens, and at the end of a street chock-full of cafés and restaurants—the perfect city escape. The owners have refurnished 17 guest rooms in a simple yet stylish manner, including cane furniture.

MANGERE (AIRPORT)

The following accommodations are within an eight-km (five-mi) radius of the airport, and each provides airport transfers.

$50-100

Airport Skyway Lodge (30 Kirkbride Rd., 09/275-4443, www.skywaylodge.co.nz) offers a swimming pool and a communal kitchen (it's also within walking distance of a couple of restaurants). The most basic rooms share bathrooms ($59 s or d), or you can stay in an en suite room ($79 s or d).

Nearby, **Traveller's International Hotel** (190 Kirkbride Rd., 09/275-5082 or 0800/800-564, www.travellersinternational.co.nz; $99–159 s or d) offers extensive landscaping around a swimming pool, complete with barbecue facility and playground.

$100-200

The faux-Tudor **Oakwood Manor Motor Inn** (610 Massey Rd., 09/275-0539 or 0800/801-555, www.goldenchain.co.nz; $135–180 s or d) is a large complex that surrounds an open courtyard. It has an outdoor pool and a small restaurant.

HOLIDAY PARKS
South

The closest camping to downtown Auckland is at **Remuera Motor Lodge,** four km (2.5 mi)

southeast of the city center (16 Minto Rd. off Remuera Rd., Remuera, 09/524-5126). It is surrounded by trees and has a large swimming pool and landscaped camping area. There are relatively few flat grassy spots for tents, but lots of space for RVs (sites $28–36 per person). Motel units range $80–130 s or d.

Avondale Motor Park (46 Bollard Ave., Avondale, 09/828-7228, www.aucklandmotorpark.co.nz; tent sites $12 per person, powered sites $14 per person, cabins and flats $50–80 s or d) is nine km (5.5 mi) southwest of the city off New North Road, close to MOTAT and the zoo. Amenities are limited but the more expensive tourist flats are excellent value.

North

Auckland North Shore Top 10 Holiday Park (52 Northcote Rd., Takapuna, 09/418-2578 or 0508/909-090, www.nsmotels.co.nz; campsites $25, dorm beds $38, basic cabins $48, en suite motel rooms $90–140 s or d). There are plenty of grassy sites, with facilities catering to campers, motor-home travelers, or those who prefer their own private cabin. All guests have the use of an indoor swimming pool, TV lounge, large communal bathroom, kitchen blocks, and laundry. To get there from the city center, cross the Harbour Bridge in the Whangarei lane. Four km (2.5 mi) north, take the Northcote Road exit (not the Northcote-Birkenhead exit) and turn left. In less than one km (0.6 mi), look for the sign and take the driveway on the far side of the Pizza Hut restaurant.

Also in Takapuna is **Takapuna Beach Holiday Park** (22 The Promenade, 09/489-7909, http://takapunabeach.kiwiholidayparks.com; tent sites $27, powered sites $30–32, on-site vans $55–70 s or d, tourist flats $95 d). As the name suggests, it's right on the beach, with some powered sites having a fantastic waterfront location. Amenities include a laundry, barbecue, and public Internet access.

Food

The food scene in Auckland has improved almost beyond recognition in the last two decades. From meat pies now filled with gourmet delicacies to a coffee culture as serious as anywhere in the world and waterfront restaurants keeping up with the latest trends, the changes have infiltrated all levels of price and style. As in North America, eating healthy has become more important in recent years, so you will find many of the better restaurants incorporating this philosophy with local produce and game, which naturally includes an abundance of seafood.

Auckland has no distinct "dining precinct," but the west side of downtown's **Prince's Wharf** and adjacent **Viaduct Harbour** have the main concentrations of upscale dining, with outdoor dining and water views as a bonus.

DOWNTOWN
Quick Bites

At **Global Sandwich** (350 Queen St., 09/303-2505), sandwiches are premade and ready to go. They also sell soup and salads. Eat at the counter or head across to the wide-open spaces of Aotea Square.

A travel writer can only take researching food so far, but for this edition I made two stops at **Pie Mania** (36 Wellesley St., 09/377-1984; Mon.–Fri. 7 A.M.–5 P.M., Sat. 9 A.M.–2 P.M.)—the first time for a chicken curry pie, the second for a Thai chili beef pie, and both were delicious.

The old Bank of New Zealand building on Queen Street hides the modern **Tower Shopping Centre,** which has a large downstairs food hall with above-average meals to go. Head to the Robert Harris Cafe (09/358-3891) on the second floor, where there are a few tables on a balcony built over the Queen Street sidewalk. Other food halls are located in the **Downtown Shopping Centre** (corner of

Albert and Customs Sts.) and **Finance Plaza** (Queen St. at Victoria St.).

Greasy spoons have never been a big part of the local dining scene, but **Brucies Burgers** (87 Victoria St., 09/366-0154; 24 hours daily), in the shadow of Sky Tower, has its regulars, including many late-night diners who stop by for a $5 burger in the early hours of the morning. A cooked breakfast is $7. It's not much to look at, but out back is a covered courtyard.

Market

Victoria Park Market (daily 9 A.M.–6 P.M.), west of downtown on Victoria Street, has food stalls scattered throughout. They sell a wide range of regular and ethnic food: everything

A concentration of upscale restaurants can be found along the western side of Prince's Wharf.

© ANDREW HEMPSTEAD

from pies and hot dogs to falafels, pasta dishes, and Chinese meals. If you're lucky, a band will be playing in the outdoor eating area, and even if it rains, you can still enjoy the food and free jazz by seeking shelter under the large table umbrellas.

Cafés

Cafés line most downtown streets. As is the case throughout New Zealand, you will be impressed by the quality and presentation of freshly brewed coffee, which is nearly always espresso and only very rarely filter-style. High Street, one block east of Queen Street, is popular with urbanites for its profusion of happening cafés. Coffee hot spots include **Columbus Coffee** (Metropolis Building, 43 High St., 09/309-5677), with coffees from around the world, and **Paneton Cafe** (60 High St., 09/303-2515). Both open weekdays at 7 A.M. and weekends at 9 A.M.

Vulcan Lane, linking High Street to the much busier Queen Street, is home to a personal favorite for breakfast—**⟨ Café Melba** (33 Vulcan Lane, 09/300-7340; Mon.–Fri. 7 A.M.–4 P.M., Sat.–Sun. 8 A.M.–4 P.M.), where service is friendly yet professional. Breakfast and lunch dishes come together with offerings such as salmon hash ($12.50), comprising poached eggs and hollandaise sauce on a bed of smoked salmon and mashed potato.

The grandly named **Mecca** (Chancery Square, Chancery St., 09/356-7028; Mon.–Fri. 7 A.M.–10:30 P.M., Sat. 8 A.M.–10:30 P.M., Sun. 8 A.M.–6 P.M.), just off High Street, has more tables outside than inside and a grand central outdoor serving area covered by a high circular roof. As one of the first Auckland cafés with Wi-Fi access and as part of a local chain renowned for top-notch coffee, this place hums day and night. With dishes such as mixed-berry-and-ricotta hotcakes and pan-fried snapper doused in hollandaise sauce, you are encouraged to stay for more than just a drink.

In the vicinity of Mecca, **Pavilion** (48 Shortland St., 09/359-9466; Mon.–Sat. from 7 A.M.) overlooks a courtyard from beside the lobby of the Royal & Sun Alliance Building. It fills with workers from the law and insurance firms above, but don't let this put you off. A popular breakfast dish is corn fritters with bacon, avocado, tomato, and chutney ($14.50).

Many of the restaurants on Prince's Wharf and around Viaduct Harbour welcome visitors to stop by for a coffee and light meal, allowing you to enjoy a waterfront setting without the high price of a full meal; **Barabra** (Prince's Wharf, 09/966-0444; daily from 8 A.M.) is one of the best choices for a coffee. Easily missed in this part of the city is the **Waterfront Café** (14 Quay St., 09/359-9914; daily 9 A.M.–9 P.M.), beside the maritime museum complex. Tiered seating means everyone has a view of the historic vessels out front, but the prime tables lie over the water. Expect to pay $12–28 for dishes as varied as salmon panini and lamb shanks with garlic mash.

Seafood

Seafood is a feature throughout Auckland, including at many of the restaurants detailed in the following *Contemporary* section. Upstairs in the Ferry Building, at **Harbourside** (99 Quay St., 09/307-0486; daily 11:30 A.M.–10:30 P.M.), it is the specialty. The menu takes its inspiration from around the world, but local seafood dominates, with dishes like clam and mussel chowder ($15) to start and mains like grilled game fish marinated in soy, ginger, and lime ($38). Crayfish, plucked live from a huge tank, are also popular; they can be steamed, grilled, or roasted—the choice is yours. New Zealand vino dominates the long wine list.

⟨ Kermadec (Viaduct Harbour, corner of Quay and Lower Hobson Sts., 09/309-0412; daily for lunch and dinner) stands out for its striking nautical-theme decor through five dining areas. For a casual meal, it's difficult to top the brasserie and starters such as king prawns and squid with papaya and honey chili dressing ($22.50). Then, for the main meal, simply choose a fish type, and then decide whether you'd like it steamed, char-grilled, or deep-fried. Mains range $22–37. Part of the same

LOCAL SEAFOOD

Snapper, hake, orange roughy, *hapuka* (groper), kingfish, tuna, and swordfish are all caught along the North Island's east coast. Oysters, mussels, crayfish, crabs, and prawns are also available. The best place to enjoy this abundance of fresh seafood in Auckland is at one of the many restaurants along the harbor. Not only do these eateries have wonderful locations for enjoying the sights, sounds, and smells of the ocean, much of the seafood comes straight from the fishing boats to the table. In the case of **Kermadec,** the fishing company owns the restaurant.

In this same part of the city are several fish markets, busiest before dawn when the trawlers have docked and local restaurateurs are searching out their favorite catch. At the **Auckland Fish Market** (corner of Daldy and Madden Sts., 09/379-1490), around 20 tons of seafood are sold by auction each morning beginning at 6 A.M. Although there's a public viewing gallery, there are plenty of reasons to return later in the day, when you'll find outlets selling seafood, a smattering of food stalls and cafés, and a cooking school. **Seamart** (corner of Fanshawe St. and Market Pl., 09/302-8989) is also open to the public. This market offers a variety of fresh fish, live crabs, and even eel, and a takeout sushi bar.

© ANDREW HEMPSTEAD

The Ferry Building has two excellent seafood restaurants.

complex is the **Two Flying Fish Café & Bar,** offering alfresco harborfront dining (a great place to sample that New Zealand classic, fish-and-chips).

Contemporary

At **Euro Bar** (west side of Prince's Wharf, Quay St., 09/309-9866; daily noon–midnight), beautiful Aucklanders gather to see and be seen, with a lucky few snatching an outdoor table to catch the last rays of evening sun as it sets over the harbor. The chef is noted for his use of organic produce and local game in dishes such as truffle and corn salad ($17.50) and rabbit loin on kumara puree ($35).

Beside Euro Bar, **Pasha** (Prince's Wharf, 09/355-0077; daily 4 P.M.–midnight) fits perfectly along the waterfront restaurant strip with a tapas menu for those looking to relax with a drink or more substantial choices like roast fish with mussels and a side of salsa ($34).

Most of the restaurants along the western side of Prince's Wharf are adult oriented, and so is **Y-Not** (Prince's Wharf, Quay St., 09/359-9998; daily from 11 A.M.), which seamlessly blends hip decor with welcoming ambience. But Y-Not also has a menu especially for children, leaving the grown-ups to dine on a mouthwatering lunchtime seafood salad or roast ostrich on a bed of steamed bok choy for dinner. Prices are reasonable all around, with most lunches under $20 and no dinner main over $30.

On the ground floor of the perfectly placed Ferry Building, **Cin Cin on Quay** (99 Quay St., 09/307-6966; daily 10 A.M.–10 P.M.) has great water views and a classical feel with high arched doorways and elegant table settings both inside and out. Start with freshly shucked oysters (from $3.50 each) then tuck into the likes of lamb cutlets infused with Asian spices or a rich bouillabaisse filled with local seafood.

Most major downtown hotels have dining rooms. One of the best of these is **Pacific Restaurant** (Rendezvous Hotel Auckland, Mayoral Dr., 09/366-3000; daily 6 A.M.–10 P.M.), a stylish space off the main lobby. The continental buffet breakfast is $18 and the cooked version is $28. In the evening, mains such as steamed game fish with bean and corn salsa are around $30.

A contemporary, innovative take on Asian-influenced cuisine can be found at **(Rice** (10–12 Federal St., 09/359-9113, Mon.–Fri. 10 A.M.–11 P.M., Sat.–Sun. 6–11 P.M.), one block uphill from SkyCity and not out of place in a glossy interior-design magazine. As the name suggests, rice features prominently, although it is a little less in-your-face than originally, when every dish and even many drinks had an association to rice. You can still order a rice tasting platter ($17.50) to start, but there's not a grain to be seen in the utterly delicious steamed orange marmalade pudding ($14).

Named for the New Zealand–born celebrity-chef owner, **dine by Peter Gordon** (Grand Hotel, 90 Federal St., 09/363-7030; Mon.–Fri. 11:30 A.M.–2:30 P.M., daily 5:30–10:30 P.M.) is a classically elegant room with lots of dark woods and perfectly presented fusion food that uses the very best local ingredients. The two-course lunch is $35, or pay that and more for a dinner main.

European

Classic European cuisine is overshadowed in Auckland by restaurants adding a local twist to region-specific cooking in a modern setting.

Limon (Prince's Wharf, Quay St., 09/358-5402; daily 10:30 A.M.–10:30 P.M.) is a perfect example. One of the hip eateries along the west side of Prince's Wharf, the menu is decidedly Mediterranean, with mains in the $22–28 range (calamari in tomato sauce, grilled lamb skewers with hummus and tzatziki) and the rhubarb and ginger pudding a delicious way to end your meal.

In an attempt to create a small back-alley restaurant as you may find in Madrid, **Tasca** (Vulcan Lane, 09/309-6300; daily 7 A.M.–10 P.M.) is a little more traditional than Limon. The tapas menu allows you to choose as much or as little as you like to eat, with most offerings in the $5–16 range (I loved the *cordero*— lamb roasted in pomegranate molasses).

Serious foodies will appreciate the **(French Café** (210 Symonds St., 09/377-1911; Fri. for lunch, Tues.–Sat. for dinner) for its perfectly presented flavor-filled contemporary European cuisine. The French Café is consistently regarded as one of the city's best restaurants, and the food combines with professional service and original artwork on sparkling white walls. The menu changes monthly, but expect to pay $35 for a main.

Mexican and South American

The **Mexican Café** (67 Victoria St., 09/373-2311; daily noon–10 P.M.) is colorfully decorated with traditional Mexican motifs and has a small outdoor patio. The food is good and inexpensive, with most mains in the $18–22 range.

Some of Auckland's freshest and most flavorful Mexican food is prepared at **Mexicali** (137 Quay St., 09/307-2419; Mon.–Fri. 8 A.M.–9 P.M., Sat.–Sun. 8 A.M.–10 P.M.), on the eastern side of Prince's Wharf. Each dish is made from scratch, yet the prices don't reflect the extra attention and care (mains $13–18). Delicious margaritas and Mexican coffee add to the appeal.

Wildfire (Prince's Wharf, Quay St., 09/353-7595; daily noon–midnight) is a Brazilian *churrascaria,* or barbecue restaurant, featuring favorite dishes from the south of the country.

Pay $32.50 before 6 P.M. or $44.50 after for unlimited food, including beef, pork, chicken, and lamb, carved at the table from long skewers of meat that has been marinated then slowly char-grilled over hot coals.

Chinese

Close to SkyCity, **Food Alley** (9–11 Albert St., 09/373-4917; daily 10:30 A.M.–10 P.M.) is filled with food stands selling plates of Asian food for under $7 and draft beer for $4.

Yum cha (also called dim sum in New Zealand, although there is a difference), the Chinese lunchtime tradition that allows you to choose from a trolley as it's wheeled past your table, is popular throughout Auckland. Expect bamboo baskets of steaming goodies such as dumplings, won ton, and spring rolls, as well as a huge array of sickly-sweet and savory desserts.

At **Ding How Chinese Restaurant** (55 Albert St., 09/358-4838; Mon.–Fri. 11:30 A.M.–2:30 P.M., Sat.–Sun. 9:30 A.M.–2:30 P.M., and daily from 5:30 P.M.), *yum cha* is a traditional affair and always busy with Asian families. Dinner mains range mostly $16–24, although you'll pay more for classic Peking duck, for which Ding How is best known.

Not much English is spoken at the **Mandarin Seafood Restaurant** (47 Hobson St., 09/377-2886) but *yum cha* is ridiculously inexpensive—and besides, not knowing what you're getting is half the fun.

New Orient Restaurant in the Strand Arcade (233 Queen St., 09/379-7793; Mon.–Fri. noon–2:30 P.M., daily from 6 P.M.) offers the ubiquitous Chinese buffet lunch ($20) and dinner ($28).

Thai

You'll find inexpensive westernized Thai restaurants scattered throughout downtown and the suburbs. One of the better choices is **Mai Thai Restaurant** (corner of Victoria and Albert Sts., 09/366-6258; Mon.–Fri. noon–3 P.M., Mon.–Sat. 6–10:30 P.M.), upstairs in the yellow building between Queen Street and

SkyCity. The set lunch is $18, while the dinner menu features pad Thai for $13 and duck, prawns, and shrimp dishes all under $20.

Moving up in style, there are a few upscale places that offer more traditional Thai cooking at reasonable prices relative to other top city restaurants. One of these is **◖ Khao** (corner Chancery and O'Connell Sts., 09/377-5088; Mon.–Fri. noon–3 P.M. and daily 5:30–10 P.M.), at street level of the imposing Chancery Towers, a Gothic Revival building dating to 1925. The restaurant itself is anything but historic, with a stylish open-plan setting. Prawn cakes ($10) make a delicious starter and you can stick with the seafood theme by ordering whole snapper ($25). The curries are also good, and average $20.

The menu at **Wangthai** (96–102 Customs St., 09/358-4131; Mon.–Fri. noon–2:30 P.M., daily 6–11 P.M.), one block back from Viaduct Harbour, is stacked with traditional northern Thai cooking. If you are looking for something different, try *pla chu chee,* steamed fish with coconut cream curry ($22).

Korean

Walk along the western side of Prince's Wharf, beyond the "restaurant strip," and you soon reach **The Koreans** (Prince's Wharf, Quay St., 09/355-6770; daily 5–11 P.M.), which doesn't take full advantage of the location but is nevertheless a good place to indulge in food that goes beyond namesake Korea to include the cuisine of Thailand, Japan, and China. In typical buffet style, the emphasis is on quantity rather than quality and service; for $34, you get to sample lots of seafood at a reasonable price.

SkyCity

This massive complex on the corner of Victoria and Federal Streets (09/363-6000) features a number of eateries. The first one you'll spy is **Rebo,** a stylish street-level café serving up bistro-style fare such as gourmet pizza daily from 8 A.M. The buffet spread at **Fortuna** (daily for lunch and dinner) is extensive, and the food decent; lunch is $20–24 (noon–2:30 P.M.) and dinner is $30–35 (5:30–8:30 P.M.). Kids pay $1.50 per year of their age. Overlooking the foyer of SkyCity is **Ming Court,** a small Chinese restaurant open daily for dim sum lunch ($18 all-you-can-eat) and à la carte dinner.

Immediately above the main observation decks of the Sky Tower is **Orbit** (Sat.–Sun. 10 A.M.–3 P.M. and 5:30–10:30 P.M., Mon.–Fri. 11:30 A.M.–2:30 P.M. and 5:30–10:30 P.M.), an upscale revolving restaurant with creative dishes such as prawn and capsicum fritters and maple-and-soy-marinated venison. Above Orbit is the **Observatory,** a buffet restaurant open daily for lunch (adult $39.50, child $3 per year of age) and dinner (adult $57, child $4 per year of age).

PARNELL

You'll find many of Aucklanders' favorite restaurants in the Parnell area. Named for a group of 1960s psychedelic rockers, **⟨ Strawberry Alarm Clock** (119 Parnell Rd., 09/377-6959; Mon.–Fri. 7:30 A.M.–5 P.M., Sat.–Sun. 9 A.M.–4:30 P.M.) attracts an eclectic crowd ranging from students to local business owners. Exposed brick walls, a painted concrete floor, and worn timber furniture all add to the funky atmosphere. The menu features lots of healthy fare, as well as cooked breakfasts and some deliciously innovative salads. Farther up the hill, **Verve** (311 Parnell Rd., 09/379-2860; daily from 7:30 A.M.) also offers a generous breakfast, as well as attractive sandwiches and interesting salads.

With a leading chef running the kitchen, stark black-and-white decor, and a reputation as a city hot spot, **Metropole** (223 Parnell Rd., 09/379-9300; daily for lunch and dinner) had its heyday in the early 1990s. But it has seen a renaissance of sorts, with the addition of exotic dishes such as filet of kangaroo accompanied by tamarind-curried potatoes ($32).

Continuing up the hill, **Non Solo Pizza** (259 Parnell Rd., 09/379-5358; 2 P.M.–midnight) offers gourmet pizzas, but as the name suggests, "not only pizza," with choices as varied as a modern take on moussaka ($19.50) and

steaming bowls of pasta for up to four diners to share (from $13 per person).

Athidi (323 Parnell Rd., 09/358-2969; daily from 5:30 P.M.) features contemporary East Indian cuisine in a smart setting (terrace seating is a delight). The menu isn't large, but it features classics like butter prawns in *masala* served with basmati rice ($31). Vegetarian delicacies include *Navrattan Korma*—mixed vegetables stir-fried in a cashew-and-almond-flavored gravy—for $17.

Just south of Parnell, in Newmarket, **Bodrum Cafe** (2 Osborne St., 09/529-1931; Tues.–Sun. from 6 P.M.) has a wide selection of Turkish and Middle Eastern dishes starting at $15, including a creative chicken moussaka ($21).

PONSONBY

Don't let a local calling this neighborhood "Ponsnobby" put you off experiencing the dining delights of this historic suburb just west of downtown. Ponsonby Road holds dozens of hip cafés and restaurants, many of which stay open until midnight. But I'll start with breakfast—**⟨ Ponsonby Road Pies** (134 Ponsonby Rd., 09/376-6770; Mon.–Fri. 8 A.M.–6 P.M., Sat. 8 A.M.–4 P.M.) has some of the best pies in the city, including Tandoori chicken, minted lamb, and smoked fish with vegetable; all are under $5.

Thirty Nine (39 Ponsonby Rd., 09/376-5008; Mon.–Fri. 7 A.M.–4 P.M., Sat.–Sun. 8 A.M.–4 P.M.) attracts the trendy crowd by not being trendy. It's a down-home type of place with tables out front and in a private courtyard out back. The coffee here is good, really good, and really strong. Muffins, cakes, and cooked breakfasts are other highlights. **Cézanne Cafe** (296 Ponsonby Rd., 09/376-3338; daily from 7 A.M.) has an artsy vibe while **Santos Cafe** (114 Ponsonby Rd., 09/378-8431) concentrates on pouring gourmet coffee in a relaxed atmosphere.

More than one U.S. reader has written us recommending **Burger Wisconsin** (168 Ponsonby Rd., 09/360-1894; daily for lunch and dinner) for the city's best burgers. They cost from $8 each, but choices include chicken breast with avocado and bacon on a sourdough bun. Another New Zealand burger chain represented in Ponsonby is **Burger Fuel** (114 Ponsonby Rd., 09/378-6466; daily for lunch and dinner). Its politically incorrect advertising campaigns get all the attention, but, like Burger Wisconsin,

the burgers themselves, far superior to Burger King et. al., are the main draw.

Thai cuisine is a popular alternative to Chinese food in New Zealand. One of the better such restaurants is **Thai House Restaurant** (25 Ponsonby Rd., 09/376-5912, dinner only), a stylish place. Dinners start at $14.

Information and Services

INFORMATION

After passing through immigration and then customs at Auckland International Airport, you'll be ushered down the ramp into the main airport lobby. Head *left* through the crowds to the **Visitor Information Centre** (09/275-6467). It's open seven days a week from 5 A.M. until the day's last flight clears customs and immigration. The information center in the domestic terminal (09/256-8480) is open daily 7 A.M.–5 P.M.

The main downtown information center is the **Auckland Visitor Centre** at the street level of SkyCity (corner of Victoria and Federal Sts., 09/363-7182; daily 8 A.M.–8 P.M.).

Tourism Auckland operates its own information center down by the harbor at the corner of Quay and Hobson Streets (09/979-7070, www.aucklandnz.com; daily 8:30 A.M.–5 P.M.). You can also contact Tourism Auckland toll-free within New Zealand at 0800/282-552 and toll-free from Australia at 1800/888-454. By Viaduct Harbour, the **New Zealand Visitor Centre** (corner of Quay and Hobson Sts., 09/979-7005) is open daily 9:30 A.M.–5:30 P.M. Both these centers are operated by **Tourism Auckland.**

You'll find a combined **Department of Conservation/Auckland Regional Parks** information center in the Ferry Building on Quay Stree (09/379-6476; Mon.–Fri. 9:30 A.M.–5 P.M., Sat. 10 A.M.–3 P.M.). This center has all the information you need on regional parks, national parks, campgrounds, walks, and the gulf islands. In the same building is the **Fullers Cruise Centre** (09/367-9111,

www.fullers.co.nz), the best source of information on travel to the gulf islands.

The **Automobile Association,** or AA, is at 99 Albert Street (09/302-1825; Mon.–Fri. 8 A.M.–4:30 P.M.). Upon proof of any worldwide AA membership, this helpful association provides free maps, information, and general travel advice. Be sure to ask for the current *Accommodation Directory* ($12), invaluable for travel throughout the country.

At **Auckland Central Library** (Lorne St. at Wellesley St., 09/377-0209; Mon.–Thurs. 9:30 A.M.–8 P.M., Fri. until 9 P.M., Sat. 10 A.M.–4 P.M., Sun. 1–5 P.M.) you'll find a newspaper reading room with current papers from all over New Zealand, as well as some British, Australian, Canadian, and U.S. papers. As in libraries across the country, Internet access is free.

SERVICES

The main post office is in the Bledisloe Building on Wellesley Street. Arriving in Auckland on an international flight, you'll find a currency exchange outlet just beyond customs. Others are located downtown along the lower end of Queen Street. You'll get a slightly better rate at banks, which are generally open weekdays 10 A.M.–4:30 P.M. Most large hotels and stores will cash checks, but the exchange rate leans considerably in their favor (particularly in the tourist shops).

Most downtown hotels and all backpacker lodges have some kind of Internet access. **Net Central Cybercafe** (5 Lorne St., 09/373-5186) is a centrally located little café where

Internet access is $4 per hour. **Cyber Max** (Level 1, 291–297 Queen St., 09/979-2468) is also downtown.

Emergency Services

For all emergencies, call 111 or **Auckland City Hospital** (Park Rd., 09/379-7440), which has a 24-hour emergency department. For less-urgent cases, call **Auckland Metro Doctors** (125 Queen St., 09/373-4621; Mon.–Fri. 9 A.M.–5:30 P.M., Sat. 10 A.M.– 5 P.M.).

Getting There

AIR

Auckland International Airport (www .auckland-airport.co.nz), New Zealand's largest airport, is 21 km (13 mi) south of downtown. It has separate international and domestic terminals, but they are linked by a free shuttle bus. Coming off international flights, and after passing through customs and immigration, the **Visitor Information Centre** (09/275-6467) is off to the left of the reception area. Open for all international flights, it has all the obligatory maps and transportation information. Nearby you'll find a bank of accommodation phones, free Internet access, rental car desks, a gift shop, café, currency exchange, and phone rentals.

In addition to international flights, the national carrier, **Air New Zealand** (09/336-2400 or 0800/737-300, www.airnewzealand.com), serves cities and towns throughout the country, with Auckland as the main hub. For details on other international and domestic airlines, see *Getting There* and *Getting Around* in the *Essentials* chapter.

Airport Transportation

There are many ways to travel between the airport and downtown. The easiest way is by cab, which costs $50–60 regardless of the number of passengers.

Airbus (09/375-4732 or 0508/247-287, www.airbus.co.nz) picks up at both terminals and stops at major downtown hotels and backpacker lodges. The service runs every 20 minutes, takes one hour to reach downtown,

and costs adult $22 round-trip. Door-to-door service is provided by **Super Shuttle** (09/306-3960, www.supershuttle.co.nz), which charges $28 one-way for the first passenger and then $6 for each extra passenger going to the same destination. Book online or call at least one hour in advance.

RAIL

The terminus for long-distance trains is **Britomart Transport Centre,** across from the harbor at the bottom of Queen Street. These trains are operated by **Tranz Scenic** (04/495-0775 or 0800/872-467, www.tranz scenic.co.nz), with services south from Auckland to Wellington, Tauranga, and Rotorua. For more information, see *Getting Around* in the *Essentials* chapter.

BUS

Long-distance bus travel is the most popular form of public transportation for international visitors to New Zealand, and Auckland is the main hub. **Intercity** (www.intercitycoach .co.nz) has services to just about every point of the country. The depot is at the **Sky City Coach Terminal** (102 Hobson St., 09/916-6222, www .intercity.co.nz), but for the number of travelers space is limited at the terminal, with passengers lining the sidewalk during busy periods. The ticket office is open Sunday–Friday 7:15 A.M.– 6:15 P.M. and Saturday 7:15 A.M.–2:30 P.M. The terminal is also the departure point for **Northliner** (09/307-5873, www.northliner .co.nz) buses, which serve Northland.

Getting Around

Auckland has an excellent transportation network; you can get almost anywhere by bus, train, or ferry. Although the services are provided by private operators, the regional transit system is known as **MAXX** (09/366-6400, www.maxx.co.nz). A Day Pass for unlimited bus, train, and ferry transport is $14, or pay $25 for a three-day Rover pass.

BRITOMART TRANSPORT CENTRE

Incorporating Auckland's historic post office, the Britomart Transport Centre (corner of Queen and Quay Sts.) is the terminus for local (and long-distance) trains and local buses. It's a large, modern terminal with cafés, a currency exchange, a gift shop, big-screen TVs, and the **Britomart Information Kiosk** (Mon.–Fri. 7 A.M.–6:30 P.M., Sat. 8 A.M.–5:30 P.M., Sun. 8 A.M.–3:30 P.M.) all located at street level. Plans for an underground concourse linking the transport center to the ferry terminals, light rail transit, and a subway loop through downtown have been on the drawing board for years, but are yet to come to fruition.

BUS

Buses cover the entire urban area, with services radiating from the streets surrounding the Britomart Transport Centre on Queen Street at Quay Street, and from suburban hubs in New Lynn and Otahuhu. Buses run Monday–Saturday 6:30 A.M.–11 P.M. and Sunday 6:30 A.M.–7 P.M. Fares begin at $0.50 for travel within the inner city and increase in increments to $9.70 for the maximum distance traveled. **The Link** ($1.60) provides an easy way to get around downtown. This efficient service runs every 10–20 minutes daily 6 A.M.–11 P.M. (until midnight on weekends) along Quay Street, up through Parnell to the museum, and back past Aotea Square to Victoria Park Market and Ponsonby.

RAIL

TranzMetro (0800/802-802) is a computer rail service that operates as part of **MAXX** (09/366-6400, www.maxx.co.nz). It operates Mon.–Sat. 6 A.M.–8 P.M.). The three routes run from the Britomart Transport Centre west to Waitakere via Newmarket, south to Papakura via Newmarket and Penrose, and south to Papakura via Panmure and the eastern suburbs; tickets are $1.20 per stage point.

FERRY

Fullers (Ferry Building, Quay St., 09/367-9111, www.fullers.co.nz) operates a scheduled service between downtown and Devonport. Ferries depart at least every 30 minutes 6:15 A.M.–7 P.M., then hourly until 11 P.M. daily. The round-trip fare is adult $9, senior $7.60, child $4.40. Fullers also operates scheduled service to Rangitoto, Waiheke, and Great Barrier Islands. Detailed coverage on all these routes is given in the *Hauraki Gulf Maritime Park* section later in this chapter.

CAR RENTAL

Auckland has an incredible number of car rental agencies. All the major agencies are represented, but it is the small, lesser-known companies that make up the bulk (more than 80 at last count). As a result of fierce competition, rates are reasonable—it is often possible to get a weekly rate in summer of under $400 from the international companies and under $300 from the local operations.

Major agencies and their local contact numbers include **Avis** (09/379-2650), **Budget** (09/976-2270), **Hertz** (09/367-6350), **National** (09/309-3336), and **Thrifty** (09/309-0111). Each of these agencies has a desk at the airport and outlets throughout downtown.

Scotties (09/303-3912, www.scotties.co .nz), a local agency based in Mount Eden, has a variety of vehicles (and a few camper-vans) at good prices, and specializes in long-term rentals. The vehicles are newer models and reliable; each is covered by the maximum insurance available. Scotties also has an outlet in Christchurch, the perfect opportunity for a one-way trip through the country. Other local companies with outlets in Auckland and beyond include **Europcar** (09/379-5080), **Letz** (09/257-2734), **Omega** (09/377-5573), and **New Zealand Rent-a-car** (09/275-2422).

BUYING A USED VEHICLE

If you plan to be in New Zealand for two months or more, a practical option is to buy a used vehicle in Auckland, and then sell it when you leave. You can find a large selection of used vehicles advertised in the Wednesday and Saturday editions of the *NZ Herald* and the *Saturday Star*. Check out the website www.carfair .co.nz for an idea of what is available.

"Car fairs," where owners sell their own vehicles, are held throughout Auckland each weekend. You'll be surprised how many Aucklanders attend—they're almost a social gath-

ering. The largest is at Ellerslie Racecourse (Hwy. 1, Greenlane Interchange, 09/529-2233, www.carfair.co.nz; Sun. 9 A.M.–noon). Another is at Manukau City Centre (09/358-5000, Sun. 9 A.M.–1 P.M.), and at Ellerslie Racecourse (09/529-2233, Sun. 9 A.M.–noon). **Backpackers Car Market** (20 East St., 09/377-7761, www.backpackerscarmarket.co.nz) is not a dealership, but a place where travelers can buy and sell vehicles amongst themselves. Insurance and inspections are available. It's one block from the top end of Queen Street. **Scotties** (27 New North Rd., 09/303-3912, www.scotties.co.nz) often has ex-rentals for sale under $2,000.

TAXI

Flag charge for a taxi is $2.75, then $1.85 for every kilometer (0.6 mi). Taxis wait outside all major downtown hotels, at the airport, and at the Britomart Transport Centre. Companies include **Auckland Co-op Taxis** (09/300-3000), **Discount Taxis** (09/529-1000), **Hop-a-Cab** (09/355-0000), and **Taxi Combined** (0800/505-550).

Hauraki Gulf Maritime Park

Right on Auckland's back doorstep is an archipelago of 47 islands, spread out over more than 13,600 square km (5,271 sq mi) of Pacific Ocean. The islands are volcanic in origin, some having erupted as recently as 200 years ago. Most of the islands are within Hauraki Gulf Maritime Park and are administered by the Department of Conservation (DOC). Some are simply rocky islets, but a few are also inhabited, with bustling little seaside villages. They all have one thing in common—the opportunity for almost unlimited recreation. They are wonderful places to hike, swim, scuba dive, sea kayak, or just visit for a picnic.

Fullers (09/367-9111, www.fullers.co.nz) serves some of the islands with a regular and inexpensive ferry service from the piers in front of the Ferry Building on Quay Street in

downtown Auckland. Here you'll also find Fullers Cruise Centre, the place to check the ferry schedule, gather island information, and make tour and accommodations bookings. The DOC-operated **Auckland Visitor Centre** is also in the Ferry Building (09/379-6476; Mon.–Fri. 9:30 A.M.–5 P.M., Sat. 10 A.M.–3 P.M.). This is a good place to pick up brochures on the islands' human and natural history, and to make campground bookings.

RANGITOTO ISLAND

This island, dominating the horizon from along the south shore of Waitemata Harbour, is easily recognized by its symmetrical and elongated shape. It last erupted only 200 years ago, spreading jagged lava flows out from the peak for a 2.5-km (1.5-mi) radius. Rangitoto has no soil or fresh running water, yet it supports an astonishing array of native and introduced plant species, and small colonies of wallaby, deer, and many birds. On the island you can climb to the 259-meter (850-ft) summit for fabulous views by following the walking track from Rangitoto Wharf. If you're walking up (the view is worth the effort!), wear sturdy footwear and take suntan lotion and sunglasses—the glare can be intense. Several other walking tracks meander across the island. Another track follows the coast and finishes at Islington Bay, where you can catch the ferry back to downtown instead of backtracking to Rangitoto Wharf. Administered by the DOC, the island is uninhabited, so only day-trippers are permitted.

Practicalities

The first of three daily **Fullers** (09/367-9111) ferries departs the Ferry Building at 9:15 A.M. The round-trip fare is adult $20, senior $18, child $11. Walking around the island and to the summit of the volcanic cone is easy, but you can also take the tractor-train **Rangitoto Volcanic Tour** for an extra adult $30, senior $27, child $15.

MOTUTAPU ISLAND

Motutapu Island is connected to Rangitoto Island by a natural causeway, yet vegetation types on the islands completely contrast with one another. Traditionally farmland, the island currently is the subject of an ambitious DOC project to return it to its natural state. The first stage, the eradication of introduced mammals, is complete, and the introduction of endangered species has begun. The project is a long one—50 years at least. The only way to get around the island is on foot. A popular loop begins at the causeway, climbing to the island's highest point before descending to Home Bay. From this point, the trail heads north past scattered World War II gun emplacements before returning along the shoreline to the causeway. This loop is 12 km/7 mi (allow four hours).

Practicalities

The only way to stay overnight on the island is by pitching a tent at **Home Bay Campground** (09/379-6476; $6 per person), a four-km/2.5-mi walk from the Islington Bay ferry dock on Rangitoto Island. Book through the DOC. **Fullers** (09/367-9111) serves adjacent Rangitoto Island, from where it's a pleasant walk across the causeway to Motutapu.

MOTUIHE ISLAND

A DOC reserve, Motuihe has seen many uses over the years, with local volunteers now doing their best to return the island to its natural state (check www.motuihe.org.nz for volunteer opportunities). Between downtown Auckland and Waiheke Island, Motuihe's biggest attraction is two long white-sand beaches on either side of a narrow isthmus, separated by a band of sand dunes and tall Norfolk pines. One side or the other is always protected from the wind, making it attractive for sailing enthusiasts, beach lovers, and picnickers. Around the coastline lie extensive mudstone reefs, and at low tide the rock pools teem with life. Tracks take advantage of the numerous natural vantage points offering the most spectacular views. You can walk around the entire island in four hours at low tide.

Practicalities

Fullers (09/367-9111; $15) has a limited schedule to Motuihe, departing summer only, Sunday at 9:15 A.M. The return ferry departs at 3:30 P.M. All facilities cluster around Waihaorangatahi Bay (where the ferry docks); they include a kiosk, picnic tables with barbecues, and a campground. For information on camping, or to find out about water taxis serving the island, call the facility operator at 09/534-8095.

◖ WAIHEKE ISLAND

Waiheke Island, second-largest of the gulf islands (92 sq km/36 sq mi), is by far the most populous, with a year-round population of 8,000. This swells fourfold in summer as city slickers swarm over to relax on the beautiful white-sand beaches or to walk through rolling farmland and native bush. The island was settled by Maori 800 years ago, at a time when its rolling inland hills were covered with kauri forests. The kauris have long gone, to be replaced with bustling holiday villages, open farmland, and vineyards.

Sights and Recreation

The island's west end is the most built up, with an almost continuous string of villages extending eastward from the main settlement of **Oneroa** to **Onetangi**. Between the two lies a string of magnificent beaches, including picturesque **Palm Beach**. Hiking trails link all parts of the less-developed eastern end of the island (pick up a detailed description from the local information center), and a pleasant six-km (3.7-mi, two-hour) coastal track links Oneroa with Palm Beach. Return along the same route or jump aboard a bus.

Waiheke's calm waters and convoluted coastline make it ideal for sea kayaking. **Ross Adventures** (09/372-5550) charges $65 for a range of half-day trips, including one by moonlight. Kayak rentals are $20 per hour.

At the far end of the island, **Connells Bay Sculpture Park** (Cowes Bay Rd., Connells Bay, 09/372-8957) comprises 25 kinetic sculptures created by some of New Zealand's foremost artists along a sloping hillside with sweeping ocean views. Unless you are a guest at the Connells Bay lodge, access is restricted to those on a guided tour. These depart on demand mid-October to mid-April by advance reservation only. The walking tour lasts two hours and costs adult $30, child $15.

Waiheke Island Historic village (Onetangi Rd., Onetangi, 09/372-2970; Mon., Wed., and Sat.–Sun. noon–4 P.M.; donation) is small but provides an interesting diversion from more strenuous activities.

Wineries

Waiheke has a reputation for excellent wine, predominantly reds, which thrive in the warm, dry climate. Around 24 wineries are spread across the island (Waiheke even has its own winegrowers' association), but most are small, family-run affairs not open to the public. As a general rule, the emphasis is on quality rather than quantity, so you can expect to pay more than in other regions, and most wineries have adopted a charge for tasting.

The most high-profile winery is **Stonyridge** (Onetangi Rd., 09/372-8822), whose annual release of Larose—considered one of the world's finest Cabernet blends—is quickly scooped up by connoisseurs the world over, even at $150–300 a bottle. Winery tours depart weekends only at 11:30 A.M. and cost $10, which includes tasting of one red and one white. Almost all Stonyridge wine is sold by mail order; the mailing list is currently oversubscribed, so the only way to taste the wine is by visiting the vineyard. On a high point of land near the ferry dock, the **Mudbrick Vineyard** (126 Church Bay Rd., 09/372-9050; daily 10:30 A.M.–5 P.M.) is best known for its restaurant (described in the following *Food* section), but also offers tasting of their well-crafted wines for $5.

Accommodations

The wide range of accommodations can be booked through the island information center (09/372-9999). Accommodations generally are more expensive than those on the mainland, but staying in one of the backpacker lodges reduces costs considerably.

At **Hekerua Lodge** (11 Hekerua Rd., Little Oneroa, 09/372-8990; dorm $25–30, $45 s, $70 d, $110 s or d for an en suite) it's a 600-meter (0.4-mi) walk downhill to the beach from a totally private setting, surrounded by dense native bush. The modern facilities include a wide deck, deep natural-feeling rock swimming pool, bikes, a barbecue, and cozy lounge area with Internet access. (You may hear this place referred to as Waiheke Island Backpackers).

Palm Beach Lodge (23 Tiri View Rd., Palm Beach, 09/372-7763; $280 s or d) is a complex of luxurious two-bedroom Mediterranean-style villas, each self-contained and with a private balcony that affords stunning views. Rates include breakfast provisions and use of a variety of facilities.

For understated luxury, nothing on the island comes close to **Connells Bay** (Cowes Bay Rd., Connells Bay, 09/372-8957, www.connellsbay.co.nz; $350 s or d), a beautifully restored 100-year-old cottage just steps from a private beach. The cottage features two bedrooms, a lounge with log fireplace, full kitchen, and verandah with barbecue; you will need to book well in advance to secure a reservation at this highly recommended lodging.

Food

Oneroa has the island's main concentration of eateries. **Vino Vino** (153 Ocean View Rd., Oneroa, 09/372-9888; daily 11 A.M.–10 P.M.) is a popular place, both for its great food and elevated ocean views from the covered deck. Favorite dishes are the Signature Platters, perfect for sharing, and seafood delights such as a filet of monkfish pan-fried with coconut and lime ($28). In nearby Ostend, **Nourish** (3 Belgium St., 09/372-3557; daily 8 A.M.–4 P.M.) is a modern café that wouldn't look out of place in downtown Auckland. The cooked breakfast was the best I had on the island, while the rest of the day the menu features healthy choices like smoked salmon and lemon risotto.

South of Oneroa, the **Mudbrick Restaurant** (Church Bay Rd., 09/372-9050) attracts the business crowd from Auckland, who catch a ferry across the bay to enjoy a relaxed lunch among the vines. Evenings are more upscale, but the food and service are equally good, with diners enjoying dishes such as grilled duck breast smothered with a red curry and plum sauce ($32). **Veranda Cafe** (Stonyridge, Onetangi Rd., 09/372-8822; summer daily 11:30 A.M.–5 P.M., off-season Thurs.–Sun. 11:30 A.M.–5 P.M.) has a modern menu of winery classics in the $18–30 range (think chilled green pea and coriander soup, carpaccio of Wagyu beef, and an antipasto platter to share).

Information

Waiheke Island Visitor Information Centre is in the Artworks Centre (2 Korora Rd., Oneroa, 09/372-1234; summer daily 9 A.M.–5 P.M., the rest of the year until 4 P.M.). As well as providing information, the center makes accommodation and tour bookings and rents bikes. The Artworks Centre is also home to a library with public Internet access and a used bookstore.

Getting There and Around

Many island residents commute to Auckland daily, so sailings are frequent. **Fullers** (09/367-9111, www.fullers.co.nz) ferries depart the downtown Ferry Building up to 20 times daily for the 35-minute trip to the island. Round-trip fares are adult $28.50, senior $25, child $14.30. A number of packages can be booked through Fullers in conjunction with the ferry price. **SeaLink** (09/300-5900 or 0800/732-546, www.sealink.co.nz) offers weekend-only car and passenger service to the island from Wynyard Wharf, at 45 Jellicoe Street (just west of Viaduct Harbour). Fares are similar; adding a vehicle to the mix costs $125 round-trip.

Once on the island, getting around is easy. The ferry docks at Matiatia Bay, from where buses run along two scheduled routes to all corners of the island. The fare to Oneroa is $1.20 and a day pass is $10. **Waiheke Taxi** can be reached at 09/372-8038. **Waiheke Rental Cars** (09/372-8635) has an office beside the wharf at Matiatia Bay; vehicles are $50–75 per day plus 50 cents per km.

GREAT BARRIER ISLAND

Largest of the gulf islands, Great Barrier is also the most remote, lying nearly 100 km (62 mi) from downtown Auckland, but conveniently linked by boat and plane. The island is mostly wilderness, with forested ranges rising more than 600 meters (0.37 mi). Geologically, the island links to the Coromandel Ranges as part of a volcanic fault. The west coast is deeply indented, while many long sandy beaches flank the east coast. The island was first settled by Maori 800 years ago, and its nonrenewable resources, such as kauri forests, were devastated by early Europeans. Today it's a peaceful place, with 1,100 residents scattered mostly over the island's southern end. Recreational opportunities abound—hiking trails crisscross the island, hot springs invite a good soaking, the road system is suited for mountain biking, and the surrounding waters are great for scuba diving and surfing.

Practicalities

Although remote, each of the island's communities offers basic services, such as ATMs and groceries. Accommodations are limited and best booked as part of a package through SeaLink or Fullers. The island has six basic campgrounds, some accessible only on foot. All campers must be totally self-sufficient and prepared with a campstove if a fire ban is in effect.

Book campsites through the DOC (09/379-6476; $6 per person per night).

The ferry trip from Auckland with **SeaLink** (09/300-5900 or 0800/732-546, www.sealink .co.nz) takes two hours each way. Departures are once daily from downtown (Wynyard Wharf, 45 Jellicoe St.) and Half Moon Bay. The round-trip fare is adult $105, senior $84, child $72, vehicle $330. The adult fare to take the ferry one way and return by plane is $148, which makes a day trip possible. **Fullers** (09/367-9111, www.fullers.co.nz) has a summer-only service, with similar fares. **Great Barrier Airlines** (09/256-6500 or 0800/900-600, www.greatbarrierairlines.co.nz) offers scheduled flights between the international airport and the island for $90 each way. **Great Barrier Buses** (09/429-0055) meets all ferry and plane arrivals, or rent a vehicle through **Better Bargain Rentals** (09/429-0092; from $70 per day).

NORTHLAND

North of Auckland lies a spectacular region particularly appealing to sun worshippers, island hoppers, sailors, nature enthusiasts, and history buffs. Apart from a mild climate and plenty of sunshine, the north offers great beauty and variety. The Bay of Islands, where nature and history blend in an unbeatable combination, attracts the largest number of the region's visitors. The irregular 800-km (500-mile) coastline is fringed with soft, sandy beaches and sheltered coves; the bay, formed by a drowned river system, is dotted with some 150 islands. Diving thrills and sensational underwater photography await you in the crystal-clear submarine world of coral reefs and shoals of brightly colored fish, and for excitement, you can't beat a day of deep-sea fishing for the magnificent game fish that cruise the Bay of Islands

in abundance. This tropical paradise also lures both overseas and New Zealand sailors, who congregate in the bay gathering supplies, getting repairs, and soaking up the atmosphere, much as the traders and whalers did at the end of the 18th century.

A great deal of New Zealand's notable early history occurred in the north, and throughout the region (particularly in the Bay of Islands) are many well-preserved historic buildings and remains of Maori *pa*. Magnificent Ninety Mile Beach stretches as far as you can see, and if you follow the main road to the end, you come to Cape Reinga, one of the northernmost tips of New Zealand. See the clashing waves where the Pacific Ocean and Tasman Sea merge. At the southern end of Ninety Mile Beach still stand several mighty kauri forests. The north is small

© ANDREW HEMPSTEAD

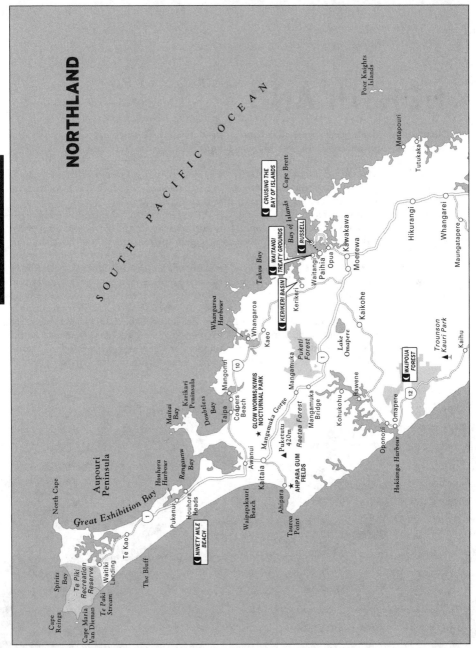

NORTHLAND

SOUTH PACIFIC OCEAN

Poor Knights Islands

Matapouri

Tutukaka

Cape Brett

Bay of Islands

CRUISING THE BAY OF ISLANDS

RUSSELL

Kawakawa

Hikurangi

Whangarei

Maungatapere

WAITANGI TREATY GROUNDS

Moerewa

Opua

Waitangi

Paihia

KERIKERI BASIN

Kerikeri

Takou Bay

Whangaroa Harbour

Whangaroa

Kaikohe

Kaeo

Lake Omapere

Trounson Kauri Park

Kaihu

Puketi Forest

Mangamuka

Rawene

Mangamuka Bridge

WAIPOUA FOREST

Karikari Peninsula

Maitai Bay

Doubtless Bay

Mangonui

Taipa

Coopers Beach

GLOW WORMS/KIWIS NOCTURNAL PARK

Mangamuka Gorge

Puketutu 420m

Raetea Forest

Kohukohu

Oponoi

Omapere

Hokianga Harbour

Aupouri Peninsula

Rangaunu Bay

Houhora Harbour

Great Exhibition Bay

North Cape

Awanui

Kaitaia

AHIPARA GUM FIELDS

Ahipara

Waipapakauri Beach

Tauroa Point

NINETY MILE BEACH

Spirits Bay

Te Paki Recreation Reserve

Cape Reinga

Cape Maria Van Diemen

Te Paki Stream

Waitiki Landing

Te Kao

The Bluff

Pukenui

Houhora Heads

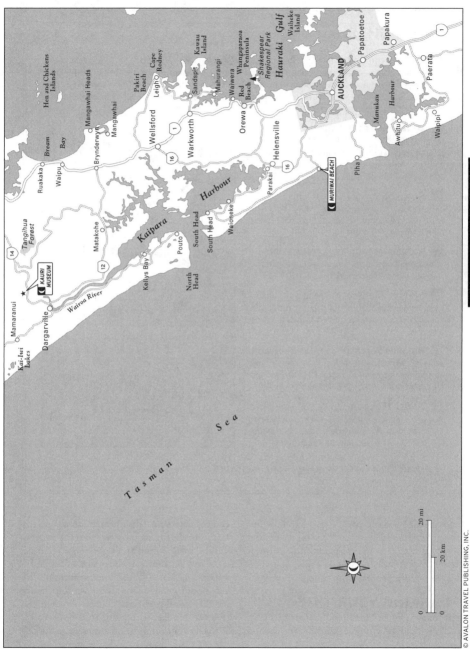

NORTHLAND

Hauraki Gulf
Waiheke Island
Papatoetoe
Papakura
Paerata
1
Paerata

AUCKLAND
Manukau Harbour
Waipipi
Awhitu

Hen and Chickens Islands
Cape Rodney
Kawau Island
Mangawhai Heads
Pakiri Beach
Leigh
Sandspit
Mahurangi
Whangaparaoa Peninsula
Waiwera
Red Beach
Shakespear Regional Park
Mangawhai
Wellsford
1
Warkworth
Orewa
Bream Bay
Brynderwyn
16
Helensville
16
Ruakaka
Waipu
Parakai
PIHA
MURIWAI BEACH

Tangihua Forest
14
Matakohe
Kaipara Harbour
Waioneke
South Head
South Head
Pouto
KAURI MUSEUM
12
Kellys Bay
North Head
Mamaranui
Dargarville
Wairoa River
Kai-Iwi Lakes

Tasman Sea

20 mi
20 km
0
0

© AVALON TRAVEL PUBLISHING, INC.

HIGHLIGHTS

◖ **Cruising the Bay of Islands:** Regardless of mainland commercialization, once your tour boat begins wending its way through uninhabited islands you'll be awestruck by the raw beauty of the landscape (page 92).

◖ **Waitangi Treaty Grounds:** An easily understood approach to explaining New Zealand's most important historic site makes a visit to Waitangi enjoyable. Ocean views and a fantastic little café are a bonus (page 93).

◖ **Russell:** Captain Cook wouldn't recognize this once-rowdy South Pacific outpost, which is now a quiet haven of upscale accommodations and fine dining (page 96).

◖ **Kerikeri Basin:** Two of New Zealand's oldest buildings lie side by side in this tranquil riverside location (page 99).

◖ **Ninety Mile Beach:** Spend a day on the beach – not sunbaking, but driving and "sand surfing" – by joining a guided tour that leads all the way north to Cape Reinga (page 104).

◖ **Waipoua Forest:** In one of the few places in New Zealand where ancient kauri remain, you can wander through a stand of 1,000-year-old trees and stare upwards in wonder (page 108).

◖ **Kauri Museum:** Once you've walked through Waipoua Forest, stop at this outstanding small-town museum to learn about the industry that almost wiped out the kauri (page 111).

◖ **Muriwai Beach:** The South Island has most of the country's accessible bird-watching spots, with one exception – this sleepy seaside village where thousands of gannets nest on offshore rock towers (page 112).

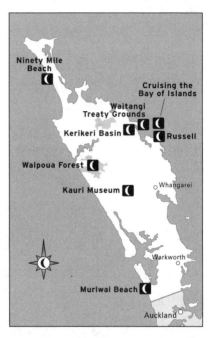

LOOK FOR ◖ TO FIND RECOMMENDED SIGHTS, ACTIVITIES, DINING, AND LODGING.

enough that you can cover it in a few days, but to spend time in its many special places deserves at least a week, especially if your interests include hiking, deep-sea fishing, or diving. Here's hoping you have the time!

PLANNING YOUR TIME

For many visitors, Northland is their first taste of New Zealand driving, and one thing soon becomes apparent—distances are in no way indicative of the time it takes to travel the narrow, winding roads found throughout the country. For example, from Auckland to the Bay of Islands is 237 km (147 mi), but even under the best conditions this trip takes over four hours (and this is on Hwy. 1, the country's main highway). For this reason, in Northland and beyond, it's always important to take note of suggested driving times, rather than just the distance between two points, when planning your time.

If your time in New Zealand is limited to two weeks and you plan on visiting both islands, an overnight trip to Paihia is probably the most sensible option. This would allow time to go **cruising through the Bay of Islands,** step back in time at **Waitangi Treaty Grounds,** and take a ferry trip to **Russell** (heading over for dinner is a popular option). Three days in Northland allows time to explore the historic buildings of **Kerikeri Basin** and take a tour along **Ninety Mile Beach.** An alternative to the beach tour would be to spend the third day returning to Auckland via the west coast, passing through the giant kauri trees protected by **Waipoua Forest** and stopping by the **Kauri Museum.** Even if you're not a keen bird-watcher, the gannet colony at **Muriwai Beach** is an eye-catching stop, as part of the journey down the west coast or as a half-day trip from Auckland.

Auckland to Whangarei

HIBISCUS COAST

Traveling up Highway 1, you quickly leave the suburbs behind and get a first taste of rural New Zealand: rich agricultural land, lush green fields, grazing sheep and cows. Greenhouses and nurseries line the roads in some areas, and roadside stalls sell fresh fruit and vegetables at good prices. The town of Silverdale, only 40 km from Auckland, marks the beginning of the Hibiscus Coast, which includes Whangaparaoa (Bay of Whales) Peninsula and stretches as far north as Hatfields Beach.

Shakespear Regional Park

At the eastern tip of the Whangaparaoa Peninsula, this park offers good bush and farm walks, and three sandy beaches safe for swimming. If you're in the area on a windy day, head for the steep cliffs near Army Bay and check out the hang-glider action. Another popular activity is shellfishing, good at low tide; place the shellfish on a barbecue and cook them until they open.

Red Beach

If you're an early riser, head for this beach before it gets light—it's spectacular at sunrise. The wet orange shells left by the receding tide reflect the sun rays, and the entire beach takes on a red glow. Also adding to the beauty are the native flax flowers and *pohutukawa* trees (covered in bright scarlet flowers at Christmas) at

TRAVELING NORTH FROM AUCKLAND

Two main highways lead north from Auckland – the fastest and most direct is Highway 1, which crosses Waitemata Harbour via Auckland Harbour Bridge then passes through Warkworth, Wellsford, and Whangarei and then on to the Bay of Islands and Kaitaia. The alternate route is Highway 16 (called the North Western Motorway within city limits) along the west coast through Muriwai Beach and Helensville. This highway rejoins Highway 1 at Wellsford, then branches west again as Highway 16 on the north side of Kaipara Harbour, closely following the west coast north via Dargaville.

BY BUS

Intercity (09/623-1503, www.intercity-coach.co.nz) runs several coaches a day from Auckland to Kaitaia via Whangarei and Paihia, the gateway to the Bay of Islands. **Northliner** (09/307-5873, www.northliner.co.nz) runs its Express Coach Service to Paihia once daily. Both companies depart from the SkyCity Coach Terminal (102 Hobson St.) in downtown Auckland.

NORTHLAND

© ANDREW HEMPSTEAD

Waves is a laidback accommodation perfectly suited to the beachside ambiance of Orewa Beach.

the southern end. The beach offers safe swimming, surf suitable for beginners, lifeguard patrol on weekends and holidays, and short rock walks at either end.

Orewa Beach

Since being bypassed by Highway 1 in 2007, the beachside suburb of Orewa, 30 km (19 mi) north of downtown, has become a bit quieter, but the long stretch of white sand is still popular (beware of the strong rip where the Orewa River meets the sea; on weekends and holidays it's patrolled by local surf club members). At the northern end you can see the remains of an ancient Maori *pa* site on the hilltop above Orewa House, and at the extreme north, over Grut's Bridge and sharply to the left, lies the entrance to **Eaves Bush.** This small reserve contains some impressive kauri trees and lots of native ferns.

Pillows Travellers Lodge (412 Hibiscus Coast Hwy., 09/426-6338, www.pillows.co.nz; dorm $25, $42–55 s, $45–59 d) is one of the many accommodations in New Zealand built specifically to cater to backpackers. You'll find a comfortable lounge, kitchen, laundry, sundeck, inner courtyard filled with greenery, and public Internet access.

 Waves (Kohu St., 09/427-0888 or 0800/426-6889, www.waves.co.nz; $155–255 s or d), within a block of the beach, has a resort-like atmosphere and modern, practical rooms filled with amenities such as luxurious bathrooms and modern kitchens. Upgrade to a premium room and enjoy extras such as a large-screen TV, high-speed Internet, and bathrobes.

Waiwera

Waiwera is a thermal resort and busy tourist area. If relaxing in hot pools sounds appealing, follow the signs from the highway to **Waiwera Infinity** (09/427-8800; daily 9 A.M.–10 P.M.; adult $22, senior $9, child $11), nestled behind a beach at the mouth of a river. The 26 indoor and outdoor pools vary in temperature

28–43°C (82–109°F), and there are private spas, water slides, a waterfall pool, a movie pool where the latest releases are shown on a big screen, picnic areas, and a food kiosk. Private spas are $30 per person for one hour, which includes general admission.

Within walking distance of the resort and with gardens extending to a quiet waterway is **Waiwera Motel** (25 Weranui Rd., 09/426-5153; from $120 s or d), with 16 modern self-contained units. Facilities include a small pool, spa, and barbecue, and kayaks for rent.

KOWHAI COAST

The Kowhai Coast stretches from Wenderholm Regional Park in the south to Pakiri Beach in the north. In between, the mighty Mahurangi River estuary has forged its way inland, allowing easy boat access to Warkworth, the main town on this stretch of coast.

Waiwera to Warkworth

Bush and beach trails offer good hiking in **Wenderholm Regional Park,** a beautiful reserve where a large variety of trees grow among the rolling green hills and back to the beach—a great spot for a picnic. You can launch your boat into the sheltered, beach-fringed harbor. The park is open daily 8 A.M.–6 P.M. **Pohuehue Scenic Reserve,** off Highway 1, is another enjoyable place for hiking. Signposted walkways lead through a spectacular variety of native trees, ferns, and exotic plantations. **Moir Hill Walkway** also starts on Highway 1, six km (four mi) south of Warkworth; it'll take you 3.5 hours to walk the six km (five to six hours round-trip). The path climbs through the trees, drops to a stream and waterfall, and again climbs to Moir Hill lookout, where great views of Hauraki Gulf await you. As an alternate return route, the track meanders back through Pohuehue Scenic Reserve.

WARKWORTH AND VICINITY

Many small family orchards grow to the south of this charming fishing village along the upper tidal reaches of the Mahurangi River (freshly picked fruit—cheaper than in town—beckons from roadside stalls), with colonial-style architecture and numerous cafés and restaurants. Warkworth (pop. 2,500) is the main town between Auckland, 70 km (43 mi) south, and Whangarei, and well worth a side trip off the main highway before you continue north.

Warkworth and District Museum

Inside this surprisingly large museum (Tudor Collins Dr., 09/425-7093; summer daily 9 A.M.–4 P.M., the rest of the year 9 A.M.–3 P.M.; adult $6, child $1) you'll find stacks of information on local history, and every nook and cranny is crammed with useful objects and curios from the past. Outside is a beautiful half-hectare (one-acre) park containing fine kauri trees—check out the two giant ones near the museum. The McKinney Kauri is 800 years old, and reaches a mere 11.89 meters (39 ft) at the first limb. The museum is accessed from the south end of town; take McKinney Road off Highway 1, turn right on Thompson Road, and follow signs.

Other Sights

SheepWorld Farm & Nature Park (09/425-7444; adult $16.50, child $7) lies four km (2.5 mi) north of town along Highway 1. The highlight of a visit is the Dog & Sheep Show (daily at 11 A.M. and 2 P.M.) that includes sheepshearing, dogs demonstrating their roundup skills, and the opportunity to bottle-feed baby lambs. Part of the four-hectare (ten-acre) complex is the Black Sheep Café, with lots of outdoor tables, a country-style store stocked with a huge collection of wool and sheepskin products, and a small petting zoo.

The **Honey Centre** on the main highway south of town at Perry Road (09/425-80039; daily 9 A.M.–5 P.M.) has the country's largest bee observatory, allowing visitors to view tens of thousands of bees hard at work making honey. There's free honey tasting and, naturally, a gift shop stocked with a wide variety of honey-related products, including royal jelly.

As early as the 1860s, Nathaniel Wilson

NORTHLAND

and his sons began to manufacture the first "Portland Cement" made in New Zealand. Abandoned in 1929, the ruins of the **Wilson Cement Works** (Wilson Rd.) are open to the public, with grand plans for an interpretive center. Currently, the riverside site is most popular for swimming, with a grassed area shaded by trees a good picnic spot.

Practicalities

Within walking distance of downtown and the river is **Walton Park Motor Lodge** (2 Walton Ave., 09/425-8149, www.waltonpark.co.nz; $105–130 s or d), where each of the spacious units has basic cooking facilities, including a microwave. Other facilities include a swimming pool, guest laundry, and restaurant offering delicious char-grilled dishes for $24–34. Take the road to Snells Beach from Warkworth and you'll eventually come to the appealing whitewashed homestead of **Mahurangi Lodge** (416 Mahurangi East Rd., 09/425-5465, www.pacificviewslodge.co.nz; $50–60 s, $80–90 d). The bed-and-breakfast, perched atop a small hill, has a sweeping verandah with great views of the surrounding lush countryside and distant ocean beaches. The two least expensive guest rooms (there are four rooms total) share a bathroom. The lodge is located around 11 km (seven mi) from Warkworth. In a rural setting above Snells Beach, the faux Tudor **Salty Dog Inn** (09/425-5588, www.saltydoginn.co.nz; from $105 s or d) provides 14 spacious and modern units, each with a king-size bed and writing desk. The in-house restaurant (daily for dinner) offers a creative menu of innovative dishes, such as pumpkin fritters ($12) for a starter, followed by lamb smothered in an apricot curry glaze with roast potato ($27) for a main.

Park by the river in downtown Warkworth, where you'll find a number of good little cafés close by. My favorite of these is **Ducks Crossing Café** (Kapanui St., 09/425-9940; daily 8 A.M.–4 P.M.), which has a homely ambience and filling lunches for $10. **Warkworth Information Centre** is downtown (1 Baxter St., 09/425-9081; Mon.–Fri. 8:30 A.M.–5 P.M., Sat.–Sun. 9 A.M.–4 P.M.).

KAWAU ISLAND

Sandspit Wharf, 6.5 km (four km) from Warkworth, is the place to catch ferries and cruise boats to Kawau Island, a delightful spot with 300 residents and a number of sandy beaches. Kawau Island was the home of Sir George Grey, governor of New Zealand 1845–1853 and 1861–1867. His residence, elegant **Mansion House,** has been restored to its former glory. Of particular note is the surrounding garden, which is filled with exotic species collected by Grey from around the world. Although most of the island is privately owned, you can walk across the lush farmland, discover small sheltered bays, and take in all the wildlife—or refresh yourself at the tea kiosk (lunches available in summer). Along with many bird species, four species of wallaby introduced by Sir Grey in 1870 continue to dominate the animal life. At the historic home, **Mansion House Café** (09/422-8903) is open for lunch through the summer holidays and on weekends October through early June, but the island has no other services.

Reubens (09/425-8006 or 0800/888-006) has regular ferries departing from Sandspit five times daily (more often during summer), taking 50 minutes to reach Mansion House Bay (adult $38, child $20).

WARKWORTH TO WHANGAREI
Dome Forest Walkway

This track, signposted on Highway 1 between Warkworth and Wellsford, climbs through Dome Forest to the Dome, a flat-topped mountain. At 336 meters (1,102 ft) it's one of the highest peaks in the area, and has great views of Hauraki Gulf. The path to the summit takes an hour; on to Waiwhiu Kauri Grove takes another 30 minutes. The path is well marked (look for the white markings on the tree trunks). Steps have been cut in the steepest sections, but the track itself remains quite steep and gets pretty slippery when wet. Ascend to Highway 1 along the same route.

A Coastal Detour

As an alternative to Highway 1 north from Warkworth, consider taking a detour east through **Leigh** and **Pakiri Beach,** rejoining the highway at Wellsford. Eight km (five mi) from the highway, Takatu Road spurs southeast along the **Takatu Peninsula.**

Along the way, the understated luxury of **Sandpiper Lodge** (Takatu Rd., 09/422-7256, www.sandpiperlodge.co.nz; $175–350 s or d) makes for a wonderful overnight stop. Set on a two-hectare property on an estuary, it features a pool surrounded by native gardens, a restaurant, and a bar/lounge. Rooms in the main lodge open to the pool and gardens while the larger, more private chalets lie right on the estuary. Rates for include breakfast, but a better value is the American-plan overnight package.

Facing the open ocean, Pakiri Beach is a long, white sandy beach. **Pakiri Beach Holiday Park** (Rakiri River Rd., 09/422-6199, www.pakiriholidaypark.co.nz; camping $15, cabins from $25) has a beachfront location with a barbecue area, modern kitchen, and games room. The least expensive self-contained cottages are $75 s or d, or pay $125 for a beachfront cottage.

North from Wellsford

At **Mangawhai Heads,** a small resort town north of Wellsford, you'll find the head of a two-hour walk along the cliffs that provides spectacular views of the offshore islands. From Mangawhai Heads, the road continues north to **Waipu Cove Beach,** popular for fishing and swimming, and rejoins Highway 1 at **Waipu.**

Continuing north, not far from Ruakaka, is the turnoff to **Marsden Point Oil Refinery,** New Zealand's only oil refinery, which refines crude oil shipped in from the Middle East. Naturally, visitors may not enter the refinery, but from the top of Pilbrow's Hill (to the south of Waipu) you can clearly see its flare. At the Visitors Centre adjacent to the main entrance (Marsden Point Rd., Ruakaka, 09/432-8194; daily 10 A.M.–5 P.M.; free) you can view an intricate model of the refinery and a documentary.

NORTHLAND

Whangarei and Vicinity

Whangarei (pop. 46,000), 130 km (81 mi) north of Warkworth and 70 km (44 mi) south of Paihia, stands alone as the only city in Northland. Founded on the edge of an extremely deep and sheltered harbor, it quickly became a thriving port. To the Maori, the harbor was known as Teranga Paraoa (Where the Whales Run). Today the harbor is a mecca for yachties from around the world—many of the brochures describe the city as the "International Yachting Centre of the North Island." Whangarei's mild climate boasts about 2,000 sunshine hours a year, 1,600 mm (63 in) of rain, and temperatures ranging from 6° to 28°C (43° to 82°F) throughout the year—the average temperature is 19°C (66°F).

SIGHTS AND RECREATION
Town Basin Marina

A few blocks from downtown, Town Basin Marina is the tie-up point for yachts from around the world, which sail up the Hatea River to Whangarei and one of New Zealand's best deepwater anchorages. An area on the basin's south side has been landscaped with gardens, and paved walkways wind through gift shops, boutiques, and cafés with outdoor eating areas. An intriguing museum at the basin is **Claphams Clocks** (09/483-3993; daily 10 A.M.–5 P.M.; adult $8, senior $6, child $4), featuring an assortment of nearly 1,000 clocks and watches contributed by Mr. A. Clapham, who made

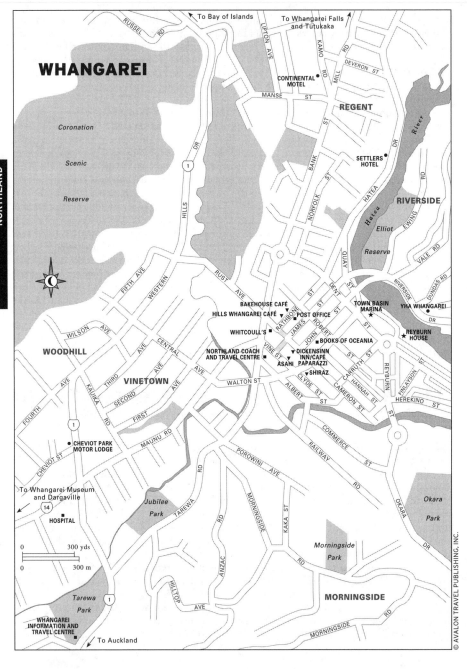

NORTHLAND

WHANGAREI

To Bay of Islands

To Whangarei Falls and Tutukaka

RUSSEL RD

LIPTON AVE

KAMO RD

MILL ST

DEVERON ST

CONTINENTAL MOTEL

MANSE ST

BANK ST

REGENT

SETTLERS HOTEL

NORFOLK ST

HATEA DR

Hatea River

RIVERSIDE

Coronation

Scenic

Reserve

HILLS DR

1

QUAY ST

Elliot

EWING RD

VALE RD

Reserve

RIVERSIDE DR

DUNDAS RD

FIFTH AVE

WESTERN

RUST AVE

DENT ST

ST

TOWN BASIN MARINA

YHA WHANGAREI

DR

BAKEHOUSE CAFÉ

HILLS WHANGAREI CAFÉ

RATHBONE ST

POST OFFICE

JAMES ST

ROBERT ST

REYBURN HOUSE

WILSON AVE

CENTRAL AVE

WHITCOULL'S

VINE ST

JOHN ST

BOOKS OF OCEANIA

REYBURN

DICKENSINN INN/CAFÉ

WOODHILL

NORTHLAND COACH AND TRAVEL CENTRE

ASAHI

PAPARAZZI

CARRUTH ST

FINLAYSON

THIRD AVE

VINETOWN

WALTON ST

SHIRAZ

CLYDE ST

HANNAH ST

HEREKINO ST

KAUKA

SECOND AVE

ALBERT ST

CAMERON ST

FIRST AVE

FOURTH AVE

1

COMMERCE ST

MAUNU RD

POROWINI AVE

RAILWAY RD

CHEVIOT PARK MOTOR LODGE

CHEVIOT ST

RD

OKARA

Okara Park

To Whangarei Museum and Dargaville

14

Jubilee Park

TAREWA RD

MORNINGSIDE

KAKA ST

HOSPITAL

RD

0   300 yds

0   300 m

Morningside Park

ANZAC

Tarewa Park

1

HILLTOP

AVE

MORNINGSIDE

WHANGAREI INFORMATION AND TRAVEL CENTRE

MORNINGSIDE RD

To Auckland

© AVALON TRAVEL PUBLISHING, INC.

many of them himself. In the courtyard out front is Australasia's largest sundial, with an interpretive panel describing how it works.

Along the river from the main concentration of shops is **Reyburn House** (Quay St., 09/438-3074; Tues.–Fri. 10 A.M.–4 P.M., Sat.–Sun. 1–4 P.M.; free), a kauri home dating to 1865 and now home to a gallery featuring the work of local artists.

Whangarei Museum and Heritage Park

This excellent museum (09/438-9630; daily 10 A.M.–4 P.M.; adult $10, child $5) is just a small part of a large complex that comprises a kiwi house, an old homestead, and 25-hectare (62-acre) grounds laced with hiking trails that lead to a stream and various waterfalls. The museum itself has a large number of Maori and European artifacts collected from throughout Northland, while **Clarke Homestead,** built in 1885, has been restored, with many of the rooms furnished as they would have been in that era. In the kiwi house, the natural cycle of day and night has been reversed so that visitors can watch these intriguing nocturnal creatures feeding and moving around at a decent hour. During the summer, local volunteers put on "live days" every second Sunday, operating a steam engine and antique farm equipment. It's on Highway 14, four km (2.5 mi) west of Whangarei—follow signs out of town to Dargaville.

Whangarei Falls

These falls are a photographer's dream. They drop 26 meters (85 ft) into a deep green pool surrounded by bush, and numerous walkways allow views from above and below. A lookout is just below the main parking lot, or you can take the one-km (0.6-mi) trail that descends to the valley floor below the falls and then loops back around the far side of the river. On a hot summer day, the upper swimming hole, directly above the falls, is a hive of activity. Local children swing out on tree ropes, or dive from the top limbs of a tree into one of the deep holes, entertaining visitors with their

© ANDREW HEMPSTEAD

Whangarei Falls

audacity. Look for the falls on the outskirts of Whangarei in the suburb of Tikipunga, next to Ngunguru Road (buses run from downtown to Tikipunga).

Tutukaka and Vicinity

Continue beyond Whangarei Falls for 30 km (19 mi) and the road emerges at a beautiful stretch of the northern coastline. **Ngunguru,** the first town along the route, sits on the edge of the Ngunguru River. A sandy beach, lots of swimming and boating action, and many holiday homes give Ngunguru its vacation atmosphere.

Tutukaka is the hub for deep-sea fishing and diving. The **Tutukaka Club,** an arm of Whangarei Deep Sea Anglers Club based at Tutukaka Marina (09/434-3818, www .sportfishing.co.nz), provides all the information on local fishing, diving, cruising, and boat chartering. The season for catching marlin, shark, or yellowtail tuna usually runs from mid-January through April, no license required. Charter boats cost $700–1,000 per day. If you're by yourself, the club tries to hook you up with a group, lowering the cost to as little as $200 per person. Line fishing, as part of a group, costs about $70 per person per day. For spectacular views of the coastline with its irresistible bays, colorful sailing boats, and shell-studded beaches, follow Tutukaka Block Road up to Tutukaka Heads.

Continuing north, the holiday town of **Matapouri** has a long, white sandy beach, calm water (perfect for swimming and snorkeling), and several other small and more private beaches—reached by wading around the rocks at the northern end. At the back of the third small beach you'll find a trail (take shoes or sandals) that passes through a rock tunnel to emerge at a beautiful cove with good snorkeling potential. Sometimes in summer the waters off Matapouri Beach become thick with plankton; local swimmers don't seem to mind, but it's a rare and unforgettable sensation to swim unexpectedly into the thick, jellylike substance when the water appears to be clear.

Around the next headland is **Sandy Bay.**

Keep your eyes peeled for the lookout and great views at Whale Bay Reserve. An easily followed cliffside trail leads from the lookout to the right. Passing through exotic natural bush and groves of *pohutukawa* trees, the trail leads down the cliffs and emerges at beautiful Whale Bay Beach. The walk from the car park to this fairly isolated beach takes about 20 minutes, but if you suffer from hay-fever allergies, this walk can be miserable in summer. After passing the road to Sandy Bay (known for good surfing—it usually boasts surfable waves when none of the other beaches do), the road swoops back inland toward Hikurangi, where it rejoins Highway 1, 18 km (11 mi) north of Whangarei.

Hiking

Several scenic reserves dot the Whangarei area. **Parahaki Scenic Reserve** contains Parahaki Mountain, with good bush walks and great views of Whangarei from its 241-meter (791-ft) summit. Two of the clearly marked walks originate from Mair Park, at the western foot of Parahaki, the third from Dundas Road at the southern foot. All converge at the summit, where the tall column of the Parahaki War Memorial stands. Ross Track features a gold mine near the summit and a waterfall near the base. About a 10-minute walk from Dundas Road (close to the Whangarei Hostel), the track takes about 40 minutes each way. Drummond Track takes about the same time to complete—it's pretty steep and features a giant kauri tree along a short sidetrack, one-third of the way down. Dobbie Track starts at Dobbie Park and takes about 50 minutes to the summit, featuring many varied views of Whangarei. On all the walks, Maori pits and old gum-digging workings add to the scenery. Regenerating kauri trees and a variety of ferns (from the tiny crepe and kidney ferns to the large tree ferns) abound along the tracks. Pick up the free *Whangarei Walks* pamphlet—a guide to Scenic Reserves and Walkways in the Whangarei district, available from the information center.

A. H. Reed Memorial Kauri Park, in the suburb of Tikipunga about five km (three mi) from downtown next to Whareora Road, is an appealing little park with a variety of trees and a choice of several paths; see the surviving remnant of a kauri forest, Wai Koromiko Stream, and a waterfall.

ACCOMMODATIONS AND CAMPING

Whangarei has about 20 hotels and motels, most of which lie along the main highway through town. The least expensive rooms start at around $80, but for a few extra bucks, there are several really nice places to stay.

Under $50

The small **Whangarei YHA** (52 Punga Grove Ave., 09/438-8954, www.yha.co.nz; dorm bed $24, twin $26) is centrally located on a hill overlooking the Hatea River and an easy five-minute walk from Town Basin. The hostel has only 27 beds, but facilities are good, including a pleasant outdoor area with a barbecue. The hosts rent bicycles and can show the way to all the local attractions.

Whangarei Falls Holiday Park (Whangarei-Tutukaka Rd., 09/437-0609 or 0800/227-222, www.whangareifalls.co.nz) is a pleasant 200-meter (656-ft) walk from Whangarei Falls, about five km (3.1 mi) northeast of town. Tent and caravan sites are $13 per person. Heated cabins cost from $20 s or d. Enjoy the spa or small outdoor pool, participate in the barbecues held on some summer nights, and check your Internet at the front-desk terminal.

$50-100

The **Continental Motel** (67 Kamo Rd., 09/437-6359 or 0800/457-634, www.continentalmotel.co.nz; $80–100 s or d) offers less expensive rates than the town's other motels and a swimming pool to complement 16 spacious units.

$100-150

Cheviot Park Motor Lodge (corner of Western Hills Dr. and Cheviot St., 09/438-2341 or 0508/243-846, www.cheviot-park.co.nz; $100–130 s or d) features 15 slightly-better-than-stan-

dard units, each with a kitchen, as well as a pool, spa, and barbecue area. And although it's on the main road, a high fence surrounds the property, affording privacy. Breakfast can be delivered to your room and a dining room opens for dinner Monday–Thursday.

Another choice just out of town is the **Settlers Hotel** (61 Hatea Dr., 09/438-2699 or 0800/666-662, www.settlershotel.co.nz; $70–140 s, $100–140 d), set among exotic gardens beside the Hatea River. The least expensive rooms are older, but the pool, patio, and barbecue area are nice touches. The in-house restaurant is open daily for breakfast and dinner, and for a Sunday brunch popular with the locals.

$150-200

If you feel like a splurge and fancy a self-contained unit with either a fantastic ocean or harbor view and use of a pool, spa, and private beach, head for 〖 **Pacific Rendezvous** (09/434-3847 or 0800/999-800, www.ocean resort.co.nz), spread over a high headland at Tutukaka, 29 km (18 mi) from Whangarei. This stretch of coast holds many accommodations, but this is by far the best. Rates range from $165 for a one-bedroom unit to $220 for a three-bedroom unit with ocean views. All are fully self-contained; other resort features include a tennis court and putting green. To get there from Whangarei, drive two km (1 mi) beyond Ngunguru, take the Tutukaka Block Road, then turn onto Motel Road and follow it to the end.

FOOD

You'll find many cafés offering good lunches and snacks at any time of the day throughout downtown.

For an inexpensive, no-frills cooked breakfast, make your way downtown to the **Bakehouse Cafe** (21 Rathbone St., 09/438-8188; Mon.–Sat. 7 A.M.–4:30 P.M.). The rest of the day, toasted sandwiches are from $3 and burgers max out at $6. A couple of doors up is **Hills Whangarei Café** (13 Rathbone St., 09/438-8761; Mon.–Fri. 7 A.M.–3 P.M.,

Sat. 8 A.M.–5 P.M.), a step up in style and substance, with breakfasts like strawberry pancakes topped with chocolate sauce ($12) and lunches that include lamb salad with papadams ($15).

Dickens Inn (corner of Cameron St. and Quality St. Mall, 09/430-0406; daily from 8 A.M.) is a Tudor-style English restaurant with a number of dining areas. The menu offers no real surprises—instead you get hearty home-style cooking in a welcoming atmosphere. The side of the Dickens Inn opens to a cobbled walkway where you'll find **Café Paparazzi** (Quality St. Mall, 09/438-2961; Mon.–Sat. 8 A.M.–4 P.M.), a Mediterranean-style café where the outdoor tables are covered by large umbrellas and the walls adorned by colorful murals. It'll cost around $20 for the salmon and prosciutto Caesar salad with a honey and banana smoothie on the side. At the back of the walkway beside the Dickens Inn, the modern look of **Asahi** (corner of Vine and Quality Sts., 09/430-3005; daily 11 A.M.–3 P.M. and from 5 P.M.) belies an inexpensive and traditional menu of Japanese favorites.

A couple of blocks east of the main downtown concentration of eateries, **Shiraz** (58 Walton St., 09/438-3112; Mon.–Sat. 11 A.M.–2 P.M., daily from 5 P.M.) is a bright space filled with the smells of traditional Indian cooking (dinner mains $12–20).

A number of stylish eateries can be found beside **Town Basin Marina,** overlooking a harbor and surrounded by landscaped gardens. Delectable fresh seafood is the highlight at **(¢ Gybe** (Town Basin Marina, Quay St., 09/430-0406; Mon.–Fri. 9 A.M.–3 P.M., Sat.–Sun. 11 A.M.–3 P.M., and daily from 5 P.M.), a two-story restaurant surrounded by Federation-style gingerbread trim. The mussels steamed Thai-style in coconut cream ($16) are an extravagant starter, while "fish of the day" ($30) is always a reliable choice for a main. Breakfast is also notable, especially the cinnamon-dusted French toast ($11.50). The best views are from the balcony.

Reva's on the Waterfront (Town Basin Marina, Quay St., 09/438-8969) also commands fine harbor views, especially tables along the verandah. The blackboard menu features pizza (from $12), salads, and seafood dishes ($17–26).

Overlooking the marina from the north side of the river is **Vinyl Cafe** (Vale Rd., 09/438-8105; Tues.–Fri. 5:30–9 P.M., Sat.–Sun. 9 A.M.–3 P.M. and 4–9 P.M.), which offers something for all tastes and budgets (think spaghetti and meatballs for $11 or braised venison with blueberry jus for $30) in a welcoming atmosphere.

PRACTICALITIES
Information
As you enter town from the south on Highway 1, make a stop at **Whangarei Information & Travel Centre** (92 Otaika Rd., Tarewa Park, 09/438-1079, www.whangareinz.org .nz; Mon.–Fri. 8:30 A.M.–5 P.M., Sat.–Sun. 9:30 A.M.–4:30 P.M.). The center has an interesting little gift shop and a café.

Whitcoull's (The Strand, Cameron St., 09/438-0819) has the usual selection of new books, but head to **Books of Oceania** (John St., 09/438-8248) and you'll find yourself surrounded by shelves chock-full of used books of local interest.

Services
Whangarei's main post office is at 16 Rathbone Street. **Surf in the City** (25 Bank St., 09/430-3540) has inexpensive Internet access. **James St. Laundromat** (66 James St., 09/430-0520) is in the heart of downtown.

Whangarei Area Hospital (09/430-4100) is on Hospital Road. **Primecare Medical Centre** (12 Kensington Ave., 09/437-9070) has a doctor on duty 24 hours daily. Next door is **Kensington Pharmacy** (09/437-3722).

Getting There and Around
It's a short 35-minute hop with **Air New Zealand** (0800/800-737, www.airnew zealand.com) from Auckland to Whangarei, but as the Auckland airport is on the south side of the city and it's only a 2.5-hour drive from downtown, flying is not that practical.

Northland Coach and Travel Centre (3 Bank St., 09/438-3206) is a stop for both **Intercity** (09/438-2653, www.intercitycoach.co.nz) and **Northliner** (www.northliner.co.nz) buses.
 Whangarei Bus (09/438-6005) charges $2–3 per sector along routes that fan out from Rose Street (by the Grand Hotel) to the suburbs and Whangarei Falls. The main car rental agencies in Whangarei are **Avis** (09/438-2929), **Budget** (09/438-7292), and **Hertz** (09/438-9790). Local taxis are operated by **Kiwi Cabs** (09/420-2299).

WHANGAREI TO THE BAY OF ISLANDS

From Whangarei, it's 70 km (44 mi) north to Paihia, gateway to the Bay of Islands.

To Paihia or Russell?

At Kawakawa, Highway 10 spurs northeast to Paihia and the Bay of Islands. If you're traveling by vehicle, it's best to decide whether to stay in Paihia or Russell before you get toOpua, where the vehicular ferry departs for Russell. It's less hassle and cheaper to leave the car in Paihia, and the passenger ferry across to Russell is short, enjoyable, and frequent. Many of the attractions in Russell are within walking distance of the ferry. However, if you want to explore Russell by road, the car ferry leaves from Opua (a 15-minute drive south of Paihia), and crosses the Veronica Channel to Okiato, from where Russell is a 10-minute drive to the north. The trip costs $17 round-trip per vehicle and driver, plus $2 per passenger. The service runs daily 7 A.M.–10 P.M. It's also possible to drive all the way from Highway 1 to Russell, avoiding the ferry altogether, but the access road, which spurs off Highway 1 at Whakapara, is unpaved, winding, and very slow going.

NORTHLAND

Bay of Islands

The Bay of Islands is one of New Zealand's most beautiful and historic areas. Situated 257 km (160 mi) north of Auckland (allow five hours by road), its irregular coastline and 144 islands are lapped by warm aquamarine waters and bathed in sunshine year-round. The mild climate of the "Winterless North" and the calm waters have made the area a sailor's paradise ever since its discovery by Captain James Cook in the 18th century. Quiet coves, soft sandy beaches, sparkling waters, and island groves of *pohutukawa* trees abound. For excitement there's the challenge of deep-sea fishing for a magnificent marlin or shark, or the chance to dive into a colorful submarine habitat.
 The main population center is **Paihia,** 70 km (44 mi) north of Whangarei and the base for cruises and fishing and diving trips, as well as a large number of accommodations and restaurants. Nearby is **Waitangi,** historically important for the signing of the Treaty of Waitangi. Across the bay from Paihia is

Russell. This delightful village is on the mainland, but road access is roundabout; most visitors arrive by passenger ferry from Paihia. **Kerikeri,** a citrus center and home to many artists and craftspeople, is a short drive from Paihia.

HISTORY
First Contacts

Captain Cook named the Bay of Islands in 1769. At that time, it was inhabited by a large Maori population, whose *pa* (fortified dwellings) studded the bay. Captain Cook's ship, the *Endeavour,* was met by a small fleet of canoes navigated by fearless warriors who came to gaze in astonishment at the huge "winged canoe." The first meeting between European and Maori was friendly; however, this changed three years later when a series of blunders by the French explorer Marion Du Fresne led to his murder by the local tribe, and in retaliation some 250 Maori were slain.

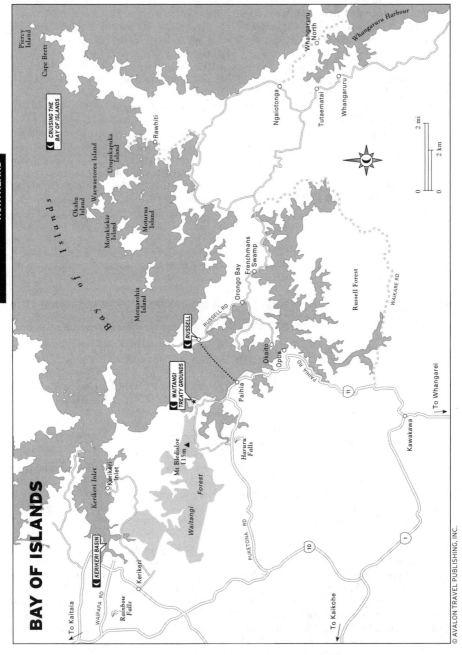

BAY OF ISLANDS

To Kaitaia

KERIKERI BASIN

Rainbow Falls

WAIPAPA RD

Kerikeri

PUKETONA RD

To Kaikohe

Waitangi Forest

Mt Bledisloe 115m

Harura Falls

WAITANGI TREATY GROUNDS

Paihia

Opua

Okaito

RUSSELL

Orongo Bay

RUSSELL RD

Frenchmans Swamp

Russell Forest

WAIKARE RD

PAIHIA RD

11

Kawakawa

1

10

To Whangarei

Kerikeri Inlet

Bay of Islands

Moturohia Island

Motuarohia Island

Motukiekie Island

Moturua Island

Okahu Island

Waewaetorea Island

Urupukapuka Island

CRUISING THE BAY OF ISLANDS

Rawhiti

Cape Brett

Piercy Island

Ngaiotonga

Tutaematai

Whangaruru North

Whangaruru

Whangaruru Harbour

2 mi

2 km

0

0

© AVALON TRAVEL PUBLISHING, INC.

NORTHLAND

Trade Center

By the end of the 18th century, the Bay of Islands had become a thriving trade center, with the whalers, timber-seekers, and traders calling in at Kororareka (present-day Russell) for supplies as well as the proverbial wine, women, and song. The migratory path of whales, unfortunately close to the northern coastline, contributed to their plunder. The tall, straight kauri trees that fringed the bay and lowlands were quickly depleted for ship masts or export to Sydney. Traders also brought predators, disease, and massive exploitation to New Zealand. In the early 19th century many missionaries arrived, and their Christian influence helped end Maori warfare.

Treaty of Waitangi

There was considerable foreign interest in New Zealand by 1831 and, in fear of take-over, a group of local Maori chiefs asked Britain for protection. In February 1840, with the ceremonial signing of the Treaty of Waitangi, New Zealand became a British colony. Within the next year, New Zealand's "capital" was set up at Okiato and named Russell, but it was soon decided that the capital should be moved to the more desirable site of Auckland. The name Russell was then transferred to the town of Kororareka, in hopes that the new name would give the "Hellhole of the Pacific" a new image.

NORTHLAND

BAY OF ISLANDS MARITIME AND HISTORIC PARK

This mostly undeveloped park, comprising about 40 sites scattered throughout the Bay of Islands, protects both scenic and historic areas. The exception to this noncommercial paradise is **Urupukapuka Island,** where Fullers makes a regular stop on most of its cruises. Here you'll find an undersea "submarine" (adult $12, child $6) and the **Zane Grey Café** (in the 1920s American author Zane Grey made the island a base for his game-fishing expeditions). A seven-km (4.3-mi/three-hour) hiking trail roughly circles the otherwise untainted island, passing secluded beaches, archeological sites, and several campgrounds.

Cape Brett (Rakaumangamanga) scenic reserve was named by Captain Cook. A 17.5-km (11-mi) track, starting at Oke Bay on Rawhiti Road, takes seven to eight hours. Classified as a hard tramp, it's recommended only for those with above-average fitness and experience (sea access is possible in calm conditions). The old lighthouse on the point was built in 1909, and the lighthouse keeper's cottage has been converted into a hut that can sleep 12, with toilet and water.

Motukawanui (Big Cavalli Island) is a large island reserve, known for its scenic track (1.5 hours) covering the length of the island. The island hut has eight bunks, a toilet, and fresh water.

Impressive **Ranfurly Bay Reserve,** at the entrance to Whangaroa Harbour, is known for rugged volcanic rock formations. The Ranfurly Bay hut provides 12 bunks, toilets, and water, and deepwater anchorage in the bay. You can hike three well-marked tracks from the bay, each providing outstanding harbor views.

PARK PRACTICALITIES

The only practical way to travel to and around the park is by boat. The cruises detailed under *Recreation* in the *Bay of Islands* section of this chapter visit the more popular spots, such as Urupukapuka Island and Cape Brett, with Fullers offering the option of spending a full day on Urupukapuka.

The best source of park information is the **Russell Visitor Centre** (The Strand, Russell, 09/403-9005; summer daily 9 A.M.–5 P.M., the rest of the year Mon.-Fri. 9 A.M.–4:30 P.M.), where you'll find interesting displays and an excellent audiovisual on New Zealand's early history. The staff provides hordes of information (including the brochure *Bay of Islands Walks*), issues camping and hut permits, and offers a list of charter operators.

RECREATION

The *real* Bay of Islands—a remote ocean wilderness accessible only by water—is beyond the region's main towns of Paihia, Russell, and Kerikeri. Along with all the services you'll need for an overnight stay, these three towns do each have their own charm, and each is covered separately later in this chapter.

◖ Cruising the Bay of Islands

Most day trips depart from in front of the Maritime Building in Paihia, but also make pickups in Russell.

Operated by **Fullers** (09/402-7421, www.fboi.co.nz), the Best of the Bay Super Cruise departs Paihia daily at 10 A.M. and Russell at 10:10 A.M., and cruises leisurely around many of the beautiful islands in the bay, the captain's commentary keeping passengers informed and amused. Following a historic route known as the Cream Trip (it once delivered cream, hence the name), the boat makes short stops at many of the islands to deliver mail and groceries to the farmers and island-caretakers scattered around the bay. The cruise also includes Cape Brett, Motukokako Island, and Cathedral Cave, and, weather permitting, the boat passes through the famous "Hole in the Rock." The cost is adult $75, child $38, including a one-hour stop for lunch at picturesque Otehei Bay on Urupukapuka Island (an optional submarine cruise is $12). Lunch itself is extra—sandwiches, filled rolls, lamb burgers, snacks, and ice cream are available—or bring your own. After lunch there's time for a quick swim or a walk up the hill for good views. This is just one of many variations offered by Fullers. If you feel like being more active (or maybe just lying on a remote beach for the day), pay for transfers to Otehei Bay (adult $35, child $18) and spend the day exploring the island.

King's Dolphin Cruises and Tours (09/402-8288, www.kings-tours.co.nz) provides a similar itinerary, with the bonus of boom-netting and swimming with dolphins included in the base cost (adult $99, child $55). This six-hour trip departs daily from Paihia (10 A.M.) and

Russell (10:10 A.M. Kings also operates *Mack Attack* (adult $70, child $35)—a 30-passenger high-speed catamaran powered by twin 600-horsepower engines—to Hole in the Rock. The round trip takes just 90 minutes.

The most unusual and stylish way to tour the bay is onboard the stunning **R. Tucker Thompson** (09/402-8430 or 0800/882-537, www.tucker.co.nz), a gaff-rigged square topsail schooner that has circumnavigated the world, taken part in Australia's Bicentenary as one of the tall ships reenacting the Australian First Fleet voyage, and starred in the TV series *Adventurer*. Take part in the sailing or just relax; you'll stop at an island (with time for swimming) and savor a barbecue lunch and then afternoon tea. Departing Russell at 10 A.M., the relaxing trip is six to seven hours long. Take a swimsuit, towel, sunblock, warm jacket, and lunch. The cost of the six-hour summer-only trip is adult $110, child $55.

Skippered by round-the-world sailor Vanessa McKay, the **Carino** (09/402-8040) is a 50-foot catamaran that departs Paihia on regularly scheduled trips through the Bay of Islands. Go day sailing (eight hours; adult $90, child $50), which includes morning and afternoon tea, fishing and snorkeling gear, swimming with dolphins, sailing lessons, and barbecue lunch on a deserted beach.

For the sailing enthusiast or would-be sailing enthusiast, **Great Escape Yacht Charters** (09/402-7143, www.greatescape.co.nz) provides two- to three-berth yachts complete with outboard auxiliary, stove, and cooking equipment. The cost is from $250 per day, or pay $590 for two day's instruction plus a three-day bareboat charter.

Fishing

The Bay of Islands is New Zealand's most popular game-fishing ground, and fishing is a year-round activity. Some say the best game fishing is in February and March, others claim June and July, but keep in mind that plenty of "big ones" are also caught in January, April, and May. Striped, blue, and black marlin; mako, thresher, blue, and hammerhead sharks;

yellowfin tuna; and yellowtail (or kingfish) cruise the waters in abundance. The most prolific big-game fish is the striped marlin; the best months are December–June. For sharks, the best time is November–May, and for tuna, it's December–March. Yellowtail are caught year-round but are mainly fished during June and July. But it's not all big-game fishing fun. Plenty of light-tackle experiences are available from smaller boats.

Paihia Wharf is a hub of deep-sea fishing activity. This town is home base to most of the local game-fishing boats, many of which can be booked through **Pacific Promotions** (09/433-9981, www.fishingpro.co.nz). A solo game-fishing charter starts at $900 per day, a share charter (maximum four people) starts at $300 per person. Non-angling passengers can go along to watch the action for considerably less.

The **Bay of Islands Swordfish Club** (09/403-7857, www.swordfish.co.nz) at both the Russell and Paihia waterfronts hosts many of the big-game fishing tournaments. Tournaments are plentiful from Tutukaka to the Bay of Islands January–June. Club officials perform the weigh-ins and record the vitals whenever a game fish is brought in. You can buy day membership for $15 before going fishing, which includes an official weigh-in and certificate and eligibility for most club trophies. Look for a crowd gathering around either Russell or Paihia wharfs, as it's likely to mean they're bringing in a magnificent game fish for a weigh-in. Records of these weigh-ins are written on blackboards by 4 P.M. daily, and displayed at both wharves. There's a good licensed restaurant at the Russell club for members, affiliated and kindred members from an overseas club, and guests of members.

Sea Kayaking

If you've always wanted to try sea kayaking, contact **Coastal Kayakers** (09/402-8105, www.coastalkayakers.co.nz). This company offers two options: a guided day trip (instruction included) with highlights that include a paddle to a deserted island, under Haruru Falls (helmet thoughtfully provided), and through a flooded mangrove forest for $75; or you can just rent a sea kayak for $10 per hour or $40 per day.

Diving

A diving hot spot was created on December 13, 1987, when the Greenpeace flagship *Rainbow Warrior* settled in 25 meters of water off the Cavalli Islands, south of the entrance to the Bay of Islands. This ship, used by Greenpeace for environmental crusades around the globe, was bombed in 1985 in Auckland Harbour by French intelligence officers trying to prevent Greenpeace from upsetting France's nuclear testing on remote atolls in the South Pacific Ocean. It was later moved north to create an artificial reef; it's now covered in brightly colored marinelife and is a feeding ground for a variety of fish. **Paihia Dive and Fishing** (09/402-7551; Mon., Wed., and Sat., departs 8:30 A.M.; $175 per person), based in Paihia, offers trips to the wreck. The cost includes the boat ride, all equipment, and two dives.

PAIHIA AND WAITANGI

Paihia (pop. 7,000) is the commercial hub of the Bay of Islands—its streets are lined with tour operators, accommodations, and restaurants. Opposite downtown is **Paihia Wharf,** the departure point for cruises, but also a great place to soak up the Bay of Islands' vacation atmosphere.

From Paihia, continue north along the waterfront to the first intersection and go straight ahead toward Waitangi (if you turn left you'll reach Haruru Falls) and one of New Zealand's most historically important sights.

◖ Waitangi Treaty Grounds

Waitangi (09/402-7437; daily 9 A.M.–5 P.M.; adult $12, child free) is the place to absorb New Zealand history and to witness the birthplace of the nation as we know it today. In the Treaty House on February 6, 1840, the Treaty of Waitangi was signed, whereby the Maori surrendered the government of their country to Queen Victoria of Britain in return for protection and "the rights and privileges of British subjects." On

© ANDREW HEMPSTEAD

Treaty House, Waitangi Treaty Grounds

first entering this historic park, don't miss the excellent audiovisual show in the Visitor Centre, then stroll through the beautifully kept grounds to the **Treaty House.** Originally designed as a home for British resident James Busby (1832–1840), drafter of the treaty, the house stands in its original condition and is open to the public. Near the Treaty House stands the intricately carved and highly decorated *Whare Runanga* (Maori Meeting House), where the local Maori discussed issues, entertained neighboring tribes, and gathered for instruction, storytelling, or games. The **Maori War Canoe,** on the other side of the reserve, is known to the Maori as *Ngatokimatawhaorua* (The Adzes Which Shaped It Twice) and is adorned with carvings, shells, and feathers. An amazing 35 meters (115 ft) in length, carved from three mighty kauri trees, it has the capacity to carry a crew of 80, plus passengers. If you're planning a visit to this area early in February, check out the annual local celebrations (commemorating the signing of the treaty; the canoe is regularly launched on these occasions.

Even if you're not a history buff, it's worth paying extra (adult $22, child $5, includes general admission) for a one-hour guided tour. Led by a Maori interpreter, these tours go beyond the interpretive panels to bring the grounds and their history to life. Adding further to the experience is **Nga Puawai o Waitangi** (Oct.–Apr. four times daily; adult $12, child $5), a cultural performance that includes the famous *haka*.

Mount Bledisloe

This mountain marks the northwest boundary of Waitangi Treaty Grounds and is an excellent vantage point. The summit lookout (115 meters/380 ft), a short walk from the parking lot, gives one of the best panoramic views of the Bay of Islands. Follow the road for 3.2 km (two mi) beyond the reserve entrance (passing the rolling fairways of scenic Waitangi Golf Club; 09/402-7713; $45).

For an alternate route back to Paihia, turn left on Haruru Falls Road to Haruru Falls, and left again at the main road (Puketona Rd.), which takes you back to Paihia.

Accommodations and Camping

Paihia has one of New Zealand's biggest concentrations of accommodations—over 40 motels and a dozen backpacker lodges within walking distance of the downtown waterfront.

Backpackers are well catered for at Paihia. **(Peppertree Lodge** (15 Kings Rd., 09/402-6122, www.peppertree.co.nz; dorm $25, $65–68 s or d) is one of the best. It has a large patio and barbecue area, lounge and deck, a quiet area stocked with books, modern kitchen, Internet access, laundry, and bikes and kayaks (no charge). Nearby, the popular **Bay Adventurer** (26 Kings Rd., 09/402-5162 or 0800/112-127, www.bayadventurer.co.nz; dorm $25, $75–115 s or d) is a purpose-built facility complete with a pool and barbecue area set in a tropical garden, a spa, a lounge equipped with a DVD player, Internet access, and a large modern kitchen.

Motels in Paihia are among the most expensive in the country, and through January prices are even higher than "high season." Try the **Dolphin Motel** (69 Williams Rd., 09/402-8170, www.dolphinmotel.co.nz; $125 s, $135 d), where there are 11 self-contained rooms close to the center of town. On the same street is **Aarangi Tui Motel** (16 Williams Rd., 09/402-7496 or 0800/453-354 from $140 s or d), with one- and two-bedroom units facing a garden area.

Aloha Garden Resort Hotel (36 Seaview Rd., 09/402-7540 or 0800/425-642, www.aloha.co.nz) is set on a two-hectare (five-acre) property complete with a pool and gardens dotted with palm trees. All rooms have cooking facilities, including the smaller studio units with a vaguely nautical theme ($149 s or d) and one-bedroom poolside suites ($189 s or d). Aloha Garden also has wireless Internet.

Like Aloha Garden, **Paihia Pacific Resort Hotel** (27 Kings Rd., 09/402-8221 or 0800/744-442, www.paihiapacific.co.nz; $185–240 s or d) is a step above the regular motels in quality, but only a few dollars more. Here, the 35 pastel-themed units open to a courtyard filled with greenery and with a small pool and spa. Other facilities include a restaurant, laundry, and tennis court.

Across the road from the beach, **(Paihia Beach Resort & Spa** (Marsden Rd., 09/402-6140 or 0800/870-111, www.paihiabeach.co.nz) is one of the Bay of Islands' premier accommodations. No expense has been spared in furnishing the luxurious units, each of which has cooking facilities and a large private balcony offering spectacular water views. Raised above street level for extra privacy are a large heated saltwater pool and spa surrounded by stone decking. Rates start at $483 s or d inclusive of breakfast and one spa treatment.

Adjacent to Waitangi Treaty Grounds, **Copthorne Hotel and Resort** (Tau Henare Dr., 09/402-7411, www.millenniumhotels.com; from $240 s or d) is a sprawling waterfront hotel with all the facilities demanded by the tour-bus crowd, including a restaurant, pool, and room service. Check the website for discounted rates that make this place decent value.

Of the several **holiday parks** in the Paihia area, none are downtown. Winning my vote as the most friendly, **Twin Pines Tourist Park** (09/402-7322, www.twinpines.co.nz; tenting $13 per person, powered sites $14 per person, cabins and self-contained flats $35–80 s, $60–d) is three km (two mi) out along Puketona Road. On the bank of the Waitangi River, adjacent to Haruru Falls (floodlit at night, and heard clearly throughout the campground), the camp has a couple of scenic walks close by (don't miss the steep three-minute bamboo trail from the camp down to the river with its built-in loveseat, view of the falls, and water access).

Beachside Holiday Park is 2.5 km from Paihia, on the road toward Opua and the car ferry to Russell (09/402-7678, www.beachside holiday.co.nz). Set on a private cove, it offers a store, game room, boat ramp and boats for rent, and the usual communal facilities. Rates for tent and caravan sites run from $25, older on-site vans are $55 s or d, and cabins start at $65.

Food

A string of cafés lines the main road through Paihia, all with water views, outdoor tables, and a beachy atmosphere that makes up for higher-priced food. Along this stretch,

(**One Hot Tuna** (Marsden Rd., 09/402-5276; daily from 10 A.M.) has fantastic fish-and-chips to go. Closer to the water is **Hansen's** (Maritime Building, Marsden Rd., 09/402-8526; daily from 6:30 A.M.), but Paihia's better restaurants are tucked out of sight from the main crush of tourists. At breakfast, **Tides** (Williams Rd., 09/402-7557; daily 7:30 A.M.–2:30 P.M. and from 6 P.M.) will keep you healthy with an oversized bowl of muesli, fruit, and yogurt ($10.50). The rest of the day, choose from dishes such as roast vegetarian lasagna ($12) or broiled lamb shanks ($22).

Among the backpacker lodges on the south side of Paihia, **Beachhouse** (16 Kings Rd., 09/402-7479; daily from 8 A.M.) has a casual South Pacific vibe, lots of outdoor tables, and occasional evening entertainment. The breakfast menu offers few surprises, but the Tribal Burger ($14), with grilled fish and mango, is delicious.

On the Waitangi Treaty Grounds and surrounded by native forest, (**Waikokopu Café** (Te Karuwha Pde., 09/402-6276; daily 9 A.M.–5 P.M.) is a world away from touristy Paihia, especially the outdoor tables with filtered ocean views. The charm extends to the menu of casual breakfasts and lunches, which changes seasonally, but includes local seafood and usually a Thai-style curry. (I had corn fritters with guacamole, salsa, and sour cream—delicious!)

On the south side of Paihia, **Only Seafood** (40 Marsden Rd., 09/402-6066; daily from 5 P.M.) is a casual seafood restaurant with mains from $25. Downstairs in the same building, **Bistro 40** (09/402-7444; daily from 6 P.M.) goes beyond just seafood and is more upscale.

Twin Pines Restaurant (Puketona Rd. at Haruru Falls, 09/402-7195; daily noon–3 P.M. and from 6 P.M.) is in an old mansion dating to the 1880s that was moved piece by piece from Auckland to the Bay of Islands. It offers Old World dining with an à la carte menu and daily blackboard specials (mains $22–28) that are traditional rather than creative, but well priced compared to downtown Paihia dining. The downstairs bar offers courtyard dining, a well-priced lunch menu, draft beer brewed in-house, and weekend entertainment.

Information and Services

Information Bay of Islands is beside the Maritime Building (Marsden Rd., 09/402-7345, www.fndc.govt.nz; daily 8 A.M.–5 P.M., in summer until 8 P.M.). This large facility has boards detailing all cruises and ferry sailings.

The post office is on Williams Road, just up from the waterfront. Around the corner is **Boots off Travellers Café** (Selwyn Rd., 09/402-6632), which has Internet access (at $9 per hour, it's not cheap). Also on Selwyn Road is a **medical center** (09/402-8407).

Getting There

Scheduled flights between Auckland and the Bay of Islands are operated by **Air New Zealand** (0800/737-000, www.airnewzealand.com) two to four times daily. The airport is inland from Paihia near Kerikeri (a $30 cab ride from Paihia). **Intercity** (09/623-1503, www.intercitycoach.co.nz) and **Northliner** (09/307-5873, www.northliner.co.nz) provide bus services between Auckland and Paihia via Whangarei for around $50 one way. All buses stop outside the Maritime Building.

(RUSSELL

Russell (pop. 1,100) is arguably New Zealand's most picturesque town. Nestled in a west-facing bay and reached by ferry, it lacks the commercialism of Paihia; the streets are lined with historic buildings and elegant cafés and restaurants.

Town Sights

Russell's many historic buildings are all within a couple of blocks of the ferry wharf, but you should start your sightseeing at **Russell Museum** (2 York St., 09/403-7701; daily 10 A.M.–4 P.M.; adult $5, child $1). This small museum contains all sorts of relics from early Kororareka (Russell's original name), a fortified Maori settlement, and gives insight into the people and the history of this colorful town. The highlight and pride of the museum is the seven-meter replica of Captain Cook's ship, the *Endeavour*, accurately reproduced down to the finest detail (Cook and his ship visited Russell in 1769).

© ANDREW HEMPSTEAD

Peaceful Russell is seemingly a world away from touristy Paihia, just across the bay.

Impressive **Pompallier** (The Strand, 09/403-9015; daily 9 A.M.–5 P.M.; adult $5) is a grand old mansion filled with historic relics. Toward the other end of The Strand stands the **police station.** Built in 1870, it has been a customs house, courthouse, and jail, and continues to serve as the Russell police station. Check out the fantastic Morton Bay Fig Tree (*Ficus macrophyllia*), with its intricately gnarled and patterned trunk, growing between the police station and the **Duke of Marlborough Hotel.** This old hotel is the proud holder of the first liquor license issued in New Zealand and was among the many "grog shops" of Russell's rowdy past. **Christ Church,** a couple of blocks back from The Strand, was built in 1847 and is the oldest standing church in New Zealand. It still bears cannonball and musket holes from the days of the Maori Wars, and the gravestones (and the stories they tell) in the cemetery are intriguing.

Flagstaff Hill

Also known as Maiki Hill, this historic landmark offers outstanding views of Russell and the Bay of Islands—great for getting oriented and watching all the boats cruising the bay. In the early 1840s, at the top of the hill, the British raised a flagstaff. Hone Heke, chief of the Ngapuhi, saw the flagstaff as a symbol of British authority (for which he had little respect). He and his warriors spent much of their time through the years chopping it down, despite British attempts to keep the flag flying. It wasn't until 1857 that a permanent reconciliation between the Maori and the British formed. At the top of the hill is a monument to these historic events. A two-km/one-mi (30-minute) track up the hill begins at the boat-ramp end of The Strand, follows the beach around to Watering Bay, and then heads up through native bush to the flagstaff. At high tide, take Wellington Street up instead of the track. By car, take Queen Street out of town and follow signs to the top.

Entertainment

There's not a lot of wild nightlife in the Bay of Islands—it's more of a wind-down-and-relax kind of place. Overlooking the beach, the **Duke of Marlborough Hotel** (The Strand, 09/403-7829; daily from 11 A.M.) is a favorite watering hole, and has been since 1840 when it was issued New Zealand's very first liquor license. In the main hotel, the **Cane Lounge** is a quiet place with an oceanfront deck and an open fire inside. The adjacent tavern is the most popular local's spot—the perfect place to enjoy a drink and soak up some of the history that permeates the surroundings.

Accommodations and Camping

Russell Top 10 Holiday Park (Long Beach Rd., 09/403-7826, www.russelltop10 .co.nz) offers the least expensive downtown accommodations. It is a well-maintained facility with well-spaced campsites ($32–38), basic cabins ($75–90 s or d), kitchen cabins ($105), and motel rooms ($170). Facilities include a TV room, a kitchen/dining complex, spotless bathrooms (metered showers complete with soft piped music), and a playground.

If you have a vehicle, consider **Wainui Backpackers** (92 Te Wahapu Rd., 09/403-8278; Nov.–Apr.; $21–26), halfway between Russell and the Opua ferry. Surrounded by magnificent bushland, it has just one three-bed dorm and one double room, but all the usual communal facilities are on hand, as well as a dinghy for guest use on the nearby bay.

Behind the waterfront are a few motels, each within easy walking distance of the main wharf, but priced higher than almost anywhere else in New Zealand. **Motel Russell** (16 Matauwhi Bay Rd., 09/403-7854, www .motelrussell.co.nz; $120–250 s or d) offers 15 uninspiring motel rooms, each with a kitchen. The one- and two-bedroom units are a good choice for families. The property's selling point is a beautifully landscaped outdoor swimming pool, one of the few in Russell.

Dating from 1899, **⟨⟨ Arcadia Lodge** (10 Florance Ave., 09/403-7756, www.arcadialodge .co.nz; $150–295 s or d includes breakfast) is an elegant accommodation high above the waterfront. Constructed from a great variety of materials collected from around the area, including kauri and wood salvaged from shipwrecks, the lodge is surrounded by extensive gardens. The six guest rooms lie on two levels; each has been elegantly outfitted in stylish furnishings and light pastels. Communal areas include a large lounge, complete with a piano and library.

The **Duke of Marlborough Hotel** (The Strand, 09/403-7829, www.theduke.co.nz; $195–390 s or d) has proudly overlooked Russell Harbour since 1840. The rooms are medium-sized and furnished casually, in keeping with the general feel of the place.

Food

The restaurants along Russell's waterfront provide many choices, but you're paying for the delightful location more than anything else. The exception is **Kamakura** (The Strand, 09/403-7771; summer 11 A.M.–3 P.M., year-round daily from 6 P.M.), where the most sought-after tables are spread around a grassed area shaded by *pohutukawa* trees and within

full view of the setting sun. The menu is filled with classic Pacific Rim dishes, such as smoked-salmon crepes ($19) to start and mains like char-grilled game fish on lemon risotto ($36).

For some of the best seafood in the Bay of Islands, reasonable prices for what you get, and a casual atmosphere, head straight for laid-back **⟨⟨ Gannets** (York St., 09/403-7990; Tues.–Sun. from 5:30 P.M.), one block back from the waterfront. Start with the seafood chowder ($13), so thick you can stand a spoon up in it, and then peruse the blackboard for daily fish specials ($24–30), or go healthy and order the prawn and pineapple salad ($28).

Information

A small information center is on the main wharf (09/403-8020; summer 8:30 A.M.–5 P.M.), or go to the DOC **Russell Visitor Centre** (The Strand, 09/403-9005; summer daily 9 A.M.–5 P.M., the rest of the year Mon.–Fri. 9 A.M.–4:30 P.M.).

Getting There and Around

Passenger ferries run regularly between Paihia's main wharf and downtown Russell (adult $9, child $4.50 round-trip). They operate at least once an hour 7 A.M.–7 P.M., with later sailings most nights. The short trip takes just five minutes, and although reservations aren't taken you can call 09/403-8288 for information. It's also possible to reach Russell by road. From Opua, four km (2.5 mi) south of Paihia, a small vehicular ferry crosses to Okiato, from where it's a pleasant 16-km (10-mi) drive to Russell. The ferry costs $17 per vehicle and driver round-trip, plus $2 per passenger. It operates daily 7 A.M.–10 P.M.

If your time in Russell is limited, jump aboard a minibus (they wait by the ferry dock) operated by **Russell Mini Tour** (09/403-7866; departs hourly 10 A.M.–4 P.M.; adult $17, child $8) for a one-hour tour of town.

KERIKERI

This historic town (pop. 5,000), 23 km/14 mi from Paihia, is well worth a visit. Once the home of Chief Hongi Hika and the Ngapuhi warriors, who conquered much of the North Island in the late 18th and early 19th centuries, it was also the site of one of the earliest missions. Kerikeri boasts impressive buildings and trees, lush agricultural land, and the attractive Kerikeri River and Rainbow Falls. It's a citrus center (the signs proclaim it "The Fruitbowl of the North"), quite obvious by the great number of orchards lining the roads between Paihia and Kerikeri, and from the delicious oranges, mandarins, and tangelos available June–January. It's also rapidly becoming an important kiwi cultivating center.

ꗸ Kerikeri Basin

The historic hub of Kerikeri is this quiet waterway north of downtown, off the main highway along Kerikeri Inlet Road. Overlooking the waterway is New Zealand's oldest European stone building, the **Stone Store** (09/407-9236; summer daily 10 A.M.–5 P.M., the rest of the year daily 10 A.M.–4 P.M.; adult $3.50). Built by the Church Missionary Society in 1832, the Stone Store once served as an impenetrable place of refuge in troubled times and as a storehouse. Still used as a storehouse today, it is under renovation. In recent times it has been used to display articles that belonged to early settlers and knickknacks from the past, and as an outlet for groceries and souvenirs. **Mission House** (same contact and hours as the Stone Store; adult $5, child $3), also known as Kemp House, was built in 1822 and lays claim to being the oldest wooden building in the country. It has been preserved by the Historic Society in much the same state as when the early missionaries lived there, and the surrounding gardens remain beautiful despite the damage caused by severe flooding in 1981. Across the road is a grassy knoll (pleasant spot for a picnic) overlooking Kerikeri Basin. The knoll is the remains of **Kororipo Pa,** a fishing base built by Hongi Hika and other Ngapuhi chiefs, where many historic meetings took place.

Rewa's village (09/407-6454; summer daily 10 A.M.–5 P.M., the rest of the year daily 10 A.M.–4 P.M.; adult $3, child $1), a recon-struction of a pre-European *kainga* or unfortified Maori village, is a short stroll up the hill facing the Stone Store. To get there, cross the bridge opposite Mission House and look for the parking lot on the left side of the road. On the other side of the road is a trail that winds through the bush and up the hillside to the village. Along the trail many of the native plants are labeled with their names and Maori uses, and at the top you'll find a variety of interesting identified structures and dwellings.

Rainbow Falls Scenic Reserve

You can easily reach the top of spectacular Rainbow Falls by road, or the bottom by foot. The water plummets 27 meters (89 ft) over eroded soft lava columns, and there are several viewing points. To get to the falls, enter the reserve off Waipapa Road about two km (1.2 mi) beyond Kerikeri Basin. The road to the falls is well signposted and there's a large parking lot; a 10-minute walk through native bush brings you to the various lookouts. From the second lookout at the top, on a sunny day, you can see how the falls got their name.

Alternatively, a four-km/2.5-mi (one-hour) one-way trail begins across the river from Stone Store; it follows the Kerikeri River, passes Fairy Pools (good swimming), and comes out at the bottom of the falls. Fairy Pools is also easily reached along a walking trail just south of YHA Kerikeri.

Arts and Crafts

Kerikeri distinctly appeals to arts and crafts collectors and music lovers. The town supports a large community of artists; spinning and weaving, ceramics, and stained-glass art are most popular (the shopping center lies off the main road to the right just before Cobham Rd.). Don't miss a stop at **Origin Art & Craft** (128 Kerikeri Rd., 09/407-1133; daily 9:30 A.M.–5 P.M.). Inside you'll discover pottery, knitwear, weaving, stained glass, leatherwork, woodwork, and furniture—it's a shopper's delight—and major credit cards are accepted, just to remove any last doubts you may have about buying up the entire shop.

NORTHLAND

Accommodations

Formerly a private residence, **YHA Kerikeri** (144 Kerikeri Rd., 09/407-9391, www.yha .co.nz; dorm beds $22, doubles $66) has just 36 beds and private kitchen-equipped cabins, but the bush setting is pleasant and the river is easily reached on foot. **Kerikeri Farm Hostel** (09/407-6989, dorm beds $22, $35 s, $50 d) is set on a seven-hectare (17-acre) orchard five km (three mi) from downtown off Highway 10. It's a small place, but the rooms are comfortable, and guests can use a relaxing lounge area and an outdoor swimming pool.

My pick of Kerikeri's many bed-and-breakfasts is the ◖ **Summer House** (424 Kerikeri Rd., 09/407-4294, www.thesummerthouse .co.nz; $225–295 s or d), an upscale lodging surrounded by one hectare (2.5 acres) of the most magnificent gardens imaginable. Overnight options include two romantic rooms and a downstairs suite with a Maori-meets-the-ocean theme.

Kauri Cliffs (Matauri Bay Rd., 09/407-0010, www.kauricliffs.com; from $1,350 s, $1,680 d) takes on the world's best golf resorts with spacious rooms filled with modern conveniences, an array of spa services and fitness facilities, fine dining, and the pièce de résistance, one of the world's top golf courses, perched high on ocean cliffs with water views on all but three holes.

Food

Several cafés lie along the main street of Kerikeri, including **Kerikeri Bakehouse** (334 Kerikeri Rd., 09/407-7266; daily 7 A.M.–5 P.M.) for pies and pastries and **Fishbone Café** (88 Kerikeri Rd., 09/407-6065; Mon.–Sat. 8:30 A.M.–4 P.M., Sun. 9:30 A.M.–2 P.M.) for good coffee and a casual sit-down meal. **Rocket Café** (Kerikeri Rd. by Hwy. 10, 09/407-3100; daily 8:30 A.M.–5 P.M.) is another recommended stop for a light breakfast or lunch.

Overlooking Kerikeri Basin, **The Landing** (215 Kerikeri Rd., 09/407-8479) has a sunny outlook and wide-ranging menu that covers all bases. It's open daily 10 A.M.–9 P.M., but the full menu is only offered 10 A.M.–2 P.M. and from 6 P.M.).

BAY OF ISLANDS TO KAITAIA

The most direct route between the Bay of Islands and Kaitaia, gateway to Cape Reinga, is to backtrack from Paihia the short distance to Highway 1, which cuts across Northland via Mangamuka Bridge.

The following section details the longer alternative, Highway 10, giving the traveler-in-a-hurry the opportunity to absorb beautiful coastal scenery while driving, yet luring the hiker and nature enthusiast into frequent stops to smell the flowers. Scenic reserves intermingled with fir tree plantations line the highway, soft white-sand beaches lead you to the ocean, and in summer wildflowers border the roads. In some areas endless rows of pine trees follow the contours of the land—planted as a windbreak, these magnificent hedges separate the rolling hills and fields into giant patchworks of color.

Whangaroa

The several small towns along Highway 10 share a relaxed atmosphere. Fishing boats, small private beaches, cottage arts and crafts, and tempting tearooms may delay your venture next to the water. Like being on the water? Take a sidetrack to Whangaroa, six km (3.7 mi) north of **Kaeo.** Beautiful Whangaroa Harbour has become a renowned spot for excellent fishing—some say it's much better than the Bay of Islands. Charter boats are always available, and in recent years local boats have captured a large number of blue, black, and striped marlin.

On the shores of Whangaroa Harbour, **Sunseeker Lodge** (Old Hospital Rd., 09/405-0496, www.sunseekerlodge.co.nz) is known for its friendly atmosphere and magnificent harbor views from its elevated location. It's the kind of place where you plan to stay a night but end up staying a week. A dinghy and fishing gear can be rented, and big-game fishing trips and harbor cruises can be arranged. Sea kayaks are also available. Travelers can camp ($12 per person) or stay indoors (dorm beds $24, private en suite rooms $70 s or d, self-contained unit $120).

Continuing north from Whangaroa Harbour, **🅒 Kahoe Farms Hostel** (Hwy. 10, 10 km/six mi north of Kaeo, 09/405-1804, www .kahoefarms.co.nz; dorm beds $20, $40 s, $50–60 d) is in a beautiful setting and it's a good base from which to explore this area of Northland. Take a short walk from the farmhouse and up a small hill on the property for great views across Whangaroa Harbour. The hosts arrange a variety of local activities, including trips to Cape Reinga.

Mangonui

The picturesque village of Mangonui, 30 km (19 mi) northwest of Whangaroa, lies on the southern edge of **Doubtless Bay,** marked as being "doubtless a bay" when Captain Cook sailed by in the late 1700s. Mangonui was originally a busy whaling base and trading station. In recent years, although the main undertaking is commercial fishing, southerners have discovered the charm of the area and the population has rapidly increased.

Ask a local for directions to the top of **Rangikapiti Pa.** The brilliant 360-degree view brings the whole area into perspective, and you can walk or drive to the top. Boats can be rented for fishing (from $20 an hour with an outboard)—though you can catch snapper, John Dory, and kingfish from the wharf on an incoming tide.

If you're looking for somewhere to stay, try the **Old Oak Inn** (66 Waterfront Rd., 09/406-0665, www.oldoakinn.co.nz; dorm $20, $80 s or d). You can't miss it—made of pit-sawn kauri and established in 1861, the two-story

whitewashed hotel stands directly across from the Magonui waterfront. The rooms are basic yet clean and comfortable, and there's a communal kitchen, lounge, and barbecue. Downstairs, a small café will lure you in for a delicious Devonshire tea ($8), a light lunch (up to $14), or seafood cuisine (from 6 P.M.; $20–32). Visit the crafts shop chockablock full of well-made kauri products, pottery, and all sorts of intriguing items. Continue along the road to the **Waterfront Cafe** (09/406-0850; daily 7 A.M.–midnight), a local favorite for seafood chowder, smoked fish pie (using fresh fish from local waters), huge addictive bacon rolls, pizzas, cappuccino, and freshly brewed coffee.

Around Doubtless Bay to Kaitaia

West of Mangonui, Highway 10 hugs the southern shore of Doubtless Bay, passing **Coopers Beach, Cable Bay,** and **Taipa,** all known for their white-sand beaches and handsome groves of *pohutukawa* trees. Coopers Beach has a campground and motor camp. Though Cable Bay's small beach is attractive to campers, it's a reserve, so camping is not permitted. After crossing the Taipa River you enter the town of Taipa, with another fairly large motor camp. Get great views of the Tokerau Beach peninsula and Cape Karikari from the Taipa area. Accessible on an unpaved road (turn off Hwy. 10 west of Taipa), the remote **Karikari Peninsula** offers more beaches and delightful coves, including **Matai Bay.**

After leaving Doubtless Bay, Highway 10 crosses a rolling rural landscape to Awanui and Kaitaia, 50 km (31 mi) from Taipa.

NORTHLAND

Kaitaia to Cape Regina

Gateway to New Zealand's northern tip is the town of Kaitaia, 110 km (68 mi) from Paihia and 330 km (205 mi) from Auckland. From Awanui, eight km (five mi) north of Kaitaia at the junction of Highways 1 and 10, it's just over 100 km (62 mi) along the spine of the Aupouri Peninsula to Cape Reinga, with the

last 21 km (13 km), from Waitiki Landing, unsealed. The alternative to the road is driving along Ninety Mile Beach, along the west side of the peninsula. The beach is not recommended for regular vehicles, but this is the route taken by bus tours—either on the outward or return trip.

KAITAIA

This bustling town (pop. 5,600) is the gateway to the far north, but also has an interesting museum and is near to the ruggedly scenic beachside town of Ahipara.

Far North Regional Museum

This excellent museum (6 South Rd., 09/408-1403, weekdays 10 A.M.–5 P.M.; $3 adult, $1 child) is a trove of information on the historical aspects of the northern region. Displays focus on ancient Maori lifestyles, including agricultural, fishing, and hunting methods and equipment, intricate feather capes and articles of clothing, and a comprehensive display of Maori carving styles and art forms. Other highlights include a display of New Zealand birds, an ancient anchor and various shipwreck articles, and a 1909–1936 photograph collection featuring kauri-gum-digging activities. Don't miss the information board at the entrance where descriptions and prices of all the latest tours up the cape are advertised.

Accommodations

In the heart of town, **Mainstreet Lodge** (235 Commerce St., 09/408-1275, www.mainstreet lodge.co.nz) is a popular budget accommodation where hospitable owners arrange tours throughout the Far North and throw the occasional *hangi* (Maori feast). Facilities include powerful hot showers, two modern kitchens, an outdoor barbecue area and pizza oven, a sunny dining room, a lounge, Internet access, laundry, and bicycles. Options include dorm beds ($25–31) or private rooms ($50–60 s, $56–64 d).

Kauri Lodge Motel (15 South Rd., 09/408-1190; $80 s, $90 d) is handily located directly opposite the information center. Each of the eight guest rooms has a kitchen, and there's a small pool for guest use.

Food

A popular gathering spot is the **Coast to Coast Bakery** (106 Commerce St., 09/408-1350; daily 9 A.M.–4:30 P.M.), where the pastry is made from scratch and the egg and bacon pie ($3) is a great way to start the day.

Dining at the **Bushman's Hut** (corner of Bank St. and Puckey Ave., 09/408-4320; daily from 6 P.M.) is more expensive than at the pubs around town, but the atmosphere is a little more sophisticated (it's all relative in small-town New Zealand) and the steaks are cooked exactly to order. **Beachcomber** (222 Commerce St., 09/408-2010; Mon.–Fri. 11:30 A.M.–2:30 P.M., Mon.–Sat. 5–8:30 P.M.) serves seafood, steak, and chicken. The food is better than the decor may suggest (dinner mains $16–30).

Information and Services

Far North Information Centre (South Rd., 09/408-0879; summer daily 8:30 A.M.–5 P.M., the rest of the year Mon.–Fri. 8:30 A.M.–5 P.M.) is by Jaycee Park.

The main street downtown is Commerce Street, on which you'll find the post office (104 Commerce St.), **Bank of New Zealand** (with ATM, 108 Commerce St.), Internet access at **Vodaphone** (84 Commerce St.,), and a laundromat (Kaitaia Plaza). **Kaitaia Hospital** (09/408-0010) and the police station (09/408-6500) are both on Redan Road, off Commerce Street heading toward Ahipara.

Getting There

Kaitaia Airport, nine km (six mi) north of town, is served by **Air New Zealand** (0800/737-000, www.airnewzealand.com) from Auckland. Cabs await all arrivals.

Kaitaia is the northernmost stop on both the **Intercity** (www.intercitycoach.co.nz) and **Northliner** (www.northliner.co.nz) bus networks. From the depot at 170 Commerce Street (09/408-0540) buses from both companies arrive and depart once daily for all points south, via Paihia and Whangarei.

AHIPARA

Spread around Ahipara Bay, 15 km (nine mi) southwest of Kaitaia and at the southern end of Ninety Mile Beach, this is a popular place for New Zealanders with four-wheel drives and those who enjoy beach fishing.

Gumdiggers Park

Just above Ahipara is Gumdiggers Park (Heath Rd., 09/406-7166; daily 8 A.M.–4 P.M.; adult $8, child $4), a stark, barren plateau that was home to hundreds of Yugoslav gum diggers in the 1890s. Vast forests of kauri trees once covered the north, but most of these forests were quickly decimated by the colonial timber-cutters of the early 1800s. Over many centuries, Kauri resin, which hardens into gum on contact with air, had dribbled down the trees, collected around the bases, and petrified under forest debris. When the timber rush finished, the gum rush began. The ground where mighty trees once stood was dug up, denuded of its gum, and made barren. By the 1890s the fossilized gum, used as a base for slow-drying hard varnishes and for making linoleum, had become one of New Zealand's major exports. Most of the gum fields of the north have been ploughed and fertilized into agricultural land, but the Ahipara Plateau has been preserved as a reminder of the past.

Accommodations and Camping

Ahipara Bay Motel (22 Reef View Rd., 09/409-4888 or 0800/909-453; from $95 s or d) is a modern motel complex overlooking the ocean. Rooms have kitchens and a couple of smaller studio units offer fantastic views. The property has a restaurant and bar, and guests can rent beach-fishing gear.

Views from the 【 **Siesta Guest House** (Tasman Heights Rd., 09/409-2011; $150–195 s or d includes breakfast) and its surrounding garden are stunning—a 180-degree panorama of the south end of Ninety Mile Beach—and the beach is only a few hundred meters away. The house has a guest wing, where the rooms feature timbered ceilings, comfortable beds, private bathrooms, writing desks, and balconies with views. On arrival, guests are treated to fresh fruit and cake.

It's just a five-minute walk to the beach from

Ahipara Motor Camp (Takahe St., 09/407-4864, www.ahiparamotorcamp.co.nz; camping $12.50 per person, dorm beds $25, cabins $45–120 s or d). Communal facilities, indoor dining, a swimming pool, and a barbecue round out the features.

KAITAIA TO THE CAPE– THE INLAND ROUTE

Most travelers who reach Kaitaia have one destination in mind—Cape Reinga. From the turnoff at Awanui, eight km (five mi) north of Kaitaia, it's 104 km (64 mi) up the Aupouri Peninsula to the cape. Traveling north, the landscape progressively gets drier. The colorful fields become scrubland, and exotic pine plantations are the only evidence of human changes to this desertlike landscape. Huge sand dunes roll in all directions, and the large saltwater marshes brim with birdlife. In March, on the mighty dunes of the north, the *kuakas* or Eastern bar-tailed godwits gather in great numbers before their annual migration to breeding grounds on the Alaskan and Siberian tundra. Much of the peninsula has been made into reserve, thus protecting it from development and other intrusion.

Waipapakauri Beach, 18 km (11 mi) north of Kaitaia and the southern access point for tours along Ninety Mile Beach, is home to **The Park** (09/407-7298 or 0800/367-719, www .ninetymilebeach.co.nz), a large and popular commercial campground. Bathroom, kitchen, and laundry facilities are communal; there's also a game room, barbecue, restaurant (with a lamb spit on weekends), and general store. Tent and powered sites are $14 per person, basic cabins with two single beds are $60 s or d, and cabins with a private bathroom and television are $80 s or d.

Houhora Harbour and Beyond

This long, narrow body of water 40 km (25 mi) north of Kaitaia makes a good stopping point on the trip to the cape. Turn east onto Houhora Heads Road to reach **Houhora Heads,** at the entrance to the harbor. Here,

NORTHLAND

Houhora Chalets Motor Lodge (Houhora Heads Rd., 09/409-8860; $70–80 s or d) offers six self-contained rooms and a swimming pool.

Continuing north, **Pukenui Lodge Motel** (Wharf Rd., 09/409-8837, www.pukenui lodge.co.nz; dorm beds $18–21, motel rooms $69–99 s or d) is on the main highway north in Pukenui, overlooking Houhora Harbour. Facilities include a game room, pool, and barbecue in landscaped grounds. Explore the beaches or go diving or fishing; you can rent a dinghy or mountain bikes at the motel, and across the road are a restaurant and café.

From Pukenui, it's 68 km (42 mi) to Cape Reinga. Take the side road west from Te Kao to **The Bluff,** an excellent area to view Ninety Mile Beach in both directions; the surf is good, and the hard, white sand is covered with shells. Offshore lies Wakatehaua Island.

The last services are at **Waitiki Landing Complex** (09/409-7508), 21 km (13 mi) from the cape, offering groceries, fuel, a laundry, and a restaurant. Camping is $18, dorm beds $20, and simple cabins $60 s or d.

❰ NINETY MILE BEACH

Abel Tasman called these northwestern shores "the desert coast." The etymology of "Ninety Mile Beach" remains unknown, although you could easily be forgiven for estimating this unbroken stretch of sand at 90 miles. The beach is actually 56 miles in length or almost exactly 90 km—the name-giver must have been an early advocate of the metric system. Huge white sand dunes reaching 143 meters (470 ft) high and six km (3.7 mi) wide fringe the beach, kept in place by mass plantings of marram grass and pine trees.

Every January, reels scream and large game fish dance in the shallows off Ninety Mile Beach as hordes of anglers compete for big-money prizes in one of the world's largest surf-fishing contests. Apart from being a shell-collector's paradise, this amazing beach is well known for good surfing conditions, particularly at Ahipara and Wreck Bay (walk around

JOURNEY OF THE DEAD

The main legend of Northland concerns the final trip of ancient Maori spirits of the dead. The legend says that after death, the Maori spirits padded up Te-Oneroa-A-Tohe (the Maori version of Ninety Mile Beach, not a direct translation) with a token of home in hand. The spirits left the token at Te Arai Bluff, then continued to Scott Point, where they climbed the highest hill and took a last look back at the land of the living. After quenching their thirst in Re-Wai-O-Raio-Po, the stream of the underworld, they trudged on to Cape Reinga. At the northern tip of this rocky promontory you can see the famed *pohutukawa* tree with its exposed root, which the spirits slid down before gently dropping into the sea. The kelp parted, and they swam to the Three Kings Island. After surfacing for a last look at New Zealand, the spirits took up the trail to Hawaiiki, their Polynesian homeland. Legend also states that the spirits of the sick sometimes got as far as Te-Oneroa-A-Tohe, but if they didn't quench their thirst at the stream the spirits returned to their bodies.

the rocks from the Ahipara access). All beach users should beware: Every now and again an unexpected roller will come way up the beach or rocks, submerging previously safe areas; keep way back from the water's edge.

Driving Ninety Mile Beach
The sand below the high-water mark along Ninety Mile Beach is concrete-hard, at times solid enough to support motor vehicles. During low spring tides a belt of about 250 meters (820 ft) of sand is considered safe under normal conditions for motoring. The main access point is the village of Waipapakauri Beach in the south and the northern pull-off point is the Bluff. Experienced 4WD enthusiasts often continue to Te Paki stream. The Automobile

Association recommends that you not drive on it for at least three hours before and after high tide. The sand is safe to *drive* on, but don't leave the car standing on wet sand for even a short time: the wheels can sink very rapidly. All rental car firms specify no driving on Ninety Mile Beach. The safest way to enjoy the unique opportunity of driving along the beach is on an organized Cape Reinga bus tour.

CAPE REINGA

The road up Aupouri Peninsula ends at an elevated parking lot 108 km (67 mi) north of Kaitaia. From this exposed promontory you get tremendous views in all directions. Looking eastward you can see **North Cape** and the **Surville Cliffs.** To the west lies **Cape Maria Van Diemen,** and on the northern horizon, 57 km (35 mi) off Cape Reinga, are the **Three Kings Islands.** This nature reserve, made up of 40 islands and rocks, is clearly visible from the cape only in fine weather. Also to the north and not far offshore is **Columbia Bank,** the point at which the Tasman Sea and the Pacific Ocean converge. Look for turbulent water and large crashing waves—in stormy weather they can reach up to 10 meters (33 ft) high. If you walk to the very tip of the cape, you'll see the famed *pohutukawa* tree, the roots of which are the legendary path for Maori spirits of the dead. Cape Reinga has no facilities, just the well-known whitewashed **Cape Reinga Lighthouse.**

Walking

The northern section of the New Zealand Walkway starts at Cape Reinga. Don't attempt any of the tracks without a map, and come adequately prepared for beach camping—there are no overnight huts. If you plan to hike all the tracks, start at the eastern end of Spirits Bay. A 28-km (17-mi) track runs from Spirits Bay to Cape Reinga, involves some steep sections toward the end, and takes about 10 hours. From Cape Reinga a 22-km (14-mi) cliff-and-beach track heads south to Te Paki Stream (look out for treacherous quicksand in this area), taking

about seven hours. The next track starts at Te Paki Stream and follows Ninety Mile Beach all the way down to Ahipara, at the south end of the beach. It takes a good two to three days to hike the entire 83 km (52 mi) to Ahipara, but you can leave the track and get back onto the main road at the Bluff (19 km/12 mi), Hukatere (51 km/32 mi), or Waipapakauri (69 km/43 mi). Many other walking tracks in Te Paki Farm Park lead to points of historical or archaeological interest and scenic lookouts—pick and choose from a short 30-minute walk to a several-day hike.

NORTHLAND

CAPE REINGA TOURS

Driving to the end of the road is only half of the Cape Reinga experience. Take one of the many guided tours and make the return (or visa-versa, depending on the tides) journey along the hard-packed sands of **Ninety Mile Beach.**

From Kaitaia, **Sand Safaris** (221 Commerce St., 09/408-1778 or 0800/869-090, www.sandsafaris.co.nz) departs daily at 9 A.M. for the cape. The tour travels along the beach in one direction, while also taking in the Te Paki Sand Dunes, Cape Reinga, east coast beaches, and Aupouri Forest. You can also try sand surfing. The cost of adult $60, child $30 includes lunch and accommodation pickups in Kaitaia. Also departing from Kaitaia is the highly recommended **Far North Outback Adventures** (09/408-0927, www.farnorthtours.co.nz). The cost is a little higher than the other options ($400 for up to five passengers), but the tour is a lot more personalized and the knowledge of guide Phil Cross is priceless.

Tours also leave from Paihia, in the Bay of Islands. **King's** (09/402-8288, www.kings-tours.co.nz) departs Paihia daily at 7:15 A.M., including all of the Sand Safaris stops in one long day tour; adult $99, child $50, optional lunch $15.

Expect to cover beaches, sand dunes, swamps, and pastureland during the various hikes, and be sure to take plenty of water, energy food, suntan lotion, and insect repellent. A large map with lengths, times, and descriptions of the various tracks is posted in Cape Reinga's parking area. For more information and maps, see the ranger at Waitiki Landing (on the main road to the cape) or call in at the Information Centre on South Road in Kaitaia. For fairly detailed maps and track descriptions, pick up the free booklet *New Zealand Walkway—Walks in the Northland District* or the *New Zealand Walkway—Far North* brochure.

Cape Camping

The closest accommodation to the cape is Waitiki Landing Complex (described earlier under *Houhora Harbour and Beyond*), 21 km (13 mi) to the south. If you don't mind roughing it for a night or two, you can camp at a couple of places farther north. Most have fresh water, some have toilets, some have no facilities at all. Try the campground at **Tapotupotu Bay**. Three km (1.9 mi) from the main road and signposted, it's down the northernmost road to the east before Cape Reinga. The campground lies at the back of a beautiful surf beach, and a park ranger supervises it during peak holiday periods from one of the resident caravans. Open all year, it operates on an honesty-box system when the ranger isn't there. Campsites are $7 per person per night, and the camp has water, toilets, and showers. A stream (considerably warmer than the ocean) runs by the campground and out to sea, and the beach, pounded by big surf, is a long stretch of golden sand with rock formations at the south end.

The campground at **Spirits Bay,** a sacred Maori area, also has water, toilets, and showers; rates are $7 per person per night. Take Te Hapua Road, then Spirits Bay Road to Hooper Point. The camping area is a long way from the main road but very handy for hikers doing the Spirits Bay to Cape Reinga Track.

Kaitaia to Auckland via the West Coast

From Kaitaia, it's 320 km (200 mi) back down Highway 1 to Auckland. The route followed below detours from Highway 1 47 km (29 mi) south of Kaitaia along the Mangamuka Road and then veers south to Hokianga Harbour, where a short ferry trip will deliver to a remote region of Northland abutting the Tasman Sea.

SOUTH TO
HOKIANGA HARBOUR
Mangamuka Gorge and Walkway

Mangamuka Gorge is a gorgeous drive, particularly on a sunny day, when you'll probably find yourself leaping in and out of the car at regular intervals, camera in hand, to capture giant tree ferns and assorted flora and fauna. Allow plenty of time to meander through all this lushness. Mangamuka Gorge Walkway starts 26 km (16 mi) southeast of Kaitaia and crosses a part of Maungataniwha Range. The route winds through the beautiful Raetea Forest and Mangamuka Gorge Scenic Reserve, emerging at Highway 1 north of Mangamuka Township. During the hike expect to traverse open farmland, dense forest, and lush native bush with its wonderland of ferns, mosses, and lichens. Climb to the radio mast atop Raetea summit (751 meters/2,494 ft) for spectacular panoramic views of North Cape and Karikari Peninsula to the north, Hokianga Harbour to the south, Bay of Islands to the east, and Tauroa Point and Ahipara to the west. At the summit, the main track doubles back and continues east—don't head south along the minor track toward Broadwood unless it's familiar;

this track fizzles out in places and it's easy to get lost in the dense bush. Keep on the main marked track at all times.

The 19-km/12-mi (six- to seven-hour) one-way trail is steep, muddy, and hard going. It's recommended for experienced hikers only, and it's best to have transportation awaiting you at the end. Wear sturdy hiking boots, and carry raingear, a change of warm clothes (the weather can turn bad quickly), food, and water—there are no streams along the ridge. To get to the western entrance take Highway 1 south of Pamapuria, turn west onto Takahue Valley Road, then turn left on Takahue Saddle Road.

Kaikohe

Highway 1 beyond Mangamuka Gorge runs south to Ohaeawai, where Highway 12 branches west to Kaikohe (pop. 3,500). The countryside around Kaikohe is scattered with historic buildings, and if you're traveling through the town, the local attraction is **Kaikohe Pioneer Village** (Recreation Rd., 09/401-0816; summer Mon.–Sat. 10 A.M.–4 P.M., Sun. 1–4 P.M., the rest of the year Sat. 10 A.M.–4 P.M., Sun. 1–4 P.M.). A re-creation of a 19th-century Northland community, the five-acre grounds contain an indoor and outdoor museum, a bush railway, the original 1864 Waimate North Courthouse building, a kauri gum collection, and Maori and pioneer artifacts.

A good option for an overnight stay is the **New Haven Motel** (36 Raihara St., 09/401-1859 or 0800/107-494, www.newhavenmotel .co.nz), just off the main road through town. Each of the 11 rooms has tea- and coffee-making facilities and a small fridge. Standard rooms are $60 s, $70 d, while one-bedroom kitchen units rent for $80 s, $90 d.

HOKIANGA HARBOUR

Stretching inland for more than 50 km (31 mi), Hokianga Harbour has forged a deep channel almost halfway across Northland to the Bay of Islands. In the early 19th century, this fiordlike harbor was lined with kauri forests and bustling with marine activity. Droves of ships sailed over from Sydney, defying the treacherous sandbars and large surf at the harbor mouth to keep up with demand for kauri timber. Once the shores had been stripped of their slow-growing forests, the timber mills closed and the ships left. Nowadays the harbor lies relatively undisturbed, slowly reverting to its original wildness and desolation. Few roads lead to the tangled mangrove forests, mighty sand dunes, and green valleys that line its shores. The peaceful beauty and quiet attracts quite a community of artists and people into alternative lifestyles; watch for out-of-the-ordinary houses, and for roadside arts-and-crafts stands where you can often pick up real bargains.

The best way to appreciate the harbor is by boat, and you'll find willing operators in Rawene, Opononi, and Omapere. Highway 1 detours east around this mighty harbor toward Okaihau, and the Highway 12 junction to Kaikohe. The shorter and more scenic route is to cross the harbor at the Narrows via car ferry and continue south down Highway 12. To get to the ferry, pass through Mangamuka Scenic Reserve, turn right at Mangamuka Bridge, and go through Kohukohu and on to the Narrows.

Kohukohu and Vicinity

For a shortcut from the north, turn south off Highway 1 at Mangamuka Bridge, then head south on Mohuiti Narrows Road to Kohukohu, a small village with many historic buildings scattered through town.

Continuing south, the Hokianga Vehicular Ferry is four km beyond Kohukohu, or follow the signs two km (one mi) past the ferry landing to the **(Tree House** (West Coast Rd., 09/405-5855, www.treehouse.co.nz; campsites $13 per person, dorm beds $19, cabins $38 s, $52 d), comprising a main building (with lots of stained-glass windows) built by the owners, along with inexpensive cabins. The atmosphere is super-relaxing and there's plenty to do around the surrounding farm and the harbor.

NORTHLAND

Hokianga Vehicular Ferry

The *Kohu-Ra* operates daily between the Narrows and Rawene. In summer it departs the Narrows every hour (on the hour) 8 A.M.–6 P.M., and Rawene every hour 7:30 A.M.–7:30 P.M. (fewer sailings in winter). Try to time it so you arrive about 10–15 minutes before the crossing—there's nothing to do while you wait (and no facilities), but you need to get in line. The crossing takes about 15 minutes and costs $14 per car and driver plus $2 per passenger each way.

Rawene

Getting off the ferry at Rawene, third oldest settlement in New Zealand (pop. 530), feels like taking a step back in time. On your way through don't miss **Clendon House** on the foreshore (09/405-7874; Nov.–Apr. Sat.–Mon. 10 A.M.–4 P.M.; adult $5). A historic building preserved by the Historic Places Trust, it was built in the late 1860s by James Clendon, ship owner, trader, and first U.S. consul in New Zealand. The house contains many of the owner's possessions and period furnishings. The **Masonic Hotel** (09/405-7822), built in 1875, is Rawene's local watering hole. You'll also find a small supermarket, a smattering of shops, takeaways, a gas station, and a post office.

Opononi and Omapere

After leaving Rawene, Highway 12 runs east to Kaikohe and Ohaeawai (where it rejoins Hwy. 1), or west to Opononi and Omapere before heading south through the kauri forests.

Situated at the mouth of Hokianga Harbour, the twin towns of Opononi and Omapere (three km apart) boast golden beaches and beautiful views up the harbor and out to sea. At Omapere you can appreciate the harbor best by cruise boat—get the details at the information center. For the best views turn off Highway 12 just south of Omapere and take the road out to South Head. Opononi became quite well known in the summer of 1955 when a friendly dolphin the locals named "Opo" came to play with swimmers every day—a

memorial statue to the dolphin stands on the oceanfront.

Affiliated with the YHA, **Okopako Lodge** (140 Mountain Rd., signposted from Hwy. 12, 09/405-8815, www.yha.co.nz; dorm beds $20, $50 s or d) is part of a working farm. It lacks modern conveniences, but the lodge has a pleasant setting and stunning harbor views. The dinner, bed, and breakfast package is $58 per person. Another budget choice, **Globe Trekkers Lodge** (Hwy. 12, Omapere, 09/405-8183; dorm $20, $50 s or d) is a modern facility with harbor views from a large deck. **Opononi Beach Holiday Park** (Hwy. 1, 09/405-8791), between the two villages but within walking distance of Opononi, overlooks the harbor and sand dunes with basic facilities that include a communal kitchen and a barbecue area. Tent sites are $12 per person, powered sites $15; small cabins with either share bath or share kitchen (none have both) are $52–65 s or d.

Beside the BP service station in Omapere, the **Harbourside Café** (09/405-8238) serves a cooked breakfast for about $10, pizza slices for $3, and burgers starting at $5. (It's probably one of the few cafés in the country without a deep fryer.)

For the rundown on the area, stop at the **Hokianga Information Centre** (09/405-8869; summer daily 8:30 A.M.–5 P.M.), on the main road between the two towns. You can also access the Internet from here.

KAURI COAST

Most of the splendid Kauri forests along Northland's west coast were logged in the 1800s, but the remaining stands and some wild west coast scenery make the journey between Hokianga Harbour and Dargaville the preferred, albeit longer, alternative to Highway 1.

⟨ Waipoua Forest

Beginning about 35 km (22 mi) south of Opononi, Highway 12 runs 16 km (10 mi) through the cool, lush greenery of Waipoua Forest, a place where time seems to stand still. Protected as a sanctuary since the 1950s, this remnant of New Zealand's once-extensive kauri forests covers an area of more than 9,000 hectares (22,240 acres) and contains five known giant trees, each estimated to be at least 1,000 years old. Apart from these giants there are 300 other species of trees, palms, ferns, and mosses, and although it's possible to enjoy the forest from the road, the best way to appreciate the grandeur is to get on some of the tracks. The forest is crisscrossed with trails; great picnic spots abound. The well-marked tracks vary from short 10-minute walks leading to particular kauri giants to longer hikes that offer a far richer assortment of sights and sounds of the forest.

From the north, the first worthwhile stop is for a short hike to 1,200-year-old *Tane Mahuta* (Lord of the Forest). Standing nearly 52 meters (171 ft) high and with a girth of 13 meters (43 ft), it's believed to be the largest kauri in the country.

Continuing south, a 700-meter (2,297-ft) trail leads through a particularly beautiful stretch of forest to *Te Matua Ngahere* (Father of the Forest). Although not as tall as *Tane Mahuta,* this kauri is renowned for its impressive five-meter-wide (16-ft-wide) diameter. Its exact age is unknown, but it may be nearly 2,000 years old. If you have the time, sit opposite the tree for a while and soak up the surroundings. The tranquil beauty of the bush and splendor of the "Father," cheerful birdsong, and buzzing cicadas create a natural high. Nearby is the **Four Sisters,** a group of kauri nestled close together.

The **Waipoua Visitor Centre** (09/439-3011; daily 8:30 A.M.–4 P.M., until 5 P.M. in summer) is off Highway 12 in the southern

NORTHLAND

THE KAURI FORESTS

The forests of Northland provide the nature lover with a wide range of native plant- and birdlife and the chance to appreciate many tree varieties. These include *rimu, rata, towai, kahikatea,* and *tawa,* though all are dwarfed by the magnificent kauri. The kauri (*Agathis australis*) is a conifer, grouped botanically with pines and firs that grow north of latitude 38 degrees south. The kauri is New Zealand's native giant – similar but less majestic trees of the same family can be found in Australia, Malaysia, the Philippines, Fiji, and other Pacific islands. The kauri is easily recognized by its tall columnar trunk (it self-sheds the lower branches), massive heavily branched crown, and thick, leathery leaves. The highly decorative bark is silvery gray in color and covered in irregular circular patterns. Another characteristic of the older kauri trees is the large mound of *pukahu,* or humus, at the base of the trunk. This mound is made up of bark, shed over several hundred years, and root systems. Note that the kauri is dependent on its surface root network for essential nutrients, and survival

depends to a large degree on not having its vital roots trampled – keep on the tracks to ensure these magnificent trees' future.

Some of the trees have been estimated at well over a thousand years old. Their rate of growth is very slow, taking 80-100 years to reach millable size. A young kauri is called a "ricker." The timber is straight grained, easily worked, durable, and very popular with carpenters and craftspeople. In the early 1800s the kauri dominated forest vegetation and covered about three million hectares (7.4 million acres) from the North Cape to Waikato. By the end of the century only one-quarter of the kauri forests remained; the trees had been cut down for shipbuilding, leached for gum, or burned when the land was cleared for agriculture.

Nowadays the policy is to preserve these ancient forests. **Waipoua Forest** and **Trounson Kauri Park,** both on Highway 12 between Hokianga Harbour and Dargaville, provide excellent examples of what all this land looked like before the arrival of Europeans.

section of the forest, to the west after crossing Waipoua River (southbound). Stop by for information on forest management, local legends, and walking tracks, and to see the cottage museum where the lifestyle of a kauri bushman is on display.

Trounson Kauri Park

This small but superb stand of kauri north off Highway 12 was deeded to the government for protection over 100 years ago. The park now totals 570 hectares (1,409 acres), and a resolute effort has been made to eradicate nonnative species such as rats, possums, and cats. This, in turn, has dramatically increased the park's kiwi population. A walking trail through the heart of the park takes about a half hour round-trip, and the highlight is the Four Sisters tree—actually two kauri trees, each with twin trunks that have grown together as one. At one point the track runs under a fallen kauri for a close-up view, and farther along you can appreciate the root system of a large 600-year-old fallen kauri from a viewing platform.

To see the park's most precious residents, join the owners of nearby Kauri Coast Top 10 Holiday Park (09/439-0621 or 0800/807-200) on their hour-long guided evening walk (adult $20, child $12). In addition to kiwis, giant *wekas* and kauri snails are often sighted.

Kauri Coast Top 10 Holiday Park

Accommodations are well spaced along this remote stretch of coastline, but there is one excellent option within the forest, **Kauri Coast Top 10 Holiday Park** (09/439-0621 or 0800/807-200, www.kauricoasttop10.co.nz), three km (two mi) along the road to Trounson Kauri Park beside a river dotted with swimming holes and filled with enough rainbow and brown trout to keep any angler happy. Tent and powered sites are all $28 and cabins and flats range $50–110 s or d. A fully equipped kitchen, three barbecue areas, a laundry, and a grocery store are on-site. You can rent kay-

aks and fishing poles, or go horseback riding for about $50 per half day. The owners also operate a popular evening walk up the road in Trounson Kauri Park.

Kai-Iwi Lakes

Continuing south from the kauri forests, turn west (toward the coast) at Maropiu on Omamari Road to access Kai-Iwi Lakes, the collective name for three brilliantly blue freshwater lakes (Kai-Iwi, Taharoa, and Waikere), great for swimming, fishing, sailing, and water-skiing. In addition, soft white-sand beaches, sheltered bays for swimming and snorkeling, rolling farmland, and lots of pine trees make this an even more attractive place. Lake Taharoa is stocked with trout and offers shoreside camping; on the banks of Lake Waikere is a water-ski club—a hive of activity on summer weekends. Two walks, to **Sandy Bay** (three km/two mi; one hour) and to **Maunganui Bluff** (1.8 km/1.1 mi), start on Kai-Iwi Lakes Road.

Dargaville

At the northern end of Wairoa River, Dargaville (pop. 4,500) was originally a busy kauri timber and gum-trading port. When the logging industry went into decline, so did Dargaville, and today it's the small commercial center for the surrounding dairy districts. The hilltop **Dargaville Maritime Museum** (Harding Park, 09/439-7555; daily 9 A.M.–4 P.M.; adult $6, child $2) displays items of local seafaring interest, the masts from Greenpeace's sunken flagship the *Rainbow Warrior,* Maori artifacts, pioneer relics, and an ancient Maori *pa.* To get there follow River Road, then turn right on Mahuta Road and follow the signs.

For self-contained accommodations and a swimming pool, head to the **Parkview Motel** (36 Carrington St., 09/439-8339, www.parkviewdargaville.co.nz; $89–145 s or d). Only a short walk from the center of town, **Greenhouse Hostel** (13 Portland St. at Gordon St., 09/439-6342; dorm beds $18, $28 s,

$44 d) is clean, friendly, and offers plenty of room to move around. The outdoor swimming pool is a bonus. Simple **Baylys Beach Motor Camp** (three km/two mi north of Dargaville then nine km/six mi west along Baylys Coast Rd., 09/439-6349; campsites $20, cabins $45 s or d) is just a short walk from an unspoiled beach.

Dargaville Information Centre (65 Normanby St., 09/439-8360, www.kauricoast .co.nz; Mon.–Fri. 8:30 A.M.–5 P.M., Sat.–Sun. 10 A.M.–4 P.M.) is on the main drag through town and has Internet access.

◖ Kauri Museum

From Dargaville, Highway 12 continues south along the Wairoa River to **Ruawai,** then veers inland to the small village of Matakohe and the Kauri Museum (Church Rd., 09/431-7417; Nov.–Apr. daily 8:30 A.M.–5:30 P.M., May–Oct. daily 9 A.M.–5 P.M.; adult $15, senior $12, child $3), which contains almost everything you'd want to know about kauri trees and gum. You'll see kauri timber, an outstanding kauri gum collection, furniture, wood flowers, old photos of lumberjacks, kauri-processing equipment, historic chain saws, and a reproduction of a colonial cottage done entirely in kauri. Volunteers Hall houses a slab of kauri from a tree milled by the landowners after it was struck by lightning in 1986. On the wall behind, this massive tree is compared to those still standing in the forest and to the largest kauri on record. Also in this section is "Transition Gateway," sculpted from kauri log that was underground for an estimated 30,000 years. Another room is paneled in all the different types of timber available in New Zealand. At the gift shop you can pick up beautifully crafted kauri products at reasonable prices.

Paparoa

Give the touristy café opposite the Kauri Museum a miss and continue seven km (4.3 mi) east along Highway 12 to ◖ **Sahara** (Paparoa Valley Rd., 09/431-6833; Fri.–Sun. 10 A.M.–

2 P.M., Thurs.–Sun. 6–9 P.M.). Within a beautifully restored 1914 bank building, the owners use local game and produce wherever possible, with the venison, pork, and kumara dishes the highlights. For lunch, the pancakes with ice cream and maple syrup were a delight. Pricing is also a delight, with dinner mains running $22–27 and wine by the glass starting at just $5.

CONTINUING SOUTH TO AUCKLAND VIA HIGHWAY 16

Highways 12 and 1 intersect at Brynderwyn, where Highway 1 continues south to Wellsford and on down to Auckland. An alternate scenic route south, Highway 16 via Helensville, branches west at Wellsford, skirting Kaipara Harbour.

Helensville and Parakai

The Helensville area, less than an hour's drive north of Auckland, boasts gentle countryside, many poultry and deer farms, and orchards and vineyards; in summer, wildflowers line the highways.

If you like hot pools and masses of people, head northwest out of Helensville along South Head Road to the town of **Parakai,** where you'll find **Parakai Springs** (corner of Parkhurst and Spring Rds., 09/420-8998; daily 10 A.M.–10 P.M.; adult $15, senior and child $8). Thermal mineral springs naturally heat the indoor and outdoor pools, so the temperatures vary a little each day—generally the outdoor pool is about 32°C (90°F), the indoor a sizzling 40°C (104°F). If you fancy whizzing down the Hydro Slide, you have to fork out an extra $9 for all-day sliding on top of admission; use of a private spa pool is an extra $5 per hour.

Next to Parakai Springs is **Parakai Springs Camping Ground** (09/420-8998), where camping is a reasonable $10 per person, or add swimming until noon the day of departure for an even more reasonable total fee of $15 per person per night. If you need a roof over

NORTHLAND

your head, consider **Mineral Park Motel** (3 Parakai Ave., 09/420-8856, www.mineralpark motel.co.nz; $95–130 s or d), where each of the eight self-contained rooms features a private mineral pool.

⟨ Muriwai Beach

South of Helensville, the only worthwhile detour before reaching Auckland is Muriwai Beach, a small village at the southern end of a windswept beach. To access Muriwai, turn off Highway 16 at Waimauku. Apart from the town's laid-back atmosphere, nesting **Australasian gannets** are the main draw. Offshore lies **Motutara Island,** where the gannets began nesting 20 years ago. The colony grew, spread to the mainland, and now numbers more than 1,000 nesting pairs. Barriers and two viewing platforms on the headland allow easy observation without disturbing the birds. The town has a beachside campground (09/411-9262; $12 per person), a general store with hot takeout food, and a golf course.

© ANDREW HEMPSTEAD

gannet colony, Muriwai Beach

WAIKATO, COROMANDEL, AND THE BAY OF PLENTY

This chapter covers a wide swathe of the North Island immediately south of Auckland, extending from the Tasman Sea in the west to the Pacific Ocean in the east. The region's largest city is Hamilton, a bustling metropolis renowned for its museum and gardens. Lush green fields dotted with dairy cows that stretch away from Hamilton in all directions are part of the Waikato Plains, one of the most productive dairying and agricultural districts in New Zealand.

To see the Central North Island's best-known tourist attraction, you'll have to descend underground to the Waitomo Caves. In keeping with the entrepreneurial spirit evident around the country, the advertising will have you believe you can't complete the "Waitomo Experience" without parting with a pile of cash. Aside from touring famous Waitomo

Caves and its glowworms, you can go blackwater (underground) rafting, abseiling (rappelling) into a limestone shaft and cave system, horseback riding, you name it.

East of Hamilton, the Coromandel Peninsula has survived the same land exploitation as the far north. It has seen both poverty and prosperity, and a dramatically fluctuating population during the last 200 years, including a mass influx of miners after gold was discovered in 1852. Today the Coromandel Peninsula is again a quiet and peaceful place, recognized for its great beauty and value as a wilderness area. The small permanent population is scattered mainly along the coastline. Although a few of the most easily reached towns (mostly along the east coast) are rapidly becoming tourist attractions, don't let the tricky gravel roads

© ANDREW HEMPSTEAD

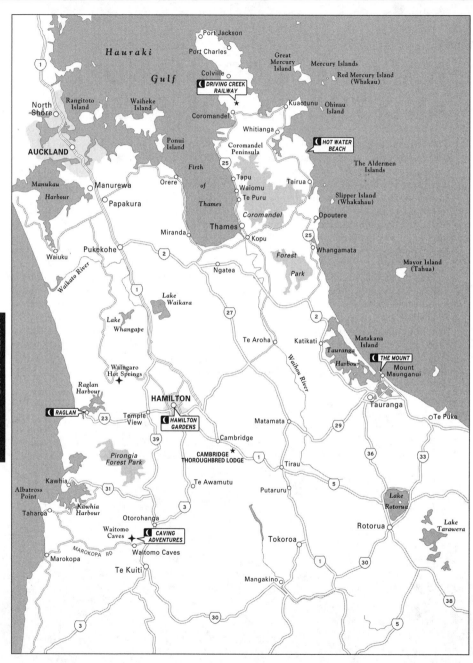

BAY OF PLENTY

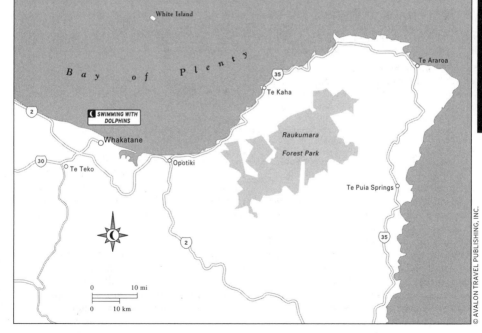

WAIKATO, COROMANDEL, AND THE BAY OF PLENTY

PACIFIC

OCEAN

White Island

B a y   o f   P l e n t y

Te Araroa

35

Te Kaha

2

SWIMMING WITH DOLPHINS

Whakatane

Raukumara Forest Park

30

Te Teko

Opotiki

Te Puia Springs

2

35

0   10 mi
0   10 km

BAY OF PLENTY

© AVALON TRAVEL PUBLISHING, INC.

HIGHLIGHTS

◖ **Hamilton Gardens:** From native forests to Japanese gardens, it's easy to spend half a day exploring this sprawling riverfront garden, but best of all, the entry is free (page 117).

◖ **Raglan:** New Zealand's quintessential surf town comes complete with world-class waves and a laid-back attitude to boot (page 123).

◖ **Caving Adventures:** You could explore Waitomo Caves on foot, but this is New Zealand, so you'll be expected to swim, rappel, and raft through the dark unknown (page 126).

◖ **Driving Creek Railway:** One man's mission is complete, and today you can ride this narrow-gauge railway to a stunning lookout point high above the forest canopy (page 132).

◖ **Hot Water Beach:** The spring water that seeps up through the sand makes for an all-natural hot tub. Bring your own spade and start digging (page 138).

◖ **The Mount:** This dormant volcano rising from the end of the beach at Mount Maunganui offers hot saltwater pools at its base and 360-degree views from its summit (page 144).

◖ **Swimming with Dolphins:** The dolphins off Whakatane encountered the first humans who suited up for this once-in-a-lifetime experience, which has become a New Zealand specialty (page 148).

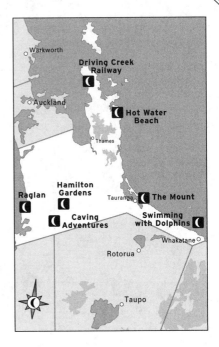

LOOK FOR ◖ TO FIND RECOMMENDED SIGHTS, ACTIVITIES, DINING, AND LODGING.

and steepness of the terrain prevent you from discovering the more beautiful, wild side of the Coromandel.

If you're hankering for a few lazy days when the only work you do is on your tan, or if you want to try your hand at various water sports, the Coromandel Peninsula has plenty to offer. However, if you're short on time and crave tourist attractions, evening action, and tons of people, you may be happier heading directly for Rotorua. Facing due north, the magnificent crescent-shaped Bay of Plenty stretches from

the Coromandel Peninsula in the west to Cape Runaway in the east. It includes several small islands, and is backed by the Kaimai and Raukumara Ranges to the south. With its mild climate, broad sweeps of golden sand, and crystal-clear waters, the bay attracts thousands of vacationing New Zealanders during the summer and reverts to a quiet resort area in winter. The fertile land produces a large variety of subtropical fruit— kiwifruit, feijoas, and tamarillos—and is well known for its citrus orchards, which supply a quarter of the country's total fruit crop.

PLANNING YOUR TIME

Travelers in a hurry zip south from Auckland to Rotorua, and if you only have two weeks to explore the entire country, you should too, maybe taking an hour or so out of your schedule in Hamilton to wander through **Hamilton Gardens. Caving adventures** are the main draw at Waitomo Caves, and adventurous souls should set aside a half day here. This region's east coast has the best beaches, but to the west, **Raglan** is renowned by surfers for its long point break. To the east of Hamilton is the Coromandel Peninsula. Seemingly lost in time, this chunk of land is mostly wilderness, with a few small towns, such as Coromandel, where an industrious potter has developed the **Driving Creek Railway.** The peninsula's east coast is all about a beachy lifestyle. Long sandy beaches, lots of sunshine, and a string of touristy towns make this region popular with New Zealanders on vacation. Aside from simply relaxing, there are a number of natural attractions worth investigating, none more unique than **Hot Water Beach,** where you can dig your own hot pool in the sand. Volcanic in origin, **The Mount** is a local landmark overlooking fine swimming and surfing beaches while **swimming with dolphins** is the highlight of a trip to Whakatane.

Hamilton and the Waikato

Travelers often miss Hamilton (pop. 140,000), center of the Waikato region, in the rush to get down to Rotorua or back to Auckland. It's on Highway 1 less than 130 km (81 mi) south of Auckland and on all public transportation routes. The city itself offers the visitor many attractions, and is an ideal base for exploring the coast near Raglan, intriguing Waitomo Caves, and the area's several forest park reserves. The Waikato River, originally the main shipping route between Hamilton and Auckland, meanders through the inner city, and along its banks are numerous parks and gardens. The east and west banks are connected by five city bridges, and footpaths run along the river on both sides. The city started out as a fairly small Maori village, Kirikiriroa, on the west bank of the Waikato.

History

The first European settlement was a military camp established in 1864, and the resulting town was named after a navy officer killed in the Battle of Gate Pa at Tauranga the same year. Hamilton has grown rapidly over the years and is now New Zealand's largest inland city.

SIGHTS AND RECREATION
Waikato Museum

This modern five-level architectural marvel (1 Grantham St., corner of Victoria St., 07/838-6606; daily 10 A.M.–4 P.M.; donation) sits beside the Waikato River (great water views from the upper level) and features Maori artifacts and sculptures, the fabulous 150-year-old carved war canoe *Te Winika,* contemporary Tainui carvings, Tukutuku weaving, and fine art exhibits, along with changing exhibitions. Part of the museum complex is the **Excite Centre** (adult $6, child $5), a large hands-on interactive science center. Don't miss the aerial sculpture, *Ripples,* which hangs between the trees outside (best viewed from the River Gallery inside). It accurately represents a pebble dropping in water—a suspended moment in time. In the museum shop pick up some high-quality arts and crafts, posters, prints, books, and art cards. Adjoining the museum is one of Hamilton's best restaurants, Canvas.

◖ Hamilton Gardens

No visitor to Hamilton should miss this garden (Cobham Dr., summer daily 7:30 A.M.–8 P.M., the rest of the year daily 7:30 A.M.–6 P.M.), and

© ANDREW HEMPSTEAD

Hamilton Gardens is a highlight of the central North Island's largest city.

not just because entry is free. Masses of roses, chrysanthemums, daffodils, camellias, magnolias, and rhododendrons; vegetable gardens; a perfume garden; trees that burst into brilliant color in autumn; and display houses sheltering tropical plants, cacti, succulents, bromeliads, and insectivorous plants can all be found through the 58-hectare (143-acre) grounds. The arrangement is subtle, with the Paradise Garden Collection comprising six gardens from around the world showing different perspectives on "perfection"—everything from a Japanese garden to American Modernist. A native garden is framed by an intricately carved *waharoa* (gateway), while down along the river is Echo Bank Bush, a native forest. The garden is south of downtown off Grey Street (Hwy. 1) toward Rotorua.

Hamilton Zoo

A place to appreciate a wide variety of animals is the 20-hectare (49-acre) Hamilton Zoo (Brymer Rd., north of the city, 07/838-6720; daily 9 A.M.–5 P.M.; $8 adult, $4 child). The main theme is conservation, and rare birds and animals are held here to establish breeding colonies, including many in a "free flight" sanctuary, where trails lead through a massive bird-filled aviary. Also on display are animals from around the world, including an ever-growing African collection.

Walking Trails

The city has three circular walking routes (brochures available at the visitor center): the **Short Historic and Scenic Walk** leads along Victoria Street, crosses Victoria Bridge, and returns along the River Walk route. The entire trip takes about 1.5 hours. The scenic three-to four-hour **River Walk,** also known as Five Bridges Walk, runs along the banks of the Waikato River. It starts from beyond Fairfield Bridge in the north and runs beyond Cobham Bridge in the south, links all five bridges, and takes in several parks and some of the older residential streets. The **One-day Scenic Walk** covers much of the River Walk route but includes several more parks and the delightful

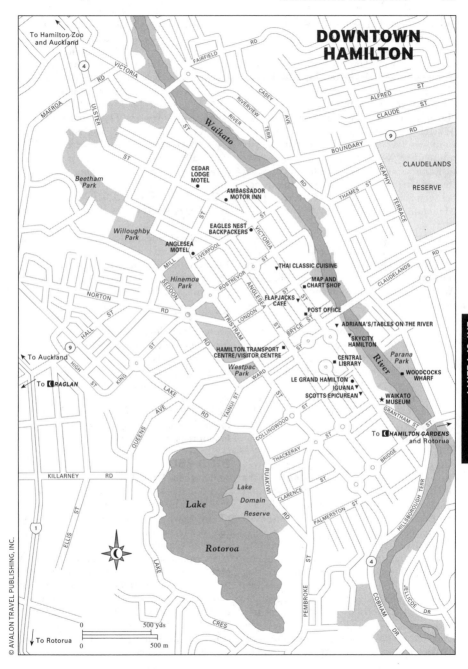

DOWNTOWN HAMILTON

To Hamilton Zoo and Auckland

VICTORIA RD

FAIRFIELD RD

MAEROA

ULSTER ST

CASEY

RIVERVIEW ST

Waikato River

RIVER TERR

AVE

ALFRED ST

CLAUDE ST

RD

BOUNDARY

HEAPHY

THAMES ST

CLAUDELANDS

RESERVE

TERRACE

Beetham Park

CEDAR LODGE MOTEL

AMBASSADOR MOTOR INN

Willoughby Park

EAGLES NEST BACKPACKERS

ANGLESEA MOTEL

LIVERPOOL ST

VICTORIA ST

CLAUDELANDS RD

Hinemoa Park

MILL ST

SEDDON

ROSTREVOR ST

ANGLESEA

LONDON ST

THAI CLASSIC CUISINE

MAP AND CHART SHOP

FLAPJACKS CAFÉ

NORTON RD

ST

TRISTRAM RD

POST OFFICE

BRYCE ST

ADRIANA'S/TABLES ON THE RIVER

SKYCITY HAMILTON

HALL ST

To Auckland 9

HIGH ST

KING ST

HAMILTON TRANSPORT CENTRE/VISITOR CENTRE

Westpac Park

WARD ST

CENTRAL LIBRARY

River

Parana Park

WOODCOCKS WHARF

To ☾RAGLAN

LAKE RD

TAINUI ST

LE GRAND HAMILTON

IGUANA

SCOTTS EPICUREAN

WAIKATO MUSEUM

AVE

ST

COLLINGWOOD ST

GRANTHAM ST

QUEENS

KILLARNEY RD

RUAKIWI RD

THACKERAY

BRIDGE

To ☾HAMILTON GARDENS and Rotorua

ELLIS ST

Lake

Lake Domain Reserve

CLARENCE ST

PALMERSTON ST

HILLSBOROUGH TERR

1

LAKE

Rotoroa

PEMBROKE ST

4

JELLICOE DR

0   500 yds

0   500 m

CRES

COBHAM DR

To Rotorua

© AVALON TRAVEL PUBLISHING, INC.

BAY OF PLENTY

grounds around Hamilton Lake; it takes five to eight hours to complete.

Karamu Walkway is a good track for panoramic views of Hamilton, Mount Pirongia (961 meters/3150 ft), Kakepuku, and Raglan. The northern end of the track starts at the eastern corner of the Four Brothers Scenic Reserve, almost at the top of the Kapamahunga Range. Take the Hamilton-Raglan Road (Hwy. 23) to the reserve. The track finishes 10 km (six mi) south of Whatawhata on Limeworks Road in Karamu, and takes about four hours; as a shorter alternative, you can walk the section between Four Brothers Scenic Reserve and Old Mountain Road in an hour.

Cruising the River

Cruise the river onboard the historic paddleboat **MV Waipa Delta** (07/854-7813). It first transported passengers between Hamilton and Auckland in the 1870s, but now offers city visitors a pleasant river trip from the Woodcocks Wharf, across the river from downtown at Memorial Park on Memorial Drive. Options include the 90-minute Lunch Cruise (departs weekends noon, weekdays 12:30 P.M.; adult $49, child $25), the one-hour Coffee Cruise (departs 3 P.M.; adult $20, child $10), and the two-hour Dinner Cruise (departs 7 P.M.; weekends adult $69, child $35, weekdays adult $59, child $29).

Entertainment

The most popular of several theaters offering live entertainment is the **Riverlea Theatre** (80 Riverlea Rd., Hillcrest, 07/856-5450), off Highway 1 southeast of downtown. The season runs April–October; check www.riverlea theatre.co.nz for a schedule.

SkyCity Hamilton (346 Victoria St., 07/834-4900, www.skycityhamilton.co.nz) is a large downtown entertainment complex facing the river. Within its modern walls are a casino, a bowling alley, three bars, and a restaurant. One of the bars, **Number Eight,** opens to a riverfront balcony and has a good-value happy hour daily 5–7 P.M. Within Hamilton's most stylish boutique hotel, **Leonardo's** (Le Grand

Hamilton, corner of Collingwood and Victoria Sts., 07/839-1994; closed Sun.) is a good choice for a quiet drink in a refined setting.

Many pubs around Hamilton have live music Wednesday–Saturday night, with cover charges at most venues on Friday and Saturday night. The **Bank Bar** (corner of Victoria and Hood Sts., 07/839-4740) is a popular drinking spot that comes alive with live and DJ music after 10 P.M. Next door, the **Outback** (141 Victoria St., 07/839-6354) attracts a younger crowd to its frenzied dance floor.

ACCOMMODATIONS AND CAMPING

Under $50

Eagles Nest Backpackers (937 Victoria St., 838-2704; dorm beds $25–28, $45 s, $58 d) is 1.6 km (one mi) north of downtown. Rooms are on the small side, but the atmosphere is congenial and it's usually not that busy.

$50–100

Most of Hamilton's 40-odd motels are on the fringes of the city, many concentrated along Ulster Street, the main route north out of the city (but bypassed by Hwy. 1). A good cheapie along this strip is **Cedar Lodge Motel** (174 Ulster St., 07/839-5569 or 0800/105-252, www.cedarlodge.co.nz; $75–95 s or d). Most of the rooms have kitchens, and there's an oversized indoor spa pool and game room.

$100–150

Ambassador Motor Inn (86 Ulster St., 07/839-5111 or 0800/800-533, www.silveroaks.co.nz; $115–165 s or d) is a large five-story motel close to downtown. All rooms have a kitchen, and facilities include a swimming pool, barbecue area, and restaurant.

Set around a courtyard and pool, **Anglesea Motel** (corner of Liverpool and Tristram Sts., 07/834-0010 or 0800/426-453, www.angleseamotel.com; $120–210 s or d) is near the downtown end of Ulster Street. All 42 units are a little plain, but are practical and spacious, and the laundry and Internet access are included in the rates.

Over $150

In the heart of downtown, you'll find **Le Grand Hamilton** (corner of Collingwood and Victoria Sts., 07/839-1994, www.rydges.com) in a historic four-story building with a restaurant and bar and wireless Internet throughout. The large rooms have an elegant Victorian charm, although you should ignore the rack rate (from $310 s or d, $335 with a view) and expect to pay from $130 online.

Part of the SkyCity complex, **Novotel Tainui Hamilton** (7 Alma St., 07/838-1366, www.accorhotels.com.au; $330 s or d) is a full-service hotel with 177 rooms and all the conveniences expected (restaurant, bar, valet parking, 24-hour room service). Dating to 1999, it was refurbished in 2005 and still has a distinctively "new" feel.

Holiday Park

On the eastern side of the city is **Hamilton City Holiday Park** (14 Ruakura Rd., Hamilton East, www.hamiltoncityholidaypark.co.nz; camping $24, dorm beds $24, cabins $55–80 s or d), where each campsite is surrounded by a high hedge. To get there, cross the central downtown bridge at Claudelands Road, turn right on Grey Street, and then turn left on Te Aroha Street. At the Peachgrove Road intersection, continue straight onto Ruakura Road.

FOOD
Breakfast and Quick Bites

Kick-start your day at **Flapjacks Café** (589 Victoria St., 07/839-5969; Tues.–Wed. 7 A.M.–3 P.M., Thurs.–Fri. 7 A.M.–10 P.M., Sat.–Sun. 8 A.M.–3 P.M.) with a stack of pancakes, U.S. style with bacon, eggs, and a dollop of maple syrup ($13.50). The smoothies here are also good.

One of the most popular local hangouts is **Scotts Epicurean** (181 Victoria St., 07/839-6680; Mon.–Fri. 7 A.M.–5 P.M., Sat.–Sun. 8:30 A.M.–5 P.M.), both for wonderful food and a welcoming ambience. At breakfast, you could order muesli with fresh fruit and yogurt ($9), while at lunch the classically simple aglio olio ($14) is a good choice.

Opening to an umbrella-shaded court-yard, the **Museum Café** (Waikato Museum, 1 Grantham St., 07/839-7209; daily 10 A.M.–4 P.M.) has premade sandwiches and salads, as well as a few simple lunch dishes under $15.

Within Hamilton Gardens, **Garden Café** (Cobham Dr., 07/856-6581; daily 10 A.M.–5 P.M., until 6 P.M. in summer) is a delightful lunch spot, especially on warm days when outside tables are set out beside a large pond. As you would expect in such a setting, the food is light and healthy, with salads and wraps mostly under $15.

Hip **Iguana** (203 Victoria St., 07/834-2280; Mon.–Fri. 10 A.M.–10 P.M., Sat.–Sun. 10 A.M.–3 A.M.) is a vast dining area with seating that ranges from bar stools to couches. The menu might not be groundbreaking in Auckland, but in Hamilton, ordering pizza topped with prawns and beef ($22.50 for two) is definitely out of the ordinary. The kitchen demonstrates its worldliness by using real bacon and anchovies in the Caesar salad ($13).

Italian

Off Victoria Street, along the access road to SkyCity, is **Adriana's** (6 Alma St., 07/838-0370; daily from 6 P.M.), a small Italian restaurant with an orange color theme extending from the facade to the tablecloths. Portions of dishes such as *gnocchi al salmone* (potato dumplings with smoked salmon, spinach, and cream sauce) are generous, although prices are a little higher than at other local restaurants.

Thai

At the far northern end of town is **Thai Classic Cuisine** (783 Victoria St., 07/839-3626; Mon.–Fri. 11 A.M.–2:30 P.M., daily from 5 P.M.), with a traditional Thai feel (think Buddha statues and gold-framed paintings). Mains, such as creamy green curry, are mostly under $20.

Upscale

The world over, dining at a museum eatery means lots of noisy children and cafeteria-quality food. But not in Hamilton, at the riverfront **Canvas** (Waikato Museum, 1 Grantham St., 07/839-2535; Mon.–Fri. 11 A.M.–2:30 P.M.,

BAY OF PLENTY

daily from 6 P.M.). In this thoroughly urban chic restaurant you could start with spring rolls with sweet chili and mint sauce ($10), then get serious with maple-rubbed salmon ($26) before ordering white chocolate and raspberry cheesecake ($10.50) for dessert.

Another solid choice for downtown upscale dining is **Tables on the River** (12 Alma St., 07/839-6555; Mon.–Fri. 11:30 A.M.–2:30 P.M., Mon.–Sat. from 5:30 P.M.), where the most sought-after tables are on a tree-shaded balcony overlooking the river. The $20 lunch attracts local businesspeople, while dinner mains range $26–32.

Across the road from Tables, you'll find lots of familiar foods at **The Post** (SkyCity Hamilton, 346 Victoria St., 07/834-4900; Sat.–Sun. for lunch, Fri.–Sun. for dinner), a typical casino-style buffet. Lunch is $17, dinner $27.

PRACTICALITIES
Information
Hamilton Visitor Centre is in the Hamilton Transport Centre (corner of Ward and Anglesea Sts., 07/834-1905 or 0800/834-100, www .waikatonz.com; Mon.–Fri. 7 A.M.–6 P.M., Sat.–Sun. 9 A.M.–5 P.M.). Lots of information is on hand, you can make onward transportation bookings, and there's a café and public Internet access.

The 200,000-book strong **Central Library** is on Garden Place (07/838-6826; Mon.–Fri. 9:30 A.M.–8:30 P.M., Sat. 9:30 A.M.–4 P.M., Sun. noon–3:30 P.M.). For specialty maps and guidebooks, drop by the **Map and Chart Shop** (636 Victoria St., 07/839-6585).

Services
The main post office is at 36 Bryce Street. Both the library and visitor center have Internet access.

Waikato Hospital is on Pembroke Street (07/839-8899). For non-emergencies, go to the **Victoria Central Medical Centre** (750 Victoria St., 07/834-0333; daily 8 A.M.–10 P.M.).

Getting There
Air, bus, and rail services converge on the city. **Hamilton Airport** is 13 km (eight mi) south of the city and is linked to downtown by the **Super Shuttle** (07/843-7778; $15 door-to-door). **Air New Zealand** (0800/737-000, www.airnewzealand.com) has direct flights from Hamilton to Auckland, Wellington, Christchurch, and Dunedin. Hamilton is also a hub for **Freedom Air** (0800/600-500, www .freedomair.com), a low-cost carrier specializing in flights across the Tasman Sea to Australia. One train a day stops at **Hamilton Railway Station** (Fraser St.) on the Auckland–Wellington route.

Go to the **Hamilton Transport Centre** (corner of Ward and Anglesea Sts.) for **Intercity** (07/834-3457, www.intercitycoach.co.nz) buses to and from throughout the North Island.

Getting Around
Busline (0800/42875463) buses head throughout the city from the Hamilton Transport Centre (corner of Ward and Anglesea Sts.), which also serves as the main visitor center and long-distance bus depot.

Car rental agencies in Hamilton include **Budget** (07/838-3585) and **Rent-a-dent** (07/839-1049).

Cabs wait outside the Hamilton Transport Centre, or call **Combined Taxi** (07/839-9099) or **Hamilton Taxis** (07/447-7477).

WAINGARO HOT SPRINGS
The sulphur-free bubbling waters of this thermal spring (Waingaro Rd., 07/825-4761, www.waingarohotsprings.co.nz; daily 9 A.M.–10 P.M.; adult $8, child $4), 42 km (26 mi) northwest of Hamilton, have been diverted into three concrete pools and down a hot-water water slide. The temperatures range 30–42°C (86–108°F). The sprawling grounds include a campground (campsites $16 per person, cabins $70 s or d, motel rooms $85) where rates include pool admission. If you're coming from the north, save some time and head directly for Waingaro. This allows you to take in both the hot springs and Raglan area attractions before reaching Hamilton. Turn west off Highway 1 at Ngaruawahia toward Glen Massey. Before

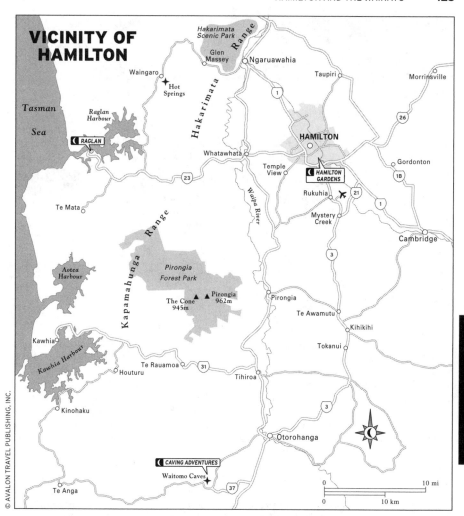

VICINITY OF HAMILTON

Hakarimata Scenic Park

Glen Massey

Ngaruawahia

Waingaro

Hot Springs

Taupiri

Morrinsville

Hakarimata Range

1

26

Tasman Sea

Raglan Harbour

RAGLAN

Whatawhata

HAMILTON

Temple View

HAMILTON GARDENS

Gordonton

1B

23

Rukuhia

21

1

Waipa River

Te Mata

Mystery Creek

Kapamahunga Range

Cambridge

3

Aotea Harbour

Pirongia Forest Park

The Cone 945m

Pirongia 962m

Pirongia

Te Awamutu

Kihikihi

Kawhia

Tokanui

Kawhia Harbour

Te Rauamoa

Houturu

31

Tihiroa

Kinohaku

3

Otorohanga

CAVING ADVENTURES

Waitomo Caves

37

Te Anga

0   10 mi

0   10 km

© AVALON TRAVEL PUBLISHING, INC.

BAY OF PLENTY

Glen Massey turn right heading for Te Akatea, continue to the Waingaro River, and turn left toward Waingaro. If you're already in Hamilton, head west along Highway 23 toward Raglan, then take Highway 22 north and continue to Waingaro Hot Springs.

◖ RAGLAN

Renowned as one of the world's greatest surfing spots, Raglan (pop. 2,800) lies 48 km (30 mi) west of Hamilton along Highway 23 at the mouth of Raglan Harbour. It is the nearest coastal resort to Hamilton, but is passed over by most sunseekers due to its lack of golden sandy beaches. Most of the year, it's a quiet little seaside town, but in summer it gets quite busy.

Sights and Recreation
Surfing takes place west of Raglan at breaks scattered along the coast. When the swell is up

BAY OF PLENTY

© ANDREW HEMPSTEAD

Raglan is one of the world's greatest surfing spots.

and the conditions are right, the breaks link up to form one of the world's longest left-hand point breaks. As Wainui Road winds southwest around the coast, it passes a number of spectacular lookouts before descending to **Manu Bay** and a grassy area perfect for relaxing and watching the surfing action. Continuing westward, the road passes through the small community of **Whale Bay,** another popular surfing spot with the renowned breaks of Indicators, the Valley, and Outsides. As well as surfing, Raglan has good harbor and surf fishing, and whitebait fishing in the local streams.

South of Raglan along the inland roads, pass through Te Mata to reach the spectacular **Bridal Veil Falls** near Lake Disappear, 21 km (13 mi) southeast of Raglan off the main road to Kawhia. Walk about 10 minutes along a bush trail to emerge at a thundering torrent of water plummeting 60 meters (197 ft) down a lava rock face into a deep pool, a popular swimming hole in summer. For an even more dramatic view, continue for another 10 minutes down the steep track to the base of the falls.

Practicalities

One of my favorite budget accommodations in New Zealand is **Raglan Backpackers** (6 Wi Neera St., 07/825-0515, www.raglan backpackers.co.nz; dorm beds $23, $52 s or d), operated by friendly couple Jeremy and Lynda Watson. This purpose-built budget accommodation lies right on Raglan Harbour and just 100 meters (330 ft) from the main street. The rooms all open to a large courtyard, complete with outdoor furniture and hammocks, while the spotless kitchen and cozy lounge overlook the harbor. There's a large selection of recreational equipment for guest use, including surfboards ($20 per day) and wet suits, canoes, bikes, and fishing tackle. The old hotel on the main street, **Harbour View Hotel** (14 Bow St., 07/825-8010; $60 s, $80 d) offers seven basic rooms. Or stay at **Raglan Kopua Holiday Park** (Marine Pde., 07/825-8283; campsites $22, cabins from $65 s or d), across an arm of the harbor from downtown, but linked by a pedestrian bridge. Overlooking the surf break, **Whale Bay Surf Bach** (9 Tohora Close, Whale Bay, 07/825-8219, www.whalebaysurf.co.nz; $160 for the entire house) is a small beach house that sleeps four in two bedrooms. It has a wonderful oceanfront location, a kitchen, and a grassed area out front for watching the surf.

The Hawaiian-born owner of **Vinnies** (7 Wainui Rd., 07/825-7273; Tues.–Sun. 8 A.M.–10 P.M.), legendary in this part of the world, offers an informal atmosphere and a blackboard menu with a bit of everything—Mexican, Thai, Italian, and more. It's a great place to just hang out, and anyone who has sampled the food keeps coming back for more. On the main street, trendy little café **Tongue and Groove** (19 Bow St., 07/825-0027) serves up a wide variety of coffee drinks, and well-prepared cooked breakfasts from $13.

Raglan Information Centre (4 Wallis St., 07/825-0556; Oct.–Apr. daily 9 A.M.–5 P.M., the rest of the year Mon.–Fri. 10 A.M.–3 P.M., Sat.–Sun. 10 A.M.–4 P.M.) is at the ocean end of the main street.

CAMBRIDGE

If you've been through rural England, Cambridge (pop. 11,000), 20 km (12 mi) southeast of Hamilton on Highway 1, will bring back memories of tree-lined avenues, immaculate flower-filled gardens, old buildings, and the traditional village green. The jade-green Waikato River runs through this scenic town, and the streets are bordered by abundant varieties of trees that meet overhead in a lush colorful archway (spectacular in late April and May when they take on brilliant autumnal colors).

Cambridge Thoroughbred Lodge

Between Hamilton and Cambridge you'll see field after field of racehorses intermingled with stud stables, which cater to an international yearling market. One of the most prominent operations is Cambridge Thoroughbred Lodge (six km/3.7 mi southeast of Cambridge on Hwy. 1, 07/827-8118), which in addition to training some of the world's fastest racehorses hosts an exhibition called New Zealand Horse Magic. It's an entertaining and informative show—good value at adult $12, child $5 for equestrian types. Call for show times (usually twice weekly through summer).

Practicalities

Cambridge Mews (20 Hamilton Rd., 07/827-7166, www.cambridgemews.co.nz; $130 s, $150 d) is an upscale motel with 12 spacious rooms, each with a kitchen, a writing desk, and a bathroom with separate shower and spa bath. It's along Highway 1 on the north side of town.

While you're in Cambridge, be sure to sample breakfast, morning or afternoon tea, or a light lunch at **All Saints Café** (8:30 A.M.–4 P.M.) above **Cambridge Country Store** (92 Victoria St., 07/827-7100). You can't miss the two-story orange-red building. The café has a large variety of assorted hot dishes, sandwiches, and salads, and the dessert specialty (among many tantalizers) is delicious orange cheesecake.

Cambridge Visitor Centre is in the town hall building (corner of Victoria and Queen Sts., 07/823-3456; Mon.–Fri. 10 A.M.–3 P.M., Sat.–Sun. 10 A.M.–4 P.M.).

WAITOMO CAVES AND VICINITY

Waitomo, 70 km (44 mi) south of Hamilton and eight km (five mi) west off Highway 3, is most famous for its caves, but it has gained a reputation in recent years as the adventure capital of the North Island. This entire area is part of an ancient seabed that was lifted up by enormous pressures from deep below the Earth's surface. Then erosion took over, with water action creating a complex system of caves, some with rivers flowing through them, others decorated with natural wonders such as stalactites.

Waitomo Museum of Caves

Start exploration at the intriguing Waitomo Museum of Caves (39 Waitomo Caves Rd., 07/878-8227, www.waitomo-museum.co.nz; summer daily 8 A.M.–8 P.M., the rest of the year daily 8 A.M.–5 P.M.; adult $5, child free). This puts you in the mood for all the other activities and gives you as much background knowledge as you desire. Displays feature local

BAY OF PLENTY

GLOWWORMS

Glowworms, New Zealand's fairy lights, twinkle by the thousands in caves and other moist and shady places, much to the wonderment of humans. The larva of a luminous gnat, the glowworm is a tiny fisherman that suspends itself from a cave ceiling or other canopy with fine, silky, sticky threads 1-5 cm long. Its tail end glows bluish-green, more brightly the hungrier it gets. It preys on bugs that breed in the mudbanks and water below the glowworm; they fly toward the light and entangle themselves in the glowworm's net. The glowworm hauls up the lines and feasts on the trapped bugs.

Proceed with caution when you enter their grottoes. They don't like loud noise; one clap and all the lights go out. They don't like bright light; shine a torch on them and the twinkles will fade. And hands off; they are fragile and a human touch will kill them.

geology, flora and fauna, spelunking, fossils, surveying know-how, skeletal remains found in nearby caves, the history of tourism in the area, preserved birds, insects, and glowworms. Don't miss the excellent audiovisual program on spelunking. The building also houses the local information center. Entry to the museum is free with paid admission to Glowworm or Aranui Caves.

The Caves

Many of the Waitomo caves are only accessible by joining a caving adventure, but three are open to the public for general viewing on a guided tour. The main attraction within **Glowworm Cave** is the magical glowworm grotto. Quietly glide through the water-filled grotto in a boat, gazing upward at the vast ceiling of twinkling lights. Tours through Glowworm Cave are run daily, generally every 30 minutes 9 A.M.–5 P.M., with extra tours at 5:30 P.M. in peak periods. Photography is not allowed in this cave. The entrance to this cave

is 500 meters (0.3 mi) west of the Waitomo Visitor Centre. Further along the road, **Aranui Cave** is definitely the more beautiful of the two caves, but lacks water and therefore there are no glowworms. The pink and white limestone formations are exquisite. Tours leave on the hour 10 A.M.–3 P.M. from the cave entrance. Both tours take 45 minutes and both cost adult $33, child $14 (or pay adult $50, child $26 for a combined ticket). No reservations are necessary and tickets can be bought from the booth at Glowworm Cave.

Known to the local Maori for over 500 years as the "Den of Dogs," but only recently opened to the public, the 1.6-km (one-mi) walking tour of **Ruakuri Cave** is more strenuous than the above tours. The entrance to the cave is a Maori burial site, so access is via a vertical passageway lined by a spiral staircase. Tours leave from the **Black Water Rafting Co.** (585 Waitamo Caves Rd., 07/878-5903) six times daily and cost adult $56, child $20.

◖ Caving Adventures

Black-water rafting began in New Zealand in the mid-1980s. It's offered at locations throughout the country, but the Waitomo experience is the original and still the best. It involves donning wet suits and helmets with headlamps, plunging into the Huhunui stream on an inner tube, and drifting along an underground river for around 90 minutes. In some places you need to get off and scramble, and in Ruakuri Cave, jump down a waterfall. Afterward a hot shower and a snack are provided. All you need to take is a swimsuit (wear it), a towel, socks, tennis or running shoes, and a waterproof camera with flash. The tour departs up to eight times daily from the **Legendary Black Water Rafting Co. complex** (585 Waitamo Caves Rd., 07/878-5903 or 0800/228-464, www.waitomo.com; $90 per person), 1.2 km (one mi) east of Waitomo village. This company offers other adventures, include Black Abyss ($175), a five-hour journey that begins with a rappel into the cave.

Competing for your tourist dollar is **Waitomo Adventures** (07/878-7788 or 0800/924-8666, www.waitomo.co.nz), best known for **Lost World Epic.** This adventure involves abseiling 100 meters (330 ft) into a limestone cave to see gold-colored stalactites, waterfalls, and glowworms. Once you reach the base of the cave, lunch is served; then it's upstream, wading, walking, swimming, and climbing through caves, vaults, and valleys to get back out. The seven-hour trip is truly an incredible experience, one that will be a highlight of your stay in New Zealand—and anyone of a reasonable fitness level can do it. The minimum age is 15 and the cost is $355 per person.

Otorohanga Kiwi House

Otorohanga, nearest town to Waitomo, is worth a stop for Otorohanga Kiwi House (Alex Telfer Dr., 07/873-7391; daily 9 A.M.–5 P.M.; adult $12, child $4), filling a valley surrounded by homes. Here you can see kiwis in the nocturnal house, walk through an enormous aviary, and see New Zealand's rare and unusual birds and reptiles in their natural habitat.

Accommodations and Camping

Also known as YHA Waitomo Caves, **Kiwi Paka YHA** (School Rd., 07/878-3395, www .kiwipaka-yha.co.nz) is a large, modern complex directly behind the museum and information center. If you don't feel like cooking in the communal kitchen, there's a great pizza restaurant on-site, as well as the usual communal facilities. Accommodation options include dorms ($26–30), private rooms ($60 s or d), and beautiful chalets with en suite bathrooms ($95–130).

Another backpacker lodge within walking distance of everything is **Juno Hall** (600 Waitomo Caves Rd., 07/878-7649, www.juno waitomo.co.nz; dorm beds $22, $60 s or d), one km (0.6 mi) east of the information center. It's a well-run operation, with a swimming pool, tennis court, and even a trampoline.

As two of the original black-water rafting guides, your hosts at ⟨ **Te Tiro** (970 Caves–Te Anga Rd., 07/878-6328, www.waitomocaves .com; $75 s, $100 d) are the perfect source of information on everything there is to see and

do around the valley (they also lead private guided tours). Accommodation is in one of two modern wooden cottages, each with a kitchen and balcony with valley views. Set on a farm 10 km (6.2 mi) west of Waitomo, the property even has its own glowworm grotto.

Once part of a government hotel chain, **Waitomo Caves Hotel** (Waitomo Caves Rd., 07/878-8204, www.waitomocaveshotel.co.nz; $70–250 s, $80–250 d) dates from 1908. It sits on a hill above Waitomo's main facility area and has its own bar and restaurant. Although it has been thoroughly renovated many times, rooms still seem a little dated, especially the smaller ones. This is where larger tour groups stay.

The area's only other motel is out on Highway 3, eight km (five mi) from the caves. **Glow Worm Motel** (07/873-8882, www.glowworm motel.co.nz; $85–110 d) has nine self-contained units, a swimming pool, and an adjacent restaurant.

Campsites are limited at Waitomo, so book in advance or register early in the day. **Waitomo Top 10 Holiday Park** (Waitomo Caves. Rd., 07/878-7639 or 0508/498-666, www.waitomopark.co.nz; campsites $16 per person, cabins with running water $55 s or d, self-contained cabins $95, motel rooms $105) spreads out across the road from the village. Amenities include a communal kitchen, barbecue area, and laundry.

Food

As well as selling groceries and souvenirs, **Waitomo General Store** (07/878-7639) has a small restaurant with good pizza from $14 and a variety of other inexpensive items to eat in or take out. **Morepork Pizzeria** (Kiwi Paka YHA, School Rd., 07/878-3395; 7:30 A.M.–10:30 P.M.) opens early for breakfast, but pizza is the specialty, with a medium ($20) serving two. The menu at the **Waitomo Caves Hotel Restaurant** (Waitomo Caves Rd., 07/878-8204; daily for dinner) is more modern than the old-fashioned dining room. Mains such as pork marinated in marmalade and ginger wine average $30.

BAY OF PLENTY

My favorite Waitomo eatery is the **Long Black Café** (585 Waitomo Caves Rd., 07/878-7361; daily 9 A.M.–5 P.M.), 1.2 km (1 mi) east of the village. It's always filled with customers coming or going from a caving adventure. Join them for a full cooked breakfast ($11), or a steak sandwich ($6.50) washed down with a milkshake. A deck overlooks the forest and inside is Internet access.

Information

From the **Waitomo Visitor Centre** (39 Waitomo Caves Rd., 07/878-8227 or 0800/456-922; summer daily 8 A.M.–8 P.M., the rest of the year daily 8 A.M.–5 P.M.), in the front of the museum, bookings can be made for cave tours and recreational activities, and the staff keeps a list of local bed-and-breakfasts.

Getting There

Intercity (www.intercitycoach.co.nz) stops outside the visitor center; the **Waitomo Shuttle** (07/873-8279) runs into Waitomo from the highway. The **Waitomo Wanderer** (03/437-0753, www.waitomotours.co.nz) operates from Rotorua and Auckland to Waitomo.

Marokopa Road

The narrow road west from Waitomo winds for 52 scenic km (32 mi) to the small coastal community of **Marokopa,** passing many natural wonders along the way. At the end of a 500-meter (1,640-ft) trail that begins 25 km (16 mi) from Waitomo, **Mangapohue Natural Bridge** is a massive arch spanning a small stream—it was once part of a mighty cave system. The trail passes under the bridge and leads to a bed of fossilized oysters. A few km farther west is **Piripiri Cave.** There are no cave tours, so you're on your own (bring a flashlight). Continuing west for two km (one mi), a parking lot marks the trailhead for a short (500-meter/1,640-ft) walk to **Marokopa Falls.** Cascading 30 meters (98 ft) over a limestone ledge, the falls are one of the most photogenic in the country. At the end of the road lies the fishing village of Marokopa. From the *very* end of the road, it's a pleasant 800-meter (2,625-ft) walk through black sand to the ocean. Early in the 1900s, when Marokopa was a bustling port town, many ships were lost attempting to negotiate the river mouth. The anchor from one such ship was salvaged and now sits in the parking lot at the end of the road.

Coromandel Peninsula

Lying equidistant from both Hamilton and Auckland and less than two hour's drive from either is the Coromandel Peninsula, a place that no hiker or outdoor enthusiast should miss. This finger of land stretches northward from the gateway town of Thames, separating the Hauraki Gulf and Firth of Thames on the west from the Pacific Ocean in the east. Like vertebrae, the rugged mountains of the Coromandel Range snake down the center of the peninsula, supporting the 72,000 hectares (177,900 acres) of wilderness and bush that make up Coromandel Forest Park. The peninsula is an area of contrasts: Along the western shores, steep, rocky cliffs terminate abruptly at the sea, while the eastern shores offer sandy beaches and private, sheltered coves. Wherever you go on the east coast you'll find beautiful beaches. If you also want peace and quiet, and maybe your own private bush-fringed cove, stay in the north. For lots of people and the bustle of a coastal resort, head for the large towns such as Whitianga and Whangamata at the southern end of the peninsula.

THAMES AND VICINITY

After crossing Waihou River, Highway 25 swings north to Thames (pop. 9,000), the gateway to the Coromandel Peninsula, 115 km (71 mi) from Auckland. In 1852 gold was found farther north in the area of the present town of Coromandel. It wasn't till 1867 that the Thames district was officially opened up for gold prospecting. In the next three years Thames boomed.

© ANDREW HEMPSTEAD

The streets of Thames are lined with historic buildings.

The rush continued until 1924, and many of the old-style buildings around town are reminders of this colorful past. Before a road link was built, Thames Port used to be the peninsula's link with the outside world, and was frequented by large riverboats and cutters. Today the port is very quiet, and caters to a small fishing fleet and many recreational boats. Thames is a commercial center for surrounding farmlands and is rapidly becoming more of a tourist attraction with its gold-rush history and close proximity to Coromandel Forest Park.

Sights

At the top end of town, where Pollen Street rejoins the highway, **Goldmine Experience** (07/868-7448; daily 10 A.M.–4 P.M.; adult $10, child $2) was the site of one of the most productive gold mines on the peninsula. You can go on an underground guided tour through a mine shaft, try gold panning ($2), as well as see a working stamper battery, a reconstructed mine manager's office, and a small museum.

The building that houses the **Thames**

Historical Museum (corner of Pollen and Cochrane Sts., 07/868-8509; summer daily 1–4 P.M.; adult $4, child $2) is more than 100 years old, and the museum features century-old printing and photographic equipment and 19th-century clothing.

Thames School of Mines and Mineralogical Museum (101 Cochrane St., 07/868-6227; summer daily 11 A.M.–8 P.M., the rest of the year Wed.–Sun. 11 A.M.–4 P.M.; adult $4, child $2) is three blocks west of the historical museum. The School of Mines was open between 1886 and 1954, teaching skills to prospective gold miners. It's now a museum, featuring an extensive collection of local and overseas mineral samples, and a working model of a stamper battery (used on quartz claims to pound quartz into powder).

Coromandel Forest Park

This 73,000-hectare (180,400-acre) park, extending along the spine of the Coromandel Peninsula, protects rugged bush-clad ranges with their ancient volcanic plugs and dense remnants of kauri forest. The park is laced with hiking tracks that vary from short walks to rugged overnight tramps in mountainous backcountry. The most easily accessed section of the park is from the Kauaeranga Valley, reached by following Banks Street east out of Thames and across the Kauaeranga River. This road winds through the beautiful Kauaeranga Valley, passing several good camping areas and four short tracks, before terminating at the starting point of some of the more difficult hiking tracks.

Accommodations and Camping

Sunkist Lodge (506 Brown St., 07/868-8808, www.sunkistbackpackers.com; camping $14 per person, dorm beds $19–24, $52–58 d) is one of Thames's appealing historic buildings left behind from gold-mining days, with a spacious upstairs verandah. Choose from dorms or single, twin, double, or triple rooms, with the use of communal bathrooms, fully equipped kitchen, dining room, TV lounge, pool table, laundry, barbecue, and garden. It's a popular place at any time of year but there's usually room—book for January and February, especially for double rooms.

Of the many motels in and around Thames, the **Avalon Motel** (104 Jellicoe Cres., 07/868-7755, www.motelavalon.co.nz; $85–130 s or d) provides the best value. At the south end of downtown and overlooking the Kauaeranga River, the Avalon features 11 kitchen-equipped units, an indoor spa pool, a barbecue area, and a laundry. A short walk from the center of town, **Rolleston Motel** (105 Rolleston St., 07/868-8091 or 0800/776-644, www.rollestonmotel.co.nz; $85–95 s, $95–120 d) is an older-style single-story motel with a pool, spa, and laundry. All rooms include a kitchen.

Coastal Motor Lodge (608 Tararu Rd., 07/868-6843, www.stayatcoastal.co.nz; $115–190 s or d) backs on the forest three km (two mi) north of Thames and features spacious self-contained cottages and chalets in a garden setting.

South of town in Totara is **Cotswold Cottage** (Maramarahi Rd., 07/868-6306,

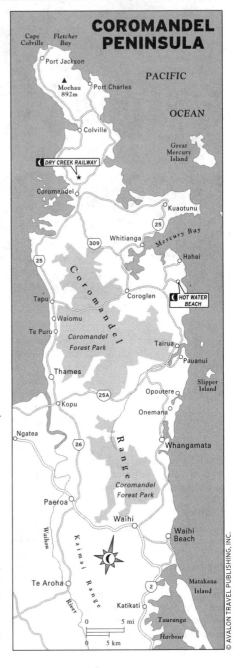

www.cotswoldcottage.co.nz; $75 s, $120–140 d). Right by the Kauaeranga River, a verandah offers a great view of the surrounding countryside. All three rooms include private bathrooms, and the rate includes a delicious cooked breakfast. Dinner is available for an extra $45 per person.

Also out of town, but to the north, is **Te Puru Coast View Lodge** (Hwy. 25, Te Puru, 07/868-2326, www.tepurulodge.co.nz; $150–175 s or d). Well signposted from the highway, it's high on a hill overlooking the town and the Firth of Thames. This Mediterranean-style accommodation has a number of rooms fronting the extensive garden, each with a private bathroom. Rates include a full breakfast, and dinner is available in the licensed restaurant on the premises.

Three km (two mi) north and closest to town is the excellent **《 Dickson Holiday Park** (Victoria St., 07/868-7308, www.dicksonpark.co.nz). On the grounds of an 1870s gold mine, it has a lush parklike camping area in a natural bush setting—a great spot to get away from it all and unwind—hiking local trails, gold panning in Taruru Stream, or relaxing at a nearby waterfall and wonderful swimming hole. In addition to the usual communal kitchen, there's a Pioneer Kitchen, a working re-creation of the rustic cooking facilities used by miners in days gone by. Other facilities include a laundry, swimming pool, bikes, trampolines, a half-sized tennis court, and a camp office selling basics. All campsites are $28, bunkroom accommodation is $22 per person, cabins (with fridge and cooking hot plate) and on-site caravans range $42–64 s or d, tourist flats (private bathroom, kitchen, TV, and radio) are $85 s or d, and motel units are $100.

Food

You'll find the usual tearooms, takeaways, and cafés throughout Thames, mostly on mile-long Pollen Street, the main shopping street downtown. A longtime favorite with locals is the **Billy Goat Cafe** (444 Pollen St., 07/868-7384; summer daily 7:30 A.M.–4 P.M., the rest of the year weekdays only), offering standard small-town fare, including cooked breakfasts (around $12) and dishes such as T-bone steak accompanied by fries and salad ($18).

At the top end of town, **Sola Café** (720 Pollen St., 07/868-8781; daily 8:30 A.M.–4 P.M.) has an earthy color scheme and an equally warm atmosphere. The vegetation goes beyond the typical, with free-range eggs used for cooking and everything made in-house from scratch. Only one or two dishes are over $10, include wheat- and gluten-free choices like cheese, corn, and potato enchiladas.

Off the main drag is **Sealey Café** (109 Sealey St., 07/868-8641; daily from 11 A.M. until late afternoon). In a renovated house with lots of outside table settings, Sealey is a great place to enjoy gourmet sandwiches accompanied by a huge side of salad.

Practicalities

Thames Information Centre (206 Pollen St., 07/868-7284, www.thamesinfo.co.nz; summer Mon.–Fri. 9 A.M.–5 P.M., Sat.–Sun. 10 A.M.–4 P.M., shorter hours the rest of the year) is at the south end of downtown (signposted from Hwy. 25). **Carson's Books** (600 Pollen St., 07/868-6301) is a great little bookstore specializing in New Zealand fiction and nonfiction.

The post office is on Pollen Street. **Thames Laundromat** (740 Pollen St.) doubles as an Internet café.

Departing Auckland, **Intercity** (www.intercitycoach.co.nz) operates a daily service east to Thames. Buses stop at Thames Information Centre (206 Pollen St., 07/868-7284) before continuing north to Coromandel. Intercity also has a direct service between Thames and Rotorua. Thames is a compact little town, and you can get just about anywhere on foot. Otherwise, call **Thames Taxis** (07/868-6037).

Thames to Coromandel

From Thames, Highway 25 northbound hugs the Firth of Thames for 40 km (25 mi) then cuts across two low-lying peninsulas before reaching the small town of Coromandel. This coastal road, perhaps most beautiful in early summer when the bordering *pohutu-kawa* trees are ablaze with red flowers, passes by rocky outcrops, picture-perfect bays, and small beaches.

Around 18 km (11 mi) north of Thames, the hamlet **Tapu** lies at the junction of Highway 25 and an unpaved road that crosses the peninsula to Whitianga. Tapu is known for its long stretch of sandy beach, shallow water, and safe swimming. Meaning "running water" to the Maori, **Rapaura** (six km/3.7 mi east of Hwy. 25, 07/868-4821, www.rapaurawatergardens .co.nz; Oct.–Apr. daily 9 A.M.–5 P.M.; adult $12, child $5) is a 26-hectare (64-acre) private estate that features waterfalls, fountains, and fish-filled ponds. The highlight is Seven Steps to Heaven, a trail that winds through lush forest to a small waterfall. Rapaura has a café and you can also stay overnight in one of two rooms in the main building ($250 s or d) or in a cottage ($145).

COROMANDEL

A quiet fishing and crafts village 60 km north of Thames, Coromandel is particularly appealing. Despite its small size (pop. 1,600), it's the business center of the far north, offering quite a variety of services—and it's the last place (other than one store at Colville) to stock up on supplies before continuing north.

◖ Driving Creek Railway

The one Coromandel attraction, which lures many visitors up the peninsula, is Driving Creek Railway (2.5 km/1.5 mi north of town, then a short distance along Driving Creek Rd., 07/866-8703). This unique narrow-gauge mountain railway was built by Barry Brickell, a well-known New Zealand potter, to serve his potteries with clay and pine wood for fuel for the kilns in the valley below. He carved a track through the forest, laying 2.5 km (1.5 mi) of line and even building the diesel-powered train himself. Nowadays you can take a ride on the train across four bridges, round a switchback, and through two tunnels to see the native kauri forest restoration project, displays, and views across Hauraki Gulf from

the Eyefull Tower. The one-hour return trip departs year-round, daily at 10:15 A.M. and 2 P.M. (additional trips in summer) and costs adult $20, senior $18, child $11. Another reason to venture out here is to browse through Driving Creek Pottery (daily 10 A.M.–5 P.M.), where you can buy the work of the resident potters, including homegrown wool, paper, and flax products.

Other Sights

Coromandel Mining Museum (900 Rings Rd., 07/866-8825; summer daily 10 A.M.–4 P.M., the rest of the year weekends only; adult $3) tells the story of the town, which boomed after 1852, when a logger discovered gold-bearing quartz in nearby Driving Creek. North of town at **Coromandel Goldfield Centre** (410 Buffalo Rd., 07/866-7933), you can see ore-crushing demonstrations for gold extraction, pan amalgamation, and plate amalgamation. Tours depart six times daily between 10:30 A.M. and 3:30 P.M. and cost adult $10, child $5.

Accommodations and Camping

South off Highway 25, **Tui Lodge** (600 Whangapoua Rd., Hwy. 25, 07/866-8237; dorm beds $22–25, private rooms $33 per person) is surrounded by grassy paddocks and citrus and macadamia orchards. If you need a ride out from town, give the owners a call and they'll collect you.

Comprising two rows of four self-contained cottages, **Colonial Cottages Motel** (1737 Rings Rd., 07/866-8857 or 0508/222-688, www.corocottagesmotel.co.nz; $95–155 s or d) is surrounded by well-tended gardens and native bush, with a covered barbecue area and pool off to one side.

Nestled high above the water and surrounded by native bush, **Buffalo Lodge** north of town (860 Buffalo Rd., 07/866-8960, www.buffalolodge.co.nz; Oct.–Apr.; $230–280 s or d) is one of the peninsula's finest accommodations. Taking advantage of its elevation, the lodge features a wide wraparound deck, with native timber dominant throughout. The four well-appointed guest rooms include thoughtful touches such as heated towel rails and plush robes. Dinner is available for an additional charge.

Overlooking the creek where New Zealand's first gold discovery was made is **(Driving Creek Villas** (21A Colville Rd., 07/866-7755, www.drivingcreekvillas.com; $295 s or d). The two units are brightly and practically furnished, yet remain elegant, with the private deck a perfect place to sip a morning coffee while listening to the resident birdlife. Highly recommended.

Coromandel Holiday Park (636 Rings Rd., 07/866-8830, www.coromandelholidaypark .co.nz; tent sites $12 per person, powered $16 per person, cabins $67–140 s or d) has a communal bathroom, kitchen, laundry, great outdoor pool, recreation room, trampoline, and barbecue. It is one km (0.6 mi) east of town toward Colville.

Food

For delicious meat pies, head to **Coro Pies** (41 Wharf Rd., 07/866-8554; daily from 5 A.M.). You know they're fresh daily—according to owner Andy Carrucan, the bakery closes each afternoon "when we've sold out." You can pick up gourmet deli products from **Tere's** (225 Kapanga Rd., 07/866-8639), including organic vegetables, fresh milk, and homemade ice cream. Complete your picnic lunch by stopping by the **Coromandel Smoking Company** (70 Tiki Rd., 07/866-8793) for smoked fish, mussels, and oysters.

There's also **Success Café** (104 Kapanga Rd., 07/866-7100; daily for breakfast and lunch), featuring lots of seafood, burgers, and sandwiches. Their advertising says "Try our Seafood Chowder" ($7.50). I did, and it's delicious. In the name of research I also sampled the seafood chowder at **Pepper Tree Restaurant** (31 Kapanga Rd., 07/866-82119; daily 10:30 A.M.–9:30 P.M.). The Pepper Tree is Coromandel's premier dining room, with a small courtyard the preferred option on a warm summer night. Along with the chowder, dishes such as snapper with paw paw and avocado ($15.50) are all very well priced.

Information

For more information on the village and areas to the north, stop by the **Coromandel Visitor Centre** (355 Kapanga Rd., 07/866-8598; Mon.–Sat. 9 A.M.–5 P.M., Sun. 10 A.M.–2 P.M.), in the old courthouse along the main road through town.

Colville

At the end of the sealed road, 30 km (19 mi) north of Coromandel, this small settlement has only one store, a restaurant, and a post office, and is the very *last* place to get supplies and petrol before heading on to the northern tip. **Colville Cafe** (2312 Colville Rd., 07/866-6690; Mon.–Sat. 9 A.M.–4 P.M.) is the local gathering spot, while the village also has a general store with petrol pumps.

Continuing North

If heading to Port Jackson is what you have in mind, expect to ford several streams (generally not too deep except after heavy rains) along this coast-hugging gravel road. You'll pass stretches of beautiful coastline with enchanting bays and excellent camping spots, and wind up at the open white sands of Port Jackson beach—lots more perfect camping spots beside crystal-clear streams, plenty of driftwood for campfires, and relatively few fellow explorers. What more could you ask for? The road leads around the top of the peninsula and ends at Fletcher Bay.

On a small hilltop farm, **Fletcher Bay Backpackers** (07/866-6712, camping $13 per person, dorm beds $16), at the northern tip of the peninsula, is one of the remotest accommodations in the country. It's easy to spend a few days here—hiking the Coromandel Track, fishing, boating, swimming, or diving. The alternative is to camp out. The DOC administers four camping areas in the vicinity of Fletcher Bay—at Fantail Bay, Port Jackson, Stony Bay, and Waikawau Bay. All have freshwater streams, but no toilets.

Coromandel Track

This seven-km (four-mi) track, part of the New

Zealand Walkway network, wanders within Cape Colville Farm Park in the far northern tip of the peninsula, from Fletcher Bay to Stony Bay. It takes about 2.5 hours each way. On this rather isolated track you traverse beach, open farmland, and bush, and are rewarded with fabulous coastal scenery. The track follows an easy grade for the most part, with only one short, steep section (marked with red disks) near the center. The small, sandy beach at Poley Bay (where a stream runs out to sea) may tempt you in for a swim, but resist the urge. Many submerged rocks lie dangerously close to the surface, and you'll find safer swimming at the end of the track. Also avoid drinking from this stream—the water is bad. Farther along, the track wanders through scrub, with the Moehau Range dominating the skyline to the west. Behind Stony Bay beach, Stony Bay and Doctors Creeks merge to form a large lagoon—a good swimming hole. A separate track leads from Stony Bay to the summit of Moehau (892 m/2,927 mi) and down the other side; allow six hours one way. The views are worth the long, hard climb, and if you're lucky you may see one of the "fairies" that Maori legends claim inhabit this area. Campsites and freshwater streams are at both ends of the track, and Fletcher Bay has toilets.

ACROSS THE COROMANDEL PENINSULA

Many roads cross the Coromandel Peninsula. The main sealed road is **Highway 25A**, which begins south of Thames at Kopu and ends 24 km (15 mi) north of Whangamata. Farther north, drivers taking the winding unsealed Tapu Hill route from Tapu to Coroglen are rewarded with views of lush valleys, clear streams, giant tree ferns, and near the top of the range, the 2,500-year-old "Square Kauri."

From the north end of the peninsula, you have two choices. The 309 Road cuts across the peninsula, while Highway 25, the route up the coast from Thames, continues beyond Coromandel as a rough unpaved road, following a remote peninsula to Kuaotunu and on to Whitianga. Allow at least one hour for these 46 km (29 mi).

309 Road

The most interesting route across the peninsula is the 32-km-long (20-mi) unsealed 309 Road between Coromandel and Highway 25 four km (2.5 mi) southwest of Whitianga (allow at least 40 minutes to an hour depending on your familiarity with curvy gravel roads); take plenty of film to capture natural bush panoramas. The first worthwhile stop is **Waiau Waterworks** (07/866-7191; summer daily 9 A.M.–5 P.M.; adult $10, child $5), where inventive owner Chris Ogilvie has created a number of interesting waterpowered machines that are dotted around his garden. At the 7.5-km (five-mi) mark, a short trail leads to **Waiau Falls**, where sparkling water cascades over a rocky ledge surrounded by dense greenery. Just 500 meters (about 0.5 mi) farther east is a grove of kauri trees that escaped logging. They are reached by a short 10-minute (each way) trail.

WHITIANGA

Whitianga (pop. 3,500), 44 km (27 mi) southeast of Coromandel and 84 km (52 mi) northeast of Thames, is the largest town on magnificent **Mercury Bay,** on the east coast of the Coromandel Peninsula. With a sheltered harbor and long, sandy **Buffalo Beach,** Whitianga is a popular holiday resort with countless holiday homes populated by a fairly large retirement community; in summer they're inundated with families on vacation. It's also a base for big-game fishing and scuba diving, and for a short time was on the world map as the home base of the small Mercury Bay Boating Club, which Michael Fay used when he challenged the America's Cup in 1988.

Sights and Recreation

From downtown, **Whitianga Water Transport** (07/866-5925; $1.50 each way) runs across he Narrows (7:30 A.M.–noon and 1–6:30 P.M.) to tranquil **Ferry Landing** (original site of Whitianga), several scenic reserves featuring ocean views and sandy beaches, and the hamlet of Cooks Beach.

Near the Whitianga side of the ferry,

© ANDREW HEMPSTEAD

Many waterfalls can be seen along the 309 Road.

Mercury Bay Museum (12 The Esplanade, 07/866-0730; daily 10 A.M.–4 P.M.; adult $4, child $1) is filled with photos and items from the days of the earliest pioneers. Highlights include relics from the HMS *Buffalo,* which was wrecked nearby in 1840, and the gigantic jaws of a white pointer shark that was estimated to weigh 1,300 kg (2,860 pounds).

Accommodations

Whitianga's many motels, backpacker lodges, and holiday parks provide quite a choice in accommodation. Rates given below are for January; outside of this month, expect discounted rates. Generally, it is the more expensive places that offer the larger discounts.

A good choice for budget travelers is **Buffalo Peaks Lodge** (12 Albert St., 07/866-2933, www.buffalopeaks.co.nz; dorm beds $22, doubles $45–65), across the road from the beach on the north side of downtown, with modern facilities, Internet access, a spa pool, and bike rentals. Another good choice is **On the Beach Backpackers Lodge** (46 Buffalo Beach Rd.,

07/866-5380, www.coromandelbackpackers .com; dorm beds $22, private rooms $46–52 s, $52–80 d). The Spanish-style building faces a large reserve, the beach, and the bay, and the enthusiastic owners offer guests the free use of kayaks, surfboards, and body boards, and have bikes for rent.

In the heart of downtown, the **Whitianga Marina Hotel** (1 Blacksmith Lane, 07/866-5818, www.whitiangahotel.co.nz; daily 11 A.M.–9 P.M.) is an old hotel that has a renovated downstairs bar and a trendy restaurant that opens to the marina. The upstairs guest rooms remain in their original state, but are good value at $50 for a double with shared bathroom to $90 for an en suite with TV.

North around the bay is the upscale **Mercury Bay Beachfront Resort** (113 Buffalo Beach Rd., 07/866-5637, www.beachfront resort.co.nz; $170–295 s or d). Each of the eight units has either a balcony or patio overlooking a garden—the only thing separating the resort from the beach.

Marina Park Apartments (84 Albert St.,

© ANDREW HEMPSTEAD

Whitianga oceanfront

07/866-0599 or 0800/743-784, www.marina park.co.nz; summer $180–450 s or d) is a modern three-story complex with a swimming pool. Each spacious room has a full kitchen with stainless steel appliances, laundry facilities, one or more separate bedrooms, and a balcony or patio with harbor views.

Food

As a seaside resort town, Whitianga has plenty of choices when it comes to casual cafés and restaurants. **Snapper Jacks** (Albert St., 07/866-5482; daily from 10 A.M.) is *the* place to get takeout fish-and-chips ($7–9). For meat pies with a difference, head to **Oliver's Deli Bakery** (74 Alberta St., 07/866-0069; daily 5 A.M.–3 P.M.) and order a smoked kahawai (fish) or creamy mussel.

Tucked away in a renovated cottage just off the main street, **Nina's** (20 Victoria St., 07/866-5440; summer daily 8 A.M.–10:30 P.M., the rest of the year daily 9 A.M.–5:30 P.M.) has good coffee and a range of light meals under $15.

Right on the water, **Salt** (1 Blacksmith Lane, 07/866-5818; daily 11 A.M.–9 P.M.) has more tables outside under palm tress than it does inside. Regardless of where you are seated the food is good, with delicious scallop chowder ($15) a warm up for a well-presented steak, veal, or chicken main ($19–29).

Information

At **Whitianga Visitor Information Centre** (66 Albert St., 07/866-5555, www.whitianga.co.nz; Mon.–Fri. 9 A.M.–5 P.M., Sat.–Sun. 9 A.M.– 4 P.M.), ask to see the photo album that tells the story about the friendly sea lion who fell in love with Clara, a local cow, back in the 1990s. The center also has public Internet access.

HAHEI AND VICINITY

Hahei, 30 km (19 mi) south of Whitianga, is best known for its sheltered soft pink beach (caused by crushed shells mixed in with the sand) and dramatic headlands with two *pa* sites at the southern end. Beyond the *pa* lie two blowholes, magnificent at high tide in stormy weather. At the northern end of Hahei Beach (signposted along Grange Rd.), a two-km/ one-mi (45-minute) one-way walk descends to **Cathedral Cove,** where you can walk through a huge sea cavern, and a magnificent white sandy beach. The *Hahei Explorer* (07/866-3910, $55 per person) is an inflatable boat that cruises around local waters to Cathedral Cove, Hot Water Beach, or snorkeling spots. **Cathedral Cove Sea Kayaking** (07/866-3877) charges $75 for a three-hour paddle or $125 for a full day on the water.

Accommodations and Food

The small village of Hahei has a choice of accommodations, a general store, and a small café. Behind the store is **Tatahi Lodge** (19 Grange Rd., 07/866-3992, www.tatahilodge .co.nz), which offers modern backpacker rooms and a small number of self-contained units. Bikes are available for rent, guests have free use of adjacent tennis courts, and the hosts can arrange all local activities. The backpacker sec-

tion is as good as you'll find anywhere in the country (dorm beds $22, $60 d). Across the courtyard are private rooms ($120 s or d) and self-contained units, with separate bedrooms and furnished in a casual yet elegant "beachy" style ($185).

The Church (87 Hahei Beach Rd., 07/866-3533, www.thechurchhahei.co.nz; $120–160 s or d) offers accommodation in 11 cottages set among wonderful gardens and surrounded by native bush. As the name suggests, a church is on the property—transformed from a small-town place of worship to an upscale restaurant that features Swiss-influenced dishes such as grilled venison ($31), as well as an equal number of lamb, pork, and seafood choices.

On the hill above town (toward Cathedral Cove) is **Spellbound** (77 Grange Rd., 07/866-3543, www.spellboundhahei.co.nz; $120–145 s, $150–175 d). Each of the three comfortable rooms in this modern bed-and-breakfast enjoys ocean views and has its own bathroom. A continental breakfast is served on an outdoor deck, and dinner is available at an extra cost.

© ANDREW HEMPSTEAD

BAY OF PLENTY

Cathedral Cove, Hahei Beach

◖ Hot Water Beach

This unassuming stretch of sand nine km (5.6 mi) south of Hahei off Hahei Beach Road hides another of New Zealand's many and varied natural attractions. And best of all, this one is free. Flooded at high tide, this area is accessible for about three hours either side of low tide, when locals and visitors alike take baths in the warm spring water that seeps up through the sand. Allow around 15 minutes to dig a hole in the sand below the high-tide mark (spades can be rented from the adjacent café), and voilà, your own private hot pool! The deeper you dig, the warmer the water.

On the way back from Hot Water Beach to Hahei, look for a sign to the left marking **Kauri Grove Walk.** This walk leads down through exotic tree ferns and native bush to a small stream, and then parallels the stream, which descends in a series of small waterfalls. Birdsong, the buzz of cicadas, and the whistling stream add to the all-around beauty. The track eventually crosses the stream and climbs into a young kauri forest. The first loop takes about 90 minutes round-trip, the track that leads to the coast is 2.5 hours one way, and the one to the coast and on to Sailor's Bay is three hours one way.

TAIRUA AND PAUANUI

Popular with vacationers, particularly in summer, the twin towns of Tairua and Pauanui are separated by a narrow tidal waterway 57 km (35 mi) south of Whitianga. Tairua, on Highway 25, is the older, more established town. Reached by ferry ($2.50 each way) or road (from Hwy. 25 south of Tairua), Pauanui is a modern subdivision punctuated by manmade canals. Just north of Tairua, keep your eyes peeled for **Twin Kauri Scenic Reserve**—two stunning kauri trees standing side by side right next to the road (easily missed if you're coming from the north—look for the small pullout).

Easterley Gallery and Garden

This beautifully located gallery (46 Ocean Beach Rd., 07/864-8677; 9:30 A.M.–5:30 P.M.) displays and sells high-quality pottery, screen-printing, basketry, painting, leathercraft, weaving, and jewelry. And don't miss a stroll along the path through the spectacular gardens. Behind the shop are fishponds surrounded by ceramic statues, more beautiful gardens, and chicken coops filled with fancy, fluffy hens and their baby chicks (send the children here while you shop).

Accommodations

Motels in Tairua are generally more expensive than elsewhere on the peninsula, but this reflects the quality more than anything else. For the atmosphere of a tropical island, consider spending the night at **Pacific Harbour Lodge** (223 Main Rd., 07/864-8581, www.pacific harbour.co.nz; $179–269 s or d), complete with palm trees and shell-lined paths as well as tastefully decorated freestanding cottages.

Across the water, **Puka Park Resort** (Mount Ave., Pauanui, 07/864-8088, www.pukapark .co.nz; from $450 s or d) is one of New Zealand's most exclusive resorts. Set among 10 hectares (25 acres) of native bush, the 47 freestanding chalets offer the utmost in luxury, with guests taking advantage of a large outdoor pool complex, café, restaurant, and bar. In relation to comparable resorts in North America and Europe (where most guests are from), the rates at Puka Park are very reasonable; packages advertised on the resort website make a stay even more so.

CONTINUING SOUTH FROM TAIRUA
Opoutere

Continue down Highway 25 south from the junction of Highway 25 and Highway 25A 11 km (6.8 mi) to Keenan's Corner, from where it's four km (2.5 mi) to the relaxed seaside village of Opoutere. **YHA Opoutere** (389 Opoutere Rd., 07/865-9072, www.yha.co.nz; dorm beds $22, $50 d) is ideally situated for hiking and beachcombing. Backed by native bush and edging a tidal estuary, this converted schoolhouse has the added bonus of being within a few minutes' walk of Opoutere Beach. The nearest shop is four km (2.5 mi) away, but the hostel shop sells a wide range of supplies, including vegetarian and health foods.

Whangamata

This popular holiday resort and retirement community of 3,500 lies at the southern end of a magnificent beach 38 km (24 mi) south of Tairua and 60 km (37 mi) east of Thames. Its great surf is popular with both serious surfers and swimmers who enjoy large waves. Whangamata (faan-ga-mata) also boasts good surf fishing. For dive and fishing charter information, continue along Port Road to the wharf, where there's an information board. **Ocean Beach,** reached via Ocean Road from the highway, is a long stretch of golden sand with offshore bush-covered islands—worth a drive out there whether you're going to catch it on film, work on your tan, or plunge into the Pacific.

Brenton Lodge (1 Brenton Pl., 07/865-8400; www.brentonlodge.co.nz; $300 s, $325 d) takes in the panorama of Whangamata and the ocean from afar. Guests stay in the main house or two garden cottages, but all enjoy fresh flowers, fresh fruit, and muffins on arrival. The grounds hold a large pool and well-tended gardens set around mature trees. Rates include a choice of cooked breakfasts.

Waihi and Waihi Beach

These two towns are crowded with vacationers and tourists in summer, but Waihi, inland at the junction of Highway 2 and 25, also has a colorful gold-mining history, with the rich Martha Mine still operating. **Waihi Gold Mining Museum** (54 Kenny St., 07/863-8386; Mon.–Fri. 10 A.M.–4 P.M., Sat.–Sun. 1:30–4 P.M.; adult $3, child $1) has a model of the mine and lots of related relics.

Waihi Beach, 11 km (seven mi) east of Waihi, is considered one of the safest beaches along the coast—it's patrolled in summer and on holidays by local lifesaving club members. **Waihi Beach Top 10 Holiday Park** (15 Beach

Rd., 07/863-5504, www.waihibeach.com; campsites $36, cabins $60–90 s or d) offers communal facilities, TV and game rooms, and a general store.

Continuing South to the Bay of Plenty

From Waihi, it's 35 km (22 mi) south to **Tauranga,** with Highway 2 paralleling Tauranga Harbour for much of the way. Tauranga and surrounding areas are covered in the following section, *Bay of Plenty.*

HIGHWAY 2 WEST FROM WAIHI

From Waihi, Highway 2 cuts back across the southern end of the Coromandel Peninsula. The first stretch of this route, to Paeroa, is quite scenic, particularly toward the Paeroa end where the highway parallels Karangahake Gorge (part of the Ohinemuri Goldfield, opened in 1875) and River, edged by large pampas grass and luxuriant tree ferns. Stop at **Karangahake Reserve** to stroll the 4.5-km (three-mi) **Karangahake Gorge Historic Walkway;** do the loop track or continue to Owharoa Falls. The track meanders along the river, passing old bridges, abandoned mining equipment and relics, and mining shafts (stay on the track)—a walk back in time. The walkway is signposted from the highway at each end—at the Waihi end, pull off to take a short amble down through another small, incredibly lush, scenic reserve to impressive **Owharoa Falls.** Several craft shops are signposted off the highway.

Paeroa

At the western end of Karangahake Gorge, Paeroa (pop. 4,000) grew as an inland port and is now a bustling rural service center at the junction of Highway 2 and 26, 38 km (24 mi) west of Waihi and 32 km (20 mi) south of Thames. The local claim to fame is Lemon and Paeroa, a soft drink that combined local mineral water and lemon. Bottled at a plant on the main street and cherished countrywide, it's

BAY OF PLENTY

no longer produced. A seven-meter-high (23-ft) L&P bottle at the southern end of town is all that's left of the legend. Of lesser fame but more interest is **Paeroa Historical Maritime Park,** three km (two mi) northwest of down-town along Highway 2. At the site of the original port, the park is the scene of an ongoing restoration project that includes the 1897 paddlesteamer *Kopu,* rescued from a silt-laden grave in the riverbed.

Bay of Plenty

Captain Cook first sailed these shores in 1769; on finding several friendly and prosperous Maori villages along the coast he was able to restock badly needed provisions, prompting him to name the area the Bay of Plenty. But the bay's history long predates Cook. According to Maori legends, nine of the original 22 emigrant canoes from Hawaiiki landed in this area, and it became home for some of the strongest and most powerful Maori tribes. You can view the remains of many *pa* along its shores. But the golden sand and crystal-clear waters are the primary attractions for visitors—including thousands of Kiwis.

TAURANGA

The city and port of Tauranga (Sheltered Anchorage) is 220 km (137 mi) southeast of Auckland and 88 km (55 mi) north of Rotorua. With a population of 90,000, it lies along a section of the large and sprawling Tauranga Harbour. Tauranga is a good place to go when you're tired of being on the road. Lots of beautiful parks and no major attractions give you the excuse to lie back and do nothing. However, if you plan to do some white-water rafting during your stay in the North Island, look into the several rafting companies based in Tauranga. Unrivaled excitement on some of the North Island's most exhilarating rivers awaits the adventurous spirit, and Tauranga is a good place to investigate a variety of trips.

Sights and Recreation

The main shopping drag in Tauranga is **The Strand,** but you can escape the hustle and bustle of the commercial center by strolling through the **Strand Gardens** on the eastern side of the street. For an enjoyable one-hour walk back a hundred years, continue to the northern end of The Strand, where the intricately carved Maori war canoe *Te Awanui* is on display, and then follow the path up to the complex earthworks of **Monmouth Redoubt.** This area, commonly called "The Camp," was the site of the original 1864 military settlement that overlooked the bay. The oval-shaped **Robbins Park,** on the knoll between the redoubt and the cemetery, has a Begonia House (open daily) and rose gardens within its grounds. For fairly graphic descriptions of Tauranga's past, check out the gravestones in the **Military Cemetery** on Cliff Road—some have quite a story to tell.

Off Cliff Road, **The Elms** (Mission St., 07/577-9772; Wed., Sat.–Sun. 2–4 P.M.; adult $5) was the original mission house built between 1838 and 1847 by the missionary Reverend Brown. The Elms is privately owned, but the grounds are open to the public dawn to dusk and the house itself is open for a couple of hours three afternoons a week.

Wet your whistle at **Prestons Kiwifruit Winery** (Moffat Rd., 07/576-8800; Mon.–Fri. 10 A.M.–4:30 P.M. and Sat. in summer). This winery offers free tastings, kiwifruit products, winery tours, and wholesale prices (wine from $12, liqueur $28). From Tauranga take Cameron Road to Highway 29 and turn right toward Hamilton. Continue for about 7.5 km (five mi), then turn left on Belk Road for another three kilometers (two mi).

The bores at Tauranga are the source of internationally known Fernland Sparkling Mineral Water, but if you'd rather immerse yourself in it than drink it, head for **Fernland**

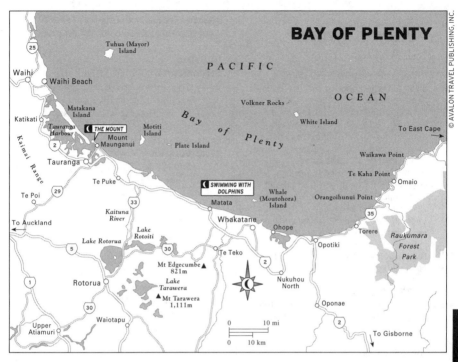

© AVALON TRAVEL PUBLISHING, INC.

Spa Thermal Mineral Springs (250 Cambridge Rd., Te Reti, 07/578-3081; daily 10 A.M.–10 P.M.; adult $5, senior and child $3.50). The water (38–40°C/100–104°F) is pumped daily from 200 meters (660 ft) beneath the ground into the main public pool and eight large private pools. From downtown (about six km/3.7 mi from the post office) follow Cameron Street to 11th Avenue and turn right; 11th becomes Waihi Road. Continue along Waihi, then turn left onto Cambridge Road.

At the bottom of a fairly steep track through native bush you'll find **Te Rerekawau Falls**—actually three beautiful waterfalls (formerly called Kaiate Falls), the third plummeting into a very deep, bush-fringed pool and popular (icy-cold!) swimming hole. It's a great place for photographers in search of slow-speed water shots. You'll need a car to get to these falls, but keep all valuables locked out of sight or with you. Take Highway 2 out of Tauranga toward Mount Maunganui, but turn right toward Welcome Bay before crossing the harbor. Continue along Welcome Bay Road, and just after the bay turn right on Waitao Road—the falls are signposted from here.

Entertainment

The Strand is lined with bars and restaurants with lots of outdoor tables—the perfect place to while away an hour or two on a warm afternoon or evening. The always-lively **Grumpy Mole Saloon** (41 The Strand, 07/571-1222) is a popular Western-style dance venue for the younger crowd. Along similar lines, **Coyote Street Bar** (107 The Strand, 07/578-8968) is a big U.S.-style saloon with a menu to match—burgers, nachos, and apple pie. **Harrington's** (10 Harrington St., 07/578-5427; Thurs.–Sat. until 5 A.M.) is a nightclub with bands on Friday and Saturday night.

TUHUA (MAYOR) ISLAND

If you're looking for somewhere to get away from just about everyone, 1,280-hectare (3,160-acre) Tuhua Island – 40 km (25 mi) offshore from Tauranga – is the place for you. Privately owned but managed by a trust, Tuhua is the remnant of an ancient volcano that last erupted approximately 6,000 years ago. It's been dormant ever since and is a quiet place, covered in native forest and inhabited by abundant birdlife such as bellbird, tui, kaka, kingfisher, and the recently reintroduced North Island robin. The surrounding crystal-clear waters are filled with marinelife and a trail leads up and over the eroded volcanic rim to two colorful lakes within the ancient crater.

GETTING TO THE ISLAND

Access to Tuhua is by charter boat from Tauranga. **Tauranga Manutere Charters** (07/552-6283, www.manutere.co.nz) and **Blue Ocean Charters** (07/578-4685, www.blueoceancharters.co.nz) provide island transfers out of both Tauranga and Mount Maunganui on demand. Expect to pay around $100 per person round-trip. You also pay a $5 per person landing fee and as the island is predator-free, visitors must unpack their day pack in the presence of a caretaker upon arrival.

Accommodations and Camping

UNDER $50

YHA Tauranga (171 Elizabeth St., 07/578-5064, www.yha.co.nz; dorm beds $22, $54 s or d) provides budget accommodation within walking distance of downtown. It has the usual communal facilities, nearby waterside walking tracks, a variety of outdoor games, and a barbecue.

Located 3.5 km (two mi) from downtown, **Bell Lodge** (39 Bell St., 07/578-6344; dorm beds $23, $50 s or d, motel room $75 s, $78 d) has excellent budget accommodations—heated bunkrooms—plus a fully equipped communal kitchen, a spacious dining room and TV area, a guest lounge, and a coin-op laundry.

$50-100

Strand Motel (27 The Strand, 07/578-5807, www.strandmotel.co.nz; $75 s, $90 d) is an old motel, but it's centrally located and a good value. It's within easy walking distance of everything, each unit has a kitchen, and the four upstairs rooms enjoy water views.

Harbour View Motel (7 Fifth Ave., 07/578-8621; $80–90 s, $95–110 d) is slightly older, but it's right on the water in a quiet location 800 meters (0.5 mi) south of downtown. Each room has a kitchen and tea- and coffee-making facilities.

$100-150

Many motels can be found on or near Cameron Street, which runs the length of the peninsula upon which Tauranga lies. One of the best of these is **Academy Motor Inn** (734 Cameron St. at 15th Ave., 07/578-9103 or 0800/782-9222, www.academymotorinn.co.nz; $125–175 s or d), with 20 self-contained units featuring many nice touches, such as hair dryers. The complex includes a swimming pool, spa pool, and barbecue area.

OVER $200

Tucked away in the Papamoa Hills, **Ridge Country Retreat & Spa** (330 Rocky Cutting Rd., 07/542-1301, www.rcr.co.nz) is an oasis of luxury surrounded by a tangle of native bush. The lavishness could be overwhelming, but it's not. Instead, you get friendly hosts, massive suites with designer bathrooms and big windows, an outdoor lap pool, spa services (extra), and an unforgettable breakfast and six-course dinner included in the rates ($690 s or d).

HOLIDAY PARKS

Silver Birch Holiday Park (101 Turret Rd., 07/578-4603, www.silverbirch.co.nz; camping $30, cabins $50–105 s or d) enjoys a quiet waterfront location four km (2.5 mi) south of downtown off Highway 2 to Whakatane (Turret Rd. is an extension of 15th Ave.). Amenities include modern communal facilities, a TV and game room, a boat ramp, use of mineral swimming pools, and a general store.

If being in town isn't a priority, plan on camping at **Fernland Spa Thermal Mineral Springs** (250 Cambridge Rd., Te Reti, 07/578-3081, www.fernlandspa.co.nz), where the overnight fee of $20 per site includes access to the hot springs.

Food

Cafés and restaurants line The Strand between Harrington and Wharf Streets opposite the harbor, with cobbled sidewalks complete with flowerbeds and old-fashioned lampposts creating the perfect atmosphere for outdoor dining.

On a sunny day on The Strand, it's hard to go past **◖ Fresh Fish Market** (Dive Crescent, 07/578-1789; daily from 10:30 A.M.) for casual outdoor dining. Right on the dock at the north end of The Strand, surrounded by fishing boats, the market offers all types of fresh and cooked fish. Fish-and-chips costs about $8. It has a couple of tables, or wander along the wharf and enjoy your meal with the seagulls.

The menu is a giveaway—Love Me Ten-Deer (baked venison medallions), Stand by Your Lamb (roasted lamb doused in mint sauce), and more—**Horny Bull** (67 The Strand, 07/578-8741; daily for lunch and dinner) doesn't take itself too seriously. But the food is good and with most mains under $30, it's a good place for a meal.

Like the surrounding eateries, **Naked Grape** (97 The Strand, 07/579-5555; daily 7 A.M.–midnight) maximizes its location with lots of outdoor tables overlooking the water. Expect to pay $12 for a stack of pancakes.

You can sit outside at **Soho** (07/577-0577; Mon.–Sat. from 6 P.M.), but the interior is one of the most stylish along the restaurant strip. You could start with beer-battered mushrooms ($15) and then order herb-crusted salmon ($30) as a main. The wine list features lots of local bottles.

For seafood without the seagulls, it's hard to beat **Harbourside** (The Strand, 07/571-0520; daily 11:30 A.M.–9:30 P.M.). Built over the water as a yacht club in 1933, the original

structure has been converted to a fine restaurant, losing none of its nautical charm along the way. Most tables enjoy harbor views, but the very best sit along a covered verandah. In addition to lots of seafood (including the delicious Harbourside Bouillabasse; $31.50), the menu features a variety of light pastas and salads for under $20.

If you can drag yourself away from the water, consider a light meal at **Sober Camel Café** (45 Grey St., 07/577-0705; daily 8 A.M.–4 P.M.), a long, narrow place surrounded by typical downtown businesses. Rich coffee is just $2, butter chicken pies are $3, and toasted paninis a bargain at just $5.

More of a restaurant than café, **Shiraz Café** (12 Wharf St., 07/577-0059; Mon.–Sat. 11 A.M.–2:30 P.M., daily from 5 P.M.) has a great little courtyard, complete with vine-covered stone walls. Main courses from the Mediterranean-inspired menu range $17.50–26, including a hearty moussaka.

Japanese restaurants are few and far between in the central portion of the North Island, with makes **Takaka** (21 Devonport Rd., 07/579-4177; Mon.–Sat. noon–2 P.M., daily from 6 P.M.) a good spot for sushi lovers.

Information and Services

The first place to head for information on Tauranga and Mount Maunganui is the **Tauranga Visitor Centre** (one block north of The Strand at 95 Willow St., 07/571-3211, www.bayofplentynz.com; Mon.–Fri. 7 A.M.–5:30 P.M., Sat.–Sun. 8 A.M.–4 P.M.). Part of the bus depot, it has brochures and tourist newspapers, and also gives out information on Tuhua Island. The **Automobile Association** has an office at the corner of Devonport Road and 1st Avenue (07/578-2222).

The post office is at 17 Grey Street. You can reach **Tauranga Hospital** on Cameron Road at 07/579-8000.

Getting There and Around

If you're short on time, **Air New Zealand** (07/577-7300 or 0800/737-300, www.airnewzealand.com) has direct flights to Tauranga from Auckland and Wellington. The airport is on the Mount Maunganui side of the city, off Hewletts Road. **Tauranga Mount Taxis** (07/578-6086, $12 per person) has a door-to-door shuttle to Tauranga and Mount Maunganui from the airport. **Intercity** (www .intercitycoach.co.nz) coaches connect Tauranga with Auckland, Thames, Hamilton, Rotorua, Whakatane, Opotiki, and Gisborne. The depot is the **Tauranga Visitor Centre** (95 Willow St., 07/578-8103).

Bay Hopper (0800/422-228) runs a local bus service through all the suburbs and to Mount Maunganui; $1.50–3 per sector, or ride all day for $6. Car rental agencies with an office in Tauranga include **Avis** (07/578-4204), **Budget** (07/578-5156), and **Rent-a-dent** (07/578-1772). Local cab companies include **Tauranga Mount Taxis** (07/578-6086) and **Citicabs** (07/577-0999).

MOUNT MAUNGANUI
Known for its wonderful surf beach and mellow vacation atmosphere, Mount Maunganui (pop. 17,000) sprawls across a low peninsula just a five-minute drive from Tauranga. Separated from that much larger city by a tidal estuary (but linked by a bridge), "the Mount," as it's usually known, is made up of row upon row of holiday homes. The real estate boom of the last decade has seen many of the older "baches" be replaced with million-dollar homes and shiny new condos, especially at the north end, where, low and behold, there's a perfectly symmetrical volcano surrounded by water on three sides.

◖ The Mount
Just by looking at its classically conical shape you can see how the Mount made an impressive Maori *pa* in the 18th and 19th centuries (you can still see the old fortifications, particularly on the southeastern side, facing town). Several walking tracks lead to the top of this 234-meter (770-ft) peak (allow 50 minutes to reach the summit), where your effort is rewarded with a magnificent 360-degree panoramic view. An easier track circles the base of the mountain; it takes about an hour to complete the circular route.

Walkers and sheep mix on the trails around Mount Maunganui.

BAY OF PLENTY

© ANDREW HEMPSTEAD

© ANDREW HEMPSTEAD

The beaches at Mount Maunganui are among the country's best.

At the foot of the volcano, unique **hot saltwater pools** (Adams Ave., 07/575-0868; Mon.–Sat. 6 A.M.–10 P.M., Sun. 8 A.M.–10 P.M.; adult $3, child $2) are the only ones of their kind in the Southern Hemisphere. The saltwater comes from a 40-meter-deep (130-ft-deep) bore, and when the water is first brought up from underground it's a sizzling 45°C (113°F). The water is cooled to a still-hot 39°C (102°F) before being pumped into the large main pool and several (hotter) smaller pools; this is a great place to soothe aching muscles and tired feet.

Beaches

The most popular beach in this area is **Mount Maunganui Beach,** directly opposite the concentration of restaurants at the north end of Marine Parade. This wide stretch of sand offers safe swimming and the distinctive volcano as a backdrop. Tiny **Moturiki Island** is linked to the mainland by a sandbar along this stretch of sand and is laced with walking tracks. The golden sands and sparkling surf stretch for almost 16 km (10 mi) southeast from this point,

and can be reached from Marine Parade on the eastern side of Mount Maunganui, and from Papamoa Beach. Additionally, small, sheltered harbor beaches run along Pilot Bay, ending at Salisbury Wharf on the western side of town.

Experienced surfers will tell you there are better breaks elsewhere, but the sandy bottom and rolling waves make the Mount one of the most popular surf spots in the country. In 2006, the first phase of **Mount Reef** was completed. One of the world's only artificial surf spots, it comprises a huge A-frame-shaped concentration of sand bags, which creates a steep, hollow wave. It's around two km (1.2 mi) down from the end of the beach opposite Tay Street. You can see all the action via a webcam at www.mountreef.co.nz. **Mount Surf Shop** (96 Maunganui Rd., 07/575-9133) rents surfboards ($30 per day) and wetsuits ($20).

Accommodations and Camping

Accommodation around the Mount is relatively expensive, especially in January, when reservations are needed far in advance.

BAY OF PLENTY

Pacific Coast Lodge (432 Maunganui Rd., 07/574-9601 or 0800/666-622, www.pacific coastlodge.co.nz; dorm beds $23–25, $70 s or d) is a large, modern, professionally operated backpacker lodge along the main road into town and a few blocks from the beach. All facilities are excellent, including a large kitchen and dining area, a TV room, a laundry, and a courtyard. The double rooms are on a different level to the dorms, and share their own bathrooms.

One of the cheapest motels is the **Blue Haven Motel** (10 Tweed St., 07/575-6508, www.bluehaven.co.nz; $80–95 s, $105–135 d). A flat 10-minute walk from the beach, the motel has nine units, each featuring a full kitchen. Out front is a grassed picnic area with a barbecue for guest use.

Right below the Mount and 200 meters (660 ft) from the beach lies **Ocean Sands Motel** (6 Maunganui Rd., 07/574-9794 or 0800/726-371, www.oceansands.co.nz; $120–185 s or d). With a striking blue-and-white interior and vaulted timber ceiling, each of its spacious units is fully self-contained.

It's impossible to miss the "twin towers" rising high above the beach. They are part of **Oceanside** (1 Maunganui Rd., 07/575-5371, www.oceanside.co.nz), with two heated outdoor pools, a fitness room, a sauna, and easy access to the downstairs cafés lining Marine Parade. The least expensive rooms ($180 s or d) don't have water views, but high up in the towers are oversized two-bedroom apartments with big balconies and even bigger views ($390).

Mount Maunganui Domain Motor Camp (1 Adams Ave., 07/575-4471; campsites $24–28 s or d) is an old-fashioned campground, with sites around the hot-water pools at the base of the Mount and on both ocean and harbor beaches.

Cosy Corner Holiday Park, four km (2.5 mi) east of the Mount (40 Ocean Beach Rd., Omanu, 07/575-5899, www.cosycorner.co.nz) has a wonderful location across the road from the beach, and a big solar-heated pool if you get tired of saltwater. Campsites are $28, kitchen-equipped cabins $60 s or d, and family units are $90 (rates rise to $40, $90, and $120 respectively over the January school holidays).

Food

The most popular cafés and restaurants are those under "the Towers" at the north end of Marine Parade, but be forewarned, finding an empty table is not easy, especially on weekends. The first to open is **Sidetrack Café** (Marine Pde., 07/575-2145; daily 6:30 A.M.–4 P.M.), with strong coffee and delicious vanilla pancakes with roast banana ($13)—a good start to the day.

Slow food—as opposed to "fast food"—is a growing worldwide movement that has found its way to Mount Maunganui in the form of **Slowfish** (Marine Pde., 07/574-7554; daily 7 A.M.–4 P.M.). Everything is healthy and made in-house, with ingredients locally sourced; organic ingredients are used wherever possible. The result? A mouthwatering eggs Florentine ($14.50), fish cakes with chili jam ($14), and poached chicken on a bed of organic greens ($15).

Sandrock Cafe (Marine Pde., 07/574-7554; daily for breakfast, lunch, and dinner) is a contemporary bistro featuring hardwood *rimu* floors and stylish timber-and-chrome furniture. The elevated deck allows for ocean views. It offers a menu featuring mostly seafood and steak; dinners range $24–32.

The usual array of cafés, bakeries, and inexpensive Asian restaurants are scattered along Maunganui Road. For homemade baked goods to enjoy inside or outside in the sunshine, try **Cottage Cafe** (373 Maunganui Rd., 07/575-3733; daily 8:30 A.M.–4 P.M.). Don't be put off by the unappealing decor; **Funky Fish** (190 Maunganui Rd., 07/574-5952; daily noon–8 P.M.) has great fish-and-chips.

Information and Services

All you really need to know is where the beach is, but for information on local accommodations, head to **Mount Maunganui Visitor Centre** (Salisbury Ave., 07/575-5099; Mon.–Fri. 9 A.M.–5 P.M., weekends in summer only).

The post office is at the back of an arcade, one shop from the BNZ Bank on the main street before you reach the Mount. **Mount Medical Centre** is at 257 Maunganui Road (07/575-3073).

Tauranga to the East Cape

TE PUKE

The largest town between Tauranga/Mount Maunganui and Whakatane is Te Puke (pop. 6,800), 20 km (12 mi) from Tauranga along Highway 2. The town, nestled in the middle of a large kiwifruit growing area, calls itself the "Kiwifruit Capital of the World," and with over 90 percent of the country's kiwifruit coming for the region, no one disputes the claim.

Sights

Kiwi 360 (82 Young Rd., 07/573-6340; daily 9 A.M.–5 P.M.; adult $20, child $10), six km (four mi) through town to the east, is a horticultural theme park in a working orchard. Admission to the park includes a ride on a kiwifruit-shaped trailer through the orchard, a tour of the packaging plant, and fruit-tasting and wine-tasting.

Next door is the **Vintage Auto Barn** (07/573-6547, Tues.–Sun. 9 A.M.–5 P.M.; adult

You'll know you're in kiwifruit country when you see this roadside attraction.

© ANDREW HEMPSTEAD

$10, child $3), with over 100 running antique vehicles.

WHAKATANE

Go to Whakatane (fah-kah-tah-nee), population 17,000, around the Bay of Plenty 100 km (62 mi) southeast of Tauranga, to enjoy the sunshine, the beaches, and the relaxed atmosphere. The best-known surf beach, **Ohope Beach,** six km (3.7 mi) east from Whakatane, attracts surfers and fishermen year-round, holidaymakers by the hordes in summer, and hikers in search of great coastal views.

Whakatane Museum and Gallery and Vicinity

Uninspiring from the street, this museum (11 Boon St., 07/307-9805; Mon.–Fri. 10 A.M.–4:30 P.M., Sat.–Sun. 11 A.M.–3 P.M.; donation) is filled with an interesting collection of Maori artifacts and displays detailing their culture and lifestyle. It also has a large collection of historical photos, a New Zealand book collection, and exhibits on European settlement.

Another interesting place well worth a visit is **Tauwhare Pa,** which is beside the highway from Ohope to Opotiki (just past the harbor). Interpretive boards along a short walkway explain how the reserve may have appeared and operated in A.D. 1700 (when most Bay of Plenty *pa* were built).

Hiking

Whakatane and the surrounding area have a reputation for very enjoyable local walkways, scenic reserves, and an island wildlife sanctuary. Ask at the information center for the helpful (and free) handouts on **Kohi Point Walkway, Whakatane Town Centre Walk, Ohope Bush Walk** (which allows hikers to walk through beautiful bush scenery from Ohope Beach to Whakatane via Ohope and Mokorua Scenic Reserves), **Lathams Hill Track, Matata Walking Track,** and **Matata Lagoon Walk** (you can see fantastic birdlife from an

BAY OF PLENTY

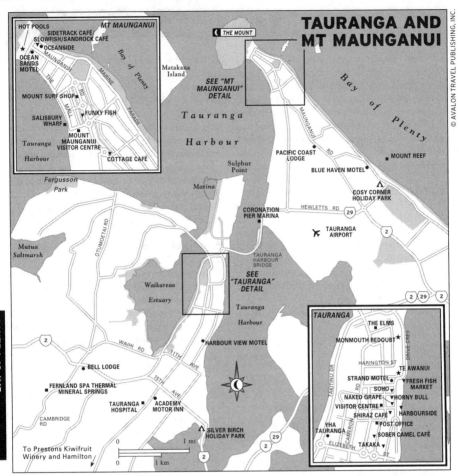

© AVALON TRAVEL PUBLISHING, INC.

observation platform). **Pine Bush Scenic Reserve** allows people with disabilities to enjoy a small remnant of *kahikatea* forest and plenty of birdlife via a wheelchair walkway.

Swimming with Dolphins

Dolphins are among the most loved of all marine mammals, and you shouldn't miss the opportunity to frolic in the open ocean with these fun-loving creatures. **Dolphins Down Under** (96 The Strand, 07/308-4636 or 0800/354-773, www.dolphinsdownunder.co.nz; $130)

offers a five- to six-hour trip out into the Bay of Plenty. During the trip you can swim with dolphins, possibly see whales (if you're lucky), and get a distant view of White Island. If you go as a spectator the cost is $90.

Accommodations and Camping

Lloyds Lodge (10 Domain Rd., 07/307-8005, www.lloydslodge.com; dorm beds $28, $56 d) is a renovated 1930s villa with just 20 beds, but facilities are good, with a library, book exchange, Internet, and a courtyard with barbecue. It's in a residential area a 10-minute walk from downtown.

On the road into town from Tauranga (just east of the Whakatane River), **Camellia Court Motel** (11 Domain Rd., 07/308-6213, www .camelliacourt.co.nz; $85 s, $100 d) is a Federation-style motel with 12 rooms overlooking gardens. Each room has a kitchen, and there's a barbecue area for those balmy summer evenings.

In a prime location across from Whakatane Wharf, **White Island Rendezvous** (15 The Strand, 07/308-9588; www.whiteisland .co.nz; $110–180 s or d) is an excellent choice for an overnight stay in Whakatane. Home to White Island Tours (see the following section, *White Island*), this accommodation comprises 24 charming units, each with a microwave and some with small kitchens. Although a little on the small side, the rooms provide good value. Wireless Internet and an onsite café add to the appeal.

Whakatane Holiday Park (McGarvey Rd., 07/308-8694, camping $26, cabins from $50) offers the usual communal facilities, a TV lounge and game room, and a swimming pool, but out of town to the east, **Ohope Beach Top 10 Holiday Park** (367 Harbour Rd., 07/312-4460, www.ohopebeach.co.nz, $20 tent sites, $22 powered sites, $45 cabins) is in a better location for beach lovers.

If you're going on toward Rotorua (or even if you're not) you may enjoy staying at **Awakeri Hot Springs** (07/304-9117, www.awakeri springs.co.nz). About 16 km (ten mi) from Whakatane on Highway 30, it has the usual holiday park facilities, with the added plus of warm mineral swim baths and hot mineral spa pools. Campsites are $25, kitchen-equipped cabins $60 s or d, and motel rooms rent for $105.

Food
Kick-start your day down along the waterfront at **PeeJay's Coffee House** (15 The Strand, 07/308-9588; daily 6:30 A.M.–5 P.M.). The base for White Island Tours, this café has a great little sunny deck off to one side. The food is surprisingly creative, with most breakfasts and lunches under $15. **Bean Coffee Roastery** (163 The Strand, 07/307-0494; Mon.–Fri. 8:30 A.M.–4 P.M., Sat. 10 A.M.–2 P.M.) is another option for a light meal and good coffee, which is roasted in-house. **Barnacles Sea Food Restaurant** (122 The Strand, 07/308-7429) is a great place for fish-and-chips—it's surrounded by seafaring relics such as fish nets and buoys. Fish of the Day is about $16 at dinner, with many other choices, much of it from local waters.

Continuing along the main road through downtown is the main wharf, and a couple of good eateries right in the heart of the ocean-going action. The name **NZ Finest** (2 The Strand, 07/307-1100; daily 10 A.M.–8 P.M.) may be a stretch, but this place does do very good fish-and-chips, with a couple of tables out on the wharf the best place to enjoy this inexpensive (under $10) meal. Next door, you'll spend more money and more time at **Wharf Shed Restaurant** (2 The Strand, 07/308-5698; daily for lunch and dinner), which delivers consistent seafood in a stylish waterfront setting. Most lunches are under $20 (the prawn and baby squid with sweet chili and passion-fruit dipping sauce was delicious) and dinners range $25–32.

Babinka (14 Kakahoroa Dr., 07/307-0009; daily for lunch and dinner) is in a distinctive blue building within a shopping-mall parking lot. But don't be put off by the location—the menu is filled with modern interpretations of classic Asian dishes, with curries around $20 and seafood blackboard specials under $25.

Information
Whakatane Visitor Information Centre (corner Kakahoroa Dr. and Quay St., 07/308-6058 or 0800/942-528, www.whakatane.com; Mon.–Fri. 8:30 A.M.–6 P.M., summer also Sat.–Sun. 9 A.M.–5 P.M.) is a sweeping modern building along the waterfront.

Getting There and Around
Whakatane Airport is on Aerodrome Road,

BAY OF PLENTY

10 km (six mi) north of town; if you don't have your own transportation, you can take a taxi (about $20 one-way). **Air New Zealand** (07/308-8397 or 0800/737-300, www .airnewzealand.com) flies from Whakatane to Auckland and Wellington. **Intercity** (www .intercitycoach.co.nz) connects Whakatane with Tauranga, Rotorua, and Gisborne via Opotiki. Buses stop outside the visitor center.

The only rental car agency in town is **Avis** (07/308-5636), with a few vehicles at the airport (reserve ahead). For a cab, call **Whakatane Taxi** (07/307-0388).

WHITE ISLAND

White Island lies about 50 km (31 mi) north of Whakatane, at the northern end of the Taupo-Rotorua volcanic fault line. This is an excellent active volcano to visit because of its intense thermal activity. Originally named by Captain Cook in 1769 for the shroud of steam surrounding it, the island continues to belch steam, noxious gases, and toxic fumes into the atmosphere. Occasional eruptions send up huge clouds of ash visible from the mainland, weather permitting. Geysers, fumaroles, holes of sulfuric acid, and boiling-water pools lie within the crater, best enjoyed from a safe distance—like from a helicopter!

Sulphur was mined on the island until an explosive landslide in 1914 killed all the miners and wiped out the mining settlement. Miners made several other mining attempts, but because of the unpredictable and violent nature of the island, abandoned all. Despite the lack of fresh water and the presence of toxic fumes, parts of the island are covered by *pohutukawa* trees and inhabited by quite a variety of birdlife. Gannets, red-billed gulls, and petrels seem to thrive in this strange environment and have made their breeding grounds on the island, now a private scenic reserve.

Visiting the Island

White Island Tours (15 The Strand, 07/308-9588 or 0800/733-529, www.whiteisland.co.nz; $160 per person) runs to the island between one and three time daily from Whakatane Wharf. The boat trip takes around 80 minutes in a stable 20-meter (66-ft) vessel. Around two hours is spent exploring the island, time enough to walk inside the crater. Lunch is included in the tour rate. You can also visit the island by helicopter. **Vulcan Helicopters** (07/308-4188 or 0800/804-354, www.vulcanheli.co.nz; $395 per person) offers the return transfer and a one-hour guided walk. Departures are on demand from Whakatane Airport.

GEOTHERMAL HEARTLAND

A volcanic fault running from White Island, in the Bay of Plenty, to Tongariro National Park, in the heart of the North Island, is one of the world's most concentrated geothermal areas anywhere in the world. Along its length is an amazing array of natural wonders, many of which have been turned into commercial attractions. In fact, the volcanic Pink and White Terraces began drawing visitors in the mid-1800s—that is, until they were destroyed by the eruption of Mount Tarawera in 1886.

The region's largest population center, Rotorua bubbles with thermal activity. All sorts of natural attractions abound throughout the city, including spectacular geysers, steaming cliffs, hot springs spurting from the ground, bubbling pools of boiling mud, and soothing mineral hot pools. Steam seems to waft out of every drain, crack in the pavement, and hole in the ground. Some of Rotorua's natural thermal energy has been tapped through artesian-type bores and other methods for central- and hot-water heating by the locals. You can pitch your tent on a naturally heated site, or marvel at the Maori who continue to use it for cooking and heating as they have done for centuries. The ever-present but soon-unnoticed smell of rotten-egg gas (hydrogen sulfide) permeates the atmosphere in all directions. Surrounding the city are magnificent bush-fringed lakes, icy-cold springs, crystal-clear trout streams, and mighty forests. The Rotorua region is also a center of Maori culture, with a great deal of New Zealand native art, architecture, song and dance, and colorful evening entertainment to offer.

Lying along the same fault line as Rotorua,

© ANDREW HEMPSTEAD

HIGHLIGHTS

Rotorua Museum: The Tudor building itself is a landmark, while inside you'll find an array of Maori artifacts and the story of past volcanic eruptions (page 156).

Whakarewarewa Thermal Valley: On Rotorua's back doorstep, this famous thermal area has spectacular geysers, Maori culture, and a village where locals live among the steaming vents and hot pools (page 157).

Wai-O-Tapu: The colorful Champagne Pool is just one highlight of this expansive thermal area (page 159).

Buried Village: Destroyed by a volcanic eruption over 100 years ago, this excavated village allows a peek at life in the shadow of a volcano (page 160).

Polynesian Spa: After a day touring the sights of Rotorua, plan on spending an hour or two doing absolutely nothing at this lakefront complex (page 162).

Volcanic Activity Centre: Curious about the whys and hows of volcanoes? This is the place to find out all the answers (page 171).

Lake Taupo: Sailing, cruising, fishing, or simply laying on a sandy beach – you can do it all at this magnificent lake with a volcanic backdrop (page 173).

Tongariro National Trout Centre: In a delightful riverside location, this trout hatchery presents visitors with the story of New Zealand's best-known fish (page 177).

Tongariro Crossing: It's a solid day's walk to traverse this hiking trail, but the volcanic views and thermal wonders en route make it all worthwhile (page 184).

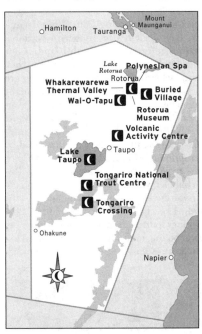

LOOK FOR ‖‖ TO FIND RECOMMENDED SIGHTS, ACTIVITIES, DINING, AND LODGING.

the Taupo region and Tongariro National Park to the south are also geothermally active. Lake Taupo is New Zealand's largest lake. Located exactly in the middle of the North Island, the crystal-clear bright-blue waters filling this volcanic crater cover a 616-square-km (238-sq-mi) area—about 42 km (26 mi) long and 30 km (19 mi) wide. White pumice beaches and sheltered rocky coves line its shores, and vast pine forests cover much of the surrounding plains and ranges. At the northeastern end of the lake, Taupo is a relaxed resort town best known as a base for lake and river trout fishing. Highway 1 follows the eastern shore of Lake Taupo, connecting Taupo and Turangi, another angler's paradise. It is possible to

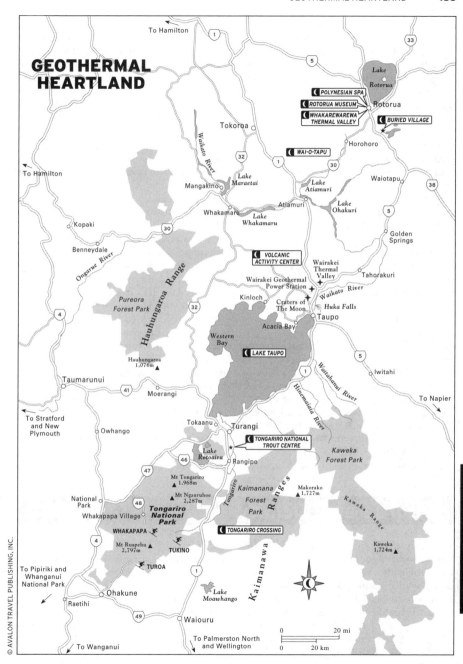

GEOTHERMAL HEARTLAND

To Hamilton

1

33

5

Lake
Rotorua

(POLYNESIAN SPA

(ROTORUA MUSEUM   Rotorua

(WHAKAREWAREWA
THERMAL VALLEY   (BURIED VILLAGE

Tokoroa

Waikato River

Horohoro

32

1   (WAI-O-TAPU

30

To Hamilton

Mangakino   Lake
Maraetai   Lake
Atiamuri   Waiotapu   38

Atiamuri   Lake
Ohakuri   5

Whakamaru   Lake
Whakamaru

Kopaki   30   Golden
Springs

Benneydale

Ongarue River

(VOLCANIC
ACTIVITY CENTER   Wairakei
Thermal
Valley   Tahorakuri

Wairakei Geothermal
Power Station

Pureora
Forest Park   32   Kinloch   Craters of
The Moon   Waikato River   Huka Falls

Acacia Bay   Taupo

Western
Bay

Hauhungaroa
1,076m ▲   (LAKE TAUPO

5

1   Waitahanui River   Iwitahi

Taumarunui

41   Moerangi

Hinemaiaia River

To Napier

To Stratford
and New
Plymouth   Tokaanu   Turangi

Owhango

(TONGARIRO NATIONAL
TROUT CENTRE

Lake
Rotoaira   Rangipo   Kaweka
Forest Park

47

46

Mt Tongariro
1,968m ▲

National
Park   48   Mt Ngauruhoe
2,287m ▲   Kaimanana
Forest
Park   Makorako
1,727m ▲   Kaweka Range

Whakapapa Village   **Tongariro
National
Park**

WHAKAPAPA   (TONGARIRO CROSSING

4   Mt Ruapehu
2,797m ▲   TUKINO   Kaweka
1,724m ▲

To Pipiriki and
Whanganui
National Park   TUROA

Ohakune   Lake
Moawhango   Kaimanawa

Raetihi

49   Waiouru

To Wanganui   To Palmerston North
and Wellington

0   20 mi

0   20 km

© AVALON TRAVEL PUBLISHING, INC.

circumnavigate the lake by taking Highway 41 from Turangi northwest to Kuratau Junction, then Highway 32 north up the western side, but most travelers continue south to Tongariro National Park. The park's three impressive peaks—Tongariro, Ngauruhoe, and Ruapehu—can be seen from as far away as Taupo, but you'll want to get closer to appreciate these mountains and the barren lava fields that surround them. In winter, thousands of outdoor enthusiasts flock to the beautiful ski fields of Mount Ruapehu. Apart from the excellent snow conditions, variety of trails, and long ski season—from late June to early November—you can't beat the views of snow-covered mountains and steaming craters.

PLANNING YOUR TIME

If you have two weeks to explore the North Island, I would recommend spending two days in Rotorua and then, depending on your interests, one day fishing at Turangi or hiking in Tongariro National Park.

Rotorua is the first destination of many travelers heading south from Auckland, but it can also be easily reached after visiting the Bay of Plenty or Waitomo Caves. Regardless of how you arrive, you should plan to spend at least two full days in this thermally active wonderland. In the town itself, you should make a point of visiting the **Rotorua Museum** and then move outdoors to **Whakarewarewa Thermal Valley,** where you can see a thermally active area up close, and see how Maori

make the most of this unique natural resource. Of the many other thermal attractions around the city, **Wai-O-Tapu Thermal Wonderland** is the most distinctive, while **Buried village** is historically worthwhile. Two other things you should fit into your Rotorua schedule are enjoying a soak at the **Polynesian Spa** and partaking in a traditional *hangi* dinner.

From Rotorua, options include heading east to the East Cape or southeast to Hawke's Bay, or south to Taupo. This chapter assumes you'll follow the latter, and in keeping with the thermal theme, Taupo delivers, but on a less commercial scale than Rotorua. It's a bustling resort town, with fantastic fishing, cruising, and swimming in **Lake Taupo.** Unlike Rotorua, many local attractions are free, including Craters of the Moon, while others, such as the interesting **Volcanic Activity Centre,** have a token admission charge. Beyond the lake is Turangi, where the main attraction, the **Tongariro National Trout Centre,** will have anglers champing at the bit to dangle a line. If you are a keen angler, this is a good low-key town in which to spend a night or two—accommodations are inexpensive and most are within walking distance of the famed Tongariro River.

Beyond Turangi are the volcanic peaks of Tongariro National Park. The park offers plenty of short walks, but for serious hikers, the **Tongariro Crossing** is a must. As you'll need a full day for this walk, plan on spending the night before your hike in or around the park.

Rotorua and Vicinity

Thermally active Rotorua (pop. 75,000), 200 km (124 mi) south of Auckland, will amaze you. Originally a wild and swampy wasteland dotted with steaming pools and mud holes, it has been inhabited by Maori since the 14th century. The Maori had been using the healing properties of the mineral hot pools for 500 years before Europeans recognized their benefits in the late 1870s. The original Maori

landowners gave 50 acres of land containing the "healing springs" as a gift to British government representatives, and the early township of Rotorua was built. In addition to the area's healing qualities, its recreational value prompted rapid development into a tourist attraction.

Today, Rotorua exists almost entirely because of tourism. The cost of visiting the major attractions will add up, but a few of the

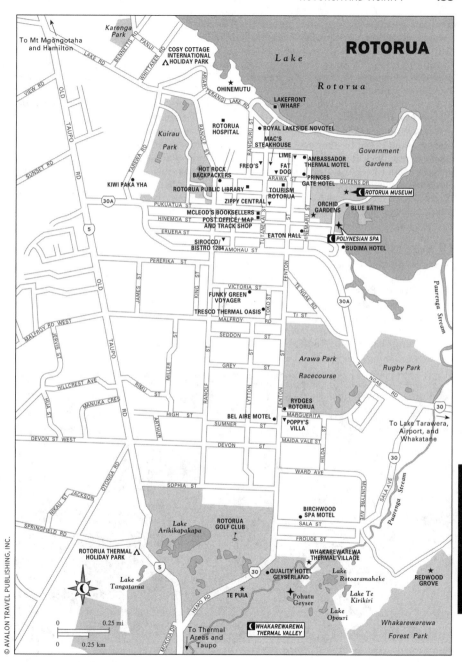

ROTORUA

Karenga Park

To Mt Mgongotaha and Hamilton

COSY COTTAGE INTERNATIONAL HOLIDAY PARK

Lake Rotorua

OHINEMUTU

LAKEFRONT WHARF

Kuirau Park

ROTORUA HOSPITAL

ROYAL LAKESIDE NOVOTEL

MAC'S STEAKHOUSE

Government Gardens

LIME

AMBASSADOR THERMAL MOTEL

FREO'S

HOT ROCK BACKPACKERS

FAT DOG

PRINCES GATE HOTEL

KIWI PAKA YHA

ARAWA ST

ROTORUA PUBLIC LIBRARY

TOURISM ROTORUA

ROTORUA MUSEUM

QUEENS DR

30A

ZIPPY CENTRAL

ORCHID GARDENS

BLUE BATHS

PUKUATUA ST

MCLEOD'S BOOKSELLERS

HINEMOA ST

POST OFFICE/ MAP AND TRACK SHOP

POLYNESIAN SPA

5

ERUERA ST

EATON HALL

SIROCCO/ BISTRO 1284

AMOHAU ST

SUDIMA HOTEL

PERERIKA ST

VICTORIA ST

FUNKY GREEN VOYAGER

TRESCO THERMAL OASIS

MALFROY RD

SEDDON ST

Arawa Park Racecourse

GREY ST

Rugby Park

FENTON

30A

TI ST

JAMES ST

KING ST

MILLER ST

RANOLF ST

LYTTON ST

TE NGAE RD

TOKO ST

MALFROY RD WEST

JERVIS ST

HILLCREST AVE

MANUKA CRES

RIMU ST

HIGH ST

BEL AIRE MOTEL

SUMNER ST

RYDGES ROTORUA

MARGUERITA

POPPY'S VILLA

TE NGAE RD

30

To Lake Tarawera, Airport, and Whakatane

DEVON ST WEST

ARTHUR ST

DEVON ST

MAIDA VALE ST

HILDA ST

30

OYONGA RD

WARD AVE

JACKSON

NIKAU ST

SPRINGFIELD RD

SOPHIA ST

BIRCHWOOD SPA MOTEL

SALA ST

MCINTYRE AVE

SALA AVE

Puarenga Stream

ROTORUA THERMAL HOLIDAY PARK

Lake Arikikapakapa

ROTORUA GOLF CLUB

FROUDE ST

WHAKAREWAREWA THERMAL VILLAGE

5

Lake Tangatarua

30

QUALITY HOTEL GEYSERLAND

Lake Rotoaramaheke

REDWOOD GROVE

TE PUIA

Pohutu Geyser

Lake Te Kirikiri

Lake Opouri

Whakarewarewa Forest Park

WHAKAREWAREWA THERMAL VALLEY

To Thermal Areas and Taupo

MOKOIA DR

HEMO RD

0   0.25 mi

0   0.25 km

© AVALON TRAVEL PUBLISHING, INC.

VIEW RD

OLD TAUPO RD

SUNSET RD

TAREWA RD

ARIKI

PANUI

BENNETT'S RD

WHITTAKER RD

LAKE RD

TE RANGI

ARIAR

RANOLF ST

RANGIURU ST

TUTANEKAI ST

HINEMARU ST

FENTON ST

natural attractions are free and, despite the year-round crowds, the unpredictable and volatile atmosphere seemingly seeping up from beneath your feet sets Rotorua apart—it's one of the exceptional areas of New Zealand that shouldn't be missed.

SIGHTS IN AND AROUND DOWNTOWN

Only a couple of the less spectacular hot spots around town have not been commercialized and are still free, including **Government Gardens,** through the impressive arches along Hinemaru Street, and **Kuirau Park.** The latter, on the west side of downtown, has public bathing pools.

◖ Rotorua Museum

Overlooking the gardens and a maze of croquet lawns is the impressive Bath House, the original Tudor Bath House building where people with joint afflictions and skin diseases came for various treatments using the soothing local volcanic mud and mineral water. Today, the building houses the Rotorua Museum

(Hinemoa St., 07/349-8334; Oct.–Mar. daily 9 A.M.–8 P.M., Apr.–Sept. daily 9 A.M.–5 P.M.; adult $11, child $5), with plans for expansion continuing through to 2012. Highlights include Taking the Cure, a fascinating display of equipment used in conjunction with mud bath therapy in this building between 1906 and 1966; displays on the Volcanic Plateau, the mighty eruption of Mount Tarawera in 1886, and the Pink and White Terraces—a famous tourist attraction of the 19th century destroyed in the eruption; and a collection of stunning historical photos. The Maori section displays intricately carved greenstone (New Zealand jade) ornaments that "have no equal in all of Polynesia," along with beautiful feather cloaks and many other objects from the past. You can also see a large display of mounted native New Zealand birds, and upstairs, a replica of a settler's cottage furnished with colonial objects.

Ohinemutu

The Maori village of Ohinemutu is at the northern end of downtown along the shores of Lake Rotorua, an easy walk from the lakefront.

Rotorua's original Tudor Bath House has been converted to a museum.

© ANDREW HEMPSTEAD

GEOTHERMAL HEARTLAND

Here you'll find steaming holes in the ground, pipes sticking out of house foundations belching steam away from the buildings, and the awesome sound of boiling water coming from deep below (a free thermal spot!). On the shore stands the beautiful Maori Anglican **St. Faith's Anglican Church** (daily 8 A.M.–5 P.M.; donation). Completely decorated with Maori art, woven wall panels, and intricate carvings, it features a particularly effective etched-glass window at the far end. Services are held on Sunday at 10 A.M. and 7 P.M. A stone's throw from the church is the 1887 **Tamatekapua Meeting House** (no public access), another good place to admire the beauty of Maori carvings inlaid with *paua* shell.

WHAKAREWAREWA THERMAL VALLEY

The best-known and closest thermal area to downtown is "Whaka," or you can try to pronounce the full name (fa-ka-ree-wa-ree-wa), which is shortened itself from Te Whakarewarewatangaoteopetuaawahiao. To get there, head south from downtown along Fenton Street for three km (two mi). Here you'll find two very different attractions—Te Puia, a huge tour bus–friendly complex that encompasses the most active geysers, and Whakarewarewa Thermal village, where around 70 Maori live a traditional life amid never-ending thermal activity.

Te Puia

Te Puia (Hemo Rd., 07/348-9047; 8 A.M.–6 P.M.; adult $28, child $14) is the biggest and most popular thermal attraction in Rotorua. It has undergone many changes in recent years, including the addition of a massive museum that opened in 2007. Just beyond the main entrance, at the **New Zealand Arts and Crafts Institute,** Maori craftspeople learn the techniques of their ancestors. Once inside the thermal area you'll see amazing geysers gushing skyward, hot-water springs, eerie boiling mud pools, and steaming silica terraces. Pohutu Geyser is particularly impressive, but "show times" are unpredictable. After

© ANDREW HEMPSTEAD

Pohutu Geyser is a highlight of Te Puia.

seeing the thermal attractions you can wander past the accurate replica of a *pa,* watch Maori women demonstrate their methods of cooking with natural steam, and take in a 45-minute lunchtime Maori Cultural Concert (daily at 12:30 P.M.). Guided tours leave every hour on the hour 10 A.M.–4 P.M., but you can cruise around the place on your own; allow at least an hour.

If admission is beyond your budget, head for the Quality Hotel Geyserland (Fenton St.) for a drink in the hotel bar. For the price of a beer you get a tremendous view of the geysers from a distance—the bar and terrace overlook Whaka, and on summer evenings after the thermal area is closed to the public, you can watch Maori kids dive from Whaka's steaming white terraces into the hot pools far below. Another good (free) view of the geyser is from the viewpoint along the Yellow Trail in Whakarewarewa State Forest Park.

Whakarewarewa Thermal Village

Much quieter than Te Puia, this is an

GEOTHERMAL HEARTLAND

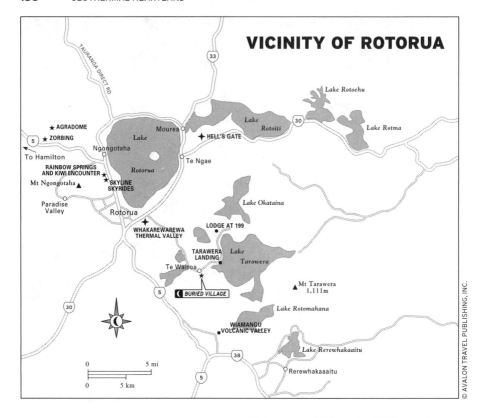

VICINITY OF ROTORUA

© AVALON TRAVEL PUBLISHING, INC.

authentic village (Tryon St., 07/349-3463 or 0800/924-426; daily 8:30 A.M.–5 P.M.; adult $23, child $11.50) where 70-odd Maori residents go about their daily life—cooking in steaming hot pools, driving the narrow roads, and living in regular houses. Of course, tourists are walking the streets, and many residents serve their needs—leading guided tours, selling arts and crafts, and dishing up traditional fare at a café. You also get a good view across to the geysers at Te Puia.

THERMAL ATTRACTIONS AROUND ROTORUA

Whakarewarewa gets a lot of attention simply because of its proximity to town, but three other commercialized thermal areas lie within a 30-minute drive of downtown.

Waimangu Volcanic Valley

Waimangu (587 Waimangu Rd., 07/366-6137; daily 8:30 A.M.–5 P.M.), 26 km/16 mi southeast of Rotorua, is a large and exciting active thermal spot at the southern end of the huge area devastated by the 1886 Mount Tarawera eruption. Take the Valley Walk (about three km/two mi) down through beautiful bushland where thousands of deafening cicadas crowd the trees in summer while you view Southern Crater, Emerald Pools, and the steaming blue-green lake of Waimangu Cauldron. The lake occupies the crater of the 1917 explosion (the last minor eruption was in 1973), and although its temperature averages 50°C (122°F), it's claimed to be the "world's largest boiling lake." Surrounded by smoldering rocks and steaming bush, and disguised by the mysterious patterns created by surface steam, the large cauldron is both majestic and eerie. Farther along you'll view Cathedral Rock and the colorful decomposing cliffs, cross Hot Water Creek, and climb to the pale blue-gray steaming waters of Inferno Lake. At the end of the Valley Walk, a bush trail (alive with native birds) leads down to Lake Rotomahana (1.8 km/one mi—largest of the 1886 craters) where you can take a tour boat (adult $35, child $7.50) to the western shores, passing the famous Pink and White Terrace sites destroyed in the big eruption. General admission is adult $28, child $7.50, although there are a number of combo options, as well as the choice of climbing Mount Haszard. To get there by road, take Highway 5 south out of Rotorua, and turn left onto Waimangu Road.

Hell's Gate

Aside from eight hectares (20 acres) of ferocious and uncanny volcanic activity (Hwy. 30, 07/345-3151; daily 9 A.M.–5 P.M.; adult $25, child $10), which you can see in 30–45 minutes, the lure of Hell's Gate is hot Kakahi Falls, which at 38°C (100°F) plummet steaming and hissing through lush natural bush—an unforgettable sight. Hell's Gate is also unique among the thermal areas in that it is set up for swimming and soaking. Known as Wai Ora Spa, you can soak in regular spa pools (adult $15, child $10, or $35 and $15 respectively with thermal-area access), but the real highlight is taking a mud bath (adult $110, child $55, with access to the spa pools and thermal area). Hell's Gate is 16 km (ten mi) east of Rotorua at Tikitere, on Highway 30 to Whakatane.

🄲 Wai-O-Tapu

Wai-O-Tapu (Hwy. 5, 07/366-6333; daily 8:30 A.M.–5 P.M.; adult $25, child $8.50) is perhaps the most colorful of all the thermal areas, but also the farthest away from Rotorua—30 km (19 mi) along Highway 5 toward Taupo. Follow the tracks past stunning Lady Knox geyser, which shoots water and steam up to 21 meters (69 ft) into the sky at

© ANDREW HEMPSTEAD

The Champagne Pool at Wai-O-Tapu is one of the region's most colorful thermal attractions.

10:15 A.M. every day (with the help of good ol' soap powder); Bridal Veil Falls, where water cascades down white, red, yellow, and green silica terraces; boiling mud pools, craters, hot and cold pools, steaming fumaroles, the orange-edged Champagne Pool, and cliffs of sulphur stalactites, just to mention some of the best-known highlights.

TARAWERA ROAD

Tarawera Road begins southeast of downtown, branching off Highway 30 and leading 17 km (11 mi) to Lake Tarawera. Along the way are a number of attractions, but the view across the lake to famous Mount Tarawera, which last erupted in 1886, makes the trip worthwhile in itself.

Whakarewarewa Forest Park

This 3,830-hectare (9,464 acre) park lying southeast of Rotorua can be accessed from Tarawera Road or from the west along Highway 5 (Rotorua-Taupo Rd.). Tree planting

GEOTHERMAL HEARTLAND

was begun right after the eruption of Mount Tarewera in 1886 to renew the attractiveness of the Rotorua region and to regain tourism lost when the main local tourist attraction—the Pink and White Terraces—was destroyed. Many species of trees were planted, but the most successful species were European larch, Corsican pine, Douglas fir, and eucalyptus species, and the easiest to grow was the radiata pine from California. You'll also come across small areas of other surviving species, such as California redwoods; the two main areas of native forest are found adjoining Lake Tikitapu and north of Kakapiko. Today the plantation is mainly managed for timber production, but the many tracks through lush native ferns and stately trees, the lake views, and the attractive picnic spots successfully put the forest on the map as a great recreational area. There's little thermal activity within the forest park boundaries—just one boiling mud pool on the southern side of Pohaturoa.

The best way to get around the park is on foot, but to learn more about the park and its history, head to the park's Visitor Information Centre (Long Mile Rd. off Tarewera Rd., 07/346-2082; Mon.–Fri. 8:30 A.M.–5 P.M., Sat.–Sun. 10 A.M.–4 P.M.).

a Maori *whare* (small house) at Buried Village

© ANDREW HEMPSTEAD

(Buried Village

In the 1880s, Te Wairoa was a small resort town that was the starting point for cruises across Lake Tarawera to the Pink and White Terraces. When Mount Tarawera erupted in 1886, it buried the village, along with many of its residents. When the Smith family moved to the site in 1931, they didn't realize the importance of what lay under two meters (six ft) of ash, but opened a roadside tearoom. When the family began farming the land, the full extent of the archeological site became apparent. Like Italy's famous Pompeii, the Buried village (07/362-8287; Nov.–Mar. daily 8:30 A.M.–5:30 P.M., Apr.–Oct. daily 9 A.M.–4 P.M.; adult $25, senior $22, child $7) was slowly excavated. A pleasant trail leads past all the major building sites, including the *whare* (home) of Tuhoto Ariki,

whose story of survival makes interesting reading. You can also see the foundations of a hotel and then walk along the river to a waterfall. Back at the entry point is a museum filled with artifacts recovered from the village. Descendants of the Smith family own and operate the site, and still offer a tasty array of goodies in the tearoom, including Devonshire tea and scones for $5.

Lake Tarawera

Tarawera Landing, on the western shore of Lake Tarawera, two km (1.2 mi) beyond the Buried village, is the departure point for cruises across the lake to Rapatu Bay. From there you can walk to Lake Rotomahana, Hot Water Beach, or the summit of Mount Tarawera. **Lake Tarawera Launch Cruises** (07/362-8595) depart daily at 10:30 A.M. and include a 45-minute stopover, enough time for a swim, and lunch. The cost is a reasonable adult $38, child $23. Also on offer is a shorter cruise (departs at 2:30 P.M.; adult $25, senior $15, child $11) with no stops.

MOUNT NGONGOTAHA

The following sights are north of downtown along Highway 5, with all but the Agrodome clustered around the base of Mount Ngongotaha. Skyline Skyrides get you high up the slopes, but the only way to the actual summit of the mountain is by road. To get there from town, take Lake Road to the Fairy Springs Road intersection and continue straight ahead onto Clayton Road. Continue along Clayton Road (past Edmund Rd. and Thomas Crescent) and turn right into Mountain Road, which winds slowly and steadily up the mountain toward the summit. Trees mar the view at the top. The best 180-degree views are from the lookout at Aorangi Peak Restaurant, which is on the way up, almost at the top.

Skyline Skyrides

Mount Ngongotaha, a 760-meter-high (2,493-ft) peak four km (2.5 mi) north of Rotorua, can be reached by vehicle, but the views are best appreciated by taking the Skyline Skyrides gondola (07/347-0027; daily from 8:30 A.M.; adult $22, child $10) up the east-facing slopes. The gondola doesn't reach the summit, but it still offers an excellent vantage point, with views extending across Lake Rotorua. Once you're at the top of the gondola, you'll find money-grabbing activities for all ages. You can ride a short chairlift, from where your downhill options are one of three luge tracks; $7.50 per run (or buy a book of tickets at a discounted rate). At the top of the gondola is a café and restaurant.

Rainbow Springs and Kiwi Encounter

Adjacent to Skyline Skyrides is this nature-lovers attraction (Hwy. 5, 07/350-0440 or 0800/724-626; daily 8 A.M.–5 P.M.; adult $23.50, child $13.50) built around crystal-clear mineral springs that provide a native home for trout. If you'd like to see just how large a rainbow or brown trout can grow, this is the place for you. Among a wide range of beautiful native ferns and natural bush, a trail leads to Rainbow Springs, a series of pools where the trout are segregated by age and size. Here you can observe a fish (and duck) frenzy by throwing in "trout food." Apart from all the pools teeming with trout there are underwater viewing ponds, native bird aviaries, deer, *tuatara* (a unique prehistoric reptile endemic to New Zealand that can live 80–100 years) and wild pig enclosures, a kiwi house, tearooms, and a decent gift shop within the grounds.

Part of the same attraction, but across the parking lot (pay and get details at Rainbow Springs), is Kiwi Encounter (07/350-0440; adult $26.50, child $16.50). This working hatchery is helping to increase numbers of New Zealand's best-loved bird by breeding and raising kiwis. Tours passing through the incubation room, nursery, and nocturnal area last 45 minutes and depart regularly between 10 A.M. and 4 P.M. (chicks can be seen hatching in summer only).

Agrodome

Anyone interested in sheep, sheepshearing, or just having a good laugh should head for one of the shows at the Agrodome (Western Rd., 07/357-1050; show times 9:30 A.M., 11 A.M., and 2:30 P.M.; adult $22, child $11), a 160-hectare (395-acre) working farm. Inside the large auditorium you'll see fine woolly representatives of all the different breeds of New Zealand sheep, tied up along the sides for petting, admiring, or making funny faces at. During the Sheep Show, each well-trained sheep runs in turn up the stairs and onto the platform while its breed and characteristics are described. When they're all gathered center stage, a talented sheepdog is put through his paces. Vocal and whistle commands have the dog barking with delight as he scampers across the flock from sheep back to sheep back (much to the obvious disgust of the woolly stars of the show), and then a sheep from offstage is sheared by a professional sheepshearer. Other Agrodome attractions include a Farm Tour (adult $28, child $13) that takes in everything from kiwifruit wine-tasting to emus and ostriches. To get there, continue north along Highway 5 beyond the sights detailed previously, and take Western Road to the right.

GEOTHERMAL HEARTLAND

SWIMMING AND SOAKING

Many accommodations boast thermally heated pools and spas; while a great bonus, they are generally clinical. Therefore I highly recommend you immerse yourself fully in the Rotorua experience by visiting one of the following places.

◖ Polynesian Spa

Polynesian Spa (Hinemoa St. by Government Gardens, 07/348-1328; daily 6:30 A.M.–11 P.M.) is on the site of the first public bathhouse built in Rotorua. Residents enclosed the spring Te Pupunitanga and used the soft waters of Whangapiporo Cauldron, later renamed the Rachel Pool. You can still see Rachel Spring boiling away at 100°C (212°F) along with several other steaming holes in the ground between the Polynesian Spa and the bathhouse—not walled off in any way, they offer free, fascinating viewing. After extensive renovation, the complex boasts several hot mineral spring pools, including Lake Spa Retreat (adult $35), comprising freeform outdoor rock pools beautifully landscaped and set right on the lake side. There are also a number of private pools, an adults-only pool, various massage services, and a café. General admission is adult $12, child $4; private pools are an extra adult $12, child $4, for 30 minutes.

Blue Baths

Also in Government Gardens, **Blue Baths** (07/350-2119; Mon.–Fri. 9 A.M.–7 P.M., Sat.–Sun. 9 A.M.–7 P.M.; adult $9, child $6) is a magnificently restored Spanish Mission–style building filled with art deco highlights. These baths opened in 1933, not for medicinal purposes, but simply for recreation. The swimming pool is set in a central courtyard, with enough architectural highlights in the surrounding building to make even a non-swimming visit worthwhile.

Wai Ora Spa

Around 16 km (ten mi) east of Rotorua along Highway 30, this spa complex is within the Hell's Gate thermal area described earlier

(07/345-3151, daily 9 A.M.–5 P.M.). Entry to the spa pools is adult $15, child $10, and soaking in unique mud baths (and then cleaning up before taking a dip in the spa pools) is adult $110, child $55.

OTHER RECREATION

Lake Cruises

At the north end of downtown, the streets converge at a large lakefront park area, which is a hive of activity and the starting point for a variety of lake cruises. Each of the operators has a booth, and you simply need to choose your favorite option. For a scenic cruise over to legendary Mokoia Island in the middle of Lake Rotorua, book with **Mokoia Island Cruises** (07/348-6634). The trip lasts two hours and includes one hour on the island, learning about its importance to the Maori and the abundant birdlife present. The trip departs four times daily and costs adult $85, child $49. The same company also offers lunch cruises (adult $60, child $30) and an evening tour that includes a barbecue dinner and cultural performance on Mokoia Island (adult $145, child $85).

White-Water Rafting

A big hit with the adrenaline-seeking crowd is rafting the **Kaituna River,** which crosses Highway 33 north of Rotorua. Along the river, a seven-meter-high (23-foot-high) waterfall is claimed to be the highest commercially rafted drop in the world. **Kaituna Cascades** (07/345-4199 or 0800/524-886), the first operator to run the waterfall, has been joined by a whole host of other companies, including **River Rats** (07/345-6543). Allow three hours from Rotorua, of which 45 minutes is spent on the river; the cost is around $80 per person. The same two companies run trips down the much tamer **Rangitaiki River,** southeast of Rotorua toward Te Urewera National Park.

Flightseeing

Sightseeing by float plane or helicopter is always a blast. If you can afford it, it truly adds another dimension to this fascinating thermal area. **Volcanic Air Safaris** (07/348-9984 or

0800/800-848) operates a large variety of scenic flights in floatplanes from the lakefront at the foot of Tutanekai Street. The eight-minute Town and Around flight ($60 per person) looks over the city and lake, but that's about it. Thirty minutes of airtime ($175 per person) is enough to travel to and over Mount Tarawera. The 80-minute excursion out to active White Island is $415 per person. Volcanic Air Safaris also operates a helicopter from the lakefront, with options ranging from a six-minute flight ($60 per person) to a three-hour trip to White Island complete with a landing ($655 per person).

Four-Wheel Driving

Mount Tarawera is the destination for a number of companies operating off-road vehicles, and because access to the mountain is restricted, it's the most practical way of seeing this recently active volcano up close. The four-hour trip offered by **Mount Tarawera Volcanic Tours** (07/349-3714; adult $121, child $71.50) is typical. After an early-morning or lunchtime pickup from Rotorua accommodations, you travel by highway through Rerewhakaaitu and climb the southern flanks of the mountain, along a narrow track that fizzles out near the summit. The lunarlike landscape above the tree line is unforgettable in itself, but then you can jump out of the 4WD and wander into a crater.

Golfing

Playing at the 27-hole Rotorua Golf Club (Fenton St., 07/348-4051) is a unique experience. The 18-hole course, known as Arikikapakapa, is the more difficult, with a Slope Rating of 123 (greens fee $60). The public nine-hole course is relatively easy, but the hot spots, steaming vents, and bubbling pools of hot mud dotting the fairways, make for an interesting golfing experience ($10 for nine holes). The course is south of downtown, opposite Whakarewarewa Thermal Valley.

Zorbing

One of the more unusual adventure activities in Rotorua—and indeed in all of New

© ANDREW HEMPSTEAD

"Zorbing," the art of rolling down a hill in a massive plastic ball, is a unique activity in Rotorua.

Zealand—is Zorbing (Western Rd., 07/357-5100 or 0800/357-5100). Another innovative Kiwi invention to relieve you of extra cash, the "Zorb" is a clear plastic sphere with enough room for one person to be strapped inside and rolled down a 160-meter (500-foot) hill. Options include a zig-zag route, or the Wash Cycle, which introduces a bucket of water to the equation. The cost is $45, with discounts for multiple runs.

NIGHTLIFE

Typical of a resort town, Rotorua has many places to drink and dance the night away. The **Pig and Whistle** (1182 Tutanekai St., 07/347-3025), in a renovated police station, is one of the most popular local drinking spots. It features a wide variety of New Zealand beers, and bands play Friday and Saturday night. This bar also has good food and an outdoor patio. **Churchill's** (1302 Tutanekai St., 07/347-1144) is an English-style pub.

Most of the big hotels have lounge-style

GEOTHERMAL HEARTLAND

bars that welcome nonguests. South of downtown, in the **Quality Hotel Geyserland** (Fenton St., 07/348-2039), the bar affords views across Whakarewarewa Thermal Valley, and you needn't be a guest to enjoy the spectacle of spouting geysers. Back downtown, the lakefront **Mallard Bar** (Sudima Hotel, 1000 Eruera St., 07/348-1174) is another good choice for hotel lounging.

Lava Bar (1286 Arawa St., 07/348-8618) features nightly drink and food specials (happy hour is 4:30–6:30 p.m.) along with video games and a pool table. It's part of Hot Rock Backpackers, so the crowd is generally young, loud, and proud.

ACCOMMODATIONS AND CAMPING

Because Rotorua revolves around tourism, it has an incredible number of accommodations offering over 14,000 guest rooms. They are spread throughout the city, but most are concentrated along Fenton Street.

Under $50

For many backpackers, Rotorua is their first stop south of Auckland, and the city offers many options. One of the best of these is **Kiwi Paka YHA** (60 Tarewa Rd., 07/347-0931, www.kiwipaka-yha.org.nz; dorm beds $24, $40 s, $56 d), a self-contained resort set on one hectare (2.5 acre) one km (0.6 mi) west of downtown. Along with the usual communal facilities, guests enjoy mineral pools, a large recreation room, and a glassed-in conservatory with barbecues, restaurant, and bar.

(Funky Green Voyager (4 Union St., 07/346-1754, dorm beds $20, $50 d) is the smallest backpacker lodging within walking distance of downtown. Offering clean, bright dorm rooms with comfortable beds and six double rooms, its well-equipped kitchen and spacious backyard add to the friendly, relaxed atmosphere. It's a short walk to city attractions, and the straightforward, environmentally conscious owner is a good source of information on attractions and backpacker hostels throughout the country.

Hot Rock Backpackers (1286 Arawa St., 07/348-8636 or 0800/462-396, www.hot-rock.co.nz; dorm beds $20, $32 s, $50 d) is the party place, with most of the action happening in the downstairs Lava Bar. It's a modern, centrally located property, with its own indoor and outdoor thermal pools, a sundeck, and a barbecue area.

$50-100

If you're looking for bed-and-breakfast-style accommodation in a central location, thermally heated **Eaton Hall Guest House** (1225 Hinemaru St., 07/347-0366, www.eatonhallbnb.co.nz) is the place to go. The friendly owners not only supply comfy beds and a delicious breakfast, they also make you feel right at home. Each room has tea- and coffee-making supplies, and guests can use a hot tub/spa and a TV room. Bed and continental or cooked breakfast is $65 s, $85 d with a shared bathroom, $80 s, $110 d with an en suite.

The least expensive motel downtown is the three-story **Ambassador Thermal Motel** (corner of Whakaue and Hinemaru Sts., 07/347-9581 or 0800/479-581, www.ambassrotorua.co.nz; $90–165 s or d). The 19 guest rooms are nothing special, but each has a kitchen and the motel features two spring-fed mineral pools, a swimming pool, and an outdoor spa.

Cruise along Fenton Street and check the discounted rates motels post out front, or reserve in advance at good-value **Bel Aire Motel** (257 Fenton St., 07/348-6076 or 0800/423-524; $90 s or d), 500 meters (0.3 mi) from downtown, where each of the eight units has a kitchen.

$100-150

Within walking distance of downtown, **(Tresco Thermal Oasis** (3 Toko St., 07/348-9611, www.trescorotorua.co.nz; $65–80 s, $110 d) is a comfortable, homey bed-and-breakfast. Each of the six thermally heated guest rooms has its own hand basin, and some have en suites. Tea- and coffee-making supplies are available in the lounge. You'll also find a washer and thermal drying room, a TV lounge, and a hot mineral pool. A hearty cooked breakfast will set you up for a day of thermally charged sightseeing.

At the south end of Fenton Street, Sala Street branches east toward the airport. Here you'll find the **Birchwood Spa Motel** (Sala St., 07/347-1800 or 0800/881-800, www .birchwoodspamotel.co.nz; $105–185 s or d), a modern complex of 13 self-contained units, each with a mineral spa. Studio units have a microwave, toaster, and tea- and coffee-making facilities while one- and two-bedroom units have full kitchens.

Overlooking Whakarewarewa Thermal Valley is **Quality Hotel Geyserland** (424 Fenton St., 07/348-2039, www.regalgeyserland.co.nz; from $135 s or d), with 66 fairly standard hotel rooms, many with views of the thermal activity. Facilities include indoor spa pools, a sauna, an outdoor pool, a small fitness room, a restaurant, and a bar; across the road is a golf course.

$150-200

Across the road from Government Gardens is the grand old **Princes Gate Hotel** (1057 Arawa St., 07/348-1179, www.princesgate .co.nz; from $165 s or d). The hotel was originally located on the east coast at Waihi, but when that town was voted dry in 1917, the owner relocated the entire building to Rotorua. The hotel has been modernized, but an old-time ambience remains. Facilities include a thermally heated pool, sauna, tennis court, restaurant, and bar.

◖ Sudima Hotel (1000 Eruera St., 07/348-1174 or 0800/783-462, www.sudimahotels .com; from $195 s or d) is excellent value, especially if you book online and book a room with breakfast for as little as $150. Offering a lakeside location within walking distance of downtown, the Sudima has well-decorated guest rooms, many with uninterrupted water views. Take a dip in the outdoor pool, relax with a wide range of spa services, sip a cocktail at the bar, or dine at the in-house restaurant and then take in a Maori concert.

Over $200

Centrally located is the seven-story **Royal**

Lakeside Novotel (9 Tutanekai St., 07/346-3888 or 0800/776-677, www.accorhotels.com .au; from $320 s or d), one of Rotorua's finest accommodations. This modern full-service hotel features a luxurious fitness/pool complex, indoor and outdoor dining, and a nightly *hangi.* Tasteful, earthy tones dominate the 199 rooms (request a lake view).

Heading south along Fenton Street you'll find a number of other upscale hotels. One of these is **Rydges Rotorua** (272 Fenton St., 07/349-0099 or 0800/446-187, www.rydges .com; from $220 s or d), with a large thermally heated indoor pool, bike rentals, a bar, and the stylish Atrium Restaurant. Many of the 135 guest rooms are sold as Deluxe Rooms and each has a private thermally heated spa bath. The rack rate for these is $275, but they are sold online for under $150.

Soak up lakefront luxury at **◖ The Lodge at 199** (199 Spencer Rd., 07/362-8122, www.199.co.nz; $695 s, $695–795 d, dinner an extra $100 per person), where the ambience is welcoming and unpretentious, yet nothing is left to chance. The guest rooms ooze warm character while public areas are adorned with luxuries like a flat-screen TV/DVD combo. Guests enjoy gourmet meals (and fudge as a nighttime snack) while outside the property slopes right to the edge of Lake Tarawera.

Holiday Parks

On the northwestern side of town, a short stroll from the lake, the excellent **◖ Cosy Cottage International Holiday Park** (Whittaker Rd., off Lake Rd., 07/348-3793, www.cosycottage .co.nz; campsites $30, cabins and flats $65–85 s or d) has been a longtime favorite for readers of this book. Amenities are all top-notch, including a well-equipped kitchen, playground, an outdoor pool, and bike rentals. Thermal extras include a soothing mineral pool, a steam barbecue, and heated tent sites.

Within walking distance of Whakarewarewa Thermal Valley and the golf course, **Rotorua Thermal Holiday Park** (Old Taupo Rd., 07/346-3140, www.rotoruathermal.co.nz; tent sites $12 per person, powered sites $14 per person, log cabins $30 s, $45 d, kitchen cabins from $50 d). It has the usual communal facilities, a game room, a camp store, a heated swimming pool, and thermal plunge pools.

FOOD

Restaurants throughout Rotorua reflect the city's thriving tourist industry, but there's so much competition around town that dining out is not as expensive as you may expect. Many older eateries in the downtown core are seemingly oblivious to the surrounding bustle, providing a good place for an inexpensive meal. One of these is **Herb's Restaurant** (1096 Tutanekai St., 07/348-3985), which has been open since the 1950s.

Cafés

The up-tempo ambience at **❮ Fat Dog** (1161 Arawa St., 07/347-7586; daily 8 A.M.–10 P.M.) attracts all types. The funky room is furnished with an eclectic array of lounges and table settings (the nursery rhymes painted on the chairs may rhyme, but aren't suitable for a nursery). Food on offer is listed on a massive blackboard—creative salads, filling pastas, thincrust pizza, healthy sandwiches—as well as well-priced wines and tempting desserts. Daily lunch specials (noon–2 P.M.) are the best deal. Follow the paw prints to the order counter.

Toward the waterfront, bright and breezy **Lime Caffeteria** (1096 Whakaue St., 07/350-2033; daily 8 A.M.–4:30 P.M.) offers the usual range of coffee concoctions and light meals away from the heart of downtown.

Head to **Zippy Central** (Pukuatua St., 07/348-8288; daily from 9 A.M.) for good, strong coffee and a variety of fresh pastries and cakes. **Freo's** (1103 Tutanekai St., 07/346-0976; Mon.–Sat. from 11 A.M.) sells pies, sausage rolls, fresh salads, seafood salad, and chocolate mousse to take away for lunch, and complete meals (such as lasagna) for $7–9 a portion or sold by the kilogram to take away for dinner.

Casual Dining

A couple of blocks from the heart of the city, **Sirocco** (1280 Eruera St., 07/347-3388; Mon.

5–9 P.M., Tues.–Fri. 10 A.M.–10 P.M., Sat. 8 A.M.–10 P.M., Sun. 8 A.M.–4 P.M.) is a pleasant little café with indoor and outdoor tables surrounded by an old restored private residence. Along with coffee and light snacks, it offers a full menu of contemporary Kiwi cuisine.

You wouldn't know from walking past, but **Bistro 1284** (1284 Eruera St., 07/346-1284; Tues.–Sat. from 6 P.M.) is an atmospheric restaurant with hearty presentations of fish, seafood, and game. Lighter eaters could order grilled scallops with tomato tortellini ($18) from the starter menu.

Mac's Steakhouse (1110 Tutanekai St., 07/347-9270; daily noon–2 P.M. and 5:30–9:30 P.M.) may be lacking in the charm department, but is all business with a meaty menu of beef, lamb, and pork. Dinner mains average $27–30. A good choice for hungry families.

Upscale

Memories Restaurant (1057 Arawa St., 07/348-1179) takes pride of place in the distinctive Princes Gate Hotel, opposite Government Gardens. The Victorian opulence of the dining room reflects the hotel's rich history, but the ambience is relatively unpretentious. Enjoy traditional dishes of lamb, duck, chicken, and pork, as well as more adventurous offerings such as blackened cajun snapper ($28.50). Aside from the full-fledged restaurant, a more casual café is open throughout the day, with some seating outside in a pleasant courtyard.

Typical of Rotorua's better restaurants, dining at **Poppy's Villa**, a colorfully decorated villa (4 Marguerita St., 07/347-1700; daily for breakfast, lunch, and dinner) is not as expensive as you might imagine. Pastas are around $20 and imaginative dishes such as Asian salmon with hot sour sauce are around $30. Save room for a slice of delicious apple and blackberry crumble ($11).

Asian and Middle Eastern

As is the case elsewhere in New Zealand, many ethnic restaurants in Rotorua seem unaffected by the pace of change, offering reasonably

THE MAORI *HANGI*

Rotorua is the best place in New Zealand to enjoy a traditional *hangi* (feast). You shouldn't miss this particular Rotorua event, which is usually held in conjunction with a Maori concert.

In a deep hole, a fire built from native timber heats a layer of stones. Onto the hot stones go a layer of leaves, then the food, then more leaves (nowadays muslin cloth replaces this second layer). Water is thrown on just before the food, the oven is closed with a layer of soil, and the steam, flavored from the wood below, cooks the food. Maori villagers cook all their food in this manner using the boxes around natural steam vents in Whakarewarewa village.

Tamaki Maori village (07/346-2823) puts on probably the most traditional *hangi* and concert performance you're likely to encounter in New Zealand. After being collected by bus from accommodations around the city, you learn from the driver that you are now actually in a *waka* (Maori canoe) approaching a *marae*, and that the group must select a "chief" for the arrival ceremony. From then on everyone

actively participates in "the challenge" (don't put your foot on that leaf!), the welcome and response, the speeches, the concert, the opening of the *hangi*, and, of course, the eating of the traditional food within the setting of a re-created Maori village. The adult $93, child $58 price includes transfers and dinner.

The several large hotels in Rotorua that put on *hangi* are better able to control the steam in their ovens, so they can open them up to put delicate foods in later to cook everything to perfection. The lamb and pork takes about three hours to cook, seafood 30 minutes, vegetables such as *kumara* (sweet potato) 30 minutes, and traditional steamed pudding about an hour in the controlled steam ovens. My fave is hosted nightly at the **Royal Lakeside Novotel** (Tutanekai St., 07/346-3888; daily from 6:30 P.M.; $75 pp), where the after-dinner entertainment includes a Maori guitarist and traditional Maori concert, which includes the fierce war dances of the men, the soft fluent *poi* dances of the women, and beautiful singing.

priced food in a casual environment. A concentration of inexpensive places to eat is along the streets running west from Fenton Street, the original part of downtown. The pick of the bunch for each cuisine includes **Hoo Wah Restaurant** (1266 Eruera St., 07/348-5271; weekdays for lunch and daily for dinner), for Chinese choices under $20; **Mr. India Tandoori Restaurant** (1161 Amohau St., 07/349-4940; Mon.–Sat. for lunch and daily for dinner), where a great chicken tandoori is $18.50; and **Wild Rice Thai** (1141 Tutanekai St., 07/348-6677; daily noon–2:30 P.M. and 5 P.M. to late), where choices include "Kiwi Hot" and "Thai Hot" for over 50 dishes.

Kebab Diner (1121 Fenton St., 07/349-0105; daily lunch and dinner) specializes in Middle Eastern cuisine; for a true experience, enjoy hummus ($6) as a starter, try a kebab ($17–19) main course, and finish off with a plate of baklava ($4.50).

Food with a View

Northwest of town, **Aorangi Peak Restaurant** (Mountain Rd., 07/347-0046; daily from 6 P.M.), aptly described as "Rotorua's restaurant complex in the sky," offers the bonus of fantastic views of the city and Lake Rotorua from Mount Ngongotaha. Seating is on two tiers, allowing views from most tables. The menu offers no real surprises. Instead, enjoy good, contemporary Kiwi cooking—such as baked venison smothered in cranberry jus for $36—in a modest setting designed to take nothing from the views. Lower on the slopes of the same mountain, access to **Cableway Restaurant** (Hwy. 5, 07/347-0027) is by the Skyline Skyrides gondola. Both the lunch buffet ($45) and dinner buffet ($57) offer lots of fresh choices. Children are charged $1 per year of age.

It's a 30-minute drive to the **Landing Café** (Tarawera Rd., 03/362-8502; daily

GEOTHERMAL HEARTLAND

9 A.M.–9 P.M.), but worth it for the views across the lake to Mount Tarawera alone. Good food is a bonus, including a massive bowl of steaming chowder ($12) and delicious crab cakes ($14).

INFORMATION AND SERVICES

Tourism Rotorua (1167 Fenton St., 07/348-5179, www.rotorua.co.nz; summer daily 8 A.M.–6 P.M., the rest of the year daily 8 A.M.–5:30 P.M.) should be your first stop upon arriving in town. It is one of the biggest and best information center complexes in the country—and it needs to be; the city entertains over one million visitors annually. The hardworking staff can advise you on everything and make bookings for tours, transportation, and accommodations. Also within the building are a Department of Conservation desk, luggage storage, a currency exchange, gift shop, Internet access, and a café. The **Automobile Association** (1191 Amohau St., 07/348-3069; Mon.–Fri. 8:30 A.M.–5 P.M.) is another good place for general travel information and maps (free for members).

At the north end of downtown, **Rotorua Public Library** (1127 Haupapa St., 07/348-4177; Mon.–Fri. 9:30 A.M.–8 P.M., Sat. 9:30 A.M.–4 P.M.) has free Internet access and a few international newspapers. **McLeods Booksellers** (1269 Tutanekai St., 07/348-5388) is a great little independent where you'll be surprised to see just how much has been written about the region. **Map & Track Shop** (1183 Hinemoa St., 07/349-1845; weekdays only) is filled with maps and specialty field guides.

Rotorua Post Office is on the corner of Hinemoa and Tutanekai Streets. Log onto the Internet at the information complex or library, or head to **Cybershed** (1176 Pukuatua St., 07/349-4965). All major banking institutions, represented on Hinemoa Street, are open Monday–Friday 10:30 A.M.–4:30 P.M. Foreign currency services are available at the banks, or at **Travelex** (Tourism Rotorua, 1167 Fenton St.). A self-service **laundry** is at 1231 Pukuatua Street.

Rotorua Hospital (Rangiuru St., 07/348-1199) is immediately northwest of downtown off Arawa Street. For a doctor or dentist call St. John Ambulance (07/348-6286), which keeps a roster of doctors and dentists available to visitors.

GETTING THERE

Rotorua Airport is nine km (5.5 mi) northeast of town along Highway 30. **Air New Zealand** (0800/737-300, www.airnewzealand.com) flies from Rotorua direct to Auckland and Wellington in the North Island, and to Christchurch in the South Island. At the airport you'll find car rental offices, a gift shop, and a phone for free local calls. **Super Shuttle** (07/349-3444) provides a door-to-door shuttle service for $15 per person to downtown. A taxi between the airport and downtown costs about $25.

Traveling by bus to Rotorua is possible with a number of companies, and arriving is convenient because the main depot is the Tourism Rotorua complex right downtown on the corner of Fenton and Arawa Streets. The main carrier into Rotorua is **Intercity** (07/348-0366, www.intercitycoach.co.nz), with services from Auckland, Hamilton, Tauranga, and Whakatane in the north. From the south, services from Napier, New Plymouth, Wanganui, and Wellington are all routed through Taupo.

GETTING AROUND

Ritchies Coachlines (07/345-5694) serves the suburbs (including south to Whakarewarewa and north to Ngongotaha). A day pass for unlimited travel is $7.

Car rental agencies in Rotorua include **Avis** (07/345-6055), **Budget** (07/348-8127), **Hertz** (07/348-4081), and **Rent-a-dent** (07/349-3993).

Rotorua is very flat, which makes it an ideal place to get around by bike. You can rent bikes at most backpacker lodges or go to **Planet Bike** (89 Grand Vue Rd., 07/346-1717).

For a cab, call **Rotorua Taxis** (07/348-1111).

Taupo and Vicinity

Taupo (pop. 22,000) lies at the head of Lake Taupo, 80 km (50 mi) south of Rotorua. After the commercialism of Rotorua, Taupo is a pleasant reprieve for your pocketbook. Although it lacks the famous large-scale thermal activity of Rotorua, there are still thermal areas around Taupo to explore, along with a whole range of sights and activities, many of which are free. Stretching north from Taupo along the Waikato River is **Wairakei Park,** in which many of the thermal sights lie—don't miss them. Taupo attracts large numbers of New Zealand vacationers year-round to take advan-

tage of its excellent lake fishing for rainbow and brown trout, sailing and water sports, and resort-like atmosphere.

DOWNTOWN SIGHTS
Taupo Museum

Behind the visitor center, this impressive museum (Story Pl., 07/376-0414; daily 10:30 A.M.–4:30 P.M.; adult $5) has undergone a transformation in recent years. The latest edition (2006) is Ora—Garden of the Well Being, a courtyard filled with lush New Zealand plants, geothermal pools, and a lizard

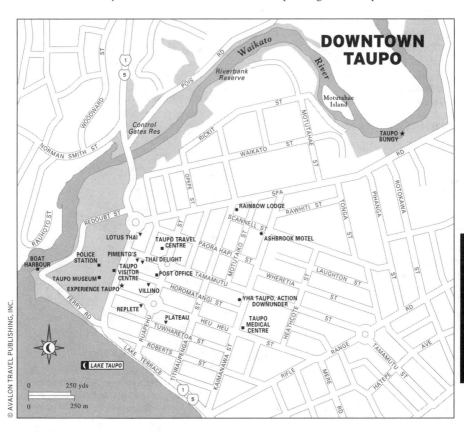

© AVALON TRAVEL PUBLISHING, INC.

GEOTHERMAL HEARTLAND

sculpture that winds its way through the greenery. Inside the museum proper is an interesting collection of historic photos, a moa skeleton, and a Maori meetinghouse. Anglers will be drawn to a display telling the story of the lake and its fish, although the highlight is a nearly nine-kilogram (19.5-pound) rainbow trout.

Cherry Island

Cherry Island (Waikato St., 07/378-9427; daily 9 A.M.–5 P.M.; adult $9, child $4), which lies in the middle of the Waikato River, is linked to the end of Waikato Street by a footbridge. This family-friendly attraction is the place to watch trout cruise by the underwater viewing windows, take a walk around the parklike island grounds to view all kinds of birds and baby animals, or check out the upstairs gallery, which features New Zealand artists. You can sit inside, or outside on the sundeck, while you enjoy food and drinks from the island tearoom. To get there take Spa Road, turn left on Motutahae Street, then turn right on Waikato Street.

WAIRAKEI PARK

This park protects both sides of the Waikato River north of town. The magnificent Waikato, longest river in New Zealand, runs northward 425 km (264 mi) from its source on the slopes of Mount Ruapehu in Tongariro National Park (this first stretch is called the Tongariro River), through Lake Taupo, to finally meet the Tasman Sea southwest of Auckland. The river pours out of the lake at Taupo, and about four km (2.5 mi) downstream hurtles with tremendous force through a narrow rock chasm and down **Huka Falls.** This massive volume of water falls in a raging torrent to a frothy, churning pool below. A footbridge and path provide access to various viewpoints overlooking the falls. You can walk to Huka Falls from town by taking the one-hour (one way) Taupo Walkway along the eastern banks of the river, off Spa Road. If you have wheels, take Highway 1 out of town to Huka Falls Loop Road and turn right. Pass Huka village and continue

along this scenic road to the various lookouts; the road eventually rejoins the main highway.

Craters of the Moon

One natural thermal area that shouldn't be missed is Craters of the Moon (Karapiti Rd. off Hwy. 1, five km/3.1 mi north of Taupo) in Wairakei Park. Apart from man-made paths through the thermal area and lookouts, everything has been left untouched. Steaming, bubbling areas lie among bush-covered hills and valleys, steam-filled craters give brief glimpses of boiling mud below, and small holes on the hillsides forcefully belch out torrents of steam. Follow the trail up the steps to the top of the hill for a great view of the thermal valley and Taupo in the distance, and continue down through the bush back to the car park. Allow about an hour to see the whole thermal area. If the area is particularly active, thermally speaking, you may find the gate closed for safety;

Craters of the Moon may not be as exciting as Rotorua's thermal attractions, but admission is free.

© ANDREW HEMPSTEAD

© ANDREW HEMPSTEAD

Wairakei Geothermal Power Station

otherwise it's generally open dawn to dusk, and admission is by donation.

Wairakei Geothermal Power Station

A little farther north from Craters of the Moon, you'll find the huge and highly developed Wairakei Geothermal Power Station, the world's first commercially viable operation to produce power from naturally occurring steam. It taps a vast underground water system heated by very hot, perhaps molten, rocks. Bores release the high pressure of the water far below, causing it to reach boiling point and produce the desired steam. At present, over 50 bores supply enough steam to generate 150 megawatts of power, or around five percent of New Zealand's total consumption. For more information and a good 15-minute audiovisual, drop by the **Geothermal Visitor Centre** (Wairakei Rd., 07/378-0254; daily 9 A.M.–4 P.M.; free) at the turnoff beside the BP petrol station. Someone is always on hand to answer questions.

Wairakei Terraces

Adjacent to the Geothermal Power Station, the entrance to Wairakei Terraces is 50 meters (164 ft) from the Wairakei Steam Pipe Bridge (on the right if you're heading south). Drive to the end of the road, passing all sorts of tame farm animals (07/378-0913; daily 9 A.M.–5 P.M.; adult $18, child $9). The main features of this natural thermal spot are the steaming pools of boiling pink, gray, and brown mud, colorful rock formations, and the surprisingly cold Wairakei Stream that flows through this hot, steamy area. You can also see a re-creation of the famous Pink and White Terraces, destroyed by the 1886 eruption of Mount Tarawera. The best time for viewing this area is after rain. Allow at least an hour to see everything.

Volcanic Activity Centre

From this research center, scientists from the Institute of Geological and Nuclear Sciences (Huka Falls Loop Rd., 07/374-8375, www .gns.cri.nz; Mon.–Fri. 9 A.M.–5 P.M., Sat.–Sun.

GEOTHERMAL HEARTLAND

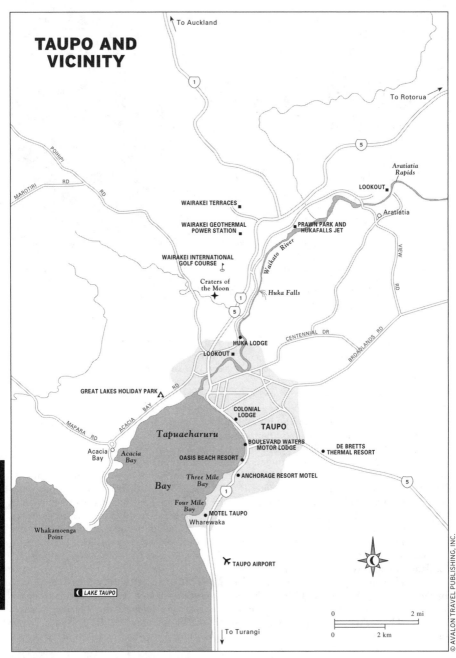

TAUPO AND VICINITY

To Auckland

To Rotorua

POIHIPI
MAROTIRI
RD
RD

Aratiatia
Rapids

LOOKOUT ■

WAIRAKEI TERRACES ■

○ Aratiatia

WAIRAKEI GEOTHERMAL
POWER STATION ■

● PRAWN PARK AND
HUKAFALLS JET

VIEW
RD

WAIRAKEI INTERNATIONAL
GOLF COURSE

Waikato River

Craters of
the Moon

Huka Falls

CENTENNIAL DR

BROADLANDS RD

HUKA LODGE ■

LOOKOUT ■

GREAT LAKES HOLIDAY PARK

RD

ACACIA BAY RD

MAPARA RD

ACACIA BAY

COLONIAL
LODGE

TAUPO

Tapuaeharuru

● BOULEVARD WATERS
MOTOR LODGE

DE BRETTS
● THERMAL RESORT

Acacia
Bay

*Acacia
Bay*

OASIS BEACH RESORT ●

*Three Mile
Bay*

● ANCHORAGE RESORT MOTEL

Bay

*Four Mile
Bay*

● MOTEL TAUPO

Whakamoenga
Point

Wharewaka

✈ TAUPO AIRPORT

◖ *LAKE TAUPO*

To Turangi

0   2 mi

0   2 km

GEOTHERMAL HEARTLAND

© AVALON TRAVEL PUBLISHING, INC.

10 A.M.–4 P.M.; adult $6, child $3) monitor the Taupo Volcanic Zone, which extends from the volcanoes of Tongariro National Park in the south to White Island in the north. A large area of the center is devoted to visitors, with a massive three-dimensional map showing all volcanic features in the area; wall displays of volcanoes, geothermal activity, and the earth's makeup; an earthquake simulator; an audiovisual of the eruption of Mount Ruapehu; working models; and a seismograph linked to Mount Ruapehu.

Prawn Park

If you've always wondered what goes on at a prawn farm, and in particular, the world's first geothermally heated freshwater prawn farm, head to Prawn Park (Huka Falls Loop Rd., nine km/six mi north of town, 07/374-8474; adult $6) for a guided tour. Although it's a viable commercial enterprise, there are plenty of things for visitors to do—try prawn fishing, play prawn golf, and dine on prawn cocktails.

◖ LAKE TAUPO

Like other bodies of water on the Central Plateau, Lake Taupo itself is a volcano, its base and surroundings involved in several gigantic eruptions 330,000, 20,000, and 1,850 years ago. During those explosions, pumice, ash, and rock debris were hurled high into the atmosphere, pyroclastic flows charred and devastated vast areas of the landscape, and the resulting crater eventually filled with water to become Lake Taupo. You'll see the remains of volcanic activity in the pumice beaches, coves of "floating rocks" around the lake, and colorful steep cliffs along Western Bay that were part of the ancient volcano.

The clear, refreshingly cold water of Lake Taupo is a joy for swimming, boating, or catching an elusive rainbow or brown trout for dinner. There are many swimming spots along the waterfront beaches, especially at the lake's edge about two km (1.2 mi) from town along Lake Terrace (almost opposite Taharepa Road). Here, Waipahihi Hot Springs bubble up into the lake, noticeably warming the water when the lake is at a suitable height. One of the best

FISHING LAKE TAUPO

Lake Taupo is generally regarded as one of the world's great trout-fishing destinations. It is not in the lake itself, however, but in surrounding rivers and streams, where dry-fly aficionados delight in challenges of casting for **rainbow** and **brown trout.** Introduced to the lake in the late 1800s, the fish consider the lake an inland sea, swimming up surrounding rivers and streams to spawn through winter months. But trout fishing with a dry fly is a definite art form, and certainly not for everyone. Without a knowledgeable guide it can be a fruitless endeavor; with a guide it can be expensive.

In Lake Taupo itself, trout feed in shallower waters during the cooler months, moving into the lake's deeper reaches through summer. To catch these fish a technique known as "downrigging" is employed. It's popular because anyone can do it, catching a pan-sized trout is almost guaranteed, and using the services of a local guide and his boat is relatively inexpensive.

When it comes to local guides, Richard Staines and his boat **White Striker** inevitably come up. He has been taking visitors out onto the lake for longer than anyone else and has an excellent reputation for ensuring that quotas are filled (three fish) within a couple of hours. On your return to the marina, you have the option of keeping and cooking the fish yourself, or Richard can recommend a local restaurant and will deliver the fish there. Then you just need to turn up at dinnertime and your fish will be cooked to your liking. The charter rate is $90 per hour for the entire boat; allow about three hours to find and fish the best spots. Richard also will take you over to Maori rock carvings at Mine Bay, which can only be accessed by boat. Book through the information center or call him direct at 07/539-4339.

GEOTHERMAL HEARTLAND

places for swimming, boating, or fishing is six km (3.7 mi) west of Taupo at **Acacia Bay.** Lie on the sandy public beach and befriend the large local duck population, swim leisurely out to the pontoon, or hire one of the rowboats, canoes, or motorboats from the friendly owners of Acacia Bay Lodge across the road.

For a pleasant several-kilometer walk, continue along Acacia Bay Road; you'll eventually reach a good track leading down through the bush to a rocky point and good fishing. Keep in mind that the road eventually dead-ends at private property—not much traffic apart from the occasional angling enthusiast or land developer.

Lake Cruises
Taupo's marina, **Boat Harbour,** lies at the mouth of the Waikato River, easily reached on foot from downtown or by road along Redoubt Street through the domain. Here you can hop on a boat for lake sightseeing, assist in sailing a fabulous yacht, or charter one of many fishing boats and/or trout guides. Local operators come together under one roof, making booking a trip easy at **Fish Cruise Taupo** (07/378-3444, www.fishcruisetaupo.co.nz), which has a booth down on the harbor. One of the vessels represented is the **MV *Ernest Kemp*,** an attractive replica of a paddlesteamer. The captain offers a fascinating historical commentary while you enjoy the lakefront; Hot Water Beach; Two, Three, and Four Mile Bays; Mine Bay and the intricate Maori rock carvings; and the serene beauty of Acacia Bay. A variety of trips are offered, including a two-hour cruise ($30). On the 13-meter (43-foot) ketch *The Barbary,* built in California in 1926 and once owned by Errol Flynn, you're encouraged to take part in the sailing activities, or you can just sit back, relax, and work on a Taupo tan. A fantastic three hours of sailing bliss costs only adult $30, child $10. Summer departures are daily at 10:30 A.M. and 2 P.M.

RECREATION
Jetboating
For speed demons, **Hukafalls Jet** (07/374-8572; adult $89, child $49) offers an exciting

30-minute jetboat trip upriver to Huka Falls. The boat departs half-hourly, on demand, from the end of Huka Falls Road in Wairakei Park. If requested, free coach transfers can be arranged from Taupo.

Taupo Bungy
Queenstown, on the South Island, is the New Zealand home of bungy jumping, but Taupo is the most popular place on the North Island to jump. If you want to plunge off a specially designed cantilevered platform 47 meters (154 ft) above the clear, cold, blue-green water of Waikato River, head out to Taupo Bungy (Spa Rd., 07/377-1135 or 0800/888-408; $99 per person, $198 tandem). This is also a good spectator sport; viewing platforms allow access to all performances.

Swimming and Soaking
Taupo Hot Springs (Hwy. 5, 07/377-6502; daily 7:30 A.M.–9:30 P.M.; adult $15, senior $6, child $4) is a good place to relax and enjoy the soothing qualities of clean hot water in attractive landscaped surroundings. In addition to the main inside and outside pools, a number of private rock pools are scattered through the native bush and cooler pools are set aside for the younger ones. If you're staying in the adjacent campground, admission is discounted.

ACCOMMODATIONS AND CAMPING
Taupo has an ever-expanding number of accommodations—more spring up along the lakeshore every year, along with timeshare after timeshare.

Under $50
Hospitable and enthusiastic hosts at **Rainbow Lodge** (99 Titiraupenga St., 07/378-5754, www.rainbowlodge.co.nz; dorm beds $24, $35–50 s, $52–62 d) provide backpackers with comfortable and relaxed accommodation in a central location 500 meters (0.31 mi) from town and the bus station. Facilities include heated rooms, a large fully equipped kitchen and living area with a pool table and

a woodstove, a sauna, off-street parking, and luggage storage. Guests can rent all sorts of recreational gear at a minimal rate: mountain bikes, bicycle gear and panniers, a canoe, tennis rackets, and fishing equipment.

A similar distance from the center of town and the bus depot is **YHA Taupo, Action Downunder** (56 Kaimanawa St., 07/378-3311, www.yha.co.nz; dorm beds $24, $55 d, $70 for an en suite). Originally a motel, the hostel features a large lounge area, raised patio, modern kitchen, spa pool, game room, and mountain bike rentals.

$50-100

The cheapest lakeside accommodation is **Motel Taupo,** but it's seven km (four mi) south of town (50 Wharewaka Rd., Four Mile Bay, 07/378-5992, www.moteltaupo .co.nz; $70 s, $85 d), with lots of outdoor space and a barbecue area all set across the road from the water. Each of the seven rooms has a kitchen.

In town but away from the lake, **Ashbrook Motel** (9 Scannell St., 07/378-5836 or 0800/828-761, www.ashbrookmotel.co.nz; $95 s or d) has nine units, each with a kitchen.

$100-150

Most of the best motel accommodations can be found along Lake Terrace. Highly recommended by readers is **⟨ Colonial Lodge** (134 Lake Terr., 07/378-9846 or 0800/353-636, www.colonial.co.nz; $110–170 s or d), a pleasant 10-minute walk from downtown and across the road from a beach. Each of the 12 units is well appointed and features a large spa bath, full kitchen, writing desk, and laundry facility.

Continuing around the lake, **Oasis Beach Resort** (241 Lake Terrace, 07/378-9339 or 0800/555-378, www.oasistaupo.co.nz; from $140 s or d) enjoys a waterfront location three km (1.9 mi) from downtown. The spacious rooms come in a variety of configurations, but each is decorated with a stylish yet casual pastel decor and enjoys water views. Amenities include a large pool, restaurant, and bar.

$150-200

Right on the lake, **Boulevard Waters Motor Lodge** (215 Lake Terr., 07/377-3395 or 0800/541-541, www.boulevardwaters.co.nz; $149 s, $169 d) is fronted by an imposing colonnaded facade. Each of the 10 units features a spa bath, king-size bed, and modern kitchen.

Farther south is the **Anchorage Resort Motel** (Lake Terr., Two Mile Bay, 07/378-5442 or 0800/991-995, www.taupomoco.nz; $160 s, $175 d), featuring a large pool complex, spa pools, sauna, and fitness room. Each room has a kitchen and private balcony overlooking the garden.

Over $200

Dating to the 1920s and long regarded as one of the world's great sporting lodges, **⟨ Huka Lodge** (Huka Falls Rd., 07/378-5791, www .hukalodge.com; $1,670 s, $2,380 d) lies on the Waikato River between Taupo and Huka Falls. The 20 rooms each enjoy private entrances that open to views extending across well-tended gardens to the river. Formal dinners are served in the main lodge or, if requested, in more private settings, such as the terrace or wine cellar. A travel writer's budget doesn't extend to this sort of luxury, but apparently it's very nice, and if you want to hobnob with the rich and famous, this is the place to do it. Rates include meals. Fishing guides cost extra, with guests whisked away to fish by 4WD, boat, or helicopter.

Holiday Parks

De Bretts Thermal Resort (Hwy. 5, 07/378-8559, www.debrettsresort.co.nz; campsites $28, cabins from $50 s or d) is a great place to stay. It has clean communal bathrooms, a bright airy kitchen and dining area with TV, play equipment for the kids, a restaurant serving buffet breakfast, and an office/store where friendly, efficient staff do bookings and sell all the basics. When you have spare time to kick back and relax, enjoy the adjacent Taupo Hot Springs.

To get to **Great Lake Holiday Park** three km (two mi) from town (Acacia Bay Rd., 07/378-5159, www.greatlake.net.nz), you need your own transportation, or call ahead and the

GEOTHERMAL HEARTLAND

friendly staff will come and get you from town. The campground offers lots of grassy, well-kept grounds for tent and caravan sites from $15 per person; standard cabins are $50 s or d, self-contained units are $75 s or d.

FOOD
Breakfast

For breakfast, it's hard to recommend anywhere but **(Replete** (45 Heu Heu St., 07/378-0606; daily 8:30 A.M.–5 P.M.) and the Complete Replete—honey-cured bacon, poached eggs, grilled mushrooms, and focaccia for $14.50. The rest of the day, this fashionable, ambitious café features an Asian-influenced menu and healthy delights such as panini bread stuffed with artichoke, Brie, and sweet Indian salsa ($11).

Casual Dining

The Express Lunch ($10) at **(Villino** (45 Horomatangi Rd., 07/377-4478; daily 10 A.M.–9 P.M.) is excellent value. There's usually a choice of dishes and all come well presented. At night the setting is more intimate, with muted lighting and candles on each table. Even though this is the trout-fishing capital of country, you won't find trout on the menu here or at any other restaurant (it's not fished commercially). But stick with the seafood theme and start with baked oysters and lemon beurre ($18.50), then get serious with seared venison and kumara ($32).

Beyond the funky fish art hanging from the walls, **Pimentos** (17 Tamamutu St., 07/377-4549; Wed.–Mon. from 5:30 P.M.) has a deserved reputation for some of the best-value (dinner mains $18–23) casual dining in Taupo.

Contemporary

The food at contemporary **Plateau** (64 Tuwharetoa St., 07/377-2425; Mon.–Fri. for lunch, daily for dinner) is consistently good—innovative and taking full advantage of local produce, but not too experimental. Lunch includes a venison burger with beetroot relish and Swiss cheese ($17.50). At dinner, you could start with duck and ginger broth ($12.50), then move on to Asian marinated pork with peanut caramel sauce ($28) for a main. Dessert is an easy choice—the passion-fruit sorbet ($11) is a delight. The wine list includes many estate and special release bottles.

Pub Fare

South of town you'll find **Ploughmans Restaurant** (Hwy. 1, Rainbow Point, 07/377-3422; daily 11 A.M.–1 A.M.). The blackboard menu changes daily but generally includes a ploughman's platter, fish-and-chips, and steak-and-kidney hot pot, each for about $10. A selection of English beers is on tap. This Tudor-style pub has a large outdoor area dotted with umbrella-covered tables, or you can drink inside at the typically English bar. Downtown, **Finn MaccCuhal's** (corner Tongariro and Tuwharetoa Sts., 07/378-6165) has a rollicking Irish ambience. **Holy Cow!** (11 Tongariro St., 07/378-0040) is a popular backpackers' hangout offering drink and food specials nightly.

Thai

If you're looking for great Thai food, **Thai Delight** (19 Tamamutu St., 07/378-9554; Tues.–Sun. 11:30 A.M.–3 P.M. and 5 P.M.–9 P.M.) is the best choice in town. All mains are under $20, including scallop and ginger stir-fry. Slightly more expensive, **Lotus Thai** (137 Tongariro St., 07/376-9497; Wed.–Fri. noon–2 P.M., Wed.–Mon. 6–9:30 P.M.) presents whole snapper cooked in red curry for $22.

PRACTICALITIES
Information

Make your first stop in town the large and helpful **Taupo Visitor Centre** (13 Tongariro St., 07/376-0027; daily 8:30 A.M.–5 P.M.), in the heart of downtown. The town and lake are promoted by **Destination Lake Taupo** (07/376-0400, www.laketauponz.com), a good contact for pre-trip planning. The **Automobile Association** office (93 Tongariro St., 07/378-6000; Mon.–Fri. 8:30 A.M.–5 P.M.) is a good source of road information and maps.

Services

Taupo's shopping area lies east of Tongariro Street. The main post office is on Horomatangi Street. Get online for a few bucks an hour at **Experience Taupo** (57 Tongariro St., 07/377-4168; daily 8:30 A.M.–6 P.M., until 8:30 P.M. in summer) or **Log On** (71 Tongariro St., 07/376-5901; Mon.–Fri. 10 A.M.–8 P.M., Sat.–Sun. 11 A.M.–8 P.M.). Both these places take bookings for local activities.

Taupo Hospital is on Kotare Street (07/378-8100). For less urgent cases, head to **Taupo Medical Centre** (corner of Kaimanawa and Heu Heu Sts., 07/378-4080).

Getting There

Taupo Airport is six km (3.7 mi) south of town, off Highway 1 to Turangi. The **Airporter** (07/378-5713; $10 per person) is a door-to-door shuttle between the airport and downtown. **Air New Zealand** (0800/737-000, www.airnewzealand.com) connects Taupo with Auckland and Wellington. Flights to all other destinations (including nearby Rotorua) are routed through these two cities.

Intercity (07/378-9032, www.intercity coach.co.nz) bus services arrive at and depart from **Taupo Travel Centre** (16 Gascoigne St., 07/378-9032), with daily services to and from Auckland, Rotorua, Hastings, Napier, Hamilton, and Wellington. A local company, **Alpine Scenic Tours** (07/386-8918), has a daily shuttle service from Taupo to Turangi, continuing south to Tongariro National Park.

Getting Around

Biking along the lakeshore is enjoyable, as is the ride through Wairakei Park. Most backpacker lodges, including Rainbow Lodge, rent bikes to guests. Otherwise, head to **Cycle World** (30 Spa Rd., 07/378-6117; $6 per hour, $30 per day) for mountain-bike rentals.

Car rental agencies include **Avis** (07/378-6305), **Budget** (07/378-9764), and **Hertz** (07/378-8056). Taxi companies include **Taupo Taxi** (07/378-5100) and **Top Cabs** (07/378-9250). The taxi stand is outside the bus station.

Turangi and Vicinity

The town of Turangi (pop. 4,000), at the southern end of Lake Taupo on the banks of the Tongariro River, used to be a small village famous for its fishing before the opening of the Tongariro Development Project. It was developed into a town in 1964 to accommodate hydroelectric construction workers, but since then it's been recognized (though little publicized) as an excellent resort area for anglers, hikers, whitewater rafters, skiers and boarders, and lovers of the great outdoors. The locals, proud of their self-proclaimed title "Heart of the Great New Zealand Outdoors," are eager to assist you in discovering their neck of the woods.

SIGHTS AND RECREATION

◖ Tongariro National Trout Centre

A place that no angling enthusiast should miss is the Tongariro National Trout Centre (Hwy. 1 four km/2.5 mi south of Turangi, 07/386-8085; daily 10 A.M.–4 P.M.). From the parking lot, a trail descends to a trout hatchery before continuing on a 1.6-km (one-mi) loop through beautiful native bush. Along the way, interpretive boards describe the various processes in maintaining the trout fishery and you can see fish swimming in the rearing ponds as well as wild trout in a stream. The highlight is River Walk Visitor Centre ($2), a small complex along the walking trail. This attractive building houses a small museum full of assorted fishing tackle used during the last hundred years, mounted trophy trout, and displays depicting the life cycle of a trout stream. Near the end of the walking trail is a fascinating underwater viewing chamber looking into the hatchery stream, where in winter you

GEOTHERMAL HEARTLAND

© ANDREW HEMPSTEAD

Tongariro National Trout Centre

can watch the spawning process, and the rest of the year watch trout of all sizes observing *you* through the window. The grounds around the hatchery are quite superb, especially in the summer when *kowhai* trees are in bloom.

Tokaanu

If you're driving around Lake Taupo, don't miss the small historic settlement of Tokaanu (five km/three mi west of Turangi) with its thermal area of boiling mud pools and hot-water cauldrons (free), and adjacent **Tokaanu Thermal Pools** (Mangaroa St., 07/386-8575; daily 10 A.M.–9 P.M.; adult $5, child $2.50), which lie along the same volcanic fault as the volcanoes of Tongariro National Park. Soak away the aches and pains of a hard day's hiking or skiing in your own private thermal pool or the main heated swimming pool.

Fishing

Turangi is the self-proclaimed "Trout Capital of the World," where you can expect to catch four-kilogram-plus trout (up to 10 pounds)

year-round. Trout are caught in local rivers and streams, as well as out on the lake. The best months for brown trout are March and April, and the best for rainbow trout are May to September. Find out about the hottest fishing spots by talking to the locals (everyone is into fishing, or knows someone who is), and check out **Barry Greig's Sporting World** (59 Town Centre, 07/386-6911) for tackle, guides, and licenses.

Naturally, many local fishing guides are ready and willing to give you a blissful day of angling on some of New Zealand's best trout rivers, with all tackle supplied and instruction if necessary. Mark Aspinall (07/378-4453, www.markaspinall.com) is based in Taupo but is knowledgeable on rivers around the Turangi area and has an excellent reputation for his guiding skills. A full day's fly-fishing, complete with equipment, lessons, lunch, and light snacks, runs $400 for one or two people.

Rafting

Rafting the Class III Tongariro River at the

GEOTHERMAL HEARTLAND

foot of the Kaimanawa Ranges is one of the most exhilarating, heart-pumping activities around, and if you're looking for this kind of action the Turangi area is a good place to try it out. Some of the Tongariro River has been harnessed for hydroelectric power generation, but the most scenic and untouched stretches still provide plenty of white-water thrills. **Tongariro River Rafting** (07/386-6409 or 0800/101-024) offers gentle family trips on the river's lower reaches for $120 (first four people, $15 each additional person), and an exciting 4.5-hour trip (two hours on the river) for $90 per person.

ACCOMMODATIONS AND CAMPING

Most of Turangi's accommodations cater to anglers. Some offer all-inclusive fishing packages, while others may have nothing more than fish-cleaning facilities.

Backpacker Lodge

Right downtown, **Extreme Backpackers** (26 Ngawaka Place, 07/386-8949; dorm beds $22, private rooms $34 s, $52 d, en suites $62) is a modern custom-built accommodation with a large communal lounge area and a private courtyard out back. Other pluses include a café, a store filled with recreation equipment, and a private shuttle for guests attempting the Tongariro Crossing (described later in the *Tongariro National Park* section). With a corrugated iron roof and imposing central tower (inside is a climbing wall), it's difficult to miss.

Motels and Fishing Lodges

The least expensive motel is **Sportsman's Lodge** (15 Taupehi Rd., 07/386-8150 or 0800/366-208, www.sportsmanslodge.co.nz; $60–80 s or d). Its rooms are basic, and kitchen facilities are shared, but it has a pleasant outdoor deck and a lounge with a log fire. The river is a two-minute walk away.

Along the same street is **Creel Lodge Motel** (183 Taupehi Rd., 07/386-8081, www.creel .co.nz; $85–110 s, $105–110 d), featuring an excellent bushland location on the banks of the Tongariro River (with some fishing holes in sight of the lodge). It has spacious private grounds, a tepid swimming pool, its own tackle shop, and a smokehouse. The 14 self-contained units are simply furnished.

A step up from these two places is the **Bridge Fishing Lodge** (Hwy. 1, 07/386-8804 or 0800/887-688, www.bridgefishinglodge.co.nz; $115–130 s or d). Dating to the 1930s, this resort was completely rebuilt in the mid-1980s and now features 24 motel rooms and seven self-contained apartments with kitchens. Enter the main lodge, and there's no doubt you're in a fishing lodge—the walls are decorated with an interesting collection of trophy fish and antique fishing rods and tackle. The Rod & Gun Restaurant will cook your catch for a small charge. It's beside the Tongariro River on the north side of Turangi (on the right as you enter town from the north).

At the top of the heap is **Tongariro Lodge,** upstream of Highway 1 (along Grace Rd., 07/386-7946, www.tongarirolodge.co.nz; $468 s, $884 d), a luxurious fishing lodge of world renown. Set on a nine-hectare (22-acre) riverfront property, it features a magnificent lounge/bar area, dining room, resident fishing guides, spa pool, tennis court, and lavish chalets. The lodge is open year-round, but is busiest May through October for the dry-fly fishing season. Rates include breakfast and dinner. River and lake guided fishing is $584 per day for two anglers.

Holiday Park

Originally built to house construction workers, centrally located **Club Habitat** (25 Ohuanga Rd., 07/386-7492, www.clubhabitat.co.nz) now provides a wide range of accommodations. The setup is mainly aimed at skiers looking for a cheap holiday, with transfers to Whakapapa provided during the winter. The rest of the year the place is fairly quiet and functions as a base for a variety of adventure activities, making it especially popular with groups. Camping is $12, dorm beds are $22, basic cabins start at $80 s or d, and motel rooms are $119. If it's quiet you'll have free run of all the facilities, including a sauna, spa, game room, bar, and inexpensive bistro-style restaurant.

FOOD

The main shopping center has a number of small-town tearooms and cafés, including **Mustard Seed Cafe** (98 Ohuanga Rd., 07/386-7377; daily from 9 A.M.). The restaurant at **Club Habitat** (25 Ohuanga Rd., 07/386-7492; closed Mondays) has a sterile atmosphere, but the food is cheap. A small cooked breakfast costs just $6, and the rest of the day they serve from a blackboard menu of basic hearty food.

Many of the fishing lodges have restaurants, and these are the best places to head for a full meal. Because trout aren't caught commercially in New Zealand, you'll need to catch your own (most local restaurants will cook up your catch—just drop it off upon returning from your fishing trip). The **Rod & Gun Restaurant** (Bridge Fishing Lodge, Hwy. 1, 07/386-8804; daily from 6 P.M.) oozes rustic appeal. It serves a wide selection of steak and seafood dishes from around $24. If you catch your own trout, the kitchen will cook it to order.

PRACTICALITIES
Information

The main source of information is **Turangi Visitor Centre** (Ngawaka Pl., 07/386-8999, daily 8:30 A.M.–5 P.M.), in the center of town opposite the shopping center. An audiovisual program on the local area is screened on request, and displays focus on fishing and forestry. Models of the Tongariro Power Development, the major contributing factor in the town's development, fill the museum area. You can also view and buy local arts and crafts, postcards, phone cards, and more; and hook up to the Internet.

Tongariro National Park

New Zealand's original national park is dramatic, spectacular, and beautiful—a restless land of contrasting elements and continuous change: rolling hills carpeted in purple heather and green and yellow tussocklands dotted with *toetoe;* dense *rimu* forest sheltering an abundance of birdlife; a desolate desert area and a lunar landscape scattered with sharp chunks of black volcanic rock; icy-cold waterfalls and bubbling hot springs; and three magnificent volcanoes that dominate the surrounding landscape—these are the images of Tongariro in summer. In winter a thick blanket of snow turns the park into a white wonderland. Backcountry explorers and ice-climbers joyfully head out into the frigid elements, skiers ride gravity down the steep volcanic slopes. Any lover of the great outdoors shouldn't miss this ancient land.

The original 6,518-acre block of Tongariro land was given as a gift to the government from Chief Te Heu Heu Tukino IV of the Tuwhare-toa tribe in 1887. The wise chief wanted to ensure that the volcanic center of the North Island would never be divided and sold in sections to the Pakeha by future Maori landowners. He believed that this area, rich in beauty and legends, should be forever enjoyed by all New Zealanders. This generous gift was gladly received by the government, which promised that the area would be left undivided and in its natural state. It officially became Tongariro National Park in 1894—one of the first national parks in the world. With the addition of much land over the years, the park has since expanded into a spectacular 188,000-acre area of New Zealand wilderness.

The only facilities within the park are in the west, at **Whakapapa village.** Nearby is the town of **National Park,** and on the park's southern outskirts is **Ohakune.** All three places offer a variety of accommodations and restaurants, coming alive with hikers in summer and skiers in winter.

TONGARIRO NATIONAL PARK

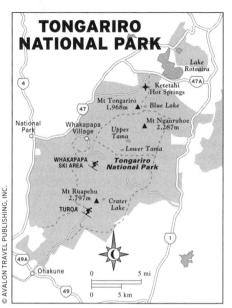

© AVALON TRAVEL PUBLISHING, INC.

THE LAND

Three major volcanoes tower above the surrounding landscape, dominating the horizon from all directions. Snowcapped **Mount Ruapehu,** the highest mountain on the North Island (2,797 meters/9,180 ft), consists of vents, lava flows, and many mudflows that have occurred over thousands of years. Eruptions (the last major one in 1996) have repeatedly ejected sulphurous water and ash from the 17-hectare (48-acre) crater onto the upper slopes of the mountain. In the past, this caused mudflows *(lahars)* to run far out onto the surrounding land, creating a distinct ring plain around the mountains, valleys, and ash-covered desertscapes. The seemingly calm but suspiciously warm and highly acidic water of **Crater Lake** continues to hide the violent nature of this volcano that smolders not far below the surface—but this doesn't deter the thousands who ski Ruapehu in winter or hike up it throughout the year.

The composite andesite volcano of **Mount Ngauruhoe** is the most easily recognized with its perfectly symmetrical cone and 32-degree slopes. It's 2,287 meters (7,503 ft) high, rises 650 meters (2,461 ft) above the southern slopes of Tongariro, and is still active. Steam wafts eerily from its crater. **Mount Tongariro,** a truncated multiple volcano, stands 1,968 meters (6,457 ft) high and contains a number of small craters. **Red Crater** and **Te Maari Craters**—the most recently active—emit steam, gas, and hot air. You can watch the volcanic activity at **Ketetahi Hot Springs** on the north side of Mount Tongariro.

Flora and Fauna

Five distinct vegetation types—mixed rainforest, beech forest, tussock grasslands, wetlands, and alpine desert—live within the park, which ranges in altitude. In the lower areas you find the large podocarp trees, broadleafs, vines, orchids, and ferns that make up the mixed rainforest—a lush and tropical home for an abundance of native birds. Birds such as the **native pigeon** (which literally stuffs itself on berry fruits), the nectar-sipping *tui* and **bellbird,** and the insect-eating **robin, fantail,** and **tomtit** are the most easily seen birds in the rainforest, along with the **whitehead** and nocturnal **kiwi.** A large variety of insects lives in the trees and among the debris on the forest floor, and the noisy **cicadas** can be quite deafening in summer. A good place to experience this kind of exotic greenery is the Ohakune area in the southwest sector of the park.

Climb to the 1,000-meter (3,281-ft) level and the rainforest gives way to mountain beech and cedar forest, where you'll see the tiny green **rifleman** (one of New Zealand's smallest birds), **silvereye,** and occasional **parakeet.** Continuing upward, the forest opens out into attractive tussock shrublands, where alpine plants, tussock, and heather are dominant. Here the **native falcon** searches for small birds and animals, the sounds of the **pipit** and secretive **fernbird** can be heard, and mice and hares scurry in the dense shrubbery.

You'll find the wetlands environment along the bogs, pond edges, stream banks, and waterfalls within the park. **Ourisia** (a delicate plant with white flowers), buttercups, daisies,

WHY THE MOUNTAINS MOVED

Maori mythology explains the location of the major North Island mountains in a vividly romantic and imaginative way. All the mightiest mountains once huddled together in the center of the North Island – Tongariro reigned as chief. They were all males, except for the beautiful forest-clad Pihanga, who stood (and still stands) at the eastern end of the Kakaramea Range between Lakes Taupo and Rotoaira. All were in love with Pihanga but she took a fancy only to the great Tongariro, who had fiercely battled the others and won. Pihanga gladly gave herself to him and the losers were forced to retreat, fleeing in anger and sorrow during the cover of darkness (mountains can move only at night) to many parts of the North Island. Putauaki traveled northeast to the Bay of Plenty, where he stopped at the northern end of the Kaingaroa Plain overlooking the Rangitaiki valley. Tauhara traveled only as far as the shores of Lake Taupo so that he could forever (masochistically) gaze back at the lovely Pihanga. Taranaki (also known as Mt. Egmont) angrily fled with great speed to the west coast, where he stopped when he reached the sea.

Many centuries passed before the mountains "came alive with fire." A great priest, Ngatoro-i-rangi, climbed Ngauruhoe to view the surrounding terrain. On reaching the top he was suddenly trapped in a terrible snowstorm, and in his fear (snow was a new and unpleasant experience) he called out for help to his priestess sisters in the north, begging them to send him fire so that he wouldn't freeze to death. Hearing his pleas, they got the fire-demons to send volcanic heat via White Island and Rotorua, the fire bursting up through the ground in many places before finally reaching the summit of Ngauruhoe. The priest sacrificed a female slave, Auruhoe, to add impact to his pleas, and when the fire burst forth he ceremoniously hurled her body into the bubbling crater. The volcano became known as "Ngauruhoe" after this gruesome incident. Tongariro was also named during this event from *tonga* (south wind – mentioned in the priest's prayers) and *rio* (seized).

and sundews live along the water's edge with freshwater crayfish and a large variety of aquatic insects. Check out the extensive bogs and intriguing plantlife on the western slopes of Mount Ruapehu, near Mount Hauhungatahi. You can still see the endangered **blue duck** (or *whio* to the Maori) in park areas around fast-flowing streams.

The deserts on the park's east side are mainly barren, an amazing contrast to the western side of the park. This is due not only to a lack of rain but also to the harsh dry winds blowing from the northwest over Mount Ruapehu. The soil is sandy gravel, the wind and temperature extremes attract little in the way of flora or fauna, and fairly frequent flash floods further desecrate the surface.

SIGHTS AND RECREATION
Viewpoints
The best and quickest way to get oriented to this magnificent volcanic area is by taking Highway 48 east from the village of National Park, which leads to **Whakapapa village,** past the Visitor Centre, and eight km (five mi) up the steep Bruce Road to Whakapapa Ski Area—from here you get spectacular views of the volcanoes and northern sector of the park.

In summer two chairlifts at **Whakapapa Ski Area** (07/892-3738) operate from Top O' the Bruce (the base village) to 2,000 meters (6,560 ft) above sea level, where you can enjoy panoramic views and lunch from the verandah of the Knoll Ridge Chalet. The lifts operate mid-December to late April, daily 9 A.M.–4 P.M.; adult $20, child $10. The safest way to continue higher is on a guided walk. Departing daily at 9:30 A.M., the walk climbs to the rim of a crater formed during the 1996 eruption. Cost (including lift) is adult $75, child $50. Hiking boots and poles can be rented at the day lodge. An interpretive trail from the top of the chairlift back down to the day lodge (90 minutes) is a more interesting alternative to taking the chair—and it's downhill all the way.

Circling the Park

A good way to admire the contrasting and varied scenery of this area is to circumnavigate the park via Highways 1, 49, 49A, 4, and 47. Highway 1, the Desert Road, is the most direct route south. If you don't have time to get into Tongariro, this is the route to take. It passes through the amazingly desolate landscape (great for dramatic photographs) on the dry, windswept eastern side of the volcanoes, and presents some craggy mountain views. To reach the most popular park attractions, head for the western side of the park. Drive clear around (just over three hours without stops, or one day to include stops at the main attractions) and you can see it all.

Easy Walking Tracks

Tongariro offers an extensive network of well-graded tracks that suit everyone from the first-timer to the serious and experienced hiker. The park has so many hiking opportunities that the best thing to do is to drop in at the Whakapapa Visitor Centre and describe the kind of terrain you'd like to see—you'll get plenty of suggestions and can load up with relevant brochures and maps.

Some of the most easily accessible shorter walks start from Whakapapa village. The shortest of these (20 minutes one way) is the **Ridge Track,** starting 100 meters (109 ft) above the Visitor Centre and leading to a lookout point above the tree line. The six-km/four-mi (two-hour round-trip) **Whakapapanui Walk** starts 300 meters (1,000 ft) above the Visitor Centre at the Whakapapa Holiday Park, follows the Whakapapanui Stream through beautiful beech forest and native bush, and ends on Highway 48, three km (1.9 mi) below the village. You can reach beautiful **Taranaki Falls,** plummeting 20 meters (66 ft) down a major lava flow, by a track starting from the Bayview Chateau Tongariro. It takes about one hour to get to the falls, up to 2.5 hours round-trip,

and the return route follows the banks of the Wairere Stream.

The 15-minute (round-trip) **Mounds Nature Walk** starts on Highway 48, five km (3.1 mi) below Whakapapa Visitor Centre. **Tawhai Falls** splashes down over the lip of a lava flow near the Whakapapanui Stream and is worth the short walk (30 minutes round-trip); the track starts on Highway 48, 3.5 km (two mi) below the Visitor Centre.

RUAPEHU BLOWS ITS TOP

Beginning in late September 1995, Mt. Ruapehu started belching ash, steam, and the occasional rock as big as a car from Crater Lake. The mountain erupted every two to three minutes in its most sustained activity since 1945. Scientists feared that it was building up to a major blast. Authorities warned residents to expect falling ash and potential water pollution from the ash and steam that shot as much as 19 km (12 mi) into the air; though they forced no one to evacuate, they closed airspace, highways, railways, and ski fields, the area's major attraction. But New Zealand tourism officials seized their chance to promote a natural wonder and encouraged tourists to take a look at the volcano – from a safe distance, of course.

Ruapehu continues to be a major attraction. You can still walk up to the crater rim, either by yourself or on a guided hike from Whakapapa Ski Area. But be aware that Ruapehu is an *active* volcano and an alpine area. The main hazard now is gas in the crater basin – continually assess the wind direction and position of any gas clouds. And the possibility of eruptions large enough to throw blocks and lake water out into the crater basin remains, as happened in October 2006, when water from the crater shot skyward up to 200 meters (640 ft).

GEOTHERMAL HEARTLAND

[Tongariro Crossing

Often described as the "finest one-day walk in New Zealand," the Tongariro Crossing is the park's most popular track. It is 20 km (12 mi) long, but takes seven to eight hours one way due to the strenuous going.

The Tongariro Crossing track begins from the end of Manatepopo Road and climbs through lava flows of varying ages, each with a different stage of regenerated vegetation. The trail then climbs steeply to a saddle between Mount Tongariro and Mount Ngauruhoe before descending to Blue Lake and the thermal area, 2.5 hours from the trail's end at the Ketetahi car park on Highway 47A. These routes cross open and exposed terrain subject to severe weather conditions—ensure you have adequate clothing and equipment. Wear sturdy boots and don't forget your swimming gear (have it on underneath if you're shy). Keep on the marked track at all times when you're in the thermal area—if the steam gets too concentrated to see, wait until it clears before you progress along the track—or you may find out firsthand how a lobster feels when it's plunged into boiling water!

Hikers with their own vehicles should park at the Ketetahi end of the trail, from where the **Mountain Shuttle** (0800/117-686, www.tongarirocrossing.com) will transport you to the trailhead at Whakapapa ($20). This service also does afternoon pick-ups for those coming off the trail and needing to be returned to National Park and Whakapapa.

Whakapapa Ski Area

New Zealand's largest ski field, Whakapapa (07/892-3738, www.mtruapehu.com) is served by 25 chairlifts, T-bars, rope tows, and platter lifts. Encompassing 400 hectares (990 acres) and 44 named runs, it has a base elevation of 1,625 meters and an impressive vertical rise of 675 meters (2,215 ft). While first-timers try their skill on the gentle beginners' slopes of Happy Valley, experts can play on slopes that test even the most experienced skiers. Snowboarders enjoy a terrain park and half-pipe. Food service is available at Top O' The Bruce,

at the Schusshaus on Hut Flat, at the top of the Waterfall Express chairlift, and at the top of the West Ridge chairlift. You'll find public shelters at the top of the Waterfall chairlift and Top O' the Bruce—the many private lodges on the field are for members only. You can rent skis, snowboards, and clothing at the base village. The season runs from mid-June with lifts operating into November. Lift tickets are $75 for adults and $5 for children.

WHAKAPAPA VILLAGE

A variety of services lie within this compact little village nestled along the western slopes of Mount Ruapehu. The village boasts a nine-hole golf course (07/892-3809; $18). Although the course is not particularly challenging, its alpine environment and the trio of snowcapped volcanoes as a backdrop prove both interesting and unique.

Accommodations and Camping

Set up for the winter rush, **Skotel Alpine Resort** (Whakapapa Village Rd., 07/892-3719 or 0800/756-835, www.skotel.co.nz)is an excellent location (behind the château) offers outstanding mountain and valley views from the verandah. Amenities include a fitness room, a TV room, indoor and outdoor saunas and spas, communal cooking facilities, and a restaurant and bar. There's nothing quite like soaking in the hot bubbling water of the spa at the end of a hard day's hiking or skiing—outside and separate from the main building but glass enclosed, it's a very appealing spot to kick back and gaze at mountains or stars while the swirling water brings your body back to life. Beds in the Hostel Wing cost $30 per person. Hotel rooms are $130 s or d, cabins $135, and chalets $160.

If you feel like an old-fashioned splurge, French château–style **Bayview Chateau Tongariro** (Whakapapa Village Rd., 07/892-3809 or 0800/242-832, www.chateau.co.nz; $175–350 s or d) is probably one of the best places in New Zealand to do it. The large and magnificent blue-roofed brick building on the lower slopes of Mount Ruapehu (you can't miss it heading up the road to Whakapapa)

© ANDREW HEMPSTEAD

Bayview Chateau Tongariro is the Tongariro National Park's premier accommodation.

is a luxury hotel and local landmark. Guests enjoy fantastic mountain views, comfortable lounges, upscale dining, a heated indoor pool, and a small fitness room. Nonguests aren't supposed to go farther than the lobby unless they pay for morning coffee or afternoon tea, or are heading for the restaurant.

Whakapapa Holiday Park is in a forest of enchanting beech trees 100 meters (330 ft) beyond the visitor center (07/892-3897). It has the usual communal facilities and a grocery store stocked with foods and essential items—open every day 8:30 A.M.–5:30 P.M. Rates are $12 per person for tent sites, $14 per person for powered sites, while cabins with shared bathrooms rent for $45 s or d and tourist flats are $65.

Food

You can buy basic foodstuffs, some canned and frozen foods, and snacks at **Whakapapa Holiday Park Store** (daily 8:30 A.M.–5:30 P.M.). On the main village road, **Fergusson's Café** (daily 8:30 A.M.–5 P.M.) serves up hot drinks and light meals.

The restaurant in the **Skotel Alpine Resort** (07/892-3719; daily 7:30–10 A.M. and 6:30–10 P.M.) has reasonable prices, but the food is nothing special. **Ruapehu Restaurant** (Bayview Chateau Tongariro, Whakapapa Village Rd., 07/892-3809; daily 7:30–10 A.M. and 6:30–9 P.M.) is the village's premier dining room. Breakfast is served buffet style while dinner is a no-jeans affair with traditional mains in the $28–38 range. The château also has a casual café with outdoor seating and two bars.

Information

The main source of park information is **Whakapapa Visitor Centre,** in the heart of the village (07/892-3729; daily 8 A.M.–5 P.M.). A lot more than just a place to get information, the center features many interesting displays describing local geology, volcanism (including an interesting look at recent eruptions), earthquakes, and flora and fauna, as well as a small skiing museum, track descriptions, and a summer interpretive program. If you'd like to see the technicolor spectacle of a volcanic eruption

GEOTHERMAL HEARTLAND

complete with awesome stereo effects, check out *The Ring of Fire* audiovisual in the theater. Equally spectacular is another audiovisual, *Sacred Gift of Tongariro*.

NATIONAL PARK

This small settlement (pop. 500) at the junction of Highways 4 and 47 is the gateway to Tongariro's western slopes and Whakapapa village, 16 km (10 mi) to the east. It holds numerous accommodations and is a stop for both Tranz Scenic and Intercity.

Accommodations

[Howard's Lodge (11 Carroll St., 07/892-2827, www.howardslodge.co.nz) is the best-value accommodation in National Park. The newer wing features comfortable rooms with private bathrooms for $72 s, $82 d. Guests staying in these rooms have use of a great lounge area and a modern kitchen. Across the parking lot and completely self-contained are rooms and facilities designed for backpackers, who enjoy the use of a private lounge and two kitchens. Dorm beds here are $22–25 and a private room is $52 s, $62 d. But what makes this place really great are the hosts. Last time I stayed here, they somehow managed to remember everyone by name, arrange track transportation, and serve up a cooked breakfast each morning ($14) and complimentary coffee and cake each evening.

Like Howard's Lodge, the other places to stay in town provide beds for all budgets. **Pukenui Lodge** (1 Millar St., 07/892-2882 or 0800/785-368, www.tongariro.cc; dorm beds $25, private room $50–65 s, $60–75 d) has a full view of the mountains from the large lounge area. The restaurant on-site serves up reasonably priced meals, which can be bought separately or as part of a package.

The **Ski Haus** (Carroll St., 07/892-2854, www.skihaus.co.nz; dorm beds $25, private rooms $70–85 s or d), like all the other places in town, is designed for the winter crowd with a spa, drying room, cozy lounge with an open fire (open from 6 P.M. year-round), and ski field transfers.

Getting There

If you're visiting Tongariro National Park and arriving by bus or train, you'll end up in town. National Park is a stop on the **Tranz Scenic** (0800/802-802) Auckland to Wellington route. Ticket prices vary considerably, but start at $85 for a one-way ticket between Auckland and National Park. **Intercity** (www.intercitycoach.co.nz) has no depot in town, but buses arrive and depart once daily in each direction for Auckland and Wellington, stopping outside the Ski Haus on Carroll Street. All Intercity buses from Auckland travel via Taumarunui, so if you are coming from the Lake Taupo area, hook up with the **Alpine Scenic Tours** shuttle (07/386-8918) for a more direct transfer.

OHAKUNE

The small town of Ohakune, 32 km (20 mi) south of National Park on Highway 49, provides the main access to the southern reaches

It's difficult to miss this oversized carrot on the road to Ohakune.

© ANDREW HEMPSTEAD

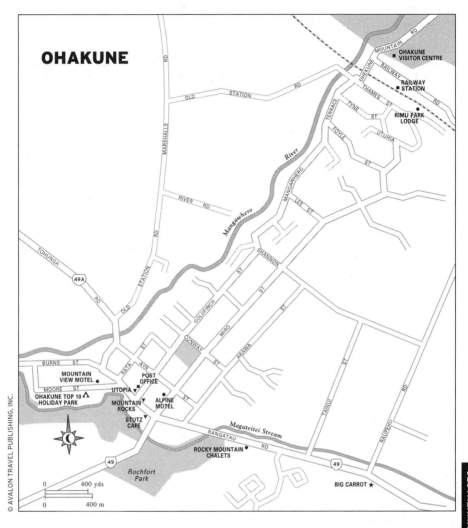

OHAKUNE

© AVALON TRAVEL PUBLISHING, INC.

OHAKUNE VISITOR CENTRE

RAILWAY STATION

RIMU PARK LODGE

MOUNTAIN VIEW MOTEL

POST OFFICE

OHAKUNE TOP 10 HOLIDAY PARK

UTOPIA

MOUNTAIN ROCKS

ALPINE MOTEL

STUTZ CAFÉ

ROCKY MOUNTAIN CHALETS

Rochfort Park

BIG CARROT ★

0   400 yds

0   400 m

of Tongariro National Park and is the jumping-off point for the Turoa ski field. Ohakune really only comes alive in winter, when the population rises from 1,500 to well over 5,000. Many businesses don't even open the rest of the year, but inquire at the information center about white-water rafting and horseback riding. The main summer draws are the hikes that radiate from Ohakune Mountain Road. Aside from winter sports, Ohakune is known for carrot farming, and the world's largest carrot lies beside the highway south through town.

Ohakune Mountain Road

Take Goldfinch Street north off Highway 49 to reach Ohakune Mountain Road, which leads back into Tongariro National Park through a subalpine forest that carpets the western side

GEOTHERMAL HEARTLAND

of the mountains. This road lends great views of Mount Ruapehu and its glaciers above as you climb, passes a couple of walking tracks to magnificent waterfalls, and terminates at Turoa Ski Field, where you get equally fabulous views of the park stretched out far below.

Along the road, **Waitonga Falls Walk** (30 minutes one way) is signposted, as is a lookout for **Mangawhero Falls. Mangawhero Forest Walk** starts opposite the Ohakune Field Centre and takes you for a one-hour (round-trip) walk through podocarp forest. The 20-meter (66-ft) **Rimu Track** also starts opposite the Ohakune Field Centre.

Turoa

In winter, Ohakune comes alive with skiers and snowboarders who spend their days at Turoa (06/385-8456, www.mtruapehu .com). This busy ski field has four chairlifts and seven surface lifts providing access to diverse terrain interspersed with small valleys and wide-open unobstructed slopes. The base of the ski field is 1,600 meters, the top is at 2,320 meters (7,610 ft), the vertical rise is 720 meters/2,360 ft (New Zealand's greatest vertical rise), and there are runs to suit all levels of experience. Turoa provides a terrain park, a half-pipe, various food outlets, a ski school, and rentals. The season runs mid-June to mid-October. Tickets are adult $75, child $50.

Accommodations and Camping

Ohakune has more than 20 places to stay, ranging from standard roadside motels to upscale lodges. Most rely on the busy ski season, when prices skyrocket and rooms need to be booked well in advance. Outside of winter, some places don't bother opening.

Rimu Park Lodge (27 Rimu St., 06/385-9023, www.rimupark.co.nz) is a charming 1914 residence offering a variety of accommodation choices. Dorm beds in the main house are $20, private rooms $45 d, while adjacent are basic cabins ($50 s or d) and a beautifully restored 1934 railway carriage converted to a double room ($75).

On the south side of the highway through town, **Mountain View Motel** (2 Moore St., 06/385-8675; $55–85 s or d) has kitchen-equipped units. Guest rooms at the **Alpine Motel** (7 Miro St., 06/385-8758, www.alpine moco.nz; $85 s or d) are medium-sized with small kitchens. Dorm beds ($17) and chalets ($135 s or d) are also available.

A great choice for families is **Rocky Mountain Chalets** (Hwy. 49, 06/385-9545, www.rockymountainchalets.com; from $120 s or d), comprising 42 freestanding units, each practically furnished and with full kitchens. Again, in wintertime it's packed; the rest of the year, you'll have the place to yourself.

Ohakune Top 10 Holiday Park (5 Moore St., 06/385-8561) provides communal facilities (the showers and electric cooking rings are coin-operated), a limited number of tent sites, and plenty of caravan sites. Centrally located, the campground is next to an attractive scenic reserve. Campsites are $30; cabins start at $65 s or d.

Food

Utopia (47 Clyde St., 06/385-9120; daily 8 A.M.–3 P.M.) features lots of light, healthy choices to eat in or take out. Open the same hours, **Stutz Café** (66 Clyde St., 06/385-8563) has basic cooked breakfasts for under $10, but the ambience isn't exactly inspiring. **Mountain Rocks** (corner Clyde and Goldfinch Sts., 06/385-9350; daily 8 A.M.–10 P.M.) is set up for the wintertime crowd, but is open year-round dishing up typical café fare in a pub-like setting.

Information

Ruapehu Information Centre (54 Clyde St., 06/385-8427) is open weekdays 9 A.M.–4:30 P.M., Sat.–Sun. 10 A.M.–2 P.M. Another good source for local information, especially if you're heading into the park, is the DOC **Ohakune Visitor Centre,** at the bottom of Ohakune Mountain Road (06/385-0010).

EASTLAND AND HAWKE'S BAY

An easy detour from the most direct route between Auckland and Wellington, Eastland and Hawke's Bay comprises the central section of the North Island's east coast. Like so many other regions of the country, it is filled with stunning, unspoiled scenery. Yet, instead of thermal attractions, snowcapped mountains, or forested wilderness, its beaches, endless vineyards, and a laidback population are what make the region popular.

The main draw away from the coast is Te Urewera National Park, a rugged interior wilderness of mountains and lakes where the sounds of running water and melodic birds are ever present. The park preserves the hauntingly beautiful land of the Tuhoe Tribe or "Children of the Mist," where legendary fairies and goblins play deep in the forest, where every tree has its own spirit, and where every rock, lake, and waterfall has a symbolic "presence." For hikers and photographers, Te Urewera abounds with mysterious and unspoiled splendor, freeing your imagination while you get back to nature.

Captain Cook took his first steps on New Zealand soil along the East Cape in 1769, naming many of the points and coves. Numerous historic landmarks commemorating his visit are interspersed with scenic lookouts all along coastal Highway 35, which passes through villages rich with Maori culture and stretches of beautiful beach with not another soul in sight. On the south side of the cape, Gisborne is the first city in the world to see the sun each day, but by this time the water is already filled with surfers, who regard local waves as among the country's best.

© ANDREW HEMPSTEAD

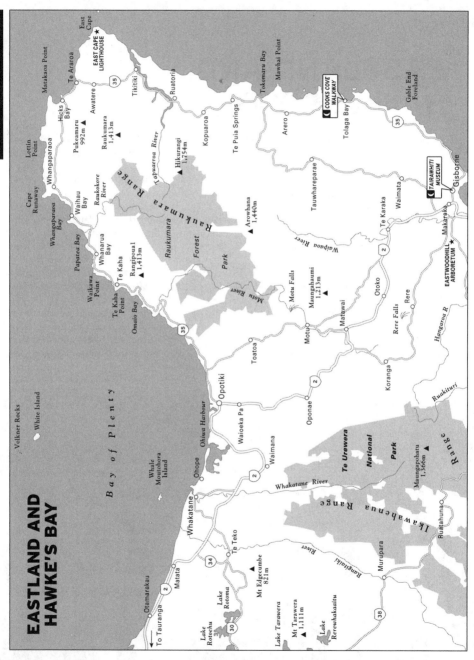

EASTLAND AND HAWKE'S BAY

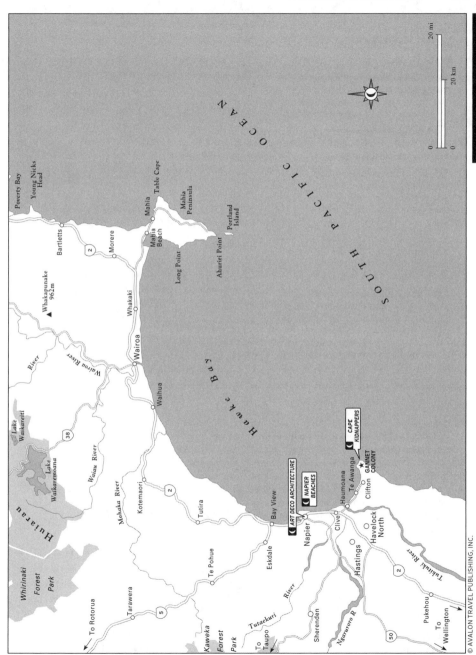

SOUTH PACIFIC OCEAN

20 mi

20 km

Poverty Bay

Young Nicks Head

Table Cape

Mahia

Mahia Peninsula

Bartletts

Morere

Mahia Beach

Portland Island

Long Point

Ahuriri Point

Whakapunake 962m

Whakaki

Wairoa

Hawke Bay

Waihua

Waiau River

Wairoa River

River

Lake Waikareiti

Lake Waikaremoana

Huiarau

Waihua

CAPE KIDNAPPERS

ART DECO ARCHITECTURE

NAPIER BEACHES

GANNET COLONY

Haumoana

Te Awanga

Clifton

Kotemaori

Mohaka River

Tutira

Bay View

Te Pohue

Eskdale

Napier

Clive

Haumoana

Havelock North

Hastings

Whirinaki Forest Park

Tarawera

Kaweka Forest Park

To Rotorua

To Taupo

Te Pohue

Tutaekuri River

Sherenden

Ngaruroro R

Tukituki River

Pukehou

To Wellington

© AVALON TRAVEL PUBLISHING, INC.

HIGHLIGHTS

[Cooks Cove Walkway: Solitude is easy to find around the East Cape, but on this rambling path over lush farmland, with the ocean ever present, you will feel like the world is a lot less crowded than it really is (page 199).

[Tairawhiti Museum: Plan on visiting this complex in Gisborne for its impressive collection of Maori art (page 200).

[Art Deco Architecture: Collectively, the buildings of Napier's downtown core are one of the world's best examples of art deco style (page 205).

[Napier Beaches: Long stretches of sand dominate the east coast of the North Island. The draw of those in Napier is that they are central to town and accommodations in all budget ranges (page 209).

[Cape Kidnappers: Jutting far into the Pacific Ocean, this peninsula is home to over 20,000 Australasian gannets (page 215).

LOOK FOR [TO FIND RECOMMENDED
SIGHTS, ACTIVITIES, DINING, AND LODGING.

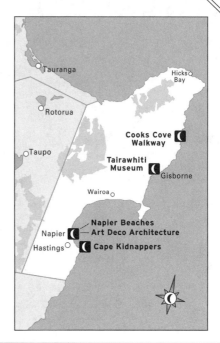

The Hawke's Bay region, to the south of Gisborne, shares the same beautiful coastline and a climate often described as Mediterranean, with lots of sunshine, cool sea breezes, and an average temperature of 21°C (70°F) in summer and 10°C (50°F) in winter. Large crowds descend on the region (especially in summer). The largest population center is Napier, which spreads along the oceanfront exuding a relaxed by-the-sea atmosphere that may tempt you to spend an extra day lounging on the beach.

I never get tired of this region's exotic bush, golden sandy beaches, and groves of ancient, gnarled *pohutukawa* trees that in summer become a magnificent mass of red flowers. There are seemingly endless opportunities for swimming and tanning, snorkeling and scuba

diving, good fishing, and gratifying, time-absorbing, colorful coastal views. No enormous foreign-owned hotels will be lining this coastline in the near future, and if you expect to find touristy towns, you'll be disappointed.

PLANNING YOUR TIME

This chapter gives you two regions for the price of one, and you should plan accordingly. As you travel south from Auckland via Whakatanethe choice at Opotiki is to take the coastal drive around the East Cape or cut across to Gisborne. The former requires a full day, but zooming right along, not taking time to relax at the many beaches, stop at the lookouts, and hike the **Cooks Cove Walkway**, defeats the purpose of taking this longer route.

Either way, you'll find yourself in the city of Gisborne, known as "the world's easternmost city." The place to learn about this geographical highlight, as well as to soak up Maori culture, is **Tairawhiti Museum.**

The major population center around Hawke's Bay is Napier. This bustling oceanfront city is a good place to kick back for a day or two, staying in one of the many accommodations suited to all budgets and enjoying a good range of restaurants. The city is best-known for its **art deco** buildings, but **Napier Beaches,** literally across the road from downtown, make it a haven for sun-lovers. The one official attraction you should plan to visit while in Napier (allow a half day) is **Cape Kidnappers,** home to an eye-popping 20,000 gannets.

Te Urewera National Park

As the largest park on the North Island (212,000 hectares/523,900 acres), Te Urewera National Park protects a remote and mountainous landscape between the Bay of Plenty to the north and Hawke's Bay to the south. The only road through the park is unpaved Highway 38, which winds its way southwest from Rotorua, climbing into the park and to **Lake Waikaremoana** before exiting the park and joining the coastal highway at Wairoa.

The Huiarau Range runs across the middle of the park, dividing the north from the south. In the northern sector the Waimana and Whakatane Rivers run northward and empty into the Bay of Plenty, and the Whirinaki River passes through the western edge of the park; in the southern sector the catchment waters of Lake Waikaremoana run southeast through several hydroelectric power stations and out to sea at Hawke's Bay. The impressive Panekiri Bluff, regularly obscured by a dense blanket of fog that appears to pour off the end and down to the water below, rises 600 meters (1,970 ft) to dominate the southern shore of Lake Waikaremoana. Waterfalls are dominant features throughout the park. Some of the most magnificent are close to the main road, or at the ends of short tracks through lush forest. In the early morning and late evening dense fog blankets the high forest peaks, and mist creeps across the lakes to swirl upward through the trees. Flapping wings and sharp notes pierce the silence, giving away the presence of a variety of birds, hard to spot among the dense greenery. You can feel the silence, and lose yourself in the beauty.

Highway 38, between Rotorua and Wairoa, is the main route through the park.

ROAD-ACCESSIBLE SIGHTS

From Rotorua, it's 179 km (112 mi) south along Highway 38 to the park boundary, from where it's another 50 km (31 mi) to the visitor center at Aniwaniwa. This section of road is unpaved and is very narrow and winding (allow at least three hours to travel between Rotorua and Aniwaniwa). From this point the road passes the park's only services and follows the shoreline of Lake Waikaremoana for 16 km (10 mi). Highway 38 then exits the park and winds its way down to Wairoa, a distance of 58 km (36 mi).

Along the section of road through the park are lookout points, waterfalls, river crossings, and other scenic stops. Here are some of the most accessible, from north to south.

Murupara to Lake Waikaremoana

Near the northwest entrance to Te Urewera, Highway 38 passes 20-meter-high (66-ft) **Totarapapa Stream and Falls** before entering typically rugged Te Urewera scenery—look on the right side of the road. You can see the beautiful **Hopuruahine Cascades and Falls** only by going down Hopuruahine Landing Road and walking back up and in the river. A huge waterfall that even the least adventurous will be able to view without getting out of the car is the fabulous 34-meter-high (110-ft-high)

WHERE THE MOUNTAIN MARRIES THE MIST

Te Urewera's past is an intriguing mixture of mysterious legends and historic facts. The original people of Te Urewera, the Tuhoe, claim descent from the symbolic union of Te Maunga, the Mountain, and Hine-Pukohu-Rangi, the Mist-Maiden. This seems quite appropriate once you've spent any time in this legendary "Land of Mist." The Maori named Urewera (burnt penis) from the time a help-less old man, Mura-kareke, was lying by a fire and accidentally roasted his privates. Urewera became the designated name of the area after this incident, and Mura-kareke's descendants traditionally acquired the tribal name "Te Ure-wera." The sound of the Maori word is defi-nitely more appealing than its translation as a name for this beautiful park!

Lake Waikaremoana was formed more than 2,000 years ago by a landslide that blocked a narrow river gorge, but local legend ex-plains its formation with much more magic and imagination. The great chief Maahu was angered by his daughter, Hau-mapuhia, and in his rage he tried to drown her. To help her escape, the gods turned her into a *taniwha* (monster) so that she could free herself from her father and burrow through to the sea before daylight (rays of the sun turn a *taniwha* to stone). In her frantic struggle she gouged out a deep area that became the "Sea of Dashing Waters." The sun came up and the *taniwha* was captured in stone to lie forever at the mouth of the Waikaretaheke River, just below Kaitawa. Sometimes jets of water shot high into the air above the rock of Hau-mapuhia and the sounds of wailing rose above it — a signal to the ancient Maori that a great storm was on its way. In recent times the waters of the Waikaretaheke River were diverted for hydroelectric power, and the hill-side slip that resulted completely buried the rock that was Hau-mapuhia.

Mokau Falls—the highway runs in a loop to-ward, over, and away from it, 11 km (seven mi) north of the visitor center.

Te Maraateatua Point (Garden of the Gods) is not marked—the signpost on the main road, between Mokau Landing and the visitor center, reads Access to Lake 5 Minutes. After traversing the very steep five-minute bush trail, you emerge at a rock- and boulder-strewn beach and a good fishing point. Walk around to the right (facing the lake) over the boulders for another 10 minutes and you'll find a beautiful sheltered cove. Small sandy areas among the rocks are suitable (and more com-fortable than they look) for a picnic lunch or camping.

Lake Waikaremoana

Translating to "Sea of Rippling Waters," this massive lake reaches a depth of 585 meters (1,920 ft). The highway follows the shoreline of its eastern arm. Continue to the visitor cen-ter at Aniwaniwa, where a wide variety of hikes leads to waterfalls, to lakes, and deep into the bush. **Hinerau's Track** starts and finishes at the visitor center, is only a half-hour walk, and gives great views of the three spectacular **Aniwaniwa (Rainbow) Waterfalls**—Moma-haki and Bridal Veil Falls (both 15 meters/49 ft), and Te Tangi O Te Hinerau (11 meters/36 ft). **Aniwaniwa Valley Walk** also starts at the visitor center, follows Old Gisborne Road for two km/one mi (a track continues to Ward's Hut), and turns down a two-minute bush track to emerge at the bottom of dazzling 20-meter (66-ft) **Papakorito Falls.** Another small track allows access to the top of these falls, but at the bottom a great swimming hole (pleasant temperature in summer) is surrounded by enormous boulders, tree ferns, and heaps of *toe toe*—a super-secluded spot for soaking up some sun.

RECREATION
Short Walks

Apart from short walks to the most accessible

waterfalls, literally hundreds of kilometers of track riddle the park. Call in at the visitor center at Aniwaniwa for brochures, track guides, and maps, or refer to the park handbook *Land of the Mist,* which contains all the short walks and a fairly detailed map.

The enjoyable **Lake Waikareiti Track** leads about 3.5 km (two mi) through dense beech forest, exotic fuchsia gullies, and sunny fern-filled glades alive with songbirds, up to a small sheltered lake (878 meters/2,881 ft) popular with hikers, anglers (an average rainbow trout is one kg/two lb), and swimmers who enjoy an icy dunking. It takes about an hour to hike up to Lake Waikareiti, less coming down, and you'll find toilets and a day shelter (no overnight stays) at the lake. The lake is dotted with six small islands, one of which, Rahui, contains a small lake of its own called Tamaiti-O-Waikaremoana—unique because of its total isolation from humans or browsing animals. Rowboats for rent on Lake Waikareiti must be paid for at the visitor center, where you can get your key, oarlocks, and directions before you set off. You can hike farther around the west shore to the sandy beach at Tawari Bay (20 minutes one way) or continue to the northern end and stay at the Sandy Bay Hut (another three hours one way). To get to the start of the Lake Waikareiti Track, cross the bridge from the visitor center and follow the highway for about 200 meters (656 ft) to the signpost.

Another good one-hour track starts at the same place as the Waikareiti Track and leads past a series of small silted lakes to **Waipai Swamp,** known for its swamp plants, sundews, and orchids. The **Lake Ruapani Track** passes through red and silver beech forests with mixed stands of *rimu, miro, kahikatea, kamahi,* and *tawari* on the way to the swamp, and the mysterious quiet of these green and serene groves is disturbed only by birdsong and fluttering wings. You can continue past the swamp for another hour and come out at the grassy verges and groves of beech trees that edge small Lake Ruapani, or continue another three hours to join the Waikareiti Track.

Lake Waikaremoana Track

Perhaps the most popular of the overnight tramps is the well-defined 46-km (29-mi) Lake Waikaremoana Track, which starts at Onepoto off Highway 38 at the southern end of the lake, crosses the spectacular Panekiri Range (great views), and then closely skirts the western shores all the way north to Hopuruahine Landing on the main highway. It takes three or four days to complete, camping out ($10 per person per night) or staying in five huts ($20 per person) along the trail. Most hikers leave their vehicles at the campground and use **Home Bay Water Taxi** (06/837-3826; $30 per person) for trailhead transfers. Before starting out, get weather forecasts, track descriptions, and maps from the visitor center.

Fishing

Anglers report excellent fishing for rainbow trout (and some brown trout) throughout the park. Lakes Waikaremoana and Waikareiti provide the easiest access for anglers, with both fly- and spoon-fishing permitted. If you want to get out on Lake Waikaremoana, hire a rowboat from the campground. If you would prefer the solitude of Lake Waikareiti, the visitor center rents rowboats and dinghies. The lakes may have easier access, but the backcountry rivers often provide better fishing. The Waimana, Whakatane, Waiau, Whirinaki, and Ruakituri Rivers are perfect for anglers. The upper reaches of the Ruakituri and Waiau Rivers and tributaries have produced some monsters in recent years—up to six-kg (13-lb) rainbow trout have been reported by gleeful anglers.

The lake fishing season runs all year; river fishing season is December 1–June 30. A license is required for fishing anywhere in the park, and can be purchased at Lake Waikaremoana Motorcamp.

ACCOMMODATIONS AND CAMPING

The only accommodation within the park is **Lake Waikaremoana Motorcamp** (06/837-3826, www.lake.co.nz; camping $10 per person, cabins and chalets $42–84 s or d), on the southeastern arm of Lake Waikaremoana one km (0.6 mi) south of the visitor center. Surrounded by tree-covered hills and right on the lakeshore, it's run by the DOC, but don't count on staying here in summer or during Easter vacation if you haven't booked up to six months ahead. Facilities include a communal kitchen, grocery store, and rowboat rentals.

Immediately south of Lake Waikaremoana, but just outside the park, **Lake Whakamarino Lodge** (The Esplanade, Tuai, 06/837-3876, www.lakelodge.co.nz; $69–100 s or d) has adequate guest rooms in three buildings, as well as a restaurant with set-price breakfast, lunch, and dinner. The big draw here is the lakefront location.

INFORMATION
Aniwaniwa Visitor Centre (06/838-3803; daily 8 A.M.–4:30 P.M.) is in the heart of the park one km (0.6 mi) north of Lake Waikaremoana Motorcamp. The center has vivid displays, plentiful reading on Te Urewera legends and local history, and detailed information on the park's natural history. Ask a staff member to put on the excellent audiovisual—it really gets you in the mood for further exploration.

East Cape

Well off the main tourist route, the East Cape is rich in Maori history and easy on the eyes. From **Opotiki,** 45 km (28 mi) east of Whakatane Highway 35 winds past unspoiled beaches, photogenic *pohutukawa* trees, and tiny towns untouched by tourism. The total distance between Opotiki and Gisborne via Te Araroa is 320 km (200 mi), but the route is as narrow and as winding as any in the country, so you should allow at least six hours, and of course more with stops.

Highway 2 from Opotiki cuts south across the interior to Gisborne, but unless time is an issue, the longer oceanfront route is recommended.

OPOTIKI
Situated on a harbor inlet formed by the junction of the Waioeka and Otara Rivers 45 km (28 mi) east of Whakatane, Opotiki (pop. 7,000) is the first and largest town around the East Cape. The beaches are the main local attraction, but stop by **Opotiki Information Centre** (corner of Elliot and St. John Sts., 07/315-8484, www.opotiki.com; daily 8 A.M.–5 P.M.) for other ideas.

Sights
Opotiki Museum (127 Church St., 07/315-5193; Mon.–Sat. 10 A.M.–3:30 P.M.; adult $2, child $1) displays locally collected items that give insight into the town's past.

The world's largest collection of specifically indigenous plants is within the low stone walls of **Hukutaia Domain,** seven km (4.3 mi) south of town. Once part of a privately owned estate, the four-hectare (10-acre) park has been maintained by the government for almost 100 years. Thousands of species are signed with lengthy descriptions. Near the center of the park is a 21-meter-high (69-ft-high) *puriri* tree estimated to be 2,000 years old.

Accommodations and Camping
At Waiotahi Beach, five km (three mi) west of Opotiki, is **C Opotiki Beach House** (Appleton Rd., 07/315-5117; Sept.–May; dorm beds $22, $40 s, $50 d). Right on the beach, this great budget accommodation has a relaxed atmosphere, a friendly host, and surfing equipment for guest use. The lodge has an open plan, with a kitchen and lounge area downstairs and dorm beds in the loft. An adjacent unit holds a couple of double rooms. Downtown, **Central Oasis Backpackers** (30 King St., 07/315-5165; dorm beds $18, $44 d) offers an appealing garden, clean spacious dorm rooms, a kitchen, and a living room. **Ohiwa Family Holiday Park** (Ohiwa

Harbour Rd., 07/315-4741, www.ohiwa holidays.co.nz) has a delightful location 10 km (6.2 mi) west of Opotiki at Ohiwa, a delightful seaside village. The campground sprawls from the protected waters of Ohiwa Harbour to a driftwood-strewn beach facing the Bay of Plenty. Campsites are $32, boxy cabins $50 s or d, kitchen-equipped flats $120, and modern motel rooms $140.

INLAND ROUTE TO GISBORNE

Highway 2 is the 148-km (92-mi) route (allow 2.5 hours) connecting Opotiki and Gisborne. The winding road passes through fern-lined gorges with riverbank rest areas and waterfall views, and by dairy farms, orchards, and vineyards that neatly patchwork the land as you approach Gisborne. The stretch of highway through **Waioeka Gorge Scenic Reserve** is a particularly magical stretch for lovers of ferns and native forest. The **Motu Gorge,** a sidetrack that runs from Matawai to Toatoa, offers wild and rugged scenery. To get in there take Motu Road, which closely follows the untamed Motu River, but take note: Although it looks like an hour's drive on the map, it really takes about a half-day—pretty hairy driving at that, and not recommended for the fainthearted. If you take this sidetrack, don't miss splendid **Motu Falls,** five km (three mi) downstream from Motu.

Eastwoodhill Arboretum and Vicinity

Off the beaten track, but a delightful detour, **Eastwoodhill Arboretum** (2392 Wharekopae Rd., 07/863-9003; Oct.–May daily 9:30 A.M.–4:30 P.M., June–Sept. Mon.–Fri. 9:30 A.M.–4:30 P.M.; adult $10, senior $8, child free) is a huge collection of trees, shrubs, and climbers not native to New Zealand—most of them are from the Northern Hemisphere. To get there from along Highway 2, continue south to Makaraka (almost on the outskirts of Gisborne), turn west toward Wairoa for five km (3.1 mi), and turn off toward Patutahi. Don't go into this township, but keep on the road to Ngatapa. It's 24 km (15 mi) from Makaraka.

After visiting the garden, continue along Wharekopae Road for 20 km (12 mi) to **Rere Falls,** within a small reserve along the banks of the Wharekopae River. The 24-meter-high (79-ft), 45-meter-wide (148-ft) falls are perhaps most impressive in winter, but in summer the deep pool at the foot is a great swimming hole and the river itself has a reputation for good trout fishing. You can cross the waterfall along a ledge at the base, which takes you behind the thundering wall of water, or at the top when it's not in flood, but look out for slippery rocks.

OPOTIKI TO TE ARAROA

Between Opotiki and **Omaio** (free campground near the Motu River; no facilities), Highway 35 is stunningly colorful, particularly in December when the *pohutukawa* trees clinging to the cliffs are covered in scarlet blossoms and the ocean alternates between deep turquoise and a brilliant blue. All along the road are places to stop for breathtaking coastal views, sandy shell- or driftwood-covered beaches, bird colonies, picturesque farmland, and rocks where you can try your luck fishing. *Pohutukawa* trees continuously splash the landscape with red and green as you continue along the coast.

Te Kaha

At Te Kaha, an old whaling port 67 km (42 mi) northeast of Opotiki, don't miss **Tukaki,** the triangular-shaped, intricately carved Maori Meeting House.

One of the most enjoyable accommodations around the East Cape is (**Waikawa Bed & Breakfast** (Hwy. 35, 07/325-2070, www .waikawa.net; $120–140 s or d), surrounded by well-manicured gardens overlooking a rocky bay and with distant views to White Island. The two rooms have en suite bathrooms, private entrances, and TV/DVD combos. Beautifully landscaped **Te Kaha Holiday Park** (Hwy. 35 northeast of town, 07/325-2894, www.tekaha holidaypark.co.nz; camping $13 per person, kitchen-equipped cabins $78 s or d, motel room $105) has a great location, just across the road from a gray sandy beach with driftwood, rocks to climb on, and, of course, *pohutukawa* trees. The park has good communal facilities, a well-stocked shop, a café, a swimming pool, a barbecue, a playground, and a TV room.

Waihau Bay

As you approach Waihau Bay from the south, don't miss a stop at the small, pleasing-to-the-eye, whitewashed **Raukokore Anglican Church** and the graveyard behind. The family graves are marked with photo-adorned stones giving all sorts of fascinating details. The **Catholic church** is almost opposite. For good fishing, head for the sandy beach near the school. The village, half a kilometer off the main road, is made up of a post office, a general store with hot takeaway foods and small information booth, a petrol station, and public toilets.

You'll pass black and gray jagged rocks with occasional patches of sand before reaching the next sandy swimming beach at **Mangatoto Bridge.**

Whangaparaoa

Two canoes from Hawaii, the *Tainui* and the *Arawa,* landed at Whangaparaoa about A.D. 1350. **Te Kura O Whangaparaoa,** the *pa* and meetinghouse, is here—you can't miss the ornately carved bright-red archway marking the entrance. Just along the road is the Cape Runaway post office. The highway then wanders up to the top of the cape through relatively uninteresting farmland. About 25 km (16 mi) from Whangaparaoa, keep your eyes peeled for gravel Lottin Point Road to the left, which, after about a 10- to 15-minute drive through grassy rolling hills, planted forests, and *pohutukawa* trees, ends at the rocky coastline, where you can clamber down to volcanic lava platforms, rock pools, and always-turquoise water. These are great spots for picnics, fishing, and diving, but remember this is private land, and camping is not allowed without first obtaining permission from the landowner.

Te Araroa

The village of Te Araroa snuggles at the base of impressive cliffs 91 km (56 mi) east of Hicks Bay. It comprises a couple of stores, a bottle shop, a service station, a post office, and takeaways. The best reason to stop here is to see and photograph the largest *pohutukawa* tree in the country (in the schoolyard at the north end of town). It's a truly amazing and awe-inspiring sight, with 22 trunks spreading out 37 meters (120 ft) and a girth of 20 meters (65 ft).

Attractive **Te Araroa Holiday Park** (Hwy. 35, 06/864-4873; tent sites $20, powered sites $24, dorm beds $20, cabins $50–70 s or d), 6.5 km (four mi) northwest of Te Araroa, has an outdoor movie theater, a general store, game and TV rooms, a playground, a fish smokehouse, and barbecue area, as well as all the usual holiday park communal facilities. Cabins sit beside the landscaped grassy camping area, which has plenty of large shade trees and a freshwater stream running through the grounds, and is only a four-minute walk from a safe, sandy beach.

East Cape Lighthouse

New Zealand's easternmost lighthouse stands at the end of a 22-km (14-mi) drive along a gravel road from Te Araroa (south end of town). This scenic road is at first sandwiched between tall cliffs and a sheer rock ledge that drops straight into the sea. It passes white-sand beaches edged by *pohutukawa* trees, then meanders inland through rolling grassy meadows filled with sheep, cows, and many horses, and a few inland sand dunes. The hike up the hill to the lighthouse is quite a workout—25 minutes of steep climbing up about 500 uneven steps—even more of a workout if you're carrying a two-year-old! However, once you've reached the top, the 360-degree view of **Hautai Beach, Whangaokeno Island** (East Island), and inland makes the effort worthwhile.

CONTINUING SOUTH TOWARD GISBORNE
Tikitiki

The next definite stop is Tikitiki to see the incredibly ornate **Anglican Church.** Although the whitewashed exterior is fairly plain, the interior is a masterpiece of Maori design—woven panels, carved faces with *paua*-shell eyes, beams covered with fern and other nature-inspired designs, benches with ends intricately carved, and stained-glass windows. Don't miss it! Tikitiki also has a store and gas station.

Tokomaru Bay

This coastal town, a stronghold of Maori culture, lies along a sandy beach and, if you follow the beachfront road north, passing old houses in various states of beauty or disrepair, you come to a scenic rocky bay backed by hills, old brick buildings (one now containing a pottery store), and a very long pier (good fishing). The town has a couple of stores, good takeout, a motel, a card phone, and a relaxed vacation atmosphere.

Budget travelers head for New Zealand's easternmost backpacker lodge, the charmingly named **Footprints in the Sand** (13 Potae St., 06/864-5858, www.footprintsinthesand.co.nz; camping $15 per person, dorm beds $20). Fronted by a classic verandah, this converted house has bright dorms, a good kitchen with help-yourself spice rack, a comfortable living area, and a backyard filled with outdoor furniture. It's only a one-minute walk from a beautiful sandy beach.

Anaura Bay

This quiet spot seven km (four mi) off Highway 35 is renowned by surfers for clean waves that peel off the adjacent headland. Before you descend to the bay, the top of the hill affords great views of an offshore island, a yellow sandy beach, green hills, and tree-covered mountains.

Anaura Bay Walkway is an easy 3.5-km (two-mi) walk through Anaura Bay Scenic Reserve. The track starts at the north end of Anaura Bay on Anaura Road, takes about 1–1.5 hours each way, and brings you back out on Anaura Road about one km south of the starting point.

Tolaga Bay

Stores, tearooms, an inn, a motel, a nine-hole golf course, and a gas station are all located here. A few kilometers south of town, turn left at the road marked Motorcamp, Cooks Cove Walkway and Historic Wharf. Continue to the end of the road, where you'll find the longest wharf in the Southern Hemisphere. This wharf used to serve the area in the days of coastal shipping. If you walk to the end (worthwhile), take a jacket. It may be sunny and warm when you start out, but by the time you reach the far end, it can be windy and quite cool. Locals jog and sunbathe along the wharf, which is popular with anglers (watch crayfish being brought up). It's a regular hive of activity, and there's always a local to talk to or something to see.

◖ Cooks Cove Walkway

For sweeping ocean views and a bit of history, head for Cooks Cove Walkway at the southern end of Tolaga Bay. This five-km (3.1-mi) walkway climbs a ridge to a lookout point (90 meters/295 ft) at the top of Tolaga Bay's southern cliffs, then follows a farm track just below the cliff tops to another lookout point (120 meters/394 ft) over tranquil Cooks Cove. Stay on the main track for the best viewing points. From here the track leads down onto Cooks Cove flats, passing the "Hole in the Wall" and the monument commemorating Captain Cook's visit to Tolaga Bay in 1769. The *Endeavour* anchored at Cooks Cove for six days to take on water, firewood, and supplies, hence the name. This easy track takes just over an hour each way. Take a windbreaker and something to drink—there's no fresh water—and wear sturdy shoes. You'll find toilets at the wharf near the beginning of the track, and there's a motor camp nearby.

Gisborne

Gisborne (pop. 35,000), 340 km (211 mi) east of Taupo and 500 km (310 mi) southeast of Auckland, is one of New Zealand's most historic cities. The hills behind Gisborne were the first New Zealand promontories sighted by Captain Cook and his crew on October 6, 1769. Nicholas Young, *Endeavour* cabin boy, was the first to see land—**Young Nick's Head** at the southern end of **Poverty Bay** was named in his honor. The crew landed at **Kaiti Beach,** where Captain Cook took formal possession of the new country in the name of His Majesty King George III. On attempting to make friends with the local Maori and restock supplies, Cook found the natives more than a little hostile, and the crew lifted anchor and left with nothing but a small amount of firewood. During the next five months they circumnavigated the new land that became known as New Zealand. As they had not been welcomed with open arms, Cook named the bay on which Gisborne now stands Poverty Bay—a name that the locals have humorously retained despite the obvious agricultural wealth of the fertile alluvial Poverty Bay flats, busy fishing fleet, and abundant natural attractions that the area presents to the explorers of today.

SIGHTS
◖ Tairawhiti Museum
This fascinating complex (18 Stout St., 06/867-3832; Mon.–Fri. 10 A.M.–4 P.M., Sat. 11 A.M.–4 P.M., Sun. 1:30–4 P.M.; donation), across the Taruheru River from downtown, has a stunning collection of Maori art and artifacts in a modern setting. Other displays cover Captain's Cook's visit and the history of New Zealand surfing. Part of the museum complex is Te Moana Maritime Gallery, contained within the wheelhouse and captain's cabin of the *Star of Canada,* which was shipwrecked on Kaiti Reef in 1912. These sections of the vessel were salvaged and turned into a house, before being moved to their present location overlooking the river. Inside you can follow the mariners' impressive contributions to the development of Gisborne through a number of whaling, shipping, and water-transportation displays, and can view hundreds of photographs with a decidedly nautical theme. Wyllie Cottage, originally built in 1872 and the oldest house in Gisborne, also stands within the museum grounds.

Historic Walking Tour
The first place to go is the Gisborne Information Centre off the main shopping street downtown. The staff gladly hands out brochures and maps, and can suggest more things to see and do than you can possibly handle. Next to the center is small **Alfred Cox Park,** dominated by the unusual sight of a large totem pole, a gift from Canada to celebrate the bicentenary of Captain Cook's first landing in 1769.

From Grey Street turn right onto Gladstone

A statue of Captain Cook overlooks the ocean at Cook's Plaza.

© ANDREW HEMPSTEAD

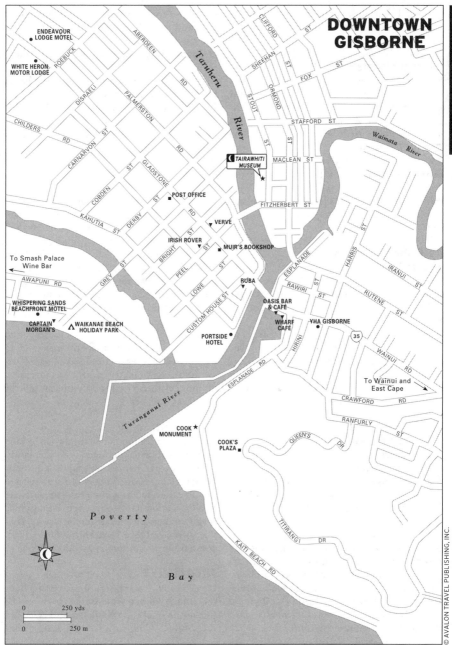

DOWNTOWN
GISBORNE

ENDEAVOUR
LODGE MOTEL

WHITE HERON
MOTOR LODGE

CLIFFORD ST
ABERDEEN
ROEBUCK
SHEEHAN
FOX
ST
STOUT
ORMOND
DISRAELI
PALMERSTON
RD
Taruheru
River
STAFFORD ST
CHILDERS
RD
CARNARVON ST
GLADSTONE
ST
Waimata River
TAIRAWHITI
MUSEUM
MACLEAN ST
POST OFFICE
COBDEN
ST
DERBY
KAHUTIA ST
RD
FITZHERBERT ST
VERVE
IRISH ROVER
BRIGHT ST
MUIR'S BOOKSHOP
To Smash Palace
Wine Bar
AWAPUNI RD
GREY ST
PEEL
LOWE
RUBA
ESPLANADE
RAWIRI ST
HARRIS
TRANUI ST
RUTENE
ST
WHISPERING SANDS
BEACHFRONT MOTEL
CAPTAIN
MORGAN'S
WAIKANAE BEACH
HOLIDAY PARK
CUSTOM HOUSE ST
OASIS BAR
& CAFE
WHARF
CAFE
VHA GISBORNE
PORTSIDE
HOTEL
HIRINI
35
WAINUI RD
Turanganui River
ESPLANADE RD
To Wainui and
East Cape
CRAWFORD RD
RANFURLY
QUEEN'S DR
ST
COOK
MONUMENT
COOK'S
PLAZA
Poverty
TITIRANGI DR
KAITI BEACH RD
Bay

0   250 yds
0   250 m

© AVALON TRAVEL PUBLISHING, INC.

Road and continue over the bridge. Veer right under the railway embankment and follow the harbor past the freezing works and wharf on The Esplanade. This road leads to **Cook Landing Site National Historic Reserve.** Surrounded by warehouses, it's not at all scenic, but the **Capt. James Cook Monument** marks the spot where Captain Cook first landed in New Zealand. From this point, a short walking path leads up Kaiti Hill to **Cook's Plaza** lookout. Take in a fantastic 180-degree view of the city; harbor; meeting of the Taruheru, Waimata, and Turanganui Rivers; and magnificent Poverty Bay. Check out the amazingly clear blue water that appears to surround Gisborne (you can also drive to this lookout point).

Te Poho-o-Rawiri Maori Meeting House

At the foot of Kaiti Hill where Queens Drive and Ranfurly Street meet is Te Poho-o-Rawiri Maori Meeting House (06/868-5364), one of the largest decorative meeting halls in New Zealand. A small Maori church lies above. The hall is usually open to the public (enter via the side door); the intricate Maori carving and *tukutuku* reedwork (done in Rotorua) are worth seeing. If it's closed, ask the caretaker who lives next door for permission to enter.

RECREATION
Town Beaches

The closest swimming spot to town is **Waikanae Beach.** A short walk from the main shopping area, it has a sandy bottom, safe swimming, and small surf, and is crowded in summer. Walk along Grey Street (same street as the information center) until you hit the sand. If you continue along beachfront Salisbury Road, Waikanae becomes **Midway Beach.** Also patrolled in summer, Midway's generally safe if you stay between the flags. "The Pipe" at the west end attracts lots of surfers. Behind Midway you'll find the **Olympic Pool Complex** (Centennial Marine Dr., 06/867-6220; summer daily 6 A.M.–8 P.M.,

the rest of the year daily 8 A.M.–6 P.M.; adult $4, child $2), with indoor and outdoor pools and a waterslide.

Sponge Bay, just north of the city around the point from downtown, is for experienced surfers only. Also popular with surfers is **Wainui Beach** (six km/four mi north of town). Continuing north is **Makorori Beach;** backed by lush farmland, this golden beach has both a reef and sandy bottom. It's not patrolled but still attracts lots of swimmers and surfers in summer; beware of rips.

Thermal Pools

One of the best places to enjoy a relaxing soak in thermal pools surrounded by lush vegetation and abundant birdlife is **Morere Hot Springs** (Hwy. 2, 06/837-8856; daily 10 A.M.–5 P.M., until 9 P.M. in summer; adult $5, child $2.50), 58 km (36 mi) south of Gisborne. Soak in the Nikau Pools (two hot pools, cold plunge pool, hot foot pool, changing rooms, showers, and toilets), in the private hot pools, in the hot indoor pool, or in the cold freshwater outdoor pool. Everything is beautifully landscaped to blend in with the forest environment. Or go for a woodland walk through the 360-hectare (890-acre) property (the tracks range from 20 minutes to 2.5 hours) to appreciate all the abundant birdlife.

Wine Tasting

After the Marlborough region, the fertile land around Gisborne produces New Zealand's largest crop of Chardonnay grapes. The information center has a wine trail map, but you should call ahead as many of the wineries are small operations not always open to the public. If you want to concentrate on the tasting, consider joining a **Taste Tairawhiti** (06/863-1285, www.gisbornewinecompany.co.nz) tour.

NIGHTLIFE

One of New Zealand's most interesting bars, the **Smash Palace Wine Bar,** is on the wrong side of the tracks (24 Banks St., off Awapuni Rd., 06/867-7769; daily from 11 A.M.). In the heart of an industrial subdivision, it's easily recognized by three Morris Minors out front and by the body of a DC3 providing shade for the beer garden. Once inside, the eclectic surroundings continue, with junk from around the world decorating the walls and floor. Even without method to this madness, it's a popular spot with locals and out-of-towners in the know. Out back is a small winery that specializes in Methode Champenoise, which along with many other local wines is available by the glass. The knowledgeable wait staff will help recommend a glass to suit your taste. Food is also available and there's often live music on weekends.

Even as the birthplace of opera diva Dame Kiri Te Kanawa, about the best music you'll find around Gisborne is from bands playing cover songs in local hotels. **Irish Rover** (99 Peel St., 06/867-1112) is one of the classier places and has decent pub grub. A few minute's drive east of town along Highway 35, **Sandbar** (Ocean Beach Motor Lodge, 7 Oneroa Rd., Wainui, 06/868-6828) opens to a tropical courtyard. Although its part of a hotel complex, locals are the main customers, with surfers especially congregating after a session at the local beach.

ACCOMMODATIONS AND CAMPING

Accommodations within walking distance of the beach are the most sought-after in Gisborne, with a couple of excellent choices down the road from downtown in Wainui. If you arrive in town without reservations and you're just looking for somewhere to rest your head for the night, cruise down Gladstone Road, which is lined with moderately priced motels.

Under $50

Across the river from downtown, but still within easy walking distance, **YHA Gisborne** (32 Harris St., 06/867-3269, www.yha.co.nz; dorm beds $24, $39 s, $52 d) is in a rambling house with a rambling atmosphere. Like all YHAs, the staff actively organizes hikes and outings.

Chill out with surfers from around the world at **Chalet Surf Lodge** (62 Moana Rd., Wainui, 06/868-9612, www.chaletsurf.co.nz; dorm beds $22, $60 d), across from Gisborne's premier surf beach. All rooms are brightly painted and there's plenty of outdoor space to stretch out and relax. The owners rent surfboards and provide lessons. Wainui is eight km (five mi) east of town along Highway 35.

$50-100

Motels lining Gladstone Road (Hwy. 35) west of downtown hover around $120 per room, but less expensive options do exist, including **Endeavour Lodge Motel** (525 Gladstone Rd., 06/868-6075; $85 s, $95 d), with a swimming pool and nine self-contained rooms.

$100-150

Separated from Waikanae Beach by only a strip of grassy reserve is **Whispering Sands Beachfront Motel** (22 Salisbury Rd., 06/867-1319 or 0800/405-030, www.whisperingsands.co.nz; $120-160 s or d). Each of the 14 rooms has a private balcony or patio, ocean view, and a small kitchen. Other facilities include a barbecue and laundry.

White Heron Motor Lodge (474 Gladstone Rd., 06/867-1108 or 0800/997-766, www.whml.co.nz; $120-175 s or d) features spacious, comfortable rooms with basic cooking facilities. It has wireless Internet throughout, and at the time of publication guests enjoyed a free round of golf at the local course. Across the road is **Teal Motor Lodge** (479 Gladstone Rd., 06/868-4019 or 0800/838-325, www.teal.co.nz; $120-180 s or d), where rooms overlook a freeform saltwater pool surrounded by gardens and outdoor furniture.

C Portside Hotel (2 Reads Quay, 06/869-1000 or 0800/767-874, www.portsidegisborne.co.nz; $135-400 s or d) is a modern condostyle complex overlooking the river mouth and within walking distance of downtown. It's a slick lodging, with a leading New Zealand designer creating a welcoming and stylish environment. Each of the 64 studio, one-, and two-bedroom units has a full kitchen and most have balconies. Other facilities include an outdoor lap pool and a fitness room.

Over $150

Out of town to the east, **Ocean Beach Motor Lodge** (7 Oneroa Rd., Wainui, 06/868-6828, www.oceanbeach.co.nz; $150–190 s or d) enjoys a wonderful location in front of one of New Zealand's best surf spots. Units, some with one and two separate bedrooms, are smartly decorated and designed perfectly for the beachside location. Each has a kitchen and opens to a tropical courtyard with outdoor dining and drinking.

Also in Wainui, and right opposite the beach, is **[one Orange** (98 Wairere Rd., 06/868-8062, www.oneorange.co.nz; $225 s or d), a well-designed open-plan studio apartment that is part of a large private residence but still has plenty of privacy. It's understated luxury all the way, with a leather couch, top-notch kitchen appliances, a Bose CD player, and a super-comfortable bed. Breakfast is included in the rates and dinner paired with local wines is available on request.

Holiday Park

Waikanae Beach Holiday Park (Grey St., 06/867-5634; camping $24, cabins $36–65 s or d) is adjacent to sandy Waikanae Beach, only 800 meters (0.5 mi) from downtown—a great spot for walking and swimming. Along with the usual community facilities (spotlessly clean), the camp has a cool room (communal fridge) with lockers and tennis courts (racket rental $5 per hour), and at the office you can rent bicycles, surfboards, boogie boards, and other equipment.

FOOD
Cafés and Quick Bites

Above Muir's Bookshop, **Bookshop Café** (62 Gladstone Rd., 06/869-0653; Mon.–Fri. 8:30 A.M.–4 P.M., Sat.–Sun. 9:30 A.M.–3 P.M.) is a quiet retreat from the busy main street (although balcony tables do give you a view of the action below). Light, healthy breakfasts and

lunches are the specialty, including delicious wraps for $7.

Verve (121 Gladstone Rd., 06/868-9095; Mon.–Sat. 8:30 A.M.–10 P.M., Sun. 8:30 A.M.–3 P.M.) has a relaxed, almost Bohemian feel, but attracts everyone from surfers to suited businessmen.

I came across **[Ruba** (14 Childres Rd., 06/868-6516; Mon.–Sat. 7 A.M.–4 P.M., Sun. 9 A.M.–3 P.M.) almost by accident, but am glad I did. Located at street level of the old Union Steamship Company, it's tucked away a half block from the river off Gladstone Street. It dishes up some of the most creative breakfasts in town (think hotcake Pavlova), and also opens earlier than other places. At lunch, expect equally imaginative cooking (sesame and pineapple prawn skewers, anyone?) under $20.

With a suitable aqua-colored exterior, **Captain Morgan's** (285 Grey St., 06/867-7821; daily 8 A.M.–8 P.M.) is a stroll from the beachfront, across from the holiday park, and close to the information center. It's a bright, casual place, with a mix of light meals and typical New Zealand café fare.

Food with a View

On the waterfront across the Taruheru River from downtown, an old row of dock buildings have been converted to restaurants. The most casual of these is **Oasis Bar & Cafe** (Shed One, 06/867-1103; daily for lunch and dinner). The decor is nothing special, but the food is fine and the outlook great. In the vicinity, the **Wharf Café** (60 The Esplanade, 06/868-4876; daily 9 A.M.–10 P.M.) features a chic interior and the same great water views. Try the seared salmon with poached eggs on an English muffin ($16.50) if it's early, or the beef tenderloin with blue cheese and peppercorn sauce ($32) for dinner.

PRACTICALITIES
Getting There and Around

Gisborne airport, on the west side of the city, is served by daily direct **Air New Zealand** (0800/737-300, www.airnewzealand.com)

flights from Auckland and Wellington. A taxi to downtown is $15.

Long-distance buses arrive and depart from Gisborne Information Centre (209 Grey Street). **Intercity** (06/868-6139, www.inter citycoach.co.nz) runs to Gisborne from Rotorua and Auckland via Opotiki and from Taupo via Napier and Wairoa.

Local cab companies are **Eastland Taxis** (06/868-1133), **Gisborne Taxis** (06/867-2222), and **Sun City Taxis** (06/867-6767). Car rental agencies with offices in Gisborne include **Avis** (06/868-9084), **Budget** (06/867-9794), and **Hertz** (06/867-9348).

Information

Gisborne Information Centre (209 Grey St., 06/868-6139, www.gisbornenz.com; Mon.– Fri. 8:15 A.M.–5 P.M., Sat.–Sun. 10 A.M.–5 P.M.) is signposted off Gladstone Road toward the beach, with plenty of nearby parking.

H. B. Williams Memorial Library (Peel St., 06/867-6709) is open Monday–Friday 9:30 A.M.–5:30 P.M., Saturday 9:30 A.M.– 1 P.M. In business for over a century, **Muir's Bookshop** (62 Gladstone Rd., 06/869-0651) is a great place to search out local literature.

Services

The post office is at 166 Gladstone Road. The information center has an Internet terminal with public access, or get online at **Verve** (121 Gladstone Rd., 06/868-9095; Mon.–Sat. 8:30 A.M.–10 P.M., Sun. 8:30 A.M.–3 P.M.), where you can check your email while enjoying the best coffee in town.

Gisborne Hospital is on Ormond Road (06/869-0500). **Kaiti Medical Centre** (Turenne St., 06/867-7411; daily 8 A.M.– 8 P.M.) deals with non-emergency medical cases. The **police station** (06/869-0200) is on the corner of Peel Street and Childers Road.

Napier and Vicinity

One of the world's best examples of the distinctive art deco style, Napier (pop. 55,000) is perched on the edge of the Pacific Ocean 210 km (131 mi) southwest of Gisborne and 150 km (93 mi) southeast of Taupo. It's another great place to enjoy sea breezes whipping through your hair and bright sun on your face, but its distinct seaside-town atmosphere and earthquake history set it apart from the other towns along the east coast.

◖ ART DECO ARCHITECTURE

The distinctive art deco building style can be appreciated throughout downtown Napier, with concentrations of buildings along Marine Parade, Herschell Street, the west end of Hastings Street, Tennyson Street, and Emerson Street. The visitor center has brochures on art deco highlights, but a better source of information is the **Art Deco Trust** (163 Tennyson St., 06/835-0022, www.artdeconapier.com; daily

9 A.M.–5 P.M.), which manages and promotes the city's unique architecture.

The trust runs its annual **Art Deco Weekend** on the second weekend of February, featuring guided walks, an antique show and auction, theater, and lots of jazz. Contact the trust for all the details.

Guided Tours

An art-deco-walking-tour brochure will set you back $4 and keep you busy for at least an hour or two. A better option is to join a guided tour. Knowledgeable locals lead a variety of these walks year-round. The **Morning Walk** (adult $10, child free) departs the visitor center daily at 10 A.M., lasts one hour, and ends at the Art Deco Trust on Tennyson Street. Lasting two hours, the **Afternoon Walk** (adult $15, child free) departs the Art Deco Trust daily at 2 P.M. and begins with a slide show.

ART DECO CITY

© ANDREW HEMPSTEAD

The Art Deco Shop, home to the Art Deco Trust, is the starting point for walking tours.

Sauntering along stately, Norfolk pine-lined Marine Parade, you will find it hard to believe that the elegant city of Napier was completely rebuilt after total destruction in the Hawke's Bay earthquake of 1931. During the earthquake the city, at that time a busy trading post, was lifted 1.8 to 2.5 meters (six to eight ft), and the salt marshes, swamps, and inner harbor were completely drained. Although there was great loss of life and almost all the brick buildings of the city collapsed, the earthquake gave the survivors an extra 4,000 hectares (10,000 acres) of land, and now the airport and a large section of Napier stand on what used to be the sea floor.

A few years before the earthquake, a world away in Paris at the International Exposition of Modern Decorative and Industrial Arts, a new bold, geometrical architectural style now known as art deco was unveiled to the world.

The 1931 earthquake coincided with the peak of this style's popularity, which is reflected in Napier's rebuilt commercial core.

© ANDREW HEMPSTEAD

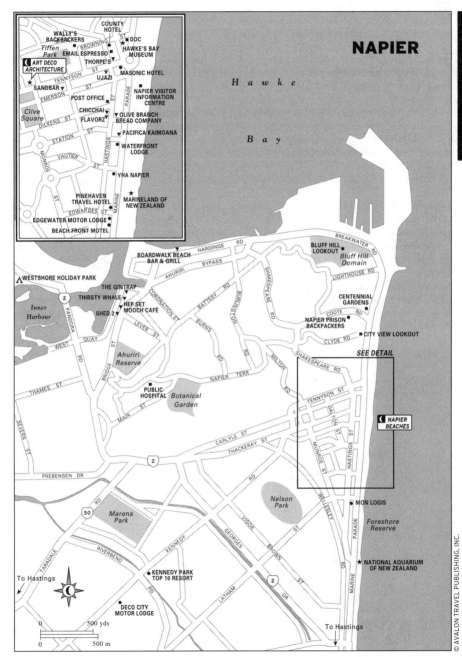

NAPIER

COUNTY HOTEL
WALLY'S BACKPACKERS
BROWNING ST
DOC
Tiffen Park
EMAIL ESPRESSO
HAWKE'S BAY MUSEUM
ART DECO ARCHITECTURE
THORPE'S
MASONIC HOTEL
TENNYSON ST
UJAZI
SANDBAR
NAPIER VISITOR INFORMATION CENTRE
EMERSON
POST OFFICE
PARADE
Clive Square
CHICCHAI
DICKENS ST
FLAVORZ
OLIVE BRANCH BREAD COMPANY
STATION
PACIFICA KAIMOANA
HASTINGS
WATERFRONT LODGE
MONROE
VAUTIER ST
YHA NAPIER
PINEHAVEN TRAVEL HOTEL
MARINE
MARINELAND OF NEW ZEALAND
EDWARDES ST
EDGEWATER MOTOR LODGE
BEACH FRONT MOTEL

H a w k e

B a y

BREAKWATER RD
BLUFF HILL LOOKOUT
Bluff Hill Domain
HARDINGE RD
BOARDWALK BEACH BAR & GRILL
BYPASS
AHURIRI
LIGHTHOUSE RD
WESTSHORE HOLIDAY PARK
THE GINTRAP
2
THIRSTY WHALE
CORONATION ST
BATTERY RD
SHAKESPEARE RD
CENTENNIAL GARDENS
Inner Harbour
PANDORA
HEP SET
SHED 2
MOOCH CAFÉ
LEVER ST
BURNS ST
BURLINGTON
COOTE RD
NAPIER PRISON BACKPACKERS
CITY VIEW LOOKOUT
QUAY
WEST RD
CLYDE RD
SHAKESPEARE RD
Ahuriri Reserve
BRIDGE ST
NAPIER TERR
MILTON RD
SEE DETAIL
THAMES ST
TENNYSON ST
PUBLIC HOSPITAL
MAIN ST
Botanical Garden
DALTON ST
NAPIER BEACHES
SEVERN ST
CARLYLE ST
THACKERAY ST
MUNROE ST
HASTINGS ST
2
PREBENSEN DR
RD
Nelson Park
MON LOGIS
50
Marena Park
VIGOR
GEORGES
BROWN
ST
WELLESLEY
PARADE
Foreshore Reserve
TARADALE
RIVERBEND
KENNEDY
To Hastings
KENNEDY PARK TOP 10 RESORT
RD
2
LATHAM
MARINE
DR
NATIONAL AQUARIUM OF NEW ZEALAND
DECO CITY MOTOR LODGE
0   500 yds
0   500 m
To Hastings

© AVALON TRAVEL PUBLISHING, INC.

MARINE PARADE

You can spend an entire day soaking up the Napier feeling by taking a leisurely walk along the attractive four-km (2.5 mi) oceanfront Marine Parade, which is lined with stately Norfolk pines. View interesting 1930s architecture on the west side of the street, nothing but ocean to the east (there's no land between Napier and Chile), or visit the many commercial attractions. Make your first stop the ideally situated **Napier Visitor Information Centre** (Marine Pde., 06/834-1911; Mon.–Fri. 8:30 A.M.–5 P.M., Sat.–Sun. 9 A.M.–5 P.M.) for a map.

Hawke's Bay Museum

For an excellent collection of Maori art, historical presentations of early Hawke's Bay, 18th- and 19th-century European antiques, and an extensive art collection, stop by Hawke's Bay Museum (65 Marine Pde., 06/835-7781; summer daily 10 A.M.–6 P.M., the rest of the year daily 9 A.M.–5 P.M.; adult $7.50, child free) for an hour or so. Art and film presentations are regularly shown in the Century Theatre. Perhaps the most remark-able feature is the audiovisual presentation of the 1931 earthquake—if you get there and find it already playing, explore the rest of the museum and come back to get the full impact of the film from the beginning. Other highlights include the dinosaur exhibit and Maori art.

Marineland of New Zealand

Marineland (Marine Pde., 06/834-4027; daily 10 A.M.–4:30 P.M.), south of the information center, is one of Napier's best-known attractions and worth a visit, but take a warm sweater even in midsummer—the wind howls through the stands where you sit facing the ocean, completely in the shade by late afternoon. Dolphins, sea lions, penguins, seals, and otters strut their stuff to a lively commentary and put on an entertaining show with the lure of tasty morsels from their trainers. You can view pens of recuperating gannets and other seabirds injured in the wild, and a well-stocked shop sells tourist paraphernalia. General admission is adult $6, child $3, but the main reason to visit is for the shows, which take place from 10 A.M. and cost from adult $11.50, child $5.50. If swimming with dolphins in the open ocean doesn't appeal to you, it's possible to do it here without getting seasick (daily at noon; $45). Another "Behind the Scenes Tour" is Touch the Dolphins (daily 9 A.M.; adult $25, child $11.50).

National Aquarium of New Zealand

Along the foreshore south of Marineland is the grandly named **National Aquarium of New Zealand** (Marine Pde., 06/834-1404; daily 9 A.M.–5 P.M.; adult $14, child $7.50). Built soon after the earthquake, it underwent massive renovations in 2002 and is now one of the largest in the Southern Hemisphere. The main aquarium—30 meters (98 mi) long by 24 meters (79 ft) wide and filled with local species, including sharks—has a clear-walled walkway winding through it for close-up viewing. On the upper floor, the continents of the world are showcased with a wide variety of exhibits, including an Australian outback diorama, the

© ANDREW HEMPSTEAD

Hawke's Bay Museum

re-creation of an African fishing village, and a Japanese garden. A diver hand-feeds many of the residents of the main aquarium daily at 10 A.M. and 2 P.M.

OTHER SIGHTS AND RECREATION
Scenic Lookouts

Just past the wildlife center at the northern end of Marine Parade, Coote Road branches off to the left, passing attractive **Centennial Gardens,** where an artificial waterfall splashes down a 100-meter (328-ft) cliff face into ponds and rock pools among flowerbeds and lawns. Coote Road continues up Bluff Hill to the **Bluff Hill Lookout** for great ocean views. (Turn right off Coote Road onto Thompson Road, then right on Lighthouse Road and follow it to the end.) If you don't have a city map it's quite easy to get lost up here, even when you're trying your best to follow the blue-and-yellow scenic drive signs. If you don't mind stumbling around in a maze of one-way streets and fascinating architecture, fancy homes, and the odd glimpse of city or sea, try finding your way to **City View Outlook** while you're in the mood. It's a great spot at night to view the city lights. Take Coote Road (off Marine Parade) to the top, turn left, then turn immediately left again onto Clyde Road, passing the Girls High School, and you *should* end up at the viewing point. (Temporarily ignore the scenic drive arrows if you're following the above directions.)

Botanical Gardens

Napier residents are understandably proud of their botanical gardens. Perfect lawns give way to beds of flowers and blooming shrubs, and paths lead through shady groves of assorted trees in this small inner-city oasis. A stream flows through the gardens and trickles down in tiny waterfalls; here and there miniature ornamental bridges or stepping-stones allow passage back and forth. The main feature is a spacious aviary. You'll find the botanical gardens in the Hospital Hill area, a couple of kilometers west of downtown between Napier

Terrace, Spencer Road, and Chaucer Road South. To get there from the visitor center, cross Marine Parade and take Emerson Street past Clive Square (it becomes Carlyle Street). Continue down Carlyle, turn right on Chaucer Road, and left on Napier Terrace. Next to the gardens is an old tree-shaded graveyard where some of the older gravestones date from the 19th century and lie abandoned or broken among grass and wildflowers.

Vineyards

If you enjoy a bit of wine-tasting, you can get more than your fill of the drink of the gods in the Hawke's Bay Wine Region—there are more than 40 wineries from which to choose. Before heading out, collect the free *A Guide to Hawke's Bay Wineries* brochure from the visitor center. It features all of the wineries in the region, and gives good road directions so you can easily find them on your map (important after a few stops). Most of the vineyards are open for tasting and buying Monday–Saturday 9 A.M.–5 P.M. (some longer). Three of the better known (all open for lunch) are **Church Road Winery** (150 Church Rd., Taradale, 06/844-2053), **Crab Farm Winery** (511 Main Rd., Bay View, 06/836-6678), and New Zealand's oldest winery (1851), **Mission Estate Winery** (198 Church Rd., Taradale, 06/844-2259).

Contact **Bay Tours** (06/843-6953, www.baytours.co.nz) for wine tours. Departing from the information center at 10:30 A.M., the basic tour visits two wineries and costs $52.50.

◖ Napier Beaches

The long stretch of shingle beach directly in front of **Marine Parade** is better for walking than for swimming. It's safe when calm, but easterly winds quickly whip up coastal breakers and rough conditions. It's patrolled on weekends until March—during the week look out for red-flag warnings on the lifesaving clubhouse. The closest sandy beach with safe swimming and light surf is **Westshore** (about two km/one mi north of city center) on the northern side of Bluff Hill. Unpatrolled **Waipatiki**

© ANDREW HEMPSTEAD

The beach parallel to Marine Parade is the perfect place for an early morning walk.

Beach, about 40 km (25 mi) north of Napier, also has good swimming, but the currents can be dangerous, particularly in easterly winds. **Waimarama Beach,** 48 km (30 mi) south of Napier, has a long stretch of sand and rolling surf but is subject to rips on the incoming tide. The safest place to swim is the area directly in front of the lifesaving club, which is patrolled on weekends until March.

Hiking Trails

You'll find several walkways in the Hawke's Bay region. **Tangoio Walkway,** 25 km (16 mi) north of Napier on the main highway to Wairoa, is the closest to the city. It winds for six km (four mi) through the native forest and pine plantations of scenic Tangoio Valley, providing a panoramic view of the bay and many waterfalls along the route. The nine-km **Tutira Walkway,** 45 km (28 mi) north of Napier, runs to and along the eastern shore of Lake Tutira, providing rugged hill-country views and (on a fine day) a view of Hawke's

Bay from the Ruahine Range all the way to Te Urewera National Park. You need sturdy boots for this track, and it's wise to take along a windproof jacket, food, and drink. **Boundary Stream Walkway,** 60 km (37 mi) north of Napier, passes through Boundary Stream Scenic Reserve; the highlight of this 12-km (seven-mi) hike is the spectacular **Shine's Falls.** Starting on Pohokura Road, it takes up to four hours to reach Heays Access Road, then another hour to the falls. (You can also start on Heays Access Road if you just want to do the four-km/2.5-mi walk to the falls.) This track demands strong boots, a windproof jacket, warm sweater (the weather can be quite unpredictable), food, and drink.

NIGHTLIFE

Younger locals tend to congregate in bars along the north end of Hastings Street and around the corner in two bars within the art deco **Masonic Hotel** (corner of Tennyson St. and Marine Pde., 06/835-8689). The latter features

EASTLAND AND HAWKE'S BAY

live music on weekends. But for a temporary home in the sun, it's difficult to go past the **Thirsty Whale** (West Quay, Ahuriri, 06/835-0028), in a converted woolshed where tables spill out onto the sidewalk overlooking the harbor. In cooler weather, the indoor section has a roaring fireplace and big-screen TVs. Along this same strip of converted warehouses is **The Gintrap** (West Quay, Ahuriri, 06/835-0199), with a similar outlook and stylish timber and pastel blue interior.

ACCOMMODATIONS AND CAMPING
Under $50
Backpackers are spoiled for choice in Napier. Close to downtown, but off a quiet back street, 🄲 **Wally's Backpackers** (7 Cathedral Lane, 06/833-7930, www.wallysbackpackers.co.nz; dorm beds $22, $55–60 s or d) combines two modernized 1920s villas to be the best choice. Rooms are outfitted with comfortable mattresses (one of the doubles has an en suite) while the large kitchen and barbecue allow plenty of room for everyone.

In a renovated beachfront house, **YHA Napier** (277 Marine Pde., 06/835-7039, www .yha.co.nz; dorm beds $25, $36 s, $50 d) is spacious, with larger-than-usual dorms and a central setting across from Marineland. A little farther south is purpose-built **Stables Lodge Backpackers** (370 Hastings St., 06/835-6242; dorm beds $24, $35 s, $48 d), with 10 rooms set around a small courtyard.

Beyond the imposing convict-hewn sandstone walls of a former jailhouse is **Napier Prison Backpackers** (55 Coote Rd., 06/835-9933, www.napierprison.com; dorm beds $22, $35 s, $54 d). Built in 1862 and decommissioned as recently as 1993, the complex has a somewhat grisly history, but the facilities today serve budget travelers well, even those who brave the original cells.

$50-100
Just down the street from the information center, **Waterfront Lodge** (217 Marine Pde.,

06/835-3429, www.napierbackpackers.co.nz; $39–59 s, $59–86 d) has a few dorm beds, but is better known for its inexpensive private rooms. From outside appearances you'd never guess that there are 14 attractively furnished rooms, a communal kitchen, a TV lounge, and a laundry beyond the front entrance.

The centrally located 35-room **Masonic Hotel** (corner of Tennyson St. and Marine Pde., 06/835-8689 or 0800/627-664, www .masonic.co.nz; $85 s, $95 d) is one of Napier's most recognized art deco buildings. The style doesn't continue to the 35 upstairs guest rooms, but staying here ensures you're close to everything.

Directly opposite the beach a few blocks from downtown, **Edgewater Motor Lodge** (359 Marine Pde., 06/835-1148, www.edge watermotel.co.nz; $95–170 s or d) is an older place with a saltwater plunge pool, a game room, laundry, and 20 smallish but comfortable units, some with separate bedrooms.

$100-150
Pinehaven Travel Hotel (259 Marine Pde., 06/835-5575, www.pinehavenbnb.co.nz; $80 s, $100 d) has a hostess who makes you feel right at home, a comfy TV lounge, tea- and coffee-making supplies, and a nonsmoking policy. There are six guest rooms with shared bath, but all with hand basins, TVs, and some with great waterfront views. Rates include a cooked breakfast.

Keeping up with the city's distinctive architectural theme, **Deco City Motor Lodge** (308 Kennedy Rd., 06/843-4342, www.decocity .co.nz; $110–190 s or d) is difficult to miss a two-minute drive west from downtown. The 31 fan-cooled rooms are fairly predictable, although the outdoor pool and playground add to the appeal for families.

As well as the old-style guesthouses along the waterfront, more luxurious bed-and-breakfasts are scattered around the city. One of these is **Mon Logis** (415 Marine Pde., 06/835-2125; $130 s, $170 d). Translating to "my dwelling," this two-story 1860s terrace house has fantastic ocean views and four splendid rooms. Rates include a breakfast basket delivered to the room.

$150-200

With a glass of local wine in hand, relax on your large balcony with ocean views at **Beach Front Motel** (373 Marine Pde., 06/835-5220 or 0800/778-888, www.beach frontnapier.co.nz; $135–185 s or d), a three-story place featuring 28 of the most modern rooms in Napier, each with a king-size bed, spa bath, and large kitchen.

Over $200

The 1909 **County Hotel** (12 Browning St., 06/835-7800 or 0800/483-468, www .countyhotel.co.nz; $250–320 s or d) is a re-stored Edwardian-era building downtown and across from the beach. Originally a council building (and one of the few buildings to survive the earthquake), it has been transformed into a boutique hotel, with a fine-dining restaurant and English-style cocktail lounge downstairs and a magnificent *rimi* stairway leading up to 18 guest rooms. Each named for a native bird, the rooms feature high ceilings, timber paneling, a tiled bathroom, and art deco–influenced decor.

Holiday Parks

The most central motor camp is in the Napier suburb of Marewa, about 2.5 km (1.5 mi) from downtown. The attractive grounds of **Kennedy Park Top 10 Resort** (Kennedy Rd., 06/843-9126 or 0800/457-275, www .kennedypark.co.nz) are adjacent to beautiful Kennedy Rose Gardens. Spacious grounds, a swimming pool, an adventure playground, and a summer children's program make this a family favorite. In summer, campsites are $16 per person and the wide range of cabins and flats range $70–175 s or d.

Westshore Holiday Park (Main Rd., Westshore, 06/835-9456; camping $28, cabins from $55 s or d) is four km (2.5 mi) from downtown but in a great location 150 meters (93 mi) from

Westshore Beach (safe swimming and good surf). It has all the usual communal facilities, an indoor spa pool (extra charge), a TV room, and an adjacent general store.

FOOD
Breakfast

Around the headland from downtown, a row of waterfront sheds once used for storing wool bales before they were exported have been converted to restaurants and bars. The basic structures remain intact, including exposed framework throughout the ceiling and worn timber floorboards. They all catch the setting sun beautifully, taking advantage of the location with lots of outdoor tables. At **Thirsty Whale** (West Quay, Ahuriri, 06/835-0028; daily from 9 A.M.), the scrambled eggs with chorizo sausage ($13) will set you up for a day of sightseeing, while the rest of the day the bar menu has an array of better-than-average pub-style dishes to share—steamed mussels in herb cream sauce and sautéed calamari with wasabi mayo are typical—for under $20. The upstairs restaurant is a little more formal (and expensive). Food at the **The Gintrap** (West Quay, Ahuriri, 06/835-0199; daily for breakfast, lunch, and dinner) includes breakfasts that appeal mostly to New Zealanders (seared lamb kidneys on toast), delicious venison burgers, and a small seafood platter for two ($28).

Cafés and Quick Bites

The café scene around Napier has improved markedly in recent years. For good, strong coffee and a variety of other caffeine-infused drinks, head to **Ujazi** (28 Tennyson St., 06/835-1490; daily 7:30 A.M.–4:30 P.M.). The menu is small but varied, offering everything from an Indonesian curry to locally caught seafood, with a couple of vegetarian dishes thrown in for good measure. In the vicinity, and a good place to take a break from an art deco walking tour of the surrounding area, is **Sandbar** (242 Emerson St., 06/835-8255; daily 8 A.M.–5 P.M.), with toasted paninis for $7 and a delicious minted roast lamb roll for $6.50.

Along Hastings Street between Browning Street and the Civic Centre is a number of inexpensive eateries, such as **Thorp's Coffee House** (40 Hastings St., 06/835-7000; daily 8 A.M.–4 P.M.) in a pleasant art deco setting. Napier isn't usually associated with sushi, but **Chicchai** (173 Hastings St., 06/835-8232; Mon.–Fri. 10 A.M.–7 P.M., Sat. 10 A.M.–3 P.M.) does it well in a casual environment with just a few tables. Sushi is all under $1.50 per piece, with seafood sourced daily from local fish shops. Continuing down the street you'll find **Olive Branch Bread Company** (216 Hastings St., 06/835-8375; closed Sun.), which fills with the delightful smells of European-style breads. **Heaven's Bakery & Café** has five Napier locations, including in the Civic Centre (Dickens St., 06/835-2030; daily 6 A.M.–5 P.M.); the chicken and Camembert pie ($3.50) is divine.

Overlooking the harbor at Ahuriri is a string of cafés and restaurants that are more than welcoming to those who just want to stop by for a coffee. Also here is **Hep Set Mooch Café** (West Quay, Ahuriri, 06/833-6332; daily from 8 A.M.), which is a little more expensive than the downtown cafés, but the coffee is good and the setting superior.

Contemporary and Seafood

The oceanfront Masonic Hotel (corner of Tennyson St. and Marine Pde., 06/835-8689) has undergone major changes in its many eateries. North American–style dining is the order of the day at **Breakers Café & Bar** (8 A.M.–9 P.M.), where you can order pancakes with maple syrup ($8.50), or have a full cooked breakfast ($14). Also in the hotel is **Acqua,** a modern brasserie with lots of seafood and an extensive wine list featuring local bottles. The oyster shooters ($18 for six) are a fun appetizer, while salmon stuffed with herb cream cheese and baked in phyllo pastry ($28) is my recommendation for dinner.

Tucked between the stylish art deco residences and accommodations along the beachfront is **Pacifica Kaimoana** (209 Marine Pde., 06/833-6335; Tues.–Sun. from 6 P.M.). The setting is simple, but the presentation of modern seafood dishes is impeccable. As it should with fresh seafood, the entire menu changes daily (look for it posted out front).

Highlights at **Shed 2** (West Quay, Ahuriri, 06/835-2202; lunch Fri.–Sun., dinner Mon.–Sat.) include a tasty Seafood Extreme Pizza ($17), steamed mussels ($12), the best Caesar salad ($13.50) in town, and a wood-fired half-chicken ($15).

Flavorz (193 Hastings St., 06/835-8477; daily noon–9 P.M.) combines flavorful cooking in a snazzy setting with many tables in a quiet courtyard. Locals are attracted by New Zealand favorites, but cuisines from around the world are represented, with Asian stir fries under $20 and gourmet thin-crust pizzas for $18.

One block north of the harborside restaurants is **Boardwalk Beach Bar & Grill** (8 Hardinge Rd., 06/834-1168; Thurs.–Sun. 11 A.M.–2:30 P.M., daily 5:30 A.M.–9:30 P.M.), where the outdoor tables are as close to the water as you can be without getting wet.

Wineries

Many of the local wineries offer delicious lunches in pleasant surroundings. Close to town, and one of the country's oldest vineyards, is **Church Road Winery** (150 Church Rd., Taradale, 06/844-2053; daily 11:30 A.M.–2:30 P.M.), where the restaurant has lots of outdoor tables and weekend entertainment in summer. Expect to pay around $25 for typical winery fare like smoked salmon asparagus salad paired with a glass of Church Road wine.

PRACTICALITIES
Information

Overlooking the beach, **Napier Visitor Information Centre** (Marine Pde., 06/834-1911, www.napiervic.co.nz; Mon.–Fri. 8:30 A.M.–5 P.M., Sat.–Sun. 9 A.M.–5 P.M.) is the first place to go for general and accommodation information, brochures, a city map, and to book all tours (including to the gannet colony) and onward transportation. The **Department of Conservation** is based at 59 Marine Parade (06/834-3111; Mon.–Fri. 9 A.M.–4:15 P.M.).

Services

The post office is at 57 Dickens Street. Send and receive email while enjoying a coffee at **Email Espresso** (6 Hastings St., 06/833-6920; Mon.–Fri. 8 A.M.–9:30 P.M., Sat.–Sun. 10 A.M.–9:30 P.M.). **Napier Public Library** is on Station Street (06/834-4180; Mon.–Fri. 9 A.M.–5 P.M., Sat. 10 A.M.–1 P.M., Sun. 2–4 P.M.).

The region's main hospital is in Hastings (Omahu Rd., 06/878-8109), with **Napier Health Centre** (76 Wellesley Rd., 06/878-8109) dealing with less-urgent medical conditions. The **police station** (06/831-0700) is on Station Street.

Getting There and Around

To get to **Hawke's Bay Airport** from downtown, take Highway 2 north to Westshore Road and turn left onto Watchman Road. **Air New Zealand** (0800/737-300, www.airnewzealand.com) has direct flights to Napier from Auckland, Wellington, and Christchurch. Shuttle buses (06/879-9766; $15) meet all flights. **Intercity** (www.intercitycoach.co.nz) buses stop at **Napier Travel Centre** (Munroe St., 06/834-2720). This company has daily services from Napier and Hastings to Auckland (around seven hours), Rotorua, Taupo, Gisborne, Wellington, and all points in between.

The following agencies have desks out at the airport, but you should reserve in advance to ensure a vehicle: **Avis** (06/835-1828), **Budget** (06/835-5166), **Europcar** (06/835-8818), **Hertz** (06/835-6169), and **Thrifty** (06/835-8818). A taxi stand is on Lower Emerson Street near Clive Square. Local cab companies include **Napier Taxis** (06/835-7777) and **Star Taxis** (06/835-5511).

HASTINGS

This large agricultural center of 50,000, 18 km (11 mi) southwest of Napier, is known as "The Fruit Bowl of New Zealand" and is Napier's twin city in the center of the vineyard region. It is known for its Mediterranean climate, fertile soil, and artesian water, and is particularly worth a visit in spring when all the colorful magnolia trees are in bloom.

Sights

The highlight of a visit to Hastings includes the many parks and gardens dotting the city, especially Te Mata. The most central is **Cornwall Park** (daily 10 A.M.–4 P.M.), well-established with 100-year-old English trees, a lake, and a begonia display. Also of interest is Oak Avenue, a stately row of trees planted along a driveway in the 1860s and now a public road. To get there from downtown, take Heretaunga Street West out of the city.

Splash Planet (Grove Rd. off Karamu Rd., 06/873-8033; summer daily 9 A.M.–6 P.M.; adult $25, child $19.50, over 65 free) is the biggest commercial attraction in Hastings. It features lots of water slides, hot pools, go-carts, mini-train rides, a skating rink, and a huge children's playground with all sorts of activities and rides.

Hiking

The 2.2-km (1.4-mi) **Te Mata Peak Walkway** starts 14 km (nine mi) south of Hastings, climbing to the 399-meter (1,309-ft) high point of Te Mata Trust Park. The trail is pretty steep (allow one hour for the uphill slog), but the summit provides magnificent views of Hawke's Bay, the Ruahine Range, and the volcanic peaks of Tongariro National Park.

Two-km (one-mi) **Monckton Walkway,** 12 km (seven mi) northwest of Takapau, passes through a steep gorge in Monckton Scenic Reserve and crosses the beautiful Tanarewai Stream with its good swimming holes. It takes about 1.5 hours round-trip; wear strong shoes. For more detailed information on any of the above tracks, pick up the individual track brochures from the information center.

Accommodations

Hastings has the usual array of standard motels, but head five km (3.1 mi) east of town to escape the ordinary at **Weldon Boutique B&B** (98 Te Mata Rd., 06/877-7551, www .weldon.co.nz; $110–120 s, $140–165 d). Dating to the early 1900s, the house has undergone a tasteful restoration with period furnishings and a distinct French Provincial style. Each of the guest rooms has its own bathroom, tea- and coffee-making facilities, and a television. Rates include breakfast in the main dining room or outside overlooking the extensive gardens. Dinner is available for $55.

Information

Hastings Visitor Information Centre (Russell St., 06/873-5526; Mon.–Fri. 8:30 A.M.–5 P.M., Sat.–Sun. 9 A.M.–3 P.M.) is in a beautiful art deco building in the heart of downtown.

◖ CAPE KIDNAPPERS

Cape Kidnappers, a dramatic bluff that forms the southern extremity of Hawke's Bay, 21 km (13 mi) southeast of Napier, is worth visiting for its natural beauty alone, but its main attraction is the four **gannet colonies,** perched precariously around its farthest tip. More than 20,000 of the birds call this site home, making it the world's largest mainland nesting place of Australasian gannets. They are members of the Sulid family (often called booby), with pale gold crowns and striking black eye markings. They arrive in July to nest and breed in several gannetries atop the high cliff plateau. Gannets lay their eggs in October and November; about six weeks later the chicks hatch. The birds start leaving in February, and by April almost all the gannets have gone. The colony is closed to the public from July 1 to mid-October so that the birds

aren't disturbed in their early nesting phase. The best time to visit the gannet colony is between November and late February.

Napier Visitor Centre (Marine Pde., 06/834-1911, www.napiervic.co.nz; Mon.–Fri. 8:30 A.M.–5 P.M., Sat.–Sun. 9 A.M.–5 P.M.) has a blackboard detailing tours, times, and costs, and its staff makes bookings. The cape can be reached in several following ways, described in the following sections.

On Foot

From Clifton, south of Napier through Te Awanga, it's eight km (5 mi) along a beautiful sandy beach to Cape Kidnappers. The walk is relatively easy, so only about two hours each way is required to reach the cape. The track follows the beach past Black Reef gannet colony and climbs the cliff. About one km beyond the reef is a rest area with water and toilets. The formed track continues up to the plateau, where you can see the gannets close up (but keep your distance so as not to disturb them). Don't forget your camera, plenty of film, suntan lotion, a hat if you burn easily, and a windbreaker.

The tide is the most important consideration for those taking the beach route; it can only be walked at low tide. The safest time to leave Clifton is no sooner than three hours after high tide and to leave the cape no later than 1.5 hours after low tide. For current tide times, call in to the Napier Visitor Information Centre. Note that the farmland between Clifton and the cape is privately owned, and the high cliffs between Clifton and Black Reef are unstable—look out for rockslides and avoid walking directly under the cliffs.

By Tractor-Trailer

The unusual, fun tractor-trailer ride is the most popular way to reach the cape. **Gannet Beach Adventures** (06/875-0898 or 0800/426-638, www.gannets.com) consists of an entourage of tractors pulling trailers along the beach at the base of the cliffs, passing the Black Reef gannet colony on the way to Cape Kidnappers. Once at the cape, you face a short but steep 20-minute climb from the end of the beach to the colony. The trip departs the signposted parking lot along Clifton Road (through Te Awanga) daily during the season, about 2.5 hours before low tide. It takes about four hours for the round-trip, with about 90 minutes of that time spent at the cape. Extra time is set aside for swimming or enjoying a picnic lunch (bring your own). The cost is a reasonable adult $33, child $19. Tours operate October–May but departure times are entirely dependent on the tides, so call ahead or check their website.

Overland

The easiest way to get to the cape is overland, crossing the privately owned Summerlee Station in a four-wheel-drive bus with **Gannet Safaris** (06/875-0888 or 0800/427-232, www .gannetsafaris.co.nz; adult $50, child $30). The 18-km (11-mi) trip takes about an hour each way, with an hour at the gannet sanctuary, with spectacular views of Hawke's Bay. To get to the starting point you'll need your own vehicle. Leave Napier on the main road south to Clive and take Mill Road to the left, following the signs to the cape along the coast road. Drive through Te Awanga and cross the Maraetotara Stream; not far after the bridge, a large sign to the right says Summerlee Station.

TARANAKI AND THE WEST

This region along the west coast of the North Island is named for one of the world's most symmetrical volcanoes, which rises majestically from forested slopes giving way to a patchwork of lush green pasture. The wave-lashed coastline is lined with black-sand beaches, significant as the place where Maori first came ashore in New Zealand. The largest population center is New Plymouth, roughly halfway between Auckland and Wellington and a six-hour drive from each. Primarily a port, this bustling seaside city is home to a magnificent museum and is dotted with gardens where rhododendrons bloom through spring.

South of the city, solitary Taranaki (formerly known as Mount Egmont) looks very similar to Japan's Mount Fuji (so much so that the peak provided a backdrop for *The Last Samurai,* starring Tom Cruise). From afar it seems to rise from the ocean, with its year-round snowy peak adding to the picture of natural perfection. It's the kind of mountain that begs to be climbed or hiked just because it's there. This dormant volcano stands loftily on Cape Egmont where the western coastline juts into the Tasman Sea, its remote location, height, and harsh climate producing interesting flora and fauna, all of which is protected within Egmont National Park. Ice and snow permanently cover the upper slopes and peak, splendid waterfalls roar over jagged lava flows to drop into deep, dark pools far below, and rivers sing over the smooth, polished rocks and dance down to the lower altitudes in a series of waterfalls.

Around South Taranaki Bight from the park,

© ANDREW HEMPSTEAD

the Whanganui River, the country's third-longest waterway, drains into the ocean. Upstream is the river city of Wanganui, where you can marvel at colonial architecture and take to the water in a restored paddlesteamer. Further upstream the river passes through Whanganui National Park. Accessible only by water, the park protects deep gorges, a blanket of podocarp forest, grasslands, and inspirational waterfalls. Casual visitors can take a jetboat tour, but for most park visitors, it is the opportunity for a wilderness canoe or kayak trip that is the main draw.

PLANNING YOUR TIME

As it's not on the main route between Auckland and Wellington, the Taranaki region is missed by travelers choosing a more easterly route through Rotorua and Hawke's Bay. If you are returning to Auckland by road, or making a loop around the entire North Island, Taranaki can easily be incorporated in your itinerary. New Plymouth, the region's largest city, has a couple of worthwhile manmade attractions, **Puke Ariki** museum and **Pukeiti,** a rhododendron garden of international fame. These two sights can easily be visited in a day, allowing enough time to marvel at the dominant natural feature, the volcanic peak of Taranaki, from different angles as you drive around its base (the **South Egmont** access provides the best mountain hiking opportunities). As you continue south toward Wellington, plan on spending an hour or so at **Dairyland,** learning about the local dairy industry, before continuing to Wanganui for a second night. The Whanganui River dominates everything about this city, but to really appreciate its history, plan on joining a cruise on the *Waimarie,* a restored paddlesteamer.

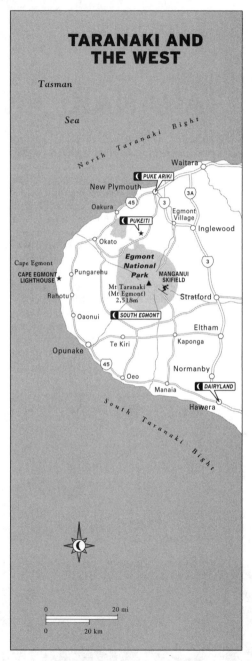

TARANAKI AND THE WEST

Tasman

Sea

North Taranaki Bight

Waitara

PUKE ARIKI

New Plymouth

3A

Oakura   45   3

Egmont Village

PUKEITI

Inglewood

Okato

Egmont National Park

Cape Egmont

CAPE EGMONT LIGHTHOUSE

Pungarehu

MANGANUI SKIFIELD

3

Mt Taranaki (Mt Egmont) 2,518m

Stratford

Rahotu

SOUTH EGMONT

Oaonui

Eltham

Te Kiri   Kaponga

Opunake

45

Normanby

Oeo

Manaia   DAIRYLAND

South Taranaki Bight

Hawera

0   20 mi

0   20 km

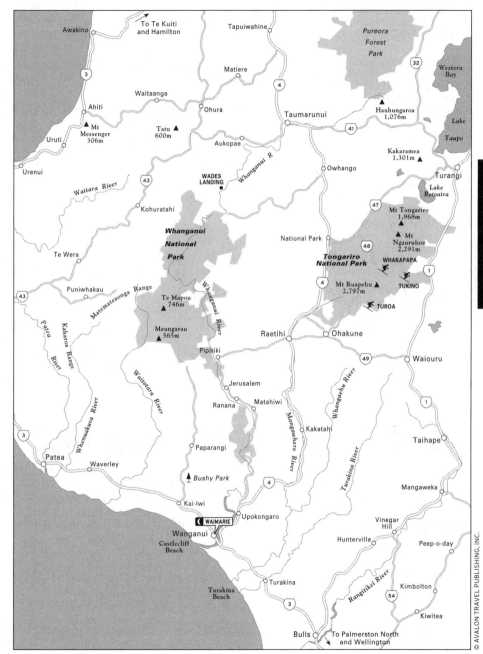

© AVALON TRAVEL PUBLISHING, INC.

TARANAKI AND THE WEST

HIGHLIGHTS

◖ **Puke Ariki:** One of New Zealand's premier museums, Puke Ariki takes a modern approach to making the natural and human history of the Taranaki region come to life (page 222).

◖ **Pukeiti:** Marvel at the world of rhododendrons at this expansive garden in the shadow of Taranaki (page 224).

◖ **South Egmont:** Of the three roads penetrating Egmont National Park, it is one leading into South Egmont that provides the best day-hiking opportunities (page 230).

◖ **Dairyland:** You've seen the endless pastureland filled with cows, now learn about the processes that result in the dairy products New Zealand is renowned for – or just stop in for a milkshake (page 232).

◖ *Waimarie:* After spending almost half a century on the riverbed, this wooden paddlesteamer was restored and now offers cruises along the historic Whanganui River (page 234).

LOOK FOR ◖ TO FIND RECOMMENDED SIGHTS, ACTIVITIES, DINING, AND LODGING.

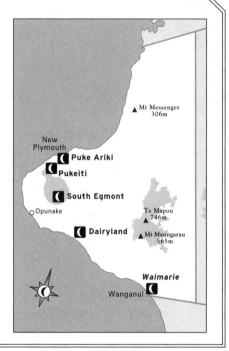

New Plymouth

On the northwest coast of Cape Egmont, 375 km (233 mi) south of Auckland, this city of 65,000 is the metropolitan and cultural center for the lush agricultural Taranaki region. The tourist brochures have aptly named it "The Garden City" for its beautiful parks and reserves (one-fifth of the urban area is green). Sandwiched between popular surf beaches along North Taranaki Bight and dominated by majestic snowcapped Taranaki to the south, the city is also recognized for its scenic beauty. Rich on- and offshore oil and natural gas fields have led to increasing affluence and development and the title "Energy Centre

of New Zealand." Apart from local city attractions, New Plymouth is an ideal base for exploring Egmont National Park, driving the coastal Surf Highway, and exploring the gently rolling hedge-divided countryside of the surrounding Taranaki dairylands.

The ocean and beaches are New Plymouth's main attraction, but on the waterfront right downtown is another impressive water-based sight—**Port Taranaki,** the largest port on New Zealand's west coast. The three main wharves, which are protected by a massive breakwater, handle five million tons of freight (everything from natural gas to timber) annually. The best

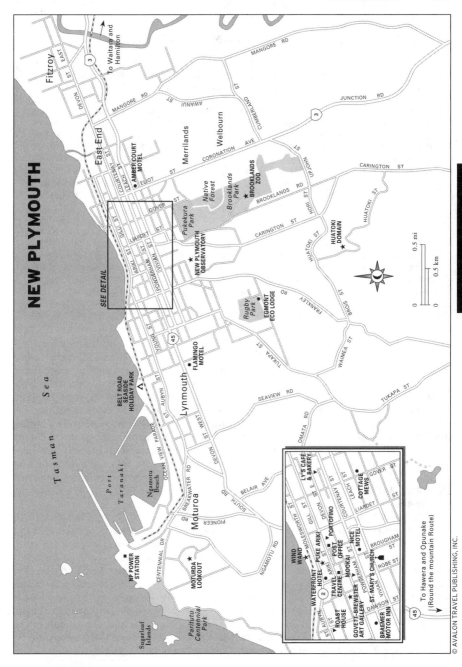

NEW PLYMOUTH

TARANAKI AND THE WEST

Tasman Sea

MANGORE RD

To Waitara and Hamilton

Fitzroy

DEVON ST EAST

MANGORE RD

AWANUI ST

JUNCTION RD

East End

Merrilands

Welbourn

CUMBERLAND

CORONATION AVE

AMBER COURT MOTEL

COURTENAY ST

LEACH ST

ELLIOT ST

Native Forest

Brooklands Park

BROOKLANDS ZOO

★

CARINGTON ST

UPJOHN ST

HORI ST

BROOKLANDS RD

GOVER ST

GILL ST

LIARDET ST

ARIKI ST

POWDERHAM ST

VIVIAN ST

Pukekura Park

★ NEW PLYMOUTH OBSERVATORY

CARINGTON ST

HUATOKI ST

HUATOKI DOMAIN ★

HUATOKI ST

SEE DETAIL

Rugby Park

★ EGMONT ECO LODGE

FRANKLEY RD

BROIS ST

0.5 mi
0.5 km
0

YOUNG ST

45

FLAMINGO MOTEL ●

TUKAPA ST

WAIMEA ST

Lynmouth

BELT ROAD SEASIDE HOLIDAY PARK

ST AUBYN ST

ST WEST

DEVON ST

SEAVIEW RD

OMATA RD

TUKAPA ST

Port Taranaki

Ngamotu Beach

OCEAN VIEW PARADE

BREAKWATER RD

BELAIR AVE

SOUTH RD

PIONEER RD

NGAMOTU RD

Moturoa

CENTENNIAL DR

★ MOTUROA LOOKOUT

NP POWER STATION ■

Sugarloaf Islands

Paritutu Centennial Park

LY'S CAFÉ & BAKERY

MOLESWORTH ST

GILL ST

DEVON ST

ARIKI ST

COURTENAY ST

LEACH ST

GOVER ST

COTTAGE MEWS ●

LIARDET ST

PORTOFINO ●

POST OFFICE

PUKE ARIKI ★

ST NICE MOTEL ●

BROUGHAM ST

WIND WAND

WATERFRONT HOTEL

2

TRAVEL CENTRE ■

MOOKAI ST

POWDERHAM ST

ST MARY'S CHURCH ●

ROBE ST

VIVIAN ST

DAWSON ST

ST AUBYN ST

ROAST HOUSE ▼

GOVETT-BREWSTER ART GALLERY ★

BRAEMER MOTOR INN ●

45

To Hawera and Opunake
(Round the mountain Route)

© AVALON TRAVEL PUBLISHING, INC.

OIL AND GAS IN THE TARANAKI REGION

The economic boom of the Taranaki region is mainly due to the discovery of oil and natural gas, both onshore and offshore. The first oil well was dug by hand in 1865 and by 1869 seven more wells had been dug along the coastline near New Plymouth. The first beam pumps were installed in the 1950s. This accelerated the rate of production, including at Ngamotu Beach, where the **Moturoa Beam Pump** is a reminder of the 33,000 barrels of oil it pumped to the surface between it was retired in 1972.

It was offshore drilling that cemented the Taranaki region as "Energy Capital of New Zealand." The first offshore well was drilled at the Kapuni Field in 1959, followed by **Maui A Field,** where natural gas was discovered in 1969. The field is 35 km (22 mi) offshore from Oaonui, 55 km (34 mi) southwest of New Plymouth (the platform can be seen from Hwy. 45), while at the mainland Maui Production Station

at Oaonui (06/758-7609), a scale model of the platform is open for public viewing. Combined with the nearby Maui B Field, discovered in 1993, the two fields are New Zealand's largest energy resource, supplying 85 percent of New Zealand's natural gas and 85 percent of the country's liquid petroleum gas (LPG). The gas is transported from the two platforms by pipeline to the production station at Oaonui, where it is used to produce electricity.

On the east side of New Plymouth at Motunui (20 km/12 mi northeast), **Methanex New Zealand** operates a synthetic fuel plant; its information center (06/754-8009; daily 8 A.M.–5 P.M.) has displays describing the process. **Chemical Methanol Plant** in the Waitara Valley (15 km/9 mi northeast of New Plymouth) offers visitors a view of the plant from a lookout on Matarikoriko Road, just off Mamaku Road.

views of the port are from Breakwater Road as it climbs westward from the city toward the old power station.

SIGHTS

Head directly for New Plymouth Information Centre (Puke Ariki, 1 Ariki St.) and collect the *City Walks* brochure. The brochure covers city parks, historic sites, Maori *pa,* swimming beaches, and general places of interest.

◖ Puke Ariki

One of the country's most comprehensive collections of Maori art and Maori, colonial, and natural history exhibits is at Puke Ariki (1 Ariki St., 06/759-6080; Mon.–Fri. 9:30 A.M.–4:30 P.M., Sat.–Sun. 1–5 P.M.; free), a magnificently modern museum across from the downtown foreshore. This world-class facility takes pride of place along the waterfront, incorporating the historic War Memorial Building, which is linked by a glass-walled "airway" across Ariki Street. Entering from the foreshore, the North Wing holds the main

lobby, the New Plymouth Information Centre, an upscale café, a gift shop, Internet terminals, and a lounge area affording magnificent ocean views. The displays, known collectively as "Taranaki Experience," are all on the upper floors, with interactive exhibits holding the attention of all ages and interests. In addition to the extensive Maori coverage, you will learn about the local oil and gas industry, the natural world before the arrival of Europeans, and the many and varied species living in the surrounding ocean.

Wind Wand

Look out across the ocean from Puke Ariki and it's impossible not to see this kinetic sculpture rising from the seawall promenade. Designed by New Zealand artist Len Lye, this 45-meter-high (150-foot-high) carbon fiber and fiberglass pole is so perfectly balanced that it stands perfectly upright—except when a breeze is blowing (truth be told, this is most of the time), when it bends up to 20 meters (66 ft) from center.

Other Downtown Sights

Two blocks west of the museum, **Richmond Cottage** (Brougham St., 06/759-6060; Fri.–Sun. 11 A.M.–3:30 P.M.; free) dates to 1854 and was occupied through the years by three prominent Taranaki families. The cottage is built of stone, unusual for a private residence of that era.

Continuing another two blocks west, the modern **Govett-Brewster Art Gallery** (Queen St., between King and Devon Sts., 06/758-5149; daily 10:30 A.M.–5 P.M.; free) has many fine art collections and changing contemporary art exhibitions.

New Zealand's oldest stone church, the Anglican **St. Mary's Church** (Vivian St. between Robe and Brougham Sts.), is also worth a quick visit. Built in 1846, the church features intricate stained-glass windows and is surrounded by pleasant gardens dotted with gravestones and memorials that tell a vivid story of the city's early days.

Sugar Loaf Islands

On the west side of downtown, around the headland from the port, is Paritutu Centennial Park, and the city's most magnificent natural feature is laid out in front of you. The Sugar Loaf Islands are the remains of ancient volcanic activity. The actual volcano has long since eroded, leaving solid cores of lava that were thrust upward more than one million years ago. One of these remaining cores, Paritutu Rock, is on the mainland. A (very) steep track leads to its summit, where the views are stunning. The islands themselves are mostly vegetated, and some show evidence of early Maori settlement. Free from mainland predators, they are a haven for birdlife, including penguins, and New Zealand fur seals breed on two of the islands.

Chaddy's Charters (Ocean View Pde., 06/758-9133; from $35) offers scheduled tours through the islands in summer.

PARKS AND GARDENS
Pukekura Park

If you enjoy beautiful parks, take a 10-minute walk from the city center to 20-hectare (49-acre) Pukekura Park—a lush urban oasis that shouldn't be missed. Paths lead through native bush and flowers, an abundance of tree ferns and exotic flowers, and along streams and lakes that provide the photographer with good scenery shots and Taranaki (the mountain) reflections. An illuminated fountain (very colorful at night) plays at the drop of a 50-cent coin, and for another coin you can enjoy an 11-meter-high (36-ft) illuminated waterfall bordered by lush ferns. The Fernery and Begonia display houses (daily 8 A.M.–4 P.M.; free) are connected by moss-festooned tunnels. The main entrance to the park is at the south end off Liardet Street.

Brooklands Park

Connected to Pukekura Park is Brooklands Park, quite a contrast with its sweeping perfect lawns and formal plantations of both introduced and native trees. Beside the main path through the center of the reserve stands an enormous *puriri* tree, thought to be more than 2,000 years old. Also within the park are the largest *karaka* and *kohekohe* trees on record, and the largest *Magnolia soulangeana* in the country. The main park entrance is on Brooklands Street (off Victoria Road). The **Bowl of Brooklands Soundshell,** a large outdoor amphitheater surrounded by native bush, lies to one side of the main gates; on the other side is the entrance to a small zoo (daily 8:30 A.M.–5 P.M.; free), best known for its comprehensive collection of colorful birds (although it is the fun-loving monkeys that will hold your attention the longest).

Barrett Domain

If viewing wildlife is your cup of tea, take a leisurely walk through 36-hectare (89-acre) Barrett Domain on the western side of New Plymouth (ask at the information center for the *Barrett Domain* brochure). Open space, native tree plantations, natural forest, and the wetland area of **Barrett Lagoon** make up this domain and wildlife refuge that attracts a large range of waterfowl, especially paradise and grey ducks, black swans, *pukeko*, pied stilt shags, Canada geese, and white-faced herons. The main entrance is on Roto Street (at least five km/three mi from downtown as the crow flies).

◖ Pukeiti

If you have your own transportation, a trip along Carrington Road is a worthwhile jaunt from downtown for Pukeiti Rhododendron Gardens (2290 Carrington Rd., 06/752-4141; Sept.–Mar. daily 9 A.M.–5 P.M., Apr.–Aug. daily 10 A.M.–3 P.M.; adult $12, senior $10, child free), one of the Taranaki region's premier attractions. This 360-hectare (890-acre) garden of international repute features New Zealand's largest collection of rhododendrons and azaleas. It is colorful at all times of the year, but the peak flowering of rhododendrons is generally September–November. Bush walks lead through spectacular gardens dominated by native forest, all kinds of birds twitter in the trees (particularly *tui* and bellbirds), and you can get outstanding views of the surrounding countryside from the summit of **Pukeiti Hill.** Refreshments, maps, brochures, postcards, slides, and plants are for sale at the gatehouse. Pukeiti is 20 km (13 mi) from downtown New Plymouth.

BEACHES

New Plymouth's city beaches stretch along the curved sandy seafront in both directions, but the best surfing beaches are at the eastern end of town. The most popular, **Fitzroy Beach,** is known for its excellent surf. It forms a continuous 1.6-km (one-mi) sweep of luxurious sand; you can reach it from Beach Street, about three km (two mi) from the city center. Farther east, about seven km from downtown (as you head for the airport), is **Bell Block Beach,** on Mangati Road, Bell Block. **East End Reserve and Beach** is west of Fitzroy Beach, at the end of Nobs Line. If you're continuing north, stop at beautiful soft black-sand **Awakino Beach.** Fed by small, clear streams, the beach is decorated with perfect shells, and the surf is just right. On the west side of the city lie the protected harbor beach **Ngamotu** on Ocean View Parade—a good place to watch yachting

and boating activities—and **Back Beach** on Centennial Drive.

About 14 km (nine mi) west of New Plymouth is the premier beach resort, **Oakura.** Head here if you just want to lie on a beautiful beach all day and soak up a tan. If you're heading northeast, plop down on one of the sandy beaches at **Waitara** (16 km/10 mi east of New Plymouth) for more tanning and swimming.

ENTERTAINMENT AND EVENTS

Bowl of Brooklands, a magnificent outdoor theater surrounded by native bush, seats hundreds; it's beside the entrance gates to Brooklands Park—call the information center for performance information and current ticket prices.

Many of the local pubs and hotels provide good entertainment a few nights a week. **Peggy Gordon's Celtic Bar** (corner of Devon and Egmont Sts., 06/758-8561) has a lively, welcoming atmosphere and bands on weekends. At the time of writing, **55** (55 Egmont St., 759-0997) was the most popular nightclub in town.

If you're in the New Plymouth area in March, check out the exact date of the annual running race, **The Mountain to the Surf Marathon** (www.energycityharriers.co.nz), which finishes at Waitara Beach, 17 km (11 mi) northeast of the city—all those sweaty bodies staggering over the finish line are quite a spectacle.

If you're lucky enough to be in New Plymouth in November, your eyes are in for one heck of a flowery spectacle. The annual **Rhododendron & Garden Festival** (06/757-9909, www.rhodo. co.nz), usually starting at the end of October or beginning of November, features flowers, flowers, and more flowers. Attend all sorts of flower-oriented events, competitions, and horticultural lectures, and visit many of the area's private homes that have spectacular rhododendron gardens.

ACCOMMODATIONS AND CAMPING $50-100

◖ **Egmont Eco Lodge** (12 Clawton St., 06/753-5720, www.mttaranaki.co.nz; dorm beds $26, $45 s, $60 d), an associate of Hostelling

International, is a modern suburban hostel two km (1.2 mi) south of the city center. Overlooking an extensive garden and small stream, it is usually pretty quiet, and with a well-equipped kitchen, comfortable rooms, and a large lounge area, it is a good choice for budget travelers. The hosts are enthusiastic about promoting the region, so ask them for ideas and you'll never be bored.

Braemar Motor Inn (152 Powderham St., 06/758-0859, www.braemarmotorinn.co.nz; $78–98 s, $88–108 d) is typical of the motels scattered through New Plymouth. The least expensive rooms are in an older wing, but units throughout the two-story complex have kitchens.

Set on sprawling parklike grounds one km (0.6 mi) west of downtown is the **Flamingo Motel** (355 Devon St. W, 06/758-8149 or 0508/352-646; www.flamingomotel.co.nz; $88–124 s or d). Guests enjoy an indoor pool, an outdoor solar-heated pool, a shaded barbecue area, wireless Internet, and laundry facilities. All the units are self-contained, many with a sliding door that opens to the garden, and some with one or two bedrooms.

On a quiet street one block from Highway 3 is **Cottage Mews Motel** (50 Lemon St., 06/758-0403, www.cottagemews.net.nz; $75 s, $95 d). Each of the five self-contained units has basic furnishings, but because it's one of the city's newer motels, they are a good value.

$100-150

Amber Court Motel, 500 meters (about 0.5 mi) east of downtown (61 Eliot St., 06/758-0922 or 0800/654-800, www.ambercourtmotel.co.nz; $105–130 s or d) has 34 kitchen-equipped units, a large indoor pool, game room, barbecue area, and playground.

$150-200

Overlooking the foreshore from a prime downtown position beside Puke Ariki, the **Waterfront Hotel** (1 Egmont St., 06/769-5301, www.waterfront.co.nz; from $190 s or d) stands out for its modern architecture and a mid-level restaurant framed by a wraparound glass wall facing the ocean. The guest rooms are stylish and simple, with the focus on comfortable beds and contemporary art.

Over $200

The name is an understatement—the **[Nice Hotel** (71 Brougham St., 06/758-6423, www .nicehotel.co.nz; $225–300 s or d) is *very* nice. A true boutique hotel (the only one in New Plymouth), the eight rooms are all about luxury, with feather duvets topping plush mattresses, stylish oversized bathrooms, and modern touches like high-speed Internet access.

Holiday Parks

Belt Road Seaside Holiday Park (2 Belt Rd., 06/758-0228, www.beltroad.co.nz; campsites $28, cabins $45–95 s or d) is just 1.6 km (one mi) from downtown and has sheltered sites on the coast overlooking Port Taranaki (west side of town). It offers communal facilities, a TV lounge, and sea views. It's close to boating, yachting, and fishing activities, and only a 10-minute walk from a municipal swimming pool.

A 10-km (six-mi) drive south from New Plymouth, **[Hookner Holiday Park** (885 Carrington Rd., 06/753-6945) provides a unique New Zealand camping experience. Set on a 100-hectare (247-acre) working dairy farm, guests are offered the opportunity to help with the milking each morning (4–5 A.M.). It is small, with 28 campsites ($22) and three cabins ($40–85 s or d), but spotlessly clean.

FOOD
Cafés, Bakeries, and Quick Bites

Devon Street is lined with small-town eateries, including **Ly's Café & Bakery** (182 Devon St., 06/769-5088; Mon.–Sat. 7:30 A.M.–5 P.M.). Don't be tempted by the menu down the back; instead, stick to the self-serve cases filled with pies, cakes, and pastries in the big, bright main room out front.

Andre's Pies (44 Leach St., 06/758-3062; Mon.–Fri. 6 A.M.–3:30 P.M.) does a classic mince pie for under $3, or get adventurous and try a steak and oyster version.

If you don't feel like eating out, but don't want to cook, head to **Roast House** (corner St. Aubyn and Dawson Sts., 06/758-1828; daily noon–2:30 P.M. and 4:30–9:30 P.M.) for a roast chicken (or lamb or beef) dinner to go for $14.

Casual Dining

Down the hill a couple of blocks from Ly's, **Mookai** (67 Devon St., 06/759-2099; Mon.– Fri. 8 A.M.–4 P.M., Sat.–Sun. 9 A.M.–4 P.M., and for dinner on weekends) offers choices as varied as spaghetti and meatballs ($13) and roasted pumpkin and bacon salad ($16).

Right in downtown, **Portofino** (Gill St., 06/757-8686; daily from 5 P.M.) is a great little casual eatery with a long menu of traditional Italian favorites. Mains range $19–30 and you'll want to save room for the delectable desserts.

Food with a View

Perfectly situated within Puke Ariki, and with ocean views, **(Arborio** (Molesworth St., 06/759-6080; daily 9 A.M.–10 P.M.) is as much a café as a restaurant, but this stylish space does offer a full lunch and dinner menu of impressive dishes such as grilled prosciutto-wrapped salmon ($27). The staff doesn't seem to mind if you linger over coffee, which makes it a good place to relax before or after a museum visit.

The service at **Salt** (Waterfront Hotel, 1 Egmont St., 06/769-5301; daily 7 A.M.– 10 P.M.), adjacent to Puke Ariki, gets mixed reviews, but one thing everyone agrees on is that the ocean views are stunning. It's a fairly small restaurant, with contemporary styling and a menu that takes a global approach to preparing New Zealand produce and game. The breakfast buffet is $20, most lunches are under $20 (the Thai pumpkin fish cakes were a treat), and dinner mains are in the $25–30 range.

Winery

One of Taranaki's few commercial vineyards, **(Okurukuru** incorporates a classic modern winery café overlooking the vines and ocean (738 Surf Hwy., 06/751-0787; Tues.–Sun. 9:30 A.M.–5 P.M., Thurs.–Sat. 5–9 P.M.). A good choice for sharing are the meat and cheese plat-

ters ($20–25), while seafood chowder ($13.50) makes for a delicious lunch or dinner starter.

INFORMATION

New Plymouth Information Centre (Ariki St., 06/759-6080; Mon.–Fri. 8:30 A.M.–5 P.M., Sat.–Sun. 10 A.M.–3 P.M.) is in the lobby of Puke Ariki, across from the ocean. There's a multistory parking lot on Ariki Street, or try your luck with the few short-term spots out front on Molesworth Street. Chances are Taranaki will remain dormant while you're visiting, but the brochures detailing contingency plans in the event of an eruption make for interesting reading. The **Venture Taranaki** website (www.taranaki.co.nz) is useful for pre-trip planning.

Connected to the museum by an elevated walkway is **Puke Ariki (New Plymouth) Library** (Ariki St., 06/759-6060; Mon.–Fri. 9 A.M.–6 P.M., Sat.–Sun. 9 A.M.–5 P.M.), with a large collection of Maori literature, a research center, and free Internet access.

SERVICES

The main shopping precinct is the **City Shopping Centre** on Gill Street. The central post office is on Currie Street. Check your email at **Computer Corner** (Richmond Gate, 1 Egmont St., 06/758-9700), at the library, or hope for an empty seat at the terminals out front of the information center. Need your laundry done? Head to **La Nuava Apparelmaster** (65 Eliot St., 06/759-1040; daily 7 A.M.–9 P.M.).

For medical emergencies, head to the **Southern Cross Hospital** (205 St. Aubyn St., 06/757-3770). **Fitzroy Pharmacy** is at 552 Devon Street (06/758-2979).

GETTING THERE

New Plymouth Airport, 12 km (seven mi) north of town (take Hwy. 3 north and it's signposted off to the left before you reach Waitara), is linked to downtown by an airport shuttle run by **Withers Coachlines** (06/751-1777, www.withers.co.nz; $14 one-way). Scheduled flights operated by **Air New Zealand** (www .airnewzealand.com) depart daily for Auckland and Wellington. **Air New Plymouth**

(06/755-0500, www.airnewplymouth.co.nz) offers sightseeing, including around Taranaki's summit.

For long-distance bus travel, go to the **Travel Centre** (19 Ariki St.), from where **Intercity** (06/759-9039, www.intercitycoach .co.nz) runs regular services south to Wanganui and Wellington, and north to Hamilton and Auckland.

GETTING AROUND

All the regular car rental agencies have offices in New Plymouth, including **Avis** (06/755-9600), **Budget** (06/758-8039), **Europcar** (06/757-3538), **Hertz** (06/755-0700), **NZ Rent-a-car** (06/758-7923), **Rent-a-dent** (06/757-5362), and **Thrifty** (06/757-4500).

For a cab call **Energy City Cabs** (06/757-5580) or **New Plymouth Taxis** (06/757-3000).

Egmont National Park

TARANAKI AND THE WEST

Take a look at a map and it's impossible not to be intrigued by the shape of this (almost) perfectly circular national park and the many rivers flowing outward to the Tasman Sea. At the center of the 33,534-hectare (86,860-acre) park is **Taranaki,** a solitary 2,518-meter (8,260-ft) peak rising magnificently from the surrounding farmland.

Taranaki is believed to have formed more than 70,000 years ago, becoming active as two adjacent volcanoes, Kaitake and Pouakai, became extinct. Through repeated *lahars* (mudflows), thousands of small rounded hills were formed across the mountain's west side. In all other directions, the *lahars* progressed as a flood and created no mounds. More recently, geologically speaking, lava regularly spilled down the mountainsides to form a series of lava cliffs and gorges. The last volcanic eruption was in 1755 (a minor affair), when ash alone was ejected onto the upper slopes. Water is another powerful and artistic element seen in all its forms throughout Egmont National Park.

Walking and climbing routes crisscross the park, ranging from short, easy walks to difficult several-day hikes to poled climbing routes to the summit. The Round-the-Mountain Track—through various vegetation zones, past dramatic waterfalls, and to scenic lookouts—is one of the most popular.

Climate

Weather around Taranaki is very changeable, and even more so on the mountain's upper slopes. A coastal location, a wide range in elevation (100–2,500 meters/328–8,200 ft), and changing wind direction are the main climatic

THE VOLCANO THAT BECAME A GOD

According to legend, Taranaki was forced to flee from his original location in the center of the North Island when he lost a battle to Mt. Tongariro over his love, Mt. Pihanga. As he angrily fled through the cover of darkness toward the west coast he gouged out the bed of the mighty Whanganui River, and on reaching the sea he traveled north to the Pouakai ranges on Cape Egmont. A spur was thrown out to anchor him and Taranaki was forced to settle there forever. The Maori had great respect for the impressive volcano, worshipping the mountain as a god and recognizing its great influence on the weather of the local region. The upper slopes were *tapu* (sacred) and they believed that the stones were part of the skull of the mountain and the shrubs were its hair. So strong was this belief that when some early European climbers brought stones and shrubs down to study, the Maori quickly replaced them on the mountain so as not to anger the spirits. The only times the Maori climbed the mountain were when they needed red ochre or to ceremoniously bury their chiefs in secret places.

© ANDREW HEMPSTEAD

Taranaki is visible throughout the region.

features affecting Egmont National Park. Long periods of fine, settled weather are common in summer; winter brings the intense, long-lasting lows that result in nasty storms.

Even if the morning is beautiful and sunny, you should check the weather forecast before venturing up the mountain. Freezing temperatures have been recorded in all months of the year. Low clouds or fog can disorient even the most experienced outdoorsperson, and the frequent combination of rain, rapid drop in temperature, and strong wind can quickly turn a pleasurable hike into a life-threatening situation of exposure and hypothermia. It is highly recommended that for longer walks or summit climbs, you leave your itinerary with your accommodation provider, or, better still, at a park visitors center. Be adequately prepared, take warm clothing, carry food and drink, observe cloud and temperature changes—particularly when venturing up to the higher altitudes—and resist trying to make the summit when the weather is obviously deteriorating.

Flora and Fauna

The combination of a wet mountain climate and periods of dry hot weather promotes a luxurious growth of vegetation, and the variations in altitude on Taranaki give rise to several distinct vegetation zones—large forest trees, small shrubs, tussocks and herbs, mosses and lichens—easily seen from any of the three main access roads. The lower slopes (about 500–900 meters/1640–2,950 ft) are covered by the broadleaf-podocarp rainforest where many varieties of native trees grow—*rimu,* northern *rata, kamahi, mahoe,* broadleaf, and tree fuchsia. Beneath the tree canopy the undergrowth is prolific—creepers grow in profusion, garlanding the smaller trees, and lush ferns, mosses, and lichens carpet the forest floor. In the 900–1,100-meter (2,950–3,610 ft) range the *totara* and *kaikawaka* (mountain cedar) trees become dominant. Above 1,400 meters (4,600 ft), you find many plants unique to the park, mostly due to the long history of volcanic disturbance and relative isolation from seed sources. A variety of small herbaceous plants, ferns (the rare *Polystichum cystostegia* flourishes only on Taranaki), and mountain daisies (two species are slightly different from those found elsewhere in New Zealand) cover the slopes just below the permanent snow line.

The park's most commonly sighted birds include the native pigeon, rifleman, whitehead, and kingfisher on lower slopes, and *tui,* bellbird, fantail, and tomtit up to about 1,300 meters (4,270 ft). You can hear shining and long-tailed cuckoos in forested areas, and see the New Zealand *pipit* on higher open slopes.

Getting Oriented

Three roads lead into the park, all branching off the inland route (Hwy. 3) between New Plymouth and Hawera. Two of these have accommodations and restaurants at the end of the road. If you plan to explore the park on foot, drive straight up the access roads. If you're not so much into outdoor activities but enjoy scenic views, take the slightly longer coastal route (Hwy. 45) for great views of Taranaki from various angles.

NORTH EGMONT

The park's closest access point to New Plymouth is south from **Egmont village.** From this hamlet along Highway 3, it's 10 km (6.2 mi) to the park boundary and then a steady climb of six km (3.7 mi) to the end of the road. Along the section of road within the park are picnic areas, lookouts, the start of several walking tracks, and, toward the end, the **North Egmont Visitor Centre** (Egmont Rd., 06/756-0990; daily 9 A.M.–5:30 P.M.) and a small café. The visitor center has natural history exhibits, a track orientation map, displays of local walks, and a summer interpretive program.

Short Walks

The easy **Nature Walk** (color-coded red) takes only 15 minutes. It starts at the southern end of the visitor center parking lot, passes through a *totara* and *kamahi* forest, gives great views over the Ngatoro Valley, and leads up to a ridge overlooking the Ngatoro Stream. The walk comes out on Translator Road—turn right, and you'll end up at the upper parking lot. The **Ngatoro Walk** (blue) takes approximately 45 minutes, and starts at the bottom eastern corner of the visitor center parking lot. After taking the first turnoff to the right, you descend

and cross the Ngatoro Streambed, then climb up through beautiful mountain cedar trees to Translator Road. Follow the road to the right for five minutes to the upper parking lot.

The longest of the short walks at North Egmont is the **Veronica Walk** (yellow, allow 90 minutes). This track starts at the western corner of the upper parking lot, crosses the slope of the mountain through *totara* and *kamahi* forest, and takes you up the mountain for great views of the Ram Stream and Pouakai Range.

Egmont Village

Egmont village is a hamlet at the northern gateway to Egmont National Park, 16 km (10 mi) from the end of the road and 12 km (seven mi) from New Plymouth. Easily recognized by the "bike fence" is **The Missing Leg** (1082 Junction Rd., 06/752-2570, www.missinglegback packers.co.nz; camping $13 per person, dorm beds $18, $48 d), a great little lodge where you can get a comfortable bed for the night and interact with the outdoor-loving owner.

EAST EGMONT

Pembroke Road spurs west from Stratford (described later in this chapter) to provide a second park access point. This 15-km (nine-mi) road takes you past numerous picnic areas and trailheads before reaching **Mountain House,** where you'll find a public shelter, toilets, motel, restaurant, and souvenir shop. From this point, the road continues climbing for three km (1.9 mi) to the **Plateau,** the park's highest road-accessible point.

Short Walks

The intriguing 15-minute **Kamahi Walk** starts at Mountain House at the direction sign (red), and winds through a magical moss-clad forest of *kamahi* trees and dense undergrowth—just the kind of place where you'd expect to find elves and goblins frolicking in the greenery. Also starting from Mountain House, the three-km (1.9-mi) **Patea Walk** (yellow) takes you through more lush forest.

For those with more time, the six-km (3.7-mi) **Enchanted Walk** is well worthwhile. Starting from below Mountain House, it crosses the Patea River and its tributaries, passes the junction with the lower track to Dawson Falls, and climbs a long ridge to the Trig at Jackson's Lookout for fabulous views; allow two hours round-trip). **Curtis Falls Track** also starts near Mountain House and crosses typically rugged volcanic land to descend into the Manganui Gorge to two spectacular waterfalls plunging over ancient lava flows. From the Plateau you can take various tracks to **Twin Falls, Wilkies Pools, Bubbling Springs,** and **Dawson Falls.**

Skiing and Snowboarding

If you're visiting in winter and looking for a totally different skiing or boarding experience, plan on spending time at **Manganui Skifield** (06/759-1119), located on the upper slopes of Taranaki. With an average slope gradient of 30 degrees, the upper terrain is challenging—in fact the incline is so steep that skiers and boarders must attach themselves to the rope tow by a belt. Another feature of the "field" (as alpine resorts are known in New Zealand) is that the entire area is covered in a layer of moss, meaning that it can operate with a very light snow cover. But there's one unusual catch to a day on the slopes of Taranaki—the lifts lie 1.5 km (0.9 mi) from the end of the road at The Plateau, meaning the only access is on foot (equipment such as skis and boards is transported by zip line, called a flying fox in New Zealand and Australia). The season generally runs June–September. Day tickets are $35 and rentals from Mountain House are $30.

Practicalities

Privately owned **Mountain House Motor Lodge** lies high up the slopes of Mount Taranaki 15 km (nine mi) from Stratford (Pembroke Rd., 06/765-6100 or 0800/668-682, www .mountainhouse.co.nz; $125–165 s or d). Accommodation is in slightly dated hotel rooms or off to one side in self-contained chalets. The in-house restaurant (breakfast, lunch, and dinner) presents simple but surprisingly good fare. Choose from the usual New Zealand favorites, such as venison or lamb, or something a little

more unusual, such as a grilled filet of kangaroo covered in a red currant sauce ($27.50). For dessert, look no further than pavlova ($8.50). The lodge also has a gift shop, bar, and ski and snowboard rentals.

◖ SOUTH EGMONT

From Highway 3, reaching the park's South Egmont unit takes the longest. Access is from the town of Eltham (described later in this chapter), 15 km (nine km) west along Eltham Road to Kaponga and then a similar distance north along Manaia Road. This stretch of paved road winds steeply up the mountainside through fantastic lush greenery and shady green tunnels where the trees meet overhead, and passes lookouts and magnificent waterfalls (at the end of short walks) before terminating at a day-use area and lodge. The **Display Centre** (daily 9 A.M.–5 P.M.) describes local flora and fauna, as well as volcanic and human history. In the immediate vicinity you'll find picnic areas, a public shelter, toilets, a lookout, and starting points of numerous tracks leading to crystal-clear streams, bubbling springs, and waterfalls.

Short Walks

Before setting off anywhere, call in at the **Dawson Falls Display Centre** and check out a detailed display showing the local track systems. **Kapuni Walk** is probably one of the easiest walks and leads to a "must-see" local attraction. Starting at the sign on the road just below Dawson Falls Lodge, the track (pink, one hour) follows the forested banks of Kapuni Stream to a view of magnificent **Dawson Falls** dropping an impressive 18 meters (59 ft) down a 1,000-year-old lava flow—you can also get down to the base by taking the steep track farther along. For great mountain views, take the short sidetrack before the falls that crosses the stream and leads to a lookout; the main track returns to the road and parking lot through mature rainforest. The circular **Konini Dell Walk** (blue, one hour) starts above the lodge, and runs along a ridge top and through a *totara* and *kamahi* forest (a favorite spot in spring for the melodic bellbirds and *tui*) to a lookout. **Wilkies Pool Walk** (red, one hour round-trip) is an easy walk upriver along Kapuni Stream to Kapuni Gorge, where water has carved an intricate channel through an old lava flow to form a series of spectacularly polished rock pools.

Hasties Walk is longer and more difficult (orange, at least 2.5 hours round-trip), but the unobstructed views of Taranaki and distant fertile plains are worth the climb. The trail starts above the Display Centre and follows a section of the Summit Track.

Practicalities

Comfortable **Dawson Falls Mountain Lodge** (23 km/14 mi from Stratford, 06/765-5457 or 0800/651-800, www.dawson-falls.co.nz) has 12 charming Swiss Alps–influenced rooms. Rates of $175 s, $275 d include meals.

New Plymouth to Wanganui

From New Plymouth it's 160 km (100 mi) south then east along South Taranaki Bight to Wanganui via Highway 3 through Stratford and Eltham. These two towns are best known as gateways to Egmont National Park, but also well worth some time for their charming small-town vibe and good array of inexpensive accommodations and eateries. The alternate route between New Plymouth and Wanganui is Highway 45, which follows the coast around the west side of Egmont National Park.

STRATFORD

Named for William Shakespeare's birthplace (street names are taken from the bard's plays), Stratford, 41 km (15 mi) southeast of New Plymouth, is the principal gateway to Egmont National Park, as well as being a worthwhile stop in itself. Many private gardens lie around the village, with most opening for the **Rhododendron Festival** each November.

Practicalities

Regan Lodge Motel (16 Regan St., 06/765-7379 or 0800/112-027; $75 s, $85 d) offers eight one- and two-bedroom units a 10-minute walk from downtown. A less-expensive option is **Stratford Top 10 Holiday Park** (Page St., 06/765-6440), adjacent to a quiet park with walks through native bush, river swimming, and a swimming pool nearby. Tent and powered sites cost $13 per person, dorm beds $18, cabins $42–60 s or d, and motel rooms $80 s or d.

At ☾ **Platinum Lodge** (535 Pembroke Rd., 06/765-5800, www.platinumlodge.co.nz; $450 s or d), a short way along the road to East Egmont, you can soak up pure luxury in one of three suites, with Taranaki rising majestically above the surrounding farmland. Whether you're sipping complimentary wine from your private courtyard, enjoying a gourmet breakfast wrapped in a plush white robe, or soaking in the jetted tub, the mountain is a constant.

The main street (Broadway) is lined with small-town eateries. Along here, at New Zealand's only glockenspiel clock (listen for tunes daily at 10 A.M., 1 P.M., 3 P.M., and 7 P.M.), duck down Prospero Place, a pedestrian mall, to reach **Collage Café** (06/765-7003; daily 9 A.M.–3 P.M.), a pleasant little eatery with covered outdoor tables. Adjacent to the café is **Stratford Information Centre** (06/765-6708; Mon.–Fri. 10:30 A.M.–4 P.M., Sat.–Sun. 10:30 A.M.–3 P.M.) and **Percy Thomson Gallery** (06/765-0917; Mon.–Fri. 10:30 A.M.–4 P.M., Sat.–Sun. 10:30 A.M.–3 P.M.), the latter filled with local artwork.

ELTHAM

Along Highway 3 south of Stratford, the distinctive peak of Taranaki is always visible to the west and a number of small villages dot the route. The first of these is Eltham, known throughout the land for its cheese. Take Upper Manaia Road west from town to **Hollard Gardens** (06/764-6544; daily 9 A.M.–5 P.M.;

donation), best appreciated in late fall, when the extensive collection of rhododendrons is in full bloom.

HAWERA AND VICINITY

Hawera, a historic dairying town at the junction of Highways 3 and 45, has a pleasant main street outfitted with cobbled sidewalks and decorative lamps—and eight traffic circles. The main attraction is the **Tawhiti Museum** (Ohangai Rd., 06/278-6837; summer Fri.– Mon. 10 A.M.–4 P.M.; donation), an eclectic collection of artifacts and displays detailing the history of the Taranaki region. In summer, a narrow-gauge railway operates around the property each Sunday. It's signposted off Highway 4 north out of town.

(Dairyland

A combination of lots of sunshine and rich volcanic soil makes south Taranaki one of the world's premier dairying areas. In this environment, two km east of Hawera, **Kiwi Co-operative Dairies** has built the world's largest dairy products manufacturing plant with a large visitor center. The numbers are staggering: The company collects milk from 4,000 farms and 750,000 cows in 100 tankers, for an annual volume of 2,500 million liters. Once at the plant, the milk is mostly processed into powder for export and use in such specialty products as Egmont Cheese, specifically developed for the U.S. market. Mozzarella cheese (the one on pizza) and protein products derived from milk are also produced. Annually, the plant manufactures 190,000 tons of milk powder alone.

At the entrance to the plant is **Dairyland Visitor Centre** (Hwy. 3, 06/278-4537; daily 9 A.M.–5 P.M.; free) featuring dairy displays, an audiovisual on the industry and plant, and a simulated tanker ride. Part of the center is a café that features delicious banana milkshakes.

Practicalities

(**Wheatly Downs Farmstay** (484 Ararata Rd., 06/278-6523; camping $15 s or d, dorm beds $28, 45 s, $65–95 d), on a farm northeast

Dairyland is a worthwhile stop – even if it's just for a delicious milkshake.

© ANDREW HEMPSTEAD

of Hawera, is a great place to experience life on a farm, hike in the surrounding bushland, or just kick back and relax. On the north side of town, **Furlong Motor Inn** (256 Waihi Rd., 06/278-5136; $88 s, $108 d) has the best regular motel rooms in town. It also has a bar and restaurant. Along Highway 3 through town, on the west side, **King Edward Park** (Waihi Rd., 06/278-8544; tent and powered sites $22, simple cabins from $40) is beside attractive gardens and within walking distance of the local swimming pool.

At the east end of downtown, **South Takanaki Visitor Centre** (55 High St., 06/278-8599; Mon.–Fri. 8:30 A.M.–5:15 P.M., Sat.–Sun. 9:30 A.M.–4 P.M.) is a good stop for northbound visitors looking for information on Egmont National Park. The adjacent concrete water tower is open during visitor center hours and for $2 you can climb to the top.

NEW PLYMOUTH TO HAWERA VIA THE COASTAL ROUTE

From New Plymouth, Highway 45 (also known as the Surf Highway) hugs the coast for 110 km (62 mi) to Hawera. Turn off Highway 45 at Pungarehu to reach **Cape Egmont Lighthouse** and a coastal lookout.

The only town along Highway 45 is **Opunake,** about halfway around the cape. Nestled behind a crescent-shaped beach and flanked by two high headlands, Opunake has safe swimming and a laidback atmosphere. A walkway leads east to the mouth of the Waiaua River and west past an old wharf dating to the 1890s to a great lookout point. One of the few accommodations along this stretch of coast is the **Opunake Motel** (36 Heaphy Rd., Opunake, 06/761-8330; $75 s, $85 d). **Opunake Beach Holiday Park** (06/761-7525; $12 per person) has campsites right on the beach.

TARANAKI AND THE WEST

Wanganui

Lazily sprawling across both sides of the slow-flowing Whanganui River, 160 km (100 miles) southeast of New Plymouth and 195 km (121 mi) north of Wellington, this historic city (pop. 41,000) has a number of interesting attractions, some of the best mid-island dining, a good choice of accommodations, and is also a central base for a day trip into Whanganui National Park.

For centuries Maori people lived in villages along the shores of the Whanganui River. Before the arrival of the first white settlers in the 1830s, the location of the city was a thriving Maori center (see sidebar "Birth of the Whanganui"). The river was an important Maori canoe route to the center of the North Island; with the Europeans came the first steamboats to puff upriver. Today most of the original villages lie abandoned, but priceless Maori artifacts found along the banks have been preserved and are on display at the downtown museum. In 1870, Town Bridge was erected over the river, which considerably opened up the

district and began a connection with Wellington in the south. The original bridge stood for almost 100 years before it was replaced with the modern Wanganui City Bridge. Today three city bridges and a railway bridge span the mighty river within city limits.

The city of Wanganui has retained the Maori spelling of what was historically Whanganui ("great wait"), while in all other references the "h" has been restored, including in the names of the river, the national park, and the region. To confuse matters further, both are pronounced the same. The correct pronunciation (wan-ga-nooey) is unlike elsewhere on the North Island where "wa" is pronounced "fa."

SIGHTS AND RECREATION
Whanganui Regional Museum
The focus of this worthy museum (corner of Wicksteed and Watt Sts., 06/345-7443; daily 10 A.M.–4:30 P.M.; adult $5, child free) is a cavernous room filled with Maori architecture, carving, art, greenstone weapons, feather

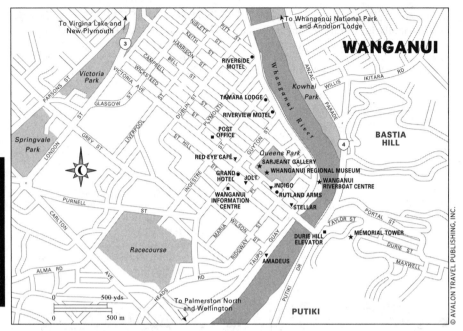

cloaks, ceremonial portraits, intriguing displays on tattooing, and the eye-catching 25-meter-long (82-ft-long) Te Mata-O-Hotoroa war canoe that carried a crew of 70. Throughout the rest of the museum there's a reconstruction of a colonial cottage and an entire Wanganui street from times gone by; a spectacular and comprehensive collection of mounted birds (see the display of moa—a huge flightless bird native to New Zealand, extinct for centuries), parrots of the world, mounted fish, whales, and animals; a shell collection; and a room full of fluorescent butterflies and moths.

Sarjeant Gallery

Also in Queens Park, this gallery (corner of Wicksteed and Watt Sts., 06/349-0506; daily 10:30 A.M.–4:30 P.M.; free) is contained in an imposing whitewashed building capped by stone dome. It holds an impressive permanent collection of 1800s European and New Zealand art, as well as excellent contemporary photography from throughout the country.

Waimarie

This 34-meter (112-ft) coal-fired paddlesteamer plied the river for 50 years before sinking at its moorings in 1952. After 40 years it was raised to the surface to begin a painstaking restoration project. The spic-and-span *Waimarie* now takes visitors on a two-hour river cruise from her berth at the **Wanganui Riverboat Centre** (1 Taupo Quay, 06/347-1863), departing daily in summer at 2 P.M. (adult $30, child $12). The Riverboat Centre is also home to a small museum (Mon.–Sat. 9 A.M.–4 P.M., Sun. 10 A.M.–4 P.M.; donation) detailing the boat's history, along with its sister ship the *Wairua*, which operates from the same wharf on a charter basis.

Durie Hill and Vicinity

Head to Durie Hill, across the river from downtown, for great views of the city, its three bridges, and the Whanganui River winding out to the coast. It's possible to reach the top of the hill by road (cross the Whanganui River from downtown, turn left, and follow the signs to "Scenic Drive View Point"), but more fun is to take the **Durie Hill Elevator.** Opened in 1925, the elevator is not a tourist attraction, but was built as an easy way for the residents of Durie Hill to reach town. To get there on foot from downtown, cross the river via Wanganui City Bridge (the main bridge) and look for the sign across Victoria Avenue. A 210-meter (690-foot) tunnel leads into the base of the hill, from where the elevator rises 66 meters (217 ft) to the top of Durie Hill. Access is free and it is open Monday–Friday 7:30 A.M.–6 P.M., Saturday 7 A.M.–5 P.M., and Sunday 10 A.M.–5 P.M.

At the top of the hill is **Memorial Tower,** built from locally quarried rock filled with fossilized seashells. A slightly claustrophobic 176-step stairway leads up 32 meters (104 ft) to an enclosed viewing platform.

Back down along the river, Victoria Avenue continues downstream to riverside **Kowhai Park,** which was planted with exotic trees a century ago. Today, it is filled with a wonderful array of playground features, including a Spanish galleon, a lime-green octopus, a giant pumpkin, the "ruins" of a castle, and a spray park.

Virginia Lake

Tranquil Virginia Lake nestles between woods, lawns, and beds of bright flowers. Although it's only one km (0.6 mi) from the top end of Victoria Avenue (about three km/two mi from downtown), the lake and grounds have a genteel parklike atmosphere. Features include a large walk-through aviary at the northwest end, colorful **Higginbottom Fountain** (startling at night), and the tropical flower- and fern-filled **Winter Gardens** (Mon.–Sat. 10 A.M.–4 P.M., Sun. 10 A.M.–5 P.M.; free). Walking tracks weave through the trees and around the lake—if you have time, follow the trail around the left side of the lake (from the road) to the small statue of *Tainui*—the romantic legend of the lake is inscribed below it.

Entertainment

The hotels and public bars do a booming business—just follow your ears to the most popular watering spots in town. A classic old pub

that has been extensively restored, the **Rutland Arms** (corner of Ridgeway St. and Victoria Ave., 06/347-7677) is a great place for a quiet beer. The **Grand Hotel** (corner of St. Hill and Guyton Sts., 06/345-0955) is a popular local drinking hole, with three stylish bars.

ACCOMMODATIONS AND CAMPING
Under $50
Tamara Lodge (24 Somme Pde., 06/347-6300, www.tamaralodge.com; dorm beds $24, $38 s, $50–60 d) features good, clean accommodations in a classic Edwardian house across the road from the river. The friendly hosts make you feel at home while you get a house tour, a map of the town, and information on what to see and do in Wanganui. Facilities include a lounge, a game room with a piano, a garden filled with palm trees and hammocks, Internet access, a barbecue area, and free use of bikes.

$50-100
The owners combined their first names to come up with the name **(Anndion Lodge** (143 Anzac Pde., 06/343-3593, www.anndion.co.nz; dorm beds $50, $65 s, $80–120 d), but they also put everything into making this accommodation the most welcoming and comfortable in Wanganui. A backpackers for grownups, it features a beautiful outdoor pool and spa, super-comfortable rooms (some with en suites), three living areas with modern entertainment systems, and a kitchen with everything from a coffee-bean grinder to a rice cooker.

The **Grand Hotel** (corner of St. Hill and Guyton Sts., 06/345-0955, www.thegrand hotel.co.nz; from $75 s, $95 d), a three-story art deco classic dating to the 1920s, has been tastefully renovated. All guest rooms have private bathrooms and downstairs are a restaurant and Irish pub.

Along Somme Parade, which follows the Whanganui River through town, are a string of motels within walking distance of downtown (they are easily confused—five start with "River"—so double-check your booking before checking in). The closest of these is **Riverview Motel** (14 Somme Pde., 06/345-2888 or 0800/102-001; $90–120 s or d), where more expensive rooms enjoy river views. Rooms at **Riverside Motel** (30 Somme Pde., 06/345-2448 or 0800/853-333; $80 s, $90 d) are similarly priced but larger.

A little farther out, **Halswell Court Motel** (59 Halswell St., 06/343-9848 or 0800/809-107; $99–109 s or d) has 20 well-appointed rooms, each with kitchen facilities and set around parklike grounds. Continuing north, beyond Virginia Lake, is **Oasis Motor Lodge** (181 Great North Rd., 06/345-4636; from $95 s or d). Rooms are self-contained and overlook a pleasant garden area. The motel also has indoor and outdoor pools.

$100-150

Rutland Arms (corner of Victoria Ave. and Ridgway St., 06/347-7677 or 0800/788-526, www.rutland-arms.co.nz; $140–175 s or d) is a restored hotel with in-house dining. Each of the eight super-spacious guest rooms has a traditional English feel, cotton sheets, reproduction period furnishings, and high-speed Internet access. Rates include a light breakfast.

If you have your own transportation and don't mind the 24-km (15-mi) drive northwest to Kai Iwi, consider staying at the beautiful **Bushy Park Homestead** (791 Rangitatau East Rd., off Hwy. 3 eight km/five mi north of Kai Iwi, 06/342-9879, www.bushypark-homestead .co.nz), an Edwardian-era home on an estate of native bushland. The rooms share bathrooms, but there's plenty of space for guests to relax—a long verandah, comfortable lounge, extensive gardens, and a network of walking trails. Rooms in the main house are $85–135 s, $105–135 d. There are also dorm beds in the old bunkhouse for $25.

Holiday Park

The **Avro Motel** (36 Alma Rd., 06/345-5279; $28) has a limited number of powered sites, each with a private bathroom, and campers have use of the motel's pool and playroom.

((Whanganui River Top 10 Holiday Park (460 Somme Pde., Upper Aramoho, 06/343-8402 or 0800/272-664, www.wrivertop10 .co.nz) is on the city-side bank of the river five km/three mi downstream from the Dublin Street Bridge. It's a great place to stay if you want to surround yourself with greenery and get a bit of rest, if you don't mind sharing your food with numerous noisy families of waterfowl. The park is situated in lush parklike surroundings with lots of trees, and the river is just a few steps away. All campsites are $16 per person, and simple riverfront cabins start at $53 s or d, but it is the cheery motel units for $120 that really shine.

Castlecliff Seaside Holiday Park (1 Rangiora St., Castlecliff, 06/344-2227, www.castle cliffholidaypark.co.nz; campsites $24, cabins $25–70 s, $45–85 d) is adjacent to a rugged black-sand and driftwood-covered beach and eight km (five mi) from downtown Wanganui. To get to Castlecliff Beach, follow Taupo Quay west onto Heads Road, continue onto Bryce Street, at the end turn right on Cornfoot Street, then turn left on Rangiora Street.

FOOD

Coinciding with a refreshing new-look main street lined with palm trees, decorative lamps, and flower-filled hanging baskets, the dining scene in Wanganui has jumped ahead in leaps and bounds over the last decade.

Cafés and Quick Bites

Jolt (19 Victoria Ave., 06/345-8840; Mon.–Fri. 7:30 A.M.–5:30 P.M.) is the quintessential city-style coffee hangout. Up the hill a couple of blocks, **Red Eye Café** (96 Guyton St., 06/345-5646; Mon.–Wed. 8 A.M.–4 P.M., Thurs.–Fri. 8 A.M.–9 P.M., Sat. 9:30 A.M.–8 P.M.) serves up a strong selection of coffee concoctions and a range of cakes, pastries, and light meals.

With a great riverfront setting that catches the morning sun, modern **Amadeus** (69 Quay St., 06/345-1538; Mon.–Fri. 8:30 A.M.–4 P.M., Sat.–Sun. 10 A.M.–4 P.M.) is a good choice for a casual lunch in the $12–18 range.

Contemporary

Overlooking Majestic Square from beside

the quiet end of Victoria Avenue, **C Indigo** (1 Maria Pl., 06/348-7459; Sun.–Tues. 8 A.M.– 4:30 P.M., Wed.–Sat. 8 A.M.–10 P.M.) is my choice for the best food in town in the hippest dining room. Early in the day, you might try the blueberry pancakes with maple syrup ($15); dinner mains are highlighted by fresh, innovative choices like sesame-crusted fish on a pumpkin risotto cake ($27).

Stylish **Stellar** (2 Victoria Ave., 06/345-7278; daily 9 A.M.–10 P.M.) is dominated by polished hardwood floors and a rustic-meets-modern decor. The wide-ranging menu includes dishes such as vegetarian curry, Thai pork noodle salad, and thin-crust pizza, all under $30.

Asian

Like towns and cities throughout the country, Wanganui has a number of Asian restaurants of varying quality. I don't profess to have tried them all, but upon a local recommendation, I had a fine dinner of typical Thai at the welcoming **Red Flame Café** (156 Victoria Ave., 06/345-2005; daily 10:30 A.M.–3 P.M. and 5:30–9 P.M.), spending less than $60 for two.

PRACTICALITIES
Information
Wanganui Information Centre (101 Guyton St. at St. Hill St., 06/349-0508; Mon.–Fri. 8:30 A.M.–5 P.M., Sat.–Sun. 10 A.M.–2 P.M.) is small, but the staff ensure a most enjoyable experience in Wanganui. They have heaps of information on the city, as well as the

Whanganui River, its reserves, and its many boat operators, and will make bookings for any trip or accommodation you desire.

Services
The main post office is at 226 Victoria Avenue. The information center has Internet access, as does **Catch 22** (62 Taupo Quay, 06/348-7610). **Wanganui Laundrette** is at 43 Hatrick Street (06/349-0600).

Wanganui Hospital (Heads Rd., 06/348-1234) has a doctor on duty 24 hours daily. **Wicksteed Pharmacy** (214 Wicksteed St., 06/345-6166) is open daily 8:30 A.M.– 8:30 P.M.

Getting There and Around
Wanganui Airport is four km (2.5 mi) west of the city center on the south side of the river. **Air New Zealand** (www.airnewzealand.com) has direct daily flights from Wanganui to Auckland and Wellington. Wanganui is on a number of **Intercity** (www.intercitycoach.co.nz) routes, with the bus depot within **Wanganui Travel Centre** (156 Ridgeway St., 06/345-4433). Regular services arrive and depart from Auckland, Taupo, New Plymouth, Palmerston North, and Wellington.

Local buses are operated weekdays only by **Wanganui Taxis** (06/345-5555) departing from Maria Place, just off Victoria Avenue. Cabs also wait at Maria Place, or call **Wanganui Taxis** (06/345-5555). Car rental agencies in Wanganui include **Budget** (06/345-5122) and **Hertz** (06/348-7624).

Whanganui River

The magnificent Whanganui River, often called "the Rhine of New Zealand," is the second-longest river and the longest navigable waterway in the country. Starting on the slopes of Mount Tongariro, the river runs a 315-km (196-mi) course north to Taumarunui and then south toward the city of Wanganui, the last 32 km (20 mi) as a wide tidal estuary

before flowing into the Tasman Sea. It's navigable as far upstream as Taumarunui, but only by shallow-bottomed jetboats above Pipiriki.

WHANGANUI RIVER ROAD
If you have a vehicle and a full day, you won't want to miss the 79-km (50-mi) scenic drive north from the city of Wanganui along the east

TARANAKI AND THE WEST

bank of the Whanganui River to the picturesque village of Pipiriki, from where you will
want to take a jetboat trip into Whanganui
National Park. From Pipiriki, the options are
to return by road to Wanganui, take an extended float trip down the river, or continue to
Ohakune and Tongariro National Park.

Services along this route are very limited (no
petrol or groceries), so plan accordingly.

To Pipiriki

The river road begins 14 km (nine mi) north of
Wanganui along Highway 4. At the junction
of the two roads, interpretive boards describe
the river's history and give general information about it. From Highway 4, the road climbs
quickly to Aramoana summit, below which
the river is laid out in all its glory. Aside from
the magnificent wilderness scenery en route,
a number of historic Maori villages are worth
a stop. The first of these is **Atene,** and then
the road passes **Koriniti,** 47 km (29 mi) from
Wanganui. This village features a number of
historic buildings transported from the original village site across the river. One km (0.6
mi) farther north is the remains of a *pa,* then
another eight km (five mi) north is a restored
flour mill.

Pipiriki

Pipiriki is the gateway to the "wilderness"
reaches of the Whanganui River (only jetboats can continue upriver) and Whanganui
National Park, and a meeting place for hikers, campers, canoeists, rafters, and jetboaters. A large Maori population used to live
across the river from the present-day village.
Then, in the early 1900s, steamboats that
could cruise the river only as far upstream as
Pipiriki brought great numbers of tourists to
what quickly became a booming resort. Today
it's again a quiet little village attracting those
who wish to explore the river and surrounding
national park. Pipiriki's era as a tourist resort
ended abruptly in 1959, when the grand Pipiriki Hotel burned to the ground; today, no
services are offered.

Accommodations and Camping

Swing into **The Flying Fox** (06/342-8160,
www.theflyingfox.co.nz; camping $15 per
person, $80–130 s or d) via an aerial tram-
way that crosses the river from Koriniti, along
Whanganui River Road (or arrive by canoe or
jetboat). Accommodations at this eco-friendly
getaway include a funky house truck or two
cabins constructed using recycled materials.

Campers looking for solitude should take
the unpaved road down to the river at **Rawana,**
where **Kauika Camp Site** (tents $10, camper-
vans $20) is little more than a clearing in the
forest with flush toilets, showers, and an older
kitchen.

Driving Tours

It takes constant concentration to drive the
narrow, winding road between Wanganui and
Pipiriki, which doesn't allow an opportunity
to take in the unspoiled scenery. Instead, even
if you have a rental vehicle, choosing to join
Whanganui Tours (06/344-2554) is a sensible
option. Operated by a local couple, this company has the contract for mail delivery along
Whanganui River Road. They always have
room for a few passengers to come along for an
interesting tour to Pipiriki and back. The bus
departs from the post office Monday–Friday at
7:15 A.M. The fare is a very reasonable $40 per
person, with the added option of a jetboat trip
for $50–95 per person extra.

WHANGANUI NATIONAL PARK

Established in 1987, 74,231-hectare (183,400-
acre) remote and relatively isolated Whanganui
National Park is divided into three major sections within the **Whanganui River** watershed.
The large, rugged, central core of the park begins at Whakahoro, and extends 92 km (57
mi) south—downstream from Pipiriki. Farther
south are much smaller sections across the river
from Pipiriki and between Ranana and Atene.
Much of the park is unmodified lowland forest.
Birds abound, particularly in the more isolated
central areas of the river valley. Brown kiwi
(one of the largest populations in the country),

fantails, grey warblers, silvereyes, tits, and North Island robins (very common) are easily spotted, as are native bellbirds, New Zealand pigeons, *tui*, and yellow-crowned parakeets. Even *kokako* sightings have been reported.

The park's focal point is most definitely the Whanganui River. With its gentle gradient, large volume of water, and 234 km (145 mi) of navigable water, the Whanganui has always been a major transport route. Today it's extensively used by canoeists, to a lesser extent by jetboaters, and is the main access into the wilderness sections of the park. Maori have lived in villages along the river for many centuries, evidenced by the many archaeological sites found in the park, and the river and adjoining forests still have important spiritual and traditional values to the Whanganui Maori people. Starting in the 1840s, European pioneers, explorers, missionaries, traders, and farmers also set up homes along the upper river.

Today, park visitors choose from a variety of energetic recreational activities—hiking, canoeing, jetboating, and fishing. But if simple sightseeing is more your thing, drive Whanganui River Road from Wanganui to Pipiriki.

Canoeing and Kayaking

Often proclaimed "the most canoed river in New Zealand," the Whanganui River is popular with paddlers from around the world. An estimated 6,000 canoeists and kayakers float the river each year. The most popular section is between Taumarunui and Pipiriki, a 144-km (88-mi) trip that takes up to five days. An easy overnight trip (and therefore popular on weekends with the locals) is the 50-km (31-mi) stretch of river between Taumarunui and Wades Landing. Usage is greatest between December and Easter, but the river is especially busy in January.

Yeti Tours (06/385-8197 or 0800/322-388, www.canoe.co.nz) has been guiding on the river for over 20 years. The company also rents gear for independent travelers. Canoes and single kayaks cost $195 for five days. These rates include transportation, life jackets, and waterproof barrels for food. Yeti also rents

camping equipment. Guided trips begin from the Hobbit Motor Lodge in Ohakune, and include transportation to and from the river, equipment rentals, and all meals. The six-day trip begins just downstream of Taumarunui, while four-, three-, and two-day trips begin at Wades Landing. The pull-out point on all trips is Pipiriki. The trips are no mad dash down the river—only a few hours a day are spent in the canoes, with plenty of time for hiking and exploring the wilderness. Prices start at $335 for a two-day trip.

Bridge to Nowhere Tours (06/348-7122, www.bridgetonowheretours.co.nz) rents canoes and kayaks. The company provides transfers upstream from Pipiriki as far as you desire; then you can simply paddle back down to the Pipiriki dock at your leisure.

Accommodations and Camping

Bridge to Nowhere Lodge (06/348-7122, www.bridgetonowheretours.co.nz) is the only accommodation actually in the park. It lies in a remote location, 21 km (13 mi) upstream from Pipiriki and perched high above the river. There's plenty to do around the property, with canoes for guest use, hiking on the nearby Matemateaonga Walkway, or simply relaxing on the deck. Accommodation is in comfortable dorms ($45) with use of a communal kitchen or in the main lodge ($125 per person includes buffet-style breakfast and dinner). Rates for one night including meals and transportation are $235 per person.

Within the park are nine huts and numerous campgrounds, many of which lie along the section of river between Taumarunui and Pipiriki, perfect for a wilderness canoe or raft trip. The huts are of a varying standard; all have bunk beds, a water supply, and a toilet, and some have cooking facilities. In summer, a Great Walks Hut & Campsite Pass is required for travelers overnighting on the river, whether you're staying in a hut or campground. Valid for four nights (the usual length of time it takes to paddle between Taumarunui and Pipiriki), the pass costs $60 if bought in advance from a DOC office.

INFORMATION

The Department of Conservation has streamlined its operation in recent years, with the **Pipiriki Field Centre** (Owairua Rd., 06/385-5022; Mon.–Fri. 8 A.M.–5 P.M.) now more of an operational base rather than an information center. A better option is **Wanganui Information Centre** (101 Guyton St. at St. Hill St., 06/349-0508; Mon.–Fri. 8:30 A.M.–5 P.M., Sat.–Sun. 10 A.M.–2 P.M.), or check online at www.doc.govt.nz.

GETTING THERE AND AROUND

The most pleasant way to get to Pipiriki is along Whanganui River Road from Wanganui. **Whanganui Tours** (06/344-2554) provides a shuttle service along this route.

The main way into and through the park is along the river. **Bridge to Nowhere Tours** (06/348-7122, www.bridgetonowheretours.co.nz) offers a four-hour tour to the Bridge to Nowhere. This famous Mangapurua Valley landmark was constructed in 1936 as part of a road that was meant to open up the area to settlers. That never happened, and today the bridge is slowly being reclaimed by the forest. The tour includes a jetboat ride, an easy 40-minute guided hike to the bridge, and tea or coffee for adult $95, child $45. **Whanganui Jet** (027/538-8687) is a little more flexible, with a day trip to the bridge and a shorter excursion downstream to the unique Flying Fox lodge the most popular options. Both companies provide a drop-off and pick-up service for hikers, or can drop paddlers as far upstream as required.

WELLINGTON AND THE LOWER NORTH ISLAND

Wellington, New Zealand's capital, spreads around a safe harbor at the southern extremity of the North Island, but there are a number of interesting options for reaching the city from points further north. Three main roads funnel traffic from the north into the Manawatu district, converging near the city of Palmerston North. If time is relatively unimportant and you want to get off the beaten track, take the inland route south that passes through scenic hilly countryside scattered with sheep, trout-filled streams, lakes, and little villages where excitement is a new face in town. The southeast area of the North Island is wild, remote, untouched (in direct contrast with the highly populated urban southwest), and well worth checking out if transportation and time are your own. The coastal route follows the Ka-

piti Coast south to the capital. Lying between the mountains of the Tararua Range and endless kilometers of golden sandy beaches littered with shells, the coastal towns naturally attract large numbers of vacationing Wellingtonians, backcountry hikers, beach bums, and a large retirement community. They are also a gateway to Kapiti Island, a favorite spot with bird-watchers.

Wellington itself is a delightful city to explore on foot. Nestled at the southern end of a large harbor, the downtown core is very walkable. From the centrally located information center, the magnificent Museum of New Zealand, Museum of Wellington City and Sea, and distinctive parliament buildings are all within striking distance. The streets rise steeply from downtown, with an abundance of Victorian

© ANDREW HEMPSTEAD

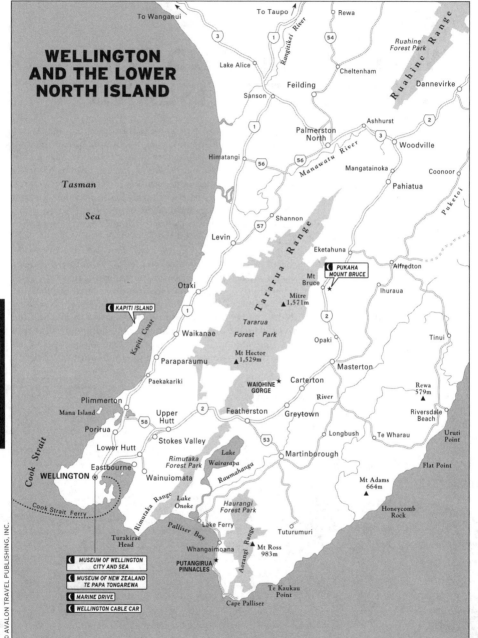

WELLINGTON AND THE LOWER NORTH ISLAND

Tasman

Sea

WELLINGTON

To Wanganui

To Taupo

Rewa

3

1

54

Rangitikei River

Ruahine Forest Park

Ruahine Range

Lake Alice

Cheltenham

Dannevirke

Feilding

Sanson

1

Ashhurst

2

Palmerston North

3

Woodville

Himatangi

56

56

Manawatu River

Mangatainoka

Coonoor

Pahiatua

Puketoi

Shannon

Eketahuna

Alfredton

57

Levin

Tararua Range

Mt Bruce

▶ PUKAHA MOUNT BRUCE ★

Ihuraua

Otaki

Mitre ▲1,571m

◀ KAPITI ISLAND

1

Waikanae

Tararua Forest Park

2

Opaki

Tinui

Kapiti Coast

Paraparaumu

Mt Hector ▲1,529m

Masterton

Paekakariki

WAIOHINE GORGE ★

Carterton

Rewa 579m ▲

Plimmerton

River

Riversdale Beach

Mana Island

Upper Hutt

2

Featherston

Greytown

Uruti Point

Porirua

58

Longbush

Te Wharau

Cook Strait

Lower Hutt

Stokes Valley

53

Flat Point

Eastbourne

Rimutaka Forest Park

Lake Wairarapa

Martinborough

Mt Adams 664m ▲

WELLINGTON ⊛

Wainuiomata

Rawmahanga

Honeycomb Rock

Cook Strait Ferry

Rimutaka Range

Lake Onoke

Haurangi Forest Park

Aorangi Range

Turakirae Head

Palliser Bay

Lake Ferry

Tuturumuri

Whangaimoana

Mt Ross 983m ▲

PUTANGIRUA PINNACLES ★

◀ MUSEUM OF WELLINGTON CITY AND SEA

◀ MUSEUM OF NEW ZEALAND TE PAPA TONGAREWA

◀ MARINE DRIVE

◀ WELLINGTON CABLE CAR

Te Kaukau Point

Cape Palliser

WELLINGTON

© AVALON TRAVEL PUBLISHING, INC.

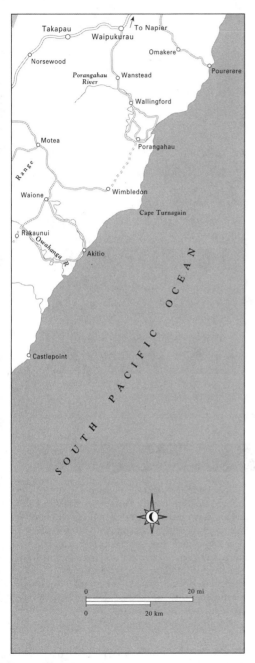

architecture and naturally pleasing spaces like the botanic garden. Wellington is renowned as a cultural center, with a surprising number of artistic offerings and pockets of café culture beckoning those willing to deviate from the main tourist trail. New Zealand's best-known author, Katherine Mansfield, was born in Wellington (and you can tour her childhood home), but the city's best-known resident is Peter Jackson, who brought high-profile movie productions including *King Kong* and the *Lord of the Rings* trilogy to the city.

PLANNING YOUR TIME

From the north, all roads lead south to Wellington, the departure point for ferries to the South Island. It is the latter that will be the most important element in planning your time in the Lower North Island. To get the best fares and to ensure a smooth transition between rental cars, ferries should be booked as far in advance in possible. With a ferry booking made, you can then work backwards in your planning. With an early-morning ferry departure from Wellington, allow at least one full day in the city and another full day reaching the capital from Wanganui, Tongariro, or Napier. On the way down south, Highway 2 via Masterton is the most scenic route, and has the **Pukaha Mount Bruce** bird sanctuary as a highlight. State Highway 1 is more direct, and passes a string of beautiful beaches along the Kapiti Coast. Nature lovers may want to schedule an extra day to visit **Kapiti Island,** either on the way down the coast or as a day trip from Wellington.

Once in the capital, it's very easy to spend a half day at the **Museum of New Zealand Te Papa Tongarewa,** which would leave the afternoon for a visit to **Museum of Wellington City and Sea,** a ride on the **Wellington Cable Car,** and a tour of **Marine Drive.**

WELLINGTON

HIGHLIGHTS

◖ Museum of Wellington City and Sea: Ensconced in a waterfront bond store, this interesting museum is filled with stories of the city's relationship to the ocean (page 245).

◖ Museum of New Zealand Te Papa Tongarewa: If you only visit one museum in New Zealand, make it this one, which tells the story of the country's natural and human history in the most interesting way imaginable (page 247).

◖ Wellington Cable Car: Rise above the crowds on this Wellington institution and you'll find yourself surrounded by beautiful gardens (page 248).

◖ Marine Drive: Escape the bustle of downtown along the coastal drive that wends its way through the suburbs past lookouts and rocky beaches (page 251).

◖ Pukaha Mount Bruce: This forested sanctuary provides a home to some of New Zealand's rarest birds (page 265).

◖ Kapiti Island: Predator-free, this beautiful island fills with the sounds of New Zealand's varied birdlife (page 269).

LOOK FOR ◖ TO FIND RECOMMENDED SIGHTS, ACTIVITIES, DINING, AND LODGING.

Wellington

Wonderful, windy Wellington, scenic capital of New Zealand and "City of a Thousand Views," perches on the edge of Cook Strait in the southwest corner of the North Island. Hemmed in by the Tararua Range to the north and the Rimutaka Range to the east, the city spills up and down bush-covered hills around the large sparkling bay of Port Nicholson. Colorful, cosmopolitan, exciting—Wellington is fun to explore whether you thrive in the great outdoors or in little seaside cafés. Sandy beaches, sheltered coves, rocky outcrops, and boat-filled marinas line Wellington Harbour, where the water is always a bright, bright blue dotted with multicolored sails. Imposing Parliament buildings, old and new, and modern skyscrapers dominate Wellington's center, in contrast to historic pioneer homes and elegant mansions that line the steep and narrow streets of the older suburbs. Scattered throughout the city are flower-filled gardens and shady parks that provide a quiet escape from the continuous hum and bustle of the busy commercial center.

According to the Maori, Wellington Harbour was first discovered in ancient times by the Polynesian navigators, Kupe and Ngahue, and it wasn't until the early 19th century that Europeans first sailed all the way into the magnificent harbor (Captain Cook missed the harbor entrance on his 1770 expedition but sailed through the heads in 1773). In 1826 Captain James Herd entered in his barque *Rosanna,* landed, and officially named the harbor Port Nicholson—the name by which it's still known today. The New Zealand Company bought the land that was to become Wellington City from the Maori in 1839, and the first settlers arrived on January 22, 1840, nowadays celebrated as a holiday throughout the region. In 1865, after much argument from Aucklanders, Wellington was chosen as New Zealand's official capital because of its central location, natural harbor, and population growth—the city became the seat of government, the harbor flourished, and banks, insurance companies, traders, and stock and land agents moved to the capital. Today, Wellington is New Zealand's third-largest city, with an urban-area population of 420,000.

Tell anyone you're going to Wellington and you're more than likely to hear horror stories about the weather—non-Wellingtonians seem to enjoy the capital city's bad reputation, rubbing it in any chance they get. Wellington's weather could best be described as...changeable. On just about any day of the year you can get bright sunshine, a sudden downpour, fog, and almost always wind. The wind, which howls in through Cook Strait, batters the city with everything from sea breezes (most days) to Antarctic gales (not too often), but no matter what the weather, there's always a scenic viewpoint, sandy beach, exotic restaurant, or snug reading nook to be found. Take a windbreaker, raincoat, and umbrella (*everyone* in Wellington has an umbrella) and you'll be ready to tackle Wellington's sights *and* elements!

DOWNTOWN SIGHTS

Like Auckland a decade before, Wellington's waterfront is undergoing much change. Linked to the visitor center and Civic Centre by a pedestrian overpass, harborside **Frank Kitts Park** was developed in the 1980s, as was the **Queens Wharf** precinct of entertainment

venues and restaurants. The waterfront art deco Ambulance Building has been extensively renovated and the early 1900 Odlin Building now provides a home to the New Zealand Stock Exchange. Next up is the revitalization of Taranaki Street Wharf and adjacent Waitangi Park, which will eventually be linked to the Museum of New Zealand by a waterfront promenade.

【 Museum of Wellington City and Sea

While Te Papa (next listing) gets all the attention, this excellent museum (Queens Wharf, 04/472-8904; daily 10 A.M.–5 P.M.; free) is also well worth a visit. Housed in a renovated 1892 bond store—where goods were held until duty was paid—it tells the story of Wellington's maritime and social history through three levels of well-planned displays. Highlights include a re-created bond store, the story of the *Wahine* ferry tragedy that claimed 57 lives in 1968, a three-story-high movie screen that can be viewed from any level, relics from local

Museum of Wellington City and Sea

© ANDREW HEMPSTEAD

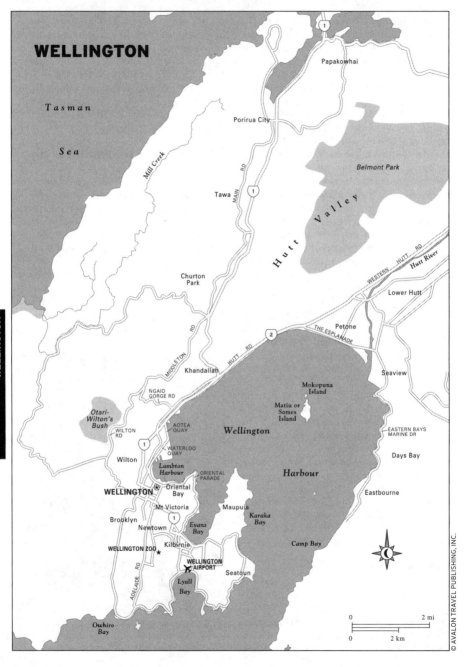

WELLINGTON

Tasman

Sea

Mill Creek

Papakowhai

Porirua City

MAIN RD

Tawa

1

Belmont Park

H u t t   V a l l e y

WESTERN HUTT RD

Hutt River

Churton Park

MIDDLETON RD

HUTT RD

Lower Hutt

THE ESPLANADE

Petone

2

Seaview

Khandallah

NGAIO GORGE RD

Mokopuna Island

Otari-Wilton's Bush

WILTON RD

AOTEA QUAY

WATERLOO QUAY

Matiu or Somes Island

Wellington

EASTERN BAYS MARINE DR

Days Bay

Wilton

1

Lambton Harbour

ORIENTAL PARADE

Harbour

WELLINGTON ✦ Oriental Bay

Eastbourne

Mt Victoria

Maupuia

Brooklyn

1

Newtown

Evans Bay

Karaka Bay

Kilbirnie

WELLINGTON ZOO ★

ADELAIDE RD

WELLINGTON AIRPORT ✈

Seatoun

Camp Bay

Lyall Bay

Owhiro Bay

0		2 mi

0		2 km

© AVALON TRAVEL PUBLISHING, INC.

shipwrecks, antiquarian maps, and antique diving equipment. The creative Telling Tales display comprises one interesting Wellington-related story from each year of the 20th century. You can also step back in time in the re-created boardroom of the harbor authority.

Museum of New Zealand Te Papa Tongarewa

Continuing around the harborfront from Queens Wharf, you can't miss New Zealand's five-story national museum (Cable St., 04/381-7051; daily 9 A.M.–6 P.M., Thurs. until 9 P.M.; free). Opened in February 1998, it rates as one of the world's finest national museums. It's impossible to get around the museum's 36,000 square meters (387,500 sq ft) of gallery in less than three hours, and a full day can easily be spent inside.

The complete history of New Zealand comes alive through a massive Maori exhibit, which tells the story of this intriguing race who arrived in New Zealand from Polynesia at least 1,000 years ago. Other exhibits include relics and engravings from Captain Cook's voyage; New Zealand's natural history, which includes interactive displays that explain the volcanic nature of the land (you can even enter a house where an earthquake is simulated); European settlement; and a number of art galleries showcasing all media. It's impossible not to be impressed by the dignity of the Waitangi display, which includes a six-meter-high (20-foot-high) backlit version of the treaty and a re-creation of a *wharenui* (long house). But you will also be amused by a gallery that highlights Kiwi inventions and creations. Near the entrance is an interactive room filled with (mostly) coin-operated simulators where visitors can try bungy jumping, water-skiing, and more. Then there are hidden gems that you stumble across—a motor bike that Kiwi world champion John Britten made in his backyard, "fossilized" possum road kill, and a cannon from Captain Cook's *Endeavour.* The museum is bordered on two sides by thousands of New Zealand native plants, with paths leading past ponds over a swing bridge above a stream, past a waterfall, and around a lagoon. A lava flow,

limestone cave, and rock-embedded fossils have also been re-created in this outdoor section of the museum.

While museum admission is free, a guided tour is highly recommended. These leave two to four times daily from the reception and cost $10.

Parliament House and the Beehive

Three totally different styles of architecture add interest to the Parliament buildings on Molesworth Street, north of the Civic Centre. The oldest of the three is a Gothic-style stone building housing the General Assembly Library; the middle building—brick, granite, and marble—houses the House of Representatives; the most modern, an 11-story circular building aptly called The Beehive, houses the ministers, their staff, and the cabinet room. At street level of Parliament House is a **Visitor Centre** (04/471-9503; Mon.–Fri. 9 A.M.–5 P.M., Sat. 9:30 A.M.–4 P.M., Sun. 11:30 A.M.–4 P.M.; free). Free tours are conducted from here Monday–Saturday on the hour (except when Parliament is in session) between 10 A.M. and 4 P.M. If you're visiting in the afternoon and a session is on (generally Tues.–Thurs.), go up to the Gallery of the Debating Chamber and see what's happening.

Historic Houses

Antrim House (63 Boulcott St., west of the Civic Centre, 04/472-4341; Mon.–Fri. 9 A.M.–5 P.M.; free) is the headquarters of the New Zealand Historic Places Trust; go there for information if you'd like to visit any of the many historic homes and buildings scattered around Wellington. The mansion itself is one of the best-preserved large townhouses of the Edwardian period, with its elegant exterior and kauri-paneled interior; the grounds and public reception areas of the house are open to the public.

Katherine Mansfield, New Zealand's best-known author, was born in a house built by her father in the historic suburb of Thorndon. The house has been lovingly restored and the garden replanted, as described by Mansfield in her book *Prelude.* Exhibits include an audiovisual

© ANDREW HEMPSTEAD

The General Assembly is housed in a distinctive Gothic-style building.

WELLINGTON

program and photos from the era. **Katherine Mansfield Birthplace** is at 25 Tinakori Road (04/473-7268; Tues.–Sun. 10 A.M.–6 P.M.; adult $5.50, senior $4, child $2).

WELLINGTON BOTANIC GARDEN

High above downtown, this garden stretches for more than 26 hectares (64 acres) over several ridges just west above the city center. Formal rose gardens contrast with wild indigenous areas and exotic tree, flower, and shrub plantations—it's a colorful tiptoe through the tulips while enjoying city views.

It's possible to drive or take a bus to the garden, but catching the cable car from downtown is the most popular way to get there.

◖ Wellington Cable Car

An excellent way to get acquainted with (and fall for) the city is to take the cable car from Cable Car Lane (off Lambton Quay, 04/472-2199) up the super-steep track to Kelburn Terminal. Three stops (a six-minute journey) along

the way allow you to discover Clifton Terrace, Talavera Terrace, and Salamanca Road, but the view from the top is by far the most spectacular. The cable car operates every 10 minutes Monday–Friday 7 A.M.–10 P.M. and Saturday–Sunday 9 A.M.–10 P.M. The one-way fare is adult $2.50, senior $1.50, child $1.

At the top of the cable car, plan on visiting the **Wellington Cable Car Museum** (Upland Rd., 04/475-3578; summer 9:30 A.M.–5:30 P.M., the rest of the year Mon.–Fri. 9:30 A.M.–5 P.M., Sat.–Sun. 10 A.M.–4:30 P.M.; free). Here you can see an interesting collection of equipment related to the history of the cable car, including Grip Car 3, one of the original cars, which has been beautifully restored.

Carter Observatory

At the highest point of the garden is **Carter Observatory** (40 Salamanca Rd., 04/472-8167; Nov.–Feb. Sun.–Tues. 10 A.M.–5 P.M., Wed.–Sat. 10 A.M.–midnight, Mar.–Oct. Mon.–Thurs. 10 A.M.–4 P.M., Fri.–Sat. 10 A.M.–11 P.M.; adult $12, senior $10,

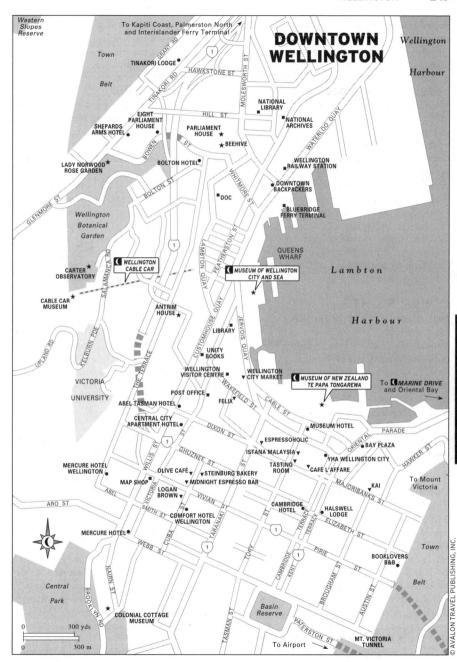

DOWNTOWN WELLINGTON

Western Slopes Reserve

To Kapiti Coast, Palmerston North and Interislander Ferry Terminal

Wellington

Harbour

Town Belt

TINAKORI LODGE

GRANT RD

HAWKSTONE ST

MOLESWORTH ST

TINAKORI RD

NATIONAL LIBRARY

HILL ST

EIGHT PARLIAMENT HOUSE

SHEPARDS ARMS HOTEL

BOWEN ST

PARLIAMENT HOUSE ★

NATIONAL ARCHIVES

WATERLOO QUAY

★ BEEHIVE

LADY NORWOOD ★ ROSE GARDEN

BOLTON HOTEL

BOLTON ST

WHITMORE ST

WELLINGTON RAILWAY STATION

GLENMORE ST

DOC

DOWNTOWN BACKPACKERS

BLUEBRIDGE FERRY TERMINAL

Wellington Botanical Garden

LAMBTON QUAY

FEATHERSTON ST

QUEENS WHARF

Lambton

CARTER OBSERVATORY ★

SALAMANCA RD

WELLINGTON CABLE CAR

MUSEUM OF WELLINGTON CITY AND SEA

CABLE CAR MUSEUM

KELBURN PDE

ANTRIM HOUSE ★

CUSTOMHOUSE QUAY

JERVOIS QUAY

Harbour

UPLAND RD

THE TERRACE

LIBRARY

UNITY BOOKS

VICTORIA UNIVERSITY

WELLINGTON VISITOR CENTRE

WELLINGTON CITY MARKET

WAKEFIELD ST

CABLE ST

MUSEUM OF NEW ZEALAND TE PAPA TONGAREWA

To MARINE DRIVE and Oriental Bay

POST OFFICE

FELIX

ABEL TASMAN HOTEL

CENTRAL CITY APARTMENT HOTEL

WILLIS ST

DIXON ST

MUSEUM HOTEL

ORIENTAL PARADE

ESPRESSOHOLIC

BAY PLAZA

HAWKER ST

MERCURE HOTEL WELLINGTON

ABEL SMITH ST

GHUZNEE ST

VICTORIA ST

MAP SHOP

OLIVE CAFÉ

STEINBURG BAKERY

MIDNIGHT ESPRESSO BAR

ISTANA MALAYSIA

TASTING ROOM

CAFÉ L'AFFARE

YHA WELLINGTON CITY

KAI

MAJORIBANKS ST

To Mount Victoria

LOGAN BROWN

VIVIAN ST

CUBA ST

COMFORT HOTEL WELLINGTON

TARANAKI ST

CAMBRIDGE HOTEL

HALSWELL LODGE

TERRACE

ELIZABETH ST

ARO ST

MERCURE HOTEL

WEBB ST

TORY ST

CAMBRIDGE TERRACE

KENT TERRACE

PIRIE ST

BROUGHAM ST

AUSTIN ST

Town Belt

BOOKLOVERS B&B

NAIRN ST

BROOKLYN RD

Central Park

COLONIAL COTTAGE MUSEUM

TASMAN ST

Basin Reserve

PATERSON ST

MT. VICTORIA TUNNEL

To Airport

0 ⊢ 300 yds
0 ⊢ 300 m

© AVALON TRAVEL PUBLISHING, INC.

WELLINGTON

child $5) featuring astronomical displays, videos, and a planetarium. The observatory is open for stargazing (weather permitting) some nights.

Lady Norwood Rose Garden

The fabulous **Lady Norwood Rose Garden** (daily dawn to dusk) is at the northern end of the Botanic Garden, where thousands of perfumed roses bloom from early November through April (quite intoxicating on a warm summer evening), and where, in spring, masses of bulbs burst into a spectacular floral display. Wander through the garden and discover a waterfall, Begonia House (daily 10 A.M.–4 P.M.), Tea House (daily 10 A.M.–4 P.M.), Camellia Garden, Sunken Gardens, Interpretive Centre in The Dell (daily Mon.–Fri. 9 A.M.–4 P.M., Sat.–Sun. 10 A.M.–4 P.M.), and many lookouts over the city.

OTHER SIGHTS
National Cricket Museum

Fans of cricket, New Zealand's most popular summer team sport, won't want to miss this museum, beneath the Old Stand at the Basin Reserve (Sussex St., 04/385-6602; adult $5, child $2). Displays are mainly centered around cricketing memorabilia related to New Zealand. There's also a cricket bat from 1743—one of the three oldest cricket bats in the world. It's open through the cricket season (Oct.–Apr.) daily 10:30 A.M.–3:30 P.M., weekends only the rest of the year.

Colonial Cottage Museum

This attractive two-story house (68 Nairn St., 04/384-9122; summer daily 10 A.M.–4 P.M., rest of the year Sat.–Sun. noon–4 P.M.; adult $5, senior $2.50, child $1.50) on a steep hill is quite a hike south from city center. Built in 1858 and slowly restored, the typically small rooms, steep staircase, and fine handcraftsmanship throughout this Victorian-era pioneer cottage give insight into life in Wellington's colonial days. From the Basin Reserve, walk west along Buckle Street to Taranaki Street and turn left. Turn right on Webb Street, left

on Thompson, right on Hankey, and immediately right on Nairn. The cottage is on the left side. Notice the mixture of assorted architectural styles in this hilly area.

Otari-Wilton's Bush

This pocket of natural forest is a 15-minute drive west of downtown at the junction of Wilton Road and Gloucester Street. Several walkways, graded and color-coded according to length and difficulty, run through this unique sanctuary "devoted solely to the cultivation and preservation of indigenous New Zealand plants." Eighty hectares (198 acres) of native bush and five hectares of cultivated garden contain more than 1,200 plant species, and the area is alive with native birds. Natural forest and cultivated gardens, rock garden and fishpond, fernery, alpine garden, and numerous picnic spots are just some of the features along the various trails. You'll often spot native wood pigeons, fantails, silvereyes, and kingfishers, along with introduced magpies, thrushes, goldfinches, and starlings; the beautiful native songbird, the *tui,* is often heard but rarely seen. To get there take a no. 14 Wilton bus from the city to the main entrance. It's open daily from dawn to dusk—to get the best out of your visit, take a picnic lunch.

Mount Victoria

The best place for orienting yourself to the layout of Wellington is from the top of Mt. Victoria (194 meters/640 ft), southeast of the city center. The summit lookout provides a 360-degree panorama and one of the best cityscapes of Wellington (unreal at night), and it's easy to get there by bus (a 15-minute ride from downtown, weekdays only) or car (get a map first). Catch a no. 20 bus at the railway station (every hour Mon.–Fri.), or on Lambton Quay, Willis Street, Cuba Street, Manners Street, or Courtenay Place. If you'd rather walk back down, several paths take at least 20 minutes through the forested town belt and suburb of Mt. Victoria, one of the oldest city suburbs (many colonial-style homes), to Courtenay Place where you can catch the bus back. If you're driving or cycling (guaranteed to get your old heart a-pumpin') from city center, take Jervois Quay south to Wakefield Street and turn left, then right on Kent Terrace and left on Majoribanks Street. Turn left on Hawker Street and follow the signs to the lookout.

Wellington Zoo

While small, Wellington's zoo in Newtown Park (Daniell St., 04/381-6750; daily 9:30 A.M.–5 P.M.; adult $15, child $6) is worth a visit for its nocturnal kiwi house and collection of *tuataras*. It also holds over 500 regular zoo animals—from cheetahs to giraffes. The zoo is four km (2.5 mi) south of downtown off Adelaide Road.

◖ Marine Drive

Thirty-km (19-mi) Marine Drive, "one of the world's best coastal drives" and a route anyone with wheels and a camera shouldn't miss, runs from **Oriental Bay** (southeast of the city center) along the inner harbor and outer shoreline to **Owhiro Bay.** The route takes you past at least 20 small bays and most of Wellington's sheltered sandy **beaches,** past built-up areas where striking homes perch on precarious sites high above the road (cable car systems lead up to some), and through surprisingly wild areas that seem quite uninhabited. The views along the route are stunning on a bright sunny day, but the locals claim that the drive is most spectacular during a southerly storm (preferably a gale). Start at Oriental Bay, an area of coffee shops, fashionable restaurants, and a strip of sandy beach where the younger set, and people-watchers in general, gather in large numbers (particularly in summer) to check each other out—it's a good place to find out the current Wellington trends in fashion, hairstyles, music, and flirting.

From Oriental Bay, Marine Drive is signposted here and there, but it really helps if you have a good, detailed map of the city center and outer suburbs to Cook Strait. The return route to the city sounds simple enough, but has the potential to become a nightmare without a map—from Owhiro Bay take the road

WELLINGTON

© ANDREW HEMPSTEAD

Marine Drive winds its way through suburban Wellington to Owhiro Bay.

through Happy Valley to the suburb of Brooklyn (about 28 km/17 mi), turn right on Brooklyn Road, go down the hill and straight ahead onto Upper Willis Street, and continue straight into the city center.

RECREATION

Several city walkway routes, devised by the Parks and Recreation Department, encourage walking through some of the most attractive areas of the "Harbour City." Pick up a city street map, the various brochures (*Northern Walkway, Southern Walkway,* and more) containing route descriptions and maps, a *Walking Around Wellington* pamphlet, and a *Discover Wellington* brochure, which contains scenic driving and walking routes; all are usually available at the Information Centre.

Red Rocks Coastal Walk

Red Rocks Walk begins south of the city center at Owhiro Bay. Although an enjoyable walk year-round, it is perhaps the most rewarding from April to early October when a colony of up to 100 New Zealand fur seals makes a rocky headland along the route its home. The seals migrate north from sub-Antarctic rookeries in April and then spend up to six months here recovering from their frantic southern breeding season. Only the bulls come north (the pregnant females stay behind) to feed and sleep (and give off a very distinct odor). They stay until October, when they return south to establish their territories in the rookeries before the pups are born. The walk to the colony and beyond begins from a quarry at Owhiro Bay (take the no. 1 bus to Island Bay and walk along the Esplanade). It is just over four km (2.5 mi) along a rough gravel road to Sinclair Head, but it's possible to drive the first three km (1.9 mi). Just before Sinclair Head is an outcrop of red rock formed about 200 million years ago when lava spewed from a volcano and then cooled on contact with water.

Makara Track

The six-km (3.7 mi) Makara Track, part of the New Zealand Walkways network, starts

and finishes at Makara Beach, 16 km (10 mi) northwest of Wellington. This popular walk lets hikers experience remote and rugged coastal scenery, fabulous views, hilly farmland, and good swimming at sheltered beaches. The "track" requires good fitness and takes about four hours round-trip; note that the inner section is closed during August and September for lambing. Wear good boots, take warm clothing (you'll be exposed to the wind, and quite possibly blown along the track in places), and carry water—there's nothing drinkable along the route. It's another good place to take a picnic. To get there from Wellington you need your own transportation and a map (the information center provides a free brochure); head for Karori Road in the western suburb of Karori West. Take Makara Road west and continue to Makara Beach, where the walkway is clearly signposted.

Kayaking

Queens Wharf, right downtown, is home to **Ferg's Kayaks** (04/499-8898), where you can rent kayaks for $10–30 per hour. Just don't challenge the owner, Ian Ferguson, to a kayaking race—he is generally regarded as New Zealand's greatest athlete ever, having won four gold medals at the Olympics in various kayaking disciplines. Instead, book a one-on-one lesson for $150 per hour.

ARTS AND ENTERTAINMENT

If you're in the mood for some action, pick up the free entertainment weekly *The Package,* which is available at venues throughout the city. An online version is at www.thepackage .co.nz. The daily newspapers list all the current movies and events, and Wellington Visitor Centre puts out the monthly *What's on in Wellington* leaflet.

Theater and Dance

Ticketek has an outlet at the **Westpac St. James Theatre** (77 Courtenay Pl., 04/384-3840) selling theater tickets, or check their website for a schedule (www.ticketek.co.nz). The grandly restored St. James is home to the

Royal New Zealand Ballet (04/381-9000) and combined with the Opera House (111 Manners St.) hosts opera, musicals, and touring shows. Beside the Museum of New Zealand Te Papa Tongarewa, **Circa Theatre** (1 Taranaki St., 04/801-7992) presents a wide variety of live theater throughout the year. Other performance venues to check out are the **Downstage Theatre** (corner of Cambridge Terr. and Courtenay Pl., 04/801-6946), with performances that range from classic to contemporary, and **Bats Theatre** (6 Majoribanks St., 04/802-4175), for cutting edge and innovative productions.

Nightlife

Bands come and go, as do venues, but some places have live music on a regular basis (good bands fetch a small cover charge). **Chicago Sports Café** enjoys an excellent location on Queens Wharf (04/473-4900). It's themed as a U.S. sports bar, and in addition to screenings of major overseas sporting events, bands play on weekends, and there's a quieter upstairs bar and pleasant courtyard. In the vicinity, the **Backbencher Pub** (34 Molesworth St., 04/472-3065) is in the heart of the politicians' territory and is especially busy at lunch and early evening.

Courtenay Place, the entertainment center of the city, has a wide variety of music venues and dance clubs. It's also popular with the younger (under 25) crowd. If any bar along this strip could be called refined, it would be the **Tasting Room** (2 Courtenay Pl., 04/384-1159), which has South Island–brewed Monteith's on tap and a better-than-average menu of dishes such as mussels steamed in green curry. Check out big and boisterous **Molly Malone's** (corner of Taranaki St. and Courtenay Pl., 04/384-2896; daily from 11 A.M.). Aside from the decidedly Irish atmosphere, bands play every Thursday, Friday, and Saturday nights, and on Monday and Wednesday nights it's "Irish night," with real Irish bands and no cover charge. The cavernous **Wellington Sports Café** (58 Courtenay Pl., 04/801-5115) has five huge TV screens showing sports from around the world. **Coyote**

Street Bar (63 Courtenay Pl., 04/385-6665) fills with serious dancers strutting their stuff to dance, hip-hop, techno, and progressive music.

With polished hardwood floors and stylish decor throughout, **St. John's Heineken Hotel** (5 Cable St., 04/801-8017), in a beautiful art deco building overlooking the harbor, is a great place for a quiet drink or meal. Off Courtenay Place heading away from downtown is **Hawthorn Lounge** (82 Tory St., 04/890-3724; Tues.–Sat. from 6 P.M.), where plush upholstery and an impressive cocktail list attract an older crowd.

Another center of nighttime action is Cuba Street. Here, **Matterhorn** (106 Cuba St., 04/384-3359; daily from 10 A.M.) is a Wellington institution. It started life in the 1960s as a Swiss café (hence the name, borrowed from an image taken by one of the original owners) and has gone through various lives before reaching its current incarnation as an unpretentious cocktail bar renowned for live music of all genres. In the vicinity is **San Francisco Bath House** (171 Cuba St., 04/801-6797; closed Sun.), which isn't a bathhouse, but rather a live music venue that is renowned for hosting popular underground acts.

Two blocks west of Cuba Street, **Bodega** (101 Ghuznee St., 04/384-8212) is a longtime favorite for local bands playing their own music to an alternative crowd. Monday features jazz and there's lots of New Zealand beers on tap and a decent menu of pub favorites.

Frontroom (5 Hania St., 04/939-1235) is a large-scale jazz venue with its own lounge bar and restaurant. You should call for a schedule as the venue hosts a variety of performances, including cabaret.

One of the capital's most popular gay and lesbian bars is **Sovereign** (Oaks Complex, Dixon St., 04/384-6024), while next door in the same building is **Pound** is a bar/nightclub with drag shows some nights.

Movies

For the latest in film, check out **Embassy Deluxe Theatre** (10 Kent Terr., 04/384-7657), a classic 1920s theater that was renovated in time to host the world premiere of *The Lord of the Rings*. **Regent on Manners** (73 Manners St., 04/472-5182) is a downtown theater showing first-run hits. **Penthouse Cinema** (205 Ohiro Rd., Brooklyn, 04/384-3157) is a modern suburban movie theater complex.

Festivals and Events

Like similar alternative theater events the world over, **Fringe** (04/382-8015, www.fringe.org.nz) attracts all types to a wide range of performances. Venues are as varied as the subject matter, but admission prices are inexpensive. The festival runs through the second half of February.

The **Cuba St. Carnival** (04/801-9390, www.cubacarnival.org.nz) celebrates the color of one of Wellington's most lively streets. Held the third weekend of February, the event features a great street market, food stalls, live entertainment, and the Illuminated Night Parade, which runs the length of the street.

In early March even years (2008, 2010, etc.), Wellington hosts the **New Zealand International Arts Festival** (04/473-0149, www.nzfestival.telecom.co.nz), which is launched with a spectacular harborfront fireworks display and continues through the month. It features Maori dancing, opera, ballet, theater, comedy, and jazz at open-air and indoor venues throughout the city.

Held over 10 days in early November, **Wellington International Jazz Festival** (04/496-5494, www.jazzfestival.co.nz) will surprise you with the quality of local talent, but the schedule also makes room for performers from the United States and elsewhere.

ACCOMMODATIONS AND CAMPING

Wellington may lack the usual array of upscale chains associated with capital cities, but it does have some excellent hotels within walking distance of downtown attractions. Overall, when coupled with a range of renovated hotels and historic bed-and-breakfasts, there is something in all budgets and for all tastes.

Under $50

Although Wellington lacks Auckland's choice of hostels and backpacker lodgings, the quality is of a similar standard and, best of all, most lie within walking distance of the city center.

As usual, **YHA Wellington City** (04/801-7280, www.yha.co.nz; dorm beds $22, doubles from $28 per person), at the corner of Wakefield Street and Cambridge Terrace, does everything well. The building used to be a hotel, and there's lots of space and facilities. Although it's quite a walk from the railway station, a supermarket and the museum are both across the road.

Opposite the railway station, **Downtown Backpackers** (1 Bunny St., 04/473-8482 or 0800/225-725, www.downtownbackpackers.co.nz; dorm beds $21–24, $58 s, $75–85 d) is in the grand old Waterloo Hotel (the queen stayed here on her 1953 Coronation Tour). This place has plenty of room for everyone, with a big lounge, TV room, and kitchen. There's also a bar, café, and tour desk.

Unlike the large-scale lodges in the downtown core, **Maple Lodge** (52 Ellice St., Mt. Victoria, 04/385-3771; dorm beds $22, $32 s, $48 d), a 15-minute walk from downtown, is more personable and quieter.

$50-100

The old **Cambridge Hotel** (28 Cambridge Terr., 04/385-8829, www.cambridgehotel.co.nz; shared bathroom $75 s or d, en suite $95) has been graciously restored, with each upstairs guestroom having a TV, fridge, tea- and coffee-making facilities, and Internet access. Downstairs is a bar and restaurant.

Above downtown, **◖ Shepherds Arms Hotel** (285 Tinakori Rd., 04/472-1320 or 0800/393-782, www.shepherds.co.nz; $85–140 s or d) has been taking in guests since 1870. Restored by the original owners' descendants, it has 14 guest rooms, some with shared bathrooms. Those with four-poster beds (the Queen Deluxe are the best value) feature modern timber furnishings, hardwood flooring, and comfortable leather couches. The hotel also has a recommended bar and restaurant.

If you plan to do your own cooking and want to be within walking distance of downtown, **Halswell Lodge** (21 Kent Terr., 04/385-0196, www.halswell.co.nz) is a good choice. The lodge comprises three buildings, each with a different type of accommodation. Small hotel rooms with shared kitchen are $89 s or d; motel rooms are $135 s, $145 d; and rooms, some with spa baths, in a restored 1920s villa are $145–160 s or d.

Out of town to the north, [(**Moana Lodge** (49 Moana Rd., 04/233-2010, www.moanalodge.co.nz; dorm beds $26, $40 s, $56–70 s or d) has a delightful waterfront location in suburban Plimmerton. The amenities—living area, communal kitchen, and more—are all of the highest standard, and kayaks are available for guest use.

$100-150

[(**Eight Parliament Street** (8 Parliament St., 04/499-0808, www.boutique-bb.co.nz, $120–185 s or d) is an upscale bed-and-breakfast in a beautifully renovated timber house high above the downtown core. Even though the house is over 100 years old, the decor throughout is decidedly contemporary, including modern furnishings in the lounge area and private courtyard. Rates include a gourmet breakfast.

Tinakori Lodge (182 Tinakori St., 04/939-3478, www.tinakorilodge.co.nz; $99–120 s, $140–170 d) has delightful owners. The nine guest rooms, some with shared bathrooms, all have plenty of character, while the inviting conservatory has tea- and coffee-making supplies and daily papers. Rates include a self-serve breakfast.

Along one of the city's most interesting streets, but still within walking distance of everywhere, is **Comfort Hotel Wellington** (213 Cuba St., 04/385-2153, www.comfortwellington.co.nz; $135 s or d), which is filled with plain but adequate guest rooms, each with an en suite and tea/coffee-making facilities. Amenities include a laundry and two streetside cafés.

Immediately north of downtown, in suburban Johnsonville, is **Capital Gateway Motor Lodge** (1 Newlands Rd., 04/478-7812 or 0800/996-996, www.capitalgateway.co.nz). This Tudor-style accommodation features spacious, well-decorated rooms and a huge spread of grassy lawn. The in-house restaurant opens for dinner Monday–Saturday. Studio units are $129 s or d, one-bedroom units rent for $149, and two-bedroom units for $190.

Farther north along Highway 1 is a number of hotels and motels within a 15-minute drive or train trip of downtown. One of the best of these is **Aotea Lodge** (Whitford Brown Ave., Papakowahai, 04/237-4257, www.aotealodge.co.nz; $120–160 s or d), which offers 38 simple yet large guest rooms, many with kitchens. The lodge also has a large swimming pool complex and a restaurant with alfresco dining.

$150-200

The centrally located **Mercure Hotel** (355 Willis St., 04/803-1000, www.mercure.com; $155 s or d) has 85 standard hotel rooms. Facilities include an indoor heated pool, a small fitness room, room service, a bar, and a restaurant.

Close to Museum of New Zealand Te Papa Tongarewa, **Bay Plaza** (40–44 Oriental Pde., 04/385-7799; $155 s or d) is a solid mid-priced choice, with fairly standard rooms, a restaurant, a bar, a laundry, free daily papers, and plenty of free parking out the back.

Central City Apartment Hotel (130 Victoria St., 04/385-4166, www.centralcityhotels.co.nz; $160–240) is exactly that—very central. Half the rooms have tea- and coffee-making facilities, while the other half have a full kitchen. The rooms all configured differently, with some studios, some one-bedroom suites, and some two-bedroom suites.

Abel Tasman Hotel (169 Willis St., 04/385-1304 or 0800/843-827, www.abeltasmanhotel.co.nz; $185 s or d, $209 with a kitchen) is an eight-story property right in the heart of the city. The 76 rooms are nothing special, but each has a writing desk, and downstairs is a restaurant. Room rates are greatly reduced on weekends.

Your host at the aptly named **Booklovers**

B&B (123 Pirie St., Mt. Victoria, 04/384-2714, www.bbnb.co.nz; $150 s, $180 d) is award-winning New Zealand author Jane Tolerton. The three handsome guest rooms each have an en suite and there are plenty of communal living areas filled with reading material. Rates include a big cooked breakfast.

Over $200

(Museum Hotel (90 Cable St., 04/385-2809, www.museumhotel.co.nz; $220–340 s or d) is a low-rise hostelry with harbor views from the top couple of stories (from $260). The hotel was originally built where the Te Papa museum now stands. Rather than demolish it to make room for the new museum, a decision was made to move it to a new site, 120 meters (390 ft) away. The move—one of the largest of an entire building ever attempted anywhere in the world—was a success. Along with a new location, the rooms underwent a major refurbishment, now featuring LCD TVs, wireless Internet, luxurious bathrooms, and original art throughout public areas.

Mercure Hotel Wellington (345 The Terrace, 04/385-9829 or 0800/288-880, www.accor hotel.co.nz; from $240 s or d) features 111 standard hotel rooms, each with modern decor and some with harbor views. Facilities include an indoor heated pool, business center, fitness room, restaurant, and bar. Disregard the rack rate, and book rooms online for around $150.

Bolton Hotel (corner Bolton and Mowbray Sts., 04/472-9966 or 0800/996-622, www .boltonhotel.co.nz; $240–360 s or d) is one of the city's finest accommodations. Luxuriously furnished in a classic yet earthy style, studios have king beds while suites have a kitchen. The hotel also features a restaurant and bar. As always with top-end hotels, check the website for deals, especially on weekends.

Holiday Parks

On the north side of downtown in suburban Johnsonville, camping with power hookups at **Capital Gateway Motor Lodge** (1 Newlands Rd., 04/478-7812 or 0800/996-996, www .capitalgateway.co.nz) is $33. Campers have use

of a kitchen and laundry, and the lodge restaurant is open daily except Sunday for dinner.

Another option is **Hutt Park Holiday Village** (04/568-5913 or 0800/488-872, www .huttpark.co.nz), around 13 km (eight mi) north of Wellington in Lower Hutt (also see listing in the *Hutt Valley and Vicinity* section earlier in this chapter).

FOOD

You'll find good cafés and restaurants almost everywhere you look in Wellington; at last count the city had more than 100 cafés alone. Concentrations of inexpensive cafés lie along Cuba Street and Courtenay Place, while the waterfront comes alive with diners in warmer weather. The downtown core also has a wide variety of ethnic restaurants—a good place for a cheap and cheerful meal.

Cafés

Right downtown, at **(Espressoholic** (128 Courtenay Pl., 04/384-7790; daily 8 A.M.–11 P.M.), the walls of this big black room are covered in murals, the staff is mostly pierced and dressed in black, and the clientele ranges from mall rats to suited businessmen. Through it all, the service is smart and surprisingly professional. But most importantly, the food is wonderful (the oversized chicken, pineapple, and camembert burger was a delight).

Once you've filled your arms with reading material from the visitor center, head to **Nui Espresso** (101 Wakefield St., 04/801-4188; Mon.–Fri. 7:30 A.M.–5:30 P.M., Sat.–Sun. 9 A.M.–5 P.M.), which is part of the same building. It offers delicious filled rolls, decent coffee and a variety of cakes. Canadians may want to stop by for a Nanaimo Bar (but someone should point out the correct spelling of this chocolate layered delight).

Sheltering under a high rise almost across from the visitor center, **(Felix** (128 Wakefield St., 04/499-5523; daily 7:30 A.M.–4:30 P.M.) has an uninspiring but modern look. Yet, the food is outstanding. For breakfast, the porridge with brown sugar and cream ($8) is a sweet treat, or go healthy and order the Power

Breakfast ($14), comprising poached eggs, cooked tomatoes, and mushrooms on a bed of greens. The rest of the day the creative fish and pasta dishes shine.

Along Cuba Street are a number of small cafés attracting loyal local clientele. Upbeat **Midnight Espresso Bar** (178 Cuba St., 04/384-7014; daily for breakfast and lunch) has a good range of coffee from around the world. A few doors down the hill is **Olive Café** (170 Cuba St., 04/802-5266), spanning two old shopfronts. The decor is very plain—the walls are whitewashed, and that's about it. Head here for a caffeine fix. Across the road, another cheap place is **Steinburg Bakery** (181 Cuba St., 04/801-5333). Just off the lower end of Cuba Street, **Dixon Street Delicatessen** (45 Dixon St., 04/384-2436) is stocked daily with gourmet breads, bagels, meats, pickles, preserves, and seafood delicacies, such as smoked salmon and mussels. Eat in or have lunch packed to go.

Te Papa Café (Cable St., 04/381-7051; daily 9 A.M.–5 P.M.) stretches around the harborside facade of the Museum of New Zealand. It's a bright, modern space, with food to match. Eggs Benedict is $14, beer-battered fish-and-chips is $14.50, or tuck into a steak sandwich for $17. On Level 4 of the museum is **Espresso** (daily 10 A.M.–6 P.M.), serving up coffee and cakes in a relaxed setting.

Behind the museum and just off Cambridge Terrace is **Café L'Affare** (27 College St., 04/385-9748; Mon.–Fri. 7 A.M.–4 P.M., Sat. 8 A.M.–4 P.M.). The epicenter of the action is the coffee-roaster, in plain view through the open kitchen. Café L'Affare imports the coffee beans, along with upscale espresso machines, and distributes them both throughout the country, so you can be assured of a good, fresh, strong cup of coffee from these guys. The food is also good, with breakfast served all day, and lunch specialties highlighted by a great Caesar salad ($11.50).

Pub Fare

Pub meals are usually filling and a good value, with the added bonus of a bar and entertainment of some sort (usually big-screen movies or rock videos weeknights, disco or live music Friday and Saturday nights).

Calling itself a "gastropub," the **Tasting Room** (2 Courtenay Pl., 04/384-1159; weekdays from 11 A.M., weekends from 10 A.M.) is a stylish space in the heart of the entertainment district. In addition to a great selection of traditional ales, you can order cheese fondue as a starter ($10 per person) and then move onto a spicy wild venison sausage main ($18), or go all out by ordering a chateaubriand for two ($65).

The historic **Shepherds Arms Hotel** (285 Tinakori Rd., Thorndon, 04/472-13207; daily 11:30 A.M.–3 P.M. and 5–9:30 P.M.) has a cozy little dining room open daily for lunch and dinner. Traditional New Zealand ingredients with a global twist are a step up from regular pub dining, while on weekends the brunch menu includes a stack of pancakes doused with Canadian maple syrup, eggs Benedict, and a gourmet cheese omelet.

Food With a View

On a sunny day, *the* place to have lunch is the waterfront—with your legs dangling off Queens Wharf—and the necessary food item is takeaway fish-and-chips. Before locating your perfect waterfront spot, head straight for the fish markets at the north end of Shed 5, a redeveloped waterfront warehouse, where you can buy freshly battered fish, chips, and coleslaw for $10. Avoid going noon–1 P.M. weekdays, when there's always a long line. In the same building is **Shed 5 Restaurant & Bar** (Queens Wharf, 04/499-9069; daily 11 A.M.–10 P.M.), a massive restaurant in a converted woolshed. It offers reasonably priced lunchtime specials and outdoor seating on the wharf. Try mussels steamed in a mild curry broth ($14.50). Dinner is a more elaborate (and expensive) affair, but seafood dominates the menu; the abalone salad is $26 while other mains range $32–38. In nearby Shed 3, **Dockside** (04/499-9900) attracts a business crowd for lunch weekdays, but is also open daily for dinner. Some of the seafood is seasonal, but dishes like seafood chowder ($17) and blackened tuna with chili and marmalade glaze ($29) are year-round highlights.

Maori

❮ Kai in the City (21 Marjoribanks St., 04/801-5006; Tues.–Sun. from 6 P.M.) is a small, welcoming restaurant featuring Maori cuisine. You will find tastes of traditional food throughout the North Island, but this is one of the other restaurants where it is a specialty, complete with a menu that explains the various ingredients. Mussel fritters, *paua* dishes, kumara and corn fritters, roasted muttonbird—everything is good and well priced (platters to share $32–40, mains $23–30). The wine list is also notable for its exclusion of all non–New Zealand wines, as well as many from Tohu Wines, a Maori-owned vineyard near Nelson.

Asian

Across from the waterfront, **Wellington City Market** (129 Jervois Quay, 04/801-8991; Fri.–Sun. 10 A.M.–5:30 P.M.) is a rabbit warren of outlets selling everything imaginable. Off to one side is the always-busy food court, where vendors serve up inexpensive sushi, whole barbecue ducks, *nasi goreng* (Indonesian rice), freshly squeezed juices—you name it.

Istana Malaysia (5 Allen St., 04/471-2909; daily for lunch and dinner) is a large place, with an inexpensive Southeast Asian menu of dishes under $20, even seafood such as garlic prawns. The setting is earthy and refined, making Istana excellent value.

Great India Restaurant (141 Manners St., 04/384-5755) looks simple from the outside, but don't let first impressions deceive you. This stylish restaurant features elegant furnishings and well-prepared dishes, of which the tandooris ($17–20) are excellent. Off Courtenay Place, **Little India** (18 Blair St., 04/384-9989) is open weekdays for lunch and daily for dinner from 5 P.M. You'll find a menu filled with curries and vindaloos ($16–21), as well as less familiar choices such as *Murg Mumtaz* ($16), a chicken-based dish which combines classic tandoori cooking with curry. And don't forget

to order delicious side dishes such as papadums, coconut-dipped banana slices, and mint chutney ($1.50–4 each).

Peking House (15 Kent Terr., 04/384-1008; Fri.–Sat. noon–2:30 P.M., daily 5:30–10:30 P.M.) serves up Beijing specialties like Peking duck. The lunch and dinner specials are good deals if you want to sample lots of everything on the menu.

Upscale

In more of the splurge category there's **Logan Brown** (192 Cuba St., 04/801-5114; Mon.–Fri. noon–2 P.M., daily for dinner). Housed in an opulently restored 1920s bank building, this restaurant has a reputation as one of Wellington's finest. The three-course table d'hôte bistro menu, offered at lunch and before 7:30 P.M., takes from the regular menu, but at the reduced price of $30. Main courses alone range $23–35 and include innovative seafood dishes, the very best cuts of beef and venison, and local delicacies such as *paua* (abalone) ravioli. The wine list includes hard-to-get New Zealand wines, as well as premium labels from around the world.

INFORMATION
Information Centers

The main source of city and regional information is **Wellington Visitor Centre** (Civic Centre, corner of Wakefield and Victoria Sts., 04/802-4860, www.wellingtonnz.com; daily 8:30 A.M.–5 P.M., until 6 P.M. in summer), and the knowledgeable staff dispenses free brochures and pamphlets on attractions, walks, accommodations, and restaurants; all the latest entertainment and transportation information; and a city street map ($1). The staff also makes bus and ferry bookings. Grab a coffee at the adjacent café and check your email at the computer terminals.

There's also an information center at the Arrivals level of the airport which remains open until around 8 P.M.

The **Department of Conservation** maintains an information center in the old Government Building (15 Lambton Quay,

04/472-7356; Mon.–Fri. 9 A.M.–4:30 P.M., Sat. 10 A.M.–3 P.M.). This is a great place to load up on park information and pick up a permit for Kapiti Island (described earlier in this chapter).

Libraries

At **Wellington Central Library** (65 Victoria St., 04/801-4040; Mon.–Thurs. 9:30 A.M.–8:30 P.M., Fri. until 9 P.M., Sat. until 5 P.M.), the first (ground) floor is devoted to fiction, the second floor contains magazines, and the third floor holds newspapers from around the world. The library also features a large travel section (third floor), a reference room, computer terminals, a café, and a bookshop.

The **National Library of New Zealand** (corner of Molesworth and Aitken Sts., 04/474-3000, www.natlib.govt.nz; Mon.–Fri. 9 A.M.–5 P.M., Sat. 9 A.M.–1 P.M., Sun. 1–4 P.M.) holds a large number of literature collections. Particularly impressive is the number of New Zealand and South Pacific books, which are held along with newspapers, magazines, and maps from throughout the region. This library also has large archives and a good website.

Wellington City Archives (28 Barker St., off Cambridge Terr., 04/801-2096, Mon.–Fri. 10 A.M.–4:30 P.M.) contains the history of the capital, from 1842 when it first became a borough, in print and audio.

Bookstores

Unity Books (57 Willis St., 04/499-4245) is an independent bookseller with a wide range of New Zealand and travel titles. **Parson's Books & Music** (126 Lambton Quay, 04/472-4587) has a similar selection, as well as homegrown music and an upstairs café. **Capital Books** (110 Featherson St., 04/473-9358) has knowledgeable staff and a good collection of non-fiction titles. The **Map Shop** (193 Vivian St., 04/385-1462, www.mapshop.co.nz) has the city's best selection of maps, including topographical maps and marine charts, as well as field guides. The chain bookstores are centered along Lambton Quay. These include **Bennetts Bookshop** (corner of Lambton

Quay and Bowen St., 04/499-3433), **Dymocks Booksellers** (366 Lambton Quay, 04/472-2080), and **Whitcoulls** (312 Lambton Quay, 04/472-1921).

Looking for out-of-print or secondhand books? Then head uptown to **Arty Bee's Books** (17 Courtenay Pl., 04/385-1819).

SERVICES

Regular shopping hours are Monday–Thursday 9 A.M.–5 P.M., Friday till 9 P.M., and Saturday 9 A.M.–1 P.M. Sunday is very quiet in downtown Wellington, although some of the touristy shops remain open. **New Zealand Post** has outlets at 280 Lambton Quay and 43 Manners Street. Get online at the visitor center, or at **Cybernomad** (43 Courtenay Pl., 04/801-5964) or **Cyber City** (97–99 Courtenay Pl., 04/384-3717).

Emergency

Wellington Hospital is on Riddiford Street, Newtown (04/385-5999). **City Medical Centre** is at 10 Brandon Street (04/471-2161), while the **After Hours Pharmacy** is at 17 Adelaide Road (04/385-8810).

GETTING THERE

Wellington is, not surprisingly, one of the easiest places in New Zealand to get to by public transportation. It has an international airport, local-bus and long-distance-coach depots, a railway station, an overseas cruise-liner terminal, a ferry terminal, a fast motorway leading in and out of the city, all the major car rental companies, and taxis.

Air

Wellington International Airport (www.wellington-airport.co.nz) is eight km (five mi) from downtown on the south side of the city. The most direct access is a tunnel leading through Mount Victoria, although the coastal drive starting from Oriental Parade is more scenic.

The Departures level is upstairs, where you find a duty-free store, bank, bookstore, and a café. Downstairs on the Arrivals level is a small information center (daily 8 A.M.–7 P.M.) and desks for all the major rental car companies. **Air New Zealand** (04/388-9737 or 0800/737-300, www.airnewzealand.com), the primary domestic carrier, has direct flights from Wellington to Auckland, Hamilton, Rotorua, Gisborne, Nelson, Christchurch, Dunedin, and many smaller towns. Other airlines flying into Wellington include **Origin Pacific** (0800/302-302), **Polynesian Airlines** (0800/800-993), **Qantas** (0800/808-767), and **Soundsair** (04/801-0111 or 0800/505-005).

Super Shuttle (04/387-8787) offers a door-to-door shuttle between the airport and downtown hotels for $15 each way. **Stagecoach Flyer** (04/801-7000) is a city-operated scheduled service that runs between the airport and downtown every 30 minutes for $9 each way. Depending on the traffic, a cab to downtown runs $25–35.

Train

The main entrance to the **Wellington Railway Station** is off Bunny Street (between Featherston and Waterloo Quay), north of the Civic Centre. Inside the station is the **Tranz Scenic Travel Centre** (Mon.–Fri. 7:30 A.M.–5:30 P.M., Sat.–Sun. 7:30–11:30 A.M.), which has long-distance train, bus, and ferry information. You'll find luggage lockers beside Platform 9; they're open daily 6 A.M.–10 P.M. and cost $1 for 24 hours.

WELLINGTON

CROSSING COOK STRAIT

From Wellington, onward southbound travel necessitates a crossing of Cook Strait to the **South Island.** Whether you get your first glimpse of landfall from aboard the ferry as it enters Marlborough Sound or through the window of a plane bound for Picton, Nelson, or Christchurch, the wild untamed landscape makes it obvious that new and very different experiences await.

FERRY

The most popular way to cross Cook Strait is by ferry. **Interislander** (04/498-3302 or 0800/802-802, www.interislander.co.nz) operates three vessels that cross year-round between downtown Wellington and Picton. These large ferries carry passengers, vehicles, and boxcars; each has an information center, cafeteria, restaurant, gift shop, newsstand, cinema ($8 per movie), bar, work desks, play room, and Club Class ($25 extra) for added comfort. The 83-km (52-mi) crossing usually takes about 3.5 hours. One-way fares are adult $65, child $42, vehicle and driver $225. These prices are for "Easy Change" bookings made from overseas or close to the time of booking. You can save quite a bit of money by booking as far ahead as possible from within New Zealand (at visitor centers, travel agencies, or by calling 0800/802-802) and being prepared to travel outside peak periods. **Bluebridge** (04/471-6188 or 0800/844-844, www.bluebridge.co.nz) is a similar operation, with a set pricing model (adult $49, vehicle and driver $169) regardless of when the booking is made. Both terminals are well signposted off Waterloo Quay in downtown Wellington. Check in your luggage up to one hour before sailing (the earlier the better if you want to avoid long lines). Ticket check-in is 30 minutes ahead of sailing, an hour if you have a vehicle.

If you're driving a rental car, call the agency and let them know your schedule. You will leave your vehicle at the Wellington terminal and another will be waiting for you at Picton. You'll need to sign a new contract, but pricing remains the same (it's still classed as a single rental period).

AIR

Flying is the quicker option, and preferred if the ocean is rough, as it often is in winter. **Soundsair** (04/801-0111 or 0800/505-005, www.soundsair.com) flies between Wellington International Airport and Picton several times a day. The fare of $79 one-way includes transfers into downtown Picton from the local airfield.

The *Overlander* is a long-distance train linking Wellington to Auckland via Palmerston North, National Park, and Hamilton, while the *Capital Connection* is a weekday-only train between Wellington and Palmerston North.

Bus

You'll find the **Intercity Terminal** at Platform 9 at the railway station, on the Bunny Street side. Intercity (www.intercitycoach.co.nz) runs from Wellington to Auckland, Hamilton, Rotorua, Tauranga, Palmerston North, New Plymouth, Wanganui—in fact, just about everywhere you want to go—with connections everywhere else. Make bookings in the railway station at the **Tranz Scenic Travel Centre** or call 04/472-5111. Intercity also stops at the Interislander ferry terminal, with a timetable designed to provide a link to departing and arriving ferries.

GETTING AROUND
Metlink

Once you're in Wellington, it's easy to get around by local transportation—bus service is excellent and numerous special fares encourage further exploration by train and bus, which come together under Metlink (800/801-700, www.metlink.org.nz). Buses run throughout the city from the railway station daily 7 A.M.–11 P.M., while the station is also the departure point for **Tranz Metro** trains running north along five routes including to Paraparaumu (Kapiti Coast) and through the Hutt Valley to Masterton in the Wairarapa. There are a myriad of fare options, with sector fares ranging $1–3.50. Day pass options include a DayTripper ($6 for travel after 9 A.M. within city limits) and a Metlink Explorer ($15 for travel to the Kapiti Coast, with kids riding for free).

The canary-yellow buses you see around downtown are running the **City Circular** route, which includes stoops at major attractions and places like the visitor center. They run Monday–Saturday 6 A.M.–11 A.M., Sunday 8 A.M.–10:30 A.M., and the fare is $3 per trip. City Circular is also included on the various Metlink passes.

Taxi

You'll find taxi stands at Wellington Railway Station, on Whitmore Street (between Lambton Quay and Featherston St.), outside the James Smith Hotel on Lambton Quay, on the Bond Street corner (off Willis St.), outside the Woolworth's Store on Dixon Street, and at the Willis and Aro Streets intersection. Taxi companies include **Gold and Black Taxis** (04/388-8888), **Harbour City Taxis** (04/388-8111), **A1 Taxis** (04/384-4444), and **Wellington City Cabs** (04/388-8000).

Car Rental

All the major car rental agencies (and many minor ones) have offices in Wellington, and a couple have outlets at the ferry terminal. The major companies don't allow their vehicles on the ferry (besides, it's expensive). Instead, you must leave the vehicle in Wellington at the ferry dock, catch the ferry across to the south island, and pick up another in Picton; let your rental company know the dates, and they'll do the paperwork. The major agencies include **Apex** (04/385-2163), **Avis** (04/802-1088), **Budget** (04/802-4548), **Hertz** (04/384-3809), **NZ Rent-a-car** (04/384-2745), **Rent-a-dent** (04/473-8789), and **Thrifty** (04/388-9494). As throughout the country, smaller companies offer competitive rates, including **Darn Cheap Rentals** (04/568-2777 or 0800/800-327, www.darncheaprentals.co.nz).

Tours

Hammonds (04/472-0869) has been showing visitors around the capital for decades. The 2.5-hour tour includes downtown highlights, Mt. Victoria, and a drive along the coastal area south of downtown. The cost is adult $50, child $25 and it departs daily at 10 A.M. and 2 P.M. from the visitor center. The company also offers a four-hour excursion up the Kapiti Coast (adult $80, child $40) and an all-day adventure out to Palliser Bay (adult $165, child $82.50, includes lunch). The latter trip includes stops at locations used for filming *The Lord of the Rings,* or join a **Flat Earth** (04/977-5805 or 0800/775-805) tour, for which film sites used for *The Lord of the Rings* are the highlight.

A fun and inexpensive way to appreciate Wellington's harbor aspect is to catch the **Dominion Post Ferry** (04/499-1282, www.eastbywest.co.nz; adult $8.50 one-way, senior $7, child $4) between Queens Wharf and Days Bay. At Days Bay visit Williams Park and the beach (favorite summertime hangouts for Wellingtonians toting barbecues and picnic lunches), look through local shops and galleries, eat at the restaurants, go for nearby bush walks, or hike along the Pencarrow Coast where New Zealand's first permanent lighthouse still stands. Many weekend sailings stop at **Somes Island,** formerly a quarantine station and now a pleasant place for a short hike.

Palmerston North

The geographical and regional center of the Manawatu region is "Palmy," a city of 65,000 on the banks of the Manawatu River 60 km (37 mi) southeast of Wanganui and 142 km (88 mi) north of Wellington. As home of Massey University, New Zealand's second-largest university, the population rises and falls with the seasons, but it's a pleasant place to visit at any time of the year and well worth a stop before continuing south to Wellington.

SIGHTS AND RECREATION

Te Manawa

This large downtown complex (396 Main St., 06/355-5000; daily 10 A.M.–5 P.M., Thurs. until 8 P.M.) cleverly combines an art gallery, museum, and science center. Admission to the former two is free, while it costs adult $8, senior $5, child $5 for entry to the science displays. The gallery will answer all your questions about what New Zealand artists are doing in the worlds of painting, ceramics, and sculpture. The museum section of Te Manawa features the history of the district from Maori to European settlements, and the beginning of the local dairy industry.

New Zealand Rugby Museum

If you're still in a museum mood, the **New Zealand Rugby Museum** (87 Cuba St., 06/358-6947; Mon.–Sat. 10 A.M.–noon and daily 1:30–4:30 P.M.; adult $5, child $2) is a must for anyone interested in New Zealand's national sport. Photographs, badges, jerseys, caps, and all sorts of rugby paraphernalia from around the world occupy this niche museum.

Parks

Palmerston North is an attractively laid out city where the emphasis has been given to shady parks and flower-filled gardens. **The Square,** a six-hectare (15-acre) park in the middle of the city, provides welcome green relief to the busy commercial center. Saunter past perfect lawns, beds of shrubs and flowers, and all sorts of trees, and don't miss the sunken gardens, floral clock, ornamental ponds and fountains, and chiming clock tower. In summer, large numbers of Palmerstonians head for The Square for lunch or afternoon tea, and throughout the year it hosts a variety of outdoor musical events.

One of the most popular city parks, **The Esplanade** (a couple of blocks south of The Square—walk down Fitzherbert Ave.) covers 25 hectares (62 acres) of bush and gardens along the banks of the Manawatu River and will appeal to all your senses. Within its boundaries is a swimming pool (06/357-2684), an aviary of native and exotic birds, rose gardens, a tropical plant conservatory, riverside nature trails, and scented gardens. The indoor pool is open daily 6 A.M.–9 P.M. Easter through October, outdoor pool open October–April. Drive through the park by entering at Park Road. Within a short walk of The Esplanade (heading east, cross Fitzherbert Ave. onto Centennial Dr.) is **Centennial Lake,** home to a large percentage

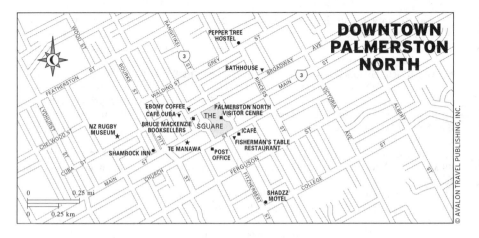

DOWNTOWN PALMERSTON NORTH

© AVALON TRAVEL PUBLISHING, INC.

of the Palmerston duck population, and a good place for a few hours' suntanning in a canoe or paddleboat (available for hire on weekends). For more park, reserve, walkway, beach, and river suggestions, ask at the information center.

South of the River

For terrific views of Palmerston North, the surrounding countryside, and (on a clear day) Mt. Ruapehu to the north and Mt. Taranaki to the northwest, take a short drive to **Anzac Park** (about four km south of the city along the southern banks of the river), where there's a lookout and observatory; cross the river at Fitzherbert Bridge and turn left on Cliff Road just before the university turnoff. **Massey University,** five km (three mi) south, is a 35-hectare (86-acre) campus consisting of an intriguing blend of historic homesteads and ultramodern architecture set in superb surroundings; from city center take Fitzherbert Street south, cross the river, and turn right on Tennent Drive. **Bledisloe Park,** on the northern campus boundary, is a quiet place for a bit of reading or a swim in a small woodland stream; it's off Tennent Drive just before the university entrance.

ACCOMMODATIONS

Backpackers can stay in a homey setting at **Pepper Tree Hostel** (121 Grey St., 06/355-4054, www.yha.co.nz; dorm beds $23, $42

s, $54 d). Bright, uncrowded dorm rooms, a well-equipped kitchen, a comfy TV lounge with piano, an outside barbecue area, and off-street parking are all provided in this lodge five blocks north of the The Square.

As a transportation hub and major convention city, Palmerston North has a great many hotels and motels, with most lining the main highways into the city. Many of Palmerston North's old hotels offer convenient, affordable accommodations, including the **Shamrock Inn** (267 Main St. W,. 06/355-2130, www.shamrock.co.nz; $55 s, $75 d), three blocks west of The Square. Each of the 20 rooms has an en suite while downstairs is a restaurant and bar.

Fitzherbert Avenue, south from downtown, holds the most motel choices, including my pick, **Kauri Court Motor Lodge** (248 Fitzherbert Ave., 06/356-6040, www.kauricourt.co.nz; $98–140 s or d), where each of the 12 units has a kitchen, Internet access, and plunger coffee. **Shadzz Motel and Conference Centre** (145 Fitzherbert Ave., 06/357-9145 or 0800/505-252, wwwshadzz.co.nz; $105–135 s or d) is a futuristic-looking black-and-white motel featuring guest rooms last revamped in 2005, each with a spa bath, kitchen, and large TV.

FOOD

Ebony Coffee (14 George St., 06/359-3303; closed Sun.) pours delicious coffee roasted at

WELLINGTON

its nearby factory. It's off the west end of The Square among many other cafés and restaurants. Also here is **Café Cuba** (corner George and Cuba Sts., 06/356-5750; daily from 8 A.M.), which has toned down its bohemian feel yet continues to serve up a delicious array of sweet treats.

Broadway Avenue, running northeast from The Square, has a number of good casual eateries. One of the best of these, **(BathHouse** (161 Broadway Ave., 06/952-5570; daily 10 A.M.–9 P.M.), features a wonderful courtyard filled with ferns and palms and with a retractable roof for sunny days. Porridge smothered in brown sugar and raisins ($10) is great for a late breakfast. Lighter options include Thai chicken curry ($20) and a memorable savory cheesecake ($28).

Fishermen's Table Restaurant (corner of Church St. and Fitzherbert Ave., 06/357-2157; daily 11:30 A.M.–2 P.M. and 5–9 P.M.) offers predictable seafood-dominated lunch and dinner menus, with dinner mains mostly under $30.

PRACTICALITIES
Information and Services
The source of all the Palmerston North information you need is the excellent **Palmerston North Visitor Centre** in The Square (06/350-1922, www.manawatunz.co.nz; Mon.–Fri. 9 A.M.–5 P.M., Sat.–Sun. 10 A.M.–4 P.M.).

Bruce MacKenzie Booksellers (51 George St., 06/356-9922) has a great collection of local non-fiction and New Zealand literature.

The post office is at 388 Church Street. **Sunshine Super Laundry** (392 Ferguson St., 06/358-6719) is open long hours daily.

Palmerston North Hospital is on Ruahine Street (06/356-9169). **Victoria Medical Centre** is at 482 Church Street (06/952-5560).

Getting There and Around
Palmerston North's **Milson Airport** is about five km (three mi) north of the city center—a $15 cab ride from downtown. **Air New Zealand** (0800/737-300, www.airnewzealand .com) has direct flights from Palmerston North to Auckland, Wellington, and Christchurch. Palmerston North is on the main north–south railway line (Auckland to Wellington). The **railway station** is off Tremaine Avenue. **Intercity** (www.intercitycoach.co.nz) provides the city with regular service from all over the North Island, with many runs requiring a bus change in nearby Bulls for a connection into the city. The main depot is the Palmerston North Travel Centre (corner of Pitt and Main Sts., 06/355-4955).

Car rental companies in Palmerston North include **Avis** (06/357-0168) and **Hertz** (06/357-0921). For a cab, call **Manawatu Taxi** (06/355-5111).

Wairarapa

Across the Tararua Range to the east of Palmerston North is the Wairarapa region, a wide swathe of pastoral land that slopes gradually to the remote southeastern coast of the North Island. Only one main road traverses the Wairarapa, Highway 2, which winds its way down from Hawke's Bay to Woodville, where Highway 3 provides a link to Palmerston North and Highway 2 continues southward to Masterton and the wine region of Martinborough, before crossing the Rimutaka Range to the Hutt Valley, gateway to Wellington.

PALMERSTON NORTH TO MASTERTON
From Palmerston North, Highway 3 makes a wide loop to the northeast through a low area of land between the Ruahine and Tararua Ranges before linking up with Highway 2. Allow 20 minutes to reach Woodville, from where it's 81 km (50 miles) south to Masterton.

Tui Brewery
This historic brewery (06/376-0815; daily 10 A.M.–4 P.M.) lies in the small village of

Mangatainoka, 36 km (22 mi) from Palmerston North. Established in 1889, Tui grew to become one of New Zealand's most successful small-town breweries. Brewing giant DB Breweries bought it in 1969, but the beer remains the same, with its distinctive taste (East Indian Pale Ale is the best known) and famously hilarious advertising campaigns revolving around the concept that male workers were drinking all the beer, so only scantily clad females are employed (check out www.tui.co.nz for sample ads). Tours depart Monday–Friday at 10:30 A.M. and 1 P.M., and Saturday at 1 and 2 P.M. The cost is $10, which includes tasting and a souvenir glass. The brewery is hard to miss; it's beside a seven-story brick tower that was once part of the brewery.

Pukaha Mount Bruce

Continuing south 40 km (25 mi) from Mangatainoka is Pukaha Mount Bruce (06/375-8004; daily 9 A.M.–4:30 P.M.; adult $8, child free), an excellent native bird reserve and breeding facility on the outskirts of beautiful **Mount Bruce Scenic Reserve.** Walk through the forest past gigantic cages cleverly constructed around trees and shrubs, and if you look hard and long enough, you'll spot all kinds of native birds, including some of New Zealand's rare and endangered birds (each cage has identifying pictures and characteristics of the birds inside). If you enjoy birdsong your ears will be in seventh heaven. The purpose of the sanctuary is to protect the rare, study and breed the endangered, and liberate the successfully bred into appropriate habitats in the wild. The complex features a large visitor center with many outstanding displays on New Zealand wildlife, a theater showing videos, a nocturnal house, a gift shop, and a café with lots of outdoor seating.

MASTERTON

Masterton (pop. 20,000) is the largest town along the inland route between Palmerston North and Wellington. It's best known for its sheepshearing competition, but also makes a good place for an overnight stop or as a base for exploring the east coast.

Sights and Recreation

The highlight of Masterton is beautiful **Queen Elizabeth II Park** on Dixon Street. Take the time to explore all the nooks and crannies of this well-established park. There's a pond and stream where you can rent large tricycle boats and duel with ducks for water space, an aviary, a sunken garden, an aquarium, miniature train rides, and a long, bouncy suspension bridge that leads over the river to a large deer park—pick long, dark-green grass on the outside of the pen and you'll soon have quite a (deer) following. If you enjoy browsing for arts and crafts, children's wooden toys, pottery, willow baskets, jewelry, wood carvings, or dried flowers, or just enjoy chatting with friendly locals, wander along Queen Street, which is lined with arty shops open seven days a week.

Ensconced in two old woolsheds, **Shear Discovery** (Dixon St., 06/378-8008; daily 10 A.M.–4 P.M.; adult $5, child $2) is a modern exhibit telling the story of sheepshearing and the characters who are household names throughout the country. What began back in the 1950s as a small exhibition at the Masterton Agricultural and Pastoral Show has grown into one of world's premier sheepshearing competitions, known as the **Golden Shears** (06/378-8008, www.goldenshears.co.nz). Competitors from around the world compete in various events over three days in early March, strutting their stuff on a massive stage. The best seats are sold a year in advance, with latecomers watching the action on a big-screen TV.

Accommodations and Food

Stay at the attractive, sheltered **Mawley Park Motor Camp** (Oxford St., 06/378-6454, www.mawleypark.co.nz; camping $10 per person, cabins $50–60 s or d), on the bank of Waipoua River (good river swimming) and you'll mostly be sharing space with vacationing New Zealanders. Facilities are all top-notch, and most cabins have kitchens.

Historic stables along the main street have been given a serious makeover to create **Tulloch Lodge** (290 High St., 06/377-5100,

WELLINGTON

www.tullochlodge.co.nz; $139–169 s or d), a contemporary, country-influenced boutique hotel. Each spacious unit has a comfortable king bed, a wall-mounted LCD TV, a kitchen, and a patio with outdoor furniture. It's a favorite with weekenders from Wellington, so you should try and stay midweek. The in-house restaurant (Mon.–Thurs. 5 P.M.–9 P.M., Fri. 10:30 A.M.–9 P.M., Sat.–Sun. 9 A.M.–9 P.M.) serves up stellar cuisine in an unpretentious room, complete with a log fire and comfortable couches. The dinner menu features dishes like seafood chowder ($10.50), mussel linguini ($14.50), and salmon roasted in a wood-fired oven ($28).

Information

Wairarapa Visitor Centre (316 Queen St., 06/370-0900; Mon.–Fri. 9 A.M.–5 P.M., Sat.–Sun. 10 A.M.–4 P.M.) is along the main road through town. If you plan to head out to the remote east coast or tour the Martinborough vineyards, this is the place to stock up on information.

SOUTH FROM MASTERTON
Waiohine Gorge

If you've plenty of time to explore scenic countryside, want good bush hiking, or are looking for your own special swimming hole or trout-fishing spot, the Waiohine Valley and Gorge is a little piece of heaven on earth. To get there from Highway 2, turn right on Dalefield Road in Carterton. The scenery all through the valley is glorious—lush green fields, good-looking sheep, crystal-clear wide Waiohine River and, farther along, the densely forested mountains of the Tararua Range on each side of the gorge. Along the road are several steep access tracks down to the deeper swimming holes in the river (and the water is *cold!*), a campground, the Waiohine Shelter, and another shelter complete with rainwater tank and raised sleeping platform. Trails lead off into the bush in all directions. A parking lot surrounded by beautiful forest lies at the end of the road, and the natural swimming holes in the river attract a

lot of local kids lucky enough to own cars that can make it that far.

Continuing South to Martinborough

On passing through **Greytown,** once the center of the Wairarapa region, don't miss **Cobblestones** (169 Main St., 06/304-9687; Mon.–Sat. 9 A.M.–4 P.M., Sun. 10 A.M.–4:30 P.M.; adult $2.50, child $1). This pioneer museum, once the site where Cobb & Co. coaches offloaded freight and passengers, has all sorts of antique agricultural machinery and buildings dating to 1857.

For another scenic ramble off the main highway, take the road just south of Greytown to Morrisons Bush, then follow the signs to the quaint town of Martinborough (but don't try this detour without a detailed map). The scenery all along the route is flat farmland (a rainbow of color in the late afternoon and early evening), and the road crosses the meandering Ruamahanga River just before entering the wide verandah-lined street of Martinborough.

MARTINBOROUGH

This small town lies in the heart of a region that has seen enormous growth in the winemaking industry in recent years. Most of the 40 local wineries are small operations, and the wines are difficult to obtain outside the area. The town of Martinborough itself is interesting, with eight streets converging on the town square, laid out as a Union Jack. Downtown, the **Colonial Museum** is open weekends and public holidays 2–4 P.M.; admission is by donation. **Hau Nui Wind Farm** (21 km/13 mi southeast of Martinborough toward Whiterock) comprises wind turbines strung along a high ridge. Prevailing westerly winds averaging 35 km (22 mi) per hour help generate enough electricity to power about 2,000 local houses.

Practicalities

Cream-colored and stylish, the ☾ **Martinborough Hotel** (The Square,

06/306-9350, www.peppers.co.nz; $275–355 s or d includes breakfast) has been extensively restored since its glory days of the late 1890s, with guest rooms set around a flower-filled courtyard. Each is decorated in colonial style and opens to either a balcony or the courtyard. If your budget doesn't extend to the hotel, plan on pitching your tent at **Martinborough Village Camping** (Dublin St., 06/306-8919; $12.50), with bike rentals and an adjacent outdoor swimming pool.

Martinborough Visitor Information Centre (18 Kitchener St., 06/306-9043; Mon.–Fri. 9 A.M.–5 P.M., Sat.–Sun. 10 A.M.–4 P.M.) is the place to pick up a winery map. Another place to enhance your wine knowledge is the **Martinborough Wine Centre** (6 Kitchener St., 06/306-9040; daily 9 A.M.–5 P.M.), which is part wine shop, part deli, part café.

TO CAPE PALLISER

Cape Palliser, the southernmost tip of the North Island, is accessible by road from Martinborough, with many interesting stops along the way. The first is **Lake Onoke,** where the waters of the Tauherenikau River and shallow **Lake Wairarapa** (known for good fishing and boating) run out into **Palliser Bay.** On the lake's eastern shore is the seaside resort of **Lake Ferry** (about 60 km/37 mi south of Martinborough), which attracts quite a crowd in summer. **Lake Ferry Holiday Park** is situated on the shores of Lake Onoke (06/307-7873). The ocean beach drops off steeply, and dangerous rips make the rugged shores of Palliser Bay an unappealing place to swim, but the swampy shores and mudflats of Lake Onoke are a bird-watcher's paradise, and good surf casting from the beach keeps anglers happy.

Inland from Palliser Bay on the way to Lake Ferry, Cape Palliser Road branches east. The first settlement along the road is Whangaimoana, which is made up of a cluster of colorful seaside baches (holiday cottages). About 12 km (seven mi) farther along this road lie the fantastic gray vertical rock pillars and intriguingly shaped cliffs of **Putangirua**

Pinnacles. The 1,000-year-old eroded rock hoodoos are 30 minutes' walk from the head of the Putangirua Stream. After returning to the road, continue the drive around the bay to **Te Kopi** and **Ngawihi,** where beaches cling to the rugged oceanfront, and tractors and boats litter the beaches. At the latter village there's a small café, and four km beyond, a massive slab of sandstone is filled with fossilized seashells. At the end of Cape Palliser Road is a **lighthouse** and a fairly large **seal colony.** The seals drag themselves out of the ocean on stormy days and rest in the long grass. An **underwater wreck** also attracts divers to these waters.

HUTT VALLEY AND VICINITY

The Hutt River valley lies hemmed in by the **Kapiti** and **Porirua** coasts to the west, the impressive **Rimutaka Range** to the east, the **Tararua Range** to the north, and the bay of **Port Nicholson** (Wellington Harbour) to the south. Although often referred to as the dormitory suburbs of Wellington, **Upper Hutt,** 32 km (20 mi) north of Wellington, and **Lower Hutt,** 14 km (nine mi) north, are cities in their own right, with a large percentage of the population engaged in either in-town manufacturing industries (biscuits, leather goods, motor vehicles, glass, plastics, electronics, to name but a few) or research work (large units of the Department of Scientific and Industrial Research are based here, along with a soil bureau and a nuclear reactor).

Sights

The residents obviously take pride in the appearance of their inner cities—they are attractively laid out and abloom with summer flowers and flowering trees and shrubs. If you're passing through Lower Hutt, feed your artistic inner self at **The Dowse** (45 Laings Rd., 04/570-6500; Mon.–Fri. 10 A.M.–4 P.M., Sat.–Sun. 11 A.M.–5 P.M.; free), which reopened in 2007 as one of the country's most innovative and interesting art spaces. The modern complex gives artists of all persuasions a chance to display their work, as well as providing performance space and workshops.

Holiday Park

If you'd rather stay in the Hutt Valley than battle your way into Wellington, the excellent **Hutt Park Holiday Village** (95 Hutt Park Rd., Seaview, 04/568-5913 or 0800/488-872, www.huttpark.co.nz) is an excellent choice for all budgets (it's 13 km/eight mi from downtown Wellington). It's a little crowded, but facilities are varied and all excellent; children especially will love the "jumping pillow," adventure playground, and games room. Campsites are $32, cabins start at $52 s or d, kitchen cabins range $64–78, and spacious motel rooms are $110.

Rimutaka Forest Park

If you're not quite ready to enter Wellington, take a sidetrack from Lower Hutt up over the hill (great views of the Hutt Valley, Wellington, and the harbor) to **Wainuiomata,** a suburb of Lower Hutt. Continue along Coast Road to scenic **Catchpool Valley,** part of Rimutaka Forest Park, where many short walks range from 30 minutes to two hours. There's safe swimming in the surrounding streams, and a campground. Stop at the information center on Catchpool Road (off Coast Rd.) about nine km (five mi) from Wainuiomata, and pick up park brochures. Longer hikes go to **Mount** Matthews (940 meters/0.5 mi) and along the **Orongorongo River** (about two hours one way)—track brochures and maps are available at the information center.

Turakirae Head

Got to see what's at the end of the road? Continue toward Turakirae Head and the **Turakirae Head Scientific Reserve**—the road ends at a parking lot. From here it's a three-km (two-mi) walk along a private road that crosses the Orongorongo River bridge and runs along the shores of Cook Strait to the reserve. Earthquakes during the last 7,000 years (the last in 1855) raised a sequence of five beaches; platforms of large boulders separate the ridges. Amongst the dense scrub and swamp vegetation and along the beaches grow all sorts of unusual flora (for the region) such as wild spaniards, a native viola, eyebright, and bamboo orchids. On the beach terraces one km farther along the cape lies a remnant of the *karaka* forest that once covered the area. The cape is particularly interesting in winter; up to 500 New Zealand fur seals colonize the point, getting into shape for the summer breeding season, when they leave for the south of the South Island. You'll also see various kinds of lizards, black-backed gulls, gannets, spur-winged plovers, swallows, yellowhammers, chaffinches, and starlings in the reserve.

Kapiti Coast

The most direct route south from Palmerston North is Highway 57 west to Levin, then Highway 1 down the gently curved sandy beaches of the Kapiti Coast to the harborside suburb of Porirua and on into Wellington. The distance between Palmerston North and Wellington is just 142 km (88 mi), but you should allow at least two hours. This route is notorious for weekend traffic jams—it can take up to four hours to reach Wellington if you are southbound at the end of a regular weekend, even longer on a long weekend.

PALMERSTON NORTH TO WAIKANAE
Levin

This town sits on the fertile Horowhenua Plain, which stretches from the foothills of the rugged Tararua Range to the Tasman Sea. The lush scenic area is the second-largest vegetable producer in the country, but is best known for its kiwifruit, berries, apples, and cut flowers. The roads at the south end of town are lined with stands selling fruit and veggies in season; quite a few of the gardens and orchards have pick-your-own specials—fun, delicious, and economical.

Otaki and Vicinity

A well-populated Maori area before European settlement in 1840, Otaki has a Maori church that shouldn't be missed. The **Rangiatea Maori Church** (on Te Rauparaha St., daily 8 A.M.–sunset) was built in 1849. It's plainer than most on the outside, but its interior is beautifully decorated with red *totara* slabs and intricately designed *tukutuku* panels representing the stars in heaven. Farther along the street is **Otaki Maori Mission** with a church and buildings from the early 19th century, and memorials and graves of early missionaries. The **Otaki Museum** (49 Main St., 06/364-6886), containing Maori artifacts and relics from the pioneering days, is at Hyde Park Craft village, about five km (3.1 mi) south of Otaki on Highway 1.

Access to marked **hiking trails** in the Tararua Range is easy from Otaki if you have your own transportation. Head south out of town, cross the Otaki River, and turn left onto Otaki Gorge Road, following it to the end. The seaside resort of **Otaki Beach,** patrolled in summer, has several campgrounds adjacent to the beach.

Waikanae

Nga Manu Nature Reserve (Ngarara Rd., 04/293-4131; daily 10 A.M.–5 P.M.; adult $10, child $4) hosts more than 50 species of native birds in 15 hectares (37 acres) of native bush and wetlands, but the main interest is breeding the once-common red-crowned parakeet. Take a short bird-spotting walk through the bush, past the aviaries and ponds and through the fernery, arboretum, and gardens comprising over 700 species of native flora. To get there from Highway 1, turn west onto Te Moana Road, then right on Ngarara Road.

Beautiful **Waikanae Beach** stretches out along the Kapiti Coast west of Highway 1 and is sheltered by offshore Kapiti Island. At the northern end of Waikanae Beach lies the wreck of the fishing trawler *Phyllis,* and if you continue north you'll come to **Peka Peka Beach,** with good surf casting and a refreshing lack of commercial development.

PARAPARAUMU

Paraparaumu is the main population center on the Kapiti Coast, with many of its residents commuting into nearby Wellington. Anyone interested in vintage cars should stop at the **Southward Car Museum** (Otaihanga Rd., 04/297-1221; daily 9 A.M.–5:30 P.M.; adult $10, child $3) and check out the 250-car collection that includes Bugattis, a de Lorean, Cadillacs with famous past owners, and an 1896 horse-drawn fire engine. Golfers may recognize the name Paraparaumu as the home course of Tiger Woods' caddy, Steve Williams, who grew up playing and caddying at **Paraparaumu Beach Golf Club** (376 Kapiti Rd., 04/902-8200; greens fee $90), a private club that welcomes visitors. A classic seaside links course, it's one of New Zealand's top layouts.

Paraparaumu Visitor Centre (Coastlands Shopping Centre, 04/298-8195; Mon.–Fri. 9 A.M.–5 P.M., Sat.–Sun. 10 A.M.–3 P.M.) is the place to pick up permits for Kapiti Island.

◖ KAPITI ISLAND

Bird-watchers and outdoor lovers should definitely plan on spending a day on this beautiful island lying close to the Kapiti Coast. Originally a stronghold of Maori Chief Te Rauparaha, the island became a whaling base, then an official bird sanctuary over a century ago. It's predator-free, meaning that native birdlife flourishes, including many species you won't likely see on the mainland, including *kokako* and *takahe.* Brightly colored parakeets are another highlight, and it is impossible not to be charmed by the call of the bellbirds.

Practicalities

Getting to Kapiti Island entails two simple

WELLINGTON

steps—getting a permit and arranging transportation (in that order). Only 50 visitors are allowed on the island each day. Permits are issued by the DOC, in Wellington (Old Government Building, 15 Lambton Quay, 04/472-7356; Mon.–Fri. 9 A.M.–4:30 P.M., Sat. 10 A.M.–3 P.M.) up to three months in advance, or at **Paraparaumu Visitor Centre** (Coastlands Shopping Centre, 04/298-8195, Mon.–Fri. 9 A.M.–5 P.M., Sat.–Sun. 10 A.M.–3 P.M.) the day before. Once you have confirmed a permit, contact **Kapiti Tours** (04/237-7965, www.kapititours.co.nz) or **Kapiti Marine Tours** (04/297-2585, www.kapitimarine charters.co.nz) for island transfers. Both companies leave from the beach at Paraparaumu, departing between 9 and 9:30 A.M., returning around 3 P.M. The cost is adult $45, child $20. You should bring lunch and drinks.

PAEKAKARIKI

Paekakariki (Hill of the Parakeet), affectionately shortened to Paekak (sounds like Piecok) by the locals, has a good sandy beach patrolled in summer—a treasure strip for avid shell collectors—and safe swimming. The other main attractions are the attractive 638-hectare **Queen Elizabeth II Park** (yes, *another* QE Park), which runs along the coast; two Maori *pa;* and **Wellington Tramway Museum** (06/292-8561; daily 11 A.M.–4:30 P.M. in Jan., weekends only the rest of the year) providing vintage tram rides ($5 adult, $2 child) from the Memorial Gates at McKays Crossing to the beach. For extensive views of the Kapiti Coast, Kapiti Island, and the South Island on a clear day, head up Paekakariki Hill Road (left off Hwy. 1 heading south) to **Summit Viewpoint.**

Accommodations

(Paekakariki Backpackers (11 Wellington Rd., 04/902-5967, www.wellingtonbeach backpackers.co.nz; $18–25) sits atop a ridge, with the small village of Paekakariki on one side and the Tasman Sea on the other. It's one of the better lodges you'll come across in your New Zealand travels (and one of the best priced), and its proximity to the capital, 40 km (25 mi) south, makes it an ideal base. Guests are greeted with a hot drink upon arrival, with the hosts explaining everything the area has to offer. The dining/lounge area overlooks the ocean, and there are four- and five-bed dorms as well as en suite doubles with private patios.

THE SOUTH ISLAND

© ANDREW HEMPSTEAD

The South Island, like the North, is a landscape

of great contrast. Spectacular scenery appears to change form, shape, or color around every bend in the road, and the variable weather and play of light and shade make it a photographer's dream. You'll find a maze of waterways separated by bush-covered peninsulas and islands edged with gold-flecked sand in the north; mighty forest-fringed glaciers inching down almost to the sea, unusual cliff formations, and gray sandy beaches pounded by the surf on the west coast; the towering snow-capped mountains of the Southern Alps; isolated glassy fiords that cut deep into remote and untouched native bush in the southwest corner; and richly colored farmland and hilly pasture-land throughout. Lakes are scattered across the South Island and, along with the trout- and salmon-laden rivers, provide excellent fishing, canoeing, swimming, and white-water rafting.

City action and nightlife are available in abundance in the

Dunedin Railway Station

© TAIERI GORGE RAILWAY

"Garden City" of Christchurch, the "Scottish City" of Dunedin, Invercargill at the base of the island, and the two bustling resorts of Queenstown and Aoraki/Mount Cook. At the foot of the South Island lies Stewart Island, carpeted in dense bush, home to all kinds of native birds and wildlife. Hike through virgin wilderness without seeing a soul for five days, cruise remote inlets, or bask on your own perfect South Pacific beach on this island where time stands still and the hum and bustle of the rat race are easily forgotten.

The main difference between the North and South Islands is weather. Temperatures are distinctly cooler in the south and the annual rainfall is much higher; the climate ranges from sunny, dry weather in the northern region to rain almost every day of the year in the southwest fiords (7.5 meters/25 ft or more per year is the norm). Unpredictable Stewart Island can experience the weather of four seasons in a single day.

windswept trees along the West Coast

© ANDREW HEMPSTEAD

MARLBOROUGH AND THE NORTHWEST

After a spectacular ride across Cook Strait (especially beautiful on a bright day), your ferry cruises up colorful Queen Charlotte Sound, one of the two major inlets of Marlborough Sounds Maritime Park. Welcome to Marlborough and the Northwest, which stretches across the top portion of South Island, from the Pacific Ocean in the east to the Tasman Sea in the west. It's a region blessed with lots of sunshine, hundreds of beaches, seemingly endless forest, and an abundance of marinelife.

The gateway to the region is the bustling port city of Picton, from where the convoluted coastline of Marlbough Sounds stretches north through a seemingly endless chain of islands. Tour boats cruise its protected waters while hikers "tramp" the many trails. Through the wine-growing region south of Picton, a coastal highway hugs the shoreline, winding past sandy beaches, rocky shores, and aquamarine waters of the scenic east coast. On the way down, stop for fresh crayfish at one of the many roadside stands, and pull off at Kaikoura. Sandwiched between the rugged Kaikoura Range and the sea, this attractive coastal town is known for whale-watching, but also offers other wildlife-viewing opportunities, empty beaches, and good surf fishing.

For those of you with plenty of time, the deliciously laid-back atmosphere of Nelson, home to many of New Zealand's best potters, weavers, and arts and craftspeople, is well worth a visit, and it's the kind of place where you're likely to meet other relaxed travelers. Continue farther northwest around Tasman Bay to the isolated and ruggedly beautiful

© ANDREW HEMPSTEAD

HIGHLIGHTS

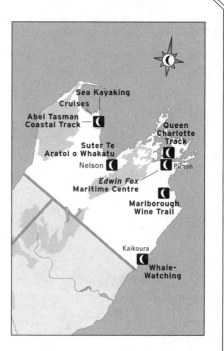

◖ *Edwin Fox* **Maritime Centre:** Walk through the world's ninth-oldest sailing boat at this waterfront museum (page 278).

◖ **Queen Charlotte Track:** Leave your pack behind and plan on staying in upscale lodges along this coastal hiking trail (page 284).

◖ **Marlborough Wine Trail:** This driving route winds its way through New Zealand's main concentration of vineyards (page 286).

◖ **Whale-Watching:** Snap that classic whale photograph with snowcapped mountains in the background on a boat tour off the Kaikoura coast (page 288).

◖ **Suter Te Aratoi o Whakatu:** Be sure to visit this modern art gallery with plenty of space dedicated to local artists (page 293).

◖ **Cruises:** No roads penetrate Abel Tasman National Park, so you'll want to jump aboard a boat to see the best of the beaches (page 301).

◖ **Abel Tasman Coastal Track:** Much like the Queen Charlotte Track, but with more sand and more crowds, this hiking trail winds along a beautiful stretch of coastline (page 302).

◖ **Sea Kayaking:** Dodge seals as you paddle the calm waters of Abel Tasman National Park, and then find a deserted beach for a picnic lunch (Page 303).

LOOK FOR ◖ TO FIND RECOMMENDED SIGHTS, ACTIVITIES, DINING, AND LODGING.

Abel Tasman National Park for outstanding paddling and coastal scenery, and on to Golden Bay, which stretches round to the far northern tip of the South Island and has secluded sandy beaches, not many people, lots of birdlife, and scenery ranging from water panoramas to rugged mountains.

Throughout Marlborough and the Northwest, the people are creative and relaxed, and make you feel right at home. Partly because of this atmosphere the region attracts a mellow crowd—even in midsummer when New Zealanders flock to the region for relaxation and outdoor adventures. Local families gravitate to the region's many holiday parks, but all types of travelers are catered to. Most towns have multiple motels and eateries, but you will want to stray from the ordinary and stay in a lodge only accessible by boat, dine among the vineyards, or grab a boiled crayfish and head down to the beach for a feast to remember.

MARLBOROUGH

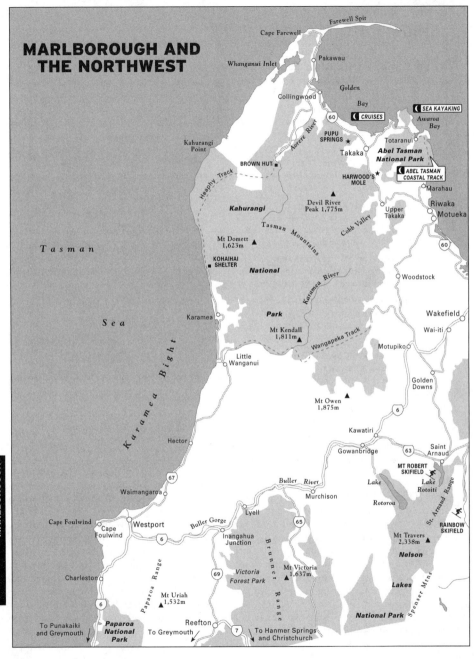

MARLBOROUGH AND THE NORTHWEST

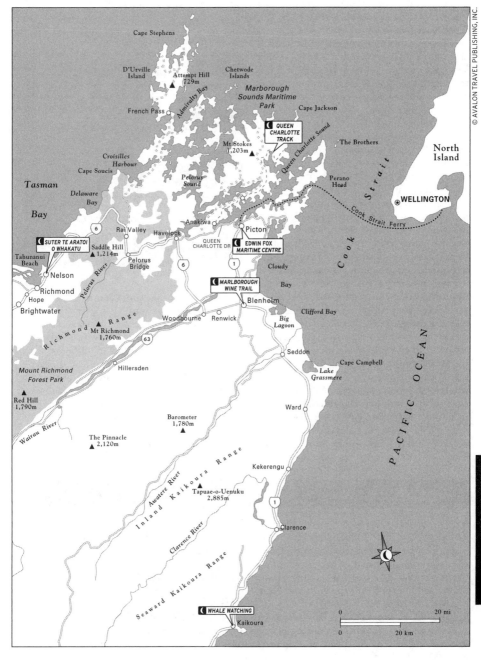

© AVALON TRAVEL PUBLISHING, INC.

MARLBOROUGH

PLANNING YOUR TIME

If you're relatively short of time to spend on the South Island, take an invaluable moment to decide what kind of scenery and activities you're looking for before racing off the ferry and into the unknown. One week is enough time to drive around the South Island, but you will be hurried and will miss lots of the highlights. An alternative is to have booked a one-way car rental between Auckland and Christchurch, and then fly back to Auckland for your return flight home. If this is your plan, you will need to be even more aware of what you want to see and do before striking off from Picton.

Upon arrival by ferry, plan on spending a half day exploring the waterfront area of Picton, including a visit to the *Edwin Fox* **Maritime Centre,** which holds one of the world's oldest ships (or save it for a pre-ferry diversion before heading back to the North Island). You will need at least one day to get onto the **Queen Charlotte Track,** but staying overnight in one of the wilderness lodges makes for an even more memorable experience. From Picton, wine-lovers heading down the east coast to Christchurch will want to schedule one or more stops along the **Marlborough Wine Trail,** while everyone should set aside a few hours at Kaikoura to go **whale-watching.** Early trips generally experience the best weather, so you could plan on spending a day meandering down to Kaikoura from the ferry, plan on a crayfish feast for dinner, and then rise early for the tour.

the beach at Kaikoura

© ANDREW HEMPSTEAD

If you do make the entire South Island loop, at some stage of your travels you'll pass through the laidback city of Nelson, where local artists display their skills at **Suter Te Aratoi o Whakatu.** Nelson is the jumping-off point for Abel Tasman National Park, a postcard-perfect wilderness of crystal-clear water, golden-sand beaches, and native forest. As a day trip from Nelson, you could either join one of the many park **cruises** or go **sea kayaking.** Stay overnight and you could do both, as well as walk a section of the **Abel Tasman Coastal Track.**

Picton

The gateway to the South Island, Picton (population 3,900) is a bustling seaside town with lots of attractions and activities, and plenty of accommodations and restaurants to choose from. All the action happens in and around the harbor, with the most popular local activities taking place on the water. Picton Harbour is a hive of activity year-round, but it's busiest during summer, when a constant stream of water taxis,

cruise boats, and privately owned watercraft heads into and out of the marina. This form of transportation is covered comprehensively in the following section, *Marlborough Sounds.*

SIGHTS
◖ *Edwin Fox* Maritime Centre

Just a few steps from the ferry terminal, this museum complex hides the world's ninth-oldest

MARLBOROUGH

ship, the 1853 *Edwin Fox* (Dunbar Wharf, 03/573-6868; daily 9 A.M.–5 P.M., until 6 P.M. in summer; adult $6, child $1). It is also the only surviving Australian convict ship and the world's oldest merchant sailing ship. In the main building you learn about the ship's history—from its launching in India, the trips made transporting convicts to Australia, and the story since its arrival in Picton over a century ago. The effort that was required to float what remained of the 44-meter (157-foot) wooden vessel across Picton Harbour in 1986 is particularly impressive. Out back of the museum is the ship herself, dry-docked and covered from the elements. Stairs lead into and around the hulk, allowing a real opportunity to get up close and personal with a priceless piece of nautical history.

Seahorse World

The admission to this aquarium beside the *Edwin Fox* (Dunbar Wharf, 03/573-6030; daily 9 A.M.–5 P.M.; adult $16, child $9) is a little on the steep side, but an admirable job has been done of telling the story of one of the ocean's most intriguing creatures. While seahorses are most definitely the stars of the show, there's also a shark tank (feeding daily at 2 P.M.), an octopus who lives in a cylindrical tank, a preserved giant squid, trout and salmon, and a touch tank.

Picton Museum

Walk down the Memorial Steps at the harbor end of High Street into the attractive flower-filled park that lines the harbor, and turn left. Just past the public restrooms you'll find the Picton Museum (London Quay, 03/573-8283; daily 10 A.M.–4 P.M.; adult $5, child $1). Displays go back to 1770, when Captain Cook sailed up Queen Charlotte Sound, and tells the story of the Maori, whaling, gold mining, and logging. It also has an impressive shell collection and the bicycle Picton's doctor got around on in 1902.

Scenic Overlooks

If you have your own transportation, cruise out to **Waikawa Bay Marina** (a 10-minute drive east of town along Beach Rd.) to see hundreds of boats clinking and twinkling in the sun.

© ANDREW HEMPSTEAD

Picton waterfront

MARLBOROUGH

Victoria Domain, an area of unspoiled bush along the headlands east of the harbor, offers spectacular views of the Picton Ferry Terminal, the sound, and Waikawa Bay. To get there from town take Dublin Street east, continue past Picton Hospital onto Waikawa Road, and go about 800 meters (0.5 mi). Turn left at Sussex Street and follow the steep road to the lookout.

You'll also find a lookout and picnic spot up on **Queen Charlotte Drive** (which leads west out of Picton toward Havelock and Nelson). You can reach it by road (take Dublin St. west and turn right at Queen Charlotte Dr.), or on foot via **Beatty's Track,** which starts near the base of Waitohi Wharf and leads up to the lookout.

Walking Trails

From town, a track follows the harbor edge east for one km (0.6 mi) and ends at sheltered **Bob's Bay**—enjoy its pleasant picnic sites and safe swimming. From here you can climb up the bush track to the headland, Victoria Domain, and a lookout for spectacular views of Queen Charlotte Sound and Picton. **Essons Valley Reservoir** is another enjoyable short walk (45 minutes one way)—particularly good in the dark when glowworms sparkle along the track. It starts at Garden Terrace at the south end of Picton and leads to forest-encircled **Humphries Dam.**

ACCOMMODATIONS AND CAMPING

As a transportation hub, Picton has a wide range of accommodations in all price brackets. If you're looking to spend a night at either end of the Cook Strait ferry trip, Picton is by far the preferred choice. If you haven't made accommodation reservations in advance (recommended, especially in summer), stop at the information center to see what's available.

Picton is also the jumping-off point for a smattering of accommodations accessible only by boat. These are covered in the following section, *Marlborough Sounds.*

Under $50

Picton has many backpacker lodges, most of which are of an excellent standard; many have bike rentals and all have Internet access.

Near the ferry terminal and associated with Diver's World, **Atlantis Backpackers** (London Quay, 03/573-7390, www.atlantishostel .co.nz; dorm beds $17–19, $48 d) features an indoor pool and free tea and coffee through the day.

Bayview Backpackers at Waikawa Bay Beach (318 Waikawa Rd., 03/573-7668; dorm beds $23, $43 s, $56 d) is bright and modern: Amenities include bunk, twin, and double rooms, a well-equipped kitchen with a microwave, a living area with a stereo, a log fire, a barbecue, free use of bicycles, and kayaks, dinghies, and catamarans for rent. It also offers free pickup and drop-off at the ferry terminal.

$50-100

Right in the center of town, within walking distance of the ferry terminal, is the brightly painted ❰ **The Villa** (34 Auckland St., 03/573-6598, www.thevilla.co.nz; dorm beds $27, $59–71 s or d), an excellent backpacker lodge with all the usual facilities, as well as free tea and coffee, free breakfast, free use of bikes, and a large backyard with a barbecue and spa pool.

Of the many motels in downtown Picton, one of the more reasonably priced, the **Ferrylink Motel** (45 Kent St., 03/573-7097, www.ferrylink.co.nz; $75–100 s or d), is a small, single-story place one km (0.6 mi) from downtown with 10 basic self-contained units, most with kitchens.

$100-150

Two blocks up from the harbor, **Jasmine Court** (78 Wellington St., 03/573-7110 or 0800/421-999, www.jasminecourt.co.nz; $125–185 s or d) doesn't look like anything special from the outside, but gets my vote as the nicest motel in town. Each room is well decorated, and has a comfortable bed and a modern kitchen. The largest suites have king beds and spa baths. Other amenities include a sauna and laundry. **The Gables** (20 Waikawa Rd., 03/573-6772, www.thegables.co.nz; $135–155 s or d) provides comfortable bed-and-breakfast rooms and a large lounge area on the upper floor of a two-story 1924 home, only a short walk from town and the marina. Breakfast is huge, and fresh fish is served when available. Also available are two small cottages at the back of the property and one down closer to the harbor. Each has a kitchen and lots of privacy.

Americano Motor Inn (32 High St., 03/573-6398 or 0800/104-104, www.americano.co.nz; $100 s, $120 d) has 26 spacious, self-contained units with TV and radio, as well as a licensed restaurant and bar, laundry facilities, a children's play area, and off-street parking.

$150-200

The **Yacht Club Hotel** (Waikawa Rd., 03/573-7002 or 0800/991-188, www.theyachtclub hotel.com; $160–300 s or d) is a high-rise waterfront hotel where most of the summertime activity revolves around an outdoor pool. Although decidedly up to date, the 35 rooms are classically styled and most have balconies. The hotel restaurant is an attractive and popular spot for a splurge.

Holiday Parks

Picton Top 10 Holiday Park (78 Waikawa Rd., 03/573-7212 or 0800/277-666, www.picton top10.co.nz; walk-in tent sites $30, powered sites $33, cabins $50–70 s or d, tourist flats $85–120) provides the usual facilities, a TV and recreation room, and a swimming pool.

Alexander's Holiday Park (Canterbury St., 03/573-6378; unpowered sites $10 per person, powered sites $14 per person, cabins $48–65 s or d) is one km (0.6 mi) from downtown (an easy 15-minute walk), in the quiet southern area of town. Waitohi Stream rushes through the attractive grounds. Alexander's has communal facilities, a TV lounge, kitchens where travelers mingle, and an office where you can

pick up information on the local area and buy basic foodstuffs, postcards, and supplies. From town, cross the railway tracks, follow Wairau Road (the sign says Hwy. 1 south) to Devon Street, and turn left. At Canterbury Street turn left, following the signs.

The next closest campground to Picton, **Waikawa Bay Holiday Park** (302 Waikawa Rd., 03/573-7434; campsites $22, cabins $45–75 s or d) has a grassy camping area and on-site caravans and cabins; it's a short drive from a food market and the bay beach.

FOOD

Picton offers a good choice of cafés and restaurants, most within a couple of blocks of the harborfront.

Cafés

For a cheap, quick breakfast or lunch, try one of the many tearooms and cafés, or **Picton Village Bakkerij** (6 Auckland St., 03/573-7082; daily 6 A.M.–3:30 P.M.), which features delicious European-style breads and pastries (great fudge slices). Moroccan lamb and chicken curry highlight the pie list, with fruit pies including pear and boysenberry also delicious.

Across the "coat hanger" bridge to the north side of the marina, turn left to the **Echo** (03/573-7498; daily 10 A.M.–6 P.M.), a 1905 cargo boat that has been converted to a café. The boat, which played an important part in Marlborough's transport industry between Blenheim and Wellington for more than 50 years, is interesting to explore in itself ($5 for non-diners).

In a restored home with hardwood floors and high ceilings, **Espresso House** (86 Auckland St., 03/573-7112; daily 11 A.M.–9 P.M.) offers a variety of good salads and open-face sandwiches.

A longtime favorite with lots of local flavors is **Le Café** (12–14 London Quay, 03/573-5588; daily for breakfast, lunch, and dinner). A full cooked breakfast is $16 and dinner mains range $19–30 (weekly fish and game specials are always reliable).

Upscale

For gourmet local seafood, steaks, and vegetarian fare, head to **Old Vault** in a renovated BNZ building (33 Wellington St., 03/573-6102; daily from 6 p.m.). Tables are in private rooms or spread around a pleasant verandah; dinners start at $22.

The finest dining in town is at the nautically themed **Chartroom** (Yacht Club Hotel, Waikawa Rd., 03/573-7002; daily for breakfast, lunch, and dinner), which has alfresco dining on a balcony overlooking the harbor. The cooking is not overly adventurous, but all bases are covered and the service is smart and professional. Expect to pay $26–34 for a dinner main.

INFORMATION AND SERVICES

Across the parking lot from the ferry terminal is **Picton Visitor Centre** (Dunbar Wharf, 03/520-3113, www.destinationmarlborough .com; daily 8:30 A.M.–5 P.M., until 6 P.M. in summer). It holds information on the entire South Island and makes bookings for all transportation. In the same building, the Department of Conservation has a desk (Oct.–Apr.) where you can get information on the Marlborough Sounds.

Picton Post Office is on High Street, next to Mariners Mall. **Bank of New Zealand** is also on High Street. **United Video** (63 High St., 03/573-7466) has public Internet access. **Picton Laundry** is at 14 Auckland Street.

For an ambulance, call 111 or 03/578-4099; for a non-life-threatening emergency, call 03/573-6405 or 03/573-6092 (local doctor). **Queen Charlotte Pharmacy** is in Mariners Mall (High St., 03/573-7927).

TRANSPORTATION

Getting to Picton from Wellington

The ferry crossing of Cook Strait is sometimes rough, and occasionally very rough, so flying between Wellington and Picton can be a welcome option. **Soundsair** (03/573-6184; $79 one way) flies over the strait up to six times daily. These flights land at Koromiko Airfield,

seven km (four mi) south of town, from where free shuttle buses run into Picton. The closest airport served by **Air New Zealand** (0800/737-300, www.airnewzealand.com) is Blenheim (28 km/17 mi south of Picton), with regular flights from Wellington.

Picton's ferry terminal, 500 meters (0.3 mi) from downtown, is the main port of entry to and exit from the South Island. Three **Interislander** (04/498-3302 or 0800/802-802, www.interislander.co.nz) ferries make up to five crossings daily from Wellington to Picton. Check the current schedule and make bookings at any visitor information center or most travel agencies. You may also book by calling or visiting Interislander's website. If you're taking a vehicle across, you need to book a space, particularly during holidays. Otherwise expect to end up in a long standby line and miss several ferries before you get on. Booking in advance is also cheaper. The pricing structure for Interislander ferry travel is complicated, but book in advance from within New Zealand for the cheapest tickets. The regular one-way fare is adult $65, child $42, vehicle and driver $225. Various discount levels apply, with a percentage of spots reserved at each fare level on every sailing. Also sailing into Picton is **Bluebridge** (04/471-6188 or 0800/844-844, www.bluebridge.co.nz), with set one-way fares of adult $49, child $25, and vehicle and driver $169.

Considering the amount of traffic these services handle, the operations are remarkably efficient and reliable. If you've left you're rental vehicle in Wellington, picking up another is a simple affair in Picton, but you should let your rental car company know your arrival time.

Onward Travel

The railway station is just around the corner from London Quay on the way to the ferry terminal. The **TranzCoastal** train departs from Picton daily for Blenheim, Kaikoura, and Christchurch, arriving at Christchurch about

5.5 hours later. Get a timetable and book tickets at the railway station (03/573-8857) or call **Tranz Scenic** (0800/872-467).

Picton is a hub for bus travel, with many companies based in town. **Intercity** (03/573-7025, www.intercitycoach.co.nz) buses arrive and depart from the Picton Travel Centre at the ferry terminal, and head west to Nelson and south along the east coast to Christchurch via Kaikoura. At least one departure daily links up with the arrival of a ferry from Wellington. **KBus** (03/578-4075) is a local company with daily service to Nelson.

Getting Around

If you've rented a car from one of the major car rental agencies on the North Island, you'll be asked to leave it at the ferry terminal in Wellington and pick up another once you've crossed Cook Strait and arrived in Picton. The agencies with cars in Picton include **Avis** (03/520-3156), **Budget** (03/573-6081), **Hertz** (03/573-7224), **Pegasus** (03/573-7733), and **Thrifty** (03/573-7387).

For a taxi, call **Picton Taxis** (03/573-6207); they also offer one- to three-hour scenic tours (up to five adults per vehicle).

Marlborough Sounds

Most of the sounds is protected as **Marlborough Sounds Maritime Park.** The park is a maze of waterways, islands with sandy beaches, and high peninsulas. Within the park boundary lie innumerable reserves, the two major inlets of Queen Charlotte and Pelorus Sounds, D'Urville Island, and Croisilles Harbour, altogether covering about 2,914 square km (1,125 sq mi) of coastline and islands. If your vehicle is reliable, you can reach many areas of the middle and outer sounds by road (some of it paved, some gravel); you can reach the more remote areas by boat only, but commercial cruises and the mail boat make regular trips everywhere. All the commercial operators (in Picton or Havelock) are willing to drop you off and pick you up at prearranged points and times, allowing one-day island exploration or a several-day hike. For information and maps of the park, head to the DOC Sounds Area Office in Picton (Auckland St., between downtown and the ferry terminal, 03/520-3002).

PICTON TO HAVELOCK

While Picton is the park's main gateway, Havelock, to the west, is the jumping-off point for Pelorus Sound. **Queen Charlotte Drive,** linking the two towns, is a winding, tortuous road along the edge of the sounds offering some of the

South Island's best waterscapes. To access this road, take Dublin Street west from High Street. Beyond the quiet settlement of **Momorangi Bay,** a side road provides access to Anakiwa and the southern end of the Queen Charlotte Track. Continuing west, another secondary road at **Linkwater** winds for almost 100 km (62 mi) into the heart of Marlborough Sounds.

Havelock

At Havelock (pop. 480) many outdoor activities await discovery—walking and hiking, cruising the sounds, mail-boat adventuring, fishing, and glowworm-viewing, to name but a few.

Budget travelers should plan on staying at **YHA Havelock** (46 Main Rd., 03/574-2104, www.yha.co.nz; dorm beds $22, $52 d), a converted classic country schoolhouse (Lord Rutherford, the first person to split an atom, went to school here). A large comfy living room, a well-equipped kitchen, spotlessly clean bathrooms, a notice board packed with useful information on the area and surroundings, and bike rentals are just some of the reasons to stay here.

Habitat Bakery & Teahouse (65 Main Rd., 03/574-2860; Mon.–Fri. 5:30 A.M.–3 P.M., Sat. 6:30 A.M.–3 P.M.) is a great little café, with full breakfasts served off to one side from the bakery counter. You can order all the usual pies and sandwiches made to order, and, in a nice touch, your cup of coffee comes with a pile of jellybeans. The local delicacy is mussels, and the best place to feast on them is **Mussel Pot** (73 Main Rd., 03/574-2824; daily 11 A.M.–8 P.M.), where a huge pile of mussels—grilled or steamed—is $17. You can also order mussel chowder ($10) and mussel salad ($12.50).

RECREATION

A track network, from 15-minute walks to several-day hikes, winds throughout Marlborough Sounds Maritime Park. Most are accessible by boat, and that's how most people enjoy the region.

◀ Queen Charlotte Track

The most popular and well-defined hiking trail, the 71-km (44-mi) Queen Charlotte Track runs along Queen Charlotte and Kenepuru Sounds from **Ship Cove** to **Anakiwa.** It winds in and out of beautiful coves, through native bushland, and to rocky headlands. What makes it particularly appealing are the many options, from hiking the entire trail to using a water taxi to access just a portion of the trail. Along the way, lodging to suit all budgets opens up even more opportunities for those not necessarily equipped for backcountry travel.

A hiker of average fitness takes about four days to cover the trail comfortably. You'll find road access at Anakiwa, Te Mahia, Portage, and Kenepuru Saddle. Sea access at Anakiwa, Mistletoe Bay, Torea Bay, Camp Bay, Endeavour Inlet, Resolution Bay, and Ship Cove allows hikers to cover as much or as little of the track as they want. The first 11 km/seven mi (four hours) of this track, from Ship Cove around Endeavour Inlet to the Kenepuru Saddle, are the most spectacular. They can be completed easily as a day trip from Picton or as an overnight excursion, staying at one of the lodges along the way. Lodge accommodations and campgrounds are spaced at short intervals along the track (no more than a seven-hour walk separates them), and all should be reserved. See *Practicalities* later in this section for information on accommodations and track transportation.

Cruising

Many commercial launch operators cruise Queen Charlotte Sound (from Picton) and Pelorus Sound (from Havelock). On these trips you'll cover an extensive area of Queen Charlotte Sound, appreciating beautiful secluded bays, isolated homesteads, old whaling stations, historic landmarks, perfect beaches, and lots of birdlife. The easiest way to find out what's available is to head down to the Picton Marina, where most operators are based. **Beachcomber Fun Cruises** (03/573-6175, www.beachcombercruises.co.nz) offers a variety of options. The Magic Mail Run departs daily at 1 P.M. For just $75, it includes a scenic trip to Torea Bay, a bus trip across to Kenepuru Sound to the Portage Resort, and the return trip to Picton. Other operators include **Cougar Line Cruises** (03/573-7925 or 0800/504-090, www.cougarline.co.nz) and **Endeavour Express** (03/573-5456, www.boatrides.co.nz). In addition to regular tours, all three companies offer day trips out to the various lodges, provide transfers for hikers, and will portage bags from lodge to lodge.

Kayaking

Adventurers shouldn't miss a chat with the owners of the **Marlborough Sounds Adventure Co.,** next to the main wharf in Picton (03/573-6078 or 0800/283-283). They offer a variety of sea kayaking trips to suit all standards and most budgets. Rent one of the kayaks and set off on your own ($40 per person per day for a single or double kayak), or take a guided trip. These range from a half-day paddle ($65) to a three-day adventure ($495), which begins with a water taxi ride to the outer sounds. According to kayakers, *this* is the only way to really appreciate the beauty of the sounds.

Diving

Scuba divers will find an abundance of natural underwater wonders throughout Marlborough Sounds, but the most popular dive site is *very* unnatural. In 1986, a Russian cruise ship, the 175-meter-long **Mikhail Lermontov,** sank near the entrance to the sounds, coming to rest on its side in around 25 meters (82 ft) of water. Today it's the world's largest diveable cruise ship, with divers able to explore its entire length and even enter the dining room. The local dive operation, **Divers World** (corner of London Quay and Auckland St., Picton, 03/373-7323), fills tanks, rents equipment, and has a charter boat stocked for divers to take you out to the best spots. Expect to pay from $140 per person for a two-dive trip, and around $250 per person to dive the *Mikhail Lermontov*, which lies a long 60-km (37-mi) boat ride from Picton.

PRACTICALITIES
Accommodations

Lodges are spread throughout the Marlborough Sounds, and because access is generally only by boat, they provide a great way to get away from it all. Each accommodation usually has a restaurant, or meals can be provided, and most offer guests the use of watercraft and fishing gear. The best way to reach them is by water taxi or on a scheduled cruise. The lodges themselves will advise you of transportation options when booking. Expect to pay $60–80 per person for the return trip from Picton.

The closest lodging to the south end of the track, **Furneaux Lodge** (03/579-8103, www .furneaux.co.nz) has a separate backpacker lodge ($30 per person), small cabins ($40 s or d), self-contained cabins ($195 s or d), and contemporary suites ($245). Spread over one hectare (2.5 acres) of gardens sloping to a sandy beach, this large complex also features a rental shop with kayaks and fishing tackle, boat charters, a restaurant, a bar, and a laundry.

Punga Cove Resort (03/579-8561, www .pungacove.co.nz), 11 km (seven mi) beyond the Furneaux Lodge but still on Endeavour Inlet, is an ideal destination in itself, or at the end of the second day on the Queen Charlotte Track. It's set at the head of secluded Punga Cove. Budget cabins with two bunk beds are $35 per person), lodge rooms are $115 s or d ($150 with en suite), and chalets, some with kitchens, are $175–225. The resort restaurant serves imaginative dishes featuring lots of local seafood.

The least expensive accommodation on

Endeavour Inlet is ⟨⟨ **Mahana Homestead Lodge** (03/579-8373, www.mahanahomestead .com; dorms $33, $75 d), a modern backpacker lodge with a wide verandah taking full advantage of a beachfront location. Rates include the use of fishing rods, kayaks, and a dinghy.

Continuing north along the Queen Charlotte Track is upscale **Bay of Many Coves Resort** (03/579-9771 or 0800/579-977, www .bayofmanycovesresort.co.nz; from $320 s or d), easily reached in one day's walk from Endeavour Inlet, or by water taxi from Picton. The guest rooms come with modern amenities like Internet access and flat-screen TVs. Surrounded by native bush, and with boats to rent, a restaurant, and a relaxing spa bath, this is naturally a popular spot.

Bay of Many Coves Resort is off the Queen Charlotte Track, but from its access point the main hiking route descends to Kenepuru Sound (accessed by water taxi from Havelock) and the **Portage Resort Hotel** (Kenepuru Rd., 03/573-4309, www.portage.co.nz). Accommodations are in bunk rooms ($35 per person) that share a communal kitchen or colorful, contemporary rooms ($170–300 s or d). Join in a wide range of activities, including fishing, diving, tennis, and hiking, or just relax in the swimming pool or delightful rock pool spa. Dining options include a restaurant and a casual waterfront café.

Camping

Within Marlborough Sounds Maritime Park lie over 20 primitive campgrounds. Facilities at each are limited to toilets and drinking water. Six of these lie along the Queen Charlotte Track, all well spaced for overnight walkers. No reservations are taken and the fee ($6 per person) is paid on an honor system.

Originally a DOC campground, **Mistletoe Bay** (Ohahau Bay, 03/573-4048, www.mistle toebay.co.nz; camping $10 per person, dorm beds $20, cabins $80 s or d, holiday home $120) is now managed by a local trust. Basic amenities include communal bathrooms, a kitchen, and drinking water. Water taxis and tour boats stop in, but it's also accessible by road 19 km (12 mi) north of Linkwater (allow one hour from Picton).

Getting There and Around

Unpaved roads lead throughout the sounds, including to many of the lodges listed above, but you'll need a reliable vehicle and a good map. Most travel through the sounds is by tour boat or water taxi. Expect to pay $60–80 round trip for lodge transfers, or a little less for hiker drop-offs. Good options for those walking between lodges are the package deals offered that include round-trip transportation, plus daily transfers of backpacks or suitcases from lodge to lodge. Day-trippers can pay for return open-jaw water transfers; for example, you could be dropped off at Ship Cove, walk along the Queen Charlotte Track to Furneaux Lodge (a 4.5-hour walk), and then catch a boat back to Picton for $60 per person. For details, contact **Beachcomber Fun Cruises** (03/573-6175, www.beachcombercruises.co.nz), **Cougar Line Cruises** (03/573-7925 or 0800/504-090, www.cougarline.co.nz), and **Endeavour Express** (03/573-5456, www.boatrides .co.nz). Also from Picton, **Arrow Water Taxis** (03/573-8229) provides on-demand transfers throughout Marlborough Sounds.

Information

The **Department of Conservation** website (www.doc.govt.nz) is the best source of pre-trip planning information. In Picton, the **Picton Visitor Centre** (Dunbar Wharf, 03/520-3113, www.destinationmarlborough .com; daily 8:30 A.M.–5 P.M., until 6 P.M. in summer) has lots of practical information on the Marlborough Sounds.

Picton to Christchurch

If you plan to whiz down Highway 1 between Picton and Christchurch, a distance of 340 km (211 mi), at a frantic pace because it looks as if there's not much to see and do, you're in for a surprise. Around Blenheim, numerous vineyards offer wine-tasting and garden settings for light meals, and galleries and pottery outlets display and sell expressive arts and crafts. As you continue south, the highway meanders along a spectacular section of coastline with ocean, beach, and mountain views. Must-see Kaikoura is a place where it's only too easy to spend at least several days exploring coastal walkways and reserves, relaxing on the beach, savoring fresh seafood, and experiencing delightful, up-close wildlife adventures with assorted marine mammals—by foot, boat, or plane.

BLENHEIM

Blenheim (pop. 26,000), 30 km (19 mi) south of Picton, is the capital of the Marlborough region and the center of a large grape-growing area. The first place to go is the **Blenheim** **Information Centre** (Sinclair St., 03/577-8080, www.destinationmarlborough.com), right in the center of town.

◖ Marlborough Wine Trail

Wine growing is relatively new to the Marlborough region, but with 50 wineries and 11,000 hectares (27,200 acres) of vines, it is now New Zealand's largest winery region, having quadrupled in production in just the last decade. Vineyards are spread throughout the region and down the coast toward Christchurch, but the main concentration is in the Wairau Valley, west of Blenheim around Renwick and beyond. In fact, 25 wineries lie within five km (3.1 mi) of each other around Renwick. Over 60 percent of plantings are Sauvignon Blanc, but Pinot Gris, Riesling, Gewürztraminer, Chardonnay, and Pinot Noir are all represented.

Visitor centers in Blenheim and Picton have maps of the Marlborough Wine Trail, or you can log on to www.wine-marlborough.co.nz.

© ANDREW HEMPSTEAD

Wineries dot the countryside surrounding Blenheim.

All the following wineries are open for tasting and sales, usually daily 10 A.M.–5 P.M.

High-profile **Cloudy Bay** (Jacksons Rd., 03/520-9140) has a wine boutique selling the company's late-harvest Riesling and signature Pelorus label. **Villa Maria** (corner Paynters and New Renwick Rds., 03/577-9530) is the country's largest privately owned winery. It is also notable as the world's first winery to be "cork free" (in 2004). The pioneer Rose family owns and operates **Wairau River Wines** (Rapaura Rd., 03/572-7950). Grapes from four vineyards have produced wines that have won over 80 awards. A café is open daily noon–3 P.M.

Marlborough Wine Tours (03/578-9515) offers personalized tours from Blenheim, with pickups from Picton on all full-day tours. Itineraries are flexible, but a three-hour tour ($39) allows for quick visits to four wineries and a five-hour tour ($49) includes light meal.

Accommodations

Most of Blenheim's backpacker lodges are designed to cater for seasonal workers rather than travelers, but **Koanui Lodge** (33 Main St., 03/578-7487; dorm beds $25, $68 d) juggles the needs of both with separate buildings opening to a courtyard.

Alpine Motel (148 Middle Renwick Rd., 03/578-1604 or 0800/101-931, www.alpine motelblenheim.co.nz; $95–130 s or d) provides good value in its nine self-contained rooms. It's west of downtown on the main road (Hwy. 6) to Nelson.

For a splurge, consider a stay at **Hotel d'Urville** (52 Queen St., 03/577-9945, www .durville.com; $298 s, $322 d). This boutique hotel is housed in a government building that has been extensively renovated but still holds its historic charm, right down to a distinctive colonnaded facade. The nine guest rooms are each very different but equally chic—request the Colour Room for bold, contrasting colors or the D'Urville Suite for a stylish nautical theme in keeping with the hotel's namesake, an 1820s explorer.

Food

Right downtown, the **((Living Room** (corner Scott and Maxwell Rds., 03/579-4777; daily

MARLBOROUGH

© ANDREW HEMPSTEAD

Hotel d'Urville

KAIKOURA

Kaikoura (pop. 4,000), 130 km (80 mi) south of Blenheim and 182 km (113 mi) north of Christchurch, has grown rapidly in recent years from a sleepy little fishing village to one of the country's premier wildlife-watching destinations. The highlight is the proximity of sperm whales, which feed within one km (0.6 mi) of the coast, but there are plenty of other opportunities to interact with nature if you have the time (and cash). Wildlife aside, the setting is nothing short of stunning, with the town fronting the sparkling blue Pacific Ocean on one side and with the steep mountains of the Kaikoura Range as a backdrop.

Sights

The many exhibits, argillite and greenstone artifacts, photographs, records, implements, and utensils on display at the **Kaikoura Museum** (14 Ludstone Rd., 03/319-7440; daily 2–4 P.M.; adult $3, child $0.50) trace the life and history of the Maori and European people and the district of Kaikoura.

7:30 A.M.–4:30 P.M.) is a modern café with excellent food, including a tasty eggs Benedict ($12.50). The pavlova ($7) dessert is also good. Many of the wineries around Blenheim serve meals, and these are the places to really tuck in and splurge. **Hunter's** (Rapaura Rd., 03/572-8489; Mon.–Fri. 11 A.M.–3 P.M., Thurs.–Sat. from 6 P.M.) has an excellent reputation for its Sauvignon Blanc and Chardonnay wines, but also for its restaurant. Morning and afternoon teas are available in an outdoor dining area, but more substantial meals—such as local green mussels steamed in the winery's own Riesling—make a meal at Hunter's memorable. Back in town, the **d'Urville Wine Bar and Brasserie** (52 Queen St., 03/577-9945; daily for lunch and dinner) is a narrow dining room with tables paralleling a long wooden bar shaped like a ship's bow and walls decorated with old maps and nautical charts. The menu features dishes such as a mouthwatering cumin-crusted rack of Canterbury lamb, as well as seasonal seafood dishes such as mussels steamed in white wine, with a hint of chili and garlic.

Continuing on the historic trail, visit **Fyffe House** (62 Avoca St., 03/319-5835; summer daily 10 A.M.–6 P.M., the rest of the year Thurs.–Mon. 10 A.M.–4 P.M.; adult $7, child $2), a colonial cottage from the 1860s when Kaikoura, then known as "Fyffe's village," was a whaling station.

Beyond Fyffe House, continue along the coast to a parking lot at the end of the road. From here, you can often see seals lazing on the rocks. This is also the starting point for a walking trail (allow 2.5 hours) that continues along the coast and then loops back through native forest high above the ocean.

C Whale-Watching

The Kaikoura coast is the only place in New Zealand where sperm whales live year-round. Therefore, visitors can usually see these impressive mammals, subject to conditions and seasonal fluctuations, whenever they visit Kaikoura—though locals say the winter months are best for viewing. The local Ngai Tahu, who have lived in the area for over 3,000 years, are

MARLBOROUGH

© ANDREW HEMPSTEAD

Snowcapped mountains form a magnificent backdrop to the beaches around Kaikoura.

the only ones permitted to operate tours. Their operation, **Whale Watch Kaikoura,** is based in a beachside railway station that has been converted to the Whaleway Station (03/319-6767 or 0800/655-121, www.whalewatch.co.nz). They operate three-hour whale-watching trips up to six times daily in search of sperm whales, orcas (summer only), humpback whales (winter only), Hector's and dusky dolphins, seals, and albatross. The cost is adult $130, child $60. Naturally, whale sightings cannot be guaranteed. Book two weeks ahead to be sure of a spot—in summer the tours are filled at least a week ahead.

The alternate way to see the whales is from above—by plane. **Wings Over Whales** (03/319-6580 or 0800/226-269) offers a 30-minute flight for a bird's-eye view of the whales (adult $135, child $75). A courtesy van will collect you from town, if needed, for the eight-km (five-mi) trip to the airfield.

Dolphins and Seals

You will probably see pods of dusky dolphins

on a Whale Watch Kaikoura tour, but the best way to get up close and personal is by swimming with them. **Dolphin Encounter** (96 Esplanade, 03/319-6777 or 0800/733-365; Oct.–Apr.) offers this experience (the first in New Zealand to do so—operators are now everywhere) that you won't forget in a hurry. The cost of the tour ($125) includes wet suit, mask, and snorkel.

Want to swim with seals? Then give Graeme or Bev Chambers of **Seal Swim Kaikoura** (03/319-6182 or 0800/732-579; Oct.–May) a call. Tours depart two to four times daily and cost $60–70 depending on the departure point.

Accommodations and Camping

Kaikoura has a large choice of excellent backpacker lodges. **Cray Cottage** (190 Esplanade, 03/319-5152, www.craycottage.co.nz; dorm beds $24, $52 s or d) is a 10-minute walk east from the information center (free pickups), but the waterfront location and modern facilities are outstanding. On the hill behind downtown

MARLBOROUGH

is **Topspot** (22 Deal St., off Churchill St., 03/319-5540; dorm beds $20, $35 s, $48 d), an old character house with a renovated modern interior—a large bright kitchen, a comfy living area (good music), a garden with deck, a barbecue, great views, and a friendly manager who offers free use of bikes.

Most motels are spread out along The Esplanade, immediately south and within walking distance of the information center. The best value of these is **Blue Seas Motels** (222 Esplanade, 03/319-5441 or 0800/507-077, www.blueseasmotel.co.nz; $110–180 s or d) with 13 self-contained units across the road from the beach.

A step up in quality is **White Morph Motor Inn** (94 Esplanade, 03/319-5014, www.white morph.co.nz). Standard rooms are $155, two-room suites are $230, and units with king-size bed and water views are $260. It features modern, spacious rooms and a seafood restaurant.

Hapuku Lodge (Hapuku Rd., 03/319-6559, www.hapukalodge.com; $390–850 s or d) is a quintessential New Zealand upscale accommodation. Rising like a mirage from the surrounding native bush, the buildings feature modern lines and lots of native woods. Inside the guest rooms are spacious bathrooms, super-comfortable beds, handcrafted furniture, and modern perks like Bose sound systems. The most expensive units are the Treehouses, with log fireplaces, king beds, and ocean views.

Within walking distance of Whale Watch Kaikoura, **Kaikoura Top 10 Holiday Park** (34 Beach Rd., 03/319-5362 or 0800/363-638, www.kaikouratop10.co.nz; camping $35, cabins $55–110 s or d, motel rooms $110) has a large grassy area for tents and vans, a number of great little cabins, a modern kitchen, a heated pool, and a playground.

Food

The one delicacy you must try in Kaikoura is locally caught crayfish (lobster). You can get it with all the trimmings in restaurants throughout town ($40–50 for half a cray), as well as enjoy it as a takeout meal (around $30 for a half). At **Continental Seafoods** (47 Beach Rd.,

03/319-5509; daily 10 A.M.–9 P.M.), a half crayfish, chips, and salad cost $30. Or choose from several fish of the day, mussels, smoked fish patties, and take it away fresh or have it cooked on the spot. Another place with less expensive seafood is **Pacifica Seafoods** (The Wharf, 03/319-5817; Mon.–Fri. 9 A.M.–5 P.M.).

Flukes Café (Whaleway Station, 03/319-7733; daily 8 A.M.–5 P.M.) features a contemporary Maori-influenced interior and an outdoor eating area overlooking the beach. The menu offers no surprises, but the setting can't be beat. Also affiliated with an adventure operator is **Café Encounter** (96 Esplanade, 03/319-6777 or 0800/733-365; Oct.–Apr. daily 7:30 A.M.–4 P.M.). Seating spills out onto the courtyard, the perfect place to enjoy eggs Benedict with smoked fish or a healthy wrap and good coffee.

Sonic on the Rocks (Esplanade, 03/319-6414; daily for lunch and dinner), easily recognized by the giant silver fish on the roof, is a casual seafood restaurant in the heart of town. Baked crayfish with all the trimmings is $89 for two, a huge bowl of wok-steamed mussels is $20, and the rich seafood chowder is $18. Moving up in style and price is **Forty Two 25 South** (146 Esplanade, 03/319-7145; daily from 5 P.M.). Again, seafood dominates, with seafood pastas for $24, fish of the day for $32, and half a cray for $40.

Information

Start your discovery at the excellent **Kaikoura Visitor Centre** (Esplanade, 03/319-5641, www.kaikoura.co.nz; summer daily 9 A.M.–5:30 P.M., the rest of the year Mon.–Fri. 9:30 A.M.–4 P.M.).

Getting There

Kaikoura has scheduled flights, but **Wings Over Whales** (03/319-6580) flies into the small airfield eight km (five mi) south of town on demand from Christchurch. The rail line runs right through town, making Kaikoura a popular stop for those traveling on the daily **TranzCoastal** service between Picton and Christchurch. For all the details, call **Tranz**

Scenic (0800/872-467). The main bus stop is in the parking lot for the visitor center on the Esplanade. Look for the board out front advertising arrival and departure times. The main operator is **Intercity** (03/364-1113, www .intercitycoach.co.nz), with daily service to Picton, Nelson, and Christchurch.

HANMER SPRINGS

Most people zoom down the east coast from Kaikoura on Highway 1, but while the alternate inland route (Hwy. 70) is longer, it provides a very different glimpse of the South Island. Around 120 km (75 mi) south of Kaikoura (allow at least 2.5 hours), Highway 70 ends at Highway 7, a major cross-island highway. From this point, it's 90 km (56 mi) south to Christchurch, but a worthwhile detour is Hanmer Springs, 43 km (27 mi) west off Highway 7. This alpine town of 700 is a popular getaway for those who enjoy soaking in thermal pools, hiking in exotic forests, fishing, or skiing. It attracts large numbers of New Zealanders and tourists year-round.

Sights and Recreation

The hot springs that feed **Hanmer Springs Thermal Pools & Spa** (Amuri Rd., 03/315-7511; daily 10 A.M.–9 P.M.; adult $12, child $6) are saline and alkaline, and the numerous indoor and outdoor pools vary in temperature 32–40°C (90–104°F). This is one of the appeals—the choice of regular hot pools, natural sulphur pools, and interconnected rock pools.

Hanmer Forest Park, one of New Zealand's oldest government-owned exotic forests, covers 16,844 hectares (41,620 acres) of land near the town; the most widely grown tree is the *Pinus radiata*. Many good tracks allow you to amble through the different types of forest to panoramic lookouts. For trail maps, stop by the **Forest Park Information Centre** (Jollies Pass Rd.; daily 9 A.M.–5 P.M.).

Practicalities

It's not too difficult to find a place to stay in Hanmer Springs—take your choice from a number of hotels and motels, tourist flats and cabins, and several good motor camps. The town also has restaurants, coffee shops, and takeaways.

Alpine Lodge Motel (1 Harrogate St., 03/315-7311 or 0800/993-377, www.alpine lodgemotel.co.nz; from $120 s or d) lies across the road from the thermal pools. Standard rooms are comfortable and self-contained but the Tower Suites ($250) provide Hanmer's finest lodging. These massive units feature circular beds, large spa baths, and private balconies.

Heritage Hanmer Springs (1 Conical Hill Rd., 03/315-7021 or 0800/368-888, www .heritagehotels.co.nz; $180 s or d), one of Hanmer's original accommodations, has undergone extensive renovations in recent years. It features landscaped gardens, a tennis court, a heated outdoor pool, and 24-hour room service. It also holds the village's premier restaurant. Check the website for discounted package deals.

Mountain View Top 10 Holiday Park is on the southern outskirts of Hanmer (03/315-7113 or 0800/904-545; camping $24–30, cabins from $45 s or d, motel rooms $120), but still within walking distance of the hot pools.

For information on the town and surrounding area, call in at the **Hanmer Springs Visitor Centre** (Amuri Ave. at Jacks Pass Rd., 03/315-7128 or 0800/733-426, www.alpine pacifictourism.co.nz; daily 10 A.M.–5 P.M.).

HANMER SPRINGS TO THE WEST COAST

From the Hanmer Springs intersection, Highway 7 climbs to 907-meter (2,980-ft) **Lewis Pass** (this route is often called the Lewis Pass Highway), then descends to the west coast. Allow six hours for the crossing, but expect to take longer if you want to stop and explore the wild, rugged South Island interior with its high mountain peaks, fast-flowing rivers, forests, and tranquil lakes.

Lewis Pass Scenic Reserve

Rediscovered by Europeans in 1861, the pass was used by generations of Maori to cross the mountains from the Canterbury coast to west coast greenstone country—the Ngai Tahu tribe used to hike over the pass, gather greenstone, then take prisoners to carry the precious rock back. Let your imagination run wild at this gorge by taking the short 25-minute one-way track starting at the Lewis Pass picnic area, which runs along the first section of the Ada Pass–St. James Walkway to Cannibal Gorge Bridge. Other tracks range from the short 10-minute **Waterfall Nature Walk** to the three- to five-day hike along the **St. James Walkway** (pamphlets available), and during the summer the rangers lead walks through the reserve.

Maruia Springs

This tiny settlement, a few km west of the pass itself, is a great place to stop for a hike, then a soak in the mineral pools of **Maruia Springs Thermal Resort** (03/523-8840, www.maruia .co.nz; daily 11 A.M.–5 P.M.; adult $15, child $8). Choices include a covered Japanese-style bathhouse, private spa pools, and outdoor pools surrounded by bird-filled native bush. You can stay overnight in pleasant hotel rooms ($169–249 s or d, includes entry to the pools). An-

other good reason to stop is to eat in the resort café. Breakfast is available 8 A.M.–9:30 A.M., lunch noon–2 P.M., and dinner 6–8 P.M.

Continuing West Toward the Coast

From Maruia Springs, it's 17 km (11 mi) to **Springs Junction,** a small hamlet with one motel, a café, a service station, and a post office. At this point, the highway divides. Highway 7 continues west to **Reefton** and Highway 65 spurs north to **Murchison,** on Highway 6. In the heart of a historic gold-mining area, Reefton offers varied opportunities for hiking, to relics of the mining era and through the surrounding wilderness, much of it protected by Victoria Forest Park. From Reefton, Highway 7 turns south, reaching the Tasman Sea at Greymouth. If you take this route, you miss one of the highlights of the west coast, Paparoa National Park, which can be reached by taking Highway 69 north from Reefton to meet Highway 6, then following the Buller River to the coast.

Nelson

Nelson (pop. 45,000), according to proud residents, has it all—over 2,500 hours of sunshine annually, beautiful beaches, top-notch wineries, a thriving arts and crafts industry, and a great selection of restaurants. Of course, visitors are invited to enjoy all of this and more, including lots of interesting accommodations and a central location for exploring three nearby national parks.

SIGHTS AND RECREATION

Trafalgar Street, which runs south from Highway 6 as it enters town from the north, is the main shopping strip, ending below an impressive cathedral that towers over downtown. Most sights are within walking distance of the centrally located information center, so park your vehicle and plan on exploring on foot.

Nelson Provincial Museum

Step off Nelson's busiest street and into this interesting museum (corner Trafalgar and Hardy Sts., 03/548-9588; Mon.–Fri. 10 A.M.–5 P.M., Sat.–Sun. 10 A.M.–4:30 P.M.; free), which features early Nelson history—displays of Maori carvings and artifacts found in the district, and objects and curios originally brought over by English settlers. A stairway leads up to a pleasant rooftop garden, from where you can look down on the bustle below.

Nelson Cathedral

Walk south from the information center along Trafalgar Street to Nelson's impressive cathedral (on Church Hill at the south end of the main shopping street, daily 7 A.M.–7 P.M. and during church services). Much of this Anglican cathedral, completed in 1925, is made of

© ANDREW HEMPSTEAD

Nelson's main shopping strip, Trafalgar Street, leads to a modern cathedral.

Takaka marble (from Takaka Hill, about 70 km/44 mi west of Nelson), and its landmark 35-meter (115-ft) tower dominates the inner-city area. Volunteer guides (on hand during the busy summer) point out the many memorials and historic links with early Nelson housed inside the cathedral.

Suter Te Aratoi o Whakatu
Reopening in early 2008 after extensive renovations and extensions, this art gallery (208 Bridge St., 03/548-4699; daily 10:30 a.m.–4:30 p.m.; adult $3, child $1) shouldn't be missed by any art lover. Along with the large permanent art collection dating back well over 100 years are varied exhibitions, films, performances, and recitals; at the excellent crafts shop you can buy top-quality pieces of local pottery, weaving, and prints. A café overlooks adjacent **Queen's Gardens,** one of Nelson's most attractive reserves containing many rare tree specimens (all named), a fernery, flowering bushes, and an ornamental pond swarming with ducks—don't miss it!

Founders Heritage Park
A collection of historic and replica buildings, this pleasant park (87 Atawhai Dr., 03/548-2649; daily 10 a.m.–4:30 p.m.; adult $5, child $2.50) lies on the northern edge of downtown. Highlights include a windmill, a chapel, a replica of Nelson's first fire station, a working general store, and horse-drawn wagons. And for those who aren't into history, there's a brewery, where you can relax with a pint of beer (see listing under *Entertainment*).

Historic Houses
Two of Nelson's oldest homes open to the public are in suburban Stoke. **Broadgreen House** (276 Nayland Rd., Stoke, 03/546-0283; daily 10:30 a.m.–4:30 p.m.; adult $3, child $0.50) is a magnificent two-story mid-Victorian "cob" house made from mud and clay mixed with straw, horsehair, and other reinforcing materials. The house, built around 1855, is set among perfect lawns and rambling rose gardens, and the interior period furnishings are an antique buff's delight.

Isel House (Main Rd., Stoke, 03/547-7529; daily 11 a.m.–4 p.m.; adult $3) is an impressive two-story wood and stone house built around 1886. Originally part of a sprawling estate, the home has been restored with period

MARLBOROUGH

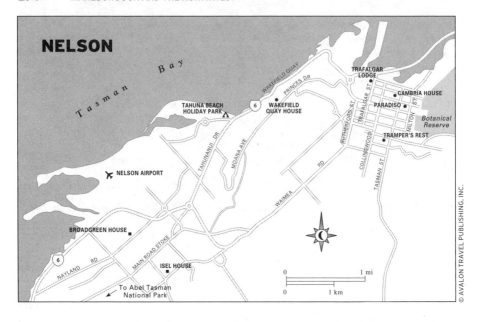

NELSON

© AVALON TRAVEL PUBLISHING, INC.

MARLBOROUGH

furnishings (including wallpaper imported from England) and is filled with priceless antiques. Although the original estate is long gone, the surrounding century-old gardens are still impressive.

Walking Trails

The many pleasant walks of varying distances around the city are described in a series of pamphlets put out by the Nelson City Council and available at the visitor center. One of the best known and most scenic is the one-km (0.6-mi) **Centre of New Zealand** track, which zigzags up Botanical Hill (148 meters/490 ft) to a lookout and monument marking the first trig station (a survey marker atop a hill) in Nelson. Start at the Botanical Reserve on Milton Street (east of downtown). **The Grampians,** another popular hike to a lookout, provides excellent views of the city and surrounding area, but note that the steep climb takes about 1.5 hours each way. The first section of the Grampian trail starts at the top (south) end of Collingwood Street in the city. The **Maitai River**

Walkway starts at the bridge near the visitor center and meanders along the river (past some good swimming holes), taking about four hours round-trip—take a picnic lunch and enjoy.

For an easy walk following the historic line of New Zealand's first railway, try the 9.5-km (six-mi) **Dun Mountain Walkway.** It starts on Tantragee Road (left off Brook St. in the suburb of The Brook, five km south of city center), finishes one km (0.6 mi) from the starting point on Brook Street, and takes about three hours round-trip.

Beaches

The closest, **Tahunanui Beach** (also called Tahuna Beach), is five km (3.1 mi) west of the city center, and is one of the safest, most popular beaches in the region. To get there from the city center take Haven Road west to Port Nelson and follow Rocks Road (Hwy. 6) along the waterfront, or catch the suburban bus (it runs every hour) from Bridge Street. This pleasant route is especially colorful in early summer, when striking *pohutukawa* trees bloom in a mass of scarlet flowers. Don't miss the incredible Aotearoa (Land of the Long White Cloud) wall mural (a Nelson Provincial Arts Council Mural Project) on the right side of Rocks Road as you follow the waterfront toward the beach.

If you don't mind a 27-km (17-mi) drive west toward Motueka, you'll be rewarded with about 12 km (eight mi) of soft golden sand, dunes, pine trees, safe swimming, and good surf casting at **Rabbit Island.** Take Highway 6 south out of Nelson, go through Richmond following signs to Motueka (Hwy. 60), and turn right at Pea Viner Corner. For more beautiful sandy beaches and fewer and fewer people, continue north to Golden Bay.

NELSON ARTS AND CRAFTS

Nelson is known throughout New Zealand for its fine, varied clays; excellent raw materials; a large community of talented, creative potters; and a vast number of outlets. Many of the clay and glaze materials (ground from naturally occurring minerals) used by potters throughout New Zealand come from the Nelson region. You can spend days visiting all the pottery shops throughout the area. For directions, pick up the free brochure *Nelson GuideBook* from the information center; it lists over 350 local artists and describes where to find them. Here are some favorites.

Nile Street, lined with some of Nelson's attractive older cottages – some dating from the 1800s – is home to many galleries. **South Street Gallery** (10 Nile St., 03/548-8117; Mon.-Fri. 10 A.M.-5 P.M., Sat.-Sun. 10 A.M.-4 P.M.) is definitely worth a stop to view its rustic interior while appreciating the works of more than 20 local artists, and maybe picking out a superb piece of the local pottery for which the gallery is renowned.

Out of Nelson to the southwest, **Craft Habitat** (corner of Main and Champion Rds. near the Stoke Bypass, 03/544-7482; Mon.-Fri. 10 A.M.-5 P.M., Sat.-Sun. 10 A.M.-4 P.M.) features an excellent selection of pottery, weaving, wood and metal products, carved bone, handcrafted baskets, fabric art, and handblown glass. You can watch many of the craftspeople actually creating their works of art. Save a few dollars for a refreshing Devonshire tea or light lunch in the **Habitat Café** (03/544-5657).

ENTERTAINMENT AND EVENTS
Nightlife
Founders Brewery (87 Atawhai Dr., 03/548-4638; daily 10 A.M.–4:30 P.M.) is my favorite place to relax with a beer in Nelson—not only is the brew tasty, there are plenty of outdoor tables in a quiet setting. On the grounds of Founders Heritage Park, the brewery uses organic ingredients, including locally grown hops and malt.

At the top end of the main street, **House of Ales** (296 Trafalgar St., 03/548-4220; daily until midnight) is a smooth-looking bar that attracts an after-work business crowd, but also a younger crowd late at night. It also offers better-than-usual pub fare and tables on the cobblestone sidewalk out front. The most popular backpacker hangout is **Shark Club** (136 Bridge St., 03/546-6630) with an outdoor beer garden, a large poolroom, and live entertainment on weekends. **Grumpy Mole** (83 Collingwood St., 03/548-1419; closed Sun.), at the corner of Bridge Street, is a Western-style bar, complete with a barn-board facade and Daisy Duke look-alike competitions. **Phat Club** (137 Bridge St., 03/548-6260) is busiest on weekends after 10 P.M., when a DJ spins dance tracks until the early hours of the morning.

Festivals
Nelson holds enough attraction to warrant a visit at any time of year, but also look out for the following annual events. **Sealord Summer Festival** (03/546-0200) extends over six weeks from the Christmas holiday break. Check at the visitor center for a schedule of lunchtime music concerts, street entertainment, a teddy bears' picnic, outdoor movie screenings, and

MARLBOROUGH

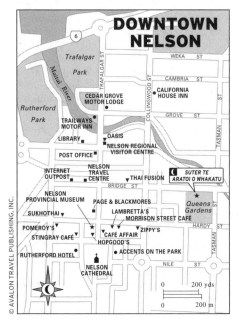

jazz concerts. On the middle Saturday of February, **Night with the Stars** opera attracts a crowd of up to 10,000 to Saxton Field, Stoke. It's a casual affair, and buses transport the masses from Nelson.

Hooked on Seafood, the fourth Saturday in March, features Nelson chefs showcasing their cooking skills at booths set up along Vickerman Street, Port Nelson; expect lots of local seafood complemented by New Zealand wines.

ACCOMMODATIONS AND CAMPING

Nelson is one of the best places in New Zealand when it comes to accommodations. With around 20 backpackers lodges, over 30 bed-and-breakfasts, and a similar number of motels, competition for business is intense—but it is you, the traveler, that benefits, with reasonable prices and high standards through all levels of accommodations.

Under $50

Backpackers are spoiled for choice, but my fave is ◖ **Accents on the Park** (335 Trafalgar St., 03/548-4335, www.accentsonthepark .com; dorm beds $24–28, $45 s, $89–99 d). Within walking distance of downtown, it has beautifully decorated (soundproofed) rooms, a greenery-filled courtyard, a bar, and a café. You'll hardly know you're staying at a backpacker lodge.

Another good choice for budget travelers is **Paradiso** (42 Weka St., 03/546-6703, www .backpackernelson.co.nz; dorm beds $18, $40 s or d), a 500-meter (0.32-mi) walk from downtown. Formerly a YHA property, it has been renovated and is surrounded by extensive gardens. It offers all the usual facilities, including a spacious kitchen, as well as a beautiful outdoor swimming pool, spa, sauna, and mountain bike rentals.

Another excellent choice is the **Tramper's Rest** (31 Alton St., 03/545-7477; dorm beds $21, $38 s, $51 d), 400 meters (0.24 mi) east of downtown. In a renovated house, this friendly lodge is small, but the facilities are of the very highest standard. No room has more than three beds, and there are no bunks.

A little farther out is the **Green Monkey** (129 Milton St., www.thegreenmonkey.co.nz; 03/545-7421), also in a renovated house. This place has two six-bed dorms ($23) and two private rooms ($56 s or d). The atmosphere is congenial, with guests having use of a courtyard and barbecue.

Out at Tahunanui Beach, four km (2.5 mi) southwest of downtown, is the **Beach Hostel** (25 Muritai St., 03/548-6817, www .nelsonbeachhostel.co.nz; dorm beds $22, $52 d). The atmosphere here is less hurried than at the downtown lodges, and the beach is a five-minute walk away. Breakfast is included in the rates. Transportation isn't a problem because the hostel offers town pickups and bikes for guest use (free), and buses heading down the west coast or out to Abel Tasman National Park stop out front.

$50-100

All the backpacker lodges have double rooms under $100, but motels in this category are

MARLBOROUGH

few and far between, especially in summer. You could try the no-frills **Anchor Lodge Motel** (7 Roto St., Tahunanui, 03/548-6007; $75 s or d), which is a couple of blocks from the beach. The six rooms each have a kitchen and there's a small pool and a barbecue area.

$100-150

A good-value motel within walking distance of downtown is **Trafalgar Lodge** (46 Trafalgar St., 03/548-3980, www.trafalgarlodge.co.nz; $105–150 s or d), opposite Trafalgar Park, which has six self-contained units and four bed-and-breakfast rooms in an adjacent villa. Even more central, **Mid City Motor Lodge** (218 Trafalgar St., 03/546-9063 or 0800/643-2489, www.midcitynelson.co.nz; $105 s, $115 d) offers 15 spacious self-contained studio units on three levels above the main shopping strip. Other amenities include a laundry and rooftop patio.

One of the better motels in town is **Cedar Grove Motor Lodge** (corner Trafalgar and Grove Sts., 03/545-1133 or 0800/233-274, www.cedargrove.co.nz; $130–180 s or d). The rooms are large and uncluttered, and even the smallest has a kitchen and TV/DVD combo. The Executive Suites are especially large.

Trailways Motor Inn (66 Trafalgar St., 03/548-7049 or 0800/872-459, www.trailways.co.nz; $145–250 s or d) boasts a peaceful location right on the Maitai River, but still within walking distance of downtown. The rooms are spacious and well furnished. They lack kitchens, but the inn has a good restaurant and a lounge bar, both opening to riverside seating.

Many more motels are southwest of downtown along Highway 6 as it passes through Tahuna Beach. Here, **Aloha Lodge** (19 Beach Rd., 03/546-4000 or 0800/462-564, www.alohalodgenelson.co.nz; $110–145 s or d) is separated from the sand by a park, and many of the rooms offer water views. Suites provide the best value. Set in vaguely Japanese-inspired towers with wraparound windows, the views are stunning. The courtyard has a barbecue area where guests tend to congregate in the evening.

$150-200

The largest downtown accommodation is the seven-story **Rutherford Hotel** (Trafalgar Square, 03/548-2299 or 0800/437-227, www.rutherfordhotel.co.nz; $165–200 s or d). It features 113 elegantly decorated rooms, a pool, spas, sauna, and fitness room, as well as a restaurant, café, and bar.

Over $200

A lovely 1905 villa enjoying an absolute waterfront setting, **☾ Wakefield Quay House** (385 Wakefield Quay, Port Hills, 03/546-7275, www.wakefieldquay.co.nz; $195–265 s, $225–295 d) is the quintessential Nelson accommodation. All rooms have water views and there's lots of outdoor space, including a verandah that is perfect for watching the setting sun. Rates include a cooked breakfast, wireless Internet, and the use of bikes. The owners also have a yacht that can be rented for $100 per hour.

If you feel like being pampered while staying in a beautifully restored old home, head directly for **California House Inn** (29 Collingwood St., 03/548-4173, www.californiahouse.co.nz; $230–295 d). Built in 1893, this elegant colonial home features five spacious guest rooms (my favorite is the over-sized Gordon Room, with an antique brass king-size bed and stained-glass windows). The cozy parlor is well stocked with reading material on Nelson and New Zealand, and you can help yourself to tea and coffee throughout the day. The breakfast menu features fresh fruit and cream, baked goodies, pancakes, blintzes, or omelets—sumptuous and different each morning.

At **Cambria House** (7 Cambria St., 03/548-4681 or 0800/548-4681, www.cambria.co.nz; $190–245 s, $235–295 d), the welcoming owner happily shares her home, offering guests six spacious guest rooms with inviting earthy color schemes and luxurious en suite bathrooms. Rates include a sumptuous

MARLBOROUGH

cooked breakfast in the attractive country-style dining room.

Holiday Parks

The center of town has no holiday parks, and if you arrive during holiday periods (especially January) without a reservation, finding a spot may be a problem. Nelson's largest holiday park is **Tahuna Beach Holiday Park** (Tahunanui Beach, 03/548-5159 or 0800/500-501, www.tahunabeachholidaypark.co.nz), 5 km (3.1 mi) from the city center—but if literally hundreds of people in close proximity to one another cause you any degree of claustrophobia, you may find the 400 tent sites and 600 caravan sites, plus cabins, a problem. It's adjacent to a sandy beach, has a shop (open daily 8 A.M.–7 P.M.) and the usual facilities. Camping is $28 and indoor accommodations range from basic cabins ($40 s or d) to wheelchair-accessible motel rooms ($100). Follow the road west along the waterfront (Hwy. 6) to Tahunanui, and turn off Rocks Road onto Beach Road.

You'll find the closest caravan sites and cabins to the city center at **Nelson City Holiday Park** (230 Vanguard St., 03/548-1445, www.nelsonholidaypark.co.nz; camping $28, cabins $40–70 s or d). It has communal facilities and a TV lounge, but no tent sites.

FOOD

Nelson brims with cafés and restaurants—take a short stroll around town and you're bound to see plenty of places likely to lure you back later for a snack or meal. If you have a particular fancy, drop by the information center and ask for a recommendation.

Cafés

Café culture is alive and well in Nelson, with cafés emphasizing quality coffee and fresh, healthy eating options. **Stingray Café** (8 Church St., 03/545-8957; daily for breakfast, lunch, and dinner) typifies Nelson's casual vibe—local artwork on the walls, lots of organic ingredients, and live music most nights. For healthy, delicious snacks, light meals ($5.50–11.50), and good music in electric blue, red, and yellow surroundings, try **Zippy's** (276 Hardy St., 03/546-6348; Mon.–Sat. 9 A.M.–4 P.M.). This is one of the better choices in town for vegetarians.

[**Lambretta's** (204 Hardy St., 03/545-8555; daily 8:30 A.M.–10 P.M.) plays up the Italian café theme with a colonnaded entrance, scooters hanging from the walls, and black-attired staff. Always bustling with locals, Lambretta's has excellent coffee, as well as dishes such as calamari and pineapple salad ($18) and a variety of single-serve pizzas under $15. Parents will appreciate the area set aside for children.

Off the main street, **Zest** (5 Church St., 03/546-7064; Mon.–Fri. 7:30 A.M.–4:30 P.M., Sat. 8 A.M.–3 P.M.) is a bright café with a delicatessen-style counter filled with gourmet goodies, including lots of locally produced items. Paninis, quiches, and creative salads range $8–15.

If it's quality coffee you're after, **Pomeroy's** (80 Hardy St., 03/546-6944; Mon.–Fri. 9 A.M.–5 P.M., Sat. 9:30 A.M.–12:30 P.M.) will deliver. The coffee is roasted in-house for cafés and restaurants throughout the region, but you can also stop by and order to go. Pomeroy's also sells specialty teas and Cuban cigars. **Morrison Street Café** (244 Hardy St., 03/548-8110; Mon.–Fri. 7:30 A.M.–4 P.M., Sat. 8:30 A.M.–3 P.M., Sun. 9 A.M.–3 P.M.) is also renowned for top-quality coffee.

With tables overlooking the river, **Oasis Café** (81 Trafalgar St., 03/548-1180; summer daily 8 A.M.–9 P.M., the rest of the year daily 8 A.M.–4:30 P.M.) provides a pleasant environment to spread out all those brochures and maps you've collected from the adjacent visitor center. Breakfasts range $10–20 while fresh favorites like sautéed scallop and bacon salad and Thai chicken curry are all under $20.

At Founders Heritage Park, the outdoor tables at **[** **Founders Brewery** (87 Atawhai Dr., 03/548-4638; daily 10 A.M.–4:30 P.M.) is the perfect place for lunch on a warm afternoon. The menu includes lots of dishes to share, as well as a tasty smoked chicken sandwich ($14), gourmet pies, and a kids' menu.

Contemporary

The themes at **Café Affair** (295 Trafalgar St., 03/548-8295; daily 9 A.M.–11 P.M.) are mixed—a modern feel, with lots of wooden furniture and a bar decorated with pioneer implements—but it works well and, most importantly, the food is good. Breakfasts include a delicious smoked fish, while evening diners gravitate to the stonegrill dining (grilling on hot stones), with everything but the scotch fillet (rib eye to North Americans) under $30.

One of Nelson's more stylish dining rooms is **Hopgood's** (284 Trafalgar St., 03/545-7191; Mon.–Fri. 9 A.M.–9 P.M., Sat.–Sun. 9 A.M.–10 P.M.). It may look like a big-city eatery, but the chef uses local and organic produce wherever possible. The ricotta pancakes smothered with strawberries and honey are a great way to start the day, while at dinner (mains $21–31) the fish and lamb dishes are reliable.

Thai

Sukhothai (89 Hardy St., 03/539-0282; daily for lunch and dinner) is an inexpensive no-frills Thai restaurant. Expect to pay under $8 for spicy Thai soups, $6.50 for delicious spring rolls, and $13–18 for stir fries and curries. With its bright-orange murals and thatched huts, **Thai Fusion** (123 Bridge St., 03/548-2988; daily 11:30 A.M.–2 P.M. and from 5 P.M.) is a little more stylish. Still, most dinner mains remain below $15, including red seafood curry and a tasty prawn and cashew stir fry.

Wine Shop

If you want to relax with a bottle of wine back at your room, talk to the experts at **Casa del Vino** (214 Hardy St., 03/548-0088; Mon.–Fri. 10 A.M.–6 P.M., Sat.–Sun. 10 A.M.–4 P.M.), a specialty downtown wine shop.

INFORMATION AND SERVICES
Information

The main source of information is the **Nelson Regional Visitor Centre** (77 Trafalgar St., 03/548-2304, www.nelsonnz.com; Mon.–Fri. 8:30 A.M.–5 P.M., Sat.–Sun. 9 A.M.–4 P.M.), which has interesting displays, a gift store, and an adjacent café. It's also a booking and transportation center, so you can get everything you need in one location. The **Department of Conservation** (03/546-9339) staffs a desk in summer, handing out information on the surrounding national parks.

Page & Blackmores (254 Trafalgar St., 03/548-9992) is a great little independent bookstore.

Services

The post office is at 86 Trafalgar Street, kitty corner to the visitor center. Get online at the visitor center or **Internet Outpost** (35 Bridge St., 03/539-1150). **Bubbles Laundrette** is at 635 Rocks Road (across from Tahuna Beach). You'll find restrooms at the cathedral steps on Trafalgar Square, and at Buxton car park, Millers Acre car park, Montgomery car park, and the Tahunanui playground.

Emergencies

For emergency ambulance, police, or fire brigade, call 111. **Nelson Hospital** is on Waimea Road (main entrance on Kawai St., 03/546-1800). Doctors at **City Care** (202 Rutherford St., 03/546-8881) are on duty daily until 8 P.M. **Prices Pharmacy** (03/548-3897; Mon.–Fri. 8:30 A.M.–8 P.M., Sat. 9 A.M.–8 P.M., Sun. 9 A.M.–8 P.M.) is on the corner of Hardy and Collingwood Streets.

GETTING THERE

Nelson Airport is right on Tasman Bay, eight km (five mi) southwest of downtown. **Air New Zealand** (0800/737-000, www.airnewzealand.com) has direct flights from Nelson to Auckland, Wellington, and Christchurch. **Soundsair** (0800/505-005) flies daily between Nelson and Wellington. **Super Shuttle** (03/547-5782) meets all arrivals and provides door-to-door service for $15 per person. A taxi to the airport is about $20 one-way.

MARLBOROUGH

It's easy to reach Nelson by bus from Picton with either **Intercity** (03/548-1538, www.intercitycoach.co.nz) or one of the many smaller shuttle services, such as **Kbus** (03/578-4075). The latter also serves Christchurch and the west coast. Meanwhile **Abel Tasman Coachlines** (03/548-0285, www.abeltasmantravel.co.nz) departs Nelson for Motueka and gateway towns for Abel Tasman National Park. Many fares are structured as day trips, with the option to add on cruises, kayaking, and other activities. All bus companies depart from the Nelson Travel Centre (27 Bridge St.; Mon.–Fri. 7 A.M.–6 P.M., Sat.–Sun. 7 A.M.–4 P.M.). Most buses also stop outside the Nelson Visitor Centre on Trafalgar Street.

GETTING AROUND

Nelson Suburban Bus Lines (03/548-3290) provides local service covering the city center, Port Nelson, Tahunanui, Bishopdale, Stoke, Richmond, and Wakefield. The downtown hub is the Nelson Travel Centre (27 Bridge St.).

Book rental vehicles well in advance, especially if arriving by air. The main agencies are **Avis** (03/547-2727), **Budget** (03/546-9255), **Hertz** (03/547-2299), **NZ Rent-a-car** (03/548-5888), **Rent-a-dent** (03/546-9890), and **Thrifty** (03/547-5563). Rent bikes from **Stewarts Cycle City** (114 Hardy St., 03/548-1666).

The friendly drivers from **Nelson City Taxis** (03/548-8225) will gladly take you on a tour of Nelson and the surrounding country, or just home from the pub.

Nelson to Abel Tasman National Park

Take Highway 6 southwest out of Nelson and, after going through Richmond, swing west on Highway 60. This scenic road along Tasman Bay passes pottery shops, weaving sheds, deer farms, and apple orchards (excellent apples in March).

If staying at a clothing-optional holiday resort sounds appealing, look for the sign to **Mapua Leisure Park** (Toru St., Mapua, 03/540-2666, www.nelsonholiday.co.nz; campsites $28–35, cabins $65, motel rooms $110–130 s or d). It's about a half-hour drive from Nelson, 15 minutes to Motueka. The camp has swimming, fishing, tennis, golf, and a beautiful waterfront café. If nudity offends you, keep driving.

MOTUEKA

Motueka (pop. 7,000) is a relaxed town nestled between the peaks of Kahurangi National Park and the white sands of Tasman Bay. Make your first stop **Motueka Visitor Centre** (20 Wallace St., 03/528-6543; daily 8 A.M.–5 P.M., until 7 P.M. in summer). The staff provides brochures, books accommodations, orders tickets, arranges horticultural tours in the local area, sells fishing licenses, and offers the latest park transportation information. Housed in a historic redbrick build-

ing along the main road, **Motueka Museum** (140 High St., 03/528-7660; Mon.–Fri. 10 A.M.–4 P.M., Sat. 10 A.M.–2 P.M.; adult $2, child $0.50) is worth a visit if it's not beach weather.

Accommodations and Food

Motueka has a range of accommodations to suit all budgets. At the top end of High Street, **Bakers Lodge** (4 Poole St., 03/528-1012, www.bakerslodge.co.nz; dorm beds $23, $66–76 d) is an excellent choice for budget travelers. A historic bakery building has been transformed for the purpose. Some double rooms have private baths and all public areas are clean, bright, and welcoming. **Equestrian Lodge Motels** (Tudor St., 03/528-9369 or 0800/668-782, www.equestrianlodge.co.nz; $120 s or d) features 15 large units, each with a modern kitchen, set around extensive gardens and a swimming pool.

For a quick snack, try one of the mouthwateringly good bakeries on the main street, such as **Patisserie Royal** (152 High St., 03/528-7200; daily 6 A.M.–4 P.M.). **Hot Mama's** (195 High St., 03/528-7039; daily for breakfast, lunch, and dinner) dishes up more substantial meals and has seats in a beautiful courtyard.

MOTUEKA TO THE PARK

After passing through **Riwaka**, Highway 60 passes the turnoff east to the beach resort town of **Kaiteriteri**, one of the best swimming beaches in the Nelson region. Here you'll find **Kaiteriteri Beach Motor Camp** (03/527-8010, www.kaiteriteribeach.co.nz; campsites $22, cabins $40–55 s or d). Features include a store, tearooms, an 18-hole mini-golf course, and trampolines, along with the usual facilities. You'll also pass the road that runs northeast to **Sandy Bay**, another good swimming beach, and **Marahau**, the southern entrance to Abel Tasman National Park.

From the turnoff to Marahau, Highway 60 continues north around the back of Abel Tasman National Park to the park's northern gateway, Totaranui. The road first ascends **Takaka Hill** (made of marble, with four major caves—the locals call this speleologist's delight "Marble Mountain"). You can take a tour of the **Ngarua Caves** (03/528-8093; Sept.–June; adult $15, child $7.50). The western entrance to the park is the 12-km (seven-km) gravel Canaan Road that leads to **Canaan**. It turns right off Highway 60 before the summit of Takaka Hill, but if you don't already know where you're headed, venture to the summit for splendid views of Kahurangi National Park, and continue down to Upper Takaka, passing the "Rat Trap" Hotel.

Abel Tasman National Park

Protecting a wild and rugged chunk of land separating Tasman Bay from Golden Bay, Abel Tasman National Park (22,139 hectares/54,710 acres) is the smallest national park in New Zealand. The focus for most visitors is the coastline, which is fronted by beautiful sandy beaches, far from any road and accessible only by boat. The park extends from **Separation Point** in the north to **Sandy Bay** in the south, and includes all the islands and reefs up to 2.5 km (1.5 mi) out to sea. Many seabirds nest in the park—shags, gannets, blue penguins, terns, oystercatchers, herons, and stilts—and you can often catch sight of seals or the occasional dolphin frolicking not far offshore.

The interior of Abel Tasman is often ignored, but adventurous hikers enjoy sculptured granite gorges and marble outcrops, icy waterfalls and polished swimming holes, impressive cave systems and an enormous vertical shaft, pockets of rainforest, isolated beaches, and lush native bush alive with birds.

No roads run through the park, but access roads lead to **Marahau** in the south, **Canaan** in the west, and **Wainui Inlet, Totaranui,** and **Awaroa Inlet** in the north. Tour boats depart from Motueka and Marahau.

SIGHTS AND RECREATION

The only way to reach the park is on foot, by cruise boat, or by kayak.

Cruises

For a good introduction to Abel Tasman National Park without hiking the tracks or driving all the way to Totaranui, take a cruise with **Abel Tasman Wilson's Experiences** (265 High St., Motueka, 03/528-2027 or 0800/223-582, www.abeltasman.co.nz). This company is run by the Wilson family, who originally homesteaded in what is now the park over 100 years ago. Their boats leave the beach at Kaiteriteri daily at 9:40 A.M., picking up passengers at Marahau before continuing into the park. The boat makes stops at many secluded spots en route, including the family's lodges at Awaroa Bay and Torrent Bay. The turn-around point, Totaranui, is reached just after midday. The round-trip cruise takes five to six hours and costs adult $56, child $26, which includes a running commentary and tea and coffee. Take your own lunch or order ahead for $14. Most people don't make the full trip, instead opting to disembark along the way to either walk a section of the coastal hiking track

Wharivwharangi Bay

SEA KAYAKING

CRUISES

Taupo Point

WHARIWHARANGI HUT

Separation Point

Mutton Cove

Anapai Bay

Golden Bay

Totaranui

Pohara

Wainui Falls

Tasman Bay

Wainui Bay

AWAPOTO HUT

ABEL TASMAN COASTAL TRACK

ANAROA HUT

Abel Head

Pikituna Range

Inland Track

Abel Tasman National Park

WAINUI HUT

BARK BAY HUT   Bark Bay

MOA PARK HUT   Cascade Falls

Canaan

CASTLE ROCK HUT

ANCHORAGE HUT

0   3 mi

0   3 km

Sandy Bay

ABEL TASMAN NATIONAL PARK

© AVALON TRAVEL PUBLISHING, INC.

(03/528-2027) runs daily water-taxi services as far north as Totaranui, dropping hikers off at Tonga and at Bark, Torrent, and Tinline Bays ($20–35 one-way). The flexible schedule allows you to spend a couple of hours hiking the coastal track and be picked up again on the same day.

Before you set out on an overnight trek on the coastal track, you must buy a **Great Walks Pass,** which must be attached to your backpack and clearly visible—you get useful track information with the pass. The pass costs $10 per person per night to camp or $25 per person for the huts. Book online at www.doc.govt.nz or pick the pass up at the DOC office in Nelson.

Short Walks

Take any of the access roads to park boundaries for a variety of short walks to scenic spots or lookouts. Coming from the south, turn northeast off Highway 60 to Sandy Bay and continue along Sandy Bay Road to Marahau. **Tinline Walk** starts from the coastal track, about two km (one mi) from Marahau car park, and loops through groves of beech, *kahikatea, pukatea, rimu,* and other native trees; it takes about 30 minutes round-trip. If you're feeling a little more energetic, follow the tracks to beautiful **Coquille Bay** (about 45 minutes one-way from Marahau car park) or to **Apple Tree Bay** (1.5 hours one-way); or take the Coastal Track to **Torrent Bay** (about four hours one-way), one of the most scenic bays in the park. From Torrent Bay, two other short walks lead to **Cleopatra's Pool** and **Cascade Falls,** and you can return by water taxi.

From Totaranui, at the northern end, a short 45-minute walk north takes you to golden **Anapai Beach,** or if you want to make it an overnighter, continue for another two to three spectacular hours to **Whariwharangi Bay** and hut. Another popular short walk is the **Waiharakeke Track.** It starts on Awaroa Road about one km (0.5 mi) south of the Totaranui turnoff and runs down to Waiharakeke Beach, taking about 1.5 hours to pass through valleys, fern-filled gullies, and crystal-clear streams to end at yet another beautiful beach.

or just relax on the beach. A popular combination is to cruise as far as Torrent Bay, then walk south to Bark Bay (allow 2.5 hours) to pick up the cruise on its return to Kaiteriteri.

Abel Tasman Coastal Track

The spectacular coastal scenery and accessibility of the Abel Tasman Coastal Track makes it one of New Zealand's most popular (and busiest) tramps. The trailheads are at Marahau and Totaranui, which are separated by 51 km (32 mi) of native bush, secluded bays, and long stretches of golden sand. The track takes three to four days, with huts and camping areas at regular intervals. Before you set out, check tide times for crossing the Awaroa and Wainui Bay inlets—posted at the ends of main roads to the park, at Totaranui, and at all coastal huts. You can cross Awaroa and Wainui Bay inlets on foot two hours each side of low tide only; Torrent and Bark Bay inlets have high-tide as well as low-tide tracks.

Abel Tasman Wilson's Experiences

MARLBOROUGH

C Sea Kayaking

An extremely popular way to discover the beauty of the Abel Tasman coastline is by sea kayak. **Abel Tasman Kayaks** (Marahau, 03/527-8022, www.abletasmankayaks.co.nz) offers kayaking options for all levels of expertise. Day trips ($99) are the most popular; you begin from the beach and paddle up the coastline to a remote spot for lunch, then out to a number of islands where seals are often spotted. Then, if the wind is right, a sail is hoisted for the return trip. The guided three-day trip with tent accommodations and all meals provided is $450. Experienced paddlers wanting to explore the park without a guide can rent kayaks for $69 per day.

Canaan

A geologically fascinating area to explore on foot is Canaan, a haven for cavers. Take Highway 60 to Takaka Hill, turn off on Canaan Road, and continue almost to the end. The winding road passes amazing granite and marble rock outcrops and ends at rocky Canaan basin. Look out for the track marker to the left leading to **Harwood's Hole,** an incredible marble-walled vertical shaft 50 meters wide and 200 meters (656 ft) deep that leads to one of the most impressive cave systems in the area. The track to Harwood's Hole is an easy 45 minutes through beech forest, but be careful around the edge of the shaft as the ground is very unstable—a fall into this hole would definitely end your vacation. From the car park at the end of Canaan Road are several other short walks, or you can join the inland track system to either Wainui or Marahau.

PRACTICALITIES

Marahau

At the southern end of the park, the small community of Marahau has a variety of accommodations. **The Barn** (Harvey Rd., 03/527-8043, www.barn.co.nz; camping $12 per person, dorm beds $26, $60 d) is right by the starting point of all the best hiking trails and just down the road from Abel Tasman Kayaks. C **Ocean View Chalets** (03/527-8232, www.accommodationabeltasman.co.nz; $128–235

s or d) are scattered along a ridge overlooking Tasman Bay at Marahau. Each handcrafted cedar chalet has a lounge area and balcony. This accommodation offers up to a 30 percent discount on room rates during the off-season. Breakfast is an additional $12, as is a picnic lunch. **Marahau Beach Camp** (Franklin St., 03/527-8176; camping $15 s and $25 d, cabins $50–60 s or d) is right by the beach and has kayak rentals, a grocery store, and a café.

Park Café (03/527-8270, Oct.–Apr. daily 8 A.M.–8 P.M.) offers ocean views and a casual atmosphere right in the heart of the village.

Accommodations Within the Park

Aside from backcountry huts and campsites, three privately owned lodges lie within the park boundaries, all on beautiful beaches. The Wilson family, operators of Abel Tasman Wilson's Experience (03/528-2027 or 0800/223-582, www.abeltasman.co.nz) has rebuilt the family homestead on its original site in Awaroa Bay. Today, **Meadowbank Homestead** offers all the expected comforts in a setting accessible only by boat or on foot. The Wilson family also operates the modern **Torrent Bay Lodge.** Overnight rates at either are adult $716, child $495, inclusive of meals.

Also at Awaroa Bay is C **Awaroa Lodge and Cafe** (03/528-8758, www.awaroalodge.co.nz; $295–400 s or d), tucked behind the sand dunes. It's a popular stopover for hikers, but a worthwhile destination in itself, with kayaks, good fishing, and a delightfully rustic sauna. For the remote location, the rooms are superb, with king beds, luxurious bathrooms, and private balconies. The restaurant here is open to both guests and day-trippers, and takes full advantage of an organic garden.

Totaranui Camping

At the north end of the park is the beachside **Totaranui Beach Camp** (03/528-8083; adult $12, child $6), with plenty of grassy campsites (no power hookups), toilets, and fresh water. It's very popular and usually booked solid

December 20–January 31 (the only period when bookings are accepted).

Information

The best source of park information is the Department of Conservation (www.doc.govt.co.nz), which operates a desk through summer in the **Nelson Regional Visitor Centre** (77 Trafalgar St., 03/546-9339; Mon.–Fri. 8:30 A.M.–5 P.M., Sat.–Sun. 9 A.M.–4 P.M.). Closer to the park, you can also get information from the **Motueka Visitor Centre** (20 Wallace St., 03/528-6543; daily 8 A.M.–5 P.M., until 7 P.M. in summer).

Getting There and Around

Abel Tasman Coachlines (03/548-0285, www.abeltasmantravel.co.nz) runs daily between Nelson and various park gateways, including Kaiteriteri, where bus arrivals are scheduled to link up with the tour boat departures of **Abel Tasman Wilson's Experiences** (03/528-2027 or 0800/223-582, www.abeltasman.co.nz). This company, along with **Abel Tasman Sea Shuttle** (03/528-9759 or 0800/732-748), provides water-taxi service throughout the park for $20–35 one-way. Both companies make pickups in Marahau.

Golden Bay

From Motueka, Highway 60 heads inland, climbing to Takaka Hill before descending into a beautiful yet sparsely populated region framed by the calm waters of Golden Bay. Missed by many travelers and much quieter than Abel Tasman National Park, it's a good spot to explore at a leisurely pace, with a mix of water and land activities to keep you busy for a day or two.

TAKAKA

Gateway to Golden Bay, Takaka (pop. 1,250) is a small inland village with an artsy feel. In town, **Golden Bay Museum** (Commercial St., 03/525-6268; daily 10 A.M.–4 P.M.; free) is contained within an old post office building along the main street. Displays cover Maori settlement, Abel Tasman's 1642 journey, local arts and crafts, and a relief map of the area.

Pupu Springs

Continue along Highway 60 north of Takaka and look for a sign on the left at Waitapu Bridge to Pupu (also known as Waikoropupu) Springs. This natural jumbo-sized freshwater spring pumps out an incredible 1.2 million liters (320,000 gallons) of icy-cold, crystal-clear water a day—the largest freshwater spring in Australasia (if not the world). At the end

of the short walking track is a large multicolored pool, calm around the edge but turbulent in the middle, where water (about 11°C/52°F) gushes and bubbles to the surface at a rate of 14 cubic meters a second. Local old-timers claim the vent is so deep that divers have been unable to find the bottom of the pool (there is no public swimming). A fascinating diagram and display near the pool gives you the rundown on the what, where, and why of the springs—don't miss the striking underwater photographs taken by adventurous divers.

If you'd like to do a short, very interesting three-km (1.9-mi) walk, continue to the end of the road (beyond the springs) to the beginning of **Pupu Walk.** About 90 minutes round-trip, the track follows an old gold-mining water race, part of which has been reused for power generation, and finishes at a weir (good picnic spot).

Practicalities

The best-located accommodations are 10 km (6.2 mi) northeast of Takaka at Pohara. Here you'll find ☕ **Pohara Beach Top 10 Holiday Park** (03/525-9500, www.pohara.com; camping $15 per person, cabins $48–65 s or d, motel rooms $105). On yet another beautiful beach (along Golden Bay, not Tasman Bay), it offers sheltered swimming and sunbathing along with the usual facilities. Back in downtown Takaka, **Anatoki Lodge Motel** (87 Commercial St., 03/525-8047 or 0800/262-333, www.anatokilodges.co.nz; $110–140 s or d) is right downtown. It features 11 spacious first-floor units, each with a kitchen, and a solar-heated pool.

The best place for a meal in Takaka is the **Wholemeal Cafe** (60 Commercial St., 03/525-9426; daily for breakfast, lunch, and dinner), which dishes up delicious home-baked goodies and full healthy meals at reasonable prices (I had the warm lamb Thai salad—delicious). Continuing beyond Takaka 17 km (10.6 mi) you'll come to the **Mussel Inn** (Onekaka, 03/525-9241; daily from 11 A.M.), which looks like a rustic old pub but actually dates to the 1990s. Most of the dishes are prepared using organic ingredients (order at the bar), the beer is brewed in-house, and you can expect live music performances on weekend evenings.

Golden Bay Visitor Centre is easy to find as you enter Takaka from the south (Willow St., 03/525-9136; Mon.–Fri. 9 A.M.–5 P.M., Sat.–Sun. 9 A.M.–4 P.M.).

COLLINGWOOD AND VICINITY

Twenty-nine km (18 mi) from Takaka and the northernmost town of any size along Highway 60 (Pakawau and Port Puponga farther north are mainly remote vacation spots), Collingwood (pop. 260) has all the services of a small resort town and is the main gateway to Farewell Spit.

Accommodations

Backpackers are well catered for at **Somerset House** (Gibbs Rd., 03/524-8624, www.backpackerscollingwood.co.nz; dorm beds $25, $38 s, $56 d), which has two dorms and three double rooms. The other option is **Collingwood Motor Camp** (William St., 03/524-8149; campsites $28, cabins from $48 s or d), on the south side of town right along the water's edge—you can pull in a fish without leaving your tent flap. It has tennis courts, bike and canoe rentals, and all the usual communal facilities.

Continuing North from Collingwood

Driving north to the end of the road is most worthwhile for scenery buffs, wildlife enthusiasts, and bird-watchers with their own wheels. The lonely road takes you along the edge of Golden Bay through wild rugged scenery chockablock with black swans, Canada geese, ducks, and shorebirds to **Pakawau** (motor camp, store, and petrol pump) and **Port Puponga.** Few homes, buildings, or signs of human life dot the road—local kids attend correspondence school. From Port Puponga, the road crosses the peninsula to the open ocean, passing **Oldman Rock,** an exposed and weathered cliff "face." At the end of the road, a one-km (0.6-mi) walking trail leads steeply over grassy hills and sand dunes to **Wharariki Beach,** where you can view the offshore seal colony of Archway Island through binoculars (largest numbers in winter). Be prepared with insect repellent, and if the weather looks ominous, carry appropriate raingear.

FAREWELL SPIT

Known as Onetahua (heaped-up sand) to the Maori, the 35 km (22 mi) of sand dunes that make up Farewell Spit are one of the country's most important wading-bird habitats. It is also regarded as the world's longest sandbar. Protected as a nature reserve by restricted access, the spit is home to banded dotterels, gannets, godwits, and royal spoonbills. A visit to the spit is not just for bird-watchers—the sight of seemingly never-ending sand dunes pushed skyward by the forces of the Tasman Sea and backed by the calm waters of Golden Bay is not soon forgotten.

Tours

Because the spit is a protected wildlife sanctuary, the only way to visit it is on a guided tour. These are operated from Collingwood by **Farewell Spit Tours** (03/524-8257 or 0800/808-257, www.farewellspit.com), which offers a 5.5-hour tour to the very end of the spit, with plenty of time for sightseeing along the way; adult $80, child $45. Ecotours take you out to a gannet colony and along prime wading-bird habitat. At least one tour runs each day, but departure times (between 6:30 A.M. and 2 P.M.) depend entirely on the tide. Without a permit and independent of the tours, you can freely walk for 2.5 km (1.5 mi) along the inner beach at the base of the spit or four km (2.5 mi) along the outer beach; anglers must obtain a permit from a DOC office to fish from the outer beach.

KAHURANGI NATIONAL PARK

If you're in search of relatively undisturbed and spectacular scenery, high mountain lakes, alpine flowers, fishing, rock-climbing, hunting, and great views, head for New Zealand's second-largest (452,000 hectares/1,117,000 acres) national park. The park is best known for the Heaphy Track, but the more accessible **Cobb Valley** is also interesting. Several hiking tracks permit access into the valley, but the short one to Bushline Hut, Lake Sylvester, and Little Sylvester Lake (about two hours one-way) is easiest. To get to the Cobb Valley from Upper Takaka, take the road to the powerhouse, and then drive another windy 13 km (eight mi) to the dam. The valley starts 28 km (17 mi) from the Upper Takaka turnoff.

Heaphy Track

The 77-km (48-mi) Heaphy Track has always been popular, but is even more so since the proclamation of Kahurangi National Park in 1996. You can travel the route in either direction, but most hikers start in the east at Brown Hut (about 35 km/22 mi south of Collingwood), walk toward the coast, and finish at the

Kohaihai Shelter (15 km/nine mi north of Karamea). The track traverses the park's vast and rugged interior, then follows the Heaphy River to the ocean, continuing south along the coast to the Kohaihai River. Swimming is not advised along the coastal section, but it's fine in the lagoons and the Heaphy River, and the Karamea offers good trout fishing. Along the way, you can expect to cross rivers by swing bridge and ford shallow streams; pass through forests, open tussock land, and **Gouland Downs** (lots of wildlife); and finish up walking along a wild, surf-pounded west-coast beach. The track takes at least three days, five to six days if you stop and smell the flowers. Seven well-equipped huts (heated, with gas cookers, bunk beds, and toilets) are situated at regular intervals. Bookings can be made online at www.doc.govt.nz or at the DOC desk in the Nelson Regional Visitor Centre (77 Trafalgar St., 03/546-9339; Mon.–Fri. 8:30 A.M.–5 P.M., Sat.–Sun. 9 A.M.–4 P.M.).

The track is in a high rainfall area so pack for rain and soggy ground. The warm summer months are the most popular time to do the track, but unless you have a good supply of insect repellent, swarms of tiny, pesky sand flies can seem to eat you alive. Many prefer to hike the track in winter when the frosts keep the sand flies and crowds away.

Kahurangi Guided Walks (03/525-7177, www.kahurangiwalks.co.nz) offers a variety of walks along the track. If you just want a taste of the park, consider a day trip up the Cobb Valley ($110), or you can complete the entire track over five days ($1,000, all-inclusive).

Nelson Lakes National Park

Nelson Lakes National Park, a mountainous area with many peaks over 2,000 meters (6,562 ft) high, lush beech forests, and bush-fringed lakes, lies inland at the northern end of the mighty **Southern Alps.** Off Highway 63, approximately 104 km (65 mi) from Nelson and 158 km (98 mi) from the west-coast town of Westport, this park is a good place

to head if you're looking for a rugged wilderness experience.

The park, with 270 km (168 mi) of hiking trails, can only be truly appreciated on foot. Because of the rough terrain, no roads run through it, but you can still reach a couple of scenic spots by car—the town of St. Arnaud (main gateway to the park), the two

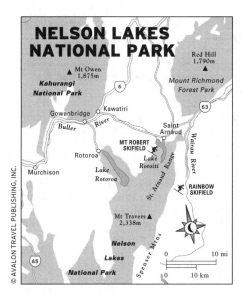

NELSON LAKES NATIONAL PARK

Flora and Fauna

Lush beech forests are the park's trademark. You can find all four beech species that grow throughout New Zealand here: Red and silver beech thrive in the lower areas, hard beech only around Rotoroa, a mixture of silver and mountain beech farther up, and mountain beech in the high-altitude areas (also in lowland low-nutrient-soil areas). These trees form a dense, dark canopy and the types of plants found on the forest floor depend on the amount of light that filters through. On a stroll through the bush, keen bird-watchers may see fantails, tomtits, robins, grey warblers, riflemen, silver-eyes, parakeets, white-bibbed *tui*, bellbirds, and *kaka*. Beautiful mixed beech/podocarp forests (native conifers) of *rata, kowhai*, and flax grow in the lower elevations around Lake Rotoroa—home for all kinds of birds including the plump, noisy native pigeon. On the main lakes, and **Rotoiti Lookout** at the end of Mount Robert Road. Short tracks put the day-tripper close to plenty of beautiful scenery, while long and more difficult tracks challenge the serious hiker.

THE LAND

This large wilderness park (102,000 hectares/252,000 acres) is sandwiched between Lake Rotoroa and Lake Rotoiti in the north and northeast, the lofty **St. Arnaud Range** on the eastern boundary, the **Spenser Mountains** in the south, and the **Ella Range** in the west. The great Alpine Fault runs right through the northern section of the park (welcome to earthquake country), crossing the northern end of Lake Rotoiti, **Speargrass Valley,** and the southern end of Lake Rotoroa. The movement of land along the Alpine Fault and glacial erosion are the two main factors in the formation of the spectacular scenery. Mighty rugged mountains and alpine tarns lie on the southeast side of the fault, and lower forest-covered ranges, ridges, valleys, deep river canyons, and two glacially formed lakes lie on the northwest side.

LYELL

In the Upper Buller Gorge, Lyell was a busy gold- and quartz-mining town of 3,000 people in the late 19th century, but today all that remains is the original cemetery, reached by a beautiful track. Where the thriving town once stood is now a historic reserve: Read about Lyell's colorful history on the display board, camp for free, or take a walk along **Lyell Walkway** (40 minutes one-way). Ten minutes from the trailhead is the fascinating original Lyell cemetery, overgrown and disguised in the bush. The graves, dating from 1870 to 1900, have old-fashioned iron fences around them and trees growing out of their centers. The gravestones tell vivid stories of the difficult lives of the gold dredgers. Don't wander off the main track, as numerous minor tracks lead to old claims, open shafts, and abandoned equipment that could be hazardous. For another perfect camping spot, head across the road from the reserve and down to the river, where there is a small grassy flat suitable for tents.

MARLBOROUGH

lakes and rivers live many varieties of waterfowl (watch for the beautiful but sadly endangered blue duck). Gulls, shags, herons, kingfishers, oystercatchers, stilts, black swans, and Canada geese are common. Above the tree line grow tough woody shrubs, colorful tussocks, and beautiful alpine flowering shrubs. Birds common at these higher altitudes include rock wrens, riflemen, pipits, and *kea.*

SIGHTS AND RECREATION
Lake Rotoiti

Lake Rotoiti, popular with boating enthusiasts and anglers chasing brown trout, is the most visited unit of Nelson Lakes National Park. Several short walking tracks start near the visitor center and take up to two hours, and longer tracks link to form a circular route around the lake (at least seven hours). For a short but rocky walk to a viewpoint 127 meters (420 ft) above Lake Rotoiti, take the **Black Hill Walk** (90 minutes round-trip), which starts at Rotoiti Lodge. It crosses a *roche moutonnée*—volcanic rock intrusion—where large lizards bask in the sun, and scrublands. If you're not feeling very energetic but enjoy lake views and all kinds of trees, try the easy (90-minute) **Peninsular Nature Walk,** which starts at the western end of the beach at Kerr Bay. The trees and shrubs along the track have been labeled, and short paths lead off the track to lookouts with views of the lake and the mountains.

The **Lakehead Track** (three hours oneway) starts at the eastern side of Kerr Bay and heads down the eastern side of the lake, passing countless bays likely to lure you off the beaten track and, in summer, into the water. If you plan to go all the way around the lake, ford Travers River near Lakehead Hut (only possible when the water is low enough) or walk from Lakehead Hut up the valley for at least another hour to the bridge. Return along the western side of the lake via **Lakeside Track.**

Getting a taste of the rugged St. Arnaud Range is possible from Lake Rotoiti via well-marked **St. Arnaud Track** (five hours round-trip). It starts at the eastern shore of Kerr Bay, climbs through beech forest, and comes out at

1,372-meter-high (4,501-ft-high) **Parachute Rocks.** From the top of the range you can see both sides of the divide—allow an entire day for this trip; you'll stop many times to absorb the magnificent scenery along the way.

Lake Rotoroa

Peaceful Lake Rotoroa is larger, deeper, and less developed than Lake Rotoiti (powerboats aren't allowed). If you feel like taking a short stroll, try the 10-minute **Flower Walk** starting 100 meters (330 ft) from the lake foreshore (on the eastern side of the Gowan River)—it offers great views of Lake Rotoroa. The **Short Loop Track** is another walk in the same area (20 minutes round-trip); it runs along the lake via Lakeside Track and back to the car park. To get to the beginning, turn left (looking toward the lake) on the road just past the Accommodation House, walk to the end of the road, and continue a short distance along **Porika Track** to the signpost where Loop Track branches off to the right. **Porika Lookout Track** climbs slowly along a ridge to a lookout with excellent views of the lake and the Travers, Ella, and Mahanga Ranges, returning down the hydro track; it takes about three hours.

One of the most beautiful "woodsy" walks in the area is the two-hour **Braeburn Walk.** Start from Braeburn Road just down from the ranger station and head south on the western side of the lake. Passing through green arches of beech/podocarp forest full of bellbirds and a wonderland of ferns, the track gradually climbs to a softly cascading waterfall, drops down to the creek, and returns along a wide path to Braeburn Road.

PRACTICALITIES
Accommodations and Food

The **Yellow House** (St. Arnaud, 03/521-1887, www.nelsonlakes.co.nz; campsites $26, dorm beds $25, $59 d), a five-minute walk from Lake Rotoiti, is a comfortable, laid-back backpacker lodge where the hosts are keen hikers. The adjacent **Nelson Lakes Motel** (03/521-1887, www.nelsonlakes.co.nz; $99–129 s or d) comprises log motel rooms, each with a kitchen and some with separate bedrooms.

If you're looking for comfort and style, **Alpine Lodge** (St. Arnaud, 03/521-1869 or 0800/367-777, www.alpinelodge.co.nz; $135–150 s or d) provides a choice of alpine-inspired motel rooms and self-contained apartments. Adjacent to the main lodge is the Alpine Chalet (dorm beds $23, private rooms $30.50 per person), suited to budget-minded travelers. The Alpine Lodge also has a café and a restaurant with a distinct alpine ambience. The latter opens daily for dinner, with selections like roasted rack of lamb smothered in freshly prepared mint sauce running $24–33. Or relax with a beer on one of the comfortable sofas around the roaring log fire in the lounge.

A member of Small Luxury Hotels of the World and one of the world's great fishing lodges, historic **Lake Rotoroa Lodge** lies on the edge of Lake Rotoroa (03/523-9121, www.lakerotoroalodge.com; $650 s, $1,100 d). It provides an elegant Victorian ambience throughout. The eight deluxe suites feature brass beds and feather quilts, while downstairs guests gather in the restaurant or bar to trade trout-fishing stories. Rates include all meals. Hiring a fishing guide through the lodge costs $675 for two people for the day.

A short drive from the park, an 1887 cob (mud) hotel has been restored and now operates as the ◖ **Tophouse** (03/521-1848 or 0800/867-468, www.tophouse.co.nz; $60 per person bed-and-breakfast, cottages $110 s or d). The Tophouse is also open for lunch ($10) and dinner ($30) with advance reservations. To get there from St. Arnaud, take Highway 63 east and look for the road north signposted Tophouse Historic Hotel.

Camping

At Lake Rotoiti are two well-established camping areas: **Nelson Lakes National Park Camp** at West Bay and **Kerr Bay Campground.** Both have cooking shelters, communal bathrooms, and coin-operated barbecues. Rates for tent sites are $20 and powered sites rent for $24.

Information

The main information source is the **Nelson Lakes National Park Visitor Centre,** overlooking Lake Rotoiti in St. Arnaud (View Rd., 03/521-1806; daily 9 A.M.–5 P.M.).

Getting There and Around

To reach the park from the northwest, take Highway 6 southwest from Nelson or Highway 61 south from Motueka. From the intersection of these highways at Kohatu, continue southwest toward Murchison and Westport. To get to the village of St. Arnaud, turn east off Highway 6 at Kawatiri Junction and follow Highway 63 to St. Arnaud.

Nelson Lakes Shuttles (03/521-1900) connects with ferry arrivals in Picton on Monday, Wednesday, and Friday, making drops at St. Arnaud and Lake Rotoroa. Use this service to travel between St. Arnaud and Lake Rotoroa. **KBus** (03/578-4075) stops at St. Arnaud on its daily run between Nelson and Greymouth.

Water taxis operate on both Lake Rotoiti (03/521-1894) and Lake Rotoroa (03/523-9199), providing hikers, fishing enthusiasts, and campers with an alternate way to explore the lakes and their foreshores, or a shortcut to hiking tracks at the far ends of the two lakes.

Nelson Lakes to the West Coast

Beginning from Lake Rotoiti, the deep, swift **Buller River** churns westward for more than 75 km (47 mi) through scrublands, meadows, and gravel flats, carving its way through rugged bush-clad mountains via the wild and beautiful Buller Gorge before draining into the Tasman Sea at Westport. Highway 6 parallels this mighty river all the way to Westport, via the picturesque town of Murchison and passing scenic reserves, abandoned settlements and relics from gold-mining days, and short walking tracks.

MURCHISON

This attractive town of 800, 63 km (39 mi) west of St. Arnaud on Highway 6, is a popular spot for travelers to break the trip between the northern interior and Westport. A peaceful atmosphere, temperatures high in summer and mild in winter, and surrounding lush meadows backed by striking mountains give Murchison a definite appeal.

Despite its unruffled appearance, the town is in an area of active faults and has an exciting geological history. On June 13, 1929, "a dense fog enveloped the town.... the church bell tolled, buildings were hurled from their foundations, and it was impossible to keep to one's feet." An earthquake, with its epicenter close to Murchison, tore the town apart, blocked rivers and roads, and destroyed all telephone communications. Hodgsons General Merchants Store was demolished in the earthquake; rebuilt on the same site, it's open for business to this day. The place to learn more about the earthquake is **Murchison District Museum** (60 Fairfax St., 03/523-9392; daily 10 A.M.–4 P.M.; donation).

Practicalities

Overnight options at **Kiwi Park** (170 Fairfax St., 03/523-9248 or 0800/228-080) include campsites for $18; basic cabins for $18 s, $30 d; tourist flats for $60–75 s or d; and five motel units for $85–100 s or d with communal kitchens and washrooms.

A service station on the original main street has been transformed into a combination rafting center and **◖ Rivers Café** (51 Fairfax St., 03/523-9009; summer daily 8 A.M.–7 P.M., shorter hours the rest of the year). The cavernous interior is scattered with furniture made from *macrocarpa* (a native wood), or you can relax in the sun at a table out front. The food is simple yet delicious café fare, including lamb and mint pie ($8), vegetarian nut loaf ($7), and lots of cakes and pastries (around $5 per serving).

BULLER GORGE

Continuing west from Murchison along Highway 6, the emerald-green Buller River pours between steep cliffs and the forested canyon of Upper Buller Gorge. At Inangahua Junction the Inangahua River joins forces with the Buller; at Berlins, a historic gold-mining settlement, the water rushes turbulently through the even more magnificent Lower Buller Gorge. The gorge has quite a colorful past—it's been the scene of major earthquakes, mighty landslides and floods, and gold-mining rushes (thousands lived along the banks in the late 19th century), and has been a formidable obstacle for early explorers, coach drivers, and road and bridge builders.

If the roadside scenery through the gorge is not enough, consider descending the river on a raft. The main local operator, **Ultimate Descents** (51 Fairfax St., 03/523-9899, www .rivers.co.nz), provides transportation from their Murchison base. Options include a four-hour family float (adult $95, child $75), an exciting adults-only trip that ends with a five-meter waterfall drop ($105), and a variety of more expensive overnight and helicopter trips.

WEST COAST

The magnificent west coast of the South Island, a narrow strip of land squeezed between the Tasman Sea and the Southern Alps, offers a taste of rock, ice, sand, and sea all at once. Well-maintained Highway 6 traverses the coast from Westport in the north to Haast Pass in the south. It's a narrow, winding road, where slow speeds are a must. But there's no rush. It's a lush, bright-green strip filled with fern and *nikau* palm, with the highway often paralleling deserted beaches and nearly always in sight of inland mountain ranges. Pull off at signposted lookouts for some of the most stunning coastal views, or wander off along one of the walking tracks signposted from the highway. Although the region has an unfortunate reputation for having rainy weather, dull skies, and an abundant summer population of sand flies, it also has extended periods of blue skies and sunshine (particularly in winter)—all you need is a bit of luck, and insect repellent smothering all exposed areas of your body.

The major attractions are all natural. The region is book-ended by the forested wilderness of Kahurangi National Park in the north and mountainous Mount Aspiring National Park in the south. The region's main highway passes through two other national parks—Paparoa, famous for its coastal rock formations, and Westland Tai Poutini, where two magnificent glaciers snake down through dense rainforest. Even if you're not feeling adventurous, the highlights of the latter two parks are all easily accessible on foot. Throughout these parks and beyond their borders the flora and fauna are varied and diverse, including towering forests

© ANDREW HEMPSTEAD

WEST COAST

HIGHLIGHTS

{(Pancake Rocks: The reasoning behind the name will become apparent as soon as you lay your eyes on this coastal geological oddity (page 317).

{(Wildfoods Festival: Even if jellied grasshopper and roast muttonbird don't sound appealing, you can at least watch the grimaces at this culinary gathering of the weird and wonderful (page 325).

{(White Heron Sanctuary: Known to the Maori as *kotuku,* these magnificent birds breed along the remote reaches of Okarito Lagoon, and access is only possible on a guided tour (page 328).

{(Lake Matheson: If you're looking for that perfect reflection shot, this is the place to search out, preferably early in the morning before the wind comes up (page 335).

{(Glacier Tours: Anyone can walk to the glaciers of Westland Tai Poutini National Park, but joining a guided tour allows you the opportunity to climb up and onto these ancient rivers of ice (page 335).

{(Haast Pass Highway: If you're driving along the west coast, this is one must-see you can't avoid – not that you'd want to. This spectacular route traverses a high alpine pass replete with waterfalls, gushing rivers, and lush rainforests (page 339).

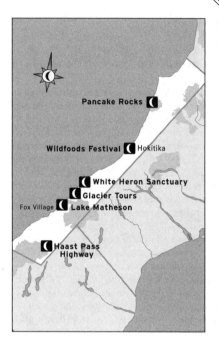

LOOK FOR **{(** TO FIND RECOMMENDED SIGHTS, ACTIVITIES, DINING, AND LODGING.

of *rimu, totara, rata,* redbeech, *kamahi, quintinia, toro, horopito,* and lancewood. On the forest floor and steep banks along the coastal highway is an incredible conglomeration of ferns, mosses, lichens, and fungi. As you'd expect, all sorts of birds thrive in this green wonderland—bellbirds, fantails, *tui, kaka, kea,* South Island robins, wood pigeons, parakeets, blue ducks, and native falcons, along with great spotted kiwis and the only breeding colony of Westland petrels in the world.

The west coast's first residents were the Maori, who used locally quarried greenstone (jade) as woodworking tools and to make jewelry. While this historic art form lives on, it was the discovery of gold that drew the first wave of European settlers. Founded in 1864, Hokitika rapidly mushroomed into the large bustling "Capital of the Goldfields." Thousands of miners flocked to the region from Australia and within a couple of years 50,000 people were living at the various gold diggings along the coast. Along with Hokitika, the old gold-mining towns of Westport and Greymouth hold most of the region's scattered population.

PLANNING YOUR TIME

The west coast of the South Island is one of the country's most remote regions. This makes it both a popular destination for those looking to escape the crowds, and also one of the first regions for travelers to bypass if time is limited. More so than anywhere else in New Zealand, traversing local highways takes a lot longer than a map may indicate. Nelson to Wanaka via the west coast is 790 kilometers (490 mi), yet this route takes at least 14 hours to drive, sans stops. Alternatives to driving include flying in and out of Hokitika from Christchurch, renting a car and spending a couple of days traveling as far south as Westland Tai Poutini, or catching the TranzAlpine Train from Christchurch to Greymouth, either as a single-day excursion or an overnight trip.

If driving is your preferred option, allow at least two days from Nelson to Wanaka, but preferably three. Two days is enough time to stop at the highlights, but certainly not long enough to really experience them. **Pancake Rocks,** an easily accessible natural attraction, can be reached on foot in just a few minutes. Most of the other west coast highlights require a little more time, including the **White Heron Sanctuary,** only accessible on a guided tour (allow half a day), and **Lake Matheson,** a 90-minute loop walk. The glaciers of Westland Tai Poutini National Park are also a short hike from the end of the road, but you should allow at least a half day to join a **glacier tour** for the full effect. The route back across from the west coast to the Otago region is via the **Haast Pass Highway,** again with enough viewpoints and short hikes to merit a full day.

Low-key Hokitika is the most interesting of the west coast towns. Renowned for its **arts and crafts,** you can spend up to a full day at one of the local studios creating your own greenstone masterpiece. One of New Zealand's most interesting and talked-about events is the **Wildfoods Festival,** held in Hokitika. It's well worth trying to coincide your travel with this one-day March event if you are in the area.

Westport and Vicinity

If you are driving south to the west coast from Nelson or Picton, the mid-sized coastal town of Westport (pop. 5,000) will be your first port of call. At one time New Zealand's largest coal-exporting port, the town's economy now revolves around tourism and cement manufacturing. Visitors are drawn by river fishing, surfing, an accessible seal colony, and the surrounding forested wilderness, but Westport also has a great museum, golfing, and a wide range of services.

Getting to Westport merits the same advice as I give elsewhere in this chapter—allow more driving time than you may imagine. The trip between the ferry terminal at Picton and Westport, a distance of 285 km (177 mi), takes almost five hours. And the route from Westport south to Wanaka is less than 600 kilometers (373 mi), yet takes over 10 hours of driving.

SIGHTS AND RECREATION

Downtown Westport lies along the east bank of the Buller River, with Coaltown at the south end. You'll need a vehicle to reach the main natural attractions at Cape Foulwind and Tauranga Bay.

Coaltown

This museum (Queen St., 03/789-8204; daily 9 A.M.–4:30 P.M.; adult $8, senior $6, child $4) is Westport's main in-town attraction. You'll find room after room of historical displays, all kinds of coal-mining equipment, films on the coal-mining industry (shown every 30 minutes), a room where special effects give the feeling of being underground in a coal mine, and an interesting collection of historical photos. Also see the colonial and maritime wings and the gold-mining exhibition. One of the rooms

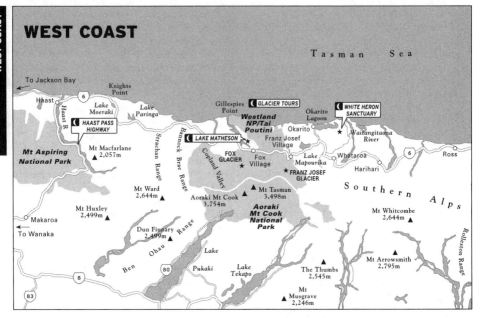

WEST COAST

features a wagon from the famous Denniston Incline, which, after completion in 1880, allowed coal to be lowered in wagons down a very steep hill by gravity—dropping 518 meters (1,700 ft) over a distance of two km (one mi) in only 4.5 minutes. The miners and inhabitants of the hill also used the wagons as their only form of transportation down to the railway in the early years.

Cape Foulwind and Vicinity

Back across the river from downtown, take Cape Foulwind Road to reach the following attractions.

Carters Beach (five km/three mi from town) is a worthwhile stop for a stroll along a sandy beach or a safe plunge in the surf.

Cape Foulwind (named by Captain Cook during a fierce storm in 1770) is a rocky promontory of granite bluffs covered in forests, wild grassy downs, and swampy streams and bogs. From the end of Cape Foulwind Road, 10 kilometers (6.2 mi) from town (go straight ahead at the Star Tavern), **Cape Foulwind Walkway**

a rare stretch of straight highway along the West Coast

© ANDREW HEMPSTEAD

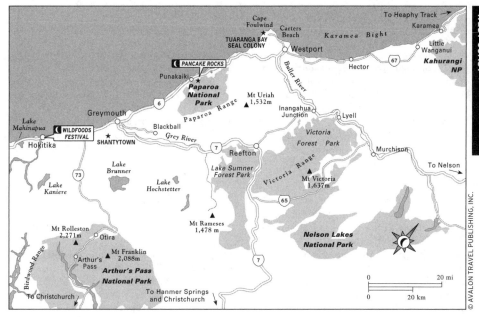

runs south over the cape's granite bluffs and undulating pasture, passes the **Tauranga Bay Seal Colony,** and finishes at the north end of sandy **Tauranga Beach.** The easy four-km (2.5-mi) walk takes just over an hour each way, and can be done in either direction. One of the best times to visit is midsummer, when you can watch new-born seals frolic on the rocks, swim gracefully in the ocean, playfully catch waves, or bask with their parents directly below.

Tauranga Bay, accessible by road, is a popular surfing spot, although the ocean can be a little rough for swimming. At the north end of the bay is the southern extent of the walkway and at the south end is a smattering of cottages protected from the wind by a rocky headland.

ACCOMMODATIONS AND CAMPING

Bazil's Hostel (54 Russell St., 03/789-6410, www.bazils.com) is a centrally located backpacker lodge where each modern dorm has its own bathroom. Rates are $22 per person, or pay $48 d for a private room with shared bath.

At the south end of Westport's long main street (on the left as you come into town), **Chelsea Gateway Motor Lodge** (330 Palmerston St., 03/789-6835 or 0800/660-033, www.chelseagateway.co.nz; $110–200 s or d) is a modern two-story motel with the nicest rooms in town.

Separated from the beach by a wide grassy park is **Seal Colony Holiday Park** (Marine Pde., Carters Beach, 03/789-6732), five km (three mi) west of town off Cape Foulwind Road. Amenities include modern washrooms, a TV lounge, and kitchen and barbecue facilities. Tent camping is $13 per person, powered sites are $18 per person, cabins are $55–95 s or d, and motel rooms top out at $130.

FOOD AND DRINK

Head to the **Rainbow Cake Kitchen** (78 Palmerston St., 03/789-7899) for a fill of pies and pastries, or to **Currtino's Yellow House** (243 Palmerston St., 03/789-8765; daily for breakfast, lunch, and dinner) for a casual café atmosphere and healthy food.

At the vaguely Irish **Bailie's Bar & Restaurant** (187 Palmerston St., 03/789-7289; daily for lunch and dinner), you can cook your own steak, then serve yourself a plateful of salad, for $18. At the northern end of the main street, the old Royal Hotel has been given a coat of black paint and the interior given a European-style makeover to create **Porto Bello** (62 Palmerston St., 03/789-5570; daily 11 A.M.–10 P.M.). At this part restaurant but mostly bar, the predictable menu of upscale bar favorites is mostly under $20, with a roast special dished up Sunday evenings.

While Westport itself offers a variety of convenient dining opportunities, I recommend heading 12 km (seven mi) west to the 《 **Bay House Cafe** (Tauranga Bay, 03/789-7133; Mon.–Fri. 10 A.M.–9 P.M., Sat.–Sun. 9 A.M.–9 P.M.) for both its food and wonderful setting. A converted 1929 holiday house, the building blends into the surrounding native bush, while taking in the wonderful sights and smells of the ocean just across the road. The creative menu includes a mix of local seafood and distinctly New Zealand dishes such as grilled lamb chops on a bed of feta and mint hash browns. Lighter meals are mostly under $15 (including a great seafood chowder) while dinner mains range $25–32. Evening reservations are recommended (especially for an outdoor table).

Monteith's, in nearby Greymouth, is famed across the country for its beer and its factory tours, but Westport has the 《 **Green Fern Brewery** (10 Lyndhurst St., 03/789-6253; Mon.–Sat. 10 A.M.–5:30 P.M.), a place that beer-lovers will remember for the sales side of the business—bring in any two-liter container (known locally as a "rigger") and pay just $1.80 to have it filled. The beer, brewed using locally grown organic ingredients, is also sold in bottles and kegs.

INFORMATION AND SERVICES

Palmerston Street, a continuation of Highway 67 through downtown, holds all the major services, including banks, the post office (corner Brougham St.) and **Web Shed** (204 Palmerston St., 03/788-8002; Mon.–Fri. 8:30 A.M.–5 P.M., Sat. 9:30 A.M.–12:30 P.M., Sun. 10 A.M.–3 P.M.) for Internet access. Just off the main street is **Westport Information Centre** (1 Brougham St., 03/789-6658, www.westport.org.nz; Nov.–Mar. daily 9 A.M.–6 P.M., Apr.–Oct. daily 9 A.M.–4 P.M.), which features photographic displays on the Buller district, racks of free brochures up for grabs, and enthusiastic staff who fill you in on all the local attractions and book tours, trips, and accommodations. If it's closed when you hit town, check the map in the window for quick orientation.

GETTING THERE

Intercity (www.intercitycoach.co.nz) stops at Craddocks (197 Palmerston St., 03/879-7819) on its daily run down the west coast from Nelson. Craddocks is also the terminus for **East West Coach** (03/789-6251) and its daily runs between Westport and Christchurch. Departing daily except Sunday from the visitor center is the **Karamea Express** (03/782-6757), which, as the name suggests, provides a link to Karamea.

KARAMEA

This small beachside community, 100 km (62 mi) north of Westport along Highway 67, is a good base for those starting or finishing the Heaphy Track through Kahurangi National Park—and an interesting detour in its own right. At **Honeycomb Caves,** 16 km (10 mi) north of the village, a wealth of moa bones make a visit worthwhile. Cave tours (adult $65, child $35) and other activities such as horseback rides and scenic flights can be arranged through Last Resort (71 Waverley St., 03/782-6617 or 0800/505-042, www.lastresort.co.nz). You don't need to spend money for other local activities, such as lazing on the beach, forest walks, and admiring intriguing limestone arches along the beach.

Practicalities

Last Resort (71 Waverley St., 03/782-6617 or 0800/505-042, www.lastresort.co.nz; camping $12 per person, dorm beds $24, shared bath $65 s or d, en suite rooms $80, kitchen units $100–140) is a large complex set around a central building that holds a café, restaurant, and bar.

PAPAROA NATIONAL PARK

Extending from the highest peaks of the Paparoa Range to the Tasman Sea, the vast majority of visitors make just one stop, to see the famously distinct **Pancake Rocks,** before continuing south or north along Highway 6. The highway through the park hugs the coastline, and is one of the most scenic stretches of driving in the country, but there's plenty to see beyond the blacktop, on the inland side of the road. Comprised mostly of soft sedimentary rock, the Paparoa Range has been weathered by wind, water, snow, and ice, creating deep limestone (karst) gorges and canyons clothed in trees and ferns. Underground drainage in this limestone region is the most unusual feature of the park—it is this, along with the dissolving action of rainwater on limestone, that sets the karst landscape apart.

Spread along the coastline 57 km (35 mi) south of Westport, the village of **Punakaiki** has accommodations, a couple of eateries, and the park visitor center, but has no gas or groceries.

☾ Pancake Rocks

The park's premier attraction is Pancake Rocks. Comprising layers of limestone and mudstone, the much-photographed ocean cliffs look like an enormous stack of wafer-thin rock pancakes. To reach them, park at the visitor center for the **Dolomite Point Walk,** a 10-minute stroll from the main highway through a wonderland of tree ferns, *nikau* palms, and northern *rata* to the rocks. On the way you pass a deep surge pool full of waving seaweed and mighty blowholes that in stormy weather boom and roar with the breaking of large waves—often unexpectedly blasting torrents of water skyward to soak startled onlookers with spray. The blowhole performs best when a large southern swell combines with a high tide.

Recreation

The visitor center has details on all the best hiking opportunities, and staff will help decide which walking tracks are best for your interests and fitness level. The trail to **Woodpecker Bay** is enjoyable, or head inland to **Fox River Caves.** The 25-km (16-mi) two- to three-day **Inland Pack Track** meanders along the historic inland road built to avoid the rugged

© ANDREW HEMPSTEAD

It's easy to see how Pancake Rocks got their name.

WEST COAST

Te Miko Coast, through spectacular limestone canyons where deep crystal-clear river pools beckon and past entrances to cave systems. If you have time to see only a little of the track, go up the Pororari or Fox Rivers to walk the beginning or end sections.

Paparoa Horse Treks (03/731-1839; Oct.–May) leads 2.5-hour rides into the Punakaiki Valley, but the highlight for most is the final stretch, along a windswept beach back to the corrals. Rates are $110 per person.

Accommodations and Camping

On the north side of the park, **Te Nikau Retreat** (Hartmount Pl., 03/731-1111, www.tenikauretreat.co.nz) caters to all budgets with a choice of accommodations in two main lodges and a selection of funky freestanding units. Rooms in the lodges (shared bath $50 s or d, en suite $65) are adequate, with one building set aside for single travelers looking for private rooms, but the real fun starts in surrounding villas hidden under a canopy of native bush. Live cheaply in the Stargazer ($30 s or d), a glorified tent, the ironically named Palace ($40 s or d),

or choose a self-contained unit ($70–80 s or d). In the same vicinity, the park's main backpacker lodge is **Punakaiki Beach Hostel** (4 Webb St., 03/731-1852 or 0800/726-225, www.punakaikibeachhostel.co.nz), a two-story residence across from the beach and within walking distance of the local tavern. Dorm beds are $24 and private rooms are $40 s, $60 d.

Paparoa Park Motel (Hwy. 6, 03/731-1883 or 0800/727-276, www.paparoa.co.nz; $130–160 s or d), overlooking the Punakaiki River and with views to Pancake Rocks from its delightful bush setting south of the information center, has seven rooms that are more woodsy than motel-like. Each spacious, self-contained unit is furnished in a simple and practical style, with lots of exposed timber.

South of the visitor center, some rooms at **Punakaiki Rocks Hotel & Villas** (Hwy. 6, 03/731-1168 or 0800/786-2524, www.punakaiki-resort.co.nz; from $125 s, $145 d) have ocean views, but across the road the larger suites are more private. This a modern complex, with services that include a restaurant open daily from 7 A.M. Continuing south 16

© ANDREW HEMPSTEAD

Punakaiki Rocks Hotel & Villas

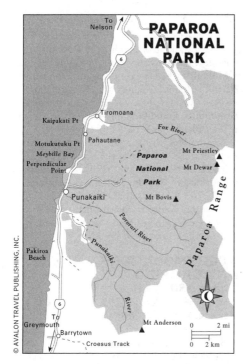

WEST COAST

© AVALON TRAVEL PUBLISHING, INC.

Operated by the DOC, **Punakaiki Motor Camp** (Owen St., 03/731-1894) is near the mouth of the Pororari River and has easy access to a wild and beautiful beach—a wonderful spot for walking. Tree-shaded tent sites are $12 per person, powered sites $13 per person, and basic cabins rent for $30 per person.

Food

If it's not overrun with the tour bus crowd, **Wild Coast Cafe** (Hwy. 6, 03/731-1873; daily 9 A.M.–5 P.M.), beside the visitor center, is a pleasant place for a snack. For more substantial meals or a quiet beer, head for **Punakaiki Tavern** (Oven St., 03/731-1188; daily for breakfast, lunch, and dinner), one km (0.6 mi) north of the visitor center.

Information

Across the road from the walkway to Pancake Rocks is **Paparoa National Park Visitor Centre** (03/731-1895; summer daily 9 A.M.–6 P.M., rest of the year daily 9 A.M.–4:30 P.M.), featuring photographic displays of the park's geology and history and an audiovisual display. Staff members provide information and maps on the park, including brochures on coastal walks to nearby caves and the most intriguing rock formations in the immediate area. In summer they hold illustrated talks at the center and run scheduled guided walks of varying lengths.

km (10 mi) is the **Beach Hideaway** (17 Cargill Rd., 03/731-1120, www.beachhideaway.co.nz; $250 s or d), comprising two beautiful cabins within walking distance of the beach. Each has a king-size bed and full kitchen.

Greymouth

At the mouth of the Grey River and originally developed as a port in the 1860s after the nearby discovery of gold, Greymouth (pop. 13,000), 100 km (62 mi) south of Westport, has grown into the largest town on the west coast. The town itself is not particularly pretty, but there's plenty of surrounding wilderness, and as the terminus of both Highway 73 from Christchurch and the TranzAlpine train, it gets plenty of tourist action.

SIGHTS AND RECREATION
Shantytown

Off the main highway at Paroa 11 km (seven mi) south of Greymouth, Shantytown (Rutherglen Rd., 03/762-6634, daily 8:30 A.M.–5 P.M.; adult $15, senior $12, child $8.50) is a historical reconstruction of a west coast gold settlement of the 1880s. Wander through the re-created town with its bank and gold-buying office, store, jail, church, hotel, hospital, printing shop, post office, pub, stables, and fire station. While all the buildings may be replicas, the gold here is real. A high-powered water jet blasts gold-bearing quartz from the hillside, a stamper battery crushes the ore, and then it runs through sluice boxes (or try your own hand at a bit of panning). Another highlight is the steam train, which runs up the valley to an active sawmill and into a claim mined since 1860.

About 15 km (nine mi) beyond the entrance to Shantytown (on a gravel road) is the start of the one-km **Woods Creek Walkway**, a 45-minute round-trip track through virgin *rimu* forest that takes you past old gold-mine tunnels, shafts (take a flashlight), and other evidence of past gold-mining activities.

Tours and Recreation

You can order beer from **Monteith's Brewing Co.** (corner of Turumaha and Herbert Sts., 03/768-4149; $10) at pubs throughout the country, but none taste as good as the ones you get to sample at the end of a one-hour brewery tour. Departures are two to three times daily.

Take a walk up through **King Domain** for good town and ocean views (preferably *before* a Monteith's beer-tasting session); the trail starts on Mount Street near the railway station. From Mawhera Quay, you can wander along **Greymouth Flood Wall** for views of the river, town, Fisherman's Wharf, and tidal estuary.

Nearby Hokitika gets all the attention for its greenstone, but one of the better places to learn about the stone and its history is Greymouth's **Jade Boulder Gallery** (1 Guinness St., 03/768-0700; daily 9 A.M.–8 P.M.; free), where a corridor leads from the main shop to a display area that holds Maori artifacts, jewelry, and a massive greenstone boulder.

ACCOMMODATIONS AND CAMPING
Under $50

Beyond the purple-and-green facade of **Duke Backpackers** (27 Guinness St., 03/768-9470, www.duke.co.nz; dorm beds $20, $33 s, $40–54 d), a converted 1873 hotel, is an equally bright and welcoming interior, which includes a downstairs bar and café. Competing with Duke for backpacker business is the well-equipped **Global Village** (42 Cowper St., 03/768-7272, www.globalvillagebackpackers.co.nz; dorm beds $22, $44 s, $54 d), beside a creek on the south side of downtown but still within walking distance. It features central heating, brightly painted common areas, free use of bikes, and a fitness room. To get there from Tainui Street (the main street) continue south onto High Street, turn right at Buccleigh Street, and then turn onto Cowper Street.

$50-100

Of the many historic downtown hotels, **Revington's Hotel** (46 Tainui St., 03/768-7055, www.revingtons.co.nz; $70 s or d) is the best choice for travelers on a budget—and you may end up in the room where Queen Elizabeth II once stayed. All 25 rooms are spacious and have a private bathroom, but facilities are basic.

© ANDREW HEMPSTEAD

Monteith's, a popular beer throughout the country, is brewed in Greymouth.

WEST COAST

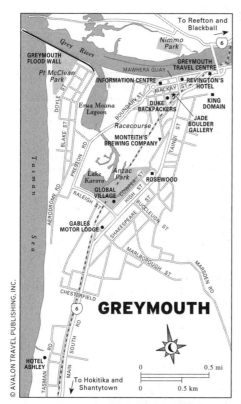

© AVALON TRAVEL PUBLISHING, INC.

$130–195 s or d) is a modern, low-rise complex offering a wide range of facilities, including a large indoor pool, fitness room, spa, sauna, bar, café, and restaurant. Each of the 60 guest rooms is spacious, and many have kitchens.

Over $150

It's worth the effort to reach **❰ Infinity Eden Lodge** (15 Tasman View Rd., 03/762-6556, www.infinityedenlodge.co.nz; $150–190 s or d), south of Greymouth near Shantytown. At this architecturally striking lodge, each of the six comfortable guest rooms opens to a paved patio from where views extend across the ocean and as far south as Mount Cook. Extras include bathrobes, Internet access, and a spa pool. A continental breakfast is included in the rates and dinner is available for an extra charge with prior notice.

For bed-and-breakfast accommodation run by a local family knowledgeable on the area, consider **Rosewood** (20 High St., 03/768-4674 or 0800/185-748, www.rosewood.co.nz; $110–150 s, $185–200 d), where the five rooms (three en suite) have comfortable beds, TV, and phone. A full breakfast is included in the rates.

Holiday Parks

The closest camping to town is at **Greymouth Seaside Top 10 Holiday Park** (2 Chesterfield St., 03/768-6618 or 0800/867-104, www.top 10greymouth.co.nz), off the main highway 2.5 km (1.5 mi) south of downtown. It's next to the beach, has a spa pool, a TV room, a grocery store, and barbecue area, and is within walking distance of a takeaway food outlet. Tent sites are $30, powered sites $34, cabins and motel rooms $50–162 s or d. The next closest, 11 km (seven mi) north of Greymouth, is **Rapahoe Beach Motor Camp** (Hwy. 6, Rapahoe, 03/762-7025, www.rapahoebeach.co.nz; camping $12 per person, caravans and cabins $38–48 s or d). Adjacent to the beach and with a small outdoor pool, it's smaller and quieter than the Top 10.

FOOD

Downtown Greymouth is dotted with cafés, but my pick for ambience is **Café 124 on**

Motels in Greymouth are not particularly cheap. At the lower end of the price scale is **Riverview Motel** (Omoto Rd., east of town off Hwy. 7, 03/768-6884 or 0508/807-060; $85–100 s or d,) with an outdoor pool, barbecue area, views across the Grey River to the Paparoa Range, and nine self-contained rooms of varying configurations.

$100-150

A step up in style from the Riverview is **Gables Motor Lodge** (84 High St., 03/768-9991 or 0800/809-991, www.gablesmotorlodge.com; $110–180 s or d), with 12 well-furnished rooms, each with a kitchen and a bath, and nice touches like plunger coffee.

Hotel Ashley (74 Tasman St., 03/768-5135 or 0800/807-787, www.hotelashley.co.nz;

THE TOWN OF BLACKBALL

The historic town of Blackball, on the inland side of the Paparoa Range 40 km (25 mi) northeast of Greymouth (north of Hwy. 7), is one of those out-of-the-way places you occasionally stumble across and never forget. Born as a supply stop during an 1866 gold rush, Blackball later thrived as a coal-mining center, then almost became a ghost town after the last mine closed in 1968. Today its few hundred inhabitants, with no visible source of income, tend to well-kept gardens, while away the time chatting on street corners, and converge on the main surviving business — the local pub. **Formerly the Blackball Hilton** (Hart St., 03/732-4705, www.blackballhilton.co.nz) — the unusual name came about after legal problems with an internationally renowned hotel chain with a similar name — is a ramshackle two-story building constructed in 1909. It appears quiet enough at first but is locally known for its raging past. The coal miners used to drink, rant, rave, and party well into the wee hours

in this hotel until the mines closed and the miners left in 1968. It has a couple of streetside outdoor tables, but you need to head inside to soak up the history and character of the building and, in turn, the town. Friendly bar staff, a huge fireplace, and antique-lined walls add to the appeal. A few years back, keen local photographers decided to make a photographic record of Blackball and its inhabitants. Ask for the photo albums at the bar — they provide a fascinating glimpse into small-town New Zealand. You'll find much to do around town, including visiting an abandoned mine, fishing, gold panning, horseback riding, or, for the more adventurous, hiking the Croesus Track. Ask for details and maps at the Hilton.

The Hilton's upper floor has been renovated and now offers single and double rooms for $55 per person, which includes breakfast, or pay $90 and enjoy dinner as well. The pub kitchen is open for meals daily at lunch and dinner.

© ANDREW HEMPSTEAD

Mackay (124 Mackay St., 03/768-7503; daily from 10 A.M.), with a few outdoor tables, although the coffee at **Smelting House Café** (102 Mackay St., 03/768-0012) is probably a little better.

Jade Boulder Café (1 Guinness St., 03/768-0700; daily 9 A.M.–5 P.M.) is part of a greenstone shop in the heart of downtown. It's a clean, contemporary space with a surprisingly creative menu featuring whitebait omelets.

The friendly staff at **Bonzai** (31 Mackay St., 03/768-4170; Mon.–Sat. from 9 A.M., Sunday from noon) dish up decent pizza ($13–28), steak, chicken, fish, and spaghetti dishes ($15–17.50). **Steamers Carvery** (corner Mackay and Albert Sts., 03/768-4193; daily noon–2 P.M. and 5–8 P.M.) draws in those looking for old-fashioned roasts ($15 per person), carved to order and served with all the usual accompaniments.

INFORMATION AND SERVICES

Greymouth Information Centre (03/768-5101; summer Mon.–Fri. 8:30 A.M.–7 P.M., Sat.–Sun. 10 A.M.–5 P.M., the rest of the year weekdays only) is in the foyer of the Regent Theatre on the corner of Mackay and Herbert Streets.

The post office is on Tainui Street (03/768-0123). The public library (corner Mackay and Albert Sts., 03/768-7684) is open Monday–Friday from 10 A.M. and has free Internet access. For the price of a coffee (or cup of tea), you can get online for free at the street-level café at **Duke Backpackers** (27 Guinness St., 03/768-9470).

Greymouth Hospital (03/768-0499) is on High Street. **Mason's Pharmacy** (03/768-7470) is at 34 Tainui Street.

GETTING THERE

Greymouth is the turnaround point for one of the world's great train journeys, the **TranzAlpine** between Christchurch and Greymouth via Arthur's Pass. The trip is popular, so reserve ahead of time at any information center or by calling **Tranz Scenic** (04/495-0775 or 0800/872-467). The schedule is set up to make a day trip possible. Trains depart Christchurch daily at 8:15 A.M., taking just over four hours to reach Greymouth, and starts the return trip after a one-hour layover. The round-trip fare is $94.

Coast to Coast Shuttle (0800/800-847) follows Highway 73 through the same valleys as the rail line on a daily run between Christchurch and Greymouth. **Intercity** (www.intercitycoach.co.nz) provides buses in all directions: north to Westport, east across the Southern Alps to Christchurch, and south to the glaciers. All services leave from the **Greymouth Travel Centre** (Mackay St., 03/768-7080).

Hokitika and Vicinity

The colorful town of Hokitika (pop. 3,800) lies beside the Tasman Sea at the mouth of the Hokitika River 40 km (25 mi) south of Greymouth. Backed by the majestic Southern Alps, surrounded by native bush, lakes, and rivers, and with architecture reflecting the "golden days" and monuments all over town, Hokitika has character, a special atmosphere, and plenty of things to see and do. Several greenstone factories turn beautiful greenstone (jade) from nearby mountains and river terraces into jewelry and carvings, and shops sell gold nuggets and jewelry and locally produced crafts.

Hokitika mushroomed into the large, bustling "Capital of the Goldfields" when gold was discovered in the area in 1864. Within a couple of years, an estimated 50,000 people were living at the various gold diggings in the area (the town itself had about 6,000 residents during the peak gold-rush period). Hokitika became a conglomeration of banks, bars, and hotels—more than 100 hotels were hastily built, most of them on Revell Street. Today, in addition to tourism, dairy farming takes place on surrounding alluvial flats, and Hokitika is also a center for sheep and cattle farming (on the

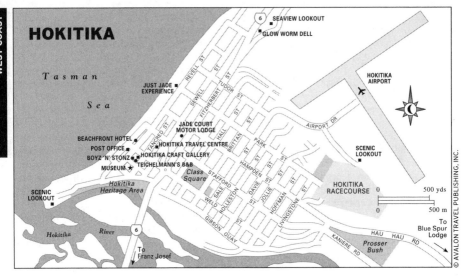

less productive land), and is home to a venison processing plant and a moss-drying factory.

SIGHTS AND RECREATION
West Coast Historical Museum
If you're interested in finding out more about the gold-rush days, visit the West Coast Historical Museum (Lower Tancred St., 03/755-6898; summer daily 9:30 A.M.–5 P.M., the rest of the year daily 10 A.M.–2 P.M.; adult $5, child $1). It features displays of old photos and sketches from the gold-mining era, a comprehensive collection of gold-mining equipment, a hall of pioneers, and an original stagecoach. Don't miss the Maori artifacts and native birds, some of which are extremely rare and possibly extinct. See the worthwhile 20-minute audio-visual on west coast life from the discovery of gold till now.

Scenic Sights
For a great view of Hokitika, distant mountains, Hokitika River, and the Tasman Sea, walk along the sandy, driftwood-strewn beach to the south end or along Gibson Quay by the river to the scenic **rivermouth viewpoint.** The view from here is particularly magnificent at

sunset, and the weathered remains of an old pier, huge boulders and rocks, and silhouetted fishermen make fascinating photo subjects. The rivermouth is also a popular place for anglers to congregate for some serious salmon fishing and some not-so-serious tale-telling. For an even grander panoramic view, head for the **Plane Table Lookout** on the road to the airport (north of town). A pointer and map indicate all the mountain peaks you can see, along with their heights. For fabulous coastal views, head up to **Seaview Lookout** and the historic kauri lighthouse built in 1879; drive north on Fitzherbert Street and turn up the hill toward Seaview Hospital—the lookout is inside the cemetery on the right.

Another free sight well worth visiting on the north side of town is the **Glow Worm Dell,** signposted along Highway 6 at the north town boundary—after dark you'll see thousands of tiny lights scattered over the 14-meter (46-ft) banks (take a flashlight to see the path and don't make any noise—noise and bright lights disturb the glowworms and their lights go out). Even if you don't have a flashlight you can easily feel your way up the path in the dark—and keep going; it's more spectacular the farther you go.

Lake Kaniere

To reach this large interior lake, head east out of Hokitika along Blue Spur Road (a continuation of Hampden St. and Hau Hau Rd.). Along the way is the **Blue Spur New Zealand Forest Lookout**—at the Forest Service notice board turn right and continue for about four km (2.5 mi). Tracks lead to old gold workings and abandoned mining equipment, parallel rivers, and pass by waterfalls and lakes.

The lake, 18 km (11 mi) east of town, is mostly surrounded by **Lake Kaniere Reserve.** An information booth where the river exits the lake has a good map of the area and details local walking tracks. There's swimming and fishing in the lake, and campsites at Hans Bay or Geologist Creek.

◖ Wildfoods Festival

This outdoor celebration (03/755-8321, www .wildfoods.co.nz) of local food has grown to become the west coast's most popular annual event and one of the county's best-known food festivals. Held the second Saturday of every March, the gathering of 20,000-plus people provides a unique opportunity to sample local cuisine from stands spread around Cass Square. Many of the dishes are simple preparations of common New Zealand ingredients, but part of the appeal is the ability of local chefs to gross out visitors with offerings such as jellied grasshopper, roast muttonbird, venison tongue, stinging-nettle soup, and pigs' eyes. For the less adventurous, there are unusual combinations (pistachio ice cream) and fun dishes (gang green donuts anyone?), as well as a smattering of international offerings. Although one of the west coast's best known businesses, Monteith's Brewing Co., is the major sponsor, there are also plenty of more exotic drinks to sample, such as Wild Mountain Moonshine and gorse wine.

SHOPPING
Greenstone Handcrafted Jewelry

Used by the Maori to make woodworking tools, locally quarried **greenstone** (the local name for what is known elsewhere in the world

© ANDREW HEMPSTEAD

a remote West Coast beach, north of Haast

as nephrite jade) is carved from lumps of rock into fine handcrafted jewelry of traditional Maori design, with many of the studios open for public viewing. The gem itself is relatively inexpensive—its value comes from the finished carving.

Rather than simply picking out a piece and moving on to the next tourist attraction, a couple of places in town let you create your own greenstone masterpiece. For those with a full day (perfect if it's raining) head to **Bonz 'N' Stonz** (16 Hamilton St., 03/755-6504), where you design your own jewelry or ornament, then grind out the basic shape, before adding the finishing touches with a sander. The cost is $95 for greenstone, or pay $75 for a *paua* (abalone) or bone carving. At **Just Jade Experience** (197 Revell St., 03/755-7612), you choose a design and carver Gordon Wells does the hard work. The piece is then handed back over and you spend up to five hours smoothing the rough edges then sanding and shining to perfection. The cost is $20–80 depending on the size and complexity of the design.

Hokitika Clock Tower marks the center of downtown.

© ANDREW HEMPSTEAD

Arts and Crafts

Hokitika is not all about greenstone. You should also take time to visit **Hokitika Craft Gallery** (25 Tancred St., 03/755-8802), a cooperative of local artists who take turns to staff the shop. Everything is handcrafted—pottery, stunning woven wall hangings, cushion covers, silk scarves, wooden works of art, sweaters, stained glass, paintings, quilts, and jewelry. Across the road, watch glassblowers plying their trade at the **Hokitika Glass Blowing Studio** (28 Tancred St., 03/755-7775).

ACCOMMODATIONS
Under $50

◖ **Blue Spur Lodge** (03/755-8445, www .bluespur.co.nz; dorm beds $23, $58 d, $75 s or d en suite, cottages $120–230) lies in a tranquil bush setting four km (2.5 mi) east of town, with views extending south to Mount Cook. All facilities at this purpose-built lodge are of the highest standard, bikes can be used for free, and canoe and kayak rentals are offered. To get

there, take Hampden Street out of town and turn left on Cement Lead Road, or call from the information center for a pickup.

Back in downtown, but with a beachfront location, **Just Jade Experience Backpackers** (197 Revell St., 03/755-7612, www.jade experience.co.nz; dorm beds $22, $50 s or d) is home to the Just Jade Experience mentioned earlier. Rates include free tea and coffee and the use of bikes.

$50-100

Having been owned and operated by four generations of the same local family, the **Beachfront Hotel Hokitika** (111 Revell St., 03/755-8344 or 0800/400-344, www.beachfronthotel.co.nz; $95–130 s or d) is a part of the local history. The rooms are fairly standard, but have been modernized (think Internet access). Downstairs are a café, restaurant, and four bars.

Also centrally located is the bright and breezy **Jade Court Motor Lodge** (85 Fitzherbert St., 03/755-8855 or 0800/755-885, www.jadecourt .co.nz; $95–130 s or d). Each spacious room has a kitchen; other extras include complimentary daily papers and a light breakfast.

$100-150
Teichelmanns Bed & Breakfast Inn (20 Hamilton St., 03/755-8232 or 0800/743-742, www.teichelmanns.co.nz; $135–240 s or d) provides six bright, cheerful rooms with king beds, a comfortable lounge area, central heating, and congenial hosts keen to extol Hokitika's virtues.

Holiday Park
Hokitika Holiday Park (242 Stafford St., 03/755-8172 or 0800/465-436) offers the usual facilities (good showers and heat lamps—aah!), plus a game room, trampoline, and adjacent shop selling basic necessities. Sites start at $11 per person, standard and economy cabins range $48–90 s or d, tourist flats are $100, and motel rooms $110.

FOOD
Hokitika doesn't have a large number of restaurants, but many tearooms and cafés serve the usual. For a delicious selection of salads, pies, quiche, light meals, pastries, and desserts surrounded by a collection of teapots, head to **P.R.'s Coffee Shop Bistro** (39 Tancred St., 03/755-8379; daily 6 A.M.–5 P.M.). Next to the town clock, **Millies Place** (35 Weld St., 03/755-8128; daily 6:30 A.M.–9 P.M.) offers everything from sandwiches and burgers to Chinese favorites.

For more of a splurge, **Stumpers** (2 Weld St., 03/755-6154; daily 7 A.M.–9 P.M.) is a slick contemporary space with a modern menu to match. Lunches are in the $10–16 range, while in the evening mains such as rib eye steak and baked rack of lamb are all under $30. **Trapper's** (79 Revell St., 03/755-5133; daily for lunch and dinner) has a rustic decor complementing a menu featuring "wild foods" such as whitebait, kangaroo, and crocodile.

PRACTICALITIES
Information
Westland Visitor Information Centre is on Hamilton Street (next to the museum, 03/755-6166; Mon.–Fri. 10 A.M.–6 P.M., Sat.–Sun. 10 A.M.–4 P.M.)

Getting There and Around
The west coast's major airport is two km (1.2 mi) north of Hokitika, served by **Air New Zealand** (03/755-8123 or 0800/737-300, www.airnewzealand.com) from Christchurch three times a day. A taxi to the airport is $8 one-way. **InterCity** (www.intercitycoach.co.nz) runs coaches north and south from **Hokitika Travel Centre** (60 Tancred St., 03/755-8557).

Local rental car companies include **Avis** (03/768-0902), **Budget** (03/768-4343), and **Hertz** (03/768-0196). For a cab, call **Hokitika Taxis** (03/755-5075).

HOKITIKA TO THE GLACIERS
Between Hokitika and Westland Tai Poutini National Park, Highway 6 passes many small lakes, accessible tracks, a few small settlements that once bustled with gold-mining activity, and mighty rivers where you can reel in brown and rainbow trout and the occasional salmon when the water is clear (many of the rivers are cloudy with glacial runoff). Farther south, the road runs by a saltwater forest, swampy areas of marshes and lagoons covered in waterfowl, then lush green paddocks backed by dark-blue mountains. As you get nearer to the town of Franz Josef on the northern boundary of the national park, magnificent snowcapped peaks loom into view.

Ross
This small but typical west coast gold town, 28 km (17 mi) south of Hokitika, has a colorful gold-mining history (kept alive in the local museum), walkways of historical interest, and several tourist attractions. Jones Creek Flat (behind Ross), a stable and productive goldfield in the early 1870s, is where New Zealand's largest gold nugget was found in 1907—nicknamed "the Honourable Roddy" after the local mayor.

The first place to go for information on local

walks is the **Ross Information and Heritage Centre**, in the old Bank of New South Wales building, uphill from the Empire Hotel (03/755-4077; daily 9 A.M.–6 P.M.). Then consider doing the two loop tracks of the **Ross Historic Goldfields Walkway.** Starting from the information center, the **Water Race Walk** is a two-km (1.2-mi) sometimes-steep loop through an old cemetery where gravestones vividly describe the hard times and tragic accidents of the 1870s (allow extra time for intriguing reading), to lookouts for good views of Ross, and past old coal-mine workings along the disused water race. The **Jones Flat Walk** (90 minutes round-trip), also starting at the information center, winds through regenerating forest along old elevator claim tailings.

White Heron Sanctuary

Continuing south along Highway 6, a sanctuary on the northern edge of Okarito Lagoon protects the breeding ground for New Zealand's only colony of white herons, or *kotuku.* These magnificent birds are distinctive for their size, pure white plumage, and elongated necks. The colony currently numbers around 100, with the birds arriving for the breeding season in late winter, hatching one or two chicks per nest, then leaving the following February. The only way to visit is with **White Heron Sanctuary Tours** (Hwy. 6, Whataroa, 03/753-4120 or 0800/523-456, www.whiteherontours.co.nz; adult $95, child $45), the only company with government permits to the sanctuary. Based at Whataroa, the company operates four tours daily November through February. Tours begin with a jetboat trip down the Waitangitaona River, then an easy 500-meter (1,640-ft) walk along a boardwalk through ancient coastal forest to the viewing area. Around 40 minutes is spent at the site. The same company also operates year-round jetboat tours and **Sanctuary Tours Motel** (cabins with shared bathrooms $60 s or d, bright motel rooms $105).

Okarito

The Okarito shoreline was the first bit of New Zealand that Abel Tasman saw in 1642. During the gold-rush era of the 1870s, the quiet settlement of Okarito flourished into a boomtown supporting 2,000 people, two banks, and many hotels and stores. Off Highway 6, today it's again a peaceful settlement on a typically wild west coast beach, and a population of just 20 souls. The tidal flats at adjacent **Okarito Lagoon,** New Zealand's largest unmodified wetland, become alive with birdlife at low tide—and you may (if you're lucky) see the rare white heron. Parts of the lagoon are flanked by *kahikatea* forest through which a maze of channels run—a fun place to explore by kayak. **Okarito Nature Tours** (03/753-4014), along the village's main drag, rents kayaks for $35 for two hours and has guided kayak trips from $65. The trick is timing your outward trip, whether guided or unguided, with the incoming tide for an easy cruise to the lagoon's farthest points.

Although the small but well-maintained **Okarito Hostel** (03/753-4124, www.yha.co.nz; $18 per person) is an associate of Hostelling International, no one seems to mind if you're not a member. It's in an 1870s schoolhouse along the main street. To get to Okarito, turn west off the main highway 12 km (seven mi) north of Franz Josef and then continue for 13 km (eight mi) along a gravel road.

Lake Mapourika

About eight km (five mi) north of Franz Josef, beautiful bush-fringed Lake Mapourika is the largest lake in Westland Tai Poutini National Park, separated from the main sector of the park by a short stretch of highway. Dark brown from rainwater filtered through the surrounding forest, the lake provides superb reflections, an abundance of birdlife, excellent salmon and trout fishing (get your license at the Franz Josef Store or park headquarters), warm swimming, and boating. It has plenty of shady picnic spots, and a free campground with fresh water and toilets at McDonalds Creek at the north end of the lake.

Westland Tai Poutini National Park

Backed by snowcapped peaks of the Southern Alps, Westland Tai Poutini covers a rugged 70-km-long (44-mi-long) 117,547-hectare (290,500-acre) area of high mountains and glaciers, lakes and waterfalls, hot springs, coastal lagoons, and icy gray-blue rivers that tumble down through dense forest to the Tasman Sea. The land rises from sea level to peaks more than 3,000 meters (9,843 ft) high, providing incredible scenery, a diverse range of habitats, plenty of birds and wildlife, and all kinds of recreational possibilities for the masses of visitors that come to this popular stretch of the west coast each year.

Most visitors center their exploration around two glaciers—**Franz Josef** and **Fox**—which are easily accessible from Highway 6. Two small resort towns, named after the two glaciers and separated by a winding 24-km (15-mi) stretch of highway, provide a wide range of services and are the staging points for glacier excursions, mountain hikes, forest and beach walks, fishing, mountaineering, ice-climbing, and flightseeing. The less adventurous or those in a hurry can appreciate some of the most striking glacier and bush scenery from the road or at the end of short tracks.

THE LAND

Thirty-km-wide (19-mi-wide) Westland Tai Poutini National Park, squeezed between the coast and the Main Divide, rises from Gillespies Beach and Okarito at sea level to the 3,498-meter (11,480-ft) summit of Mount Tasman (second-highest peak in New Zealand). The park is dominated by a massive ice field that sprawls across the top of the Southern Alps. The park's two largest glaciers (out of 60) are Franz Josef Glacier and Fox Glacier, which descend 12 km (seven mi) and 13.5 km (eight mi) respectively from permanent snowfields to dense rainforest only 300 meters (9,843 ft) above sea level—the only glaciers in the world that descend directly into lowland rainforest.

In the last ice age, 14,000 years ago, even the lowland areas were totally covered in ice. Today, most of the terrain above 1,500 meters (4,921 ft) is still covered with permanent ice and snow, with high peaks and ridges of frost-shattered rocks where up to 10,000 mm (394 in) of rain and snow fall per year. The lowland moraines and river valleys are now clothed in alpine grasslands and herbfields, shrublands, and dense coniferous rainforest. Lakes and coastal lagoons nestle in glacially formed hollows, and the entire landscape is riddled with wide gravel beds and mighty glacier-fed rivers.

Climate

The weather is as varied as the terrain in this area. Westland Tai Poutini ("Wetland" to visitors who whiz through the area in search of blue-sky "been-there" snapshots) has the reputation for dull gray skies and rainy summer days, but the winters are generally clear and cold and the scenery is dramatic. Be prepared for a downpour and cool temperatures, even in the middle of summer, and you'll be ready to make the most of your surroundings. The average yearly rainfall on the coast is about 3,000 mm (118 in) at the townships of Franz Josef and Fox Glacier, and at the foot of the mountains it can be as much as 5,000 mm (197 in) per year. Up to 10,000 mm (394 in) of rain and snow are expected above the 1,500-meter (4,921-ft) level each year.

Flora and Fauna

One of the most fascinating things about Westland Tai Poutini flora is the way the bare rock surfaces left behind by retreating glaciers are rapidly invaded through a process called "plant succession." In the early years after glacial retreat, windblown grasses and mat plants colonize the bare surfaces, and within 20 years, various shrubs, such as *tutu* and native broom that fix nitrogen from the air to form soil, have established themselves. Within the next 50 years, dense young forests of *rata* and *kamahi* trees spring up, followed by *rimu* and *miro* trees, forming the canopy of a lush podocarp rainforest. The luxuriant rainforest you drive through on the way to the glaciers also contains *kahikatea, matai,* and *totara* trees, an assortment of small shrubs, and beautiful ferns of all sizes (best appreciated on some of the short walks). Above the *rata* and *kamahi* forests, shrublands and alpine grasslands cover the slopes. Alpine herbs such as edelweiss, buttercups, and hebe grow in the higher reaches of the park, but only lichens survive on the highest rock areas below the snowline. Altogether about 600 species of plants and ferns inhabit the park.

Native birds, such as the *tui*, kiwi, bellbird, pigeon, fantail, tomtit, robin, and parakeet (ears become rapidly accustomed to ever-present rapturous birdsong), and oystercatchers and Caspian terns abound, and you'll see a number of godwits and the occasional crested grebe in the lake areas, wetlands, and coastal lagoons. White herons are prominent during their breeding season, Oct.–February. All kinds of insects creep around in the undergrowth, including termites, *weta,* and *huhu* grubs that feed on fallen trees.

THE CHEEKY KEA

A special feature of New Zealand's subalpine environment, *kea* are unique dull-green birds with red underwings and large, powerful beaks. Not the least bit afraid of mere mortals, they in fact seem to enjoy terrorizing you at times – swooping out of nowhere to land on your car or bicycle with a thud. They grab food from your fingers with no encouragement and pose obligingly for photographs, but take particular pleasure in ripping holes in bicycle seats and shredding windshield wipers. They also have a reputation for sliding down the tin roofs of mountain huts during the night, and removing shoelaces from boots left outside – such friendly little critters!

FRANZ JOSEF GLACIER

The terminal face of Franz Josef, one of two major glaciers within Westland Tai Poutini, is reached via a two-km (1.2-mi) walking trail that begins south the highway, where the village of Franz Josef does an admirable job of keeping tourists well-rested and -fed. The village, known locally as "Franz," is 137 km (85 mi) south of Hokitika, but you should allow at least two hours to negotiate the narrow, winding road between the two.

Walking Tracks

Follow Highway 6 south through the village and turn left after the Waiho River bridge onto the glacier access road. Continue for four km (2.5 mi) along this road through lush rainforest to a parking lot and interpretive shelter to get your first views. Many tracks begin from along the access road, but the busiest is the **Ka Roimata o Hine Hukatere Walk,** leading to the terminal face of Franz Josef Glacier. Taking about 40 minutes each way, the trail crosses riverbed gravel and several small streams, passes impressive waterfalls that cascade down steep glacially carved cliffs, then climbs up and over enormous boulders for great views of the glacier and the Waiho Valley. Stick closely to the marked track, watch out for possible rockfalls, and resist the urge to venture onto the ice without an experienced glacier guide—the front wall of the glacier is unstable. If you don't have enough time to hike all the way to the glacier, take the short 10-minute climb up **Sentinel Rock** for distant glacier views and examples of plants that have progressively colonized this huge rock. This trail also begins from the end of the access road.

From a small parking area back from the end of the road, the **Douglas Walk** is an easy forest walk over glacial landforms created by advances of the Franz Josef Glacier between 1600 and 1750; allow one hour for the loop. The **Roberts Point Track** branches off the Douglas Walk at the Douglas Swing Bridge. It climbs up the east side of the Waiho Valley, crossing slippery rock and side streams to a lookout high above the glacier where you get incredible long-distance views. Classified as a moderate-to-hard forest track, it takes about three hours one-way, returning via the same route (don't take a shortcut down from Roberts Point to the glacier track—it's very unsafe); wear sturdy footwear, and take a raincoat and some energy food. The **Lake Wombat Track** is an easy-to-moderate fern-lined trail through *rimu* forest to a small glacial lake where you'll hear all kinds of songbirds and see plenty of waterfowl. Signposted from the access road, allow 30 minutes each way.

The **Terrace Walk** starts opposite the Park Visitor Centre. It's an easy 30-minute round-trip forest walk, zigzagging up the terrace behind the village to the sluice face (from which a considerable amount of gold was taken), passing old gold-mining relics and finishing on Cowan Street behind Franz Josef village. A 20-minute sidetrack leads off the main track to scenic Tatare Gorge, where clear water gushes down between enormous boulders. The **Canavans Knob Rainforest Walk** is another short walk/climb for good views. The 20-minute (one-way) track starts on Highway 6, two km (one mi) south of Franz Josef, where the highway makes a sharp left turn.

Glacier Tours

Franz Josef Glacier Guides (03/752-0763 or 0800/484-337, www.franzjosefglacier.com) leads walks up to and on the glacier. Tours last four to five hours and include at least two hours exploring the glacier with crampons clipped on for safe passage of the slippery surface. The cost of this tour is adult $90, child $45, or you can upgrade to a full-day trip for adult $140, child $70. A heli-hike includes two short helicopter rides and a two-hour guided hike in the middle reaches of the glacier (adult $340, child $320). For adult $55, child $27.50, visitors can join a guided Terminal Face Walk. It doesn't involve climbing on the ice, but gives plenty of insight into the history and geology of the glacier.

Locally owned **Glacier Valley Eco Tours** (03/752-0699, www.glaciervalley.co.nz) has a less ambitious schedule of tours, including a

> # BIRTH OF A GLACIER
>
> West coast glaciers are formed by snow falling on the upper névé or snowfield (up to 300 meters/984 ft deep), squeezing out air from underlying layers to create firn or soft ice; when most of the air is forced out, dense blue ice is formed. The enormous mass of ice moves downward with the force of gravity (up to five meters/16 ft a day has been recorded in Westland), creating great pressures deep within the ice as it's crushed against the underlying terrain; the glacier cracks into ravines and crevasses up to 100 meters (330 ft) deep as it spills slowly downward. You can hear its movement at the terminal face – cracking and creaking ice, and rushing glacial melt-off. The glaciers are always either advancing or retreating – the terminal face retreats if the melt rate (due to warm rain) exceeds the snowfall at the head of the glacier, and advances if ice replacement (due to heavier snowfalls or colder temperatures than normal) exceeds melt rate.
>
> Although both Franz Josef and Fox have retreated dramatically overall during the last 200 years (during the last major glacial advance they swept all the way out to the sea), in recent years they've been advancing – a total of 1.8 km (one mi) since 1984. In 1994 the glaciers advanced nearly 200 meters (656 ft) – that's nearly five meters (16 ft) a day. Glaciologists predict this trend will continue for a few more years, even though the long-term trend is retreat.

guided walkup to the glacier and beyond the public barrier to the terminal face (adult $55, child $27). The company also operates similar tours to Fox Glacier and Lake Matheson from Franz Josef.

Flightseeing

On a clear day, the sky above the glacier is filled with flightseeing craft, with helicopters departing from a helipad within walking

WEST COAST

© ANDREW HEMPSTEAD

Flightseeing is the easiest way to get up close to a glacier.

distance of the village and fixed-wing planes departing from an airstrip south of town toward Fox Glacier. Seeing the glaciers and mountain peaks from the air is unforgettable in fine weather, and although it's expensive, it's worth every cent. Book yourself on an early-morning flight (it's worth waiting an extra day to accomplish this)—the skies are most likely to be clear early, often rapidly clouding over as the day progresses. **Glacier Helicopters** (03/752-0755 or 0800/800-732, www .glacierhelicopters.co.nz) and the **The Helicopter Line** (03/752-0767 or 0800/807-767, www .helicopter.co.nz) offer a similar range of options, starting with a 20-minute flight with a glacier landing for $180 per person. Expect to pay around $250 for a 30-minute flight over both glaciers and a landing, and $350 for a 40-minute trip that includes Mount Cook.

Fixed-wing service is provided by **Air Safaris** (03/752-0716 or 0800/723-274), which offers a 50-minute Grand Traverse flight over both glaciers and around Mount Cook for adult $260, child $180.

Accommodations and Camping

While the tour bus crowd is paying over $300 per night to stay in the largely anonymous **Franz Josef Glacier Hotel,** you, the savvy traveler, will have made advance reservations at one of the following choices.

The standout accommodation for me is **Rainforest Retreat** (Cron St., 03/752-0220, www.rainforestretreat.co.nz), in a beautiful forested setting one block from the highway and with rooms to suit all budgets (including campers; see listing in *Holiday Parks*). Facilities include a restaurant, a bar with an outdoor pool table, an outdoor spa tub, a laundry, and a covered barbecue area. Backpackers gravitate to the largest building, where dorm beds are $25, private rooms are $65–85, and there's a modern kitchen filled with stainless steel appliances. Motel rooms are $149 s or d, but worth the extra money are the spacious and modern Tree Lodges ($199 s or d), with kitchens, mini-conservatories, beautiful bathrooms, and decks. For families and small groups the two- and three-bedroom Tree Houses have even more room.

At **Glow Worm Cottages** (27 Cron St., 03/752-0172 or 0800/151-027, www.glow wormcottages.co.nz) the 4- and 6-bed dorms ($22 and $24 respectively) each have their own bathroom and kitchen. Other options are private rooms with shared bath ($50 s or d) and fully self-contained units with full kitchens ($100). Amenities include a cozy common area with a log fire, a hot tub, and bike rentals. **Franz Josef Glacier YHA** (24 Cron St., Franz Josef, 03/752-0754, www.yha.co.nz) offers over 100 beds in a bush setting. Comfortable dorms are $28, private rooms with shared bath sell for $50 s or d, and self-contained family units are $198. Both these places are within one block of the highway.

Alpine Glacier Motor Lodge (Condon St., 03/752-0226 or 0800/757-111, www.alpine glaciermotel.com; $135–155 s or d) has 24 comfortable rooms, with it worth the extra bucks for a king bed and small balcony.

One block behind the main commercial strip, **Punga Grove** (Cron St., 03/752-0001 or 0800/437-269, www.pungagrove.co.nz; $180–250 s or d) provides comfortable motel rooms decorated in a pleasing mix of natural colors and with a king bed, in-floor heating, and gas fireplace. Each opens to a private balcony surrounded by bird-filled native rainforest. Guests also have use of a spa, pool, and small forest-cloaked conservatory.

Surrounded by lush farmland two km (1.2 mi) north of the village, **Westwood Lodge** (03/752-0111 or 0800/741-111, www.westwood lodge.co.nz; $320–370 s or d includes breakfast) is an upscale bed-and-breakfast offering luxurious guest rooms with king-size beds and plush duvets, a billiards room, a lounge with fireplace, and a deck.

Franz Josef Top 10 Holiday Park (03/752-0735 or 0800/467-897; tent sites $19, caravan sites $20, self-contained cabins $55–65, motel rooms $95), beside Highway 6 one km (0.5 mi) south of Franz Josef, offers many accommodation options, and more: The kitchen and living area (with TV) and the comfy lounge room are particularly good places to meet fellow travelers; the bathrooms are clean and spacious, with

plenty of hot water, disabled facilities, and a baby's bathroom; and there are plenty of coin-operated washing machines and driers.

In the village itself is **Rainforest Holiday Park** (Cron St., 03/752-0220, www.rainforest holidaypark.co.nz), where powered camp-sites surrounded by rainforest cost $17.50 per person. This place is part of Rainforest Retreat (described earlier), and campers have access to the same range of excellent facilities as other guests.

Food

To find a place to eat, just take a stroll through the village—it's small enough that you can easily *see* what's happening. **Fern Grove Food Centre** (daily till 8 P.M.), on the main road next to the souvenir shop, sells groceries, dairy foods, fruit, and veggies. **Guzzi Alfresco** (Alpine Adventure Centre, Hwy. 6, 03/752-0047; daily from 8 A.M.) serves up good coffee and light meals—it's the perfect place to hang out on a rainy day. It also has public Internet access.

Within the Rainforest Retreat complex, 🄲 **Monsoon** (Cron St., 03/752-0220; daily 7–10 A.M. and 4:30–9 P.M.) is a delightful L-shaped space with a bar in one wing and restaurant tables filling the other. A breakfast pie is $6.50 and full breakfast $16. In the evening, check the blackboard for daily specials in the $20–28 range, or stick to favorites like fish-and-chips for $13. Either way, the pavlova ($5) is a dessert must.

Blue Ice Café (Hwy. 6, 03/752-0707; daily for lunch and dinner), toward the south end of the commercial strip, is a step above the usual café fare and decor, although you'll want to finish up before the seasonal-worker crowd arrives to drink and dance the night away. Pizza is the specialty, while other mains such as roast venison topped with red-onion jam are around $30.

Information

Westland Tai Poutini National Park Visitor Centre is beside the highway at the south end of town (03/752-0796; summer daily

8:30 A.M.–6 P.M., rest of the year daily 8:30 A.M.–noon and 1–5 P.M.). The center has all sorts of fascinating displays, a stunning photograph/art gallery, all the reading material and maps you could possibly need, friendly staff, and indigenous arts, crafts, pottery, and photographs for sale in the lobby. Ask about the summer schedule of guided walks.

Getting There and Around

Intercity (03/752-0164, www.intercitycoach .co.nz) buses to Franz Josef run from Hokitika, Greymouth (with connections from Christchurch), Queenstown, and Wanaka. The bus stops outside Glacier Scooter Safaris, on the main street, with one service daily in each direction. No shuttles run between Franz Josef and Fox Glaciers; instead you must take the Intercity bus.

Franz Josef has no rental cars or taxis, but **Glacier Valley Eco Tours** (03/752-0699) has a regular shuttle between the glacier and town for $10 per person round-trip.

FOX GLACIER

Fox Glacier is no less spectacular than Franz Josef, but the associated village is smaller and more low-key than its neighbor 24 km (15 mi) to the north. The glacier itself is slightly closer to the road, making reaching the terminal face an easier proposition than at Franz Josef.

Walking Tracks

To get to the glacier from Fox Glacier village, take the main highway south just over one km (0.6 mi), then turn left before the bridge over the Fox River onto the glacier access road. Continue for three km (1.9 mi) to the end of the road, where the track to the glacier terminal starts. The access road itself is interesting, as it takes you through green tunnels of overhanging *rata* and *kamahi* trees covered in ferns and mosses. You get glimpses of the icy Fox River, with its huge potholes filled with turquoise water, areas of quicksand (warnings posted), and towering vertical rock cliffs. From the end of the road it takes around 30 minutes of easy walking to the glacier's terminal face.

Wear comfortable shoes, keep on the marked track, watch out for rockfalls, and resist the urge to venture onto the ice—it's unsafe without a glacier guide.

Along the access road, **River Walk** is signposted to the south (right). This easy 30-minute (one-way) track takes you over a long, narrow suspension bridge (built in 1929) that literally sways in the breeze (great views of the rushing icy-cold Fox River far below), and on through *kamahi* forest to meet the end of Glacier View Road. Where this road ends (it is accessible by vehicle from Hwy. 6 on the south side of the Fox River), the 40-minute (one-way) **Chalet Lookout Track** starts. Once the main glacier access track, nowadays it gives views only of the terminal face and lower icefall. Also along this road is the **Moraine Walk,** taking 40 minutes round-trip to meander through impressive tree ferns and *rata* forest, showing the effect of glacial advances during the 17th and 18th centuries (a good rainy-day option).

Between the village and the glacier turnoff is **Minnehaha Walk,** a short and easy loop (allow 20 minutes) following Minnehaha Stream through typical park rainforest chockablock with beautiful ferns—it's a good walk to keep in mind for a wet day, and if done at night (take a flashlight), thousands of tiny glowworms light up the rainforest.

Three km (two mi) south from Fox Glacier village, just beyond Thirsty Creek, is the four-hour (one-way) track up the slopes of **Mount Fox.** The track climbs steeply through native bush to a viewpoint at 1,022 meters (3,353 ft) to give impressive views of the Alps, glacier, and coast.

Copland Valley Track

For experienced and well-equipped backcountry enthusiasts only, this three-day tramp links the west coast to Mount Cook village and includes a tricky crossing of Copland Pass, which is notorious for bad weather. A less-ambitious option is to hike the first section of the track, starting 26 km (16 mi) south of Fox Glacier. The first 20-km (12-mi) section to Welcome Flat takes about six hours, and hikers are rewarded with hot springs and a hut. From this point, it's 10 km (6.2 mi) across rivers, over grasslands, and through rainforest, before emerging at Douglas Rock Hut. The tricky 14-km (nine-mi) alpine climb from Douglas Rock to Hooker Hut in Aoraki/Mount Cook National Park takes about eight hours, followed by an easier four- to five-hour walk down the Hooker Valley to end in Aoraki/Mount Cook village. Before setting out, get the rundown at park visitor centers in Westland Tai Poutini or Aoraki/Mount Cook National Parks.

Lake Matheson

One of the most delightful (and photographed) lake-and-mountain panoramas in all of New Zealand is accessible at Lake Matheson, off Cook Flat Road (which branches west off Hwy. 6 in Fox Glacier village). The lake is renowned for outstanding reflections (on a calm day—morning is best) of 3,744-meter (12,280-ft) Mount Cook and 3,498-meter (11,480-ft) Mount Tasman. The trail around the lake is beautiful in itself, but you need to reach the

The view of Lake Matheson with Mount Cook in the distance is one of New Zealand's most scenic panoramas.

© ANDREW HEMPSTEAD

lake's far end for the famously scenic viewpoint froma small lake-level deck. The loop is four km (2.5 mi) and takes around 90 minutes. Back at the trailhead, Matheson Café (described later in *Food*) is perfectly located for an after-walk meal or snack.

Gillespies Beach

Cook Flat Road ends 22 km (14 mi) from Highway 6 at Gillespies Beach, which was once the site of a short-lived gold rush. A trail near the lagoon mouth follows an early miners' track through a cliff tunnel and down to the beach (20 minutes one-way), or take a side-track at the tunnel for a 10-minute climb to a trig survey marker for superb views. You can also walk north along the beach (allow three hours round-trip) to a **fur seal colony,** returning through beautiful Waikukupa State Forest. You can get near the seals, but don't disturb them or get between the seals and the ocean.

Glacier Tours

While you can easily reach Fox Glacier by yourself, joining a guided tour has many advantages—most notably that you will be equipped with crampons that allow you to safely climb onto and around the glacier. In business since 1928, **Fox Glacier Guiding** (03/751-0825 or 0800/111-600, www.foxguides.co.nz) operates from a base on the ocean side of Highway 6 as it passes through town. Most popular is the half-day guided hike, with walkers climbing above the glacier, then descending and scrambling across the ice. This tour departs twice daily (9:05 A.M. and 1:35 P.M.) and costs adult $79, child $46. For the less adventurous, the shorter Terminal Face Walk is adult $35, child $17.50. Other options include a daylong ice-climbing course, heli-hiking, heli-skiing (spring only), and an overnight helicopter trip to remote Chancellor Hut. Boots, socks, winter coats, and transportation are included in the price of all tours.

The same two companies operating out of Franz Josef, **Glacier Helicopters** (03/751-0803 or 0800/800-732, glacierhelicopters.co.nz) and **The Helicopter Line** (03/751-0767 or 0800/807-767, www.helicopter.co.nz), also fly from Fox Glacier. A 20-minute flight and landing on Fox Glacier is $180 per person while a longer flight that loops past both glaciers is $250.

Accommodations and Camping

In the heart of the village, **Ivory Towers** (Sullivan Rd., 03/751-0838, www.ivory towerslodge.co.nz; dorm beds $24, $45 s, $58 d, $80 en suite) comprises three separate buildings (none of which is a tower), each with a few rooms, central living area, kitchen, and shared bathroom.

Fox Glacier Inn (39 Sullivan Rd., 03/751-0022, www.foxglacierinn.co.nz; $70–105 s or d) offers adequate budget accommodations in small rooms with twin or double beds. Breakfast costs an extra $13.50 and dinner is $29 for two courses.

Several park-at-your-door motels lie along Cook Flat Road leading west from the village to Lake Matheson. Closest to the highway is the **Rainforest Motel** (Cook Flat Rd., 03/751-0140 or 0800/724-636, www.rainforestmotel.co.nz; $115–150 s or d), comprising 12 self-contained units set on pleasant grassed grounds with a barbecue area off to one side. A little further along, **Lake Matheson Motel** (Cook Flat Rd., 03/751-0830 or 0800/452-243, www.lake matheson.co.nz; $115–160 s or d) is still only a short walk back to the services of the village. The rooms are very appealing, especially the spa units ($130 s or d). All have kitchens, or guests can cook up a storm in the barbecue area.

Continuing toward the ocean, **Fox Glacier Holiday Park** (Cook Flat Rd., 03/751-0821, www.foxglacierholidaypark.co.nz) spreads over open farmland where the views extend back across town to the mountains. Cabins start at $56, or pay $100 for a self-contained unit. Campsites are $28–30 s or d.

The standout upscale accommodation is the **Te Weheka Inn** (Hwy. 6, 03/751-0730 or 0800/313-414, www.weheka.co.nz; $328 s, $348 d, includes breakfast). Each of the spacious rooms has a contemporary feel, a luxurious bathroom with plush towels and a separate shower and bath, an ironing facility, Internet access, and a private balcony with comfortable outdoor furniture. It's at the northern edge of the village, within walking distance of local restaurants and booking offices.

Food

Part of the Fox Glacier Guiding complex on Highway 6 in the middle of the village, the **Hobnail Cafe** (03/751-0005; daily 8 A.M.–5 P.M.) has a relaxed and welcoming ambience. A cooked breakfast is $16, or try healthy mains like the warm chili and chicken salad for $16.

At the Lake Matheson trailhead, off Cook Lake Road, **Matheson Cafe** (03/751-0878; daily 8 A.M.–5 P.M.) takes full advantage of the mountain panorama with large windows and a few outdoor tables. It's a bright, contemporary space with café fare such as gourmet sandwiches, salads, and soups.

For dinner, coach drivers herd the tour bus crowd to the restaurant at the **Glacier Country Hotel** (Hwy. 6, 03/751-0847; daily from 5 P.M.) to pay upwards of $37 for an unremarkable main. Much better, and just around the corner, is **Plateau Café & Bar** (Sullivan Rd., 03/751-0058; summer 8 A.M.–9 P.M., the rest of the year 11:30 A.M.–9 P.M.), a low-key place with a few outdoor tables set along the sidewalk. Prices are relatively reasonable and choices are as varied as deep-fried kumara with honey-mustard dressing and a Malaysian-inspired salmon and mussel *laksa* (curry).

Information

The park's main visitor center is in Franz Josef, but the **Department of Conservation** maintains an office at the north end of the village (03/751-0807; Mon.–Fri. 9 A.M.–4:30 P.M.) where you can get trail and weather information.

Getting There

Fox Glacier is a turnaround point for Intercity buses, so if you're either northbound or southbound, you must change buses here. All services stop at **Alpine Guides** along Highway 6 (03/751-0701). By bus, it's four hours north to Greymouth and eight hours south to Queenstown over Haast Pass and via Wanaka.

Haast Pass to Wanaka

From Fox Glacier, it's 264 km (164 mi) south along the coast and then east over Haast Pass to Wanaka. No different from anywhere else on the west coast, the road is narrow and often winding. Allow at least five hours to get to Wanaka, or a full day with stops.

FOX GLACIER TO HAAST

Between Fox Glacier and **Lake Paringa,** Highway 6 moseys along through lush tree ferns and forest in almost every shade of green imaginable, passing rugged headlands, desolate pebble beaches covered in driftwood, and the odd lonely farm hacked out of the bush. Surrounded by ferns and forest (in what seems like the middle of nowhere), Lake Paringa is deceptively tranquil but teems with brown trout and quinnat salmon—an angler's paradise. The lake used to be the end of the road before the opening of the Haast route, yet despite the traffic that nowadays whizzes through, it's still a quiet spot for outdoor enthusiasts. You'll find DOC campsites just off the road south of the housing development.

Lake Moeraki

Lake Moeraki is another beautiful lake known for its distinct glacier-blue color and good fishing. Take the easy 40-minute (one-way) bush walk along **Monro's Track** to the coast, where you'll find sandy beaches interspersed with rocky headlands; the track starts near the lake outlet. You'll find a number of pleasing campsites around the lake. Overlooking a fast-flowing stream at the outlet of the lake is the upscale **Wilderness Lodge Lake Moeraki** (03/750-0881, www.wildernesslodge.co.nz; $475 s, $720 d). The lodge, owned by Dr. Gerry McSweeney, a well-known naturalist and one of New Zealand's leading conservationists, provides comfortable accommodations in recently revamped rooms and a riverside restaurant. Rates include meals prepared using seasonal game such as *cervena* (farmed venison), and accompanied at din-

ner by fine New Zealand wine. A number of fabulous guided outdoor activities can be booked through the lodge, such as rainforest walks (free), a canoe trip from the lake to the sea ($78), fishing trips (rates on application), and wilderness walks to see seals and penguins ($88). Lodge guests have the free use of canoes, life jackets, and rowboats (rent fishing gear).

Knights Point and Ship Creek

Southbound from Lake Moeraki, Highway 6 quickly reaches Knights Point, where a lookout provides some of the most spectacular ocean views accessible by road anywhere along the west coast. About five km (3.1 mi) south of Knights Point the highway crosses Ship Creek. The creek is named for the remains of a ship which until recently were visible on the beach. Believed to be from the *Schomberg of Aberdeen,* the largest wooden ship ever launched from Britain, when the vessel floundered off the Australian coast in 1885 the passengers and crew escaped, and it was never seen afloat again. Shifting sands have covered the relics, but it's an interesting stop, with unique rock formations where the creek flows into the ocean. Stretching south from Ship Creek is a 50-km-long (31-mi-long) beach that is part of New Zealand's largest sand dune system.

HAAST

This town, where the Haast River drains into the Tasman Sea and Highway 6 makes a sharp turn away from the west coast, lies just 120 km (75 mi) south of Westland Tai Poutini National Park, but allow at least two hours for the trip.

Haast Visitor Centre

A lot more than a place to add to your brochure collection, this metallic architectural wonder (corner Hwy. 6 and Jackson Bay Rd., 03/750-0809; Dec.–Mar. daily 8:30 A.M.–7 P.M., the

© ANDREW HEMPSTEAD

Haast Visitor Centre

rest of the year daily 9 A.M.–4:30 P.M.) holds exhibits that catalogue the natural history of the **South-West New Zealand World Heritage Area.** Combing Westland Tai Poutini, Mount Aspiring, and Fiordland National Parks, UNESCO recognized the importance of these forests, mountains, and coastline to create an integrated 2.6-million-hectare (6.4-million-acre) World Heritage Site in 1990.

Accommodations and Food

Beyond Haast Visitor Centre, Highway 6 veers inland and a side road leads to the small township of Haast. Here, **Wilderness Accommodation** (03/750-0029, www.wildernessaccommodation.co.nz) provides all the backpacker necessities, including comfortable dorms ($24) and private rooms with shared bath ($45 s, $55 d) surrounding a covered courtyard. Motel rooms ($95 s or d) in a newer wing share their own communal kitchen. Another choice for those on a budget

is **Haast Beach Holiday Park** (Jackson Bay Rd., 03/750-0860), where camping is $22–26 and basic cabins are $50 s or d. The campground is 14.5 km (nine mi) south of Haast Junction at Okuru.

At Haast Junction (opposite the visitor center) is the **World Heritage Hotel Haast** (Hwy. 6, 03/750-0828 or 0800/502-444, www.worldheritage-hotel.com), a low-rise complex of regularly revamped motel rooms (from $105 s or d). Amenities include a barbecue area, laundry facilities, and Internet terminals. Also here is the **Frontier Café & Bar** (daily for breakfast, lunch, and dinner), with surprisingly good food and an evening buffet ($35).

Between Haast Junction and Haast is **McGuires Lodge** (Hwy. 6, 03/750-0020 or 0800/624-847, www.mcguireslodge.co.nz; $110–180 s or d), with 19 smartly furnished rooms in six configurations, including units with separate bedrooms. Each has a fridge and toaster. Part of the complex is a café (daily

8 A.M.–2 P.M.) and restaurant (daily 5–9 P.M.). Prices could be a little lower, but the fish-and-chips (in the café; $18) was absolutely delicious. Dinner in the restaurant includes creative mains ($26–30) such as poached cod doused in a creamy chardonnay and lemon dressing.

Jackson Bay

The road out to Haast Beach Holiday Park continues for another 40 km (25 mi) to Jackson Bay, a small fishing village nestled under Jackson Head. Long sandy beaches and coastal views on one side of the road and dense bush and swampy areas backed by magnificent, steep, tree-covered mountains on the other make an interesting detour from the highway.

◖ HAAST PASS HIGHWAY

Although this highway (Hwy. 6) was completed as recently as 1960, for centuries prior west coast Maori traveled over the pass they knew as *Tioripatea* ("the way ahead is clear") to trade greenstone. Linking Haast and Wanaka, it is a 146-km (91-mi) route of great beauty. In less than three hours of driving, the scenery changes from lush west coast greenery to the snowcapped peaks and deep river gorges of Mount Aspiring National Park, the Gates of Haast and Haast Pass (563 meters/1,850 ft), mighty lakes with sparkling blue-green water, and open space extending to the horizon. It's best not to drive it at night (you'll miss all the scenery) or when you're in a hurry—there are many one-lane bridges and some narrow stretches with sharp corners and steep drop-offs where it's almost inevitable you'll meet a large semi-trailer around a blind turn.

East from Haast

From Haast, the highway follows the crystal-clear, turquoise Haast River, which is joined by the large Landsborough River; then the road crosses a bridge with fantastic mountain views before passing **Pleasant Flat,** where there's a picnic spot and short walk (five min-

utes) to a river viewpoint. From Pleasant Flat to **Rainy Flat,** Highway 6 winds through a small northeast section of **Mount Aspiring National Park.** Continue to **Thunder Creek Falls** and take the short forest track—here the water drops an impressive 30 meters (100 ft) from a small notch in the rock. About two km (1.2 mi) farther along the road at the Gates of Haast bridge, the Haast River roars down a gorge full of enormous schist boulders. **Haast Pass** is the lowest on the Main Divide at 563 meters (1,850 ft) and from here to **Makarora Gorge** lies some of the best scenery along the entire route. Rivers meander like silver ribbons in and out of dense bush and hills, through large flats covered in woolly "grass cutters" (sheep) for as far as the eye can see. One of many worthwhile stops is to take the short trail to **Blue Pools,** deep bodies of water within the Blue River that are often filled with trout; allow 15 minutes each way from the signed parking area just south of the pass.

Makarora

Beyond Haast Pass, the road begins a long and gradual descent to Lake Wanaka, passing through the eastern extent of Mount Aspiring National Park. As the highway exits the pass, it comes to Makarora, a small service center overlooking the Makarora River Valley. This is the starting point for a one-day wilderness excursion called the **Siberia Experience** (03/443-8351, www.siberiaexperience.com; $245), which comprises a 25-minute flight over Mount Aspiring National Park, a landing in the Siberia Valley, then a three-hour wilderness walk to a jetboat for an exciting return trip to Makarora. The adventure is offered by **Southern Alps Air** (03/443-8666 or 0800/345-666), which also operates flightseeing tours to Milford Sound (90 minutes; $320).

Across from the airstrip, **Makarora Wilderness Resort** (03/443-8372, www .makaroa.co.nz) has campsites ($12 per person), dorm beds ($22), private rooms with shared bathrooms ($50), and A-frame chalets ($95 s or d). Part of the same complex are a restaurant (daily 8 A.M.–9 P.M.), general store, and service station. Beside the resort is **Makarora Visitor Centre** (03/443-8365, Mon.–Fri. 8 A.M.–5 P.M., daily during summer holidays), a DOC facility for Mount Aspiring National Park (the main park information center is at Wanaka). Even when it's not staffed, you can walk around a glass-enclosed 3-D map of the park.

Makarora to Wanaka

The road from Makarora to Wanaka emerges to a landscape of wide-open tussock-covered hills and water, water, water as it first runs along the eastern shores of shimmering bright-blue **Lake Wanaka,** one of the largest southern lakes. Along with good trout fishing, the lake-shores provide many ideal spots for free camping, and generally a good supply of driftwood for campfires (make sure you have an adequate supply of insect repellent in summer).

The highway crosses The Neck (between Lake Wanaka and Lake Hawea), then parallels the hilly western shores of equally beautiful **Lake Hawea,** descending to its southern shores and through the small town of Hawea to **Wanaka,** which is covered in the *Otago* chapter.

CHRISTCHURCH AND CANTERBURY

Most visitors come to New Zealand to experience the wonders of nature and the intrigues of Maori culture. Christchurch has neither, but still manages to hold its own as one of the country's top tourist destinations. Largest city on the South Island, capital of the province of Canterbury, and New Zealand's second-largest city (pop. 330,000), Christchurch conjures vivid images of what are perceived to be some of the best aspects of typical English charm—striking Gothic architecture and fine stone buildings, lush green parks and flower-filled gardens, grassy banks and drooping willow trees along the meandering Avon River, and droves of Christ's College schoolboys in black-and-white uniforms and straw boaters cycling home at the end of the day. One hectare in every eight in Christchurch is a public park, reserve, or recreation ground. Lush greenery and gardens abound everywhere you go, always well maintained and usually chockablock with flowers—hence the well-deserved title "Garden City." Christchurchians must surely have more green thumbs concentrated in their area than in the rest of the country.

The remnant of two huge volcanoes attached to the mainland by a gravel plain, rugged Banks Peninsula lies immediately southeast of Christchurch. Trails over craggy peaks and through deep valleys and forest remnants (most take about a day and are best done in summer), good swimming at sandy beaches along the sharply indented coastline, small towns nestled in striking crater harbors, and an overall island-getaway atmosphere make the peninsula an ideal place for a day trip from

© ANDREW HEMPSTEAD

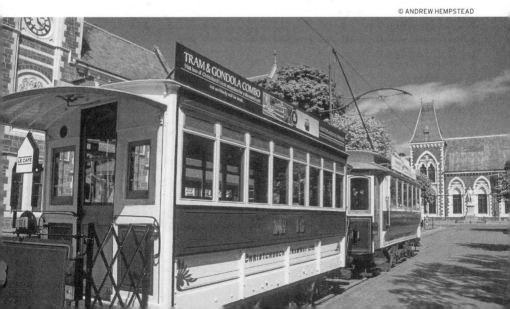

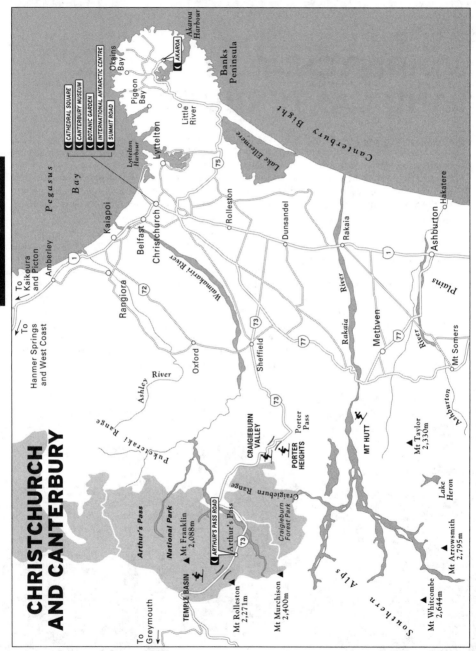

CHRISTCHURCH AND CANTERBURY

CHRISTCHURCH

AKAROA

Akaroa Harbour

Banks Peninsula

Okains Bay

Pigeon Bay

Little River

Lyttelton

Lyttelton Harbour

- CATHEDRAL SQUARE
- CANTERBURY MUSEUM
- BOTANIC GARDEN
- INTERNATIONAL ANTARCTIC CENTRE
- SUMMIT ROAD

Canterbury Bight

Lake Ellesmere

75

Rolleston

Dunsandel

Rakaia

Hakatere

Ashburton

1

Pegasus Bay

Kaiapoi

Belfast

Christchurch

Waimakariri River

Rakaia River

Rakaia

Plains

Methven

Mt Somers

Amberley

To Kaikoura and Picton

1

Rangiora

72

Oxford

Ashley River

Puketeraki Range

Sheffield

73

77

Mt Hutt

Mt Taylor 2,330m

Ashburton River

77

Lake Heron

To Hanmer Springs and West Coast

To

CRAIGIEBURN VALLEY

PORTER HEIGHTS

Porter Pass

Craigieburn Range

Craigieburn Forest Park

MT HUTT

Arthur's Pass

National Park

Mt Franklin 2,088m

ARTHUR'S PASS ROAD

Arthur's Pass

73

Mt Arrowsmith 2,795m

TEMPLE BASIN

Mt Rolleston 2,271m

Mt Murchison 2,400m

Southern Alps

Mt Whitcombe 2,644m

To Greymouth

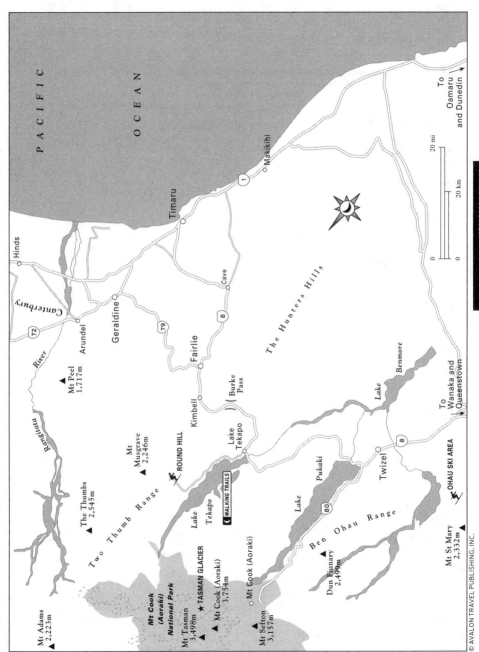

© AVALON TRAVEL PUBLISHING, INC.

CHRISTCHURCH

HIGHLIGHTS

Cathedral Square: In the shadow of a magnificent Gothic cathedral, the heart of Christchurch pulses with action day and night (page 349).

Canterbury Museum: Step back in time at this large museum that explores the region's natural and human history (page 350).

Botanic Garden: Large tracts of Christchurch are set aside as parkland, including this riverside park on the edge of downtown (page 352).

International Antarctic Centre: Transport yourself to the world's most remote continent (page 353).

Summit Road: Buckle up for an exciting drive through the mountains circling Christchurch's southern city limits (page 354).

Akaroa: A slice of France on the South Island, this seaside village is *très beau* (page 367).

Arthur's Pass Road: Passing through a patchwork of farms before entering the mountainous wilderness of Arthur's Pass National Park, this is New Zealand at its best (page 371).

Walking Trails: Hit the trails of Aoraki/Mount Cook National Park for the true alpine experience (page 381).

LOOK FOR **(** TO FIND RECOMMENDED SIGHTS, ACTIVITIES, DINING, AND LODGING.

Christchurch—though you might find yourself staying longer. Spreading out from Christchurch to the west are the flat patchwork-neat fields of the Canterbury Plains, the orderly design broken only by rivers and streams, and the lakes and coastal marshes in the southwest. Beyond the plains rise the Southern Alps. Pockets of these dramatic mountains are protected in areas such as Arthur's Pass National Park and Aoraki/Mount Cook National Park, both paradises for outdoor enthusiasts, climbers, hikers, and naturalists.

PLANNING YOUR TIME

Christchurch is a transportation hub, and so most visitors find themselves passing through the city at some stage of their South Island travels. If time is limited, I'd suggest a one-way car rental between Auckland and Christchurch, and then a flight out of Christchurch back to Auckland. This allows as much or as little time as you need to see the South Island, but cuts out at least two day's travel time returning to Auckland.

Regardless of how you arrive in Christchurch,

or what your onward travel plans are, a full day of city sightseeing is easy to fill. This allows time to blend with the crowds in **Cathedral Square,** visit **Canterbury Museum,** wander through the **Botanic Garden,** spend at least two hours at the **International Antarctic Centre,** drive the **Summit Road,** and enjoy a night out at one of the city's many top restaurants. With two nights booked in Christchurch, you could take a day trip out to the seaside village of **Akaroa.** With a third night, plan on traveling **Arthur's Pass**

Road and into the mountains of Arthur's Pass National Park (or take the famous TranzAlpine train). The main route south from Christchurch is Highway 1 along the coast through Timaru to Dunedin, from where you can loop through Otago and Southland and either cross over to the west coast or return to Christchurch via an inland route that provides access to Aoraki/ Mount Cook National Park, where **walking trails** put you within sight of New Zealand's highest mountain.

Christchurch

Christchurch was founded in 1850 by the Canterbury Association as a planned Church of England settlement. The first group of settlers started a typically "English" community in the new land. They successfully combined the old-English aspects they previously enjoyed with the aspects of a new land—a look and feeling that Christchurch has always retained. This gives the city its unique atmosphere— one that needs to be felt to be appreciated. Its flat terrain is ideal for walking and cycling, and an excellent public transportation network makes exploring its special nooks and crannies a snap. The central city area bustles with activity, but a short hop from Cathedral Square and you're strolling along a beautiful river with quacking ducks the only sound. Then several blocks later, you're passing house after house with spectacular "English" flower gardens—it's hard to believe you're still in the center of a city (in England, blocks this large would be out in the suburbs). Although the large international airport has made Christchurch the principal gateway to the scenic wonders of the South Island (or "Mainland" according to South Islanders), the city itself (and its many cultural offerings) is a New Zealand attraction that you shouldn't miss.

SIGHTS
The downtown core is a mix of history and highrise centering on Cathedral Square. All

major attractions are within walking distance of this central square, including the tree-lined Avon River, which winds its way through downtown. Across the river from Cathedral Square is

Playing chess is a popular activity in Cathedral Square.

© ANDREW HEMPSTEAD

CHRISTCHURCH

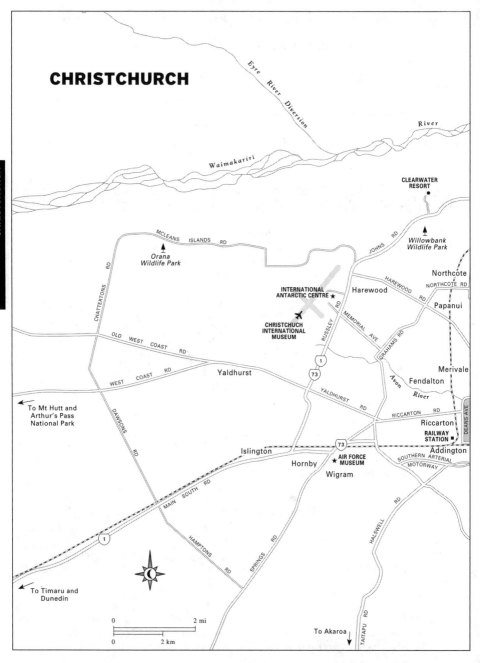

CHRISTCHURCH

Eyre River Diversion

River

Waimakariri

CLEARWATER
RESORT

MCLEANS ISLANDS RD

JOHNS RD

Willowbank
Wildlife Park

Orana
Wildlife Park

CHATTERTONS RD

Northcote

HAREWOOD RD

NORTHCOTE RD

INTERNATIONAL
ANTARCTIC CENTRE ★

Harewood

Papanui

CHRISTCHUCH
INTERNATIONAL
MUSEUM

OLD WEST COAST RD

RUSSLEY RD

MEMORIAL AVE

GRAHAMS RD

Yaldhurst

WEST COAST RD

1

73

Merivale

Avon
River

Fendalton

To Mt Hutt and
Arthur's Pass
National Park

DAWSONS RD

YALDHURST RD

RICCARTON RD

DEANS AVE

Riccarton
RAILWAY
STATION ■

Islington

73

Addington

Hornby

AIR FORCE
MUSEUM ★

SOUTHERN ARTERIAL

MOTORWAY

Wigram

MAIN SOUTH RD

HAMPTONS RD

SPRINGS RD

HALSWELL RD

1

To Timaru and
Dunedin

0   2 mi

0   2 km

To Akaroa

TAITAPU RD

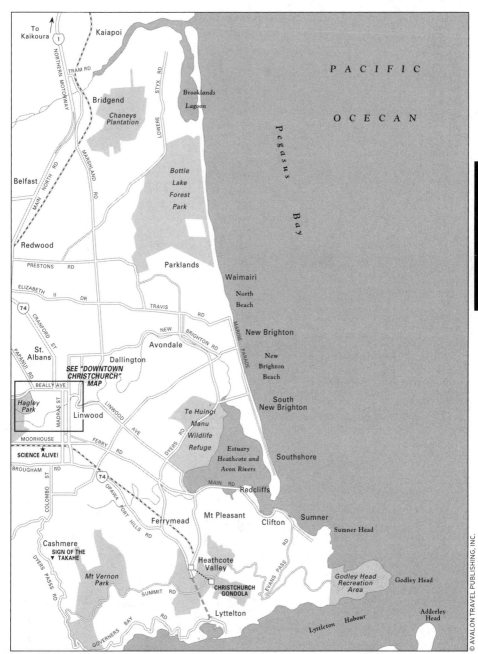

To Kaikoura

Kaiapoi

PACIFIC

OCECAN

NORTHERN MOTORWAY

TRAM RD

STYX RD

Brooklands Lagoon

Bridgend

Chaneys Plantation

LOWERE

MAIN NORTH RD

MARSHLAND RD

Belfast

Bottle Lake Forest Park

Redwood

Pegasus Bay

PRESTONS RD

Parklands

ELIZABETH II

DR

74

CRANFORD ST

PAPANUI RD

St. Albans

TRAVIS RD

NEW BRIGHTON RD

Waimairi

North Beach

New Brighton

MARINE PARADE

Avondale

Dallington

SEE "DOWNTOWN CHRISTCHURCH" MAP

BEALLY AVE

MADRAS ST

Hagley Park

Linwood

LINWOOD AVE

New Brighton Beach

South New Brighton

MOORHOUSE

SCIENCE ALIVE!

FERRY RD

DYERS RD

Te Huingi Manu Wildlife Refuge

BROUGHAM ST

COLOMBO ST

74

OPAWA

PORT HILLS RD

Ferrymead

Estuary Heathcote and Avon Rivers

MAIN RD

Redcliffs

Southshore

Mt Pleasant

Clifton

Sumner

Sumner Head

Cashmere

SIGN OF THE ▼ TAKAHE

DYERS PASS RD

Mt Vernon Park

SUMMIT RD

CHRISTCHURCH GONDOLA

Heathcote Valley

EVANS PASS RD

Godley Head Recreation Area

Godley Head

GOVERNERS BAY RD

Lyttelton

Lyttleton Habour

Adderley Head

© AVALON TRAVEL PUBLISHING, INC.

CHRISTCHURCH

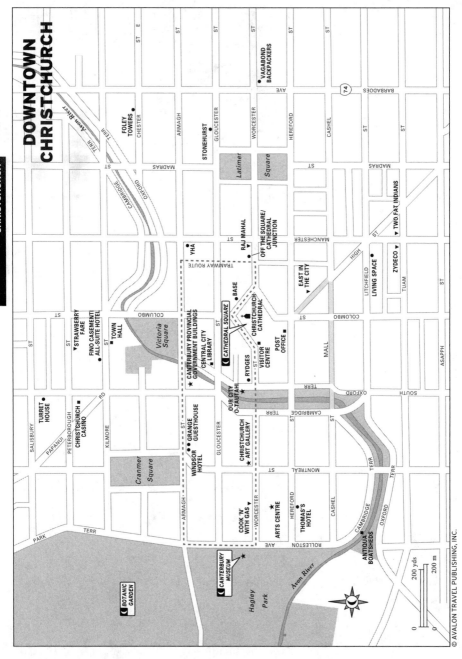

DOWNTOWN CHRISTCHURCH

Avon River

VAGABOND BACKPACKERS

FOLEY TOWERS

STONEHURST

Latimer Square

TWO FAT INDIANS

RAJ MAHAL

YHA

OFF THE SQUARE/ CATHEDRAL JUNCTION

ZYDECO

LIVING SPACE

EAST IN THE CITY

BASE

STRAWBERRY FARE

FINO CASEMENT/ ALL-SUITE HOTEL

TOWN HALL

Victoria Square

CANTERBURY PROVINCIAL GOVERNMENT BUILDINGS

CENTRAL CITY LIBRARY

CATHEDRAL SQUARE

CHRISTCHURCH CATHEDRAL

POST OFFICE

RYDGES

VISITOR CENTRE

TURRET HOUSE

CHRISTCHURCH CASINO

GRANGE GUESTHOUSE

OUR CITY O-TAUTAHI

WINDSOR HOTEL

CHRISTCHURCH ART GALLERY

Cranmer Square

COOK 'N' WITH GAS

ARTS CENTRE

THOMAS'S HOTEL

ANTIGUA BOATSHEDS

CANTERBURY MUSEUM

BOTANIC GARDEN

Hagley Park

Avon River

200 yds

200 m

© AVALON TRAVEL PUBLISHING, INC.

the Arts District, with the city's main museum and art gallery. Sights outside the central core are spread out and you will need your own vehicle or to use public transportation. Some attractions, such as the Christchurch Gondola, provide a shuttle service from downtown.

🄲 Cathedral Square

This large pedestrian-only plaza with its trees, flower-filled planters, pigeons, and striking cathedral in the heart of downtown is the best place to begin your exploration of the city. It's home to the **Christchurch and Canterbury Visitor Centre,** but is also a great place to soak up some of the city's rich heritage, sit and people-watch, dine at surrounding cafés, or just chill out and soak up some sun.

Cathedral Square's most famous resident, soap-box orator **The Wizard,** has been informing, humoring, annoying, and plain-out manipulating his captivated audience since 1974. Controversial, whimsical, and interesting, he is a bona fide tourist attraction—one that has been officially declared a "living work of art"

and the "Wizard of New Zealand." The Wizard (his legal name) has been making less frequent appearances in recent years. When he does come out, it's usually only in summer, on Tuesdays at 1 P.M.

Christchurch Cathedral

Christchurch Cathedral (03/366-0046; Mon.–Fri. 8:30 A.M.–7 P.M., Sat.–Sun. 9 A.M.–5 P.M.) is the centerpiece and dominant feature of Cathedral Square. Completed in 1904 and built of stone from local Canterbury quarries, topped by a 64.5-meter (210-ft) spire of Australian hardwood and copper, this striking cathedral was quite the pioneer triumph of the day. Holy Communion is held every day, but the most enjoyable time to visit is during Choral Evensong (during the school term, Fri. at 4:30 P.M.) when the Boy Choristers sing—your ears are in for a treat. For a fabulous view of the city (and on a clear day, the distant Southern Alps), climb the 134 narrow stone steps up through the bell chamber to the balconies at the top of the tower ($4).

© ANDREW HEMPSTEAD

Christchurch Cathedral

Southern Encounter Aquarium and Kiwi House

Enter this attraction (Cathedral Square, 03/359-0581; daily 9 A.M.–4:30 P.M.; adult $14, senior $12, child $5) through the visitor center. The documentary highlighting New Zealand's marinelife is a highlight; you can also see creatures such as eels and seahorses. A diver feeds the eels at 11 A.M.

Our City O-Tautahi

Ensconced in a distinctive 1887 redbrick building beside the Avon River just west of Cathedral Square, Our City O-Tautahi (corner Worcester St. and Oxford Terr., 03/941-7460; Mon.–Sat. 10 A.M.–4 P.M.; free) describes the growth of Christchurch as it relates to the local environment while also displaying details on future redevelopment projects—it's as much a place for locals to learn about what's going on in their city as it is for out-of-towners.

Canterbury Provincial Government Buildings

Also known as the Provincial Chambers (03/366-1100; Mon.–Sat. 10:30 A.M.–3 P.M.), these buildings beside the Avon River on the corner of Durham and Armagh Streets are fine examples of Christchurch's Gothic architecture. Until 1876 each province governed itself; the chambers, built between 1858 and 1865, were the main government buildings for Canterbury province. Today the last remaining provincial buildings in New Zealand, they're sources of both historical and architectural interest. From Cathedral Square walk north two blocks along Colombo Street, turn left at Armagh Street, walk another block, and then cross the river.

◖ Canterbury Museum

This museum on Rolleston Avenue at the entrance to the Botanic Gardens (03/366-5000; daily 9 A.M.–5:30 P.M.; donation) had its beginnings as early as the 1870s, when moa bones were traded from local Maori for display. Today the highlight of the museum is the Maori Hall filled with artifacts of early Maori

culture from the Moa Hunting era. The museum also features the Hall of Birds (one of the best mounted bird displays in the Southern Hemisphere), an Egg Wall (with hundreds of eggs arranged from small to large), Asian art, furniture and fashions throughout the ages, a reconstruction of a colonial Christchurch street from the 19th century, and the fabulous Antarctica displays (pioneer polar explorer Robert Scott visited Christchurch in 1901 and 1910 on his Antarctic expeditions—see his statue standing on the banks of the river at Worcester St.). You can have a light meal or snack in the upstairs Museum Café.

Arts Centre

Formerly Canterbury College, the attractive old neo-Gothic buildings in the heart of the Cultural Precinct at the west end of Worcester Street have become a large cultural and community center, providing entertainment to suit just about everyone.

The college's most famous alumni is Ernest Rutherford, the New Zealand scientist best

Canterbury Museum

© ANDREW HEMPSTEAD

CHRISTCHURCH

and bars. During the day, stroll in and out of the many crafts, music, book, and wooden-toy shops, and watch the potters, cane and stained-glass workers, and candlemakers creating their works of art. To get to the Arts Centre from Cathedral Square, walk four blocks west along Worcester Street toward the Botanic Gardens; it's on the left.

Christchurch Art Gallery Te Puna O Waiwhetu

The magnificent Christchurch Art Gallery (corner of Worcester and Montreal Sts., 03/941-7300; daily 10 A.M.–5 P.M., Wed. until 9 P.M.; free) is a modern architectural wonder, with a curved glass exterior the gateway to eight galleries. The collection of over 5,000 pieces is the largest in New Zealand and includes many historic paintings as well as touring exhibitions. The gallery is also home to the recommended Alchemy Café (see listing later in *Food*) and a gift shop filled with arty books and souvenirs. Outside is the Sculpture

© ANDREW HEMPSTEAD

the courtyard of the Arts Centre

known as the first person to split the atom. Rutherford's other achievements were many—he was the first to accurately date the age of Earth, developed the world's first smoke alarm, held the record for length of wireless transmission, and developed the first primitive submarine detection system. During Rutherford's time at the college, he used a cloakroom to conduct experiments. Now known as Rutherford's Den (Worcester St., 03/363-2836; daily 10 A.M.–5 P.M.; donation), this room and five others tell the story of his early years in New Zealand and his later achievements.

The Arts Centre is also a working outlet for some of New Zealand's most acclaimed artists and craftspeople. The center's North and South quadrangles and cobblestoned boulevards provide the perfect venue for a wide variety of entertainment—from jazz, blues, and classical music to stiltwalkers, jugglers, and street theater. It's the kind of place where you can quickly lose an entire day amidst intriguing entertainment and a variety of shops, or eating up a storm at the smattering of cafés

© ANDREW HEMPSTEAD

Modern architecture is a defining feature of Christchurch Art Gallery Te Puna O Waiwhetu.

AVON RIVER

Gently meandering through the city and particularly noticeable in the city center, the delightful Avon River is Christchurch's dominant natural feature. Grassy daisy-dotted banks, weeping willows and old oak trees, ducks and trout, and small ornate bridges linking the main streets lure office workers and visitors out into the sunshine for tea breaks or lunch, or just to appreciate the peaceful, almost rural atmosphere that permeates the city center. See some of the inner city's most historic and modern buildings, statues, and other items of interest along the Avon River by taking a 90-minute riverside stroll between Cathedral and Victoria Squares.

Enjoy the river from water level on a **punting** trip. Of traditional English design but built locally, punts depart on demand 9 A.M.-6 P.M. from the Worcester Street bridge (west of Cathedral Square) and the Antigua Boat Sheds at the south end of Rolleston Avenue. The cost for a 30-minute ride is adult $16.50-20, child $8-10. Also at Antigua Boat Sheds (03/366-0337), you can rent kayaks ($8 per hour), canoes ($16 per hour), paddleboats ($15 per 30 minutes), and rowboats ($15 per 30 minutes).

Garden, where the "art" includes motivational speeches broadcast through speakers.

Centre of Contemporary Art

After selling its permanent collection to the city in the mid-1990s, COCA (66 Gloucester St., 03/366-7261; Tues.–Fri. 11 A.M.–5 P.M., Sat.–Sun. noon–4 P.M.; donation) was extensively renovated and now showcases the work of New Zealand artists, including displays of paintings, sculpture, prints, photography, weaving, ceramics, woodcarvings, batik, glassmaking, and jewelry. The Canaday Gallery offers paintings, prints, and weavings for sale. To get there from the north end of Cathedral Square, walk west along Gloucester Street and cross the river.

▌ Botanic Garden

One of the best places to appreciate the profusion of vegetation within easy walking distance of the central city is the Botanic Garden (7 A.M. until one hour before sunset; a bell is rung at closing time). Stroll through grounds bordered by the gently meandering Avon River; through the rose, rock, and azalea gardens; past an area full of New Zealand native plants; and into all the individual conservatories (daily 10:15 A.M.–4 P.M.) featuring tropical, flowering, and alpine plants, cacti and succulents, ferns, and spectacular orchids. Seasonal displays feature the most beautiful flowering trees, daffodils, azaleas, rhododendrons, and bedding plants. The **Botanic Garden Information Centre** (03/941-7590; Mon.–Fri. 9 A.M.–4 P.M., Sat.–Sun. 10 A.M.–4 P.M.; free) features displays, horticultural information, botanical books, and souvenirs. To get to the Botanic Garden from Cathedral Square, walk west along either Worcester Street or Hereford Street—the main entrance is off Rolleston Avenue close to Christ's College and the museum and art gallery.

Hagley Park

Hagley Park, the enormous park that borders the Botanic Garden to the north, south, and west, has kilometers of excellent walking, jogging, and cycling tracks, and is a venue for all kinds of organized sports. The park covers an area of about 180 hectares of woods and playing fields (separated from the Botanic Gardens by the Avon River, but bridges allow access), and is divided into two main north and south sections by Riccarton Avenue. If you want a bit of exercise or enjoy watching other people sweat, this is the place. Entrance from the inner city to North Hagley Park is from Rolleston Avenue, and to South Hagley Park from Hagley or Riccarton Avenues.

Mona Vale

Built in 1904, this historic mansion (entry from Fendalton Rd. or Mona Vale Rd., 1.6 km/one mi west of Cathedral Square, 03/348-9660; Oct.–Apr. daily 9:30 A.M.–4 P.M., May–Sept.

daily 10 A.M.–3:30 P.M.) is surrounded by 5.5 hectares (14 acres) of traditional English-style gardens. Visitors are invited to stroll through the grounds for free, absorbing the beauty of conifers, maples, rhododendrons, camellias, magnolias, ericaceous plants (members of the heath family), herbaceous perennials and annual bedding displays, roses, dahlias, fuchsias, herbs, irises, and the Bath House featuring seasonal displays of cool greenhouse plants. The Avon River, home for hundreds of ducks eagerly awaiting handouts, meanders lazily through the gardens, and punt rides are offered from the jetty in front of the homestead. Within the homestead, a café serves traditional teahouse fare.

Science Alive!

This hands-on science and technology museum (392 Moorhouse Ave., 03/365-5199, www.sciencealive.co.nz; Sun.–Thurs. 10 A.M.–5 P.M., Fri.–Sat. 10 A.M.–6 P.M.; adult $12, senior and child $8), on the southeast side of downtown, is designed to appeal mostly to children. Favorite hangouts include the Black Hole nighttime mini-golf, the brainteasers in Brain Drain, and Kidz Zone for kids under seven.

International Antarctic Centre

There can be no better location than Christchurch for the world's best Antarctic-related display (at Christchurch International Airport on Orchard Rd., 03/358-9896; Oct.–Mar. daily 9 A.M.–7 P.M., Apr.–Sept. daily 9 A.M.–5:30 P.M.; adult $30, senior $28, child $20, with Hagglund ride adult $48, senior $46, child $36). After all, Robert Falcon Scott began his ill-fated expedition to the South Pole from here in 1910. Many other Antarctic explorers used Christchurch as a base throughout the years and, in the 1950s, the United States followed suit, basing southbound aircraft and ships here. The International Antarctic Centre primarily serves as an operating base for the New Zealand, U.S., and Italian Antarctic programs, but also holds a large public facility incorporating resources collected by the center's programs, along with those of Australia,

Russia, Britain, and Japan, to give visitors an insight into all aspects of the continent through the eyes of those who live and work there.

Starting with the exciting human history of Antarctica, the first display, a seven-minute show, gives a feeling of what the earliest Antarctic explorers must have experienced—right down to howling winds and the Southern Aurora. After the show is over, you step inside a realistic simulation of a room at Scott Base, with up-to-date notices, the weekly newsletter, rosters, and weather reports all pinned to the walls (check out the local rules of the base golf course). Then it's on to displays showcasing natural and geological history, flora and fauna, and life today at the various bases—including a re-creation of an Antarctic field camp—and to a theater where *Great White South,* an awe-inspiring 13-minute audiovisual, shows continuously. Beyond the main display area is Little Blue Penguin Encounter, which focuses on the story of the world's smallest penguin (it's about 40 cm/16 in tall). Around two dozen of these intriguing little creatures are on display, with an underwater viewing window providing a different perspective of their swimming skills. Then, outside, you are invited to take a ride in the Hagglund, a Swedish-designed vehicle that is the workhorse of all Antarctic bases.

Once back in the main foyer, you can browse through the Antarctic Shop, boasting the world's largest choice of Antarctic-related items, or go to the 60° South Cafe and Bar. The second Sunday in October is Antarctic Festival Day; most activities take place in the center grounds and across the road at the airport, where Antarctic aircraft are displayed.

Willowbank Wildlife Reserve

The focus at Willowbank (Hussey Rd., Harewood, 03/359-6226; daily 10 A.M.–10 P.M.; adult $20, senior $11.50, $6 child), a large wildlife park, is New Zealand wildlife. The kiwi house is the largest in the country, but these rare birds also inhabit a two-hectare (five-acre) spread of native bush. The facility stays open after dark, allowing visitors to see the birds when they are most active. Adding to the appeal for evening visitors is a restaurant (adult $57, child $35.50 for park entry and a buffet dinner) and the Ko Tane Maori Cultural Performance (adult $36, child $20). Willowbank is north of the airport off Johns Road.

Orana Wildlife Park

Lying 18 km (11 mi) north of downtown is 80-hectare (200-acre) Orana Wildlife Park (McLean's Island Rd., Papanui, 03/359-7109; daily 10 A.M.–5 P.M.; adult $19, senior $17, child $7), New Zealand's largest wildlife park. The main reason to venture out here is for the large collection of native birds and *tuataras,* but you'll also enjoy the many African animals, including giraffes, lions, zebras, and antelopes. The highlight for many is the Lion Encounter Ride, in the back of a caged truck.

Christchurch Gondola

A free shuttle bus connects Christchurch Gondola (03/384-0700; daily 10 A.M.–9 P.M.; adult $22, child $10) with Cathedral Square, or you can catch a no. 28 Lyttelton bus, or drive out along Ferry Road southeast of the city to suburban Heathcote. Why go there? Outstanding 360-degree views of the city, Banks Peninsula, Canterbury Plains, and distant Southern Alps from the Summit Complex, perched on the rim of an extinct volcano. It puts everything into perspective. Also at the top is the Time Tunnel, an easy-to-follow description of the forces that created the surrounding landscape. Two one-hour walking trails, a big-screen audiovisual, two restaurants, and a souvenir shop are other reasons to make the excursion. Gondola admission combined with a day pass for the tram system is adult $30, child $12.

Air Force Museum

Airplane buffs should find their way out to Wigram on the south side of the city to feast their eyes and let their spirits soar at Air Force Museum (Harvard Ave., Hornby, 03/343-9532, www.airforcemuseum.co.nz; daily 10 A.M.–5 P.M.; adult $15, senior $9, child $5), worth every cent for flying enthusiasts. Aside from studying extensive displays featuring the history of New Zealand aviation, watch a movie on the same in the small theater, marvel at the interactive displays (including an ejection seat), then wander at will around a large number of beautifully displayed aircraft spanning the age of aviation. Adding to the authenticity of Air Force Museum are the guides—they are all World War II veterans. Allow two hours if you like reading all the details. Access to the museum is from the main highway south (to Timaru), near the Springs Road turnoff.

◖ Summit Road

For great views of the seaside suburb of Sumner, Lyttelton Harbour, the Seaward Kaikoura Range to the north, Christchurch City, checkerboard Canterbury Plains, and the distant snowcapped Southern Alps, take the 45-km (28-mi) scenic Summit Road circuit. From the city center, follow High Street east onto Ferry Road heading along the Avon River Estuary through the seaside suburbs of Redcliffs and Sumner. At Sumner, take Wakefield Avenue then Evans Pass Road to an intersection where Summit Road branches to the left and Sumner Road leads down to Lyttelton. Taking the Summit Road option, be sure to stop at the **Bridle Path,** the route early colonists took from Lyttelton Harbour over the steep hills to the flat, grassy Canterbury Plains and Christchurch. The route is narrow and winding, and not for the fainthearted, but the views are well worth the mental strain. A limited number of viewpoints dot the route, although it passes under the gondola and access is not possible to the upper terminal.

To return to the city from along Summit Road, turn right at Dyers Pass Road and continue down through Victoria Park with its impressive rock gardens to the **Sign of the Takahe** (200 Hackthorne Rd., 03/332-4052; daily noon–4 P.M. and from 6 P.M.), a distinctive Gothic building and a great place to stop for afternoon tea or lunch. To get back to downtown from this point, continue through the attractive suburb of Cashmere via Dyers Pass Road or Hackthorne Road onto Colombo Street, which leads back to Cathedral Square.

© ANDREW HEMPSTEAD

Views from Summit Road are stunning.

Lyttelton

Over the hill from Christchurch, Lyttelton (pop. 3,000) is a working port, with hilly streets ending at the harborfront, where many century-old commercial buildings remain. The **Visitor Centre** (20 Oxford St., 03/328-9093; daily 9 A.M.–5 P.M.) has brochures detailing historical highlights. Also here, the *Black Cat* (17 Norwich Quay, Jetty B, 03/328-9078; adult $49, child $20) operates harbor cruises—searching out dolphins and viewing natural features around the bay. The trip lasts two hours.

RECREATION
Beaches

Christchurch has lots of sandy swimming beaches but the tidal currents can be dangerous—it's safest to swim in the patrolled areas between flags, and with friends. The closest beach, **New Brighton,** is eight km east, reached by a no. 5 city bus. **North Beach** is 10 km (six mi) east (no. 19 bus); **South Brighton** is also 10 km (six mi) east (no. 5S bus); and **Sumner** is 11 km (seven mi) southeast (no. 3 bus). **Lyttelton Harbour** has a number of scenic beaches, and **Corsair Beach,** a 15-minute walk from Lyttelton, has excellent swimming. If getting to the beach is part of the fun, consider taking a short 15-minute launch ride from Lyttelton across Lyttelton Harbour to Diamond Harbour and its beach (refreshments available). The launch crosses the harbor several times a day (less frequently on weekends and public holidays—note return times).

Bicycling

One of the most enjoyable and fun ways to discover the flat terrain and lush beauty of Christchurch is on a bicycle—and many roads have special cycling lanes. Both **Cyclone Cycles** (245 Colombo St., 03/332-9588) and **Wheels & Deals** (159 Gloucester St., 03/377-6655) charge around $30 for one day, $45 for two days, $60 for three days.

ARTS AND ENTERTAINMENT

To find out what's on around the city, call in at the Christchurch and Canterbury Visitor Centre, where you can pick up all the free tourist guides and ask locals where the best action

CHRISTCHURCH

is. Daily newspapers have an entertainment page with cinema and theater listings, along with the venues for bands and cabarets, music recitals, and performances. On the back page of the Wednesday and Saturday *Christchurch Press* are all the entertainment venues. Also pick up the free *Christchurch and Canterbury Visitors' Guide,* which has an extensive "What's On in Canterbury" section covering art, music, theater, sports, and special events.

As usual, **Ticketek** (Town Hall, 86 Kilmore St., 03/377-8899, www.ticketek.co.nz) has a monopoly on selling tickets to all manner of events and concerts.

Performing Arts

For theater, ballet, cinema, classical, jazz, and folk music, head straight for the Arts Centre at the west end of Worcester Street. The **Arts Centre Visitor Centre** (Worcester St., 03/363-2836; daily 9:30 A.M.–5 P.M.) is the place to make general inquiries and bookings. Theater performances ranging from classical Shakespeare to modern playwrights, with special emphasis on New Zealand plays, are put on in the **Court Theatre** (03/963-0870, www.courttheatre.org.nz)—enjoy dramas, comedies, tragedies, and farces for about $20; the theater bar and coffee bar in the foyer are open before and after all performances and during intermission. Lunchtime concerts are featured every Friday at 1:10 P.M. in the Great Hall, profiling New Zealand and international musicians from a wide variety of musical disciplines.

The **Town Hall** (86 Kilmore St., 03/377-8899) hosts local theater, orchestra, and a variety of other performing arts. This building is also the home of **Ticketek. Isaac Theatre Royal** (145 Gloucester St., 03/331-9452, www.isaactheatreroyal.co.nz) has undergone extensive restoration to now provide a beautiful venue for theater, ballet, and musical concerts.

Cinemas

Cinemas can be found throughout the city, including **Hoyts** (392 Moorhouse St., 03/366-6367) and **Regent on Worcester**

(94 Worcester St., 03/366-0140). For art-house movies head to **Arts Centre Cinemas** (Worcester St., 03/366-0167).

Casino

Christchurch Casino (30 Victoria St., 03/365-9999; Mon.–Wed. 11 A.M.–3 A.M., the rest of the week 24 hours daily) offers gamblers blackjack, roulette, mini baccarat, Sic Bo, stud poker, keno, and more than 300 slot machines. There's also a dress code—no jeans or T-shirts.

Nightlife

You'll find bands in hotels and bars throughout the city almost every night of the week and always on weekends. Scan the papers, listen to the radio for advertisements, or check the information centers to find out current venues and prices.

Oxford Terrace holds the main concentration of bars and nightspots, all with lots of outdoor tables overlooking the river. **Ferment** (130 Oxford Terr., 03/377-9898) and adjacent **Liquidity** (128 Oxford Terr., 03/365-6088) are typical—busy during the day with the business crowd and then filling with a younger audience for dancing until the wee hours. A good place for a quiet beer at any time is the **Tap Room** (124 Oxford Terr., 03/365-0547), featuring contemporary decor highlighted by an impressive beer tank behind the main bar. This bar is owned by Monteith's, a west coast brewer of national repute, and it's this company's "craft beer" that makes the Tap Room a worthwhile stop.

Another concentration of bars is at the corner of Manchester and Cashel Streets, on the southeast side of Cathedral Square. One of the most popular spots with the under-20 crowd is the Western-style **Grumpy Mole** (03/371-9301) bar and nightclub. Those who appreciate beer may like to sample the large selection at the **Loaded Hog** (corner of Manchester and Castel Sts., 03/366-6674), a bar with loads of atmosphere in a working natural brewery. It features four beers on tap, including Red Dog Draught.

Step out of the bustle of Cathedral Square and into the peace of the **Font Bar** (Heritage

Christchurch, 28 Cathedral Sq., 03/377-9722), which has a long list of cocktails and a menu of healthy eating.

Twisted Hop (6 Poplar St., Lichfield Lanes, 03/962-3688) specializes in brewing traditional British-style ales, all on tap in the street-level pub. It's open daily from noon and there's live jazz on Wednesday. Another boutique brewery is **Dux De Lux** (Arts Centre, corner of Hereford and Montreal Sts., 03/366-6919). As is the case throughout the city, the outdoor tables are popular during the day while night sees reggae or rock performers hit the stage.

The bars detailed above along Oxford Terrace have a nightclub atmosphere after midnight, or head to **Base** (92 Struthers Lane, 03/377-7149) for dancing to house, trance, or whatever the hottest dance music of the day is. This place is renowned for its laser light show and booming sound system.

Festivals and Events

The city's biggest summer gathering is the **World Buskers Festival** (03/377-2365, www.worldbuskersfestival.co.nz) at outdoor venues such as Cathedral Square, the Arts Centre, and Oxford Terrace over 10 days in late January.

The city bursts with color during the **Festival of Flowers** (03/365-5403, www.festivalofflowers.co.nz) the second week of February.

Through the second week of November, Christchurch plays host to the **Royal New Zealand Show** (03/343-3033, www.theshow.co.nz), which is held at the Canterbury Agricultural Park on Curletts Road. Dating to 1859, this historic gathering includes traditional events such as dog trials, horse racing, wood chopping, and sheep and cattle judging, but modern agriculture is also catered to, with wine and cheese competitions and exotic animals such as ostriches on display. The Friday of the show is a provincial holiday.

ACCOMMODATIONS AND CAMPING

Like cities the world over, Christchurch has pockets of motels throughout city limits. One such grouping is around the intersection of Bealey

and Papanui Roads, just over one km (0.6 mi) northwest of Cathedral Square, where you can expect to pay $100–150 for a double room with a kitchen. But I recommend staying downtown, where all accommodations are within walking distance of Cathedral Square. As always, check the websites of the bigger hotels for online rates up to half the quoted rack rate.

Under $50

As with New Zealand's other large cities, what Christchurch lacks in quality backpacker lodges it makes up with the large number of inexpensive beds available. **Foley Towers** (208 Kilmore St., 03/366-9720; dorm beds $18, en suite $52 d), across from the river one km (0.6 mi) from Cathedral Square, is an attractive old guesthouse with well-kept gardens, a stone's throw from the river and a short stroll from city center. It has a dining room, a comfy guest lounge, luggage lockers, a sunny backyard, no TV, and limited off-street parking.

Vagabond Backpackers (232 Worcester St., 03/379-9677; dorm beds $21–24, $35 s, $52 d) is another good choice. This small lodge four blocks east of Cathedral Square features comfortable beds, a pleasant courtyard, and a laundry; most beds are in twin rooms and no room has more than four beds.

$50-100

Three blocks from Cathedral Square, **Stonehurst** (241 Gloucester St., 03/379-4620, www.stonehurst.co.nz; dorm beds $26, private room with shared bath $60 s, $70 d, en suites from $75) is a modern complex with an outdoor pool, barbecue area, two communal kitchens, a laundry with TV, and a reception selling pizza, pasta, and booze.

If you stayed at the Auckland version of **Base** (56 Cathedral Sq., 03/982-2225, www.basebackpackers.com; dorm beds $26–28, $60 s or d, $80 s or d en suite), the set-up will be familiar—lots of young travelers, a female-only Sanctuary floor with upgraded everything (dorms $28), a barbecue area, and busy but clean and modern communal facilities.

Two blocks north of Cathedral Square is

YHA Christchurch City Central (273 Manchester St., 03/379-9535, www.yha.co.nz; dorm beds $26, $68–120 s or d). This large, modern hostel lies within easy walking distance of all the downtown sights and many of the best cafés and restaurants. It features more than 160 beds, including many in single and double en suite rooms.

Many of Christchurch's old downtown hotels have been knocked down over the years, and those that haven't have been converted for other uses. An exception is **Thomas's Hotel** (36 Hereford St., 03/379-2536, www.thomas hotel.co.nz; dorm beds $30, $65 s, $75 d, en suite hotel-style rooms $109 s, $129 d), opposite the Arts Centre. Rooms are basic, and most share bathrooms, but all have a TV and phone. Guests have use of a communal kitchen, lounge, an outdoor barbecue area, and Internet access; the more expensive rooms have an en suite bathroom.

One of the least expensive downtown bed-and-breakfasts is **Turret House** (435 Durham St., 03/365-3900, www.turrethouse.co.nz; $95–150 s or d), a 10-minute walk from Cathedral Square. In one of the city's large old homes (built in 1885) the owners provide spacious, elegant rooms with private bath and a continental breakfast. Get to know the other guests at the evening wine and cheese get-together or at breakfast, or relish complete privacy—whichever you choose.

$100-150

Stonehurst (241 Gloucester St., 03/379-4620, www.stonehurst.co.nz; $115–240 s or d) encompasses almost a full block a five-minute walk southeast of Cathedral Square. In addition to the backpacker section detailed above, it offers adjacent motel rooms, much larger Superior Studios with kitchens ($125 s or d), and one-bedroom apartments for $170. Guests have use of an outdoor pool, laundry, and barbecue area.

If you're looking for modern, facility-filled accommodation in a central location, it's impossible to go past **⬛ LivingSpace** (96 Lichfield St., 03/964-5212, www.livingspace .net), which is halfway between a backpacker

Stonehurst is one of Christchurch's best-value accommodations.

© ANDREW HEMPSTEAD

lodge and full-service hotel, and fills the niche perfectly. The style throughout is slick and contemporary, with lots of big bright art on the walls. Facilities include three commercial-style communal kitchens, a guest lounge on each floor, a laundry, secure parking ($10 per day), two small movie theaters, a library and reading room, and a downstairs restaurant and bar. The smallest rooms $119 s or d) are on the small side, but Premier Studios ($129 s or d) are larger and have kitchens. Or reserve a two-bedroom ($150) or three-bedroom apartment ($180).

A longtime favorite with travelers on a budget, 500 meters from Cathedral Square, is the grand old **Windsor Hotel** (52 Armagh St., 03/366-1503 or 0800/366-1503, www.windsor hotel.co.nz; $89 s, $128 d), offering shared bathrooms, free tea and coffee, a laundry, a full cooked breakfast (6:30–9 A.M.), and a congenial adult atmosphere. It's often full, so book well in advance (many Antarctic workers use this hotel as a base before flying south).

Next door to the Windsor is the 1895

Grange Guesthouse (56 Armagh St., 03/366-2850 or 0800/932-850, www.thegrange.co.nz; $110–135 s, $125–180 d), a rambling mansion set back from the road with eight tastefully decorated rooms, adjacent apartments, an attractive guest lounge, and off-street parking.

The largest concentration of motels is found northwest of downtown along Bealey Avenue and Papanui Road. Each has units with separate bedrooms from around $150, making them good value for families looking to be close to downtown.

Along this strip, you'll find good value at the **Southern Comfort Motel** (53 Bealey Ave., 03/366-0383 or 0800/655-345, www.southern comfort.co.nz; $105–230 s or d) featuring 21 spacious units, each with a basic but modern kitchen and many with one or more separate bedrooms. The Southern Comfort also boasts an outdoor swimming pool, a barbecue area, and wireless Internet.

In the vicinity, **Avenue Motor Lodge** (136 Bealey Ave., 03/366-0582 or 0800/500-283, www.avenuemotorlodge.co.nz; $110–180 s or d) has 14 self-contained rooms of a similar standard, some with private patios furnished with outdoor furniture.

Near the above mentioned properties, but closer to Hagley Park, **Colonial Inn Motel** (43 Papanui Rd., 03/355-9139 or 0800/111-232, www.colonialinnmotel.co.nz; $125–189 s or d) provides comfortable units, each with a sunny bed-living room, kitchen, tea-making supplies, fridge, TV, and plenty of space to stretch out.

$150-200

◖ Off the Square (115 Worcester St., 03/374-9980 or 0800/633-843, www.offthesquare .co.nz; $158–338 s or d) proves yet again that New Zealand is miles ahead of the competition when it comes to providing travelers with practical accommodations at a sensible price. None of the 38 rooms in this boutique hotel above Cathedral Station are the same, and none are square. Some are designed for families (think bunk beds), some for tall people, others for those with pets. A Provision Wagon supplies the necessities (pizza, beer, fresh milk, and

more), or you can order in advance and have it waiting for your arrival. The style is New York–chic throughout, from the ever-changing art gallery in the lobby to loft apartments. There are also many thoughtful extras, such as an IT consultant on call to help with wireless Internet problems and rooms outfitted with practical lighting and beds topped with pure wool blankets.

Pavilions Hotel (42 Papanui Rd., 03/355-5633 or 0800/805-555, www.pavilionshotel .co.nz; from $185 s or d) is northwest of Cathedral Square (within walking distance of the casino). It has 120 simply furnished but modern rooms, an outdoor swimming pool, spa, a small restaurant open daily for a buffet breakfast, and a cocktail bar. Superior Studios, with a kitchen, are the best value.

For travelers arriving or departing Christchurch International Airport, the **Sudima Hotel Christchurch Airport** (Memorial Ave., 03/358-3139 or 0800/783-462, www.sudima hotels.com; $160–240 s or d) is an excellent choice. Located opposite the airport and linked by an on-demand shuttle, the main draw is a beautiful outdoor pool and hot tub. You can cook up a storm at the outdoor barbecue, or dine at the in-house restaurant. Check the website for packages that include breakfast and entry to the International Antarctic Centre for around $170 d.

$200-250

Chateau on the Park (189 Deans Ave., 03/348-8999 or 0800/808-999, www.chateau-park .co.nz; from $240 s or d) gives the feeling of being miles from the hustle and bustle of downtown Christchurch. In addition to the adjacent Botanic Garden, the hotel has its own two-hectare (five-acre) garden, including a plot of alpine species and a small planting of pinot noir wine grapes. It features 193 comfortable rooms with garden views (check the website for free upgrades and multi-night discounts) as well as a swimming pool and bike rentals. The Chateau also has an in-house English-style pub and a casual restaurant with outdoor seating. Book online and pay under $200 with breakfast.

For resort-style living on the edge of the city, consider **Clearwater Resort** (Clearwater Ave., Harewood, 03/360-1000 or 0800/688-7444, www.outrigger.com; from $245 s or d), set on 188 hectares (465 acres) mostly taken up by a world-class golf course that hosts the annual Clearwater Classic (part of the U.S. Nationwide Tour). In addition to golfing (greens fees $130), amenities are typical of a resort—tennis, spa services, bike rentals, restaurants, and bars—but as this is New Zealand, you can also fish for trout in spring-fed streams. Many of the better rooms are built over a manmade lake, including the oversized Lakeside Rooms.

Over $250

Overlooking the river, three blocks from Cathedral Square, is **Rydges Christchurch** (corner of Worcester St. and Oxford Terr., 03/379-4700 or 0800/446-187, www.rydges.com; $310 s or d). Call direct or check the Internet for discounted rates.

Fino Casementi All-Suite Hotel (87–89 Kilmore St., 03/366-8444 or 0800/696-963, www.scenic-circle.co.nz; $330–380 s or d) is furnished in the style of Europe's best hotels and with rates to match. Each of the large one- and two-bedroom suites has a full kitchen and private balcony. At street level is a restaurant and bar.

Millennium Christchurch (14 Cathedral Sq., 03/365-1111 or 0800/645-536, www.millenniumchristchurch.co.nz; $350–510 s or d) is a 179-room full-service hotel at the heart of downtown. Facilities include a fitness room, sauna, business center, currency exchange, and underground valet parking.

The prime location alone makes (**Heritage Christchurch** (28 Cathedral Sq., 03/377-9722 or 0800/936-936, www.heritagehotels.co.nz; from $360 s or d) an excellent choice for visitors looking to combine city sights with night lights. The hotel combines the Old Government Building with a "tower wing." The former has guest rooms decorated in an elegant heritage style while the latter offers contemporary styling in larger suites, many with one or two bedrooms. The Heritage also offers all the

amenities of a full-service hotel—valet parking, room service, an indoor lap pool, a business center, and a bar and restaurant.

Charlotte Jane (110 Papanui Rd., 03/355-1028, www.charlotte-jane.co.nz; $395–495 s or d), north of downtown, is in an 1891 home built for a sea captain and named for one of the ships that transported Christchurch's early settlers from England. Superbly refurbished without losing any of the original charm, each room features polished timber paneling, a writing desk, a comfortable bed, and a fireplace. Rates include welcome drinks upon arrival and a full cooked breakfast the following morning.

Holiday Parks

Within walking distance of Cathedral Square, **Stonehurst** (241 Gloucester St., 03/379-4620, www.stonehurst.co.nz; $26) has a few power hookups for camper-vans, but this is more for convenience than anything else.

If you don't mind being 10 km (six mi) east from city center and prefer to be closer to the ocean, make reservations at **South Brighton Motor Camp** (Halsey St. off Estuary Rd., 03/388-9844, www.southbrightonmotorcamp.co.nz; tent sites $22, powered sites $24, cabins $52–75 s or d). It's an old-fashioned place, but it faces a quiet estuary and the beach is a three-minute walk.

Christchurch Top 10 Holiday Park (39 Meadow St., Papanui, 03/352-9176 or 0800/396-323, www.christchurchtop10.co.nz; campsites $35–40, basic cabins $55, self-contained cabins from $90, motel rooms $110–155) is five km (3.1 mi) north of downtown, off Highway 1 near the junction of Cranford Street. Amenities include a sauna, spa, indoor swimming pool, wading pool, trampolines, a jumping pillow, two barbecue areas, bike rentals, and Internet terminals.

If you're approaching from the north, consider staying 14 km (8.7 mi) north of Christchurch at **Spencer Beach Holiday Park** (Heyders Rd., Spencerville, 03/329-8721; camping $12 per person, cabins $42–60 s or d, self-contained flats $80). Spread through a large tract of native bush and within walking distance of a beach, this campground sets up well for children.

FOOD
Cafés and Desserts

In centrally located Cathedral Square, give the American chain a miss (you can drink their coffee back home) and cross to the other side of the visitor center to the **Yellow Rocket** (Cathedral Sq., 03/365-6061; Mon.–Fri. 7:30 A.M.– 6 P.M., Sat.–Sun. 8 A.M.–6 P.M.) for good coffee in a bright, fun-loving atmosphere. Aside from caffeine, bagels are the specialty here, with the cosmic-themed menu including simple cream cheese bagels ($4) to a gourmet smoked chicken and cranberry version ($6).

If you're heading out to the Cultural Precinct from Cathedral Square, **Daily Grind** (78 Worcester St., 03/377-6288; daily from 7 A.M.) is a good stop for a quality coffee to drink in or order to go. Away from the busiest part of downtown (one block south of Cathedral Square), I had a decent cup of coffee at **Café D'Fafo** (137 Hereford St., 03/366-6083).

 Seasons (Cathedral Junction, Worcester St., 03/366-5204; Mon.–Fri. 7:30 A.M.–10 P.M., Sat.–Sun. 8 A.M.–10:30 P.M.) is a funky little café, necessarily triangular in shape to fit between dividing lines of Christchurch Tramway. A few tables line the outside walls under the canopy of Cathedral Junction while inside is a central communal table filled with newspapers and magazines. There's a simple buffet breakfast ($14), big muffins ($3), good coffee ($3), and an array of sandwiches and wraps made to order.

Surely nothing can be more romantic than reaching your lunch spot via a punt ride down the willow-lined Avon River. The **Boatshed Café** (Antiqua Boat Sheds, 2 Cambridge Terr., 03/366-5885; daily 7 A.M.–6 P.M.) is perfectly located for just such an arrival. You can order a picnic hamper ($14.50) to enjoy along the riverbank, or talk your way to an outdoor table and feast on barbecue blackened fish with melon salsa. Lunches are all under $20.

New Regent Street between Gloucester and Armagh Streets is a pedestrian-only thorough-fare lined with a funky array of heritage buildings with pastel facades. The retail shops are mostly old fashioned, as is the **Swiss Café** (3 New Regent St., 03/365-5557; daily for breakfast and lunch). This one-man show is crammed with Swiss kitsch, and has a menu to match—fondues, bratwurst, and more. A little further along, there's been a café where **Veronica's** (27 New Regent St., 03/371-7219; Mon.–Fri. 7:30 A.M.–3:30 P.M., Sat. 9 A.M.–2:30 P.M.) now operates since 1946. And although the facade has changed little in over half a century, the range of café fare (premade sandwiches, wraps, and rolls) is all fresh and healthy.

Those with a sweet tooth shouldn't miss a stop at **Strawberry Fare Restaurant** (114 Peterborough St., 03/365-4897; Mon.–Fri. 7 A.M.–midnight, Sat.–Sun. 9 A.M.–midnight). Delectable treats such as White

AFTERNOON TEA

The delightful English tradition of afternoon tea can be enjoyed at locations around Christchurch. Expect fresh scones with cream and jam, finger sandwiches, an array of cakes, and not a tea bag in sight. For beautiful park surroundings, head for **Gardens Restaurant and Tea Kiosk** (in the center of the Botanic Garden, 03/366-5076). It's open for lunch and dinner, with Devonshire tea served between meal times.

West of downtown, **Mona Vale** (63 Fendalton Rd., 03/348-9660; Oct.-Apr. daily 9:30 A.M.-4 P.M., May-Sept. daily 10 A.M.-3:30 P.M.) is a century-old riverside mansion surrounded by immaculate gardens. In this relaxing environment, morning and afternoon tea (from $8) are served daily. Eat in the garden or the gracious homestead dining room with Avon River views.

An atmosphere-soaked spot to have traditional Devonshire tea is the **Sign of the Takahe** (Summit Rd., Cashmere, 03/332-4052; daily noon-4 P.M.), a distinct Gothic-style roadhouse built at the beginning of the 20th century.

Chocolate Fantasy (a chocolate biscuit tower filled with mousse) that go straight to the thighs range $8.50–15. Just reading the menu is a mouthwatering affair. However, the owners also serve breakfasts (delicious blueberry pancakes) for $6–16, and savory dishes throughout the day—try their salmon and phyllo parcel for $19.50, smoked salmon and dill pots for $20, or cheese plate for $15.50 before diving into dessert.

Asian

Originally a farmers market, an art deco building on the south side of Cathedral Square has been converted to **East in the City** (266 High St.; Mon.–Sat. 10:30 A.M.–8 P.M.), a food court where the cuisine of China, Japan, Cambodia, Indonesia, Singapore, and Thailand is represented.

Inexpensive Thai is the order of the day at **Manee** (241 Manchester St., 03/377-9983; daily from 11 A.M.). A mixed tempura starter is just $6, soups are around $10, and all mains are under $20, including *yum pla muek*, a calamari salad spiced up with lemon juice and chili.

On the eastern side of Cathedral Square, on Worcester Street, **Sushi on the Road** (33 Cathedral Sq., 03/374-6431; daily 8 A.M.–9 P.M.) serves up packs of sushi to go from around a buck a piece.

Aiki Organic (599 Colombo St., 03/366-1178; closed Wed.) adds a twist to standard Japanese dining by offering a wide variety of vegan and gluten-free dishes, with organic ingredients used wherever possible, including in most of the vegetable and meat dishes. Prices are a little higher than most casual Japanese restaurants, but regulars swear by the freshness and composition of each dish. The tempura chips are a starter that will have even meat eaters wanting more, while mains such as curried vegetables ($21) and teriyaki salmon ($29) showcase the restaurant's style. Highly recommended.

The name hints at the approach—**Two Fat Indians** (112 Manchester St., 03/371-7273; daily for dinner) is a casual, contemporary

restaurant, sans Indian music and garish gold decor, and with diners more likely to order a pint of English-style ale over Chai tea. The food, though, does have its origins in traditional Indian dishes, including fish *molee*, a rich and mild seafood dish cooked in coconut milk ($17).

In the vicinity of the fat guys, **Raj Mahal** (corner Manchester and Worcester Sts., 03/366-0521; Tues.–Sun. 4:30–10 P.M.) is also a contemporary Indian restaurant, with the difference being that the food is more traditional. The menu is divided by region and waitstaff are knowledgeable on the different cooking styles associated with each part of the country. All mains are under $20, but you should budget for a few condiments (mango chutney is a must).

Southern

For New Zealanders, Cajun and Creole cooking is a novelty, which makes **Zydeco Café & Bar** (113 Manchester St., 03/365-4556; Mon.–Fri. 9 A.M.–10 P.M., Sat.–Sun. 5:30–10 P.M.) a perennial favorite with locals. Southern classics include jambalaya, gumbo, barbecue pork ribs, and blackened fish with a citrus and coriander yogurt sauce ($28). Most starters are $15 (including spicy sausages with a honey wine sauce). The rooftop patio is especially popular in summer.

Upscale

Out of town and with panoramic views from the top of Christchurch Gondola (03/384-0700) is the casual **Summit Café** (daily 10 A.M.–9 P.M.) and the full-dining **Pinnacle** (dinner only). As you'd expect at this tourist-oriented location, the menus have wide appeal, offering everything from sushi to Caesar salad. Don't let that put you off, though. Many choices in Pinnacle have a distinctive Kiwi flair, including venison, salmon, and lamb dishes in the $27–33 range.

A similar distance from downtown as the gondola but farther to the west is **Sign of the Takahe** (Summit Rd., Cashmere Hills,

CHRISTCHURCH

© ANDREW HEMPSTEAD

Sign of the Takahe restaurant

03/332-4052; lunch daily 10 A.M.–4 P.M., dinner daily from 6 P.M.), a castlelike structure built as a roadhouse in the early 1900s. Although it was never completely abandoned, a massive effort at restoring the grand property has successfully turned this landmark building into a fine restaurant. Enjoy tempura-fried quail as a starter and then move on to grilled venison with truffle polenta ($34).

Arts Centre Eateries

The very popular 【 **Dux De Lux** in the Arts Centre (Arts School Building, 41 Hereford St., 03/366-6919; daily 9:30 A.M.–midnight) is a good place for either lunch or dinner. The menu showcases lots of local produce and is made up almost entirely of seafood and vegetarian dishes, including some such as Greek Salad Without Feta that are pointedly vegan. The menu also includes lighter meals perfect for sharing, such as kumara chips with sour cream and plum sauce ($6.50), and desserts such as mango and ginger wontons ($13.50). The restaurant is part of a larger complex, with an in-house brewery and three different bars offering inexpensive meals; there's

free live music a few nights a week starting at 8:30 P.M.

Also in the Arts Centre is **Annie's Wine Bar and Restaurant** (South Quad, Arts Centre, 03/365-0566; daily 11 A.M.–11 P.M.), offering lots of New Zealand favorites, along with an extensive range of South Island wines by the glass or bottle. The atmosphere is informal and rustic. Both these Arts Centre restaurants have outdoor dining.

Behind the glass facade of the Christchurch Art Gallery Te Puna O Waiwhetu is **Alchemy Café** (corner of Worcester and Montreal Sts., 03/941-7300; daily from 9:30 A.M. for breakfast and lunch, Wed.–Sat. from 6 P.M. for dinner). The food reflects modern cooking trends and uses mostly New Zealand produce. At lunch you can chose from grilled lamb salad or beer battered fish-and-chips with Caesar salad, both around $20.

In an 1894 villa, 【 **Cook 'N' with Gas** (23 Worcester St., 03/377-9166; Mon.–Sat. from 6 P.M.) is a fashionable bistro with snappy service and well-informed waitpersons. Expect an ever-changing menu that may include such delights as roast belly of pork served on roast apple salad ($31). The wine list is dominated by local and Australian offerings. The three-course table d'hôte is good value at $55.

Tramway

Every evening at 7:30 P.M., a renovated 1926 tram departs Cathedral Junction (Worcester St.) filled with diners at the **❖ Christchurch Tramway Restaurant** (03/366-7511). It runs the same circuit as the regular trams, but instead of jumping on and off, you stay aboard for a limited but tasty menu of New Zealand specialties. The fixed-price menus range from $56 for three courses to $115 for five courses paired with beer and wine. Children are welcome, but those age six and over pay full price.

INFORMATION AND SERVICES
Information

Overlooking Cathedral Square from the southwest corner is **Christchurch and Canterbury Visitor Centre** (03/379-9629, www.christchurch.org.nz; daily 8:30 A.M.–5 P.M., extended summer hours). Upon entry, head left to search through the brochures and make travel bookings for onward travel. On the right is a desk dedicated to making transportation and tour bookings within Christchurch, a gift shop, and a currency exchange. Keep walking straight ahead and you'll find yourself at the Southern Encounter Aquarium and Kiwi House (described earlier under *Sights*).

The Department of Conservation's **Christchurch Conservation Information Centre** (133 Victoria St., 03/371-3706; Mon.–Fri. 8:30 A.M.–5 P.M.) is the place to find out about South Island parks.

Central City Library (corner of Gloucester St. and Oxford Terr., 03/941-7923; Mon.–Fri. 10 A.M.–9 P.M., Sat.–Sun. 10 A.M.–4 P.M.) is home to the Aotearoa New Zealand Centre, a literary and photographic resource focusing on New Zealand. The library also has a good selection of newspapers and magazines from around the world, and Internet access is free with advance reservations.

Independent from the chain bookstores is **Scorpio Books** (79 Hereford St., 03/379-2882)

and **Easts Books** (236 High St., 03/377-0197), both with a good range of New Zealand fiction and nonfiction. The latter also has a café. **Smith's Bookshop** (133 Manchester St., 03/379-7976) and **Dymock's** (105 Cashel St., 03/377-8250) are part of national bookstore chains. Each has a section devoted to New Zealand nonfiction and another to maps. Secondhand bookstore **Pacific Bookshop** (137 Manchester St., 03/366-8659) features a small collection dedicated to mountaineering in New Zealand. **Natural History Books** (11 New Regent St., 03/365-7188), also known as Arnolds Books, was for sale at the time of publication, but for 20 years has been the city's premier outlet for used natural-history books.

Services

The main post office is at 140 Hereford Street. All downtown hotels and backpacker lodges have some kind of public Internet access, or head to centrally located **Blah Blah** (77 Cathedral Square, 03/377-2381; daily 8:30 A.M.–10 P.M.), with row upon row of computers with public Internet access. This place also has phonecards (and a bank of phones) with inexpensive international rates, webcams, laptop stations, luggage storage, and mobile phone rentals.

Banks are generally open Monday–Friday 10 A.M.–4:30 P.M. (foreign transactions close at 3 P.M.), but a few stay open longer on Friday nights. There is a foreign exchange bureau in the visitor center, or go to **Travelex** (730 Colombo St., 03/366-2087).

Head to **Imagelab** (corner Manchester and Welles Sts., 03/379-7179), a few blocks southeast of Cathedral Square, or **Photo Warehouse** (207 Durham St., 03/366-3151), which both sell a wide range of digital supplies and have facilities for printing and downloading images to disk.

Emergency and Medical

Christchurch Hospital (03/364-0640) is on Riccarton Avenue and Oxford Terrace, west of city center and south of the Botanic Gardens. At **After Hours Surgery** (corner of Colombo St. and Bealey Ave., 03/365-7777) visitors can get same-day appointments if necessary. Centrally located pharmacies include **Victoria Square Pharmacy** (748 Colombo St., 03/379-2049) and Hanfins City Pharmacy (272 High St., 03/366-8071).

The city **police station** (03/379-3999) is on the corner of Hereford Street and Cambridge Terrace.

GETTING THERE

Getting to and from Christchurch is easy. An excellent highway network leads to and from the city, it has a bustling national and international airport, and it's well served by major coach companies and by rail from Picton in the north, Greymouth in the west, and Invercargill and Dunedin in the south.

Air

Over four million passengers annually pass through busy **Christchurch Airport** (www.christchurchairport.co.nz), 12 km (seven mi) northwest of Cathedral Square. Naturally, **Air New Zealand** (0800/737-300, www.airnewzealand.com) offers flights to all major centers throughout New Zealand, as well as direct flights to the Australian gateways of Sydney, Melbourne, and Brisbane. Other airlines using the airport include **Air Pacific,** offering a winter-only service to Fiji; **Qantas** flies between Christchurch and Sydney; **Singapore Airlines** to Singapore; and **Korean Air** to Seoul. Within the International and adjoining Domestic Terminals are a currency exchange, shops and boutiques, showers, various eateries, major car rental agencies, lockers, and a visitor center (daily 7:30 A.M.–8:30 P.M.).

The pleasant 15-minute route to the airport through leafy suburbs with glimpses of beautiful gardens through hedges and white picket fences is well served by shuttles and taxis. The least expensive way to travel between the airport and downtown is with **City Flyer** (03/366-8855; adult $8, child $5). Buses depart every 30 minutes Monday–Friday 6 A.M.–11 P.M., Saturday–Sunday 7:30 A.M.–11:30 P.M.). The downtown pickup point is Cathedral Square out front of the visitor center.

Super Shuttle (03/365-5655; $15 per person) offers a door-to-door pickup/return service to all points of the city. Bookings are essential (for pickup before 7 A.M., book by 10 P.M. the day before). A cab between downtown and the airport costs around $30.

Train

Christchurch Railway Station (Mon.–Fri. 9 A.M.–5 P.M., Sat.–Sun. 7–9:15 A.M.) is in the suburb of Addington, three km (two mi) from the city center (approach from Whiteleigh Ave., then Clarence St.). One of the most spectacular train rides in New Zealand is on the **TranzAlpine** (panoramic windows, onboard commentary) between Christchurch and Greymouth through Arthur's Pass. If you're short on time, take the Arthur's Pass Day Excursion. The other route, the **TranzCoastal,** links Picton and Christchurch; it takes around six hours and runs daily. Both trains are operated by **TranzScenic** (0800/872-467, www.tranzscenic.co.nz).

Bus

Christchurch Travel Centre is located just west of Cathedral Square (123 Worcester St., daily 6:45 A.M.–7:30 P.M.). This is the departure point for all **Intercity** buses (03/365-1113, www.intercitycoach.co.nz), including north to Picton, where direct connections are made with the ferry to Wellington. The city is also a hub for many smaller shuttle buses. One of these is **Atomic Shuttles** (03/322-8883) with services to Picton, Dunedin, and Queenstown. The advantage of Atomic and other small companies is their door-to-door service.

GETTING AROUND
Christchurch Tramway

Trams ran through the downtown streets of Christchurch for the first 50 years of the 1900s and were reintroduced in 1995 on a 2.5-km (1.6-mi) loop through Cathedral Square, over Worcester Bridge to the Cultural Precinct and the gateway to Hagley Park, then back toward downtown past the casino and library. It then heads south along pedestrian-friendly New Regent Street and through Cathedral Junction before reentering Cathedral Square. It's a good, fun way to experience downtown, but if you need to travel a short distance, walking is much quicker. The trams operate 9 A.M.– 6 P.M. (until 9 P.M. in summer) and cost adult $13, child free, for two days' unlimited travel. For more information, contact Christchurch Tramway (03/366-7830).

Bus

Metro (03/366-8855, www.metroinfo.org.nz) contracts bus services to various local operators, but all come under the same fare structure— $1.30–2.50 per sector. A Metrocard costs a minimum of $10 and allows you to swipe the card per sector, or ride all day for $3.80. From the City Bus Exchange on Columbo Street at Cashel Street buses radiate out to all suburbs. In addition to regular buses, many routes are branded: The Shuttle is a free inner-city bus departing every 10 minutes; Orbitor bypasses downtown completely to make a circuit around the outer suburbs; bright-orange Metrostar buses link major shopping malls; City Flyer shuttles passengers between downtown and the airport; and Midnight Express is exactly that—a late-night bus running along four routes until 4 A.M.

Car Rental

Like Auckland, Christchurch has dozens of car rental agencies. Well-known names include Apex (03/379-6897), Avis (03/379-6133),

Jump aboard the Christchurch Tramway to get around downtown.

Budget (03/366-0072), Hertz (03/366-0549), NZ Rent-a-car (03/358-1358), Omega (03/377-4558), and Thrifty (03/353-1940). Scotties (03/348-2002) is one of the local operators (also with an Auckland office) with an inexpensive yet reliable fleet of vehicles.

Taxi

Cab companies in Christchurch include Blue Star Taxis (03/379-9799), Christchurch Taxis (03/379-5795), First Direct Taxis (03/377-5577), and Gold Band Taxis (03/379-5795).

Banks Peninsula

Jutting into the Pacific Ocean southeast of Christchurch, this dramatic peninsula is volcanic in origin. The landscape is appealing in a rugged, untamed way, yet the land is dotted with small villages, vineyards, and country-style accommodations. The main settlement is Akaroa, 85 km (53 mi) from Christchurch along Highway 75, where the influence of early French settlers is still apparent.

If you like getting off the beaten track, get a detailed map of the peninsula and then, in one direction, take roads other than the main route to Akaroa. You'll be traveling narrow (in some places almost one lane), twisty, steep, often gravel roads with fabulous views around every bend, and you'll need a reliable car unless you're a fairly masochistic bicycle rider. On the way back, take the main road, which also offers great scenery.

© ANDREW HEMPSTEAD

CHRISTCHURCH TO AKAROA

Pigeon Bay

This is just one of the many picturesque little villages waiting to be discovered around the peninsula, reached by sealed road from the main route or by gravel road from the north-west. A campground along the edge of a peaceful bay, a schoolhouse, and a boat club are all you'll find, but it's also the starting point for the five-hour **Pigeon Bay Walkway** that leads to Wakaroa Point. The track starts by the boat club (parking available); no camping is permitted along the track.

Okains Bay

If you have your own transportation, visit another secluded getaway—the small township of Okains Bay on the northeast side of the peninsula, 83 km (52 mi) from Christchurch but only 25 km (16 mi) from Akaroa. Here you'll find a beautiful sandy beach with lots of shells and safe swimming, boating, fishing,

large caves to explore around the bay, scenic walks, and great views. Check out the small campground (no showers), equally small general store, post office, and **Okains Bay Maori and Colonial Museum** (03/304-8611; daily 10 A.M.–5 P.M.; adult $6, child $2), featuring colonial and Maori culture. By car take Highway 75 toward Akaroa, but at Hilltop take the Summit Road (sealed) instead of the lower road down to Akaroa, and eventually turn left on Okains Bay Road.

◖ AKAROA

This picturesque seaside town (pop. 800) on Akaroa Harbour has a colonial village appearance with late-Victorian architecture, quaint cottages, narrow streets, cosmopolitan shops, and French and English street signs and place-names. The original Akaroa colonists came over from France in 1840 on the *Comte de Paris*. Once a whaling settlement, Akaroa is now recognized for its plentiful commercial,

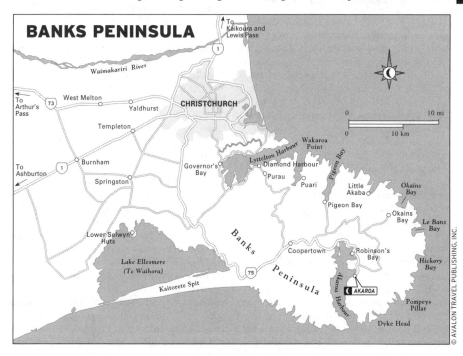

BANKS PENINSULA

To Kaikoura and Lewis Pass

Waimakariri River

To Arthur's Pass — 73 — West Melton — Yaldhurst — CHRISTCHURCH

Templeton

To Ashburton — 1 — Burnham — Governor's Bay — Lyttelton Harbour — Diamond Harbour — Wakaroa Point

Springston — Purau — Puari — Little Akaba — Pigeon Bay — Okains Bay

Lower Selwyn Huts

Lake Ellesmere (Te Waihora)

Banks — Coopertown — Robinson's Bay — Okains Bay — Le Bans Bay — Hickory Bay

75 — Peninsula — AKAROA — Akaroa Harbour

Kaitorete Spit — Pompeys Pillar — Dyke Head

0   10 mi
0   10 km

© AVALON TRAVEL PUBLISHING, INC.

CHRISTCHURCH

CHRISTCHURCH

© ANDREW HEMPSTEAD

Bank of New Zealand building, Akaroa

sport, and recreational fishing. Stroll around town soaking up the atmosphere, dangle a fishing line from the wharf, take a launch ride on the harbor, visit the local museum, or sample sole, grouper, *tarakihi*, crayfish, or gurnard cooked to perfection. Try a variety of fish at the takeaway fish shop, or at one of the many restaurants.

Sights

Akaroa is the kind of place you can easily browse on foot. Meander through scenic reserves and waterfront parks where benches have been strategically placed to take best advantage of water and mountain views. Head along the waterfront to the sparkling, whitewashed **Akaroa Head Lighthouse** or through **Akaroa Museum** (corner of Rue Lavaud and Rue Balguerie, 03/304-1013; daily 10:30 A.M.–4 P.M.; adult $3, child $1) to see historical displays, videos, and audiovisuals. Akaroa has many beautiful old buildings dating from the 1840s to 1860s, and even the new buildings have been designed to blend in with the old. Galleries,

arts-and-crafts shops, and homes with spectacular gardens along quiet streets or up little alleyways add to Akaroa's general appeal.

Recreation

Take a variety of cruises on Akaroa Harbour with the **Black Cat** (Akaroa Wharf, 03/304-7641). The most popular tour departs daily at 1:30 P.M. (with an extra 11 A.M. departure Nov.–Mar.), heading out in search of seals, dolphins, and sea birds. Stops are made at natural sea caves and a salmon farm. The two-hour cruise costs adult $52, child $32. This company also has a trip on which you can swim with the dolphins (adult $105, child $55) and charter boats for fishing.

Akaroa Adventure Centre (62 Rue Lavaud, 03/304-8709) rents sea kayaks ($12 per hour or $30 per half day), mountain bikes ($8 per hour or $20 per half day), and surfboards ($24 per day).

Another natural attraction is the **Banks Peninsula Track** (03/304-7612, www.bankstrack.co.nz), a 35-km (22-mi) walking trail that winds around the rugged volcanic coastline of the southeast bays, starting and ending in Akaroa. The track is unique because it is almost entirely on private property, and a limited number of hikers are allowed at any one time. For $125 per person (two-day) or $225 (four-day), transportation to the first hut, hut accommodation, landowners' fees, track registration, and a booklet describing the track are provided.

Accommodations and Camping

Chez La Mer (50 Rue Lavaud, 03/304-7024, www.chezlamer.co.nz; dorm beds $23, $53 s, $56–76 d) is a fantastic budget accommodation in a historic hotel building on the main road, a short walk from the center of Akaroa. Offering facilities of a high standard, it features a private garden courtyard, free continental breakfast, a couple of rooms with en suites, and knowledgeable hosts who have plenty of suggestions to keep you on the peninsula at least a couple of days.

Opposite the main wharf and above a trendy

little café is **L'Hotel** (75 Beach Rd., 03/304-7559, www.lhotel.co.nz; $120–140), comprising five equally stylish self-contained units, each with a balcony with water views.

Driftwood Motel (56 Rue Jolie, 03/304-7484 or 0508/928-373, www.driftwood.co.nz; $130–240 s or d) enjoys a waterfront location a short walk from downtown Akaroa. The 12 units are modern and well equipped—each has a large kitchen and private balcony, making this accommodation an excellent value. Breakfast delivered to the room is $12–16 per person and kayaks can be rented out front.

Akaroa's most intriguing accommodation is **Tree Crop Farm** (south through town, 03/304-7158, www.treecropfarm.com; $299 for the first night, $199 for additional nights), which is dotted with romantically rustic cottages. The sprawling property blends native gardens with wildflower-filled meadows, and is laced with walking trails. Breakfast is included in the rates, and guests are encouraged to bring pizza ingredients or their meat and fish to cook in the outdoor wood-fired oven.

Akaroa Top 10 Holiday Park (96 Morgans Rd., 03/304-7471, www.akaroa-holidaypark .co.nz; tent sites $30, powered sites $34, cabins $45–55 s or d, self-contained flats $75–95) can be very crowded in summer, with tents squashed into every spare spot—check out your allocated site before paying.

Food

Plenty of places to eat lie along the main street, most with their menus conveniently displayed outside. **Akaroa Bakery** (51 Beach Rd., 03/304-7663; daily 7:30 A.M.–4 P.M.), across from the waterfront, sells all kinds of bread, cakes, and pastries, and sandwiches and salads

to take away or eat there. It also serves breakfast from $8 with bottomless cups of coffee or tea.

Named for an American buccaneer, **Bully Hayes Bar and Café** (57 Beach Rd., 03/304-7533) is one of Akaroa's best little restaurants, although it's not cheap. In keeping with its namesake, a notorious sea captain who sailed into Akaroa in the 1860s, it features a nautical theme. A full cooked breakfast is $17, and main courses the rest of the day range $20–36.

If you're heading back to Christchurch along the main road, **◖ French Farm Winery** (French Farm Valley Rd., 03/304-5784; daily 10 A.M.–4 P.M.) has a restaurant with alfresco dining on a beautiful terrace overlooking the bay. The winery itself has eight hectares (20 acres) of vines, mostly Chardonnay and Pinot Noir grapes, that thrive on dry, north-facing slopes. The menu is classic French Provincial (mains $18–25), but you can order thin-crust gourmet pizza from the adjacent pizzeria for a more casual dining experience. Either way, the homemade cheesecake is a delightful way to end your lunch.

Information

Akaroa Information Centre (corner of Rue Lavaud and Rue Balguerie, 03/304-8600, www.akaroa.com; daily 9 A.M.–5 P.M.) is opposite the main wharf, kitty corner to the museum.

Getting There and Around

Akaroa Shuttle (0800/500-929; one-way $15, round-trip $20) provides twice-daily summer service between the Christchurch and Canterbury Visitor Centre and Akaroa. The rest of the year, trips depart at least once daily.

Arthur's Pass National Park

New Zealand's fourth-largest national park, Arthur's Pass protects a magnificent concentration of mountain peaks west of Christchurch. One of the park's best features is the accessibility of scenic and hiking highlights. It takes around two hours to drive the 160 km (100 mi) between Christchurch and the park's only settlement, Arthur's Pass. Along the way, the highway passes scenic lookouts, short walking trails, longer hiking tracks, and a multitude of spectacular sights for the more energetic. Beyond the village, the road descends steeply to the west coast, from where it's north to Greymouth or south to Hokitika.

THE LAND

Situated at the southern end of the major earthquake zone, Arthur's Pass National Park ranges in altitude from 245 meters (803 ft) in the Taramakau River Valley to the highest peak, **Mount Murchison** (2,400 meters/7,870 ft). The mountainous landscape has obviously been glacially carved, deeply eroded by rivers carrying enormous loads of gravel and shingle, and weathered by an often harsh and unsettled alpine climate. But first impressions can be misleading as you cruise through the low valley floors craning your neck upward. From the highway the "mountains" appear to be steep forest-covered

CHRISTCHURCH

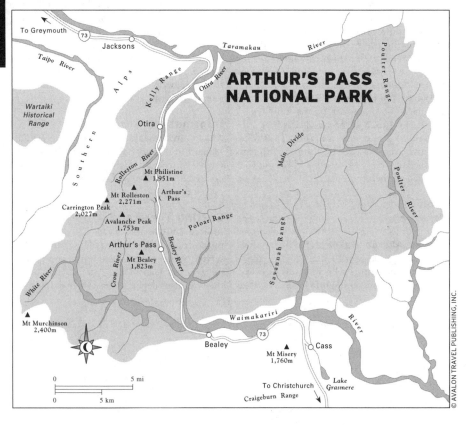

© AVALON TRAVEL PUBLISHING, INC.

THE BUILDING OF ARTHUR'S PASS ROAD

The building of Arthur's Pass Road and the railway that followed is a vivid piece of New Zealand pioneering history. As you drive this magnificent road, let your mind wander back to the 1860s: Imagine the brave mountain explorers who hunted for a suitable pass, colorful gold miners, wild and crazy stagecoach drivers, highly skilled road engineers, and 1,000 courageous men who blasted their way through Otira Gorge in the winter of 1865 with picks, shovels, road drills, and bare hands to bring the road into reality.

The first European to make the crossing between Christchurch and the west coast was Arthur Dobson in 1864, although Maori had used this route for generations prior. It was the discovery of gold on the west coast that originally spurred construction of a road over

the pass, with the first stagecoaches making the 270-km (170-mile), 36-hour journey over Arthur's Pass in 1866.

At the same time, engineers accomplished some amazing feats as the railroad inched its way from both the east and the west toward the historic underground **Otira Tunnel.** Through the use of air drills and explosives, the railway builders finally joined the two ends of the railroad in the 81.5-km (51-mi) tunnel in 1918, and the first train thundered through in 1923. Stagecoach travel quickly lost its popularity with the completion of the railroad. You can still see the original Cobb & Co. Seddon Coach that ran between Arthur's Pass and the Otira railheads in the 1890s until the tunnel opened; it's on display in the visitor center in the town of Arthur's Pass.

hills with snowcapped peaks behind them, but a full half of the park landscape consists of towering mountains. The forces that continuously mold the landscape are visible and awesome—mighty rivers in flood tossing huge boulders as though they were pebbles, earthquake-triggered rock falls and landslides careening down cliff faces, and with the heavy snowfalls of winter, avalanches crashing down the mountainsides to line the valleys below.

Flora and Fauna

The park's flora is particularly interesting to naturalists: The range in altitude and difference in rainfall from the wetter west to the drier east is apparent in the large diversity of plantlife. On the western flood plains, you'll find podocarp forests of *matai, miro, rimu, kahikatea,* and *kamahi,* clothed in tree ferns and clematis, mosses, and fungi. As you climb higher, *rata* and mountain *totara* become more abundant. Every couple of years in midsummer, the slopes of Otira Gorge are totally covered in the scarlet flowers of the *rata*—a beautiful sight. Beech trees dominate the eastern forests, and wild orchids grow on the forest floor. The timberline ends abruptly, giving

way to subalpine scrub. Up in the rocky alpine areas grow the beautiful white and yellow edelweiss, in the herb fields the anisotomes, alpine daisies, violets, gentians, snowberries, mosses and lichens, and in the alpine bogs, fascinating insect-eating sundews. The subalpine and alpine flowers are best appreciated in their summertime bloom between mid-November and late February.

You'll see and hear many kinds of birds throughout the park. In the river beds and valley flats you'll often see pairs of striking black and white-headed paradise ducks, and banded dotterels, pipits, oyster-catchers, black-fronted terns, and Canada geese. The *tui, morepork* (owl), shining cuckoo, yellowhead, and parakeet dwell in the bush. The cheeky *kea* lives in the upper forests and open slopes, and the rock wren also appears in the higher altitudes.

◖ ARTHUR'S PASS ROAD

Arthur's Pass Road (Hwy. 73) is the highest and most spectacular highway across the Southern Alps—the only crossing over the rugged Main Divide between Lewis Pass in the north and Haast Pass in the south. The 250-km (155-mi) sealed and well-maintained highway connects

Christchurch with the old gold-mining town of Kumara on the west coast. Apart from passing through a variety of awesome landscapes just to get to the other side, many people travel this route to explore, hike, climb, and ski the mountains of magnificent Arthur's Pass National Park, which surrounds the highway about 150 km (93 mi) west of Christchurch.

From Christchurch, the road traverses the fertile flatland of the Canterbury Plains, then climbs steeply to the stark and desolate landscape of **Porter's Pass** (945 meters/3,100 ft) and through the lunar-like landscape of **Castle Hill,** which is dotted by weirdly shaped limestone formations (some with overhangs covered in Maori charcoal drawings that are thought to be 500 years old). The scenery changes dramatically as the road enters the mountain beech–covered hills of **Craigieburn Forest Park,** then changes yet again as you enter bare eroded hills, passing **Lake Pearson.** Continuing into the mountains, the scenery along Highway 73 becomes even more spectacular. The hills give way to craggy mountains covered in trees almost to the tops (and snow in winter) as the road curves around the northern end of the Craigieburn Range following the mighty Waimakariri River into Arthur's Pass National Park.

As you drive through the park, more incredible snowcapped mountains loom above, in front, and beyond, beckoning alpine explorers and nature lovers to pull off the road and stay for a while. Picnic shelters, camping spots, and walking tracks are clearly signposted along the route to **Arthur's Pass.** The highway continues through the Bealey Valley to cross Arthur's Pass, where rugged mountains covered in natural bush flank the roadway. Crossing the Otira River, the road takes you through the old railway town of **Otira,** and then the scenery subtly changes yet again as the road joins the Taramakau River. Descending steeply, you soon leave the Southern Alps behind and enter a lush valley with dense natural bush, scrub, and grass typical throughout Westland. Arthur's Pass Road finishes at **Kumara Junction,** where it meets Highway 6, which runs north to Greymouth and south to the old gold town of Hokitika.

HIKING

The park's network of trails covers a wide range of scenery, flora, and fauna. For any of the shorter walks, pick up the appropriate booklets at the visitor center for information on the flora and fauna you'll see en route. The brochure *Walks in Arthur's Pass National Park* has a good map showing all the short walks. Remember, the weather can change rapidly in this alpine area—be prepared.

Walking Trails

Arthur's Pass Village Historic Walk takes just over one hour, and informative plaques along the trail provide a good introduction to the significance of linking the east and west coasts by road and rail. It starts by the visitor center.

One of the most spectacular sights in the park, worth seeing under any weather conditions at any time of year, lies at the end of the short **Devils Punchbowl** trail. The track starts on the east side of Highway 73, 500 meters (0.3 mi) north of the visitor center, and takes you 1.5 km/one mi (30 minutes) one way to an impressive waterfall that cascades down a gorge into a large rock basin 100 meters (330 ft) below. Starting from the same parking lot is a two-km/1.2-mi (40 minutes) one-way track to the **Bridal Veil.** It takes you through beech forest to the Bridal Veil Lookout for views of Arthur's Pass village and the Bealey Valley. **Dobson Nature Walk** is a great track to take if you enjoy subalpine and alpine flowers. It starts on Highway 73 opposite the Dobson Memorial and takes about 30 minutes for the shorter of two loops. **Cockayne Nature Walk** follows Kelly's Creek and takes you through a diverse area of typical west coast plants and flowers. It starts on Highway 73 at Kelly's Creek, north of Otira.

The easiest way to get into the subalpine environment is on the trail used in winter to access the ski field in **Temple Basin.** It wanders up the bluffs through subalpine scrub to the alpine grasslands of a basin from where you earn sweeping views of Mount Rolleston, Mount Philistine, Mount Barron, Phipps Peak, and many other snowcapped beauties; allow one hour each way, plus additional time to explore the bluffs and ridges above the ski lifts. To get to the start of the track, take Highway 73 north from Arthur's Pass village for four km (2.5 mi). Another track from which to appreciate distinctly different vegetation zones is the **Carroll Hut** track. The climb is fairly heavy going uphill through *rata* and *kamahi* forest and subalpine scrub, onto tussock grasslands that surround the hut, but it's worth the effort. The track starts at Kelly's Creek, north of Otira (by Cockayne Nature Walk).

Craigieburn Valley Ski Area

New Zealand's equivalent to hidden gems such as Mad River Glen (Vermont) and Red Mountain (Canada) is Craigieburn Valley Ski Area (03/365-2514, www.craigieburn.co.nz), around 100 km (62 mi) west of Christchurch. This private club field with three rope tows has no snowmaking, no grooming, no ski rentals, and no fancy base lodge. In fact it doesn't have much of anything. What it does have is the unchallenged reputation as the country's steepest alpine resort. There are no beginner runs whatsoever; instead, trail classifications include "Tricky" and "Suicidal"—enough to make any self-respecting skier or boarder's heart pound. The vertical rise is 560 meters (1,837 ft), with 400 hectares (1,000 acres) of marked terrain spread over two basins. Lift tickets are adult $55, child $35. Accommodation at the on-hill lodge is adult $75–90, child $40, inclusive of meals. You must bring your own sleeping bag and help with chores before hitting the slopes. The turn-off is along Highway 73, three km (1.9 mi) beyond the Porter Heights access road.

Other Ski Fields

The closest alpine skiing to Christchurch is at

Porter Heights (03/318-4002, www.porter heights.co.nz). Located an hour's drive (89 km/55 mi) from Christchurch near Springfield, the resort features an impressive 670-meter (2,198-ft) vertical rise served by five lifts; views from the slopes extend across the Canterbury Plains. Facilities include a café, rentals, and on-hill accommodations. Lift tickets are $46 adult, $22 senior, and $23 child.

Temple Basin (03/377-7788, www.temple basin.co.nz), west of Arthur's Park village, provides skiers and boarders with downhill thrills—that is, those willing to hike up to the ski field itself. Add to the views some excellent downhill slopes (a narrow and steep main run between Mount Temple and Mount Cassidy and nursery slopes on Mount Cassidy), three rope tows, 320 hectares (791 acres) of terrain, and a season generally running June–September. To get to the ski field, leave your vehicle at the Temple Basin parking lot, eight km (five mi) west of the village, then walk the well-graded but steep track (an hour or so depending on track conditions and your level of fitness) the rest of the way. Ski equipment and packs are transported up by the Goods Lift. On-hill rentals are available. Tickets are adult $45, child $30. Most skiers stay at least one night, in basic bunkroom accommodation that costs $60 per person inclusive of breakfast and dinner.

ACCOMMODATIONS AND CAMPING

YHA Arthur's Pass (Hwy. 73, 03/318-9258, www.yha.co.nz; dorm beds $21–23, $56 d) accommodates 39 people in two dorms and three double rooms, but during the summer, particularly January, this place fills quickly. Along with the usual communal facilities is a large day room/living area (left open in bad weather) with a log fire. Across the road is **Mountain House** (03/318-9258, www.trampers.co.nz; dorm beds $24–26, $59 s, $62 d, self-contained cottage for up to six $180). This popular backpacker lodge features friendly owners, a congenial atmosphere, a laundry, barbecue, and a ton of information on local outdoor attractions.

CHRISTCHURCH

On the south side of the village but still within walking distance, you'll find the **Alpine Motel** (Hwy. 73, 03/318-9233, www.apam.co.nz; $85–120 s or d), providing seven units with kitchen, private bath, and TV.

In the heart of the village, **Trans Alpine Lodge** (Hwy. 73, 03/318-9236 or 0800/506-550, www.arthurspass.co.nz; $120 s or d) offers 14 appealing, comfortable rooms with private facilities and TV. Rates include a light breakfast. Trans Alpine also has a few campsites ($25) and a cabin for backpackers (dorm beds $25).

Camping at the public day shelter in Arthur's Pass village, on the east side of Highway 73 opposite the visitor center, is $5 per night. Other designated campgrounds are at **Klondyke Corner,** eight km (five mi) to the south, and **Kelly's Creek,** 20 km (12.5 mi) north. All are signposted along the main highway and have day shelters, toilets, and fresh water.

FOOD

It's best to stock up on supplies in Christchurch or Greymouth, find a place with a kitchen, and whip up your own culinary delights. If you're not in a whipping mood, however, try the **Store and Tearooms** (Hwy. 73, 03/318-9235; daily 8 A.M.–8 P.M.), which has good selection of home-baked pies and sandwiches. Across the road is the **Wobbly Kea** (Hwy. 73, 03/318-9101; daily 8 A.M.–9 P.M.), another option for a casual meal. There's also a restaurant in the **Trans Alpine Lodge** (Hwy. 73, 03/318-9236), open daily for breakfast, lunch, and dinner.

INFORMATION

All park services can be found in the village of Arthur's Pass, 160 km (100 mi) west of Christchurch. The main source of park information is the **Arthur's Pass National Park Visitor Centre** (03/318-9211; daily 8:30 A.M.–4:30 P.M.), on the west side of Highway 73 as it enters the village. The highlight is a large room crammed with fascinating displays on the park's geology, flora, fauna, human history, and climate. Read about the discovery of gold in Westland, the resulting construction of the road and railway over Arthur's Pass, and the colorful coaching era.

GETTING THERE AND AROUND

Tranz Scenic (0800/872-467) operates the **TranzAlpine** train between Christchurch and Greymouth via Arthur's Pass. After crossing the Canterbury Plains, the train begins to climb, then enters the spectacular Waimakariri Gorge, passing through a series of tunnels, before reaching the village. Tranz Scenic offers a variety of one-day and overnight packages from Christchurch for $119–159. The train departs Christchurch daily at 8:15 A.M., and two hours later you're in Arthur's Pass—with five hours to spend before the return train.

Coast to Coast Shuttle (0800/800-847) and **Atomic Shuttles** (03/322-8883) operate between Christchurch and Greymouth, stopping at Arthur's Pass along the way. The Christchurch pickup point is the visitor center at Cathedral Square.

Christchurch to Aoraki/Mount Cook

METHVEN

The alpine resort town of Methven (pop. 1,100) lies southwest of Christchurch inland from Highway 1 across the Canterbury Plains on Highway 77 and directly south of Arthur's Pass National Park. As the gateway to one of the South Island's premier ski fields, Methven is busiest in winter, but there's plenty to do year-round. Most summer recreation takes place in the **Mount Hutt Forest,** west of town, which is laced with hiking trails. Other local activities include jetboating through the Rakaia Gorge, golfing, hot air ballooning, and mountain biking.

Mount Hutt

At 1,680 meters (5,510 ft), the elevation of

Mount Hutt ski field (03/302-8811, www .nzski.com) is not particularly high, but with modern lifts, views across the Canterbury Plains, and a five-month-long season (longest in the Southern Hemisphere), it's the most popular alpine resort within the vicinity of Christchurch. The resort has a vertical drop of 672 meters and is served by nine lifts, including one quad chair and one triple chair. Lift tickets are adult $84, senior and child $45.

Practicalities

Many local accommodations are only open in winter; the following two are year-round operations. Budget travelers are drawn to **Skiwi House** (30 Chapman St., 03/302-8772, www .skiwihouse.com; dorm beds $22, $50 d), a converted residence, for its congenial atmosphere and central location. Just north of the main downtown intersection, **Brinkley Village Resort** (03/302-8885, www.brinkleyvillage .co.nz; $95–155 s or d) is Methven's premier accommodation. Appealing mostly to the winter crowd, it features 80 modern, self-contained units; half are studios and the other half have two bedrooms. Other amenities include a restaurant with alfresco dining, bar, hot tub, tennis court, barbecue area, and playground.

For maps of the local forest and to book activities, stop at **Methven Visitor Centre** (121 Main St., 03/302-8955, www.methveninfo .co.nz; winter daily 8 A.M.–6 P.M., the rest of the year Mon.–Fri. 9 A.M.–5 P.M., Sat.–Sun. 11 A.M.–4 P.M.).

CHRISTCHURCH TOWARD TIMARU

South of Christchurch, Highway 1, the main coastal route, passes through the agricultural plains of South Canterbury and North Otago, linking the two largest South Island cities, Christchurch and Dunedin. Although most drivers complete the 360-km (224-mi) route in less than five hours, Aoraki/Mount Cook National Park, to the west, is an inviting detour.

Ashburton

This town, 87 km (56 mi) south of Christ-church and 77 km (48 mi) northeast of Timaru, is a good place to stop, stretch your legs, and grab a bite to eat. Along with the beautiful trees, gardens, and lake of **Ashburton Domain** (on the other side of the railway, off West St. between Willis St. and Walnut Ave.), trees and impeccable gardens are all over the city. The locals take particular pride in their "green" downtown square (Baring Square) with its ornamental tree garden, flower display, and refurbished **town clock** in a specially designed tower. A great number of the historic buildings and churches are made of brick—Ashburton once had a thriving ceramics industry. At **Ashburton Visitor Centre** (corner of East and Burnett Sts., 03/308-1064, www.ash burtoninfo.co.nz; Mon.–Fri. 8:30 A.M.– 5:30 P.M., Sat.–Sun. 10 A.M.–1 P.M.), friendly staff will fill you in on all the things to do in the town and farther afield.

Salmon and sea-run trout thrive in **Ashburton River** just south of the city, and many anglers make Ashburton their base while they fish the Rakaia River to the north and the Rangitata River to the south. If you like to hike, fish, and camp out, walk the 19-km (12-mi) **Ashburton Walkway,** which runs along the east side of Ashburton River to the river-mouth and beach at Hakatere. A free camping area with toilets (the river is the only source of water) is halfway along the walkway; prearrange a return ride (no public transportation at the coastal end) or be prepared to walk the same route back to town.

TIMARU

On the southern fringes of the Canterbury Plains, 77 km (48 mi) south of Ashburton, Timaru (pop. 27,000) is one of the country's busiest ports. Before and during the building of the port (beginning in 1877), ships were frequently wrecked as they tried to get close to shore to transfer cargo through the surf by small boat. Timaru's many local industries include a tannery, brewery, and textiles and milling companies (many give free tours—get details at the Timaru Visitor Centre); there are many "green spots" scattered throughout the city;

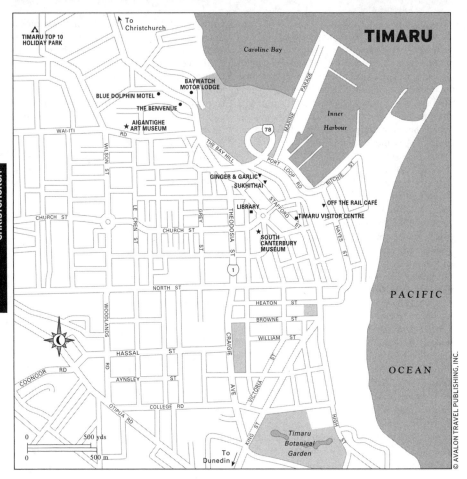

and you'll find an interesting mixture of modern and traditional architecture (the Landing Service Building, built in 1870, is the oldest of its kind in the Southern Hemisphere). Timaru also produced the famous racehorse, Phar Lap, that won all the major races in Australia and the United States in the late 1920s and early '30s (a statue of Phar Lap stands in the paddock at Washdyke where he was born).

Sights and Recreation

All kinds of local Maori artifacts and items relating to the settlement and development of the South Canterbury region are on display at **South Canterbury Museum** (Perth St., 03/684-2212; Tues.–Fri. 10 A.M.–4:30 P.M., Sat.–Sun. 1:30–4:30 P.M.; donation), along with photographs showing the step-by-step building of Timaru's artificial harbor, and information on Maori rock drawings in the district.

Aigantighe Art Museum (49 Wai-iti Rd., 03/688-4424; Tues.–Fri. 10 A.M.–4 P.M., Sat.–Sun. noon–4 P.M.; donation) has collections of New Zealand and British paintings, and English and continental china.

To absorb some outdoor culture, relax in

the greenery around the art gallery and view all the stone sculptures, or head for Timaru's **Botanical Gardens** on the south side of the city (entrance on Queen St., off King St., the main route south), a lush area of bush and flower gardens interspersed with ponds, an aviary, fernery, greenhouses, and an education center.

Timaru's most popular gathering point is **Caroline Bay,** a sandy beach with safe swimming, an aviary, miniature golf, tennis courts, picnic spots, and a large expanse of grass along the seafront.

Accommodations and Camping

Many motels line Highway 1 (Evans St.) north of downtown. One of the least expensive is **Blue Dolphin Motel** (40 Evans St., 03/684-4589 or 0800/866-835; $85–110 s or d), with 11 smallish one- and two-bedroom self-contained units. There's also an outdoor swimming pool and barbecue area.

Adjacent to the park that lines the shore of Caroline Bay is **Baywatch Motor Lodge** (7 Evans St., 03/688-1886 or 0800/929-828, $98–128 s or d).

Across the road from the Baywatch, **[** The **Benvenue** (16–22 Evans St., 03/688-4049 or 0800/104-049, www.benvenuehotel.co.nz; $112–150 s or d) features 30 brightly decorated kitchen-equipped units, each with a king bed. Some of the standard rooms have a balcony for no extra cost, but the VIP Suite ($140) is an even better deal. Amenities include a heated pool, a bar, and a restaurant with bay views.

Timaru Top 10 Holiday Park (154 Selwyn St., 03/684-7690 or 0800/242-121; campsites $26, cabins $45–72 s or d, motel rooms $100) is two km (1.2 mi) north of downtown. Amenities include the usual communal facilities, a canteen, TV room, and spa. From the north end of town at Evans Street (the main road), turn right on Hobbs Street, and then left on Selwyn Street.

Food

In the downtown railway station opposite the visitor center, **Off the Rail Café** (Station St., 03/688-3594; daily for breakfast and lunch)

remained open after the suspension of passenger rail service through town. Which is a good thing-the coffee is excellent and the light, mostly healthy cooking is well priced.

Along the main street, **Sukhothai Restaurant** (303 Stafford St., 03/688-4843; Mon.–Sat. 11 A.M.–2 P.M. and 5–10 P.M.) is a decent small-town Thai restaurant with all dinner mains under $20 and most seafood mains under $15.

Savvy locals and travelers in the know head to **Ginger & Garlic** (335 Stafford St., 03/688-3981; daily noon–2 P.M. and from 5 P.M.) for Timaru's most appealing dining experience. The service is professional yet friendly, the food healthy and reasonably priced (dinner mains $18–28), and the water views are free.

Information

For a city map and general information, drop by **Timaru Visitor Centre** (12 George St., 03/688-6163, www.southisland.org.nz; Mon.–Fri. 8:30 A.M.–5 P.M., Sat.–Sun. 10 A.M.–3 P.M.).

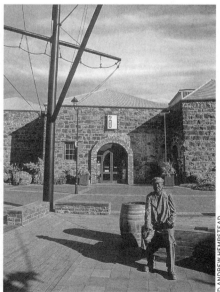

Timaru Visitor Centre

© ANDREW HEMPSTEAD

ASHBURTON TO MACKENZIE COUNTRY

Fairlie

The first town along this route is Fairlie, with pleasant tree-lined streets and a small museum through town to the west. An excellent health-food restaurant, the **Sunflower Centre** (03/685-8258), provides tasty vegetarian meals and snacks and sells homegrown vegetables, bulk health-food supplies, and a variety of handicrafts.

To Burke Pass

West of Fairlie, Highway 8 is lined with bright purple, pink, yellow, coral, and cream-colored lupines. It's an amazing sight when they're all in bloom (January is usually one of the best months for this vivid display). Randall Froude, an internationally renowned artist, has a studio and gallery in **Kimbell,** the last village before Burke Pass. In the vicinity, 19 km (12 mi) from Fairlie, Keith and Margaret Walker operate **Dobson Lodge** (RD 17, 03/685-8316, www.dobsonlodge.co.nz; $70–100 s, $120–160 d), a two-story stone building with a cedar-shingled roof and views to Mount Dobson. Rates in-

clude a light breakfast; dinner by prior arrangement is an additional $25 per person.

MACKENZIE COUNTRY

This plateau of high country lies immediately east of the Southern Alps. Highway 8 passes through the heart of the region, passing Lake Tekapo and Twizel on its way to Otago.

Lake Tekapo

Beautiful Lake Tekapo is always a deep milky-blue from "rock flour," finely ground particles of glacial sediment from glaciers high in the Southern Alps. Highway 8 skirts the lake's southern edge, passing through the small lakeside village of Lake Tekapo (pop. 330), which lies halfway between Christchurch and Queenstown, making it a good overnight stop (and saving the high accommodation prices of Aoraki/Mount Cook National Park, if that's the way you're headed). Wander along the lakefront for views across the water and tussock-covered hills to the snowcapped Southern Alps. The lake is a lot larger than it looks, extending for 32 km to the north and reaching depths of over

Church of the Good Shepherd, Lake Tekapo

© ANDREW HEMPSTEAD

120 meters (400 ft). The simple 1935 **Church of the Good Shepherd,** a memorial to pioneer runholders of Mackenzie Country, stands on the lakeshore east of the outlet—the view from its east window is best in the early morning or late afternoon when the light is just right.

YHA Lake Tekapo (3 Simpson Lane, 03/680-6857, www.yha.co.nz; $17–21 per person), billed as "the hostel with the million-dollar view," is right on the lakefront west of downtown. Separated from the lake by nothing more than tussock grass is **Lake Tekapo Scenic Resort** (03/680-6808, www .laketekapo.com; dorm beds $25, motel rooms $160–230 s or d). Although the penthouse suite is a long way from luxurious, it does offer a large, modern space complete with two bedrooms, a full kitchen, and private entrance. The resort's **Reflections Restaurant,** with lakefront seating, is open throughout the day. The other large lakefront lodging, **Goodley Resort Hotel** (Hwy. 8, 03/680-6848 or 0800/835-276, www.tekapo.co.nz; $125–165 s or d), has a swimming pool, spa, laundry, and a restaurant with a good buffet breakfast.

Lake Tekapo Motels and Holiday Park (Lakeside Dr., 03/680-6825 or 0800/853-853) offers excellent showers (and a special baby bath), communal kitchen and dining area, and laundry. Campsites with stunning lake-through-the-trees views are $13–15 per person, dorm beds $26 s, $65 d, basic cabins are from $55 d, tourist flats are $80 d, and motel rooms are $140 d.

Twizel and Vicinity

Beyond the southern end of Lake Pukaki, Twizel (pop. 1,200) is the gateway to Aoraki/Mount Cook National Park, 60 km (37 mi) to the north.

Originally built as construction housing for the Upper Waitaki Hydropower Development Scheme, Twizel has since grown into the second-largest town in the Mackenzie Basin. The scheme involves the Waitaki, Benmore, and Aviemore Dams; Lakes Tekapo, Pukaki, and Ohau (linked by canals to provide water for power stations); and Lakes Ruataniwha and Benmore (largest earth dam and man-made lake in the country).

The wilderness west of Twizel is protected as 49,000-hectare (121,000-acre) **Ahuriri Conservation Park,** which protects a population of *kaki* (black stilts), the world's rarest wading bird. Access to the park is limited to those in four-wheel drives, but you can see the birds at the **Kaki Visitor Hide,** a series of hides built on ridges above the breeding aviaries within a Department of Conservation complex. Tours last one hour and cost adult $12.50, child $5. To book, contact the **Twizel Visitor Centre** (Market Place, 03/435-3124, www.twizel.com; summer daily 9 A.M.–7 P.M., the rest of the year Mon.–Sat. 9 A.M.–5 P.M.).

Stop for the night about four km (2.5 mi) south of Twizel at enormous **Lake Ruataniwha Holiday Park** (Lake Ruataniwha, 03/435-0613; camping $15 per person, cabins from $25 per person).

Twizel to Wanaka

From Twizel, Highway 8 continues its tortuous southward journey to Otago and the resort towns of Wanaka and Queenstown; allow three and four hours respectively for this trip.

Many winter travelers heading south from Twizel miss a great little alpine resort in the Ben Ohau Range, **Ohau Snow Fields.** This small resort has an impressive vertical rise of 425 meters (1,400 ft) with three surface lifts over 125 hectares (310 acres). Lift tickets are adult $58, child $23. At the beginning of the access road and operated by the same people who own the ski field, 75-room **Lake Ohau Lodge** (03/438-9885, www.ohau.co.nz; $57–140 s, $78–155 d) offers simple yet comfortable lakefront accommodations in four wings of varying comfort levels. Rates include breakfast and dinner is also available.

Continuing south, the village of **Omarama** lies in the Waitaki Valley, where Highway 83 parallels the Waitaki River for just over 100 km (62 mi) to Oamaru, on the east coast. Highway 8, meanwhile, climbs the bleak tussock-covered hills of 971-meter (3,190-ft) **Lindis Pass** then descends to the Otago goldfields town of Cromwell and on to Queenstown.

Aoraki/Mount Cook National Park

CHRISTCHURCH

This park, one of the South Island's major tourist attractions, preserves a spectacular alpine area of great beauty—well worth the 60-km (37-mi) trip off the beaten track by road from the main route between Christchurch and Queenstown. With its snowcapped mountains, glaciers, river valleys, and incredibly fresh air, Aoraki/Mount Cook National Park is a popular playground for climbers, hikers, photographers, and skiers who catch planes up to the tops of glaciers for unforgettable experiences in the Southern Alps.

THE LAND

The beautiful Maori word Aoraki (High Mountain to the West) is the name of the first-born son of Rakinui, the sky father, and now incorporated as part of the official name of both the mountain and the park. Towering above the surrounding snowcapped mountains and glaciers at 3,744 meters (12,280 ft), ma-

jestic Aoraki/Mount Cook, when viewed from the south, rises in a perfect pyramid that's both impressive and easily recognized.

Aoraki/Mount Cook National Park, encompassing 70,013 hectares (173,000 acres) of the **Southern Alps,** is a long, narrow area of rugged snow-covered mountains and glaciers, 65 km (40 mi) long and only 20 km (13 mi) across at its widest point. The terrain ranges from river flats under 750 meters (2,460 ft) above sea level to 140 peaks over 2,100 meters (6,890 ft) high, including 22 peaks that soar to more than 3,050 meters (10,010 ft). New Zealand's three tallest mountains—Aoraki/Mount Cook at 3,744 meters (12,280 ft), Mount Tasman at 3,498 meters (11,480 ft), and Mount Dampier at 3,440 meters (11,290 ft)—are grouped together in the heart of the park. Because of the high, rugged terrain, more than one-third of the entire park is covered in permanent snow and ice, and huge glaciers are a natural attrac-

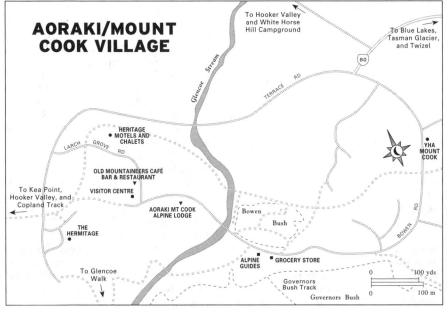

AORAKI/MOUNT COOK VILLAGE

To Hooker Valley and White Horse Hill Campground

To Blue Lakes, Tasman Glacier, and Twizel

Glencoe Stream

80

TERRACE RD

HERITAGE MOTELS AND CHALETS

LARCH GROVE RD

YHA MOUNT COOK

OLD MOUNTAINEERS CAFÉ BAR & RESTAURANT

VISITOR CENTRE

To Kea Point, Hooker Valley, and Copland Track

AORAKI MT COOK ALPINE LODGE

Bowen

Bush

BOWEN RD

THE HERMITAGE

ALPINE GUIDES

GROCERY STORE

To Glencoe Walk

Governors Bush Track

0   100 yds

0   100 m

Governors Bush

© AVALON TRAVEL PUBLISHING, INC.

© ANDREW HEMPSTEAD

CHRISTCHURCH

Kea (alpine parrots) are found throughout the park.

tion. The gigantic **Tasman Glacier,** 27 km (17 mi) long and up to three km (1.9 mi) wide, is one of the world's largest glaciers outside the polar regions (view it from Hwy. 80 as you enter the park).

FLORA AND FAUNA

More than 300 species of native plants have been identified within the park boundaries, from tiny ferns, herbs, mosses, and grasses to shrubs and trees. The park's lower elevations literally spring to life in summer (mid-November to the end of February), when flowering plants put on their best show. Most of the alpine flowers are white, blending in with the snow and ice of their harsh environment—the most striking is the **Mount Cook lily,** identified by its pure white petals, a yellow center, and shiny saucer-shaped leaves. In December the mountain daisies put on a terrific display in the alpine scrub and grasslands. Only a small area of what was once a large silver beech forest remains at **Governor's Bush** behind Aoraki/Mount Cook village—in this grove you can

also see mountain *totara,* mountain three-finger, broadleaf, and the occasional lancewood.

Birds are everywhere, about 40 species all told: riverbed birds such as black-backed gulls, pied oystercatchers, paradise ducks, and banded dotterels; bush birds such as native pigeons, tomtits, fantails, riflemen, grey warblers, and *morepork;* and alpine birds such as New Zealand falcons (rare), rock wrens (also rare), pipits, and *kea* or alpine parrots (cheekiest and most familiar). Dull green in color with scarlet underwings and a black heavy-duty beak, the *kea* has a reputation for unlacing boots, tearing holes in bicycle seats, and sliding down tin roofs just for fun—hold onto your food when they're hanging around.

RECREATION
🄲 Walking Trails
Though the park has many short walks around the village and along the surrounding valleys to excellent viewpoints and other scenic attractions, it does not provide much in the way of major hiking tracks. Because of the rugged

CHRISTCHURCH

© ANDREW HEMPSTEAD

Mount Cook is New Zealand's highest mountain.

alpine terrain, the park is much more satisfying for serious climbers and experienced mountaineers than for hikers. However, the "short walks" are the only way to grasp a little of the park's natural beauty, varying from a 10-minute bush walk by the village to a 4.5-hour one-way hike through the Hooker Valley for magnificent views of Aoraki/Mount Cook and the Hooker Glacier. Pick up the handy *Walks in Aoraki/Mount Cook National Park* brochure ($1) at the visitor center; it contains a map of the village and brief descriptions and approximate times of each walk. Many of the walks also have individual brochures, which aid in identifying native plants and items of natural history along each route.

If you have your own transportation, head out of Aoraki/Mount Cook village onto Highway 80 and turn left on Tasman Valley Road (the second road to the left after leaving the village). This long gravel road takes you along the western banks of the braided Tasman River, passing beech forest, Wakefield Falls, walking tracks, and picnic spots, and continues beside the Tas-

man Glacier to Husky Flat. From the end of the road, take the short trail to an overlook of **Blue Lakes** (allow 20 minutes each way), which are green rather than blue, but still spectacular. **Tasman Glacier Lake Track** branches off Blue Lakes Track and continues to the top of the moraine wall for tremendous views of the entire terminal area of the Tasman Glacier, Aoraki/Mount Cook, and Mount Tasman—it's well worth the 30-minute (each way) walk.

Mountaineering and Guided Walks

The first European attempt to climb Aoraki/Mount Cook was in 1882, but it wasn't until 1894 that Clark, Fyfe, and Graham finally conquered the summit. This alpine region is considered one of the best mountaineering areas in the world, offering all levels of climbing possibilities among tall peaks of varying difficulty. High-altitude huts equipped with radios, stoves, cooking and eating utensils, and some blankets lie scattered throughout the park—get more information and pay overnight fees at the visitor center; before attempting any climb, be sure to first notify park personnel, and also sign out on leaving the area.

Alpine Guides (03/435-1834, www.alpine guides.co.nz) provides guided mountaineering services, as well as equipment rental. For those without climbing experience, but a reasonable level of fitness, consider joining the company on a guided climb to the summit of Sebastopool, a full day excursion with an elevation gain of 750 meters (2,500 ft). The cost is $130. This company also guides hikers across the **Copland Valley Track** to the west coast.

Flightseeing

All kinds of flightseeing experiences are available by fixed-wing plane or helicopter within the park—most similar to those at Franz Josef and Fox on the west coast, and just as expensive. However, it's the only way to really see this area, so splurge if you haven't already. **Air Safaris** (03/680-6880) features "The Grand Traverse" from Glentanner Park Centre, a 50-minute flight that takes in Aoraki/Mount Cook and crosses the divide to the famous glaciers and rainforest of the west coast before returning via the Canterbury Plains; adult $295, child $200. **The Helicopter Line** (03/435-1801 or 0800/650-651) has flights that vary from a 20-minute Alpine Vista for $200 per person to a 45-minute circumnavigation of Aoraki/Mount Cook, the major peaks, and a snow landing for $400, departing from the helipad at Glentanner Park, along the access road to the village. The activities desk in the foyer of The Hermitage (call 03/435-1809 and ask for the activities desk) makes reservations for many of the flightseeing tours and has all the latest brochures and current prices.

AORAKI/MOUNT COOK VILLAGE

You can't get lost in Aoraki/Mount Cook Village, but the quickest way to orient yourself to your surroundings is to drive to the end of the road. Depending on which route you take, you'll either end up at The Hermitage, a historic hotel where you can fight your way through the bus tours and collect a free map and brochures from the activities desk in the main foyer, or you'll reach Aoraki/Mount Cook National Park Visitor Centre. The village (pop. 120) exists primarily to serve tourists.

Accommodations and Camping

The very popular **YHA Mount Cook** (corner of Bowen and Kitchener Drives, 03/435-1820, www.yha.co.nz; dorm beds $26) is open year-round and has excellent facilities including sauna, a log fire, barbecue, facilities for the disabled, and a well-stocked shop. From November to May the staff puts on barbecues most nights. Book as far in advance as possible because there are only 72 beds and they fill fast, especially in summer.

The newest addition to the local accommodation scene is ◖ **Aoraki/Mount Cook Alpine Lodge** (Bowen Dr., 03/435-1860, www.aoraki alpinelodge.co.nz; dorm beds $39, $144–200 s or d), a perfectly placed accommodation with a welcoming and congenial ambience. Facilities include a communal kitchen, a large lounge and fireplace, and a laundry.

All other village accommodation is owned and operated by one company. The flagship property, the **The Hermitage** (03/435-1809 or 0800/686-800; www.mount-cook.com; $445–685 s, $520–770 d includes breakfast), has a colorful history, having opened in 1884 and been destroyed twice—once by flooding and once by fire. It boasts one of the finest views of any accommodation in the country and recently underwent $15 million renovations, which included a new foyer aligned toward Mount Cook, magnificently framed by floor-to-ceiling windows. Within the hotel are an activities desk, a gift shop, two restaurants, a café, and a bar. Each of the 170 rooms is starkly elegant, taking nothing away from the views. Across from the main hotel complex, **Heritage Motels & Chalets** (same contacts; $240–275 s or d) fills with tour groups most nights.

HOLIDAY PARKS AND CAMPGROUNDS

Part of a working sheep station overlooking Lake Pukaki, **Glentanner Park Centre** (03/435-1855, www.glentanner.co.nz; tent sites

$13 per person, powered sites $15 per person, dorm beds $25, cabins $60–95) is a full-service tourist complex along the park access road, 22 km (14 mi) south of Aoraki/Mount Cook village, far enough from the mountains that the weather can be remarkably better. Along with the usual holiday park communal facilities, there's a general store and restaurant.

Aside from the sites at Glentanner Park Centre, the DOC maintains **White Horse Hill Campground** (adult $6, child $3). It's in the Hooker Valley, 1.8 km (1.1 mi) from the village. The campground and adjacent picnic area have running water and flush toilets in summer, a rainwater tank, pit toilets in winter (a coin-operated shower is available at the Public Shelter in the village), and plenty of space for tents on a grassy hillside (self-registration). Note that the campground is exposed to prevailing inclement weather conditions and the normally dry creekbed can become a raging torrent during a storm—if you leave your tent there during the day, be sure it's well staked and not close to the creek. To reach the campground, head out of the village on Highway 80 and take the first road to the left.

Food

Adjacent to the visitor center is the highly recommended (**Old Mountaineers Café Bar & Restaurant** (Bowen Dr., 03/435-1890; daily for breakfast, lunch, and dinner), the natural hangout for outdoorsy types. There are picnic tables out front and an infectious vibe inside, and you can order full breakfasts, hearty soups, healthy salads, stacked sandwiches, and simple dinner mains from $18.

Other dining options are limited to the tour-isty Hermitage properties. In the main hotel (03/435-1809), the **Alpine Restaurant** is a cavernous, casual dining room. The breakfast buffet (6–9 A.M.) is $30. The lunchtime buffet (11:30 A.M.–2 P.M.) is $26 and from 6 P.M., the expansive dinner buffet costs $50. Views from the hotel's more formal **Panorama Restaurant** (summer only daily from 6 P.M.) are priceless. Dinner choices start at $28, while dishes such as pan-fried salmon served on a bed of kumara and accompanied by stir-fried vegetables average $35.

Information and Services

Aoraki/Mount Cook National Park Visitor Centre (03/435-1186; summer daily 8:30 A.M.–6 P.M., the rest of the year daily 8:30 A.M.–5 P.M.) holds displays representing a complete record of the park from its creation to modern-day tourism, mountaineering, and skiing activities.

Within Aoraki/Mount Cook village you'll find a post office, a grocery store, petrol, and the Alpine Guides office (03/435-1834) and store (rental and sales, information on climbing instruction, and guide services, open daily).

Getting There

The only road access into Aoraki/Mount Cook National Park is Highway 80, which dead-ends in Aoraki/Mount Cook village. **Intercity** (03/365-1113, www.intercitycoach.co.nz) runs a day excursion from Christchurch to Aoraki/Mount Cook village, as well as regular services from all points on the South Island. On all scheduled Intercity services that make the detour to the park, a one-hour "lunch" stop is made in front of the Hermitage.

OTAGO

The province of Otago stretches from the Pacific Ocean to the Southern Alps, encompassing a bustling university town, abundant wildlife attractions, abandoned gold-rush towns, a never-ending patchwork of farmland, two major resort towns, and a wilderness of glaciated peaks and unspoiled lakes.

Highway 1 down the east coast from Christchurch is the main route into Otago. This wide, easy-to-drive highway passes through pleasant rural and coastal towns, including historic Oamaru and intriguing natural features such as the Moeraki Boulders. Otago's largest city is Dunedin, renowned for its grand architecture and the nearby natural wonders of the Otago Peninsula, which is one of the few places in the world where albatrosses can be seen by casual observers.

From Dunedin, most travelers turn west, to Queenstown. Founded after gold was discovered on the Shotover River, the ensuing boomtown could have easily slipped into oblivion, but for one thing—its stunningly scenic location, overlooking a glacial lake and surrounded by the jagged peaks of the Remarkables. In the last 20 years, Queenstown has made its mark as one of the world's premier resort towns. In addition to old-fashioned adventures such as hiking, fishing, and skiing, Queenstown draws adrenaline junkies who arrive in the thousands to spend their cash on bungy jumping, white-water rafting, jetboating, and parapenting (jumping off a mountain with a parachute-like glider). But Queenstown isn't all about adventure—visitors can step back in time at the gold-rush town of Arrowtown,

OTAGO

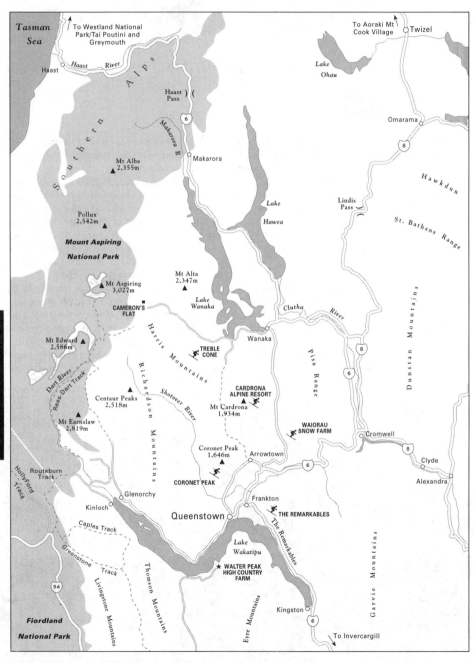

Tasman Sea

To Westland National Park/Tai Poutini and Greymouth

Haast

Haast River

Haast Pass

6

Makarora R

Makarora

Mt Alba 2,355m

Pollux 2,542m

Mount Aspiring

National Park

Mt Aspiring 3,027m

Mt Alta 2,347m

Lake Wanaka

CAMERON'S FLAT

Mt Edward 2,586m

Harris Mountains

Dart River

Rees-Dart Track

TREBLE CONE

Wanaka

Richardson Mountains

Shotover River

CARDRONA ALPINE RESORT

Mt Cardrona 1,934m

Centaur Peaks 2,518m

Mt Earnslaw 2,819m

WAIORAU SNOW FARM

Coronet Peak 1,646m

Arrowtown

Hollyford Track

Routeburn Track

Kinloch

Glenorchy

CORONET PEAK

Frankton

Queenstown

THE REMARKABLES

Caples Track

Greenstone Track

Lake Wakatipu

The Remarkables

94

Livingstone Mountains

Thomson Mountains

★ WALTER PEAK HIGH COUNTRY FARM

Fiordland

National Park

Eyre Mountains

Kingston

6

To Invercargill

To Aoraki Mt Cook Village

Twizel

Lake Ohau

Omarama

8

Hawkdun

Lindis Pass

St. Bathans Range

Lake Hawea

Clutha   *River*

Dunstan Mountains

8

6

Pisa Range

Cromwell

8

Clyde

Alexandra

Garvie Mountains

Southern Alps

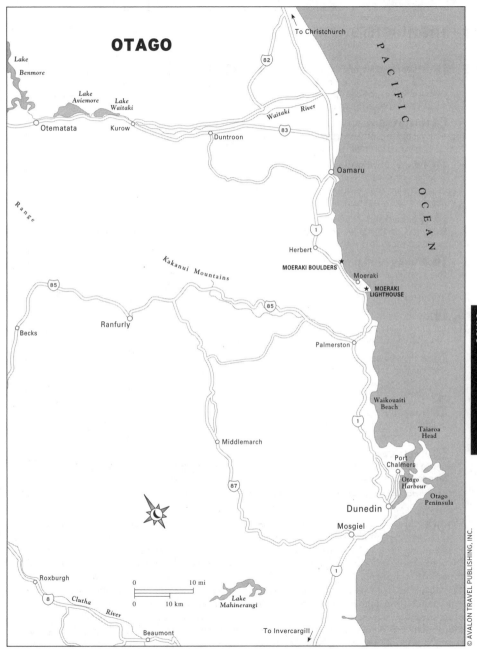

OTAGO

Lake
Benmore

Lake
Aviemore Lake
Waitaki

To Christchurch

82

P
A
C
I
F
I
C

Otematata Kurow

Waitaki River

83

Duntroon

Oamaru

O
C
E
A
N

Range

1

Herbert

MOERAKI BOULDERS

Moeraki

MOERAKI
LIGHTHOUSE

Kakanui Mountains

85

85

Becks

Ranfurly

Palmerston

Waikouaiti
Beach

1

Taiaroa
Head

Middlemarch

Port
Chalmers

Otago
Harbour

87

Otago
Peninsula

Dunedin

Mosgiel

Roxburgh

1

0   10 mi

8

Clutha

0   10 km

River

Lake
Mahinerangi

Beaumont

To Invercargill

OTAGO

© AVALON TRAVEL PUBLISHING, INC.

OTAGO

HIGHLIGHTS

◖ Historic Oamaru: A concentration of historic stone buildings makes downtown Oamaru one of the best-preserved century-old streetscapes in the country (page 389).

◖ Moeraki Boulders: Clusters of concretions along a remote stretch of beach make for an interesting diversion (page 391).

◖ Otago Peninsula: Penguins and albatrosses are the main draw, but there's also stunning coastal scenery and even New Zealand's only castle (page 397).

◖ Skyline Gondola: Rise above it all on this steep gondola that provides sweeping lake and mountain views (page 404).

◖ Bungy Jumping: It all started in Queenstown and today you have a choice of jump sites, including the original Kawarau Bridge (page 406).

◖ Jetboating: Fast and furious, these locally designed boats will amaze you with their versatility and speed (page 408).

◖ Arrowtown: Away from the crush of Queenstown, this gold-rush town is filled with historic homes and pleasant walking trails (page 418).

◖ Puzzling World: All ages will love this unique attraction, which blends intrigue and frustration (page 421).

◖ Treble Cone: It's downhill all the way at one of the Southern Hemisphere's premier alpine resorts (page 424).

◖ Siberia Experience: This unique adventure combines a spectacular flight, a quiet walk through the wilderness, and an exciting jetboat ride (page 429).

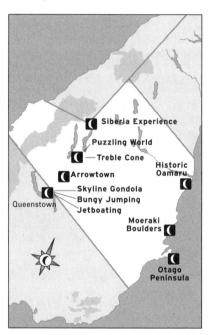

LOOK FOR ◖ TO FIND RECOMMENDED SIGHTS, ACTIVITIES, DINING, AND LODGING.

stay in world-class resorts, and dance the night away at trendy nightclubs.

If kicking back in the sunshine on a lakeshore beach or trying a new sport is your definition of fun, head north from Queenstown to Wanaka, which enjoys the same magnificent mountain setting, but without the ritz and glitz of its neighbor. Though Wanaka is a smaller, more sedate version of tourist-oriented Queenstown, hordes of vacationing New Zealanders

and a good number of tourists are attracted to Wanaka in summer for the beaches, boating, and water-skiing. In winter, they come to ski and board at three world-class resorts, including the only one in the world dedicated to free skiing. Rising majestically across the lake from Wanaka are the snowcapped peaks of Mount Aspiring National Park. This is an area of rugged snowcapped mountains, glaciers, and hanging valleys, with wide rushing rivers and open grassy flats—a wild and untouched paradise for backcountry hikers, mountaineers, climbers, photographers, and bird lovers.

PLANNING YOUR TIME

Otago appeals to all interests and caters to all budgets. This makes deciding where to spend most of your time (and money) a personal decision. If you're on a two-week trip through the South Island, you'll have enough time to explore **Historic Oamaru** and wander through the **Moeraki Boulders** on the way south to Dunedin. You should plan on spending at least one night in this city and then a full day admiring the wildlife of the **Otago Peninsula.** From this point, the natural routing is to continue through the Southland region then pause in Queenstown for a couple of nights before heading over the Southern Alps to the west coast. If you only have a week in the South Island and are looking for resort-town action, your focus

will be in Queenstown, a seven-hour drive (or one-hour flight) from Christchurch. Regardless of how you arrive, two days is enough time to ride the **Skyline Gondola** and for the adventurous to try **bungy jumping** and **jetboating.** Close by, but seemingly a world away, quiet **Arrowtown** is a good place to escape Queenstown's commercialism. The smaller resort town of Wanaka is on the way over to the west coast, but well worth the detour for its laidback lifestyle. While children will gravitate to **Puzzling World,** you should also incorporate the **Siberia Experience,** a flying/walking/jetboating wilderness combo, into your itinerary.

Peak season in Queenstown and Wanaka is winter, when skiers and snowboarders from throughout New Zealand and Australia are drawn to the slopes of five resorts, including **Treble Cone,** where steep slopes and views that seemingly extend forever combine to create a memorable winter vacation.

North Otago

OTAGO

OAMARU

Creamy-white stone buildings, wide tree-lined streets named after the rivers of Great Britain, and well-kept gardens give a distinctive air to Oamaru, 87 km (54 mi) south of Timaru and 117 km (73 mi) north of Dunedin. This commercial center of 12,000 is a popular base for anglers fishing for quinnat salmon in the Waitaki River. **Oamaru stone,** a white granular limestone, has been used for many of New Zealand's most important buildings, including the customhouse in Wellington and the town halls in both Auckland and Dunedin; Weston, five km (3.1 mi) west of Oamaru, is the limestone industry center.

◀ Historic Oamaru

Park at the south end of downtown and plan on spending at least an hour admiring the grand stone buildings that line the main street and beyond. North of the visitor center, the grand old athenaeum (library) building houses the **North**

Otago Museum (60 Thames St., 03/434-1652; Mon.–Fri. 10:30 A.M.–4:30 P.M., Sat. 10 A.M.– 1 P.M., Sun. 1–4:30 P.M.; free). Displays cover geology, natural history, and Maori and early European settlement of North Otago, and feature the extraction and uses of Oamaru stone. Other impressive main street structures include the courthouse, post office, and National Bank. On the south side of the visitor center, duck down Itchen Street toward the waterfront and then explore Harbour Street, a narrow alley lined with stone buildings used as warehouses in the 1870s and 1880s.

Blue Penguin Colony

Oamaru's best-loved natural attraction is the blue penguin colony (Waterfront Rd., 03/433-1195; daily from 9 A.M.), which has made a home in an old quarry along the south side of the harbor. Much work has been put into re-introducing native flora to make the site as natural as possible, and "breeding boxes" have

© ANDREW HEMPSTEAD

OTAGO

Oamaru's main street is lined with grand stone buildings.

been placed throughout. For years penguins have nested here, but only in recent years have their numbers increased (they are now successfully protected from predators by a surrounding fence). Each night, just as the sun sets, the penguins—up to 200 on a busy night—return from a day of feeding on fish to wander up the beach, crossing a lighted area in front of a grandstand to get to their nesting area. Also at the site is a visitor center, but to see the nightly parade you'll pay adult $17.50, senior $15.75, child $6. A Behind the Scenes tour is adult and senior $10, child $2. Birds are present year-round, but their numbers are highest September–February.

Bushy Beach

Across South Wanbrow Reserve from the Blue Penguin Colony is Bushy Beach, home to New Zealand's northernmost breeding colony of yellow-eyed penguins. You can reach Bushy Beach along a trail that climbs up and through the reserve from the end of Waterfront Road (allow 40 minutes each way), or drive to the beach along Bushy Beach Road. Great numbers of seabirds frequent the area, along with a variety of coastal vegetation and sealife on the benches and platforms protected from the pounding surf. You can see (or hear) the penguins almost year-round from the walking track and viewing shelter. The best time to see them coming out of the surf is late afternoon/early evening.

Accommodations and Camping

Across from an outdoor swimming pool, a one-minute stroll from Oamaru Gardens, and five minutes from downtown, **YHA Oamaru** (corner of Reed and Cross Sts., 03/434-5008, www.yha.co.nz; $21) is perfectly situated for an overnight stay. All beds in this restored villa are in five-bed dorms and these's a red kettle on the picket fence out front so you'll know when you've arrived.

Ambassador Motor Lodge (296 Thames St., 03/437-2146 or 0800/437-2146, www.ambassadorlodge.com; $95–140 s or d) is a complex of 11 well-equipped rooms, each with a large kitchen, Internet access, and some with spa baths.

Built in the early 1880s, the expansive Oamaru stone facade of the **Kingsgate Hotel Brydone** (115 Thames St., 03/434-0011, www.millenniumhotels.com; $159–249 s or d) hides 50 spacious guest rooms decorated in a contemporary style that doesn't hint at the historic surrounds. Book online and pay $160 for a Junior Suite, complete with a king bed and luxurious bathroom.

Oamaru Top 10 Holiday Park (Chelmer St., 03/434-7666 or 0800/280-202; campsites $14 per person, cabins $45–70 d) has a pleasant location next to Oamaru Gardens; children will love the playground along the street. Aside from the usual facilities, there's a spacious, comfortable TV room and lots of information on the local area in the office. From Severn Street, the main road from the south, take Cross Street, then turn left on Chelmer.

Food

Oamaru has a good number of reasonably

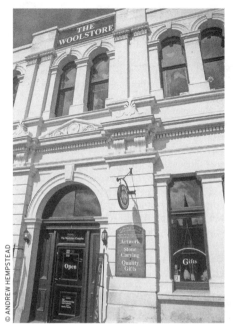

The Woolstore Café is in this historic building behind the Oamaru Visitor Centre.

Information

Oamaru Visitor Centre (Thames St., 03/434-1656, www.tourismwaitaki.co.nz; Mon.–Fri. 9 A.M.–5 P.M., Sat.–Sun. 10 A.M.–4 P.M.) is in the heart of the historic precinct at the south end of the main street.

MOERAKI BOULDERS

Thirty-eight km (24 mi) south of Oamaru, just south of Hampden, Highway 1 passes a short gravel road that leads to the boulder-shaped Moeraki Boulders Restaurant. From there various tracks lead down to the beach and into unique **Moeraki Boulders Scenic Reserve.** Just to the north, along sandy Moeraki Beach, you come to what at first looks like a group of extra-large turtles washed up on the sand. On closer inspection you find a great number of round, perfectly smooth, gray boulders of varying sizes (up to four meters round) with a cracked design, scattered haphazardly along the sand and sticking out of the cliffs almost as if they're being "born"—some have split apart into several gigantic pieces. Made of carbonate

priced eateries, including the **Woolstore Café** (1 Tyne St., 03/434-8336; daily 9 A.M.–8 P.M.), in the restored Woolstore Complex. Eggs Benedict is $14 and lunches range a reasonable $10–15. Across the road is another restored building, the **Criterion Hotel** (3 Tyne St., 03/434-6247), which reopened in 1998 after being closed for over 90 years. Extensive renovations include to the downstairs bar, which is a popular local drinking spot.

A couple of doors up from the visitor center is **Steam** (7 Thames St., 03/434-3344; daily 8 A.M.–4 P.M.), a simple space at street level of an old stone building, and with a few tables out front. The coffee is the best in town. **T-Bar** (Kingsgate Hotel Brydone, 115 Thames St., 03/434-0011, www.millenniumhotels.com), open daily from 6:30 A.M. (7 A.M. on weekends), offers a typically wide-ranging hotel menu in a long, narrow room decorated in a stylish historic theme.

Moeraki Boulders

of lime, silica, alumina, and peroxide of iron, the boulders were formed by chemistry on the seafloor about 60 million years ago through the slow accumulation of lime salts around a small core; the cracks are filled with yellow calcite crystals. They "appear" from the beach and cliffs behind as the mudstone in which they lurk is eroded by the sea. According to Maori legend, the boulders were food baskets and water casks from one of the great canoes from Hawaiiki wrecked off Shag Point at the south end of Katiki Beach. These magnificent boulders were once found all over the beaches in this area (volcanic boulders lie on **Katiki Beach** a few km to the south, but they're older and smaller); sadly, most have been carried off as souvenirs—only the largest and heaviest boulders remain, and the area is now protected as a scientific reserve.

CONTINUING SOUTH

From the boulders, it's 21 km (13 mi) south along Highway 1 to Palmerston, from where Highway 85 spurs inland to Queenstown (260 km/161 mi), a four-hour drive. Continuing south, it's 56 km (35 mi) to Dunedin from Palmerston.

Between Moeraki and the boulders, a short detour leads to **Shag Point.** At the end of the road, a lookout provides sweeping ocean views. Fur seals often pull themselves up onto the rocks below, and yellow-eyed penguins can be seen ambling up the adjacent beach at dusk.

If you're not in a hurry to reach Dunedin, consider overnighting at **Waikouaiti Beach Motor Camp** (186 Beach St., 03/465-7366; tent sites $18, powered sites $22, cabins from $45), beside the beach 16 km (10 mi) south of Palmerston.

Dunedin and Vicinity

Second-largest city in the South Island (pop. 110,000) and capital of the Otago region, Dunedin (pronounced Dun-EE-din) sprawls around the head of bustling **Otago Harbour** 360 km (225 mi) south of Christchurch. With its well-planned city center, hilly suburbs and harbor views, Victorian-era stone buildings decorated with spires and turrets, stately homes, historic statues and memorials, and well-kept parks and flower gardens, the self-proclaimed "Rhododendron City of the South Island" has plenty of living history, lots to see and do, and a distinct appeal of its own.

Dunedin is also the gateway to the scenic **Otago Peninsula,** northeast of the city center. The peninsula is an enjoyable place to tootle around for a day—for views, spectacular beaches and towering cliffs, farmland separated by century-old stone walls, and birdwatching. At **Taiaroa Head** (the northeastern tip), the albatross colony and a beach full of yellow-eyed penguins are two Dunedin sights you shouldn't miss.

Otago Harbour was a popular whaling ground long before the first European whaling station was officially established at the Maori village of **Otakou** in 1840. In late 1847 the Free Church of Scotland established a Scottish settlement at Otago under the leadership of William Cargill and Rev. Thomas Burns (nephew of famous Scottish poet Robert Burns). The following year **Otago** (the European mispronunciation of Otakou) was chosen as the official name for the settlement, and "New Edinburgh" as the name for the new town—the latter was greatly criticized for its lack of originality and replaced by the Gaelic name for Edinburgh, Dun Edin.

The discovery of gold in Otago in 1861 brought numerous gold diggers, along with bankers, hoteliers, and great wealth to Dunedin, and within a couple of years public works and enterprises had flourished to the extent that the city became the commercial and industrial heart of the country. It became, in 1882, the first city in New Zealand to set up a freezing works and send frozen meat to England; it was the first city to use kerosene

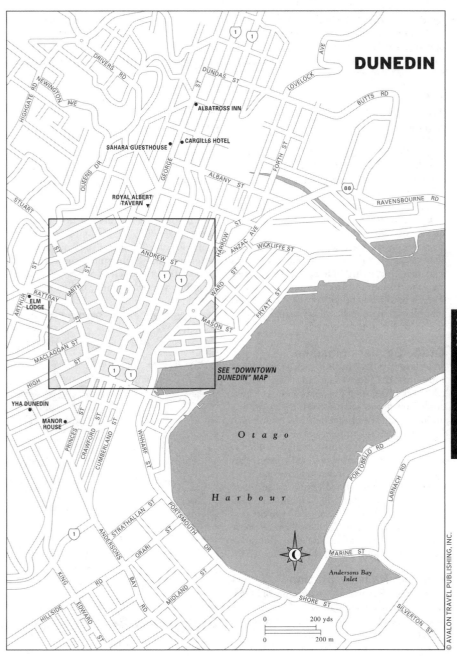

DUNEDIN

DRIVERS RD

NEWINGTON AVE

HIGHGATE RD

DUNDAS ST

LOVELOCK AVE

BUTTS RD

● ALBATROSS INN

● CARGILLS HOTEL

SAHARA GUESTHOUSE ●

QUEENS DR

GEORGE

FORTH ST

ALBANY ST

STUART

ROYAL ALBERT
TAVERN ▾

RAVENSBOURNE RD

88

HARROW

ANDREW ST

ANZAC AVE

WICKLIFFE ST

WARD

SMITH ST

1 1

WARD

FRYATT ST

RATTRAY

ARTHUR

● ELM
LODGE

MASON ST

MACLAGGAN ST

ST

HIGH

1 1

**SEE "DOWNTOWN
DUNEDIN" MAP**

YHA DUNEDIN ●

MANOR ●
HOUSE

PRINCES

CRAWFORD ST

CUMBERLAND ST

WHHARF ST

Otago

1

STRATHALLAN ST

PORTSMOUTH DR

ANDERSONS

ORARI

Harbour

PORTOBELLO RD

LARNACH RD

KING

BAY

RD

MIDLAND

MARINE ST

*Andersons Bay
Inlet*

HILLSIDE

EDWARD

ST

SHORE ST

SILVERTON ST

| 0 | 200 yds |
| 0 | 200 m |

OTAGO

© AVALON TRAVEL PUBLISHING, INC.

lighting, the first place in the country to use a cable tramway, and the first successful developer of a hydroelectric works (which prompted the government to further develop hydroelectric power throughout the country).

SIGHTS
The Octagon
In the heart of downtown, the attractive eight-sided Octagon is a great place to people-watch (especially around lunchtime). Situated around the Octagon are the **Dunedin Visitor Centre,** art gallery, civic center, library, a cathedral, and, one block back, the town hall, public library, and post office.

Dunedin Public Art Gallery (30 The Octagon, 03/477-4000; daily 10 A.M.–5 P.M.; free) lies on the west corner of the Octagon. Founded in 1884, the gallery has two claims to fame—first, it's the oldest art gallery in New Zealand, containing an extensive collection of foreign paintings and one of the most important New Zealand collections; second, it holds the only Monet in the country.

Otago Settlers Museum
In a classic art deco building, this jam-packed museum (31 Queens Garden, 03/477-5052; Mon.–Fri. 10 A.M.–5 P.M., Sat.–Sun. 1–5 P.M.; adult $5) features photos, costumes, furniture, antique medical and dental instruments (which look like great instruments of torture!), a portrait gallery, a gold-mining exhibit, a pioneer cottage and blacksmith's shop, a penny-farthing bicycle, horse-drawn vehicles, a tram, a display devoted to "the forgotten sex and early feminists of New Zealand," and much, much more—it's the kind of place where you can easily spend several hours. The excellent reference library and Research and Reading Room are open to the public during the week.

Dunedin Railway Station
The Flemish Renaissance architecture of Dunedin's spectacular train station on Anzac Avenue at the east end of Stuart Street is something to see whether you're catching a train or not. When you first see its white Oamaru stone facings,

polished granite pillars, covered colonnade and "carriageway," and stunning clock tower, you think you've seen it all. But the highly decorated interior of the main foyer is even more intricate, with a tiled mosaic floor featuring the steam train and the old New Zealand Rail symbol (NZR), Royal Doulton china cherubs frolicking in foliage around the upper walls, and beautiful stained-glass windows with steam trains puffing toward you from every angle. The station was completed in 1907, and the architect, George A. Troup, won the Institution of British Architects Award for this amazing design.

As well as the departure point for the Taieri Gorge Railway, the railway station is worth visiting for the **New Zealand Sports Hall of Fame** (03/477-7775; daily 10 A.M.–4 P.M.; adult $6, child $3), where you can learn about national heroes in the sports you may expect (cricket, rugby) as well as others you may not (yachting, wood-chopping, and more).

First Church, Dunedin

© ANDREW HEMPSTEAD

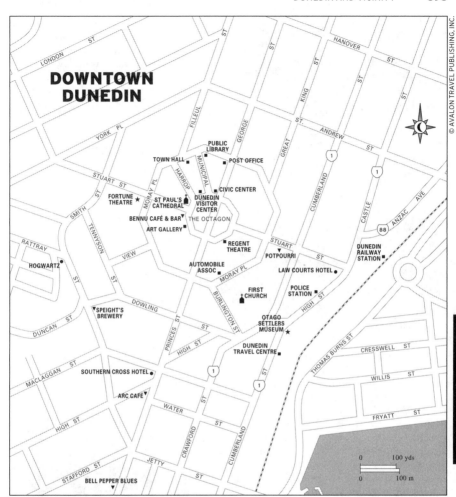

© AVALON TRAVEL PUBLISHING, INC.

DOWNTOWN DUNEDIN

OTAGO

Olveston

A one-hour guided tour of this stately 35-room home (42 Royal Terr., 03/477-3320; adult $14.50, child $5) is definitely worth the admission—to see all the antique furniture, paintings, and priceless art objects; the gleaming kitchen filled with functional implements, crockery, and silverware; and the maids' and butlers' quarters. You hear the history of the house and its people as you move from room to room. Built for the Theomins between 1904 and 1906, the perfectly maintained Jacobean-style house was kept in the family until 1966, when they gave it to the city. A tour takes you back to the days of early 20th-century Dunedin, giving you a taste of what it was like to live in style—or *serve* those living in style. The house is a 20-minute uphill walk from city center. Tours depart daily at 9:30 and 10:45 A.M., noon, and 1:30, 2:45, and 4 P.M.

Otago Museum

Museum freaks can spend hours wandering

© TAIERI GORGE RAILWAY

Dunedin Railway Station

established buildings covered in ivy, as well as modern buildings, green lawns and flower gardens, and Leith Stream, which meanders through to Otago Harbour (follow the creek and you end up at a boat harbor). Call the information center (03/474-3300) to organize a guided tour. To the north lies Dunedin's

TAIERI GORGE RAILWAY

The Taieri Gorge Railway (03/477-4449, www.taieri.co.nz) winds its way west out of the city through a remote section of Otago. Originally built as a link to interior goldfields, the railway has been restored, along with a number of historic carriages. Today, the train passes through tunnels, over viaducts, and along a narrow valley for 77 km (48 mi) to Middlemarch. Departing daily at 9:30 A.M. from Dunedin Railway Station, the round-trip costs $75. Children are free when accompanied by paying adults. Other options include a one-way train trip to Middlemarch and then a bus ride through to Queenstown (adult $115, child $58), and a shorter return trip between Dunedin and Pukerangi (departs daily at 2:30 P.M.; $67 round-trip).

around enormous Otago Museum (Great King St., 03/474-7474; daily 10 A.M.–5 P.M.; free), with its outstanding collection of Polynesian art (largest collection in New Zealand). Visit the halls on Melanesia, the Maori culture, world civilizations, furniture and ceramics, cameras, coins and medals, lions and primates, birds, small animals, and marinelife. The museum also features a Southern Land, Southern People display and a maritime hall. One section of the museum, **Discovery World** (adult $6, child $3), has an admission charge, but this hands-on science center will keep kids amused for at least an hour. It includes various illusions, sporting challenges, and a piano you can play with your feet. The museum is two km (1.2 mi) north of the Octagon.

University of Otago

The university grounds off Cumberland Street (north of city center) are an agreeable place to wander. You'll pass attractive, well-

© TAIERI GORGE RAILWAY

beautiful Botanic Garden and to the east are Logan Park and University Oval.

Speight's Brewery

To visit Dunedin's historic 1876 **Speight's Brewery** (200 Rattray St., 03/477-7697) you'll need to join a tour. These depart Monday–Thursday at 10 A.M., noon, 2 P.M., and 7 P.M., and Friday–Sunday at 10 A.M., noon, 2 P.M., and 4 P.M. The tour costs adult $17, senior $14, child $6.

Parks and Gardens

Well-planned Dunedin has no shortage of "green spots" around the city. New Zealand's first **Botanic Garden** (north end of George St.; daily dawn to dusk) features formal lawns interspersed with trees and native bush, magnificent flower displays, trails, an aviary and, in the center, the Visitors Education Centre. The Rhododendron Dell in springtime bloom is a multicolored feast for your eyes—Dunedin is famous for its springtime flowering shrubs. Stop by the Botanica Restaurant next to the Winter Gardens for fruit juice, tea, or a light lunch. Drive through the gardens via Lovelock Avenue from the south or Signal Hill Road from the north, or catch a bus heading north up George Street from the Octagon to the northwest boundary of the Botanic Garden. All down the west side of the city are parks, gardens, and sports grounds, known as the **Town Belt,** and on the northeast side of the city is **Logan Park.**

◖ Otago Peninsula

Two main roads run along the peninsula: the high Highcliff Road (good views) and the low Portobello Road along the waterfront (a bird-watcher's delight)—both join at the small settlement of **Portobello** (pub, general store and hot takeaway foods, café, and public telephone). Other than these, the peninsula is relatively noncommercial—buy your lunch, drinks, and munchies in the city before you venture up the peninsula.

To get the most out of the peninsula by car, take the high route first, and after visiting Taiaroa Head via Portobello Road, return to the city by the low route. To get to the peninsula from city center, take Highway 1 south and turn left on Andersons Bay Road, which becomes Portobello Road. Buses to Portobello depart from Centre City New World on Cumberland Street Monday–Friday (frequently) and Saturday (considerably less frequently); for times, call 03/477-9238.

GLENFALLOCH WOODLAND GARDEN

Are you a gardening nut, particularly into azaleas, rhododendrons, or fuchsias? Enjoy hand-feeding peacocks and all kinds of semi-tame birds? Then these gardens (430 Portobello Rd., 03/476-1006; daily during daylight hours; adult $3, child $1) originating in 1873 and their pioneer homestead (1871), eight km (five mi) from the city, are more than worth the effort to find. The grounds are spectacular in spring; in summer they're noted for colorful fuchsia displays. Take some of the short walks through the trees passing a stream and beautiful woodland gardens. Pottery is made and sold in the Potters Cottage (1–4 P.M.) and there's a café open daily for lunch.

LARNACH CASTLE

If you've always wondered what it would be like to live in a genuine castle, wonder no longer. Built in the early 1870s by extravagant banker, businessman, and politician William Larnach, Larnach Castle (145 Camp Rd., 03/476-1616; daily 9 A.M.–5 P.M.; adult $20, child $10) sits in 15 hectares (37 acres) of bush and gardens, 13 km (eight mi) from Dunedin city center—a grand and extravagant stone mansion built along Scottish baronial lines, filled with original marble, Venetian glass, plaster, and woodcarvings collected by Larnach from all over the world. You can wander through the castle and grounds at will, spending as much or as little time as you want; most of the rooms are not roped off so you can actually enter each one and let your imagination run free. Don't miss climbing the narrow stone steps to the top of the tower for incredible views, waltz into the café for a Devonshire

OTAGO

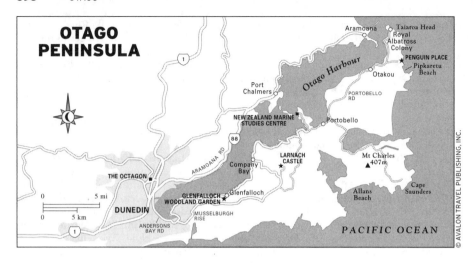

OTAGO
PENINSULA

Aramoana
Taiaroa Head
Royal Albatross Colony
PENGUIN PLACE
Pipkaretu Beach
Otago Harbour
Otakou
Port Chalmers
PORTOBELLO RD
NEW ZEALAND MARINE STUDIES CENTRE
Portobello
88
LARNACH CASTLE
Mt Charles ▲407m
Company Bay
THE OCTAGON
0   5 mi
0   5 km
DUNEDIN
GLENFALLOCH WOODLAND GARDEN
Glenfalloch
Allans Beach
Cape Saunders
MUSSELBURGH RISE
ANDERSONS BAY RD
ARAMOANA RD
PACIFIC OCEAN

© AVALON TRAVEL PUBLISHING, INC.

OTAGO

tea (served till 4:30 P.M.) or lunch, then stroll through the gardens, stopping to check out the stables and dungeon.

NEW ZEALAND MARINE STUDIES CENTRE

Operated by the University of Otago, this complex (Hatchery Rd., 03/479-5826) lies on a narrow peninsula near Portobello. Primarily a marine education center, it incorporates a public facility that allows for a behind-the-scenes look at life under the surrounding waterways. It features the sealife of New Zealand's southern waters, with live specimens, interactive displays, and shallow tanks re-creating the habitat of coastal marinelife. Guided tours depart daily at 10:30 A.M. (adult $18, child $9), or call for a schedule of other programs.

PENGUIN PLACE

When Howard McGrouther bought a sheep farm on the Otago Peninsula, little did he realize that he would become instrumental in a struggle to save the **yellow-eyed penguin,** the world's rarest penguin. As soon as a small colony began nesting among his grazing sheep, he set out to protect the birds and to ensure that, while they nested on his property, the species would survive. Since the land is devoid of

suitable vegetation for nesting, McGrouther constructed special breeding boxes. Predators were trapped, and sick and injured birds were nursed back to health—and now the colony is growing. To support this private conservation

© ANDREW HEMPSTEAD

yellow-eyed penguin

project, the McGrouthers have encouraged visitors to view the penguins. Camouflaged trenches lead to a series of blinds scattered through the colony, allowing visitors to view the penguins at extremely close range without disturbing them. The birds are most active around dusk, on cooler days, and when nesting, but tours (10:15 A.M. until sunset; adult $35, child $16) with knowledgeable guides are run year-round. Bookings are essential at 03/478-0286, or make them through the visitor center.

ROYAL ALBATROSS COLONY

The colony of royal albatrosses at **Taiaroa Head** (03/478-0499; adult $30, child $15) is the only colony in the world on inhabited mainland. If you're lucky enough, you'll be there when the birds are flying (they need winds of at least 15–20 knots to take off but can land with very little wind—the afternoon is best). The all-white birds with black wings at Taiaroa are great albatrosses—true seabirds; with wingspans of more than three meters (10 ft), these large, bulky birds waddle on land but are magnificent fliers. The parent albatrosses (currently around 20 nesting pairs that mate for life) arrive at the colony late in September, build a nest, lay an egg early in November, and share incubation duty for about 11 weeks. The chick hatches by the end of January and the parents take turns guarding it for the first 40 days, feeding it by regurgitation, and caring for it for several months before they bid it farewell and take off to sea. The nine-month-old chick first tests its wings in late September. It takes off in a strong wind with no practice flight, and then it's gone for the next three to four years, during which it circumnavigates the pole—never landing, feeding in flight and on the sea surface.

You may see albatrosses circling overhead from the parking lot, but venturing inside and joining a tour is highly recommended. On arrival at the reception building you're given an informative talk on the albatrosses and their way of life, then taken up a short trail to the observatory and viewing room to see the nests

(binoculars help) and the birds flying on windy days. The tour includes a visit to historic Fort Taiaroa, a defense station established in 1885 to protect the port from a Russian invasion that never came. **Pilots Beach** just below the headland is a popular place for **fur seals**—you can walk down to it for close-up views.

RECREATION
Walking Trails

For panoramic views of the city, harbor, and Otago Peninsula, consider hiking the five-km (3.1-mi) **Pineapple Skyline Walkway.** The track starts at the car park off Flagstaff Whare Flat Road, takes about two hours (going downhill toward the city), and finishes at the end of Booth Road in the northern Dunedin suburb of Glenleith; you can walk it in either direction, depending on whether you want to go uphill or down. For information on public transportation to the track, as well as details of other hiking tracks in the area, head to the visitor center.

Tunnel Beach Walkway is another very popular short walk, starting seven km (4.3 mi) south of the city off Blackhead Road. Taking about one hour, the walkway meanders down to striking sandstone cliffs, arches, stacks, and caves, and to a stairway through a rock tunnel leading down to Tunnel Beach. Access to the walkway is not permitted during lambing season (Aug.–Oct.).

ARTS AND ENTERTAINMENT

Bands playing rock 'n' roll, Top 40, and alternative music appear all around Dunedin in the pubs and hotels—just follow your ears. Dunedin is well known throughout New Zealand for its alternative and grunge musical contributions. Two venues feature this particular kind of Dunedin music: the **Crown Hotel** (179 Rattray St., 03/477-0132) and **Arc Café** (135 High St., 03/474-1135). The latter is the quintessential Dunedin music venue, with a typical student crowd, acoustic jams, and, sometimes, local bands recording live performances for a CD. Near the university, **Captain Cook Tavern** (354 Great King St., 03/474-1935)

OTAGO

has bands playing most nights and gets very crowded. Back toward the city, **Royal Albert Tavern** (387 George St., 03/477-2952) is another live music venue, with an Irish house band on Monday night.

When the pubs close, the under-25s looking to dance the night away head to **Bath St.** (1 Bath St., 03/477-6750; Tues.–Sat.).

The **Regent Theatre** (The Octagon, 03/477-8597) presents a wide variety of local and visiting performers, plays, ballet, and grand opera. At the **Town Hall** (Moray Pl., 03/474-3614) you can attend performances by local opera companies and acting groups, and various musical events. Go to the **Fortune Theatre** (231 Upper Stuart St., 03/477-8323) for professional theater—see the back of the daily newspaper for details or call the box office.

ACCOMMODATIONS AND CAMPING
Under $50
A five-minute uphill walk from the Octagon and close to the Speight's Brewery, **Hogwartz** (277 Rattray St., 03/474-1487; dorm beds $23–27, $38 s, $56 d, $66 en suite) is a smaller backpacker lodge in a restored historic home. In addition to all the usuals, amenities include a log fire, piano, and book exchange.

YHA Dunedin (71 Stafford St., 03/474-1919, www.yha.co.nz; dorm beds $24, $60 d), also known as Stafford Gables, is a large Tudor-style building in a handy central location on the southwest side of the Octagon. Check-in is after 2 P.M.

◖ **Elm Lodge** (74 Elm Row, 03/474-1872 or 0800/356-563, www.elmwildlifetours.co.nz; dorm beds $25, $41 s, $56 d) is an excellent backpacker accommodation providing bright cheerful rooms with views of Otago Harbour, an equipped kitchen, comfy living room with TV, well-kept garden, and barbecue area—all the comforts of home only a 10-minute walk from the Octagon. The friendly owners also do bookings for most local activities, rent bikes, and can arrange good-value (and very popular) nature tours of Otago Peninsula and other local sights.

Colonial **Manor House** (28 Manor Pl., 03/477-0484, www.manorhousebackpackers .co.nz; camping $15 per person, dorm beds $24, $55 d) is like a home away from home, yet with all the facilities you hope to find: a very spacious and rather grand living room, a modern kitchen, good showers, laundry, and a bush setting. It's a short walk (about five blocks) from city center.

$50-100
Comfortable **Sahara Guesthouse** (619 George St., 03/477-6662, www.dunedin-accommodation .co.nz; $85–120 s or d with breakfast; $95–140 s or d for self-contained motel units) has a pleasing decor, TV lounge, tea- and coffee-making supplies, and a laundry.

One of a few graciously restored downtown hotels is the **Law Courts Hotel** (65 Stuart St., 03/477-8036, www.lawcourtshotel.co.nz; $60 s, $99 d), with 24 comfortable but basic guest rooms scattered around the top three floors of an 1880s building. Rates include a light breakfast, or you can upgrade to a cooked version for $5.50 per person.

Dunedin's least expensive motels are along Musselburgh Rise, on the way out to the Otago Peninsula. One of the best of these is the **Arcadian Motel** (85–89 Musselburgh Rise, 03/455-0992 or 0508/272-234, www.dunedin motel.co.nz; $85 s, $88 d); there are a couple of inexpensive two-bedroom units ($125 s or d) perfect for families.

$100-150
Built in the early 1900s, the **Albatross Inn** (770 George St., 03/477-2727 or 0800/441-441, www.albatross.inn.co.nz; $85–100 s, $100–160 d) offers accommodation in eight Edwardian-style rooms, each with hardwood floors and high ceilings. Unlike many bed-and-breakfasts, each room in the Albatross has a private bathroom, TV, and telephone. A complimentary breakfast is served in a bright and breezy room on the ground floor.

The most interesting place to stay when you're in Dunedin is **Larnach Castle** (03/476-1616, www.larnachcastle.co.nz), on the Otago Peninsula 13 km (8 mi) from downtown.

Accommodation is in the re-creation of a colonial farm building (12 en suite rooms; $240–270 s or d) or converted stables (six rooms with shared facilities and a TV lounge; $130 s or d), and the beautiful 15-hectare (37-acre) grounds become almost your own private garden. Tea- and coffee-making facilities are provided and breakfast is included in the rates. Dinner is an additional $54.50 per person.

Over $150

A few blocks north of the Octagon (near the Otago Museum) is **Cargills Hotel** (678 George St., 03/477-7983 or 0800/737-378, www.cargills.co.nz; $155–250 s or d). Each of the 50 rooms is large, and comes complete with a selection of plants, wireless Internet, and a writing desk. The hotel also features a restaurant that opens to a peaceful outdoor courtyard.

Beyond suburban St. Kilda, and overlooking the long expanse of St. Clair Beach, is the **(Esplanade Motel** (14 Esplanade, 03/455-1987, www.esplanade.co.nz; $175–250 s or d), where the most expensive rooms have king beds, beautiful bathrooms, kitchens, and balconies with sweeping ocean views.

If you're in search of a full-facility hotel, complete with 24-hour café, a fitness center, laundry, underground parking, hairdresser, restaurants, and souvenir shop, try the **Southern Cross Hotel** (118 High St., 03/477-0752 or 0800/696-963, www.scenic-circle.co.nz; $280–530 s or d).

Holiday Parks

You'll find a couple of holiday parks within a reasonable distance of the city center.

Dunedin Holiday Park (Victoria Rd., St. Kilda, 03/455-4690 or 0800/945-455, www.dunedinholidaypark.co.nz; tent sites $14 per person, powered sites $18 s, $28 d, cabins $42–85 s or d, motel rooms $98) is five km (3.1 mi) south of downtown, but within earshot of the waves rolling onto St. Kilda Beach.

Aaron Lodge Top 10 Holiday Park (2.5 km/1.6 mi west of the Octagon at 162 Kaikorai Valley Rd., 03/476-4725 or 0800/879-227, www.aaronlodgetop10.co.nz; tent sites $32, powered sites $35, cabins 46 s or d, tourist flats $78, motel rooms $145) is similar, and meals are available in nearby restaurants. Take Stuart Street west from the Octagon and follow it uphill until it becomes Kaikorai Valley Road.

FOOD

Café culture flourishes in Dunedin, with a dozen or more cafés within a stone's throw of the Octagon.

Cafés

One block back from the center of the Octagon, the emphasis at **(Mazagram Espresso Bar** (Upper Moray Pl., 03/477-9959; Mon.–Fri. 8 A.M.–6 P.M., Sat. 10 A.M.–2 P.M.) is on quality coffee, which is roasted in-house. But with just four tables (and a few more on the sidewalk), finding a place to sit can be difficult at peak times.

Strictly Coffee (23 Bath St., 03/479-0017; Mon.–Fri. 8 A.M.–5 P.M.) also has its own roastery, but as it's along a narrow alley (on the east side of the Octagon), most out-of-towners miss it. That's a shame, because the coffee is as good as it gets in Dunedin.

For a little more choice than the recommended coffee hangouts, **Tangente Café** (111 Moray Pl., 03/477-0232; Mon.–Fri. 8 A.M.–3:30 P.M., Fri.–Sat. until 9 P.M.) is a good place for breakfast. The Sourdough Extreme, a delicious vegetarian dish topped with a poached egg and hollandaise sauce ($11.50), is a particular treat. The rest of day, healthy choices include a pumpkin-based fettuccini topped with feta and ham ($16.50).

Open daily for breakfast and lunch, **Café Nova** (29 The Octagon, 03/479-0808; Mon.–Fri. from 7 A.M., Sat.–Sun. from 8:30 A.M.) attracts more of a business and tourist crowd than the places detailed above. It's part of the Dunedin Public Art Gallery, and is separated from the lobby by a glass wall.

Gourmet Goodies

Everyday Gourmet (466 George St., 03/477-2045; Mon.–Fri. 9 A.M.–6 P.M., Sat. 10 A.M.–3 P.M.) has a few indoor seats, but many customers eat on the run, ordering deli meals to go and delicious cinnamon hot chocolate, while visitors are drawn to gift packs of New Zealand delicacies.

A recommended stop on your way out to the Otago Peninsula is the delightfully named **《 Who Ate All the Pies** (12 Prince Albert Rd., St. Kilda, 03/456-1062; Tues.–Fri. 10:30 A.M.–6 P.M.), where the savory pies are an absolute treat (try ostrich, kumara, and caramelized red onion for something different).

Who Ate All the Pies is also represented at the **Otago Farmers' Market** (Anzac Ave., 03/477-6701; Sat. 8 A.M.–12:30 P.M.), along with local farmers selling fruit and vegetables and gourmet food producers selling everything from organic beer to specialty meats.

Italian and Mexican

Just off the Octagon, **Etrusco** (8 Moray Pl., 03/477-3737; closed Mon.) is at street level of the impeccably restored Savoy Building. The theme is upscale Italian, yet prices are reasonable, with most pastas under $20 and gourmet single-serve pizzas in the $20–23 range.

Continuing up the hill is **Bennu Café & Bar** (12 Moray Pl., 03/474-5055; Mon.–Sat. 11 A.M.–11 P.M., Sun. 5–11 P.M.). In a restored brick building, with original plaster ceilings and a warm European atmosphere, the restaurant features mainly Mexican and pizza dishes (the antipasto platters are delicious; from $12).

Local Cuisine

Many locals regard **Bell Pepper Blues** (474 Princes St., 03/474-0973; Mon.–Sat. from 6 P.M.) as Dunedin's finest dining experience. The menu of modern New Zealand cooking is overseen by local celebrity chef Michael Coughlin, whose best-known dishes incorporate venison (although the bread and butter pudding smothered in rum and Belgian chocolate is worthy of mention also).

Pub Fare

For steak, lamb chop, chicken, or fish bistro meals under $15 in comfortable, cozy Scottish surroundings, head for the **Royal Albert Tavern** (corner of London and George Sts., 03/477-8035; daily for lunch and dinner). On Monday night, Irish bands are the featured entertainment.

Vegetarian

Along Stuart Street, downhill from the Octagon, are many trendy little cafés, including vegetarian restaurant **Potpourri Natural Foods** (97 Lower Stuart St., 03/477-9983; Mon.–Fri. 9 A.M.–8 P.M., Sat. 11 A.M.–3 P.M.; from $11 for lunch or dinner). This place serves a large variety of health foods, Mexican meals, fresh salads, light meals, and desserts.

South of the Octagon, across from the Southern Cross Hotel, the **Arc Café** (135 High St., 03/474-1135, Mon.–Sat. noon–11 P.M.) has a bohemian atmosphere and a menu dominated by vegetarian and vegan choices—an omelet and side salad is $10, a tofu dog is $5.50, and vegetarian lasagna is $9.

INFORMATION

The excellent staff at **Dunedin Visitor Centre** (48 The Octagon, 03/474-3300, www.cityof dunedin.com; Mon.–Fri. 8:30 A.M.–5:30 P.M., Sat.–Sun. 9 A.M.–5:30 P.M.) happily provides sightseeing information, city maps, and accommodation and restaurant suggestions.

Originally funded by Andrew Carnegie, **Dunedin Public Library** (230 Moray Pl., 03/474-3690; Mon.–Fri. 9:30 A.M.–8 P.M., Sat.–Sun. 11 A.M.–4 P.M.) has a section devoted to local literature. Browse through a huge collection of used books at **Scribes** (corner of Great King and St. David Sts., 03/477-6874).

SERVICES

The post office is on the north side of the Octagon at 251 George Street. **Dunedin Public Library** (230 Moray Pl., 03/474-3690; Mon.–Fri. 9:30 A.M.–8 P.M., Sat.–Sun. 11 A.M.–4 P.M.) has free Internet access, or pay a few bucks an hour to get online at **Arc Café** (135 High St., 03/474-1135) or **A1 Internet Café** (149

George St., 03/477-5832). Most of the banks are around the Octagon and along George and Princes Streets. For travelers checks and foreign cash exchange, go to **Travelex** (346 George St., 03/477-1532).

The staff at **Sudz** (4 Howe St., 03/477-7421; Mon.–Fri. 8:30 A.M.–5 P.M., Sat. 8:30 A.M.–12:30 P.M.) does complete laundry services for you, or you can do it yourself.

Emergencies
Dunedin Hospital (201 Great King St., 03/474-0999) is three blocks north of the Octagon. For less urgent cases, head for **After Hours Doctors** (95 Hanover St., 03/479-2900, daily 24 hours). The **Urgent Pharmacy** (03/477-6344, Mon.–Fri. 6 A.M.–10 P.M., Sat.–Sun. 10 A.M.–10 P.M.) is in the same building.

GETTING THERE AND AROUND
Getting There
Dunedin Airport is 26 km (16 mi) south of the city center. Get there with **Kiwi Shuttles** (03/473-7017) for $15 per person each way. **Air New Zealand** (03/479-6594 or 0800/737-300, www.airnewzealand.com) has direct flights out of Dunedin to Wellington, Christchurch, and Auckland.

Intercity (03/474-9600, www.intercity coach.co.nz) buses run from Dunedin to Queenstown via Roxburgh and Cromwell; also to Christchurch, Invercargill, Te Anau, and Milford Sound. Buses terminate at the **Dunedin Travel Centre** (205 St. Andrews St.). Many smaller companies serve Dunedin, often using the information center as a departure point. These include **Catch-a-bus** (03/479-9960) with one service daily to Queenstown, Wanaka, and Te Anau.

Getting Around
Local transit is operated by three local companies, with timetables available at the visitor center.

Car rental agencies in Dunedin include **Avis** (03/486-2780), **Budget** (03/474-0428), **Hertz**

(03/477-7385), **National** (03/442-5887), **NZ Rent-a-car** (03/477-3895), **Pegasus** (03/477-6296), **Rent-a-dent** (03/477-7822), and **Thrifty** (03/456-3600).

For a taxi to the airport or a variety of sightseeing tours, contact **City Taxis** (03/477-1771), **Dunedin Taxis** (03/477-7777), or **Otago Taxis** (03/477-3333).

Tours
Dunedin is a large and hilly city. If you don't have a vehicle, a good way to get to all the major attractions is aboard the **Otago Explorer** (0800/322-240), which has a hop-on, hop-off service that does a one-hour loop to all the major attractions. The cost is adult $20, child $10. The same company runs a 3.5-hour Wildlife Tour out to the Otago Peninsula (Nov.–Mar.; adult $70, child $35), and a full-day tour that includes the above two tours as well as time at Larnach Castle (Nov.–Mar.; adult $130, child $65).

Citibus (03/477-5577) offers a Heritage Tour passing 15 attractions in a little over an hour (adult $18, child $9). The four-hour Otago Peninsula Tour (adult $75, child $38) doesn't include admissions to Glenfalloch, Woodland Garden, Larnach Castle, Penguin Place, and Royal Albatross Colony.

The best way to appreciate the beauty of Dunedin's harbor and the Otago Peninsula is by boat. A cruise with **Monarch Wildlife Cruises** (03/477-4276 or 0800/666-272) on the MV *Monarch* lets you experience the harbor while hearing about its marinelife, folklore, and history. Wildlife often sighted includes seals, penguins, and albatrosses. Boat one way and bus back for adult $75, child $40. The longer version (7.5 hours) takes in all the major sights and includes admissions to Glenfalloch, Woodland Garden, Larnach Castle, Penguin Place, and Royal Albatross Colony for adult $180, child $100. Refreshments and accommodation pickups are included. Boats depart from Dunedin Harbour Basin, on the corner of Wharf and Fryatt Streets.

OTAGO

Queenstown and Vicinity

Backed by the craggy Remarkables range, Queenstown (pop. 9,000) nestles along the edge of Queenstown Bay on the northeast shore of **Lake Wakatipu,** 280 km (175 mi) west of Dunedin and 530 km (330 mi) southwest of Christchurch. Beautiful Lake Wakatipu is the second largest of the southern glacial lakes (only Lake Te Anau is larger) at 77 km (48 mi) long and almost five km (3.1 mi) wide. Although several rivers feed it (the Rees and Dart are largest), only the Kawarau River drains this always-blue, crystal-clear lake. With a colorful history steeped in gold, outstanding scenery in all directions, and modern-day notoriety as the "Adventure Capital of the World," Queenstown is the most popular and attractive resort town in New Zealand.

From all over the world everyone from backpackers to celebrities congregates in this cosmopolitan melting pot, and although tourism

© ANDREW HEMPSTEAD

Look for this oversized Moa statue along the Queenstown waterfront.

is the main industry, the resort has somehow managed to retain a friendly, small-town atmosphere. Its drawbacks? Irresistible outdoor adventures and heavy-duty nighttime partying require an understanding credit card company at home—come here for a couple of days and, time and budget permitting, you're more than likely to stay a couple of weeks.

SIGHTS
The Waterfront

The best way to appreciate the Queenstown atmosphere is on foot. Start at the waterfront end of the pedestrian-only **Queenstown Mall** (also called The Mall)—a great place to people-watch, listen to accents, and meet fellow travelers. Walk east along Marine Parade into **Queenstown Gardens** (colorful any time but spectacular in autumn) and follow the walkway around the point. An interesting stop before the gardens is **Williams Cottage.** Built on the shore of the bay in 1864, it was once the home of shipwright John Williams and stayed in his family for more than a century.

From the main jetty at the end of Queenstown Mall you can watch fat trout and enormous eels cruise the clear water below while you feed the large, always-hungry duck population, or enter **Underwater World** (Marine Pde., 03/442-8437; 9 A.M.–7 P.M.; adult $5, child $3) and "catch" the action from a viewing lounge five meters (16 ft) underneath.

◖ Skyline Gondola

To orient yourself to the entire area, hop on the Skyline Gondola (Brecon St., 03/441-0101; daily 9 A.M.–10 P.M.; adult $20, child $9) for the steep ride up Bob's Peak to an observation deck 450 vertical meters (1,475 ft) above town with outstanding panoramic views of Queenstown, Lake Wakatipu, and the Remarkables. At the upper terminal is a café, restaurant (buffet lunch adult $28, child $14, dinner adult $49, child $23), theater, and gift shop. In the theater, sit back

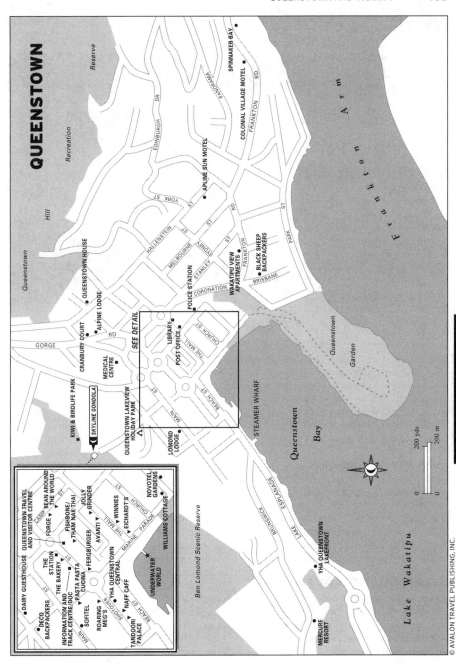

QUEENSTOWN

Recreation Reserve

Queenstown Hill

Frankton Arm

SPINNAKER BAY

COLONIAL VILLAGE MOTEL

APLINE SUN MOTEL

FRANKTON RD

PANORAMA DR

EDINBURGH DR

YORK ST

HALLENSTEIN ST

MELBOURNE ST

SYDNEY ST

STANLEY ST

CORONATION RD

QUEENSTOWN HOUSE

ALPINE LODGE

CRANBURY COURT

GORGE RD

MEDICAL CENTRE

KIWI & BIRDLIFE PARK

SKYLINE GONDOLA

QUEENSTOWN LAKEVIEW HOLIDAY PARK

POLICE STATION

SEE DETAIL

LIBRARY

POST OFFICE

THE MALL

CHURCH ST

MAIN ST

BEACH ST

WAKATIPU VIEW APARTMENTS

BLACK SHEEP BACKPACKERS

BRISBANE ST

FRANKTON RD

PARK ST

LOMOND LODGE

STEAMER WHARF

Queenstown Garden

Queenstown Bay

BRUNSWICK ST

LAKE ESPLANADE

YHA QUEENSTOWN LAKEFRONT

MERCURE RESORT

Lake Wakatipu

200 yds
200 m
0

Ben Lomond Scenic Reserve

MARINE PARADE

THE MALL

CHURCH ST

SHOTOVER ST

BEACH ST

MAIN ST

CAMP ST

BEAN AROUND THE WORLD

QUEENSTOWN TRAVEL AND VISITOR CENTRE

FORGE

FISHBONE/ THAM NAK THAI

JOLLY GRINDER

WINNIES

AVANTI

FERGBURGER

PASTA PASTA CUGINA

NOVOTEL GARDENS

EICHARDT'S

WILLIAMS COTTAGE

UNDERWATER WORLD

DAIRY GUESTHOUSE

DECO BACKPACKERS

INFORMATION AND TRACK CENTRE/DOC

THE STATION

THE BAKERY

SOFITEL

ROARING MEG'S

YHA QUEENSTOWN CENTRAL

NAFF CAFF

TANDOORI PALACE

OTAGO

© AVALON TRAVEL PUBLISHING, INC.

© ANDREW HEMPSTEAD

OTAGO

the Queenstown waterfront

and enjoy *Kiwi Magic* (adult $10, child $5), a goofy film featuring the spectacular beauty of New Zealand, with more than a splash of Kiwi Humor. A dry land **luge** run (two rides for $10) higher up the hill provides a little extra excitement: Take the fast track for the thrill (although this is relative in Queenstown) or the slow track for the views.

Kiwi and Birdlife Park

Near the gondola base, this wildlife park (Brecon St., 03/442-8059; summer daily 9 A.M.–7 P.M., the rest of the year daily 9 A.M.–6 P.M.; adult $16, child $6) is a small slice of nature on the edge of town. You can view kiwis in their natural habitat in the nocturnal house and all sorts of endemic birds in parklike surroundings.

ADRENALINE ADVENTURES

Queenstown is one of the most scenically situated towns in all of New Zealand, but it is adrenaline adventures such as bungy jumping, jetboating, white-water rafting, and parapenting that draw the crowds.

It is easy to be overwhelmed by the number of options. Before you arrive, the website www.queenstownadventure.com can give you a good overview of all the different activities. Once in town, take time to visit one or more of the downtown booking agents representing local operators. The main concentration is at the corner of Shotover and Camp Streets, where you'll find **The Station** (03/442-4007 or 0800/286-495), home to bungy booking desks as well as massive video screens showing footage of jumping, rafting, and jetboating.

◖ Bungy Jumping

Bungy jumping is one of the most popular activities in Queenstown and provides thousands of people with unforgettable memories. And once they've "jumped," many come back for more. If *you* relish the idea of diving off a canyon-spanning bridge high above a river, free-falling on the end of an elastic rope, then plunging into icy water before rocketing back toward the bridge for another fall (or two, or three, until momentum subsides), *and* surviving to tell the tale, Queenstown is the place to get your thrills.

The procedure at each of the following jumps is the same. After working out how much rope is needed, experienced operators wrap your ankles with a towel and then with the incredibly springy rope (similar to the rope used by mountain climbers). You're helped out onto a small platform and told to look straight ahead as you dive off, and then a large crowd of not-so-brave onlookers enthusiastically does a community countdown to encourage you to take the plunge. Afterward you're scooped into a boat, released from the life-saving rope, and taken to shore to walk the trail to the top for your designer bungy-jumper T-shirt (you have to jump to get one).

New Zealander A. J. Hackett, who started it all, now operates four commercial jumps in Queenstown. His first commercial operation, and the world's first, began in 1988 at the old **Kawarau Suspension Bridge** spanning the beautiful Kawarau River, 23 km (14 mi) east of Queenstown along Highway 6. The Kawarau jump costs $150, which includes a shirt, video, and transportation from

A SHORT HISTORY OF BUNGY JUMPING

Bungy jumping originated as a test of manhood on the South Pacific island of Vanuatu, where young men would throw themselves off a bamboo tower with nothing more than a vine tied around their ankles. The vine stopped their fall, just centimeters from the ground.

Various daredevils imitated the feat over the years, but it was New Zealander A. J. Hackett and his speed-skier pal Henry Van Asch who got the world's attention by jumping off the Eiffel Tower in the summer of 1987 with only a latex rubber cord separating them from fame or a very public death. The following year, Hackett opened a commercial bungy jumping site on an old suspension bridge over Queenstown's Kawarau River. The enterprise was an immediate success and led to the construction of a custom-built bridge over the Shotover River. Today, Hackett also operates jumps from the Skyline Gondola and from a gondola over the Nevis River; for a time in the mid-1990s you could also jump from a helicopter over Lake Wakatipu.

Hackett has spread his wings beyond New Zealand and you will see his name on jumps in Las Vegas, Panama, Germany, Macau, and Bali. Over 1,000,000 otherwise ordinary folk have experienced the adrenaline rush of a lifetime with Hackett's company, and there's no place better to add your name to the list than Queenstown. Or maybe you'd just like to check out his website: www.aj-hackett.com.

© ANDREW HEMPSTEAD

OTAGO

Queenstown. Expanding the notion of bungy jumping as a spectator sport, the **Kawarau Bungy Centre** (03/442-4007; daily 9 A.M.– 6 P.M.; free) is buried in the cliff face overlooking the bridge. A circular ramp leads from the parking lot above through a huge room filled with big-screen TVs and bungy memorabilia to the main floor, which opens to a viewing deck. Even if you're not jumping, it's a great place to hang out, maybe with a glass of local wine from the bar or a snack from the café. The **Secrets of Bungy Tour** ($40) is a behind-the-scenes look at how bungy jumping works.

Another Hackett jump is the **Nevis Highwire** off Skippers Canyon Bridge. Accessible only by 4WD, this 134-meter-high (440-ft-high) jump drops into a narrow and spectacular section of the canyon. It costs $210, which includes a shirt and transportation from Queenstown. This jump, from a glass-bottomed gondola, has a six-second-plus free fall. It also has a unique twist at the end—once you've bounced a couple of times, pull a release pin and swing around and into a sitting position—a perfect way to enjoy the view.

Finally, and closest to Queenstown, there's **The Ledge,** where you can plunge from a platform at the top of Skyline Gondola; $150 includes the gondola ride and a shirt. The actual bungy cord isn't very long (47 meters/154 ft), but the jump still gets the adrenaline flowing.

All Hackett jumps can be booked at **The Station** (corner of Shotover and Camp Sts., 03/442-4007 or 0800/286-495, www.ajhackett.co.nz).

🌊 Jetboating

Jetboat tours from Queenstown combine power, maneuverability in just inches of water, and skilled drivers to provide a thrilling ride through impressive river and canyon scenery. If you haven't already been on a jetboat, this is the place! Jetboats are operated on the wide, tree-lined, swift-flowing **Upper Kawarau River,** the turbulent and exciting **Shotover River** with its narrow rocky gorge and incredible scenery, and the **Lower**

Shotover River with its wide shingle riverbeds, tree-lined narrow sections, and varied terrain. Most trips last 30 minutes to an hour or so; some leave from the downtown Queenstown waterfront while others provide transportation to launch sites.

Shotover Jet (03/442-8570 or 0800/746-868) gives you one of the biggest adrenaline rushes for your money. The 30-minute trips depart every 15 minutes from Arthur's Point and include a ride to the launch site for adult $100, child $60. Operating on the tamer Kawarau River from Queenstown's Town Pier, **Kawarau Jet** (03/442-6142 or 0800/529-272; adult $89, child $49, for one hour) was the world's first commercial jetboat operation. **Twin Rivers Jet** (03/442-3257) also operates on the Kawarau, and trips are longer and less expensive than the Shotover.

White-Water Rafting

Queenstown is the self-proclaimed "Rafting Capital of New Zealand." Rivers are numerically classed from one (easy) to six (unraftable)—in the Queenstown area it's more than likely that, even if you're a total beginner, you'll be rafting a Class IV or Class V river. Trips are on the **Kawarau River** with 15 km (9 mi) of large-volume water and four thundering rapids, and on the **Lower Canyon** of the **Shotover River** with 17 km (11 mi) of Class IV roaring rapids, twisting and churning through spectacular rugged scenery to end by shooting 170 meters (560 ft) through the completely dark, narrow-walled Oxenbridge gold-miners' tunnel and down a waterfall—this trip takes guts and is the most popular. Rafting trips take 3.5–4 hours and cost about $90–130; all companies provide helmets, life jackets, and wet suits (a necessity—the water is icy), and you need to wear a swimsuit, wool socks and sandshoes or tennis shoes (some companies provide rubber booties), and a lightweight waterproof jacket. Forget the camera unless it's waterproof and floats.

Stop by Queenstown booking agents for a rundown of options, or contact **Queenstown Rafting** (35 Shotover St., 03/442-9792 or

0800/723-8464), **Extreme Green Rafting** (03/442-8517), or **Challenge Rafting** (03/442-7318 or 0800/423-836).

Flightseeing

All local flights leave from Queenstown Airport, northeast of town, near Frankton. There are shorter flights over the city, but most flights head farther afield. One of these includes a 30-minute flight across the Southern Alps to Milford Sound, a boat cruise, and the return flight for adult $380, child $255. To see the stunning mountain scenery of Mount Aspiring National Park from above, consider a 70-minute flight (adult $380, child $255) that takes in the best of the park. Flightseeing companies based at the airport include **Glenorchy Air** (03/442-2207) and **Air Fiordland** (03/442-3404 or 0800/103-404).

The Helicopter Line (03/442-3034) offers trips from the helipad by the airport that include the popular 30-minute circuit that takes in the Remarkables, Coronet Peak, and Skippers Canyon before following the Shotover River back down to Queenstown for $250.

Skydiving

If you'd rather jump out of a perfectly good airplane for kicks, contact **nzone** (35 Shotover St., 03/442-5867 or 0800/376-796). The basic tandem jump ($245), from 9,000 feet, comprises a 30-second free fall and then up to seven minutes "under the canopy." There are extra charges to have someone freefalling beside you with a still camera ($185). Jumping from a plane is intimidating enough for most people, but in the Queenstown tradition of upping the adrenaline ante, nzone offers jumps from 12,000 feet ($295) and 15,000 feet ($395). From the latter, the free fall takes almost a minute and speeds of 200 km (120 mi) per hour can be reached.

Paragliding and Hang Gliding

Another way to take to the sky for a one-way-down flightseeing adventure is by tandem paragliding from the top of the Skyline Gondola. This involves a trip up the gondola, a 15-

paragliding high above Queenstown

© ANDREW HEMPSTEAD

OTAGO

minute walk to the launch area, instruction in the handling of a paraglider (a rectangular, very maneuverable parachute that acts like a wing), followed by an airborne plunge off a hill with your guide. The cost is $185, inclusive of the gondola ride. For details, contact **Queenstown Tandem Paragliding** (03/441-8581 or 0800/759-688).

SkyTrek Tandem Hang Gliding (03/442-6311) offers yet another way to experience the mountain scenery from above. Once you're at the designated launch site (dependent on wind conditions—usually Coronet Peak or The Remarkables), a short briefing on glider operation is given before your 10- to 30-minute flight. The cost of the flight, $185, includes transfers from Queenstown and a photo from a camera mounted on the wing.

OTHER RECREATION

Not everyone comes to Queenstown looking to jump off a bridge or out of a plane, but those activities are so prevalent it is easy to miss a number of less-adventurous recreational options.

Walking Trails

The best place to get information about the many local walking trails, as well as the more serious overnight options (such as the Routeburn Track, described in the *Southland* chapter), is the Department of Conservation's **Queenstown Visitor Centre** (37 Shotover St., 03/442-7933; Dec.–Apr. daily 9 A.M.–6 P.M., May–Nov. daily 9 A.M.–5 P.M.). In the same building is the **Information and Track Centre** (37 Shotover St., 03/442-9708, www.infotrack .co.nz), which is where you go to find out the practical aspects of local walks, such as track transportation.

The **Queenstown Hill Walk** (3 km or 1.9-mi one way, one-hour each way) is a great way to absorb the scenery as you steadily climb to a vantage point for 360-degree views of Ben Lomond peak, the Skyline Gondola, Queenstown, and much of Lake Wakatipu. From the summit you can also see Coronet Peak, the Crown Range, Lake Hayes, Frankton Arm Peninsula, and the bare, craggy Remarkables Range. The track starts at the east end of Edgar Street.

The five-km (3.1-mi) **Frankton-Queenstown Walkway** wanders along the Frankton Arm shoreline of Lake Wakatipu, with views of the Remarkables and Cecil and Walter Peaks on the far side of the lake, and of Peninsula Hill. The 1.5-hour walk starts at the east end of Peninsula Street in Queenstown, passing a harbor bustling with boating activity and the fronts of private properties before reaching the north end of Frankton Recreation Reserve on the lakefront (return by bus).

Ben Lomond Walkway is a challenging 10-km (6.2-mi) climb through forest and grassland to the 1,746-meter (5,730-ft) summit of Ben Lomond. From here you can see Mount Cook in the distant northeast, Mount Aspiring and Mount Earnslaw to the north, the Remarkables and Lake Wakatipu to the southeast, Arrow Flats and Lake Hayes to the east, and Moke Creek and gorge and Moonlight Creek to the north. The track starts and finishes on Lomond Crescent (west end of Queenstown) via Skyline access road and takes about seven hours round-trip; wear sturdy shoes and take a warm jacket for the summit—the weather can change very quickly. On the return trip you can take the sidetrack to the Skyline (signposted) and catch the gondola down for a few bucks.

OTAGO

© AVALON TRAVEL PUBLISHING, INC.

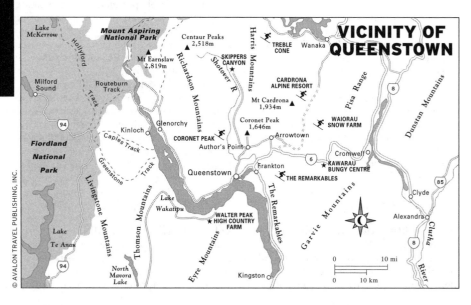

To get more out of walking trails around Queenstown, consider hiking with an experienced local guide. **Guided Walks NZ** (03/442-7126, www.nzwalks.com) charges adult $98, child $55 for an easy three-hour guided hike along the shore of Lake Wakatipu and adult $215, child $95 for a full day on the famous Routeburn Track.

Four-Wheel Driving

Filled with history from the gold-rush days, **Skippers Canyon,** north of Arthur's Point, is a hub of adrenaline activities but worth visiting in its own right. Gold was first discovered on the Shotover River, which flows through the canyon, in 1862 and was mined until the early 1990s. **Nomad Safaris** (03/442-6699) and **Queenstown Heritage Tours** (03/442-5949) offer great four-hour tours of the canyon. The adult $120, child $60 price includes four-wheel-drive transportation from Queenstown taking in Hell's Gate and Heaven's Gate; driving along Pincher's Bluff, the Blue Slip, and Devil's Elbow to Bridal Veil Falls; and crossing Skippers Bridge to the site of Skippers township. Also try your hand at gold panning.

TSS *Earnslaw*

One of the most leisurely ways to appreciate Lake Wakatipu is on the historic vintage coal-fired steamship TSS *Earnslaw,* a Queenstown landmark. Known as "The Lady of the Lake," since 1912 she's carried supplies and stock to remote farms, and in recent times, taken visitors on tours. The most popular cruise is to **Walter Peak High Country Farm** on the far side of the lake. This high-country sheep and cattle station offers sheepdog displays, sheep-shearing and wool-spinning demonstrations, horseback riding, and viewing of the only fold of highland cattle in the country. This 3.5-hour cruise departs daily for the farm, passing the spectacular scenery at the head of the lake; adult $82, child $34 includes a barbecue lunch. The TSS *Earnslaw* also departs regularly on a 1.5-hour **Midday Cruise** around Queenstown Bay and up Frankton Arm for adult $40,

child $15. Each night at 6 P.M., the **Evening Cruise** offers the option of tucking into the "Great Kiwi Carvery" at Colonels Restaurant at Walter Peak High Country Farm; adult $102, child $52. Book all these cruises through **Real Journeys** (Steamer Wharf, Beach St., 03/249-7416).

WINTER ACTIVITIES

Queenstown was traditionally a winter resort town, and it has only been in the last two decades that its popularity as a year-round destination has grown. Skiers and snowboarders from New Zealand and Australia flock to the slopes of the two local ski fields, with two additional ski fields in nearby Wanaka (see *Wanaka* section later in this chapter) from July through September.

Coronet Peak

A 30-minute drive north of Queenstown, Coronet Peak (03/442-4620, www.nzski.com; adult 89, senior and child $47) has no on-hill accommodation, but it's a very busy commercial resort suited mostly to beginners and intermediate skiers. One six-seater chair, one quad, a double, and three surface tows serve 280 hectares (700 acres) of treeless, rolling slopes. Snowmaking takes over where Mother Nature leaves off, making the season somewhat more reliable than in years past. The spread-out base lodge has ski, snowboard, and clothing rentals; a restaurant; self-service cafeteria; and various boutiques. To get to Coronet Peak, take Gorge Road north out of Queenstown for about eight km (five mi), then turn up Skippers Road—it's another eight km (5 mi) or so of sealed road to the sprawling parking lot.

The Remarkables

Owned by the same company that operates Coronet Peak, The Remarkables (03/442-4615, www.skinz.com; adult $84, senior and child $45) is tucked behind the mountain range of the same name east of Queenstown. Surrounded on three sides by towering jagged peaks, the base area is at 1,730 meters (5,680 ft), higher than Coronet Peak, and therefore

OTAGO

with somewhat more reliable snow. Three chairlifts and two surface lifts open up 220 hectares (540 acres) and 350 vertical meters (1,150 ft) of mostly intermediate and easier expert terrain. These statistics don't really give The Remarkables justice as the more experienced skiers and boarders climb or traverse to access surrounding off-piste slopes or take the Homeward Run, which ends along the access road. One thing that you definitely shouldn't miss is the short climb from the top of the Snow Basin chair to a lookout for views over Lake Wakatipu and Queenstown. Rentals, clothing, and meals are available in the day lodge. From Queenstown, follow Highway 6 through Frankton and around Lake Wakatipu to the signposted access road. From this point, it's 14 km (9 mi) along a steep, winding, and often muddy road to the base area.

Invincible Snowfields

If you thought a day schussing down the slopes of Coronet Peak or The Remarkables was as far as you could get from the mega-resorts of North America and Europe, think again. High in the remote Richardson Mountains west of Queenstown, where the only access is by helicopter, an entrepreneurial local has built a single 700-meter-long (2,300-ft-long) rope tow that opens up 230 hectares (570 acres) of intermediate terrain. Beside the tow is a two-story hut. The lower level holds a kitchen and lounge with open fire while upstairs is reserved for sleeping. For information on packages and heli-transfers, contact Invincible Snowfields (03/442-9933, www.invincible.co.nz).

NIGHTLIFE

Queenstown really hops at night—in summer and during the winter ski season, bands play in pubs and nightclubs around town almost every night, particularly on weekends—just follow your ears.

Younger locals gravitate to **Red Rock Bar and Café** (48 Camp St., 03/442-6850), which isn't the most stylish bar in Queenstown, but the beer and food is cheap, especially during the 4–6 P.M. happy hour, when a beer is just

$3.50. A backpacker hot spot, **The Edge** (corner of Camp and Man Sts., 03/442-4144) has drink and food specials most nights.

Tucked away on Searle Lane, **Barmuda** (03/442-7300) attracts moneyed locals and anyone else who can find the place. Another stylish but hidden gem is **Bardeaux** (Eureka Arcade, 03/442-8284), a wine bar with an open fire and a long list of New Zealand wines.

Pog Mahones (14 Rees St., 03/442-5382) has a large two-story deck, packed day and night through summer. Inside, Irish bands play most nights. Another pub-style place is **Dux de Lux** (14 Church St., 03/442-9688), a small stone building with its own in-house brewery and live music on weekends.

Fun and funky, **Chico's Restaurant and Bar** (in Queenstown Mall, 03/442-8439) is very popular with all ages and occasionally provides live entertainment.

The most stylish spot for a drink is **Eichardt's House Bar** (Marine Pde., 03/441-0450), in a historic downtown hotel that is also one of New Zealand's most exclusive accommodations.

You'll find DJs spinning until dawn at **Subculture** (below Dux de Lux at 14 Church St., 03/442-7685), while **Surreal** (7 Rees St., 03/441-8492) is a little more alternative.

The **Skyline Restaurant** (Skyline Gondola, Brecon St., 03/441-0101) has a bar with great views and there's often live entertainment in the main dining area.

If you have your own transportation or don't mind taking a taxi, head to **Arthur's Point Tavern** (461 Gorge Rd., Arthur's Point, 03/442-8007), which is especially busy as an après-ski stop in winter.

ACCOMMODATIONS AND CAMPING

You can get anything you want in Queenstown—from basic rooms that share bathrooms to luxurious first-class international-standard hotel rooms. Pick your price range and go from there.

Room rates in Queenstown fluctuate greatly throughout the year. All rates quoted below are for a standard double room in summer

(Dec.–Feb.). Rates are higher in busy winter season (late June–late Sept.) and lower the rest of the year. Regardless of the season, use the Internet to find the best rates.

Under $50

In the heart of downtown and just one block back from the lake, **YHA Queenstown Central** (48 Shotover St., 03/442-7400, www.yha.co.nz; dorm beds $25, $95 s, $105–115 d) is a well-run backpacker lodge where the private rooms all have en suites. Further along the waterfront, **YHA Queenstown Lakefront** (88–90 Lake Esplanade, 03/442-8413, www.yha.co.nz; dorm beds $23–26, $68 d) is larger (around 150 beds), but has more space to move around.

Opposite Queenstown Lakeview Holiday Park, **Deco Backpackers** (52 Man St., 03/442-7384, www.decobackpackers.co.nz; dorm beds $24, $27–29 d or twin, en suites $70 s or d) is a small, friendly place with a relaxed vibe and a quiet garden.

$50-100

Centrally located is **Black Sheep Backpackers** (13 Frankton Rd., 03/442-7289, www.blacksheepbackpackers.co.nz; dorm beds $26, $60 d). Rooms in this converted low-rise motel are large (with up to 10 dorm beds in each). Facilities include a pool room, bar, spa pools, and a communal kitchen.

A two-minute walk from town is smaller **Alpine Lodge** (13 Gorge Rd., 03/442-7220, www.alpinelodgebackpackers.co.nz; dorm beds $26, $58 d), with just 26 beds, and **Hippo Lodge** (4 Anderson Heights, 03/442-5785, www.hippolodge.co.nz; camping $15 per person, dorm beds $26, $38 s, $65–80 d), in the same vicinity.

Overlooking Steamer Wharf, **Thomas's Hotel** (50 Beach St., 03/442-7180, www.thomashotel.co.nz; dorm beds $35, $89–149 s or d) is in the heart of the action. It mainly caters to backpackers, but has double rooms with en suites, and a couple of spacious corner rooms with lake views. All private rooms have a TV, fridge, and tea- and coffee-making facilities. The hotel also holds a café, laundry, and bike rentals.

$100-150

Many of Queenstown's mid-priced motels have been replaced in the last decade, while others, such as ◖ **Colonial Village Motel** (136 Frankton Rd., 03/442-7629 or 0800/226-652, www.colonialvillage.co.nz) are in transition. At the time of publication, nine older motel-style units were clinging to a steep hillside ($110 s, $115 d). Each has a kitchen and lake and mountain views that will make you think you're paying a lot more than you are. Note that these rooms are only accessible via very steep steps. At the top of the property is Earnslaw View Apartments ($275–415 s or d), a row of modern units with even better views.

Back toward town, **Wakatipu View Apartments** (14 Frankton Rd., 03/442-7463, www.wakaview.co.nz; $115–190 s or d) comprises 12 chalet-style units with kitchens.

Another decent choice in this price bracket is **Alpine Sun Motel** (18 Hallenstein St., 03/442-8482 or 0800/101-914, www.alpinesun.co.nz; $105–125 s or d), with small, comfortable self-contained units within walking distance of downtown. A two-bedroom unit for $160 is one of the better deals in town for families.

Moving up slightly in style and closer to downtown than the other options detailed above, **Lomond Lodge** (33 Man St., 03/442-8235, www.lomondlodge.com) has self-contained units from $125 s or d, but I recommend upgrading to the lake-view rooms ($145), which also have balconies. Out back is a peaceful garden with a barbecue for guest use.

$150-200

Along Gorge Road toward Arrowtown, **Cranbury Court** (19–23 Gorge Rd., 03/442-6483 or 0800/269-666, www.cranbury.co.nz; $160–320 s or d) is a French Provincial–style motel of 23 self-contained units, each with one or more bedrooms, sliding doors opening to a private courtyard, and an impressive entertainment system.

$200-250

Stella Resorts Group (www.stellaresorts.co.nz) manages nine properties in town, including

OTAGO

BreakFree Alpine Village (633 Frankton Rd., 03/450-2000 or 0800/275-373; $211–265 s or d), where the modern units come with kitchens, TV/DVD combos, air-conditioning, and balconies with lake views. Alpine Village is along the lake five km (3.1 mi) toward from Frankton.

In modern ◖ **Queenstown House** (69 Hallenstein St., 03/442-9043, www.queens townhouse.co.nz; $225–295 s or d, villas $395–895), you'll find a luxurious "homey" atmosphere and eight bright, individually country-style furnished rooms each with a private bathroom, lake or mountain views, and a king-size bed. The adjacent "villas" have plenty of room to move around and balconies with lake views. Breakfast is a grand affair in the elegant dining room, and each evening guests can indulge in a complimentary wine and cheese platter.

$250-300

Modern and stylish **Mercure Resort** (Sainsbury Rd., 03/442-6600 or 0800/444-422, www.accorhotels.co.nz; $250–380 s or d) is a self-contained resort on the main road into Queenstown overlooking magnificent Lake Wakatipu. The 148 rooms are fairly standard, but with the views, a large outdoor heated pool, fitness room, two tennis courts, three eateries, and shuttle service to downtown and the airport, it provides good value, especially with discounted online rates.

Tucked below the busy road between Queenstown and Frankton, **Spinnaker Bay** (151 Frankton Rd., 03/442-5050 or 0800/005-577, www.spinnaker.co.nz) offers unimpeded views across the lake to the Remarkables and an indoor pool. Each well-appointed unit features separate bedrooms, a modern kitchen, and a wood-burning fireplace. Rates range from $295 s or d for a one-bedroom unit to $325 for three bedrooms.

$300-400

Built back in the 1920s, ◖ **Dairy Guesthouse** (10 Isle St., 03/442-5164 or 0800/333-393, www.thedairy.co.nz; $360–390 s, $390–420 d)

incorporates a dairy (general store) and adjacent house. Converted to an upscale bed-and-breakfast, the setting is halfway between country and contemporary, with 13 well-appointed rooms, a courtyard with an outdoor fireplace, and wireless Internet throughout. The rates include a cooked breakfast.

$400-500

Novotel Gardens Queenstown (corner Marine Pde. and Earl St., 03/442-7750 or 0800/444-422, www.accorhotels.co.nz; $430 s or d) features more than 200 well-appointed rooms surrounding a courtyard filled with gardens and outdoor furniture. The hotel's smart-casual restaurant is open for breakfast and dinner, but in summer it's a barbecue in the courtyard that draws the biggest crowd. Disregard the rack rates, and look to pay around $200 online.

Over $500

At the apex of local luxury, **Sofitel Queenstown** (8 Duke St., 03/450-0045 or 0800/444-422, www.accorhotels.co.nz; $975 s or d) fulfills the needs of the rich and famous looking to stay in downtown Queenstown with a company known around the world for its elegant accommodation. The 82 oversized guest rooms are outfitted with everything from LCD TVs to espresso machines while guests are tended to by professional, confident staff. Online rates occasionally dip below $500.

Once a grand country estate, **Remarkables Lodge** (595 Kingston Rd., 03/442-2720, www .remarkables.co.nz; $990–1,475 s or d) lies south of town on the road to Te Anau. While none of the building's character was lost during restoration, no expense was spared either, and today guests enjoy a heated swimming pool, hot tub, snooker room, tennis court, library, and comfortable lounge with a log fire. Guests take meals in an elegant dining room that opens to a courtyard and the pool, and the lodge is licensed to serve alcohol. Each of the six guest rooms, as well as the Garden Suite (originally a shepherd's cottage), are individually decorated, feature king-size beds, and boast luxurious private bathrooms. Rates include a gourmet breakfast, pre-dinner drinks, a three-course dinner, and airport transfers. **Eichardt's Private Hotel** (Marine Pde., 03/441-0450, www.eichardtshotel.co.nz; $1,275–1,495 s, $1,375–1,595 d) is quite simply one of New Zealand's finest accommodations. Dating to the gold-rush era and damaged by flooding in 1999, this historic property across the road from the lake was saved from the wrecking ball and now offers five huge guest rooms, each with king beds, heated floors, and luxurious bathrooms. Rates include breakfast and evening wine-tasting in the parlor.

Holiday Parks

Queenstown Lakeview Holiday Park (Upper Brecon St., 03/442-7252 or 0800/482-735, www.holidaypark.net.nz) is a large campground with many rules and regulations to keep the crowd in order. Aside from the usual communal bathroom, kitchen, and laundry, there's a fully stocked shop on the premises. Tent sites are $16 per person, powered sites $18 per person, and modern self-contained units range $90–110 s or d.

At **Queenstown Top 10 Holiday Park Creeksyde** (Robins Rd., 03/442-9447 or 0800/786-222), campsites have been developed around a central building that has modern bathrooms, kitchen, laundry, and spacious lounge with TV and video. Rates are the same as Queenstown Lakeview Holiday Park.

FOOD

In a town changing so rapidly, it's amazing that many of the best cafés and restaurants have been around for a decade or more. You'll find the best of these recommended below, along with the latest hot spots.

Cafés and Quick Bites

Naff Caff (66 Shotover St., 03/442-8211; daily for breakfast and lunch) opens early for good coffee, muffins, and cookies. At lunch, a wide range of breads is stuffed with healthy filings for $6–9. Other places to get a caffeine fix include **Bean Around the World** (11 Athol St.,

03/441-2440; daily from 7:30 A.M.); **Forge** (18 Athol St., 03/409-0346; daily 8 A.M.–3 P.M.), a small place that catches the morning sun; and **Jolly Grinder** (22 The Mall, 03/441-8588; daily from 8 A.M.), a hole-in-the-wall place also serving cooked breakfasts.

Vesta (Marine Pde., 03/442-5687; daily 9 A.M.–5 P.M.) is within a tiny cottage that has changed little since 1864. Most surprisingly it's located across from the lake in the heart of downtown. The main business is selling homewares, but Vesta has an espresso machine and a few outdoor tables—the perfect escape from the surrounding commercialism.

For cakes, pastries, and meat pies, head to **The Bakery** (15 Shotover St., 03/442-8698; daily 6 A.M.–6 P.M.)—the steak, garlic, and mustard pie is a treat.

Burgers and Pizza

Fergburger (42 Shotover St., 03/441-1232; daily 10:30 A.M.–5 A.M.) is a trendy spot that is busiest when the surrounding bars and nightclubs close. A regular burger is $8.50 while options like Sweet Bambi (venison with Thai plum chutney) sell for up to $14. It's an order-at-the-counter place with a few chairs along wall counters.

You'll hear the bustle before walking up the narrow stairs leading to **Winnies** (7 The Mall, 03/442-8635; daily from noon), which fills with casual diners looking for gourmet pizza and a good time. The most sought-after seats are on the balcony, but on warm nights the entire roof is retracted. The menu includes all the usual suspects, as well as tasty combos such as chicken, cranberry, and brie. A single-serve pizza is $14.50, a medium $23.50, and a large $28.50.

Cow Restaurant (Cow Lane off Beach St., 03/442-8588; daily noon–11 P.M.) has undoubtedly the best pizza in town, an open fireplace that's very appealing when the evenings get chilly, good music, and a jovial, laid-back atmosphere as guests wait around the fire for their turn to sit and tuck in. A large variety of pizza sizes and combinations range $15–30, various spaghetti dishes are $12–17, and crisp

OTAGO

green salads, homemade soup, garlic bread, and desserts complete your meal. It has a BYO license (the bottle shop in Cow Lane has a great selection of cold wines and beers), and is very popular with the locals—expect to wait for a table, or go in early (5:30 P.M.), put down your name, and return later.

Asian and Middle Eastern

For reasonably priced Thai, consider **Tham Nak Thai** (7 Beach St., 03/441-3585; daily for lunch and dinner), where nearly every main is under $20. The dishes are more traditional than your average small-town Thai restaurant, but the menu is marked with English translations and heat indicators.

Part of a South Island chain, **Tandoori Palace** (62 Shotover St., 03/409-2845; daily from 5 P.M.) has a relaxed and inviting atmosphere. Predictable mains such as butter chicken and lamb vindaloo are all under $15, although you'll want to order sides like papadums and mango chutney.

Habebes Lebanese Takeaways (in Wakatipu Arcade off Rees St., 03/442-9861; daily from 10 A.M.) has excellent kebabs (meat- and salad-filled rolls) for $6.50–10, and an assortment of other Lebanese delicacies—all tasty, all reasonable in price.

Italian

One of many Italian restaurants in Queenstown is **Avanti** (20 The Mall, 03/442-8503; daily 7 A.M.–10 P.M.). Like other popular restaurants in town, you can't just walk in and get a table, but the wait is usually worthwhile. Typical Italian fare and seafood dishes (fresh from the sea on Wednesday) are the specialties, though if you take a look at the desserts you may beg to differ. The atmosphere is relaxed and jovial and the service is excellent. Expect to pay $24–34 for a dinner main.

Another great Italian place, this one a little more casual, is **Pasta Pasta Cucina** (6 Brecon St., 03/442-6762), a long, narrow restaurant with lamb spaghetti bolognese for $17, venison stroganoff for $20, and smoked salon and corn pasta for $25. The pasta is made in-house.

Local Cuisine

In a gold rush–era cottage, **Roaring Megs** (53 Shotover St., 03/442-9676; Tues.–Sun. from 6:15 P.M.) has been one of Queenstown's favorite restaurants for over a quarter of a century. The menu has changed with the times, and is now filled with modern interpretations of classic Kiwi dishes. Soups ($10) are creative and hearty, while mains such as baked venison with poached pear and beetroot confit range $28–36. Save room for the chocolate mousse ($11.50).

Like Roaring Meg's, 【 **Gantley's** (seven km/4.3 mi north of town on Arthur's Point Rd., 03/442-8999; daily from 6:30 P.M.) is in a goldrush–era building. This elegant dining room features crisp white-linen tablecloths, muted lighting, and attentive service. The food is equally classy; start with the Caesar salad, complete with anchovies and warmed croutons ($16.50), before moving onto mains including blackcurrant and herb crusted rack of lamb ($38). Gantley's wine list is regarded as the finest in New Zealand.

While most restaurants clamor for high-traffic locations, 【 **The Bunker** (Cow Lane, 03/441-8030; daily from 5 P.M.) is so assured of its reputation for top-notch cooking it does just fine with little fanfare down a back alley. The menu is filled with the latest trends in modern New Zealand cooking (think caramelized duck breast with pineapple and cherry sauerkraut). It's also one of the town's most expensive restaurants, with starters to $29 and mains ranging $30–48.

Seafood

Queenstown is a long way from the ocean, but **Fishbone Bar & Grill** (7 Beach St., 03/442-6768; daily from 5:30 P.M.) does seafood well, in a bright and breezy space and at a reasonable price. Oysters, whitebait, and muttonbird are all seasonal, while salmon smoked over a cedar plank ($11) is a year-round starter and fish burgers ($20) and shark vindaloo ($25) are typical of the mains.

Boardwalk Seafood Restaurant (Steamer Wharf, Beach St., 03/442-5630; daily from

6 P.M.) is excellent in all regards. The menu changes with the seasons, but there's always a wide variety of starters, such as seafood chowder (from $12.50), and a daily fish special that may be barbecued *hapuka* smothered in a garlic-based mayonnaise ($35). Although the Boardwalk is a touristy, upscale restaurant, the setting is unpretentious and presentation of food stylish.

Food with a View

At the upper terminal of the gondola, **Skyline Restaurant** (Brecon St., 03/441-0101; daily for lunch and dinner) holds 300 diners on two tiers, with most tables having fantastic views of Queenstown and its reflections twinkling in the lake far below. The tourist-oriented buffet is $28 at lunch and $49 at dinner; gondola extra. For something a little less substantial, head for the gondola café, which opens to a table-filled terrace.

INFORMATION

Destination Queenstown (www.queens town-nz.co.nz) promotes the town around the world. Once you arrive, head for the **Queenstown Travel and Visitor Centre** (corner of Shotover and Camp Sts., 03/442-2800, www.queenstown-vacation.com; daily 8:30 A.M.–5 P.M., longer hours in summer).

For information on Mount Aspiring and Fiordland National Parks, regional hiking-track details, maps, trail conditions, and hut passes, visit the Queenstown Visitor Centre of the **Department of Conservation** (37 Shotover St., 03/442-7933; daily 8:30 A.M.–5 P.M.). Next door is the **Information and Track Centre** (37 Shotover St., 03/442-9708, www.infotrack .co.nz), for more of the same plus walking-trail transportation information and bookings.

Queenstown Library (10 Gorge Rd., 03/441-0600; Mon.–Sat. 10 A.M.–5 P.M.) has newspapers from throughout New Zealand as well as free Internet access.

SERVICES

A shopper's delight, Queenstown has an incredible variety of stores selling handcrafted articles such as sheepskin, wool, leather, and suede goods; local pottery; greenstone jewelry; and Maori woodcarvings. There's also innumerable outdoor clothing and camping outlets, ski and snowboard shops, and all manner of chic boutiques.

The post office is on Camp Street near the top of the Queenstown Mall. Send and receive email at **Budget Communications** (upstairs in O'Connell's Shopping Centre, 309 Camp St., 03/441-1562) or **Internet Outpost** (27 Shotover St., 03/441-3018).

Emergency

For an ambulance call 03/441-1600. For medical care, go to **Lakes District Hospital** (20 Douglas St., Frankton, 03/441-0015) or the **Queenstown Medical Centre** (9 Isle St., 03/441-0500; Mon.–Fri. 8:30 A.M.–9 P.M.). **Bradley's Pharmacy** (03/442-8338) is open daily 8 A.M.–10 P.M.

GETTING THERE

Air

Queenstown Airport is nine km (5.6 mi) east of town at Frankton, flanked by the Remarkables to the south, Richardson Mountains to the north, and Lake Wakatipu to the east. Flying into Queenstown is an unforgettable experience—the approach is awe-inspiring and knuckle-clenching at the same time. **Air New Zealand** (0800/737-000, www.airnewzealand .com) has direct flights linking Queenstown to Auckland, Christchurch, and Wellington (don't plan to travel between Queenstown and the southern cities of Invercargill and Dunedin by air—these flights are routed through Christchurch). **Qantas** (0800/808-767) has direct flights between Sydney, Australia, and Queenstown.

Super Shuttle (03/442-3639) is at the airport for all arrivals. This is a door-to-door service costing $12 per person each way. You can save a few bucks by catching the scheduled **Connectabus** (03/441-4471), which departs the airport six times daily for the top of Queenstown Mall ($7). A cab between downtown and the airport runs about $25.

OTAGO

OTAGO

Bus

To find out schedules and current prices, and to book ongoing transportation, call in at **Queenstown Travel and Visitor Centre** (corner of Shotover and Camp Sts., 03/442-4100), which is also the booking office and pickup point for **Intercity** (www.intercity coach.co.nz) buses. From Queenstown, Intercity has regular buses to Christchurch, via the west coast to Greymouth and Nelson, and through Te Anau to Invercargill and Dunedin. Many small shuttle companies provide service to Queenstown. With an extensive timetable is **Atomic Shuttles** (03/442-8178); its shuttles link Queenstown with Dunedin, Christchurch, Greymouth, and Picton. **Real Journeys** (Steamer Wharf, Beach St., 03/249-7416 or 0800/656-501) offers transport from Queenstown to Te Anau and Milford Sound, with packages including cruises the best deal.

To get to Arrowtown, consider **Arrow Express** (03/442-1900), which departs five times a day from the top of Queenstown Mall.

Tracknet (03/249-7777, www.tracknet.net) is designed for hikers, but everyone is welcome to jump aboard their shuttle buses, which depart the corner of Shotover and Camp Streets for all major walking tracks, Te Anau, Milford Sound, and Invercargill.

GETTING AROUND

The local transit bus is **Connectabus** (03/441-4471), which runs daily along three routes: to Sunshine Bay, to the airport, and to Arrowtown. Sector fares range adult $5–7, child $2–4.

Car and Bike Rentals

The main car rental agencies are **Avis** (03/442-3808), **Budget** (03/442-9274), **Hertz** (03/442-4106), **NZ Rent-a-car** (03/442-7465), **Rent-a-dent** (03/442-9922), and **Thrifty** (03/442-3532). A recommended local company is **Queenstown Car Rentals** (03/442-9220).

Vertigo Bikes (4 Brecon St., 03/442-8378) rents mountain bikes from $12 per hour.

Taxi

Queenstown taxi companies include **Taxi Alpine** (03/442-6666) and **Queenstown Taxis** (03/442-7788).

Queenstown Water Taxi (03/442-8665) runs from the Marine Parade wharf to all points of Lake Wakatipu, including the golf course ($25 per person) and Walter Peak ($120 per boat).

◖ ARROWTOWN

Magnificent scenery abounds in all directions from Queenstown, but for a scenic 28-km (17-mi) drive that ends at one of New Zealand's most picturesque towns, head north out of Queenstown on Arthur's Point Road to Arrowtown (pop. 2,200), which began as Foxes, a wild and unruly gold-mining settlement, when gold was discovered in the Arrow River in 1862. A memorial marks the "golden" spot, an 800-meter (2,600-ft) walk upstream from the present township. The river was soon famous as one of the richest alluvial goldfields

The peaceful Arrow River was once a hive of activity.

© ANDREW HEMPSTEAD

in the world, attracting hordes of miners from everywhere.

Sights

More than 60 of Arrowtown's gold rush–era buildings remain, many along narrow Buckingham Street, which is also home to the **Lakes District Museum** (49 Buckingham St., 03/442-1824; daily 8:30 A.M.–5 P.M.; adult $5, child $1). Beyond this downtown core, you can appreciate the original gold-mining character by strolling along the tree-lined streets of miners' cottages, or wandering down to the river, where it's easy to spend at least an hour reading the interpretive boards and wandering along tree-lined walking trails. Also down along the river is the **Chinese Settlement** (Villiers St.; donation), where a number of huts have been restored. If you feel like trying your luck at panning for gold, rent a pan from the visitor center.

For an enjoyable walk from Arrowtown, consider walking 13 km (8 mi) up the Arrow River (about 30 river crossings) to the ghost town of **Macetown.** There's not much left, but the three remaining buildings and machinery of a once-thriving gold town are protected. Allow six to eight hours for the round-trip.

Accommodations

A five-minute walk from downtown, **Poplar Lodge** (4 Merioneth St., 03/442-1466, www .poplarlodge.co.nz; dorm beds $23, $55 s, $62 d, en suite cottage $95 s or d) is a two-story purpose-built backpacker lodge with pleasant gardens.

Perfectly priced between a backpacker lodge and the more-expensive Millbrook is **Shades of Arrowtown** (9 Merioneth St., 03/442-1613, www.shadesofarrowtown.co.nz; $100–200 s or d), a quiet complex of nine units set around parklike surroundings. Some have kitchens and everyone has use of a laundry and barbecue area.

Millbrook (Malaghan Rd., 03/441-7000 or 0800/800-604, www.millbrook.co.nz), New Zealand's original resort and residential community, continues to expand. Guests enjoy one

© ANDREW HEMPSTEAD

Arrowtown is filled with historic buildings.

of the country's premier golf courses (guest greens fees $45; $135 for non-guests), a fitness room, tennis courts, an indoor swimming pool, and a variety of cafés and restaurants. Accommodation choices range from spacious hotel rooms, each with a private balcony fireplace and walk-in wardrobe ($390 s or d), to luxurious estate homes ($2,250). Check the Millbrook website for multi-night packages that include golf and spa services.

Food

Do what the locals do and start your day at the **Arrowtown Bakery** (Ballarat Arcade, Buckingham St., 03/442-1589; daily 8 A.M.–4:30 P.M.) with an espresso. The food is all fresh and tasty—scones, apple strudel, and venison pies all get top marks.

Dating from the gold rush, the **New Orleans Hotel** (27 Buckingham St., 03/442-1745; daily from 7:30 A.M.) is a traditional pub squeezed between other historic buildings along the main street. Cooked breakfasts are around $15, a roast dinner is also $15, and other mains are

OTAGO

around $25. The downstairs bar opens to outdoor tables overlooking the river.

Back when horses were the main form of transportation, overnight guests at the New Orleans Hotel would tether their mount across the road in an old stone building that has been converted to **Stables Restaurant** (28 Buckingham St., 03/442-1818; daily for lunch and dinner), a casual dining room with outdoor tables set back from the street.

Information

Arrowtown Visitor Centre (49 Buckingham St., 03/442-1824; daily 8:30 A.M.–5 P.M.) shares space with the museum. It's at the east end of the main street, but it's easiest to park down by the river.

Getting There

Intercity (03/442-8238, www.intercity coach.co.nz) stops in Arrowtown on request, but a better option is **Arrow Express** (03/442-1900), which departs five times daily from the top end of Queenstown Mall for Arrowtown. The round-trip fare is adult $25, child $10.

GLENORCHY

A super-scenic 50-km (31-mi) drive west from Queenstown brings you to the head of Lake Wakatipu and Glenorchy (pop. 220), a small village that seems a world away from the commercialism of Queenstown. For outdoor enthusiasts, Glenorchy is best known as the starting point for a number of overnight walking trails, such as the **Routeburn Track** (see *Fiordland National Park and Vicinity* in the *Southland* chapter), but it offers plenty of other activities.

The picturesque drive along Lake Wakatipu alone is worth the trip out from Queenstown, but the scenery only gets better beyond the village, where a rough road leads into the Rees and Dart Valleys, used for locations in the *Lord of the Rings* trilogy—Ithilien, the Misty Mountains, Wizard's Vale, Isengard, and more. The local visitor center has brochures detailing short walks in this area.

Horseback Riding

Signposted from the center of the village, **Dart Stables** (Coll St., 03/442-5688) offers guided trips through high-country farmland with magnificent mountain views and along remote river valleys. A two-hour ride to the delta where the Rees and Dart Rivers drain into Lake Wakatipu is adult $105, child $95, but the most popular option is the five-hour Ride of the Rings (adult $155, child $145 including transportation from Queenstown), which traverses numerous *Lord of the Rings* filming sites.

Jetboating

If you're looking for a combination of wind-whipping-through-your-hair excitement, outrageously beautiful mountain scenery, and a small, friendly group, I recommend **Dart River Safaris** (03/442-9992 or 0800/327-8538) over the more commercial operations operating out of Queenstown. These trips start with a thrilling 90-minute jetboat ride, after which it's a peaceful 30-minute walk to the highway from where a shuttle bus transports you back to Glenorchy. The cost is adult $179, child $89.50 (adult $209, child $104.50 from Queenstown).

Accommodations and Food

◖ **Glenorchy Hotel** (Mull St., 03/442-9902, www.glenorchynz.com) provides cheerful private rooms with old-fashioned decor, gorgeous views, and a communal TV lounge. Rates are $85–115 s or d, with the less expensive units sharing a bathroom. Backpackers are catered to in comfortable dormitories costing $22 per person per night. You'll find the usual communal facilities at **Glenorchy Holiday Park** (Oban St., 03/442-9939; tent sites $9 per person, powered sites $10 per person, cabins $32 s or d, self-contained lakeside cottages $80 s or d), plus a camp store, storage for hikers doing the tracks, transportation to the tracks, and jetboat tours.

Glenorchy Café (Mull St., 03/442-9958; Oct.–May daily 7 A.M.–8:30 P.M., the rest of the year breakfast and lunch only) has an appealing outdoorsy vibe, and lots of outdoor tables—the perfect spot to enjoy the summer sun. The restaurant in the **Glenorchy Hotel** (Mull St., 03/442-9902) receives great raves from *everyone* who has eaten there. It offers typical no-frills, hotel-style dining, with hearty portions and friendly service.

Practicalities

Many Queenstown tour operators include Glenorchy in their itineraries, or you can get there on the **Backpacker Express** (03/442-9939). Buses run in either direction at least once every two hours, continuing beyond the village to all trailheads.

The **Glenorchy Visitor Centre** (03/442-0303; summer daily 8:30 A.M.–5 P.M., the rest of the year Mon.–Fri. 8:30 A.M.–5 P.M.) is at the corner of Mull and Oban Streets.

QUEENSTOWN TO FIORDLAND NATIONAL PARK

There are three ways to get to Fiordland National Park from Queenstown: via Highway 6 to Te Anau (180 km/112 mi); by air to Te Anau or Milford Sound; or, for the adventurous, by foot on the Routeburn Track. If you have your own transportation, take the main road northeast out of Queenstown to Frankton, then Highway 6 south between the Remarkables and Lake Wakatipu.

Kingston, at the south end of the lake, is the starting point for trips on the **Kingston Flyer** (03/248-8848; adult $40, child $20), a vintage steam train that runs along a historic section of track to Fairlight. Pullman green carriages with original wood interiors, black metal and polished brass engine, plume of black smoke, shrill whistle, and staff in period costume take you back to the days of the early 1900s when the Flyer first ran between Kingston and Gore. The round-trip takes 90 minutes and costs adult $40, child $20. Departures are October–April daily at 10 A.M. and 1:30 P.M.

Continuing south from Kingston, you come to **Lumsden**—an angler's paradise with five trout-filled rivers crisscrossing the countryside within a relatively short distance of town. Just before Lumsden, Highway 94 branches west to Te Anau, Manapouri, and Fiordland National Park, and east to Gore.

Fiordland National Park is detailed in the *Southland* chapter.

Wanaka and Vicinity

Encircled by mountains and nestled at the southern end of the crystal-clear, bright-blue waters of **Lake Wanaka,** the four-season resort town of Wanaka (pop. 7,000) lies 70 km (43 mi) northeast, but seemingly a world away, from Queenstown. You can reach Wanaka from Queenstown via Cromwell, but the most direct route is the Crown Range Road (also known as Cardrona Valley Rd.), which climbs from Arrow Junction, 20 km (12 mi) east of Queenstown along Highway 6, into a treeless alpine environment and passes the historic gold-rush town of Cardrona before descending to Wanaka, which rivals Queenstown for scenic setting. The approach from the west coast is equally scenic, with Highway 6 winding over the Haast Pass to Lakes Wa-naka and Hawea, a distance of 140 km (87 mi) from Haast.

Wanaka has always played second fiddle to its more famous neighbor in the tourism stakes, but the town is in the middle of a mini-boom, with lots of new development and a growing realization that the region has a lot going for it, including the combination of year-round wonderful weather and beautiful scenery.

SIGHTS

Wanaka has a few official attractions, but the main draw is outdoor recreation, which is covered in the following sections.

◀ Puzzling World

Three km (1.9 mi) east of town, Puzzling

© ANDREW HEMPSTEAD

Leaning Tower of Wanaka, Puzzling World

World (Hwy. 6, 03/443-7489; daily 8:30 A.M.–5:30 P.M., until 8 P.M. in summer; adult $10, child $7) is easily recognized by the Leaning Tower of Wanaka rising from the front entrance. Stop at this popular local attraction to lose yourself in a 1.6-km (one-mi) three-dimensional maze of wooden passages, under- and over-bridges, room where you appear taller than in reality, a Tilting House, and a hall of holograms that can tease you for 30 minutes to several hours. At the adjoining puzzle center, all kinds of puzzles are demonstrated and you're encouraged to try them out yourself.

New Zealand Fighter Pilots Museum

New Zealand provided the Allies with the largest number of airmen per capita during World War II, so it's not surprising that the country also holds one of the world's largest collections of airworthy World War II airplanes, housed at Wanaka Airport (Hwy. 8, 12 km/7.5 mi east of Wanaka, 03/443-7010; daily 9 A.M.–4 P.M.; adult $10, child

$5). In addition to 50-odd restored planes from both world wars—complete with colorful descriptions of the pilots who flew them and historical photos of all the action—it shows World War II film footage, has interactive computer programs, holds a roll of honor that remembers each of New Zealand's fighter pilots, and showcases an assortment of military and vintage machines.

Every second year (even years) over the Easter long weekend, Wanaka hosts **Warbirds over Wanaka** (03/443-8619, www.warbirds overwanaka.com; day passes $40–60), one of the world's premier vintage airshows.

Rippon Vineyard

One of New Zealand's most photogenic wineries is **Rippon Vineyard** (246 Mount Aspiring Rd., 03/443-8084; daily Dec.–Apr. 11 A.M.–5 P.M., July–Nov. 1:30–4:30 P.M.), four km (2.5 mi) west of town. Otago is the world's southernmost wine-growing region, but a high spring rainfall followed by long, dry summer days produces perfect grapes come harvest time. Rippon has 14 hectares (35 acres) of producing vines. The grapes are mostly Pinot Noir and Riesling. Aside from tasting, there's Golfcross (golf played with an oval ball) and an outdoor music festival on the first weekend of February (even-numbered years only).

SUMMER RECREATION
Walking Trails

Both local visitor centers have copies of *Wanaka Walks and Tracks* ($1), detailing trails in and around Wanaka. One of the most popular, with both walkers and cyclists, is the **Millennium Walkway,** which begins from the downtown lakefront and follows the lake west for three km (1.9 mi) to Waterfall Creek.

Eely Point Walk also starts downtown, but leads off in the opposite direction to Eely Point (20 minutes one-way).

For fabulous panoramic views, climb to the top of **Mount Iron** (527 meters/1,730 ft) in Mount Iron Reserve, off the main highway into town. The reserve is known for lizards, abundant birdlife, and semi-arid vegetation.

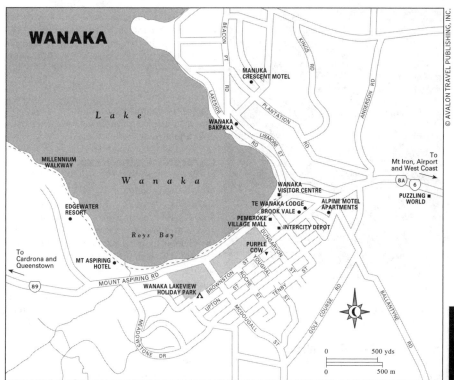

WANAKA

© AVALON TRAVEL PUBLISHING, INC.

OTAGO

Return along the eastern face for a 1.5-hour round-trip.

The more energetic, in search of an even better view, can climb to the top of **Roy's Peak** (1,585 meters/5,200 ft)—you can see almost the entire lake, its islands, the rivers flowing in and out, plus a spectacular view of Mount Aspiring and surrounding glaciers and valleys. This eight-km (five-mi) track (allow three hours each way) starts six km (3.7 mi) along Mount Aspiring Road west of town. (The trail is closed Oct.–Nov. for the lambing season.) Farther along Mount Aspiring Road is **Diamond Lake.** A signpost on the right side of the road marks the beginning of a short trail (15 minutes one-way) to the lake.

Eco Wanaka Adventures (03/443-2869) offers a large number of outdoor adventures, including a hiking trip to Rob Roy Glacier for $180, and a cruise/walk combo to Mou Waho Island for $130.

Water Activities

In a lakefront building across the road from downtown, **Lakeland Adventures** (100 Ardmore St., 03/443-7495) is a clearing center for all lake activities. The fastest of these is a jet-boat ride on the *Clutha River Jet.* The exhilarating 60-minute trip departs daily every hour and on demand and costs adult $75, child $35. Fishing charters chasing rainbow and brown trout cost around $300 per boat for two hours, which includes all the equipment. This company also rents canoes, kayaks, aqua-bikes, small motorboats, and mountain bikes.

Sample kayaking down the Hawea or Clutha Rivers with **Alpine Kayak Guides** (03/443-9023). These trips cost $120 for a full day,

© ANDREW HEMPSTEAD

The Wanaka waterfront is lined with willow trees.

OTAGO

including transportation from Wanaka. Easier half-day floats are adult $75, child $35.

SKIING AND SNOWBOARDING
Wanaka is central to two alpine resorts, the world's first dedicated free skiing resort, and New Zealand's premier cross-country-skiing facility.

In downtown Wanaka, **Racers Edge Planet Snow** (99 Ardmore St., 03/443-7882) has ski, snowboard, chain, and winter-clothing rentals.

◖ Treble Cone
Encompassing 550 hectares (1,359 acres), Treble Cone (20 km/12 mi west of Wanaka off Mount Aspiring Rd., 03/443-7443, www.treblecone.co.nz; adult $99, senior and child $50) is the South Island's largest ski field, with plans in place for a gondola linking the resort to the main road in the valley far below. Treble Cone has open, uncrowded slopes that suit mostly intermediate and advanced skiers and boarders; basins of powder; lengthy natural half-pipes; tremendous lake views; and a warm, sunny season generally lasting from late June to the end of September. Lifts include a six-seat detachable chairlift, as well as one quad chair and three surface lifts. Experienced skiers and boarders gravitate to Saddle Basin, or climb higher than the lifts to the 2,000-meter (6,560-ft) summit, for more diverse and longer runs. Snowmaking is restricted to the beginner's area, while off to one side is a terrain pipe. No on-hill accommodations are provided, but the day lodge has ski and snowboard rentals, a café, and a ski school.

Cardrona Alpine Resort
Cardrona (34 km/21 mi south of Wanaka off Cardrona Valley Rd., 03/443-7411, www.cardrona.com; adult $77, senior $41, child $39) is a lot mellower than its neighbor. With a base area some 300 meters (980 ft) higher than Treble Cone, the snow is somewhat more reliable. Three chairlifts and four surface tows service mostly beginner and intermediate terrain spread over 320 rolling hectares (790 acres). The resort also has a half-pipe, terrain park, ski and snowboard school, rentals, and a variety of apartment accommodations ($200–530 per night).

Snow Park
Turn off Cardrona Valley Road just north of Cardrona, 20 km (12 mi) south of Wanaka, to access the **Snow Park** (03/443-9991, www.snowparknz.com; day passes $75), the world's first alpine resort dedicated to freestyle skiing and boarding. A quad chair accesses dozens of jumps, a rail park, pipes, and a boardercross run. As you may expect, music blares from massive speakers and the crowd is mostly young and loud. Base village facilities include a café, restaurant, bar, dorm accommodation ($30 per person), and ski-in, ski-out apartments (from $180 s or d).

Waiorau Snow Farm
Along the same access road as the Snow Park, Waiorau Snow Farm (Cardrona Valley Rd., 03/443-7542, snowfarmnz.com) is exactly that—a snow-covered farm. The difference between this and the surrounding snow-covered farms is that in winter it is transformed

into a world-class cross-country-skiing facility. Over 55 km (34 mi) of groomed and ungroomed trails lace the 500-hectare (1,235-acre) property. The epicenter of the facility is a magnificent timber structure that holds a rental shop, restaurant, bar, and en suite accommodation. Trail passes cost adult $30, child $15, inclusive of insurance, which in charming NZ lawyer-speak is "in case something bad happens to you." Ski, boot, and pole rental is $25–35.

Heli-Skiing and Boarding

For an unforgettable experience, consider heli-skiing in the Harris, Richardson, or Buchanan Mountains—3,000 square km (1,158 square mi) in total—with **Harris Mountains Heliski** (03/442-6722, www.heliski.co.nz). Experienced guides cater to small groups of skiers of all abilities—but strong intermediate skiers get the most out of it. These adventures start at $760 for a three-run day, or pay $975 for seven runs.

ENTERTAINMENT AND EVENTS
Nightlife

A number of bar/restaurant combos with outdoor tables line Ardmore Street, across from the lakefront. Perfect for an afternoon or evening drink, they all have regular bar menus and a relaxed, friendly ambience. At the east end of the strip, **Shooters** (145 Ardmore St., 03/443-4345) also has a log fire, pool tables, and a dance floor.

Away from the lake, **Woody's** (33 Ardmore St., 03/443-5551) is a sports bar with pool tables and big-screen TVs. In the same building is the more refined **Barluga** (33 Ardmore St., 03/443-5400), with a large outside fire pit.

If you're driving between Queenstown and Wanaka, do what generations of locals have done and stop for a drink at the 1865 **Cardrona Hotel** (Cardrona Valley Rd., 03/443-8153), where gold-rush history has been preserved. The hotel has a delightful beer garden, serves hearty meals, and also has a few guest rooms. In winter, this place is standing-room-only.

Events

Every second year (even years) over the Easter long weekend, Wanaka hosts **Warbirds over Wanaka** (Wanaka Airport, 03/443-8619, www.warbirdsoverwanaka.com; day passes $40–60), one of the world's premier vintage airshows. In addition to a continuous flow of flybys, the event features a trade show, exhibitions, and food supplied by local restaurants.

ACCOMMODATIONS AND CAMPING
Under $50

With an alpine ambience, **C Purple Cow** (94 Brownston St., 03/443-1880, www.purplecow.co.nz; dorm beds $24–26, $69–75 d) is two blocks from the lakefront and central to downtown. The dorm rooms have a maximum of four beds, each with a private bathroom, but most of the rooms are doubles or twins. Other features include a pool table, TV room, table tennis, comfortable beds, and a commercial-style kitchen.

Wanaka Bakpaka (117 Lakeside Rd., 03/443-7837, www.wanakabakpaka.co.nz; dorm beds $24, $28 s, $60 d) provides panoramic views of the lake and surrounding mountains from the lounge. This place is popular with hikers and doesn't get the busloads of noisy travelers that the larger lodges do. You can also rent bikes, canoes, and kayaks.

$100-150

Manuka Crescent Motel (51 Manuka Crescent, 03/443-7773 or 0800/626-852, www.manukacrescentmotel.co.nz; $100–170 s or d) offers 12 moderately sized units, each with a kitchen, set around pleasant gardens and a small swimming pool. The more expensive units have one or two separate bedrooms.

Down the hill toward town, you'll find **Alpine Motel Apartments** (7 Ardmore St., 03/443-7950 or 0800/822-284, www.alpinemotels.co.nz; $115–210), which offers rooms of a similar standard. Facilities here include a pleasant picnic and barbecue area, a laundry, and playground.

BrookVale (35 Brownston St., 03/443-8333

OTAGO

or 0800/438-333, www.brookvale.co.nz; $100–180 s or d) provides studio units (one double bed and one single bed with separate bath and kitchen) and one-bedroom units. Guests also have the use of kitchen and laundry, a color TV, and a spa pool.

$150-200

A restored relic from the gold rush, the **(Cardrona Hotel** (Cardrona Valley Rd., 03/443-8153, www.cardronahotel.co.nz; $165 s or d) is nestled in a picturesque valley 24 km (15 mi) south of Wanaka toward Queenstown. The rooms are separate from the original hotel, but each has a welcoming, heritage style and all modern conveniences. It's a good spot to get away from it all, and the hotel bar and restaurant is a friendly place to hang out.

Mount Aspiring Hotel (two km/1.2 mi west of downtown along Mount Aspiring Rd., 03/443-8216, www.wanakanz.com; studio $168 s or d, one-bedroom unit $250) has bright, spacious timber rooms with private bath, balcony, breakfast-making supplies, and LCD TV. Some have a spa bath, and some have lake and mountain views. The inn also has a laundry and Tilikum Restaurant, specializing in Pacific Rim cuisine.

Built of local timber and stone and taking advantage of the surrounding mountain panorama, **(Te Wanaka Lodge** (23 Brownston St., 03/443-9224, www.tewanaka.co.nz; $195–225 s or d) is suitably alpine in ambience and design. The 12 spacious rooms each have a private balcony or verandah and are stocked with plush bathrobes, thick duvets, and a range of toiletries. In the garden, the hot tub takes center stage under an old walnut tree. You'll be welcomed with afternoon tea and a big gourmet breakfast the next morning will set you up for a day of outdoor recreation.

Over $200

Continuing around the lake from the Mount Aspiring Hotel is **Edgewater Resort** (Sargood Dr., 03/443-8311, www.edgewater .co.nz; $220–325 s or d), a sprawling resort with a mix of hotel rooms and one-bedroom

units. Amenities include tennis courts, a putting green, a swimming pool, a spa, and mountain bike rentals. The in-house restaurant opens daily for a buffet breakfast and nightly from 6:30 P.M. for à la carte dinners.

Off Highway 6, east of Wanaka, **(RiverRun** (Halliday Rd., 03/443-9049, www.riverrun .co.nz; $320–460 s or d) is an upscale bed-and-breakfast set on 200 hectares (500 acres) of farmland running right down to the Clutha River. The country-style lodge features elegant furnishings, with lots of exposed timber and stylish earthy tones throughout. Each room has a luxurious bathroom, views, robes, and real cotton sheets. A cold and cooked breakfast and non-alcoholic drinks are included in the rate. Dinner is $85 per person extra.

Holiday Parks

Within walking distance of the town and the lake **Wanaka Lakeview Holiday Park** (212 Brownston St., 03/443-7883, www.wanaka lakeview.co.nz; campsites $13 per person, cabins $40 s or d, self-contained tourist flats $60–80) has all the usual communal facilities, including a shaded barbeque area.

If you have your own transportation and don't mind staying out of town, head for the popular **Glendhu Bay Motor Camp** (Mount Aspiring Rd., 03/443-7243). Attracting large numbers of swimmers, water-skiers, and boaters, it's on the lakefront at beautiful Glendhu Bay, 11 km (6.8 mi) west of Wanaka, which is renowned for magnificent views of Mount Aspiring. The campground has 450 campsites ($12 per person), 10 very basic cabins ($17 per person), communal facilities, a large kitchen, canoe rentals, and a grocery store.

FOOD
Cafés and Bakeries

Opposite the lake, **Pembroke Village Mall** (139 Ardmore St.) has several cafés, including **Doughbin Bakery** (03/443-7290), which serves a large variety of delicious baked goods, including one of the better steak pies I've ever tasted and a mutton pie, which is definitely an acquired taste. Doughbin is open daily 10 A.M.–6 P.M. but stays open 24 hours through summer.

Kai Whakapai Café (Ardmore St., 03/443-7795; daily from 7 A.M.) is a casual café with healthy dishes at reasonable prices. It's also a good place to relax with just a coffee and slice of divine banana cream pie.

Quick Bites and Outdoor Dining

Ever-popular **Relishes** (99 Ardmore St., 03/443-9018; daily 9:30 A.M.–3 P.M. and from 6:30 P.M.) serves tasty lunches for less than $15, and all dinners (except the venison) for less than $30 in a cozy country-style atmosphere with a few outdoor tables.

You can relax in the sun with a coffee at **Café Gusto** (1 Lakeside Dr., 03/443-6639; daily from 8 A.M.), but the main draw is creative, healthy cooking in a bright, casual room overlooking the lake. If none of the daily pasta specials (usually under $20) take your fancy, try the venison burger ($16.50).

The character-filled **Cardrona Hotel** (Cardrona Valley Rd., 03/443-8153; daily for lunch and dinner), built in the mid-1860s during the Otago gold rush, has been beautifully restored and now offers visitors driving between Wanaka and Queenstown everything from cold beer to full meals. Have a drink at the original brass bar, eat inside surrounded by items from the gold-rush days, or enjoy your meal outside in the garden. Everything is well priced, including a hearty meal of lamb sausages ($18.50) or venison medallions on roasted pumpkin ($21).

Mediterranean

The aptly named **White House** (33 Dunmore St., 03/443-9595; daily 11 A.M.–11 P.M.) is a casual restaurant with lots of outdoor seating in a courtyard. The Mediterranean-inspired menu uses local produce combined with exotic spices. Mains are all under $30.

Seafood

Above the Bank of New Zealand, **Capriccio** (123 Ardmore St., 03/443-8579; daily from 6 P.M.) is a longtime local favorite for Italian and seafood dishes in a casual atmosphere. But

you don't have to appreciate pasta to enjoy this restaurant—it also whips up chicken, pork, steak, and lamb, and desserts with an Italian flair. Mains range $21–28, or choose a live crayfish from the tank for $40.

Reef (145 Ardmore St., 03/471-7185; daily noon–2 P.M. and 5:30–9 P.M.) is a big, confident restaurant across from the lake. As the name suggests, the extensive menu is dominated by seafood and the color scheme is suitably aquatic. You could start with deep-fried calamari ($12.50) and then get serious with a whole grilled fish ($26.50) or Indian fish curry ($25.50). For lighter appetites, there's a smoked salmon salad ($26).

PRACTICALITIES
Information

Wanaka Visitor Centre (100 Ardmore St., 03/443-1233, www.lakewanaka.co.nz; daily 8:30 A.M.–5 P.M.) is in a log building along the lakefront. **Mount Aspiring National Park Visitor Centre** (corner of Ballantyne and Ardmore Sts., 03/443-7660; Nov.–Apr. daily 8:30 A.M.–4:30 P.M., the rest of the year weekdays only) offers all types of displays featuring the adjacent national park, documentaries, and trail condition reports.

Services

Wanaka Post Office is on Ardmore Street. Check your email at **Bits & Bytes** (corner of Helwick and Brownston Sts., 03/443-0400).

Wanaka Medical Centre (03/443-7811) is at 21 Russell Street. **Aspiring Pharmacy** is at 29 Helwick Street (03/443-7986).

Getting There and Around

Air New Zealand (0800/737-300, www.airnew zealand.com) flies five times daily between Christchurch and Wanaka while **Aspiring Air** (03/443-7943) is mostly a flightseeing operation, but also has scheduled flights to Queenstown for $135 each way. The airport is along Highway 8 12 km (7.5 mi) east of town. **Alpine Coachlines** (03/443-7966) meets all incoming flights and charges $10 per person for the ride downtown. **Intercity** buses (03/443-7885, www.intercitycoach.co.nz) stop along Brownston Street at Helwick Street, with daily service provided to Queenstown, up the west coast to Franz Josef and Fox Glaciers, and east to Christchurch. **Wanaka Connexions** (03/443-9122) links Queenstown and Wanaka. This company stops outside the visitor center.

Wanaka is a compact little town, which makes getting everywhere on foot easy. It's also relatively flat for biking. Rent mountain bikes from **Lakeland Adventures** (100 Ardmore St., 03/443-7495) and **Mountain Bikes Unlimited** (99 Ardmore St., 03/443-7882). **Wanaka Taxis** (03/443-7999) is on call 24 hours daily.

MOUNT ASPIRING NATIONAL PARK

The second-largest national park in New Zealand at 161 km (100 mi) long and 32 km (20) wide, Mount Aspiring National Park covers 355,540 hectares (878,600 acres) of the southern end of the Southern Alps. In the center of this mountainous park, spectacular **Mount Aspiring** (3,027 meters/9,930 ft), a pyramid-shaped peak of snow and ice that the Maori called Tititea (Upright Glistening Mountain), towers above a sea of mighty peaks and more than 50 named glaciers. The park's northern boundary is the Haast River and Haast Pass Highway (Hwy. 6), which winds down the river to the west coast.

Vegetation varies from dense forests of silver beech, *rimu, matai, miro,* and *kahikatea* to alpine meadows of snow *totara,* alpine daisies, heaths, hebes, Giant Mountain buttercups, and mountain flax. The park is known for its abundant birdlife. On the valley floors are riverbed inhabitants such as migratory black-backed and black-billed gulls, black-fronted terns, South Island pied oystercatchers, banded dotterels, and spur-winged plovers. In the forests live migratory shining cuckoos, *morepork, tui,* and yellow-fronted parakeets. Considerably fewer birds thrive in the high alpine regions, but you're likely to see cheeky *kea* (alpine parrots), along with rock wrens and pipits. The rarely seen blue duck has been spotted in some of the park valleys.

Matukituki Valley

Mount Aspiring Road leads west from Wanaka past Glendhu Bay for 47 km (29 mi) to **Cameron's Flat**—the start of a walking trail up the east branch of the Matukituki River to Glacier Burn, Junction Flat, and Aspiring Flat. The easy two-hour (one-way) **Glacier Burn Walk** starts at the flat and climbs through beech forests to a saddle with excellent views of peaks and hanging glaciers, and at the head of the valley are impressive bluffs, waterfalls, and lots of birds.

Around 6.5 km (four mi) beyond Cameron's Flat following the west branch of the Matukituki River, you come to a parking lot at **Big Creek,** the trailhead for the **Matukituki Valley Track.** This easy 2.5-hour (one-way) trail leads along river flats to Aspiring Hut. For a beautiful alpine valley hike and outstanding scenery at the end, sidetrack off the Matukituki Valley Track onto the **Rob Roy Stream Walk.** Cross the Matukituki River on the swing bridge, and follow the track up past the gorge at the stream mouth and through lush fern-filled forest to the valley head, where you can see the south face of Rob Roy (2,606 meters/8,550 ft) and its glacier, sheer bluffs, and waterfalls; it's two to three hours one-way.

Makarora Valley

Haast Pass Highway (Hwy. 6), which cuts across the park's northeast corner, links Wanaka and the west coast town of Haast (see the *West Coast* chapter). A number of short walks are signposted along the highway. Take the 20-minute **Makarora Bush Nature Walk** through a forest, starting near the Makarora Visitor Centre. For alpine plant-viewing or a full-day trip and excellent panoramas, start on the Nature Walk track and branch off onto the **Mount Shrimpton Track.** This relatively steep track takes about 3.5 hours (you need to be fit) to climb through silver beech forest to the tree line, and then up to a knob overlooking the Makarora Valley for views of the park's highest peaks.

For an alpine view that takes much less effort than many of the tracks, visit the **Cameron**

Creek area (11 km/6.8 mi north of Makarora) and take the 10-minute walkway to a lookout. The gradient is easy; all ages can manage this one. Another short walk, starting nine km north of Makarora, leads to the intriguing **Blue Pools** on the Blue River; allow 15 minutes each way.

Another popular walk is on the 1.5-hour (one-way) **Bridle Track** from the top of Haast Pass to Davis Flat, following sections of the old Bridle Track, the original link between Otago and the west coast.

Siberia Experience

A world away from the commercialism of Queenstown, the Siberia Experience (03/443-8351 or 0800/538-945, www.siberiaexperience .com) combines adrenaline elements with the wilderness of Mount Aspiring National Park. This four-hour adventure begins and ends at Makarora, 65 km (41 mi) north of Wanaka. First up is a scenic 25-minute flight, which is followed by a 2.5-hour walk through the remote Siberia Valley, from where a jetboat whisks you back down the Wilkin and Makarora Rivers to Makarora.

Guided Walks and Mountaineering

If you'd like to hike up the Matukituki Valley to Shovel Pass for spectacular views of

MOUNT ASPIRING NATIONAL PARK

OTAGO

© AVALON TRAVEL PUBLISHING, INC.

© ANDREW HEMPSTEAD

Haast River and Mount Aspiring National Park

Mount Aspiring, and you need a guide, contact Geoff Wayatt of **Mountain Recreation** (03/443-7330, www.mountainrec.com). One of New Zealand's most experienced mountaineers, Wayatt offers a three-day low-elevation trek for $645, which includes transportation, guiding services, accommodations in a remote mountain hut, and food. For those looking at a mountain-climbing adventure, the company guides to the summits throughout the park, including Mount Aspiring (three or four days for $3,300).

Flightseeing

Aspiring Air (Wanaka Airport, Hwy. 8, 03/443-7943 or 0800/100-943) provides reasonably priced flights, including a spectacular 50-minute flight over snowcapped mountains and glaciers of Mount Aspiring National Park for adult $200, child $135.

Practicalities

For casual park visitors, the best plan is to spend a day driving north from Wanaka, admiring the scenery and walking the short trails leading off Highway 6. You could then return to your Wanaka accommodation, or continue through the park to Haast and the west coast.

The alternative—and it's a good one—is to stay at **Makarora Wilderness Resort** (Hwy. 6, Makarora, 03/443-8372, www.makarora .co.nz; camping $12 per person, dorm beds $22, cabins $69 s or d, self-contained units $95), overlooking the Makarora River 65 km (41 mi) north of Wanaka. In addition to accommodations, the resort has a friendly restaurant open daily for breakfast, lunch, and dinner (mains $20–22), a grocery store, and petrol pumps.

Beside Makarora Wilderness Resort is the DOC **Makarora Visitor Centre** (Hwy. 6, 03/443-8365; Dec.–Mar. daily 8 A.M.–5 P.M.). It's not always staffed, but a small display room with a 3-D park map is usually open. Another source of information is **Mount Aspiring National Park Visitor Centre** (corner of Ballantyne and Ardmore Sts., Wanaka, 03/443-7660; Nov.–Apr. daily 8:30 A.M.–4:30 P.M., the rest of the year weekdays only).

SOUTHLAND

This southernmost area of the South Island is a landscape of hills, lush sheep pastures, plains liberally crisscrossed by trout-filled rivers, large forest parks, and a wild, rugged coastline. Much of the land is protected by Fiordland National Park, a remote area of deep fiords and magnificent waterfalls, rugged mountains covered in dense beech forest, large lakes and rivers, and three small settlements that cater to visitors. The park is home to famously photogenic Milford Sound, where visitors line up by the busload for boat tours, but there are many lesser-known highlights, such as Doubtful Sound. But Fiordland is best known for its walking tracks. More than 500 km (311 mi) of developed tracks of varying standards and difficulty crisscross the park. You can walk the five major hiking tracks—

Milford, Routeburn, Hollyford, Kepler, and Dusky—either independently, staying in basic huts where you provide everything yourself, or with a guided group staying in more comfortable backcountry lodges that include bedding, meals, and hot showers.

The main economic and industrial center of Southland is Invercargill, the country's eighth-largest city and departure point for traveling across Foveaux Strait to Stewart Island. Bluff, 27 km (17 mi) south of Invercargill, is the region's chief port and harbor. In the remote southeast lies the unspoiled scenic region of the Catlins. The central Southland town of Gore is the region's second-largest town—its location near many of the best trout rivers makes it an excellent place to kick back and get into some real fishing.

© ANDREW HEMPSTEAD

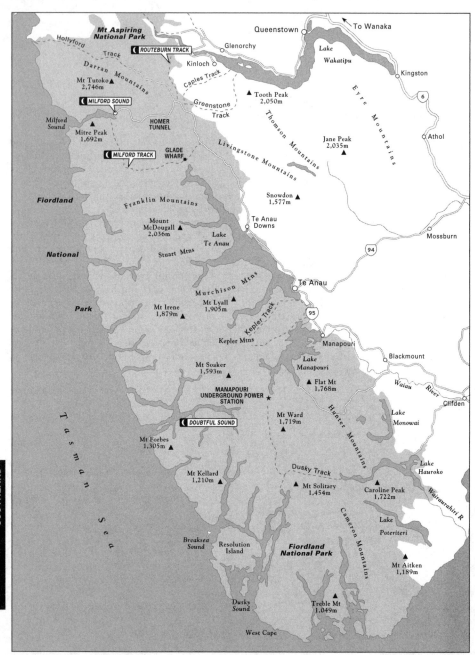

SOUTHLAND

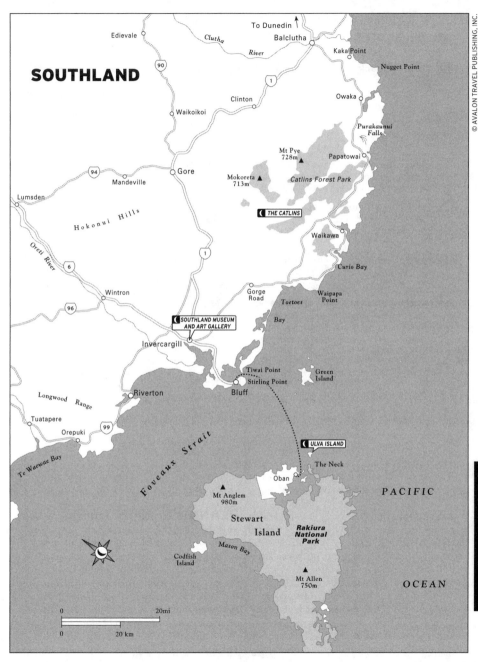

© AVALON TRAVEL PUBLISHING, INC.

SOUTHLAND

To Dunedin
Edievale
Clutha
Balclutha
Kaka Point
River
Nugget Point
90
1
Clinton
Owaka
Waikoikoi
Purakaunui Falls
Mt Pye
728m ▲
Papatowai
94
Gore
Mokoreta
713m ▲
Catlins Forest Park
Mandeville
Lumsden
Hokonui Hills
(THE CATLINS
Waikawa
Oreti River
Curio Bay
1
6
Gorge Road
Waipapa Point
Wintron
Toetoes
96
Bay
(SOUTHLAND MUSEUM AND ART GALLERY
Invercargill
Tiwai Point
Green Island
Stirling Point
Bluff
Longwood Range
Riverton
Tuatapere
(ULVA ISLAND
99
Orepuki
The Neck
Te Waewae Bay
Foveaux Strait
Oban
PACIFIC
Mt Anglem
980m ▲
Stewart
Island
Rakiura National Park
Codfish Island
Mason Bay
Mt Allen
750m ▲
OCEAN
0   20mi
0   20 km

SOUTHLAND

HIGHLIGHTS

◖ Milford Track: Generally considered one of the world's greatest hikes, the four-day "tramp" will be a highlight of your time in New Zealand (page 440).

◖ Routeburn Track: While the Milford gets all the glory, this overnight walk traverses equally scenic terrain (page 441).

◖ Milford Sound: In a fiord of monumental proportions, tour boats cruise past waterfalls, wildlife, and distinctive Mitre Peak (page 442).

◖ Doubtful Sound: It takes a boat-bus-boat combo to reach this remote corner of Southland, but the scenic isolation is unparalleled (page 445).

◖ The Catlins: Sea lions, a fossil forest, and abundant birdlife are just a few of the surprises along this remote stretch of coast (page 450).

◖ Southland Museum and Art Gallery: With most of the region's attractions being outdoors, this large museum makes an ideal rainy-day diversion for its natural-history displays (page 453).

◖ Ulva Island: Easily accessible by water taxi, this remote outpost of untamed wilderness is alive with birdlife (page 458).

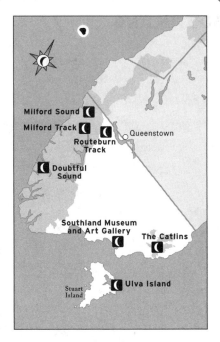

LOOK FOR ◖ TO FIND RECOMMENDED SIGHTS, ACTIVITIES, DINING, AND LODGING.

The third and southernmost of New Zealand's main islands, little-developed Stewart Island is home to one settlement of island-dwellers, supported mostly by fishing and a growing tourism industry. Heading over to Stewart Island is like taking a giant step back in time—the locals depend on rainfall for water, some depend on generators for electricity, and there are few roads. It's not the place to go for lively evening entertainment—residents and visitors alike tend to go to bed early so they can make the most of the daylight for outdoor activities. Go there to revel in scenery and solitude, to hike through bush and along endless sandy beaches, and to cruise remote inlet waters.

PLANNING YOUR TIME

Most two-week escorted tours include a brief excursion to Southland, and independent travelers can, too. The most common scenario is taking a cruise on **Milford Sound** as part of a (long) day trip from Queenstown. If you can spend at least a couple of days in Southland and have your own vehicle, you should plan on also driving through to Milford Sound for the cruise, and combine this day with time in **The Catlins.** Three days is an ideal amount of time in the region, as it allows you time to also include a cruise on remote **Doubtful Sound.** Invercargill's **Southland Museum and Art Gallery** is also worth visiting for an hour or two, or maybe longer on a rainy day.

My suggestion for allowing three days doesn't include one of New Zealand's best-known outdoor activities—walking the **Milford Track,** which takes four days and requires reservations to be made well in advance. The nearby three-day **Routeburn Track** is equally as scenic, but a little less regulated, making it a good alternative. Finally, Stewart Island extends the Southland wilderness theme. You can fly in and out in a day, but this defeats the purpose of traveling to the southernmost end of New Zealand. Instead, plan on staying at least one night, which will allow enough time to take a boat tour to the bird-filled **Ulva Island,** join a kiwi-spotting tour, and feast on local seafood.

Fiordland National Park and Vicinity

The vast, remote Fiordland region in the southwest corner of the South Island is made up of Fiordland National Park and the towns of Te Anau and Manapouri, which lie just outside the park boundary. In a country that has spectacular scenery from top to bottom, Fiordland is one of the most majestic areas—the kind of place where you constantly hear the words "breathtaking," "spectacular," "awesome," and "magnificent." Though you can expect dull skies or endless days of rain and drizzle, keep in mind that the scenery is at its most dramatic after heavy rain. Although tour boats and flightseeing planes provide easy access to remote corners of the park, it is the walking tracks that are most famous. Outdoor enthusiasts from around the world are drawn to the famous Milford Track, although many say the Routeburn, Hollyford, Kepler, and Dusky Tracks are equally scenic.

THE LAND

Fiordland National Park covers a remote area of more than 1.2 million hectares (3 million acres) of forest-covered mountains, pristine fiords, lakes, enormous waterfalls, and rivers in the southwest corner of the South Island. It's the largest national park in the country (and one of the largest in the world), stretching from Martins Bay and the Hollyford Valley in the north to Preservation Inlet in the south, from the large Lakes Te Anau and Manapouri in the east to 14 fiords along the heavily serrated western coastline. The rocks of Fiordland are among the most ancient in the country, and the mountains you see today were uplifted during the past 15 million years, then carved into sheer valleys, large hollows, and fiords up to 40 km (25 mi) inland during several periods of glaciation—the last ending only 14,000 years ago. After the ice melted, the sea flooded the coastal valleys and the inland hollows, forming the mighty Lakes Te Anau and Manapouri, and Lakes Monowai, Hauroko (deepest lake in New Zealand at 462 meters/1520 ft), Poteriteri, and Hakapoua. In recent times the ice and snow have been largely replaced by an enormous amount of rain.

Climate

The climate ranges from mild to severe at any time of year. It's generally warm (but never hot) in the lower altitudes. The heaviest rainfall is recorded on the west coast, where the annual average in some places is 8,000 mm (315 in); Milford Sound annually receives more than 7,200 mm (283 in). The coldest months (and best time to visit if you're hoping for drier weather) are May–August—frost collects east of the ranges, and the road to Milford Sound is usually open.

Flora and Fauna

Because of the high rainfall, just about everywhere you look you see flowing water and lush greenery. Rich, dark-green beech forest with a luxuriant understory of prolific ferns,

SOUTHLAND

shrubs, mosses, and lichens carpets the land-scape. Throughout much of Fiordland, the forest clings precariously to steep rock faces, roots entwined in a thin spongy pad of peat and moss that retains the heavy rainfall and allows understory plants to thrive. Red, silver, and mountain beech are the three dominant species in the forest, with the podocarps *rimu, miro,* and Hall's *totara* scattered through the lowland forest, and *matai* and *kahikatea* found in swampier areas. In late spring and early summer the high slopes come alive with flow-ering alpine shrubs, daisies and buttercups, and other alpine herbs. Above the tree line, small mountain lakes (tarns) and bogs surrounded by deep peat, white-flowered donatia, and alpine grasses dot the land.

A great variety of both native and introduced birds thrives here—ask at the visitor center for the pamphlet *Fiordland Birds And Where To Find Them.* The most unusual local birdlife are the four kinds of flightless birds. The noc-turnal South Island brown kiwi, *weka, kakapo* (a large, nocturnal, yellow-green ground parrot on the brink of extinction), and *takahe* (a large blue and iridescent green bird with scarlet bill and feet, one of New Zealand's rarest birds) all live in Fiordland National Park. You can see a mounted *kakapo* and *takahe* at the visitor center in Te Anau. The Murchison and Stuart Mountains, west of Lake Te Anau, where most of the few remaining *takahe* survive, have been designated as a refuge, with no public access, to ensure that the birds survive in their natu-ral habitat. Along the fiords live great numbers of penguins—the Fiordland crested penguin the most predominant—and New Zealand fur seals are common.

Warning: Sand flies are tiny black insects that inflict painful bites that swell and itch and cause great discomfort. They're most annoying in calm weather and around dusk, and insect repellent is at times more of a "must have" for the outdoor enthusiast than food.

TE ANAU

Te Anau (pop. 1,800), the gateway to Fiordland National Park, is 175 km (109 mi) southwest of Queenstown along Highway 6 and then High-way 94. Adjacent **Lake Te Anau** is backed by the rugged, glacier-carved mountains of Fiord-land National Park and Milford Sound is just up the road. Te Anau is a shortened version of the Maori word Te Ana-au (Caves of Rush-ing Waters). The caves are on the other side of the lake—rediscovered relatively recently, they've become one of the most visited local attractions. Centrally located with a range of accommodations to suit all budgets, Te Anau is a good base for exploring the many natural attractions of the park, and Milford Sound is less than a three-hour drive through magnifi-cent scenery.

Sights

The **Fiordland National Park Visitor Centre** (Lakefront Dr., 03/249-7924; daily 8 A.M.–5 P.M., summer until 8 P.M.; free) is a Depart-ment of Conservation facility on the Te Anau waterfront. It is the main source of information for all Fiordland tracks, but also holds inter-esting park displays, screens a documentary, carries track and weather conditions, and sells topo maps and trail guides.

A 10-minute walk along the waterfront from the visitor center, **Te Anau Wildlife Centre** (Te Anau–Manapouri Rd., 03/249-7924; daily dawn to dusk; free) is home to some of New Zealand's most colorful and intriguing birds, including *takahe* (there are only about 150 of these rare flightless birds left in the wild), *weka,* parakeets, aviary birds, and waterfowl, as well as fish.

Local Walks

Even if you're not up for the Kepler Track, there are a number of easy alternatives begin-ning from the same trailhead—the Lake Te Anau Control Gate, which lies along Te Anau–Manapouri Road (you can walk there from town along the lakeshore beyond the wildlife center in 50 minutes). At the lookout and con-trol gates, **Riverside Walk** runs north for four km (1.5 hours) one-way to Brod Bay, across the lake from Te Anau. Beyond Brod Bay, a trail branches west and climbs to the summit

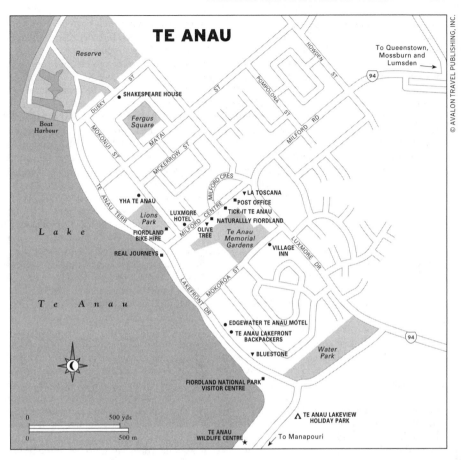

of **Mount Luxmore** (allow 10 hours for the round-trip from the control gates). Also from the control gates, you can walk for three hours along the Waiau River to Rainbow Beach.

Kepler Track

This circular 67-km (42-mi, three to four days) track, which opened in 1988, is the latest to be constructed in the park. Starting between Te Anau and Manapouri at the Lake Te Anau Control Gate, it follows the shore of Lake Te Anau, then climbs past limestone cliffs and above the tree line for panoramic views. From the Mount Luxmore Hut, the track climbs through stunning alpine scenery, wanders through beech and podocarp forest, and along Lake Manapouri, then meanders along the Upper Waiau River to the original starting point. The full circuit is suitable for hikers with above-average fitness, although everyone can enjoy *some* sections of the track; access has been provided for those wishing to fish and climb. In summer take water for the alpine section (it can be very dry), and be prepared in winter for snow and adverse weather conditions that can close the alpine stretch.

Three serviced huts ($40 per person per night) equipped with mattresses, water, flush

© AVALON TRAVEL PUBLISHING, INC.

SOUTHLAND

toilets, heating, and gas cooking and lighting lie at regular intervals along the track. The Kepler Track is a Great Walk and, therefore, requires a Great Walks hut pass available at any local DOC office.

The track officially starts and ends a 45-minute walk from the Fiordland National Park Visitor Centre, but you can catch the **Kepler Water Taxi** (03/249-8364) from downtown Te Anau to Brod Bay ($20 per person one way), cutting just over five km (3 mi) off the total distance. **Tracknet** (03/249-7777) provides hiker transportation to the control gates, as well as to Rainbow Beach, along the Waiau River, 10 km (6 mi) from the trailhead.

Lake Cruises

Start at **Real Journeys** (1 Lakefront Dr., 03/249-7416 or 0800/656-501) for cruise and tour information and tickets, brochures, and maps. Be sure to ask about the various discount packages and current specials before you hop on a boat. A cruise across Lake Te Anau to the limestone caverns of **Te Ana-au Caves** (adult $54, child $15), with an underground waterfall and glowworm grotto, is one of the best cruises for the price. The 2.5-hour trip departs several times a day.

Accommodations and Camping

One block back from the lake, **YHA Te Anau** (29 Mokonui St., 03/249-7847, www.yha .co.nz; dorm beds $24, double and twin $62) is a modern, well-equipped backpacker lodge with bonuses such as an outdoor barbecue area, hammocks, and a well-stocked library. Another recommended choice for budget travelers is **Te Anau Lakefront Backpackers** (48 Lakefront Dr., 03/249-7713 or 0800/200-074, dorm beds $18, doubles $22 per person), a short lakeside walk from downtown. Facilities include a cozy kitchen, dining room, living room with TV, a laundry, barbecue area, solar-heated pool, off-street parking, and free use of bikes.

Shakespeare House (10 Dusky St., 03/249-7349 or 0800/249-349, www.shakespeare house.co.nz; $100 s, $120 d) has eight appealing en suite rooms, a bright breakfast room, a great glassed-in porch that stretches along the front of all the rooms, Internet access, and tea- and coffee-making supplies.

Te Anau has lots of motels, but rooms in summer are mostly over $100. One of the best values is **Edgewater Te Anau Motel** (52 Lakefront Dr., 03/249-7258 or 0800/433-439, www.edgewatermotel.net.nz; $90 s, $130 d) in a central position between downtown and the visitor center. Each of the 16 units has a kitchen, and guests have free use of canoes and a barbecue area.

In the heart of the shopping district, the **Village Inn** (Mokoroa St., 03/249-7911 or 0800/249-7911, www.thevillageinn.co.nz; $135–180 s or d) stands out for its pioneer-village facade. Beyond the barn board, you find large, elegantly decorated rooms, some with kitchens, and a bar and restaurant.

Around 200 meters from the lakefront, the **Luxmore Hotel** (Town Centre, 03/249-7526 or 0800/589-667, www.luxmorehotel.co.nz; $175–325 s or d), with 180 rooms, is the largest place in town. This full-service hostelry underwent a serious revamp in 2006 and offers spacious but standard rooms, a café, a restaurant, and a bar.

🌙 Te Anau Lakeview Holiday Park (03/249-7457, www.teanauholidaypark.co.nz) is beyond the park visitor center on the road out to Manapouri. It lies among plenty of trees in a beautiful lakeside setting one km (0.6 mi) from downtown. Within the grounds are tennis courts, sauna, volleyball court, comfortable bar and outdoor beer garden, TV, barbecue areas, and a boat ramp. Vehicles ($80 per day plus 30 cents per km/0.6 mi), bikes, and golf clubs are available for rent. Tent and caravan sites are $14–15.50 per person, cabins start at $58 s or d, self-contained tourist flats near to the lake are $105, and motel rooms sell for $120.

Food

Naturally Fiordland (62 Town Centre, 03/249-7111; Mon.–Thurs. 8 a.m.–3 p.m., Fri.–Sat. 8 a.m.–9 p.m.) is a great place to hang out on a sunny day (outside tables are set around a courtyard), or just to relax over a specialty pizza and glass of local wine.

Small and inviting **La Toscana** (108 Milford Rd., 03/249-7756; daily from 6 P.M.) is the place to go for no-frills, reliable Italian fare. Prices are from $16 for spaghetti bolognese to $24 for a large Quasitutto pizza, and homemade desserts and ice cream sundaes are all around $6. **Olive Tree** (52 Town Centre, 03/249-8496; daily for lunch and dinner) is another inviting café, with a few tables on a private terrace. Focaccia-bread pizzas ($15–18) shine brightest, with lots of vegetarian choices.

Bluestone (Kingsgate Hotel, 20 Lakefront Dr., 03/249-7421; daily 6:30–9 A.M. and 6–9 P.M.) offers a modern, café-like setting. It's a good place for a hearty breakfast (continental buffet $14, full buffet $20), while dinner mains range $22–34. **Hilights** (Luxmore Hotel, Town Centre, 03/249-7526) has similar hours and ambience, with a buffet breakfast and dinner.

Information and Services

Make your first stop in town the **Fiordland National Park Visitor Centre** (Lakefront Dr., 03/249-7924; daily 8 A.M.–5 P.M., summer until 8 P.M.).

The police station, post office, and bank are all on Town Centre, the main thoroughfare through downtown. **Te Anau Medical Centre** (Luxmore Dr., 03/249-7007) is open Monday–Friday only.

Getting There and Around

Air services to and from Te Anau are operated by **Air New Zealand** (03/249-7516 or 0800/737-300, www.airnewzealand.com); all flights are routed through Queenstown. Planes arrive and depart from a small airfield seven km (4.3 mi) south of Te Anau on the road to Manapouri. Shuttle buses ($7 per person one-way) meet all flights.

Tick-it Te Anau (70 Town Centre, 03/249-7505 or 0800/107-505) is the local transportation agent, and also the depot for **Intercity** (www.intercitycoach.co.nz) bus services to Milford Sound, Queenstown, and Dunedin. The trip to Milford Sound takes just under three

hours, with a timetable that allows a two- or four-hour stop in Milford Sound (enough time for a cruise). **Real Journeys** (03/249-7416 or 0800/656-501) operates buses between Queenstown and Te Anau, with services continuing to Manapouri and Milford Sound to link up with the company's various cruises. Again, the schedule allows for a day trip from Te Anau. **Tracknet** (03/249-7777 or 0800/483-2628, www.tracknet.net) operates throughout the region, including to Queenstown, with a service designed mainly for hiker drop-offs.

For single or tandem bicycle and mountain bike rentals head for **Fiordland Bike Hire** (7 Mokonui St., 03/249-7211) and expect to pay from $6 per hour, $18 half day, $39 full day. The local cab company is **Te Anau Taxi & Tours** (03/249-7777).

TE ANAU TO MILFORD SOUND

Scenic Highway 94 leads north from Te Anau, ending after 119 km (74 mi) at Milford Sound. With your own vehicle, you can stop for the many scenic points and short hiking trails en route, but even on an Intercity or Real Journeys bus the trip to Milford Sound is breathtaking. Many appealing camping spots run by the DOC are marked along the highway. All have toilets and picnic tables. Pay in the honesty box; $5 adult per night.

Stock up on film and insect repellent, and set off as early in the morning as possible—cloud cover usually forms as the day progresses, and in summer it's a case of beating the bad weather; allow at least 2.5 hours each way without side trips. In winter the road may occasionally be closed because of inclemency—get current road conditions from the Fiordland National Park Visitor Centre (Te Anau).

Te Anau Downs

Te Anau Downs, 27 km (16.7 mi) north of Te Anau, is the launch point for boats transferring hikers to the Milford Track trailhead. A 10-minute walk from the dock, **Te Anau Downs Motor Inn** (03/249-7811 or 0800/500-805; $110–140 s or d) has lakefront rooms, each with a kitchen, as well as a restaurant, bar,

SOUTHLAND

and public Internet access. This accommodation is closed in winter. Part of the same complex is the excellent **Grumpy's Backpackers** (03/249-8133 or 0800/478-6797), where dorm beds sell for $25 and private rooms with shared bath for $68 s or d.

◖ Milford Track

Often referred to as "the finest walk in the world," the 53.5-km (33-mi) Milford Track starts at Glade Wharf, at the north end of Lake Te Anau, and ends at Sandfly Point, on Milford Sound. Hikers here follow in the footsteps of the earliest pioneers, passing through river valleys surrounded by magnificent mountain scenery, climbing up and over 1,073-meter (3,520-foot) **Mackinnon Pass,** and opting for a sidetrack to breathtaking **Sutherland Falls,** which plunges 580 meters (1,900 ft) in three cascades—New Zealand's highest waterfall and the world's fourth-highest. The trailhead is Glade Wharf, from where the trail follows the Clinton River to its source, Mintaro Lake, before making a steep ascent to the alpine environment of Mackinnon Pass. The side trip to Sutherland Falls is in this vicinity, then it's downhill all the way, paralleling the Arthur River to Sandfly Point and Milford Sound. The longest day on the trail is the last, when 18 km (11 mi) is covered in 5–6 hours.

The track is strictly regulated: It *must* be hiked south to north, hikers *must* spend one night in each of the three huts (it's a four-day hike and cannot be lengthened or shortened—it's all about crowd control), and no camping is permitted along the track—you must stay in the huts. You should also be prepared for wet weather.

The track is very popular and space is limited to 40 walkers starting from Glade Wharf each day. These spots usually book out months in advance. Bookings are taken from July 1 for the following season (late Oct. to mid-Apr.). The easiest way to apply for a pass is online at www.doc.govt.nz. You can also contact the Great Walks Booking Desk (Department of Conservation, P.O. Box 29, Te Anau, 03/249-8514). The booking fee and hut pass is adult

$120, child $60. You must complete the form (one per group) and return it along with total payment. Receipts are sent out, but you must pick up the actual pass from the Fiordland National Park Visitor Centre in Te Anau.

The total cost for transportation to and from the beginning and end of the track from Te Anau is $155—a bus to Te Anau Downs ($20), a boat to Glade Wharf ($60), then from the north end of the track a boat to Milford Sound ($30) from where buses run back to Te Anau ($45). Transportation can be booked and paid for on the DOC form that reserves your spot on the track. The alternative is to contact **Tracknet** (03/249-7777, www.tracknet.net) or **Info & Track** (37 Shotover St., Queenstown, 03/442-9708, www.infotrack.co.nz).

Ultimate Hikes (03/441-1138 or 0800/659-255, milfordtrack.co.nz) offers guided walks along the Milford Track. This option is a much more expensive alternative to independent tramping, but it's perfect for those who want to walk the track but lack the equipment or experience to do it alone; there is also less need to book so far in advance. The cost of $1,750–2,100 includes transportation from Queenstown, four nights in comfortable backcountry lodges, and all meals. This same company offers a day hike along the southern portion of the track for $165.

North from Te Anau Downs

Beyond Te Anau Downs, Highway 94 enters Fiordland National Park then reaches **Mirror Lakes** (55 km/34 mi from Te Anau), which are worth a stop; a short wooden plank walkway runs through a forest alive with bellbirds, along several small lakes that mirror all that's around them on a still day.

Continuing north, at beautiful **Lake Gunn** you can camp surrounded by trees along the edge of the lake. For the best views of the lake and the Livingstone Mountains, take an early-morning hike along the short **Black Lake Track** that runs along the west side of the lake at the south end.

At **The Divide,** the lowest east–west pass in the Southern Alps (531 meters/1740 ft), the popular Routeburn Track leads overland to Lake Wakatipu, and not much farther along the highway, Hollyford Valley Road leads off the highway to **Gunn's Camp** (also known as Hollyford Camp), where Murray Gunn displays a collection of relics that his father accumulated over 50 years of tramping and exploring through the Fiordland wilderness. You can also buy petrol and basic supplies and camp (no facilities). A cabin with a wood-burning stove and hand basin is $35 s or d. With no power or telephone, a night at Gunn's Camp is Southland at its remotest—but waking up to Fiordland songbirds and a fabulous mountain panorama is worth it.

🄲 Routeburn Track

The magnificent 33-km (20.5-mi) Routeburn Track passes through high mountain scenery in both Fiordland and Mount Aspiring National Parks. It runs between the road out to Milford Sound and Routeburn Road, at the north end of Lake Wakatipu (access from Queenstown). Highlights include spectacular Routeburn Gorge, innumerable waterfalls, subalpine lakes, and views from high alpine meadows that extend west across the Darran Mountains. At the trail's high points (up to 1,280 meters/4,200 ft), the weather can be severe, and it can snow at any time of year.

Like the Milford Track, huts and campsites must be booked in advance for the main tramping season from November to April, but unlike the Milford, the Routeburn can be hiked in either direction and there is no limit to the amount of time you can spend on the track. The Great Walks Pass costs $40 per person per night for hut accommodation (most hikers spend two nights on the trail), while campers pay $12 per person per night. Bookings can be made over the phone, in writing, or at any local DOC office.

Tracknet (03/249-7777, www.tracknet.net) provides shuttles to and from either end of the track from Queenstown and Te Anau. **Info & Track** (37 Shotover St., Queenstown, 03/442-9708, www.infotrack.co.nz) is an excellent source of information on transportation and current trail conditions.

Hollyford Track

Although a relatively easy walk, the 56-km (35-mi, four days) Hollyford Track passes through remote territory in the far north of Fiordland National Park. Most hikers begin at the northern trailhead, Martins Bay (accessed only by air), and walk in a southerly direction back to civilization (recommended, as inclement weather often prevents air access to Martins Bay). At Martins Bay, the Hollyford River drains into the Tasman Sea; this river is followed the entire distance, flanked to the west by the snowcapped Darran Mountains and for 15 km (nine mi) by deep Lake McKerrow. Because the Hollyford is a low-level track, it can be hiked any time of the year. The remote coast around Martins Bay is well worth an extra day's worth of exploration before setting off.

The six huts along the track ($5 per person per night) hold up to 20 bunk beds. No bookings are required, but hut tickets must be bought in advance from the Fiordland National Park Visitor Centre in Te Anau.

Hollyford Track (03/442-7789, www.hollyfordtrack.co.nz) is a local company offering three-day guided walks, including accommodations and meals at backcountry lodges, and all transportation for $1,655. The southern trailhead, at the end of Hollyford Valley Road 18 km (11 mi) from the Te Anau–Milford Sound road, can be reached by bus with **Tracknet** (03/249-7777, www.tracknet.net); $42 each way from Te Anau. Independent hikers can book transportation, including flights, through **Info & Track** (37 Shotover St., Queenstown, 03/442-9708, www.infotrack.co.nz).

Continuing to Milford Sound

From Hollyford Valley Road to Homer Tunnel, Highway 94 veers westward and passes through some of the most magnificent scenery to be found in New Zealand.

The 1.2-km (0.7-mi) **Homer Tunnel** is another local feat of engineering (built on and off between 1935 and 1954), descending at a grade of one in ten through a mountain to the **Cleddau Portal** on the other side—drive through it with care, as it can get foggy and

SOUTHLAND

icy inside. Cross the Cleddau River, then look out for a track leading to the **Chasm,** a sight you shouldn't miss; a 10-minute walk takes you to two fascinating viewpoints. From the Chasm to Milford Sound, the road descends steeply through the **Cleddau Valley** between sheer rock walls that become endless waterfalls after a good rain. After several river crossings you pass the local airstrip and the road ends abruptly at the head of Milford Sound.

◖ MILFORD SOUND

Milford Sound (the original Maori name was Piopiotahi, meaning Single Thrush, taken from a legend) is actually a 16-km-long (10mi-long) fiord—a glaciated valley carved well below sea level, flooded by the sea when the ice melted. The sound is one of New Zealand's best-known attractions, popular for its raw beauty, splendor, and accessibility (reached by road, air, or by hiking the Milford Track). The most famous landmark is pyramid-shaped **Mitre Peak,** a magnificent sheer-faced mountain soaring 1,692 meters (5,551 ft) straight out of the sea about halfway along the sound on the south side. As in all fiords, the deepest point is at the head rather than the entrance of the sound—in Milford the water plunges 265 meters (869 ft) to the sound's deepest point off Mitre Peak. Dolphins, fur seals, an occasional Fiordland crested penguin, crayfishing boats, and tourist launches share the sound's deep dark waters, but you never lose the feeling of being at the bottom of the world.

At the end of Highway 94 nestle the few buildings that make up the tourist center of Milford Sound, along with a smattering of fishing boats and sightseeing launches in the small protected port. It's a busy place throughout the day, with a never-ending stream of buses and cruise boats swapping passengers at the wharf. Early and late in the day, it's a much quieter place. One of the reasons is the lack of places to stay—there are only lodges, one of which is restricted to hikers coming off the Milford Track with Ultimate Hikes.

© ANDREW HEMPSTEAD

Mitre Peak is easily recognizable on a boat tour of Milford Sound.

© ANDREW HEMPSTEAD

cruising on Milford Sound

Weather

The rainfall here is almost unbelievable. More than seven *meters* (23 ft) fall on average per year (the highest recorded fall for one day was 250 mm/9 in) and it's one of the wettest places in New Zealand—you can pretty much expect to see Milford Sound in rain or drizzle. However, the scenery is at its most dramatic in stormy weather, particularly during a downpour. Because of the lack of soil, water almost instantaneously cascades down the cliffs, turning into waterfalls up to 100 meters (328 ft) wide, throwing plumes of spray high into the air. The clouds cover the mountaintops, the mist comes down, and you swear the waterfalls are falling straight out of the sky. The sound also has distinct moods that change with the weather—it can be serenely beautiful on a sunny day when the reflections are mirror-perfect (in winter), mysteriously shrouded in low clouds and mist, or downright spectacular in the rain.

Cruises

The best way to see Milford Sound is to take a cruise past some of the main sights while you listen to the skipper's vivid commentary—even in bad weather when you can't see anything. As you slip through the glassy waters craning your neck back to see vertical rock walls soaring 1,500 meters (4900 ft) above (and dropping 265 meters/870 ft below sea level), feeling the spray from torrents of water plummeting straight into the sea, you can understand why Rudyard Kipling described Milford Sound as the "eighth wonder of the world." Pass delicate **Bridal Veil Falls,** come in close to impressive **Stirling Falls,** which the skippers claim they use as a boatwash, and observe fur seals lying on the rocks at aptly named **Seal Point.** Another well-known sight is the two-, sometimes three-tiered **Bowen Falls,** dropping 162 meters (530 ft) from a hanging valley into the sound—after heavy rain, the water arches way out into the sound, sometimes completely obstructing visibility.

Real Journeys (03/249-7416 or 0800/656-501, www.realjourneys.co.nz) offers the greatest variety of cruises. The most popular are aboard

SOUTHLAND

the MV *Milford Haven* and MV *Milford Monarch* up the sound and to the Tasman Sea (allow two hours). Including coach fare from Te Anau to Milford Sound, the cost is adult $142, child $70; from Queenstown the trip costs adult $205, child $95. Other optional add-ons include lunch ($15–28) and admission to an underwater observatory (adult $24, child $12).

If sailing is more to your fancy, the MV *Milford Wanderer* and MV *Milford Mariner* are other Real Journeys vessels worth considering. Day cruises depart daily for a 2.5-hour cruise ($60). At the end of every day, these two vessels turn around and head back out onto the sound for an overnight trip. The *Wanderer* has four-bed-dorm accommodation for 60 passengers ($205 per person) while the *Mariner* also sleeps 60 ($612 s, $700 d), but in private cabins with en suite bathrooms. In both cases, the fare includes dinner, overnight accommodation, and breakfast while you see the sights at a time of day when there's little other boat traffic on the water.

Red Boats (03/441-1137 or 0800/657-444, www.redboats.co.nz) has up to 10 boats departing daily for a nine-km (six-mi) trip to the head of the sound, with a stop made at the observatory (adult $60, child $15). Tea and coffee is complimentary with Red Boats, and meal options ranging $15–28 are available if preordered. In conjunction with Great Sights, a bus-cruise combo from Queenstown is $205 per person. The Queenstown departure makes for a very long day (over 10 hours); therefore the option is given to fly one way and take the coach the other ($535).

Sea Kayaking

Milford Sound Sea Kayaks (03/249-8500 or 0800/476-726) offers guided sea kayaking trips along the edge of the sound. The four-hour trip is $135. If you're coming off the Milford Track, you can arrange for kayaks to paddle back into town. The 20-minute paddle is a unique way to finish one of the world's great walks.

Short Walks

Several short walks from Milford provide excellent views of the sound. **Bowen Falls Walk** starts at the rock face by the jetties in Freshwater Basin, follows the shoreline, and comes out at the first view of the falls (which provide the hotel with water and drive a small hydroelectric plant). It's about a 30-minute walk; take a waterproof jacket. **Look-out Track** starts at the west end of the hotel and leads up a steep flight of steps to a lookout for magnificent views of the sound (five minutes); the more experienced can continue up the steep ridge for another hour or so to two more viewpoints. The track then descends to the road that leads to the tourist boat jetties.

Accommodations and Camping

Accommodation in Milford Sound is limited to basic backpacker accommodation and a lodge only open to clients of Ultimate Hikes. Other options include the campgrounds back toward Te Anau or an overnight stay aboard one of the cruise boats (described earlier).

Back about one km (0.6 mi) from the water (off the main road down a short road alive with glowworms at night) is **Milford Sound Lodge** (03/249-8071, www.milfordlodge.com). Although it's been upgraded in recent years, it's fairly basic. On the other hand, considering they have a monopoly on accommodation, prices are fair. Facilities include a communal bathroom and kitchen, guest lounge with cozy open fireplace, sauna, shop with tramping supplies, and restaurant open for breakfast and dinner. Camping is $18 per person, dorm beds $28, and double rooms with shared bath $70 s or d.

Getting There

Flying into Milford Sound is very weather-dependent. Most people fly into Milford Sound as part of a tour (see *Cruises* earlier in the *Milford Sound* section) from Queenstown. To get the best out of a day trip to Milford Sound, consider flying one way and catching a bus the other. It's a long day (including a five-hour bus trip) but worthwhile. Expect to pay over $500 for this trip, which includes a cruise. Flights from Queenstown are provided by **Air Wakatipu** (03/442-3148), **Glenorchy Air**

(03/442-2207), and **Air Fiordland** (03/442-3404 or 0800/103-404). Expect to pay around $175 for a 70-minute flightseeing trip over the sound (no landing) from Queenstown.

Intercity (03/249-7559, www.intercity coach.co.nz) and **Tracknet** (03/249-7777) offer scheduled bus service from Te Anau to Milford Sound. **Real Journeys** (03/249-7416 or 0800/656-501) has a variety of options for travel between Queenstown or Te Anau and Milford Sound, including round-trip bus transportation from Te Anau to the sound and a cruise for $142.

MANAPOURI

The small settlement of Manapouri (pop. 220), 19 km (12 mi) south of Te Anau, nestles at the mouth of the Waiau River on the shores of Lake Manapouri, second-deepest lake in the country at 443 meters (1,453 ft) and often described as "New Zealand's most beautiful lake." Backed by the snowcapped Kepler Mountains, its crystal-clear waters dotted with forest-covered islands, the lake *is* beautiful, and offers excellent brown and rainbow trout fishing, boating, and swimming. Organized cruises and charter boats cross the lake, and a number of short walks lie close to town. Manapouri is also the gateway to Doubtful Sound, accessible only by tour boat.

In the late 1960s and early '70s Lake Manapouri was the subject of a large-scale conservation battle when the government proposed raising the lake level 12 meters (40 ft) for a hydroelectric scheme—which would have destroyed its natural beauty. More than a quarter-million concerned New Zealanders (a lot of people when you consider the total population is just over four million) signed a petition opposing the destruction of the lake, and the incoming Labour Government in 1972 pledged that the lake would be left alone—the power station at West Arm was lowered 213 meters (700 ft) underground instead.

Manapouri Underground Power Station

At the far end of the lake, this is the power station that was built in a victory for protesters over 30 years ago. Constructed over a 10-year period to provide power for the Comalco aluminum smelter at Bluff (south of Invercargill), the entire power station is underground, and no dams are required to drive the massive turbines—just an exceptionally high rainfall—more than 8,000 mm (315 in) annually. As part of the lake cruise (described in the following *Doubtful Sound* section), you're driven by coach down an eerie two-km (1.2-mi) spiral tunnel into the heart of a mountain for views of the machine hall carved out of solid granite rock. A guide gives a lighthearted but detailed commentary on power production, the seven turbine-driven generators, and the two 10-km (6.2-mi) tailrace tunnels that take the water all the way to Deep Cove.

◖ Doubtful Sound

The most popular cruise from Manapouri is to Doubtful Sound with **Real Journeys** (on the riverfront at Pearl Harbour, 03/249-6602 or 0800/656-502; Oct.–Apr.). It's an eight-hour tour, which begins with a boat trip 30 km (19 mi) to West Arm at the far end of Lake Manapouri, stopping to visit the Manapouri Underground Power Station. The next stage is a wilderness bus trip over 700-meter-high (2,300-ft-high) **Wilmot Pass** to **Deep Cove,** followed by a cruise to the mouth of remote Doubtful Sound (actually a glacier-formed fiord, misnamed by Captain Cook). Geographical center of Fiordland National Park, the still waters of the fiord (broken only by penguins, dolphins, and the occasional rock lobster fishing boat), fantastic reflections, sheer 1,500-meter (4,900-ft) mountain walls, hanging valleys, and tumbling waterfalls combine to make a lasting impression. The cost is adult $230, child $55 ($240 and $64 respectively from Te Anau), and an optional lunch is $14.50–23 extra.

Adventure Kayak & Cruise (03/249-6626 or 0800/324-966, www.fiordlandadventures .co.nz) offers a more personalized tour along the same schedule as Real Journeys, but with sea kayaking and lunch included. It's a

© ANDREW HEMPSTEAD

Doubtful Sound from above

full-day trip, departing Manapouri at 7:40 A.M. and not returning until 6:10 P.M. that evening. This tour costs $195, with the option to camp overnight in Doubtful Sound for an additional $30. The company rents camping gear for $40 per night.

Short Walks

Various short walks start across the mouth of the Waiau River from Manapouri. Based in town right across the river from the main trailheads, **Adventure Charters** (03/249-6626) offers inexpensive transfers across the narrow body of water. The alternative is to rent a rowboat ($25 per day) or canoe ($45 per day) from this company and leave it tied up on the other side. The popular 3.5-hour **Circle Track** follows the shoreline before climbing a ridge to lookouts for excellent views of Hope Arm, Monument, Back Valley, Mount Titiroa, and Garnock Burn. The three-hour **Pearl Harbour-Hope Arm Track** branches off the Circle Track leading past a lagoon and swamp, and crosses the Garnock Burn to a lakeside beach and hut. The **Back**

Valley Track takes about three hours, branching off the Hope Arm Track to the Back Valley and Garnock Burn. Continue for another hour along Stinking Creek to **Lake Rakatu** for good bird-watching, fishing, and an excellent campsite on the far side of the lake (dinghy provided for public use).

The **Hope Arm-Snow White Track** starts at the hut at the head of Hope Arm, then climbs and descends for longer hikes in the Upper Garnock Burn Valley, where the hunting is good; it's about 3.5 hours one-way. You can reach the fairly difficult **Monument Track** only from the beach at the head of the bay (north of Monument in Hope Arm)—get there by boat from Pearl Harbour. The 2.5-hour track climbs steeply to a point above the tree line (be very careful on the crumbly rock and narrow ledges), where you get superb views of Lake Manapouri and the surrounding area; wear sturdy boots and take warm clothing.

Dusky Track

The 84-km (52-mi) Dusky Track links Lake

Manapouri to Lake Hauroko. The track traverses long valleys and crosses two alpine passes on its winding route between the two lakes. Most hikers make a 12-km (7.4-mi) sidetrack to Supper Cove at the head of Dusky Sound, a long fiord that deeply indents the southwest. The track is only suitable for fit, experienced, well-equipped hikers willing to allow five to nine days to do the track.

Eight huts ($5 per person per night) lie along the track. Hikers need to take a stove and fuel (dry firewood is hard to find). To get to the Lake Manapouri trailhead requires a boat trip from Te Anau. Hikers go as passengers on the tour to Doubtful Sound ($40 one-way). For schedules, contact **Real Journeys** (03/249-7416, www.realjourneys.co.nz). From the south, **Lake Hauroko Tours** (03/226-6681, www.duskytrack.co.nz) offers a variety of options from Tuatapere, including minibus and launch transportation to the southern trailhead for $80 per person. Departures are November–April on Monday and Thursday.

Accommodations and Camping

Manapouri Lakeview Motor Inn (68 Cathedral Dr., 03/249-6652, www.manapouri.com) is one km (0.6 mi) north of the post office on the main road to Te Anau. Overlooking the lake, this 55-room complex offers small, basic rooms with shared kitchen ($40 s, $70 d) and pleasant motel rooms with semi-private patios overlooking the lake ($110–120 s or d). The inn also has a bar, café, liquor store, and Internet terminal.

Manapouri Lakeview Motels and Motor Park (03/249-6624), a couple of hundred meters farther north along the road to Te Anau, also has motel rooms ($120 s or d). The eccentric owner has a vast collection of items scattered around the property—everything from a row of Morris Minor autos, to an airplane, to a game room chock-full of working pinball

machines from the last four decades. Other accommodations here include campsites ($22–24), cabins (from $55 s or d), and comfortable tourist cabins with kitchens ($90 s or d).

Don and Joy MacDuff, who once called a remote island on Doubtful Sound home, own **The Cottage** (Waiau St., 03/249-6838, www .thecottagefiordland.co.nz; $130 s or d), a delightful accommodation surrounded by English-style gardens and with river views. The three guest rooms have en suite bathrooms while two open to the gardens and one has a private deck. Breakfast is an extra $10 per person.

■ **Murrell's Grand View House** (Murrell Ave., 03/249-6642, www.murrells.co.nz; $275 s, $295 d), built in 1889 as a guesthouse, is the most comfortable accommodation in Manapouri. The old rambling house boasts wide verandahs, three homey guest rooms (each with private bathroom), mountain views, and extensive flower gardens. The house is a stone's throw from the beach and only a short stroll from the store and post office. Friendly Robert and Philippa Murrell are the fourth generation of Murrells to run the guesthouse; if you want to know anything about the area, talk to Robert. Rates include breakfast delicacies such as venison sausages and homemade marmalade (not together). The entrance is difficult to spot—look for the sign and the tall hedges across the road from the general store.

Food

Manapouri is definitely not a tourist town. The closest town of any size with a number of cafés and restaurants is Te Anau (19 km/12 mi north). There's a café beside the post office and another under the Real Journeys office by the river (daily 8 A.M.–4 P.M.). **Manapouri Lakeview Motor Inn** (68 Cathedral Dr., 03/249-6652) has a café, a restaurant, and a bar with occasional evening entertainment.

Te Anau to Invercargill

SOUTHERN SCENIC ROUTE

The Southern Scenic Route officially begins in Te Anau. It passes through Manapouri, following the eastern boundary of Fiordland National Park to **Tuatapere,** then meanders along a wild stretch of coastline to Invercargill, the largest center in Southland. This route is only slightly longer than the inland route (via Lumsden) to Invercargill, but the scenery makes it worthwhile—gentle rural landscapes liberally dotted with sheep, contrasting rugged peaks to the west, access roads to remote lakes and walking tracks in Fiordland National Park, and several small coastal towns seemingly perched at the end of the world.

Clifden and Lake Hauroko

When at Clifden, 85 km (53 mi) south of Te Anau, don't miss the impressive suspension bridge built in 1902 over the Waiau River, and the system of limestone caves nearby. From Clifden, an unsealed road runs west for 30 km (19 mi) to Lake Hauroko, deepest lake in New Zealand. Seventeen km (10.5 mi) along this road lies an outstanding stand of *totara* trees—including one of the largest known *to-tara,* believed to be more than 1,000 years old. Lake Hauroko is drained by the Waiau River, which drops 200 vertical meters (660 ft) in its 27-km (17 mi) run to the ocean. **Hump Ridge Jet** (03/225-8174, www.humpridgejet.co.nz) provides an exciting ride across Lake Hauroko and down the river to the ocean. The return trip takes four hours and can be combined with a four-hour trek to an abandoned viaduct for $175, or $190 with lunch.

Tuatapere

This small farming town of 700 was once the center of a large timber industry that supported the area for decades (visit the Tuatapere Domain to see what the area *used* to look like). The town is an excellent base for embarking on a number of tracks in the remote southern end of Fiordland National Park—an area that is relatively quiet in comparison with the north of the park.

Basic rooms, a few with en suites, are available at the **Waiau Hotel** (47 Main St., 03/226-6409, www.waiauhotel.co.nz; $35–50 s, $45–55 d), which is also the best place in town for meals. **Tuatapere Camping Ground**

© ANDREW HEMPSTEAD

windswept trees along the coastal road to Invercargill

(on Peace St., 03/226-6626) provides tent and caravan sites for $18 s or d and a cabin for $45 per night. Other options for campers include the Domain, or, farther out, a DOC campground at Lake Monowai.

At **Tuatapere Information Centre** (Orawia Rd., 03/226-6739; daily 9 A.M.–4 P.M.) staff enthusiastically describe everything there is to see and do in the area and help organize transportation to all trailheads.

South Coast Track

Beginning at Bluecliffs Beach at Te Waewae Bay, this walking track traverses a wild stretch of coastline to **Port Craig,** which, in the 1920s, was the location of New Zealand's largest sawmill. Logs were cut farther west, then brought to the mill along a rough track that crossed four steep-sided valleys over which massive viaducts were constructed. The **Percy Burn Viaduct** was the largest at 125 meters (410 ft) long and a dizzying 36 meters (118 ft) above the valley floor. It has been repaired and re-decked, allowing trampers to continue west to the mouth of the Wairaurahiri River (a jetboat service can be organized to Lake Hauroko; contact **Hump Ridge Jet** at 03/225-8174; www.humpridgejet.co.nz). Along the trail are three huts, including the old Port Craig schoolhouse. More detailed information is available from Tuatapere Information Centre (03/226-6739).

Hump Ridge Track

The 53-km (33-mi) Hump Ridge Track has been improved to alleviate "overcrowding" on the South Coast Track. It branches north at the end of Bluecliffs Beach, following an old logging road and climbing steadily to a hut just below the tree line. The track then follows a ridge from where you get spectacular views of the southern reaches of Fiordland National Park and Te Waewae Bay before descending to Lake Hauroko. For track details contact **Tutapere Hump Track Trust** (03/226-6739, www.humpridgetrack.co.nz), based at Tuatapere Information Centre. This nonprofit group organizes track accommodations, transportation, and equipment rentals.

Riverton

Historic Riverton (pop. 1,800), oldest settlement in the south and once the base for sealers and whalers, lies at the mouth of the Aparima River, 38 km (24 mi) west of Invercargill. A popular fishing resort, it has safe sandy beaches and good fishing. Nearby **Riverton Rocks** is another seaside resort with safe beaches. The small **Wallace Early Settlers Museum** (172 Palmerston St., 03/234-8520; daily 2–4 P.M.) displays items from pioneer days, and acts as the local information center.

◖ Riverton Rock Guesthouse (136 Palmerston St., 03/234-8886 or 0800/248-886, www.riverton.co.nz; $95–145 s or d) offers comfortable lodgings in a restored hotel dating to 1863. The Fireside Forest, complete with two beds and a log fire, is $135 s or d (although the bathroom is shared). Furnishings and facilities throughout are of the highest standard, and guests have use of a kitchen and lounge, both overlooking the river.

Through town to the south, the **Beach House** (126 Rocks Hwy., 03/234-8274; daily for breakfast, lunch, and dinner) is a contemporary space with lots of local seafood and a heated patio. Expect to pay from $18 for a dinner main.

TE ANAU TO GORE

The most direct route between Te Anau and Invercargill is to take Highway 94 to **Lumsden,** then veer south on Highway 6 along the Oreti River. But if you're agriculturally minded, have your own transportation, and enjoy scenic sidetracks off the main tourist drag, continue east from Lumsden on Highway 94, crossing fertile plains and sheep country to Gore.

Mandeville

Mandeville, 42 km (26 mi) east of Lumsden, is home of the **Croydon Aircraft Company** (03/208-9755)—a must-see for any aircraft enthusiast. They specialize in restoring vintage aircraft, oftentimes from scratch and including rebuilding engines and recalibrating instruments. Visitors are encouraged to wander around the enormous hangar where volunteers patiently work on de Havilland, Tiger Moth, Fox Moth, Dragon Fly, and larger Dominie planes. Adjacent to the hangar and airfield is **The Moth** (03/208-9662, Tues.–Sun. for lunch and dinner), a historic hotel refurbished with an aviation theme.

Gore

The regional urban center of Gore lies on the banks of the **Mataura River,** 66 km (41 mi) northeast of Invercargill. The river is renowned worldwide for its brown trout fishing, but even if you're not into angling, the town's wide streets, attractive stone architecture, and many parks and gardens give this busy town of 8,500 its appeal. Anglers flock from afar to dangle their lines in the Mataura River and its myriad streams and to explore the fishing possibilities of the **Mimihau, Pomahaka, Oreti,** and **Waikaia Rivers** in the surrounding region; get your hot tips and a license at any sporting goods store downtown.

Gore Historical Museum (corner of Norfolk St. and Hokonui Dr., 03/208-7032; Mon.–Fri. 9 A.M.–5 P.M., Sat.–Sun. 1–4 P.M.; donation) is crammed with local history, including one display dedicated to the moonshiners who once plied their trade in the surrounding hills. The museum also serves as the local information center. five km (3.1 mi) west of Gore is **Croydon Bush,** a reserve where you can view native flora while wandering at will along tracks through grassland, forest, and valleys crammed with lush ferns. Formal **Dolamore Park,** with its contrasting lawns and flower gardens, lies next to the reserve.

A five-minute walk from downtown, the river, and the museum, **Riverlea Motel** (48 Hokonui Dr., 03/208-3130; $95–135 s or d) offers 10 clean and comfortable rooms, each with a kitchen. On the south side of downtown, **Gore Motor Camp** (35 Broughton St., 03/208-4919) offers communal facilities, tent sites for $20, powered sites for $24, and cabins for $45.

❰ THE CATLINS

The alternative to zipping down Highway 1 to Invercargill from Gore is to follow Highway 1

east toward Dunedin, then cut back along the coast to Invercargill on Highway 92 through the remote, beautiful Catlins coastal region. From Dunedin, the most direct route to Invercargill is via Gore, but if you have plenty of time and like to get off the tourist track, this coastal route (Hwy. 92) will only add a couple of hours to the journey. That said, many of the coastal highlights detailed below are off the main highway, so you should allow at least a full day to make the most of this wildly scenic region. Meander through the podocarp-hardwood forests that make up **Catlins Forest Park,** getting tempting glimpses of isolated sandy beaches and rugged coastal scenery; sidetracks to the coast are worthwhile, especially **Cannibal Bay** north of Owaka and **Jack's Bay**—cliffs, grassy hills, a perfect golden-sand surf beach, and a 30-minute track to 55-meter-deep (180-ft-deep) Jack's Blowhole in the middle of clifftop pastures—south of Owaka. Birds abound in the Catlins, the rivers provide all types of trout fishing and whitebaiting in season (get your license at local sporting goods stores), and sea-fishing for blue

Hooker's sea lions often drag themselves ashore along the Catlins Coast.

© ANDREW HEMPSTEAD

SOUTHLAND

CATLINS WILDLIFE TRACKERS

Owned and operated by Mary and Fergus Sutherland, Catlins Wildlife Trackers (03/415-8613 or 0800/228-5467, www.catlins-ecotours.co.nz) offers numerous options for making the most of the Catlins. Most popular are two- and four-day packages ($345 and $690 respectively) that include accommodation at their Papatowai lodge, all meals, and day trips throughout the region, searching out wildlife such as penguins, sea lions, elephant seals, and Hector's dolphins while also hearing about the area's geology, climate, and human history. Travel is by minibus, but most of the time is spent exploring and learning to view nature from a perspective that will be new to all those except the most deeply committed ecotourist.

For the more adventurous, pay just $35 to hike the Top Track over coastal private property. The cost includes an information kit and an overnight stay in an old trolley bus decked out with bunk beds. Finally, the company rents out a number of self-contained cottages through the Catlins ($70-135 s or d).

cod is popular along the coast. Historic, scenic, and recreational reserves line the road—most providing short scenic nature walks, lookouts, campgrounds (limited facilities) or picnic areas, and toilets and fresh water.

Balclutha to Papatowai

The first worthwhile detour is to **Nugget Point.** To get there, turn off Highway 92 seven km (4.3 mi) south of Balclutha and follow the road for 21 km (13 mi), passing through the picturesque seaside community of **Kaka Point.** For the last one km (0.6 mi), the road climbs steeply to a parking lot, from where an exposed walking track leads to **Nugget Point Lighthouse,** built in 1869. Bird- and sealife abound around the point. Southern fur seals bask year-round on the rocks below, elephant

seals and Hooker's sea lions frequent the area, penguins breed here, and gannets, shags, and shearwaters nest and feed around the point.

Back on Highway 92, between Owaka and Papatowai, keep your eyes peeled for the sign to **Purakaunui Falls,** a great little track for stretching your legs. A five-to-ten-minute stroll from the flat, grassy, camping area takes you to a viewing platform overlooking these pleasingly asymmetric falls.

Across from a shell-covered beach, **Papatowai Motor Camp** (30 km/19 mi southwest of Owaka on Hwy. 92, 03/415-8565; tenting $8 per person, powered sites $9 per person, cabins $32 s or d) has the usual communal facilities as well as tearooms and a general store. For a more private hideaway in the trees, consider staying at **Tautuku Lodge** (03/415-8024; from $25 per person per night) in 550-hectare (1360-acre) Lenz Reserve, six km (3.7 mi) south of Papatowai beside the Fleming River. Owned by Forest and Bird Southland, the property features a six-bed lodge with bathroom and well-equipped kitchen; a bathroom block; an attractive four-bed cabin with kitchen, lounge, and large deck; and a tiny two-bed A-frame cabin with basic kitchen. Several walks and tracks of varying lengths start at the lodge. It's signposted on the main road, but because it's understandably popular, it's best to book with the caretaker.

Continuing West from Papatowai

As the road leaves Papatowai, it passes through Catlins Forest Park, with all the coastal and scenic reserves and walking tracks well signposted. The first worthwhile stops are **Waipati Beach** and **Cathedral Caves;** from the parking area it's a 15-minute walk to the beach, and a 25-minute walk through native bush and along the beach to impressive caves that resemble an English cathedral (accessible only at low tide; tide tables are posted at the turnoff from Hwy. 92). About seven km (4.3 mi) farther along the road, watch for the sign to **Chaslands Farm Motor Lodge** (Waipati Rd., 03/415-8501; $75 s, $85 d)—one of the best accommodation deals in the Catlins. You get

SOUTHLAND

© ANDREW HEMPSTEAD

a lighthouse along the Catlins Coast

a motel unit that's like a small home away from home in a farm setting. You may find large woolly sheep mowing the grass by the swings or snoozing under the trampoline. Each unit has bedrooms with linen and towels provided, a bathroom, a fully equipped kitchen with refrigerator (bring your own food), and a living room with TV. The friendly owners provide a free bottle of milk, and plenty of information on the Catlins.

Curio Bay and Vicinity

Turn off the highway 35 km (22 mi) west of Papatowai and drive through Waikawa to reach Curio Bay, one of the highlights of the Catlins. This bay is protected from the prevailing southerly winds by high cliffs to the south. From the end of the road, the high headland provides a panoramic view across the bay (scan the bay's calm waters for dolphins, which often frolic near the shore). To the south, the cliffs drop dramatically to a wide ledge and the raging southern ocean. Follow the cliff line westward and you'll come across Petrified Forest signs, leading to **Curio Bay Scientific Reserve,** where there are a lookout, interpretive boards, and wooden stairs that lead down to a flat rock platform cluttered with petrified tree stumps. If it's low tide, don't just stop at the lookout. You need to be actually on the rocks to really appreciate all the petrified tree logs and stumps that make up one of the world's best examples of a Jurassic fossil forest.

You can camp along the cliff top at Curio Bay, but facilities are limited (no showers or kitchen; $6 per person per night) and the weather can deteriorate rapidly. Excellent value is (**Waikawa Holiday Lodge** (Waikawa, 03/246-8552; $50 s or d), a small place with just three guest rooms, but the lounge is cozy (with a log fire) and the communal kitchen well equipped. The hosts live elsewhere in the village, so call ahead and they'll meet you at the lodge, show you around, and tell you everything there is to do and see in the region.

Invercargill and Vicinity

Invercargill, largest city of Southland and one of the world's southernmost cities, is a well-planned metropolis of 49,000. Originally settled by Scottish people, Invercargill has wide tree-lined streets named after Scottish rivers, many beautiful parks and reserves (the acreage of parks per population is the highest in New Zealand), and plenty of reasonable places to stay, though it's not the place to come for titillating tourist attractions or exciting nightlife.

Intensive farming is practiced on the plains stretching inland from the city—this productive and obviously prosperous region produces more than six million lambs a year, 36 million kg (79 million lbs) of wool, two million bushels of wheat, 6,000 tons of potatoes, and 5,000 tons of cheese. The bulk of the region's

SOUTHLAND

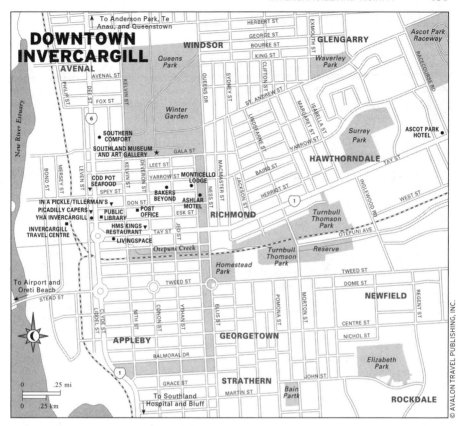

wealth comes from more than eight million sheep, though the dairy factories; small seed producers; timber mills; fertilizer, cement, and freezer works; a paper mill; a coal mine; and an aluminium smelter are all major contributors.

SIGHTS AND RECREATION
◖ Southland Museum and Art Gallery

On the northern edge of downtown, this pyramid-shaped museum (Victoria Ave., 03/219-9069; Mon.–Fri. 10 A.M.–5 P.M., Sat.–Sun. 10 A.M.–5 P.M.; donation) stands 26 meters (85 ft) high with a 50-meter (160-ft) base. The biggest attraction within this distinctive structure is the gallery dedicated to Antarctica, featuring *Beyond the Roaring Forties Subantarctic Experience,* a stunning 25-minute audiovisual on the islands ($4), a subantarctic garden, and a historical display. The museum also features items from the province's early days, a collection of Maori artifacts, and a fascinating "tuatarium," one of the only places in the country where you can see live *tuatara* in a closely simulated native environment. The *tuatara* looks like a lizard but is actually the only surviving species of the Sphenodontia order of reptiles, once widespread but now found only on about 30 islands off the northeast coast of the North Island and Cook Strait. Described as New Zealand's "living fossil," the *tuatara* has an undetermined lifespan but it's believed that it lives to be at least 100 years old. This tuatarium is the only place in the world with a regular captive breeding

SOUTHLAND

© AVALON TRAVEL PUBLISHING, INC.

© ANDREW HEMPSTEAD

Climb to the top of the water tower on Leet Street for city views.

program. If you watch the *tuatara* for quite some time, you may actually see one of them move—maybe Henry, who is more than 115 years old, or Lucy, who is over 50 years old.

Queens Park

Eighty-hectare (200-acre) **Queens Park** (on Queens Dr.) is a peaceful green spot in the central city, the perfect place to while away some time, especially on the weekend when everything closes. Wander past perfect lawns under all kinds of native and exotic trees; visit the large aviary, statuary, gardens, and duck ponds; and if you're feeling energetic, follow the fitness trail.

Anderson Park

Originally a farm, Anderson Park (McIvor Rd., 03/215-7432; daily 10:30 A.M.–5 P.M.; donation) features 20 hectares (50 acres) of native bush that has remained virtually unchanged and a garden of exotic trees. The original farmhouse is now an art gallery with an impressive collection of early New Zealand land-scape paintings. The park lies seven km (4.3 mi) north of Invercargill.

Short Walks

Before Invercargill was built, the entire area was natural bush—see how it used to be in **Waihopai Scenic Reserve,** 34 hectares (84 acres) on the city's northern outskirts, with a 2.8-km (1.7-mi) walk along the Waihopai River (it starts on Hwy. 6 at Gladstone Terr. and finishes on Racecourse Rd.; one hour one-way), or at 120-hectare (300-acre) **Seaward Bush** southeast of Invercargill.

Sandy Point Reserve, west of the city along **New River Estuary,** is another good area for short bush walks with views of the estuary, Invercargill, and several protected beaches. Get information and brochures on walking tracks around the city and the region at the DOC Field Centre in the State Insurance Building (Don St., 03/214-4589).

Oreti Beach, 9.5 km (5.9 mi) west of the city along the shores of Foveaux Strait, is a long sweep of sand excellent for walking; on a clear day, you can see Stewart Island. The water is warmer here than along many South Island beaches, thanks to a warm current from Australia.

ENTERTAINMENT AND EVENTS

Invercargill is not the most exciting place in New Zealand for evening entertainment—unless you enjoy drinking in the many hotel bars around town. The hotels and liquor stores in the city are operated by Invercargill Licensing Trust, a local authority founded in 1944 when liquor licensing was re-established after 38 years of prohibition, with members elected by the community; all profits are used to remodel the hotels or for community projects. The **Frog 'n' Firkin** (31 Dee St., 03/214-4001) is one of the friendlier pubs in town, and occasionally has live music. The **Embassy** (112 Dee St., 03/214-0050) is Invercargill's premier nightclub. For something a bit tamer, contact the **Invercargill Musical Theatre** (176 Don St., 03/218-4440, www.imti.co.nz) for a mix of professional and amateur performances.

SOUTHLAND

On the second weekend of February, the city springs to life for the **Invercargill Summer Festival** (www.invercargillsfestival .co.nz). A street parade, running races, live music, and outdoor movie screenings take place all over town.

ACCOMMODATIONS AND CAMPING
Under $50
Southern Comfort (30 Thomson St., 03/218-3838; dorm beds $21, $45 s, $50 d) shines brightly for excellent services and friendly hosts. In one of the city's many leafy suburbs, it's an easy walk to the museum and downtown. All the usual facilities are provided, everything is modern, the building is immaculately clean, and guests have free use of a few bikes.

Also known as Tuatara Lodge, the world's southernmost YHA property, **YHA Invercargill** (30 Dee St., 03/214-0954, www .yha.co.nz) has all the usual facilities in a converted villa, including a booking desk for onward travel. Dorm beds are $23, private rooms $65 s or d, and the double en suite is $85.

$50-100
You'll think you're paying a lot more than you really are at ◖ **LivingSpace** (15 Tay St., 03/211-3801, www.livingspace.co.nz; $80–110 s or d), a slick hotel-like accommodation in the heart of downtown. The rooms are bright, ultra modern, and almost minimalist, with facilities that include kitchenettes, high-speed Internet, and a work desk. A lounge and small movie theater are available for guest use.

Combining a location close to downtown and good-value rooms is the **Ashlar Motel** (81 Queens Dr., 03/217-9093 0800/274-527, www .ashlarmotel.co.nz; $85–120 s or d), with nine self-contained, well-kept rooms. Breakfast and dinner are available for an extra charge. Other moderately priced motels line Tay Street (Hwy. 1) east of downtown and North Road (Hwy. 6) north of downtown.

Across Otakaro Park toward downtown from the Ashlar, **Montecillo Lodge** (240 Spey St., 03/218-2503; $80 s, $100 d) is an attractive house built in 1895. The rooms in the original building, along with a dining room and lounge, are appealingly old-fashioned. Rates include breakfast and dinner is available for an extra $20 per person.

Over $100
The **Ascot Park Hotel** (corner of Tay St. and Racecourse Rd., 03/217-6195, www.ilt.cop .nz/ascot) is a sprawling complex just under four km (2.4 mi) east of the city. It's designed mainly as a conference center but has a heated pool and spa, landscaped gardens, and multiple restaurants and bars. Accommodations are in spacious self-contained motel-style rooms ($125 s or d) or in more upscale hotel rooms ($175–190 s or d).

Holiday Park
The most central of Invercargill's campgrounds is **Invercargill Caravan Park** (on Victoria Ave. off Dee St., the main highway north, 03/218-8787). One km (0.6 mi) north of city center, it's next to a track where greyhounds are trained some mornings (free entertainment) and raced two evenings a month. The camp has communal facilities, a TV lounge, and a general store. Tent sites in the large, grassy camping area are $10 per person, powered sites are $12 per person, comfortable cabins start at $40 (definitely worth the extra bucks when it's raining), and a few bunk beds are $15 per person.

FOOD
On the east side of downtown, **Bakers Beyond** (198 Spey St., 03/218-6911; Mon.–Sat. 8 A.M.–4 P.M.) has the best pies in town. They use top-notch ingredients such as venison, and also offer wholemeal pies with creative fillings such as a chicken, cranberry, and camembert combo.

The menu at **Picadilly Capers** (38 Dee St., 03/218-1044; daily 11 A.M.–9 P.M.) offers traditional fare, with the specials board getting slightly more creative. The setting is modern, but pleasantly unfocused with a variety of seating styles. Around the corner, the food at **In a Pickle** (16 Don St., 03/218-7340; Mon.–Fri. 8 A.M.–4 P.M., Sat.–Sun. 11 A.M.–4 P.M.) is better than the setting may suggest. Expect to pay under $10 for delicious pancakes at breakfast and freshly made quiche at lunch.

Oyster lovers *must* sample Foveaux oysters—the region's delicacy. Old-fashioned and centrally located, **Cod Pot Seafood** (136 Dee St., 03/218-2354; daily for lunch and dinner) has battered oysters and the usual choice of seafood to eat in at the booths or takeout.

A good place for healthy dining is **(** Tillermans Café Bar** (16 Don St., 03/218-9240, Mon.–Fri. for lunch, Tues.–Sat. for dinner). Sit in an airy room surrounded by elegant antique furniture while you munch on sandwiches and mixed salads, the hot dish of the day (whole foods, vegetarian, seafood, chicken), sushi, or fresh fruit salad. There's live music (from classical to blues) most weekends.

Locals flock to **HMS Kings Restaurant** (82 Tay St., 03/218-3443; Mon.–Fri. 11:30 A.M.–9:30 P.M., Sat–Sun. 5–9:30 P.M.) for a semi-splurge in a very nautical atmosphere—lots of wood, portholes filled with shells, knotted rope, and life preservers. Tasty dishes average $22 (the Fisherman's Platter for $24 has a good selection of deep-fried seafood), and the portions are enormous.

Most folks dine out so they *don't* have to cook, but doing so can be fun also. At **Big Willy Rustlers Bar & Grill** (Newfield Tavern, Centre St., 03/216-7313; Thurs.–Sun. from 4:30 P.M.), choose your meat of choice and cook it yourself on the large barbecue. A T-bone with potato and salad is $17.

PRACTICALITIES
Information
For information on Invercargill and all of Southland, call in at the **Invercargill Visitor Information Centre,** located within Southland Museum (Victoria Ave., 03/214-6243, www.invercargill.org.nz; Mon.–Fri. 10 A.M.–5 P.M., Sat.–Sun. 10 A.M.–5 P.M.). **Venture Southland Tourism** (www.visit.southlandnz.com) is another source of local information.

Services
The post office (03/214-7700) is at 51 Don Street. **Invercargill Public Library** (Dee St., 03/211-1444; Mon.–Fri. 9 A.M.–8 P.M., Sat. 10 A.M.–1 P.M., Sunday 1–4 P.M.) has a solid collection of local literature. Internet access is free, but you should call to reserve a terminal. No reservations are necessary at **Global Byte Café** (150 Dee St., 03/214-4724), but you pay $4 per hour to get online.

Southland Hospital (Kew Rd., Kew, 03/218-1949) is south of the city center. **Invercargill Urgent Doctor** (103 Don St., 03/218-8821) is open Monday–Friday 5–10 P.M., Saturday and Sunday 8 A.M.–10 P.M.

Getting There and Around
The airport is 2.5 km (1.6 mi) from the city center, with downtown transfers provided by **Spitfire Shuttles** (03/214-1851, $5 each way). **Air New Zealand** (03/215-0000 or 0800/737-300, www.airnewzealand.com) flies from Invercargill to Dunedin and Christchurch direct. Flights to all other points are routed through Christchurch. **Intercity** (03/214-6243, www.intercitycoach.co.nz) provides regular bus services from Te Anau, Queenstown and Lumsden, Dunedin and Gore, terminating at the Invercargill Travel Centre in the railway station on Leven Street.

Passenger Transport (03/218-7108) buses depart from opposite the old post office on Dee Street and head to all corners of the city daily except Sunday 10 A.M.–2:30 P.M. Travel on the city-center loop is free while beyond this you pay adult $2, child $1 per sector. Car rental agencies with offices out at the airport include **Avis** (03/218-7019), **Budget** (03/218-7012), and **Hertz** (03/218-2837). Local taxi companies are **Blue Star** (03/218-6079) and **Taxi Co.** (03/214-4478).

BLUFF
At the end of Highway 1, 27 km (17 mi) south of Invercargill, lies Bluff, the South Island's largest port, and home base for fishing fleets that cruise the south and west coasts for fish, crayfish, and delicious Foveaux Strait oysters (commonly called Bluff oysters). The Maori called Bluff Motu-Pohue, or Island of Pohue, after a giant white convolvulus that flowers yearly on Bluff Hill.

Sights and Walks

At the *very* end of Highway 1 (or at the beginning—Cape Reinga, north of Auckland, lays claim to being the "end" of Hwy. 1) is **Stirling Point**—and an often-photographed sign giving distances to far-flung destinations around the world.

For panoramic views of the harbor, Foveaux Strait, and Stewart Island, head to the lookout atop **Bluff Hill** (265 meters/870 ft)—particularly enjoyable in the evening when the waters far below are dotted with fishing boats on their way home. Starting from Stirling Point, the 6.6-km (4.1-mi) **Ocean Beach Track** follows the coastline around Bluff Hill for magnificent views of beaches and offshore islands, crossing small gullies into open pasture with views of farmland and the coastline; allow 2.5 hours one-way.

New Zealand Aluminium Smelters Ltd. (Tiwai Point, 26 km/16 mi south of Invercargill, 03/218-5440) is one of the world's largest aluminium smelters (no, not a spelling error— "aluminum" is a trademarked North American bastardization of the proper spelling), and a vital part of Southland economy. The bauxite is mined and refined in northern Australia, then shipped to New Zealand for smelting. The facility runs free two-hour tours three times a week, but you need to book a space, have your own transportation out there, and wear a long-sleeved shirt, long pants, and closed-toe shoes. Although the smelter is at Bluff, access is along Tiwai Road, which branches off Highway 1 eleven km (6.8 mi) south of Invercargill.

Practicalities

Bluff has no motels. Instead, consider **Land's End** (10 Ward Pde., 03/212-7575, www.landsend.net.nz; $100 s, $140–150 d), overlooking the ocean from a hilltop position at Stirling Point. This white two-story lodge has seven guest rooms, each with an en suite bathroom. Rates include a cooked breakfast. Adjacent, the **Drunken Sailor Cafe** (03/212-8855; daily at 10 A.M. for lunch, Sat. only for dinner) has stunning views over Foveaux Strait. Seafood features prominently with chowder ($11) and fish dishes, such as battered flounder ($15.95), are reasonably priced. The menu even includes an American Sandwich ($12), which is basically a BLT—just what you've traveled to the end of the road at the opposite side of the world for.

Stewart Island

Stewart Island is the third and most southerly of New Zealand's main islands, separated from the South Island by shallow, 24-km (15-mi) **Foveaux Strait.** Called Rakiura (Land of the Glowing Skies) by the Maori, it is a peaceful place, whose appeal lies in its natural beauty (over 75 percent of the island is protected as a national park), well-maintained walking tracks, and abundant seafood.

Including outlying islands, Stewart Island covers an area of 1,746 square km (674 sq mi). The island, almost triangular in shape, stretches 65 km (40 mi) from north to south, 40 km (25 mi) from east to west, and its deeply indented coastline is about 755 km (470 mi). Most of the island is mountainous and hard to penetrate, with short, sheer gullies and steep ridge systems, but it's fringed with bays and sandy beaches.

Oban (pop. 400), the island's only settlement, home of fishermen, vacationers, and island devotees, lies nestled along the protected shores of Halfmoon Bay, on the east side of the island. Ferries and scheduled flights provide a link to the mainland while in Oban itself you'll find a range of services (except a bank), accommodations, and eateries.

SIGHTS AND RECREATION

Oban is the principal settlement, nestled along the sandy shores of Halfmoon Bay. Most of the island's 400 permanent residents live at Halfmoon Bay, and the 50-boat fishing fleet is anchored here. A variety of short tracks start in

SOUTHLAND

Oban, and several beautiful beaches lie within walking distance of town.

Oban

If you're able to spend only a day on Stewart Island (not long enough), you'll find lots of things to do in and around Oban. Your first stop should be the **Stewart Island Visitor Centre** (Main Rd., 03/219-0002, Jan.–Mar. Mon.–Fri. 8:30 A.M.–7 P.M., Sat.–Sun. 9 A.M.–7 P.M., the rest of the year Mon.–Fri. 8:30 A.M.–5 P.M.), which has general island information, hiking trail brochures, and displays (don't miss the mounted *kakapo*, an almost-extinct nocturnal parrot).

BIRD SANCTUARY

High rainfall, mild winters, and fertile soil combine to create lush forests across Stewart Island, with *rimu, miro, totara,* ferns, mosses, scented native orchids (30 species), and a wealth of native plants. This setting is home to the Stewart Island brown kiwi, which is larger than its mainland relatives and has a longer beak and legs. But the main appeal for visitors is that unlike other kiwis, it feeds during the day (usually for an hour after sunrise and before sunset), creating the unparalleled opportunity to see this iconic creature in its natural habitat. A couple of smaller offshore islands provide a home for *kakapo,* a flightless, nocturnal parrot. Perilously close to extinction in the 1980s, there are now a little less than 100 in existence, with most living on uninhabited islands around the Stewart Island coast. Also resident are *kaka,* parakeets, Stewart Island robins, fernbirds, dotterels, pied shags, Stewart Island shags, and yellow-eyed penguins. The forest abounds with bush birds – *tui,* bellbirds, pigeons, parakeets, cuckoos, *kaka,* brown creepers, fantails, tomtits, grey warblers, and finches. Along the shores you find oystercatchers, herons, black-billed gulls, blue penguins, Hooker's sea lions, and fur seals.

Rakiura Museum (Ayr St.; Mon.–Sat. 10 A.M.–noon, Sun. noon–2 P.M.; adult $2, child $0.50) houses a fascinating collection of historic relics relating to the island's whaling, sealing, timber milling, and pioneering past; Maori art; and information on the island's modern fishing industry.

Walking Tracks

Find out where all Stewart Island's 150 km (93 mi) of tracks lead by picking up the *Stewart Island Day Walks* brochure at the visitor center. It's packed with useful information, and has directions and descriptions for all the day tracks close to Oban. The most rewarding of these is to **Observation Rock,** particularly splendid at sunset.

Longer tracks take you into some of New Zealand's most beautiful bush. Locals say that as long as you can hike with a pack for at least four hours nonstop, you're fit enough to do the tracks on Stewart Island. Tracks in the northern sector of the island are especially intended for experienced hikers, winding along the picturesque shoreline and deep into the dense interior. The most popular long-distance walking track, the **North-West Circuit,** meanders along the northern coast of the island, taking 7–10 days to complete—add several extra days if you sidetrack to Mason Bay (a reliable kiwi-spotting spot) on the west coast.

◖ Ulva Island

All manner of cruises can be taken from Oban, with Ulva Island, in Paterson Inlet, the most popular destination. The island is predator-free and has been a bird sanctuary since 1922. Hiking trails lead to all corners of the island, and the habitat remains natural. Water taxis run over to the island regularly (about $25 per person round-trip), or take a guided tour. Typically, a tour includes a stop at the island and a visit to a salmon farm. If you want to spend more time on the island, ask to be left behind and you can get picked up on the boat's return from the farm. All trips leave from the wharf at the south end of Golden Bay Road. **Stewart Island Adventures** (03/212-7700) operate a large vessel, with lots of onboard facilities, on a 2.5-hour tour that includes a short walk on Ulva Island. Departures are September–April daily at 11:30 A.M. and the cost is adult $59, child $29.50. **Ruggedy Range Wilderness Experiences** (03/219-1066, www.ruggedyrange.com) offer a variety of options for visiting Ulva Island, including as a day trip from Invercargill.

Sea Kayaking

The calm waters of Paterson Inlet are perfect for sea kayaking. The inlet lies a couple of kilometers by road south of Oban, offering endless opportunities for a wilderness trip with its convoluted shoreline, many small islands, and a number of DOC huts. **Stewart Island Sea Kayak Adventures** (03/219-1080) rents single and double kayaks for $30 per person per day and can arrange drop-offs anywhere around the inlet.

Golfing

On the outskirts of Oban, **Ringa Ringa Golf Course** (03/219-1269; green fees $5) boasts just six holes, but the fact that it's farther south than any other golf course in the world makes it a popular attraction.

ACCOMMODATIONS

Accommodations on the island are limited, so make bookings before arriving. That said, they span the entire length of the price spectrum.

$50-100

Centrally located **Jo and Andy's B&B** (Morris St., 03/219-1230) is good value at $40 s, $60 d, in rooms with shared bath and access to cooking facilities. As a bonus, a cooked breakfast is included in the rates.

Built in 1927, the venerable **South Sea Hotel** (03/219-1059, www.stewart-island.co.nz) overlooks Halfmoon Bay and has a restaurant and lounge. The 16 guest rooms in the original building share bathrooms ($60 s, $80 d), but a couple have water views ($90 s, $100 d). Adjacent are more modern if smallish motel rooms for $135 s or d.

Over $100

In a forested setting, **Rakiura Retreat** (Horseshoe Bay Rd., 03/219-1096, www.rakiuraretreat.co.nz; $100 s, $150 d) lies just over one km (0.6 mi) north of the ferry dock. Each of the five rooms has a kitchen and one or two bedrooms.

Port of Call (Leask Bay Rd., 03/219-1394, www.portofcall.co.nz; $250 s, $285 d), is a modern bed-and-breakfast operated by sixth-generation islanders. Running right down to the ocean, the 20-hectare (49-acre) property is surrounded by bird-filled bush and encompasses an 1870s stone cottage. Only one room is offered for overnight guests, meaning you'll have full access to the comfortable lounge with an open fire and plenty of local literature. Rates include a light breakfast and complimentary hot drinks, fruit, and cookies throughout the day. The same family also rents a downtown cottage ($160 s or d) and a forest-encircled bach ($250).

FOOD

If you like fresh fish, Stewart Island is a culinary delight. The residents live off the sea, and although a thousand sheep graze the backcountry and deer are widespread, crayfish and blue cod are the main sources of income and diet. At **Four Square Supermarket** (Elgin Terr., 03/219-1069; Mon.–Fri. 9 A.M.–5:30 P.M., Sat.–Sun. 10 A.M.–noon) you can buy regular groceries, picnic lunches, and hot takeout meals. **Justcafe** (1 Main Rd., 03/219-1567; daily 8 A.M.–8 P.M.) has good coffee, a range of cakes and pastries, and other homemade goodies, such as quiche.

Up the hill from the ferry dock, **Church Hill Café** (36 Kamahi Rd., 03/219-1323; daily 10 A.M.–9 P.M.) offers fantastic ocean views from its elevated location. Seafood dominates the menu, with dinner mains in the $22–30 range. **South Sea Hotel** (03/219-1059, noon–2 P.M. and 6–8 P.M. daily) offers surprisingly good food to be enjoyed at the bar, in the dining room, or at tables out front. Start with the seafood chowder ($9), and then choose a local specialty, such as battered blue cod with tartar sauce ($20) or grilled crayfish ($32). Less adventurous seafood treats, such as chowder, oysters, and mussels, are good for a lighter meal. A separate bar menu is less expensive but offers many of the same choices.

GETTING THERE

There are two ways to get to the island—by a 20-minute flight from Invercargill or a one-hour ferry crossing from Bluff. If you can afford the time and expense, ferry one way and fly the other for a broader experience.

Until 1980, when an island airstrip was developed, seaplanes landed right in Oban Bay. Today, **Stewart Island Flights** (03/218-9129 or 0800/843-475, www.stewartislandflights .co.nz) offers three scheduled flights daily between Invercargill Airport and the island; bus transfers to Oban are included in the airfare. The one-way fare is $90, or pay $155 round-trip (discounts for seniors, students, HI members, or those prepared to go standby). Packages offered by Stewart Island Flights include a same-day return fare, including a 90-minute bus tour, a boat trip, and lunch combined with flights for $230. The baggage allowance on all flights is just 15 kg (33 lbs) per person.

Stewart Island Experience (03/212-7660 or 0800/000-511, www.stewartislandexperience .co.nz) operates two passenger-only catamarans between Bluff and the main wharf at Oban up to five times daily (reduced winter sailings). The crossing takes an hour and costs adult $51, child $25.50 each way. If you need vehicle storage in Bluff, it's available for $8 per day. (The strait is very shallow and can become extremely rough at a moment's notice. The ferry makes crossings, weather permitting, but it can still get uncomfortably rough. If you're susceptible to seasickness, take drugs.)

GETTING AROUND

Stewart Island has only 32 km (20 mi) of roads, and in the village of Oban everything is within walking distance of the harbor, so getting around is not a problem. **Oban Taxis** (03/219-1456) and **Sam & Billy the Bus** (book through Stewart Island Travel at 03/219-1269) offer short island tours along the road system for $20 per person. Highly recommended, these are a great introduction to the island. As the name suggests, Oban Taxis also runs a cab service around the island's short road system. **Stewart Island Travel** (03/219-1269) has a couple of small cars that they rent for $50 per half-day and $70 per full day.

INFORMATION AND SERVICES

A good website for pre-trip planning is www .stewartisland.co.nz. Once on the island, head to the **Stewart Island Visitor Centre** (Main Rd., 03/219-0002, Jan.–Mar. Mon.–Fri. 8:30 A.M.–7 P.M., Sat.–Sun. 9 A.M.–7 P.M., the rest of the year Mon.–Fri. 8:30 A.M.–5 P.M.). In addition to general tourist information, the DOC maintains a desk where you can learn about walking tracks and view interesting island displays.

Some businesses accept credit cards, but there are no banks or ATMs on the island, so stock up on cash before leaving Invercargill. The small post office is on Elgin Terrace. Between the waterfront and the visitor center, **Justcafe** (1 Main Rd., 03/219-1567; daily 8 A.M.–8 P.M.) has Internet access. In the recreation of a fisherman's cottage, **The Fernery** (Golden Bay Rd., 03/219-1453) is crammed with island souvenirs emphasizing the natural history of Stewart Island. It's the place to buy living ferns, souvenirs, cards, books, delicate silk scarves, dressing gowns, and prints—all with a fern theme. **Halfmoon Bay Library** (Ayr St.) is open Wednesday 2–3:15 P.M. and Friday–Saturday 11 A.M.–noon.

For medical needs, head to the **Stewart Island Health Centre** (Argyle St., 03/219-1098; daily 10:30 A.M.–12:30 P.M.).

BACKGROUND

The Land

About 150 million years ago New Zealand was just a small part of the supercontinent called Gondwanaland, consisting of present-day Australia, Antarctica, India, Africa, and South America. About 70 million years ago, New Zealand separated from Australia and Antarctica. Geographically isolated and uninhabited by humans until A.D. 700 (at the earliest), New Zealand reveals its unique natural history in its unusual animals and plants, which have long since disappeared elsewhere.

GEOGRAPHY

Volcanoes

The Pacific and Indian-Australian tectonic plates meet along a line of collision that runs through present-day New Zealand, producing the Taupo Volcanic Zone in the North Island and Alpine Fault in the South Island. Volcanic and geothermal areas smolder along the Taupo Volcanic Zone from the Bay of Plenty to the central North Island. Three volcanoes dominate this area: **Mount Ruapehu** and **Mount Ngauruhoe**, both active, and dormant **Mount Tongariro**.

© ANDREW HEMPSTEAD

Mount Ruapehu erupted continuously from September 1995 to late 1996, rocketing ash, steam, and car-sized rocks into the sky from the volcano's Crater Lake. About 50 km (31 mi) offshore from Whakatane in the Bay of Plenty lies **White Island,** an active volcano often obscured by clouds of steam. Discovered and named by Captain Cook in 1769, White Island erupts ash intermittently to this day. On the west coast the dormant cone of **Mount Taranaki** towers over the Taranaki Volcanic Zone, and farther north, both Auckland and the Bay of Islands are classified as separate volcanic zones. The waters of **Lake Taupo** lie in an enormous deep crater in the center of the North Island—the area has a violent history of volcanic eruptions, though the last one was nearly 19 centuries ago. You'll find no volcanoes active within the last 2,000 years on the South Island, but you can see remains of the colossal twin volcanoes that formed Banks Peninsula, south of Christchurch.

Mountains, Glaciers, and Lakes

Although the North Island offers impressive volcanoes and mighty Lake Taupo, the South Island is really the place to go for snowcapped mountain scenery and perfect lakes set in idyllic surroundings. Most of New Zealand lies at least 200 meters (656 ft) above sea level, but the tallest peak, **Mount Cook** (3,754 meters/12,316 ft), rises among the magnificent **Southern Alps,** spine of the South Island. Spectacular glaciers are scattered throughout the landscape—the mighty **Fox** and **Franz Josef** are still easily accessible from the main route down the west coast. In other areas of the South Island are U-shaped valleys, moraines, and deep lakes left behind by glaciers of earlier ice ages. New Zealand's numerous lakes vary greatly in size and depth, many of the largest concentrated in the South Island and fed by glaciers and snowpacks of the Southern Alps. Many fast-flowing rivers and meandering streams follow the contours of the land. Extensive flat plains of rich alluvial soil deposited by these rivers provide plenty of valuable agricultural land; vast gravel plains, such

as those found in the South Canterbury region of the South Island, are predominantly used as sheep country.

The Coastline

New Zealand's coastline offers a bit of everything. Sand stretches as far as the eye can see in some areas, such as **Ninety Mile Beach** at the tip of the North Island; in other areas, such as the **Bay of Islands** in the northeast of the North Island and **Marlborough Sounds** at the South Island's northern tip, deep coves and sheltered bays dotted with tiny islands fringe the coast. The west coast of the South Island is lined with rocky cliffs, blowholes, caves, and rugged surf beaches where seals haul themselves ashore; in the far southwest corner, 14 magnificent fiords deeply indent the coastline, and along a small section of the east coast, several sandy beaches are strewn with large, perfectly circular boulders. For sandy beaches and warm, aquamarine waters, stay in the north; for rugged surf-swept beaches, intriguing rock formations, and deep, mirror-surfaced fiords, head south.

CLIMATE

New Zealand has an oceanic, temperate climate; although it varies from subtropical in the north to almost subarctic in the mountainous areas of the south, overall it's relatively mild. Seasonal variations are not pronounced: summers never get uncomfortably hot; winters are mild, with snow usually confined to the high country and southern lowlands. Rainfall levels vary throughout New Zealand; winter tends to be the wettest season—but not so wet that it should be avoided. If you're coming from the Northern Hemisphere, keep in mind that the seasons are opposite—spring is September through November, summer December through February, autumn March through May, and winter June through August.

North Island

The North Island tends to be warmer and drier than the South Island, though the highest mountain peaks often have snow year-round. It has an average rainfall of 130 cm (51 in) and prevailing westerly winds. **Auckland** (where most visitors enter New Zealand) averages a summer temperature of 23°C (73°F) and a winter temperature of 14°C (57°F). **Wellington,** perched on the edge of Cook Strait, generally receives slightly colder weather, with temperatures ranging from 26°C (79°F) in summer to 2°C (36°F) in winter. The capital also has a reputation for windy weather, at times making the ferry trip between the two main islands unforgettably rough.

South Island

The differences in temperature and weather in each area are more pronounced in the South Island. The pressure systems travel west to east (the Southern Alps have a noticeable "wet" and "dry" side), the lows dumping considerable rain and cold temperatures on the west side of the mountains; snow is a permanent fixture on the highest peaks. On the east side of the Southern Alps the rainfall can be as low as 30 cm and temperatures are a good deal warmer. On the east coast, **Christchurch** averages temperatures in the low 20s C (low 70s F) in summer and

AVERAGE DAILY TEMPERATURES AND ANNUAL RAINFALL

LOCALITY	JANUARY	JULY	RAINFALL
North Island:			
Bay of Islands	25°C/77°F	15°C/59°F	1,648 mm/65 in
Auckland	23°C/73°F	14°C/57°F	1,268 mm/50 in
Rotorua	23°C/73°F	12°C/54°F	1,511 mm/59 in
Napier	24°C/75°F	13°C/55°F	780 mm/31 in
Wellington	20°C/68°F	11°C/52°F	1,271 mm/50 in
South Island:			
Nelson	22°C/72°F	12°C/54°F	999 mm/39 in
Christchurch	22°C/72°F	12°C/54°F	658 mm/26 in
Queenstown	22°C/72°F	8°C/46°F	849 mm/33 in
Dunedin	19°C/66°F	10°C/50°F	772 mm/30 in
Invercargill	18°C/64°F	9°C/48°F	1,042 mm/41 in

Note: Temperatures are maximum

MOUNTAIN WEATHER

As the mountains generally run north-south and the pressure systems move west-east, the worst weather hits the highest barrier – the Southern Alps. Rivers and streams can flood rapidly from snowmelt and rain, avalanche risks increase dramatically, and temperatures drop quickly. Watch for an increase in wind strength and the formation of large sheets of cloud. Also watch for clouds gathering over the lee side of the ranges – and expect rain. Gale-force winds, snow, or blizzards can come with these storms at *any time of year* in the mountains. The **New Zealand Mountain Safety Council** (www.mountainsafety.org.nz) suggests three important rules to follow: Be aware of approaching bad weather (expect it in the mountains); be adequately prepared with warm wind- and waterproof clothing; and don't cross flooded rivers – wait until they subside (generally as quickly as they flood).

For current weather forecasts, check the local newspaper or tune in to local radio or TV stations. If you're in a national park, the visitor center has the latest local weather forecast. For avalanche information, consult the **Backcountry Avalanche Advisory** (www.avalanche.net.nz), an online report of backcountry conditions throughout New Zealand.

low teens (low 50s F) in winter. **Dunedin,** farther south, averages 19°C (66°F) in summer and 10°C (50°F) in winter. **Invercargill,** New Zealand's southernmost city, experiences slightly colder temperatures. Snow is relatively common in the southern lowlands as well as the higher hills, and occasionally falls even at sea level.

ENVIRONMENTAL ISSUES

New Zealand is well known for its stance on environmental issues, including being the first country to ever announce itself a nuclear-free zone, which to this day includes the policy that no nuclear-powered ships are allowed into its waters. Damage to natural plant species caused by grazing sheep and cattle is enormous, but rather than bare ground, the result of their introduction by Europeans is a carpet of "beautiful" green grass hiding the real damage.

Signed in 1991, the **New Zealand Forest Accord** ended decades of conflict between the forestry industry and environmental groups. It put an end to the haphazard harvest of native forests while recognizing the importance of plantations.

Currently wind farms produce 320 megawatts of electricity, enough to power around 140,000 households. Wind farms are scattered around the country, with one of the more accessible near Levin in the southern portion of the North Island.

Parks

Covering more than 2.1 million hectares (5.2 million acres) of the country, 14 of New Zealand's most beautiful areas have been set aside for total preservation in their natural state and designated national parks. They offer vast areas of untouched wilderness where hikers, mountaineers, anglers, hunters, and flora and fauna enthusiasts are in their element. In the North Island lie **Te Urewera, Tongariro, Egmont,** and **Whanganui National Parks;** in the South Island are **Abel Tasman, Kahurangi, Nelson Lakes, Arthur's Pass, Westland, Paparoa, Aoraki/Mount Cook, Mount Aspiring, Fiordland,** and **Rakiura National Parks.** Three maritime parks, **Bay of Islands** and **Hauraki Gulf Maritime Parks** in the North Island and **Marlborough Sounds Maritime Park** in the South Island, preserve some of the most spectacular and accessible coastal scenery, and dozens of scenic reserves and forest parks, used for conservation, recreation, and timber production, contain some of the best bush scenery in the country.

All the national parks, reserves, forest parks, and state forests are under the jurisdiction of the **Department of Conservation** (DOC), created on April 1, 1987, by the Conservation Act. The department manages the land and wildlife, promotes the conservation of natural and historic resources, protects endangered species, produces educational and promotional material, and fosters recreation and tourism in conjunction with conservation. The best way to obtain information on a particular area or park is to visit local DOC offices scattered throughout the country or check their website, www.doc.govt.nz.

Worthwhile Organizations
In addition to the Department of Conserva-

tion, two publicly funded organizations are active in the fight to save New Zealand's natural wonders. **Greenpeace** (09/630-6317, www.greenpeace.org.nz) may have been formed in Canada, but it gained world renown after its flagship, the *Rainbow Warrior,* was blown up in Auckland Harbour by French government agents. The **Royal Forest and Bird Protection Society** (04/385-7374, www.forestandbird.org.nz) may keep a lower profile than Greenpeace, but it has been instrumental in the preservation of native flora and fauna. With 40,000 members, "Forest and Bird" is New Zealand's largest conservation organization.

Flora and Fauna

New Zealand's long isolation from other continents is responsible for unique developments in plant and animal life. Before humans arrived, much of the country was covered in dense tangled forests and heavy undergrowth alive with native birds, many flightless. With the introduction of grazing animals, much of the undergrowth was thinned out; early settlers felled the forests, and introduced predators chased many unique birds into extinction.

FLORA
Today, the remaining native forests, known locally as "the bush," are lush wonderlands of subtropical appearance. Ferns, mosses, and lichens carpet their floors, tree ferns grow up to 10 meters (33 ft) high, and twining creepers, *nikau* palms, palm lilies, tree ferns, and many species of native trees intermingle to form a dense green canopy overhead. For fern lovers, New Zealand is a delight. Ferns (one of the country's national emblems) seem to grow everywhere—on trees, along rivers and streams, on hillsides, and in open areas, and the more than 150 species range in size from filmy two-cm (0.79-in) ferns to impressive 15-meter (49-ft) tree ferns.

© ANDREW HEMPSTEAD

There are more than 150 species of ferns in New Zealand.

Trees
Altogether 112 native tree species grow in New

© ANDREW HEMPSTEAD

Cabbage trees are common throughout
New Zealand.

Zealand among the dense undergrowth and large areas of scrub (mainly *manuka* or tea-tree). A few ancient kauri pine (*Agathis australis*) forests can still be appreciated on the North Island, growing naturally only north of latitude 39 degrees south. These magnificent trees grow up to 53 meters (174 ft) high, losing their lower branches to become long bare cylinders of intricate design with large bushy tops. They were the favorites of the forest for Maori war canoes—a vast canoe could be chiseled out of one tree trunk. Unfortunately, they were also the favorites of early shipbuilders and settlers, who rapidly depleted the forests without much thought to the future—the kauri takes about 800 years to mature. Nowadays, these impressive trees survive in relatively few areas, towering above the other trees in small groves or randomly in the bush. Two areas in Northland, northwest of Dargaville, are worth a special visit just to see these giants—**Waipoua Forest Park,** with two very famous trees (one is estimated to be at least

2,000 years old), and the small but beautiful **Trounson Kauri Park.**

Most of New Zealand's flowers are white- or cream-colored. However, native flowering trees and shrubs add red and yellow highlights to the evergreen flora of New Zealand. A few of the most spectacular flowering trees are the *pohutukawa, rata,* and *kowhai.* The striking *pohutukawa* (*Metrosideros tomentosa*), or New Zealand Christmas tree, is a mass of scarlet flowers in December. The *rata* (*Metrosideros robusta*), another vividly colored tree also covered in red blossoms, is initially a parasitic vine, growing up a host tree (and often strangling it) until it has grown roots and become a tree in its own right. The bright-yellow hanging blossoms of the *kowhai* (*Sophora tetraphera*) bloom in all their glory during spring. Large beech (*Nothofagus*) forests with little undergrowth cover upland areas, and vast areas of land throughout New Zealand have been planted with exotic trees for timber, thus saving the remaining indigenous trees. The most common nonnative tree is the radiata pine. It flourishes here, growing to complete maturity within 35 years—a popular tree with the timber industry.

Flowers

At least three-quarters of New Zealand's flowering plants are endemic. Orchids are abundant, adding multihued splashes of color to the landscape. About 60 species thrive in the lowland forests and countless beautiful parks and gardens. The alpine flowers are vastly different from those of other countries, with about 500 species of flowering plants found only in New Zealand's alpine areas. Large, white mountain daisies (genus *Celmisia*) are the most common; the beautiful Mount Cook lily (*Ranunculus lyallii*) is the largest of the buttercups. A rather strange growth called vegetable sheep (*Raoulia eximia*), a large, low-to-the-ground, cushion-like plant covered in white hairs, grows only in the South Island and is easily mistaken for a sheep from a distance. Apart from the abundance of native wildflowers, New Zealanders also take great pride in their gardens. If you're a flower fancier, stroll through any of the suburbs (particularly of Hamilton, Cambridge, New Plymouth, Napier, and Christchurch) to see a great variety of both indigenous and exotic plantlife, tended with obvious TLC (most New Zealanders are born with green thumbs). Botanical gardens, reserves, and beautiful parks (called "domains") are found in most cities, and are highly recommended as part of any walking tour.

FAUNA
Birds

Until humans arrived these islands had no native land animals. However, the country was alive with birds, no fewer than 250 species. A perfect balance of nature existed between vegetation and birdlife, but when humans set foot on the islands they brought rats, cats, and dogs; introduced mammals and birds; and began clearing native habitat. Many native birds, unable to adapt to the foreign predators, became extinct.

The best-known creature of New Zealand is the nocturnal kiwi, a flightless bird found nowhere else in the world—the national emblem of New Zealand. It has a round body covered in dense, stiff feathers (looks like shaggy fur from a distance), strong legs (kicks out when frightened), no tail, tiny invisible wings, a long beak, and a piercing call—"ki-wi." It's not easy to find a kiwi in the bush, but you can see them in a simulated natural environment in the many excellent nocturnal houses throughout the country.

Other native birds include the *tui* (with its beautiful song), bellbird (its crystal-clear call is like the ping-pong of a door bell), fantail, *kaka, kea, pukeko, morepork,* and wood pigeon. The *kaka* is a shy brown-and-green parrot. The *kea,* a dull brownish-green parrot with red underwings and a hooked beak, lives in the high country and is commonly seen in the Southern Alps as it scavenges around campsites.

The *takahe,* a rare bird unique to New Zealand, is found mainly in Southern Fiordland. Large, flightless, and blue and green with red feet and bill, it was thought to be extinct until a small colony was rediscovered in 1948. Since then, 120 *takahe* have been found and are now protected in a restricted area in the Murchison Mountains.

The *weka,* another flightless bird, is as bold as the *kea* but not as common. Found in the west coast forests of the South Island and the Gisborne area of the North Island, it also helps itself to the food and property of campers.

Introduced birds include the blackbird, thrush, magpie, chaffinch, sparrow, skylark, myna, white-eye, and goldfinch.

Insects and Reptiles

Of the numerous forms of insect life found throughout the country, one of the most audible is the cicada. Twenty or so species of cicada live in New Zealand, mostly above the timberline. Often mistaken for that of crickets, their song in the summer heat is an incredibly loud, raspy, clicking noise—one that seems to intensify in the evening—a distinct part of the summer atmosphere in New Zealand.

The *tuatara,* a lizardlike reptile, now inhabits only about 30 islands off the country's coast (see live ones in the Southland Museum Tuatarium in Invercargill). It is believed to live at least 100 years, has a distinctly prehistoric appearance, and is often referred to as a "living fossil."

Mammals

The *wild* animals in New Zealand are descended from pigs, goats, opossums, rabbits, weasels, ferrets, and deer released by European settlers. Some of these—especially deer, rabbits, goats, and opossums—adapted to their new environment so well that they rapidly became an environmental problem and are to this day hunted to control their populations.

Of eight species of deer, the red deer is the most common and widespread. When first released it had an abundant food supply (rapidly destroying the native forest undergrowth) and no predators, and its numbers increased rapidly. Commercial hunting from helicopters began

© ANDREW HEMPSTEAD

New Zealand fur seal

in the 1960s, followed by profitable heli-hunting with live capture for deer farms. Hunting is still encouraged, but in recent years controlled deer farming has become a valuable part of the economy. The deer are raised for meat, breeding stock, and their antlers, which when in velvet are sold to the Asian market to be crushed and used as an aphrodisiac.

History

EARLY INHABITANTS
The Moa-Hunters

Exactly when the first Polynesians arrived in New Zealand is unknown. Maori legends claim the Polynesian navigator Kupe first sighted New Zealand in the 10th century, naming it Aotearoa, "Land of the Long White Cloud" (one of many translations), but archaeological evidence suggests that an archaic Maori population originating in Polynesia may have been established in New Zealand as early as A.D. 700. The first arrivals were hunters—stalking flightless birds, predominantly the large, emulike moa (now extinct)—gatherers,

and excellent fishermen. No evidence suggests that the moa-hunters were a warrior society. Their camps were originally concentrated in the South Island, but by the 12th century they also inhabited the North Island.

Classic Maori Society

By the 13th and 14th centuries, a new kind of Polynesian culture began to replace moa-hunter society. Dwindling moa caused an increasing dependence on other fowl and fish. Legends speak of the arrival at this time of East Polynesians and the "Great Migration" of the 14th century. Crossing the Pacific in

many large canoes, they came from the Society Island Group (Hawaiiki of Maori legends), where overpopulation, food shortages,
and war had been a part of everyday life. Most
present-day Maori claim their descent from
these legendary canoe voyagers. With the new

arrivals came a change in lifestyle. About 40
tribes developed, each a territorially based social unit; subtribes were based on kinship and
ancestral descent. Cultivation of the fleshy *kumara* (sweet potato) became important; since
the *kumara* needed warmth and sunshine to

MAORI ART

The most important and sacred Maori art was
sculpture, predominantly wood but also jade,
ivory, and whalebone. Trained in the art from
an early age, the best carvers of early Maori
society became men of high rank. Only men
could become carvers – women, regarded as
inferior, were not even allowed to watch the
carvers at work. The canoe (*waka*), meeting
house (*whare whakairo*), and food storehouse
(*pataka*) were the main vehicles for Maori relief
sculpture. Enormous pieces of indigenous timber were deeply carved into highly decorative
spiritual designs, both on the interior and exterior. Well-preserved woodcarvings, decorative

interior panels of woven reed, and painted rafters are best seen in *marae* or meeting grounds
throughout the country, and all the major museums feature Maori art. All useful items of
the Maori were covered in abstract designs,
inspired by plants (a fern design is fairly common) or symbols, and inset with abalone shell.
The human body, in particular the sacred head,
was the major figurative element. Profiles with
birdlike heads were *manaia* (evil beings).

The *tiki*, a spiritual carving of human form
representing the Maori conception of the
beginning of life, was worn as a good-luck
pendant – it has been mass-produced in all
mediums for tourists. Unfortunately, a lot of
Maori art is now machine-made and you have
to search for hand-carved original pieces. One
of the best places to see hand-carved works is
Te Puia, in the Whakarewarewa Thermal Valley, Rotorua, the home of Maori culture. Other
areas where you can find carvers in action are
the far north and the east coast of the North
Island, and in the town of Hokitika on the west
coast of the South Island.

BODY ART

The Maori also decorated their bodies, a custom that the earliest European visitors found
particularly intriguing. Apart from wearing
flax cloaks and kilts decorated with woven
borders, tufts of colorful feathers, or dog hair,
they adorned themselves with beautiful greenstone pendants, ear pendants, and combs. The
men painfully carved intricate symmetrical designs (*moku*) into their faces and thighs with
tiny chisels filled with paint, and the women
tattooed their lower lips and chins. Nowadays
you see few authentic tattoos (only on the
elderly), but they're still effectively painted on
for ceremonial occasions.

© ANDREW HEMPSTEAD

ancient art displayed in the Maori village
of Ohinemutu, in the city of Rotorua

flourish, the Maori spread to the north of the North Island.

The new Polynesian culture placed great emphasis on a strict warrior code. The Maori took pride in being fierce warriors. *Pa* (fortified villages) were skillfully built on tops of hills or ridges, with at least one side blocked by a natural barrier such as a river or the sea; fences and trenches further protected the thatched cottages within from enemy attack. *Mana* (prestige) and *utu* (retribution) were important qualities. If one Maori insulted another, the offended family would demand *utu*, eventually leading to war.

The focus of community life was the *marae* (central square) in front of the large, intricately carved meeting house (today the term also covers the meeting house itself and any auxiliary buildings). Maori leaders were usually hereditary chiefs or priests. The people were governed by strong family loyalties and religious beliefs and traditions. *Tapu* (sacred) was a positive force from the gods—certain places, acts, and people were *tapu*. *Noa* was the opposing negative or evil force; together these elements regulated every area of Maori life.

To the Maori, all nature was alive and had magic or supernatural powers; the people lived in harmony with the land, respecting it as property of the gods. They had many gods; different gods looked after such things as the sea, forests, and crops. With no written language, they passed on their tribal history through song and dance, storytelling, and arts and crafts. They were (and still are) excellent craftspeople, expressing great symbolism in their intricate, decorative carvings. Rituals were another important part of life. Some, such as offering the first fish of a catch to the god Tangaroa and first bird to Tanemahuta, are still performed. Those rituals associated with traditional arts such as weaving and carving, and with Maori ceremonial gatherings, are strictly maintained and an integral part of society today.

EUROPEAN DISCOVERY AND COLONIZATION
Tasman and Cook
The Dutch navigator Abel Tasman is believed to have been the first European to discover Aotearoa in 1642. Seeking a great unknown continent in the South Pacific with which to trade, he stumbled across the west coast of the South Island. He named the new land "Staten Landt" to honor the States-General of the United Netherlands, and because he thought it might be connected with Staten Landt, an island off the tip of South America. Tasman's theory was disproved within the year, and the name was changed to "Nieuw Zeeland"—no doubt after the Dutch island province of Zeeland. In one encounter with the Maori, several of his men were killed, and Tasman sailed away disillusioned by the lack of friendly trading prospects.

In 1769 the British navigator Captain James Cook landed on the east coast of the North Island. He was also in search of the vast unknown continent, but for scientific purposes. On arrival at Gisborne, Cook also had misunderstandings with the natives that led to bloodshed, but he persevered, circumnavigating both islands, charting the coastline in great detail, and concluding that most Maori were helpful and friendly. Cook took possession of "New Zealand" for Britain, and New Zealand became known to the world. Many French explorers followed Cook, some for scientific reasons, some for trade.

Whalers and Sealers
Within 30 years of Cook's discovery, other Europeans sailed to New Zealand shores and began a period of great exploitation. Whaling stations sprang up around the coast, sealers slaughtered the colonies along the southern shores (almost to extinction), and loggers drastically cut magnificent kauri trees for shipbuilding. Trade in whale oil, sealskins, timber, and flax began with New South Wales in Australia. In the late 1820s, Kororareka (now called Russell) in the Bay of Islands became the first European settlement—a refuge for whalers, sealers, adventurers, and escaped Australian convicts, it earned the name "Hell-hole of the Pacific." With the traders came disease, alcohol, and muskets, all of which had devastating impact on the Maori.

Intertribal Wars

The musket was of great interest to Maori warriors and quickly became a coveted weapon. The warriors welcomed the traders and their muskets, and Maori society was irrevocably changed. Hongi Hika, chief of the Northland Ngapuhi tribe, was the first to recognize the weapon's potential. With its aid he, followed by other great chiefs, slaughtered many rival tribes throughout the North Island. As the wars spread to the south, many tribes began trading for muskets, eventually equalizing the balance of power. With the realization in the 1830s that the weapon was annihilating the race, the Maori gradually ended the intertribal wars.

Colonization

Missionaries of many denominations spent the early 1800s establishing missions. Many recognized the exploitation of the Maori by the Pakeha (white people) and tried to protect them. They also taught the Maori the latest European agricultural techniques. Until 1832 there had been no law and order in New Zealand. James Busby, a New South Wales civil servant, was the first to be sent over from Australia as "British resident" to protect the Maori from further exploitation and establish some order. Busby had an impossible task and no police; he became known as "a man-of-war without guns." When he proved ineffective, Captain William Hobson was sent from Britain in 1840 to be lieutenant-governor and to unite the Maori chiefs with Britain by extending British sovereignty to New Zealand. On February 6, 1840, Hobson, representatives of the Crown, and a number of leading Maori chiefs signed "The Treaty of Waitangi." New Zealand became a British colony. Though this made land available for European settlement, it also specified that all property belonged to the Maori and guaranteed that it could not be taken without their consent and/or payment. It gave them the "rights and privileges of British subjects." Though the treaty was meant to protect the Maori, it later became obvious that they had not fully understood the document

they had signed. Colonists began flooding into the new country.

The Land Wars

The early Europeans found the concept of Maori land use and ownership hard to comprehend. The kumara fields and burial grounds made sense, but tapu areas, and land specifically designated for fishing and hunting, were considered a waste of good agricultural land. The land belonged to entire tribal groups, and consent for a change in ownership had to be agreed upon by all—new occupations had previously occurred only by conquest. At first the Maori were eager to "sell" their land (they thought they were selling the "shadow of the land" like a lease) for money and alcohol. However, the growing number of colonists demanding land put increasing pressure on the Maori, and the ideals of the Waitangi Treaty were soon overlooked. As the European population grew and the Maori became increasingly reluctant to sell land, antagonism also grew. Fighting broke out in 1843 and continued sporadically as more settlements were established. Between 1860 and the early 1880s, war raged between the Maori tribal chiefs and government troops over land purchase (even the Maori were divided—some tribes joined the government side to even old scores with rival tribes), and the fighting spread across the central regions of the North Island.

The Maori lacked any kind of unifying nationalism, and tradition forced them to prove they were the best fighters; against artillery, they had no chance. Ancestral land was confiscated from "rebel tribes" and given as a reward to "friendly tribes," further destroying unity. Land was also given to military settlers who fought for the government, or was sold to recoup some of the cost of the wars. In 1862, Land Courts forced the Maori to name 10 owners, and then only one owner, of each block of land—this destroyed any remaining unity and made it relatively easy for crooked land agents to buy the land for less than its worth with money or alcohol. Traders deliberately let the Maori run into debt, forcing them to sell or go to jail. By 1982 only 4.5 million hectares (11.1 million acres) of land remained under Maori ownership—some of it leased to settlers, the rest too rugged to be useful.

Wool and Gold

While the North was at war, the South Island forged ahead. The small Maori population was still eager to sell land. Settlement spread rapidly and farmers established many large sheep runs on the vast areas of tussockland. Thousands of sheep, predominantly merino for their fine wool, were shipped from Australia. Between 1850 and 1880, many Australian squatters came over to lease large areas of tussockland for their flocks. This became known as the "wool period." However, sheep scab came with the Australian flocks, killing thousands of sheep, and in the 1860s, a plague of rabbits forced many runholders into abandonment and bankruptcy. Some turned to rabbiting as the export in rabbit skins soared.

In 1861, gold was discovered in the South Island's Otago district. The rush lasted for less than a decade, but for those years the Shotover River became "the richest river in the world," soon followed by the Arrow River. The discovery attracted thousands of miners from the goldfields of California and Australia, further stimulating growth and establishing the south as a commercial and industrial center. Railways and roads were built. After the rush in Otago, miners moved to the west coast, where Hokitika temporarily became a busy port.

Administration

Auckland had been chosen as the capital in 1840, and Wellington, New Plymouth, Nelson, Dunedin, and Christchurch were founded during the next 10 years. In 1852 direct rule from Britain ended, marking the beginning of "self-government." New Zealand's central government was made up of a governor appointed by London, a Legislative Council appointed by the governor, and a House of Representatives elected by the people. The country was divided into six provinces—Auckland, New Plymouth, Wellington, Nelson, Canterbury, and Otago, each with its own government. In 1865, Wellington replaced Auckland as capital of New Zealand, and by 1873, four more provinces had been added—Hawke's Bay, Marlborough, Westland, and Southland.

Trade

In 1882 the introduction of refrigeration produced a major change in farming. Many of the big wool runs were abandoned as farmers recognized new export possibilities. Many turned to meat and dairy production. The high country became the merino area for wool production, the hill country became lamb-breeding land, and fat-lamb farms were developed to breed lambs specifically for export. With the introduction of refrigerated cargo ships, Britain and Europe became eager consumers of the meat, and New Zealand entered the overseas market as a major food producer.

THE TWENTIETH CENTURY
Social Welfare

The 20th century became the era of advanced social legislation. Two major political groups, the Liberal and Labour Parties, emerged in 1890. The Liberal Party held power until 1912, introducing many changes in social policy. Its first landmark legislation was the introduction of the Old Age Pension. New Zealand was the first country in the world to give women the vote (1893). In 1894 the world's first form of compulsory state arbitration for industrial disputes was introduced. The Liberals successfully combined capitalism with socialism, and New Zealand became a country of progressive social policies. With the interruption of World War I and the following Depression, it was not until the first Labour government in 1935 that New Zealand again took up the social welfare banner. The Social Security Act was introduced, guaranteeing free health care, education, and welfare benefits for all. Sickness pensions, low-cost housing, and a 40-hour workweek were introduced over the years, and in 1972, the Accident Compensation Act was passed, insuring all people against accidental injury. These were the foundations of New Zealand's modern welfare state.

World Wars

During World War I, New Zealand sent 100,000 troops to support Britain—16,000 were killed, 45,000 wounded in action. After World War I, New Zealand became a member of the League of Nations. In World War II, 150,000 New Zealanders joined the Allied War effort; more than 11,000 were killed and 17,000 wounded. After World War II, ties with "the mother country" weakened. New Zealand claimed full independence in 1947. For most of the years between 1949 and 1978, the National Party held power. National and Labour have been the two major parties in recent years.

Modern Maori

For years New Zealand has been promoted as a country of racial harmony, though there's considerable unrest and ongoing land disputes between some Maori and Pakeha—problems that date from the Treaty of Waitangi. The Maori population grew rapidly with improved health opportunities and social education, but the adjustment to urban life further weakened Maori culture. By 1962 the Maori annual growth rate was more than twice the Pakeha rate—and one of the highest in the world. Pakeha had to adjust to an increasingly assertive, fast-growing Maori and Polynesian population. Maori language, arts and crafts, and song and dance are taught in schools all over the land, and many Maori are looking back to the ways of their ancestors, searching for their identity and regaining a culture that had been submerged in the ways of the Pakeha. Although many New Zealanders are showing a renewed interest in *Maoritanga,* the Maori way of life, resentment between Maori and Pakeha continues to escalate. Despite protest from present-day Pakeha landowners, an increasing number of Maori plan to reclaim land they believe was wrongfully stolen years ago. They have rejected government intervention in the form of a lump-sum payment. They want only the land they believe is rightfully theirs.

Economy and Government

ECONOMY

The New Zealand economy is trade-oriented. Traditional trading partners—Australia, the United Kingdom, and the United States—have been joined by many Asian countries, including Japan. Agricultural exports of dairy, meat, and wool products—worth $17 billion annually to New Zealand—dominate the economic pie, but forestry, horticulture, manufacturing, and tourism are growing in importance.

Agriculture

New Zealand's major source of income is agriculture. It has developed advanced techniques to use the country's rugged land, including specially designed aircraft to replace land machinery. Of the country's 80,000 farms, approximately 55,000 are on the North Island and 25,000 are on the South Island. Many areas are highly mechanized. About 50 percent of total export income comes from meat, dairy products, and wool; the land supports some 48 million sheep and 4.5 million beef cattle. New Zealand is one of the world's largest exporters of lamb and mutton, has an ever-expanding beef industry (about 75 percent of which is produced on the North Island), and supplies about 90 countries with meat (the major markets are the U.K., Russia, Japan, the United States, and Canada).

New Zealand is one of the largest and most efficient exporters of dairy products. The combination of a good growing climate, stable rainfall, and lush grass year-round has produced an average herd of about 120 cows; most of the four million dairy cows in the country are Jerseys or Friesians. Butter (mostly to the U.K.) and cheddar cheese (mostly to Japan and the U.K.) are the major dairy exports, but casein (mainly to the U.S.) and skim-milk powder (to a wide variety of countries, mainly in Asia) are also in demand. The industry generates 32 percent of total

© ANDREW HEMPSTEAD

Sheep farms dominate both islands.

agriculture revenue. New Zealand's rich and creamy dairy products are among the best in the world—one taste and you'll be convinced.

Sheep are a predominant part of the landscape throughout the whole of New Zealand. New Zealand is the second-largest producer of sheep (after Australia) and largest supplier of medium-to-coarse crossbred wool (for carpets, upholstery, and clothing) in the world, with an average flock of about 1,800 sheep. In North Island hill country, sheep are farmed for their wool; the fertile lowland farms (up to 25 sheep per hectare) specialize in lamb and mutton production. Teams of sheepshearers travel around the country from woolshed to woolshed, many shearing more than 200 sheep each a day (don't miss any opportunity to watch shearers in action—their speed and dexterity are really something). Most of the medium-to-coarse crossbred wool used for carpet making and knitting yarn comes from Romney sheep; the fine wool used for soft fabrics and high-quality yarn comes from merino sheep.

Venison (often called cervena in New Zealand) is an important export. The country's 4,000 deer farms hold 1.8 million deer, half the world's population of farmed deer. Around 75 percent of deer meat is exported and when combined with the value of antlers and hides, the industry is worth over $200 million annually to the local economy.

Most of the crops—**wheat, barley, maize, oats, vegetables, berry fruit,** and **tobacco**—are grown for the local market. Horticultural exports are dominated by fresh fruit, comprising 14 percent of the local agricultural economy. The citrus export industry has grown dramatically as kiwifruit, tamarillos, feijoas, and passion fruit have increased in popularity worldwide; apples and pears are also important exports. Orchards in the north produce apples, apricots, peaches, plums, nectarines, berry fruit, cherries, lemons, and oranges, mostly for local consumption, but increasingly for export. Other important crops include malting barley, herbage seeds, some herbs, grass seed, and clover seed. Hops and tobacco leaf (plus orchard fruit) are grown for the local market in the warm, sunny Nelson area of the South Island.

Forestry

After agriculture, forestry is New Zealand's next important industry, pumping $3.3 billion annually into the local economy. More than 27 percent of the country is covered by forest—about 1.8 million hectares (4.4 million acres), equivalent to seven percent of total land area, of production plantation forest and 6.2 million hectares (15.3 million acres) of indigenous forests. As native trees are very slow-growing, they are used for special purposes only. The planted forests of exotic radiata pine (known as Monterey pine in the U.S.) are the major suppliers of New Zealand's timber. Radiata grows rapidly here, producing a high amount of usable wood per tree. In addition to 20 million cubic meters (2.2 million cubic ft) of unprocessed logs annually, forest export products consist of wood pulp and chips, paper, building boards, plywood, veneers, and various oils. Australia, the United States, Japan, and Taiwan are New Zealand's largest customers of forest-product exports.

Energy and Minerals

New Zealand does not have large mineral

deposits and so relies heavily on imported raw materials to manufacture chemicals. Imported petroleum supplies almost 60 percent of New Zealand's energy needs; hydroelectricity, natural coal and gas, solar energy, and geothermal steam supply the rest. New Zealand's lone oil refinery is at Marsden Point, Northland. Jointly owned by the country's five major petroleum companies, it refines crude oil supplied from seven offshore fields. Nuclear power is not foreseeable in New Zealand's future; the country's objective is to harness its own natural power resources. Newer ventures include oil refining, aluminum smelting, ironsand deposit mining, processing New Zealand's offshore oil and gas condensates, and processing associated with steel and glass production. Schemes to change natural gas into synthetic petrol are promoted and encouraged by the government, and solar units to heat household water are increasing in popularity as an alternative to electricity.

At Lake Grassmere in Marlborough, the first solar salt works in the country converts seawater from a manmade 688-hectare (1,700-acre) lake into household and industrial salt through evaporation.

Coal is the most commonly mined mineral, with an estimated 15 billion tons present. Currently 42 mines extract 5.2 million tons annually.

Tourism

Tourism is a major part of the New Zealand economy. In fact, it is the top earner of foreign exchange and is worth a total of $6.6 billion annually to the economy. **Tourism New Zealand** does an excellent job of developing facilities while maintaining the natural and cultural aspects of the country; the department also promotes New Zealand overseas through trade shows and on their website (www.newzealand .com). The **Tourism Industry Association of New Zealand** (www.tianz.org.nz) represents over 4,500 tourism-oriented businesses across the country.

Visitor numbers are growing exponentially, with 1.9 million visitors arriving in 2006. The majority are from Australia (890,000 annually);

however, more and more visitors from Great Britain (310,000), the United States (230,000), Japan (160,000), and Korea (95,000) are discovering New Zealand.

GOVERNMENT

New Zealand is a sovereign independent state, its government based on the British parliamentary system. The head of state, Queen Elizabeth II of Britain, is represented in New Zealand by a resident **governor general.** Appointed for five years, he's advised by the ministers of cabinet.

Since 1950, the New Zealand Parliament has had only one chamber, the **House of Representatives.** Made up of 120 members, this number includes four Maori members elected by the Maori population. The House of Representatives is primarily responsible for

POLITICAL PARTIES

Currently, eight political parties have representatives in New Zealand Parliament, but two parties dominate. **Labour** was formed in 1916 and has had more impact on the country than any other party. It was Labour who led the world with its anti-nuclear stance in the 1980s, but it was also Labour that was in power leading up to economic turmoil in the late 1980s. The Labour Party is currently in power. Created in the 1930s when Liberal and Reform parties merged, the **National Party** led New Zealand through much of the 1990s. The Nationals created an economic blueprint that has been mimicked around the world for curtailing public spending. Along the way, exports increased and the economy boomed.

Other parties of note include the right-leaning **New Zealand First,** established in the 1990s by high-profile former National Party minister Winston Peters; the **Maori Party,** established in 2004 and quickly gaining over four percent of the vote at the last general election; and the always high-profile **Green Party.**

The federal government is based in Wellington.

keeping the government in check; no tax or expenditure can be made until the proposed bill has been read, debated, and authorized. The governor general gives final authorization, and if approved by all these channels, the bill becomes law.

Elections are held every three years, but a government may request an earlier election to vote on a topic of national importance. The party that wins the most seats becomes government; its leader automatically becomes **prime minister.** The leader of the other major party is called the leader of the opposition. The **cabinet** is made up of the prime minister and selected ministers of his party; they form policy, promote legislation, and become the heads of the **Departments of State.** Cabinet ministers and other government members are together called the **Caucus.**

The 40 or so federal government departments are staffed by members of the **Public Service** who retain their jobs despite government changes. The departments provide services for the country: mail, telephone, media, transpor-

tation, education, finance, health, housing, and other services. The official government website is www.govt.nz.

Local government consists of elected officials in 12 regions and 74 districts.

The judiciary has four levels: Formed in 2004, the **Supreme Court** is the ultimate authority, the **High Court** deals with major crimes and important claims, the **Court of Appeals** is exactly that, and **District Courts** deal with all minor offenses. There are also special courts dealing with family, youth, and Maori land issues.

Voting and Republicanism

The voting age is 18. In 1893 New Zealand became the first country in the world to give women the right to vote. Registration to vote became compulsory in 1924—though not obliged to actually vote, more than 80 percent usually do.

New Zealanders are split on whether they would like New Zealand to become a republic within the Commonwealth. Debate has been ongoing since the 1960s.

People and Culture

At the last national census (2006) New Zealand's population numbered 4.027 million. This is up from 3.8 million in 2001, from 3.2 million in 1981, and 2.4 million in 1961. Of the total population, 67 percent are of European descent, 565,000 (14.6 percent) are Maori, Asians number 354,000 (9.2 percent), and Pacific Islanders number 265,000 (6.5 percent).

New Zealand census numbers do not include expatriates (New Zealand citizens living overseas), a number which is estimated to be around 600,000 at any one time. The vast majority of these (460,000) live in Australia. These two countries have an informal and unique arrangement that allows citizens to live and work in either country.

DEMOGRAPHICS

The population is unevenly distributed between the two main islands. Historically the South Island has always had a smaller population than the North Island (except for during the gold-rush era), but at the last census there was a slight trend south, most notably to the Canterbury region. Today, 3.1 million New Zealanders live on the North Island while just over one million live on the South Island. In the 1960s, New Zealanders began to migrate in large numbers from the rural areas to cities in search of better opportunities, but this has been reversed in recent times and the populations of regions such as Northland and Otago are experiencing faster population growth than the cities.

MAORI

After a colorful history of racial resentment and resulting land wars, today the Pakeha (Caucasian people) and Maori live in relative harmony compared to people in other parts of the world, though there's been increasing unrest over land disputes in the last few years—disputes that originated in the 1840s with the signing of the **Treaty of Waitangi.** Intermarriage has increased dramatically in the last four decades, leaving very few full-blooded Maori

in New Zealand. It's estimated that one out of twelve New Zealanders is at least half-Maori in origin, and many more are part Maori. No longer do you find the modern Maori wearing ceremonial costume, cooking in boiling pools, and living as they are depicted on postcards. Only those involved in the tourist industry continue to give this picture of Maori life—mainly in Rotorua, where visitors enjoy authentic performances of the fierce *haka* (war dance) of Maori men, the graceful *poi* dance and beautiful singing of the women, traditional arts, crafts, and carving.

An estimated 60 percent of the Maori population live in main urban centers. The Maori had difficulties adjusting to urban life and Pakeha ways, and began to lose their culture and tradition. Recognizing these problems, the government and Maori themselves introduced programs to ease the situation. Out of these programs came a growing Maori nationalism and an eventual upsurge of Pakeha interest in *Maoritanga,* the Maori way of life. Today the Maori language, traditions, arts and crafts, music, and dance are taught in schools throughout New Zealand, and there is an increasing national interest in preserving the once-fading Maori culture. A cultural concert of Maori songs, chants, games, and graceful dances is a colorful spectacle that shouldn't be missed, especially when combined with a *hangi* (Maori feast). Men perform fierce war chants (*haka*) and women sing and perform graceful flowing dances, twirling *poi.* Rotorua is the best place to go to appreciate Maori culture in all its forms, past and present.

PACIFIC ISLANDERS

In New Zealand, "Pacific Islander" is a term used to describe people—mostly Polynesians—from islands in the South Pacific, a region which has strong cultural, social, and economic ties to New Zealand. The term does not include people from the fringes of the Pacific Ocean, such as Australians, Filipinos, or

Japanese. There is even a name for the culture that Pacific Islanders have developed in New Zealand—Pasifika Aotearoa.

The migration of Pacific Islanders to New Zealand began of course with the arrival of the first Polynesians over 1,000 years ago. In the last 50 years, migration from the islands to New Zealand has increased markedly for a variety of reasons ranging from better employment prospects to escaping from natural disasters such as cyclones. Over half of all Pacific Islanders living in New Zealand were born in Samoa, while over 110,000 New Zealanders claim Samoan heritage. The next largest group is Tongans, of which 18,000 living in New Zealand were born in Tonga. The Cook Islands have particularly strong ties to New Zealand, including a currency based on the New Zealand dollar. The entire population of the Cooks Islands numbers around 21,000, yet 15,000 people living in New Zealand were born in the islands and 51,000 New Zealanders are of Cook Island descent. Niueans are typical of other Pacific Islanders who live in New Zealand; the entire population of Niue, a tiny coral atoll between the Cook Islands and Tonga, is rather generously quoted at 1,400, yet there are over 5,000 Niue-born New Zealand residents and over 20,000 New Zealanders consider themselves Niuean in descent.

RELIGION

Around half of New Zealand's population identify themselves with Christianity, but a majority of these two million people do not attend regular church services. Around 75 percent of Christians are fairly evenly split by three denominations—Anglican, Catholic, and Presbyterian—while Methodist, Latter Day Saints, Protestant, and Baptists make up most of the remaining 25 percent. Two denominations that have seen an increase in membership are Ratana and Ringatu, which blend Christian values with Maori beliefs. A little over one percent of the population is affiliated

with Eastern faiths such as Islam, Hinduism, and Buddhism. Over 40 percent of New Zealanders nominated no religious affiliation in the last census (2006), and the remaining six percent polled objected to the question.

Because New Zealanders as a whole are not a pious people, it is interesting that the national anthem is *God Defend New Zealand*.

LANGUAGE

The common language of New Zealand is English, which 96 percent of the population speaks fluently. The Maori have their own melodic language, mainly heard in songs and chants and on ceremonial occasions. However, some Maori phrases, such as *Haere mai* (welcome) and *Haere ra* (farewell), have been adopted by Pakeha and integrated into general use. With the renewed interest in Maori culture, the Maori language was made an official language of New Zealand in 1974. At the last census, four percent of the population were recorded as fluent Maori speakers.

Beautifully descriptive Maori place-names are scattered throughout New Zealand. Places were often named after particular events, such as Taumatawhakatangihangakoauauotamateapokaiwhenuakitanatahu—"the place where Tamatea, the man with the big knees, who slid, climbed and swallowed mountains, known as 'landeater,' played his flute to his loved one." (There's also a longer version, claimed to be the world's longest place-name.) The Maori language was entirely oral until the early missionaries recorded it in a written form. The sounds broke down into eight consonants: h, k, m, n, p, r, t, w; five vowels: a, e, i, o, u; and two combinations: wh, and ng. "Wh" is pronounced as f, "ng" is a nasal sound, as in siNG. All words end in a vowel, and each syllable has equal stress. Many words are Maori pronunciations of English words, but they look Maori, such as *motaka* (motor car). The easiest way to say Maori words is to pronounce each syllable phonetically.

ESSENTIALS

Getting There

AIR

The only practical way to get to New Zealand is by air. Ticket prices vary greatly between airlines and depend on how and where you buy your ticket (see the sidebar *Cutting Flight Costs*), but one thing you can't control are seasonal fluctuations in prices. Low season (also called "off peak") in the Northern Hemisphere is high season in the Southern. To benefit from departing at low-season prices, you must leave the Northern Hemisphere between June and October. If you head for New Zealand in December or January, you pay high-season (also called "peak") prices, generally considerably higher.

However, high, shoulder, and low-season fares are not standardized throughout all airlines—call them and find out their seasons.

Before you buy your ticket, check the prices on special passes for domestic air travel within New Zealand—some passes are valid only if bought overseas or in conjunction with an international ticket.

Air New Zealand

The national airline, Air New Zealand (09/366-2400 or 0800/737-000, www.airnew zealand.com), started life as Tasman Empire Airways Limited in 1940 and was rebranded as

© ANDREW HEMPSTEAD

CUTTING FLIGHT COSTS

In today's topsy-turvy world of air travel, finding the cheapest fare and best-suited route can be a challenge. The Internet has changed the way many people shop for tickets, but even if you use this invaluable tool for preliminary research, having a travel agent that you are comfortable in dealing with – who takes the time to call around, does some research to get you the best fare, and helps you take advantage of any available special offers or promotional deals – is an invaluable asset in starting your travels off on the right foot.

In the first instance, though, to get an idea of what your agent should be able to come up with, go to the **Air New Zealand** website (www.airnewzealand.com), search using a range of dates, and check out the pages of special offers. Also look in the travel sections of major newspapers – particularly in weekend editions – where budget fares and package deals are frequently advertised. **Flight Centre,** which began as a discount airline ticket agency, has spread its wings around the world and now guarantees to match any other published fare. This company combines easy-to-navigate websites with travel agencies in towns and cities across the United States,

Canada, Great Britain, Australia, and New Zealand. Contacts include www.flightcenter. us (U.S.); www.flightcentre.ca (Canada); www. flightcentre.co.uk (Great Britain); www.flightcentre.com.au (Australia); and www.flightcentre.co.nz (New Zealand).

Many cheaper tickets have strict restrictions regarding changes of flight dates, lengths of stay, and cancellations. A general rule: the cheaper the ticket, the more restrictions. Most travelers today fly on APEX (advance-purchase excursion) fares. These are usually the best value, though some (and, occasionally, many) restrictions apply. These might include minimum and maximum stays and unchangeable itineraries (or hefty penalties for changes); tickets may also be nonrefundable once purchased.

Edward Hasbrouck's *The Practical Nomad: Guide to the Online Travel Marketplace* (Avalon Travel Publishing, 2007) is an excellent resource to working through the maze of online travel-planning possibilities.

When you have found the best fare, open a **frequent flyer** membership with the airline you'll be flying on – **Air New Zealand,** part of the Star Alliance, has a popular program that makes rewards easily obtainable.

Air New Zealand in 1965, then privatized in 1989. Today, it boasts one of the world's most modern fleets, with top-notch service, and a great spread of well-priced flights to New Zealand from Australia, Asia, and North America. The airline also has a distinct kiwi flavor, with local food and drink, the screening of quirky New Zealand movies, and friendly yet professional service. On international flights, every Economy passenger has their own on-demand entertainment system, or you can upgrade to Premium Economy for extra legroom and business-class food service. Business class features lie-flat beds.

Air New Zealand offers flights to Auckland from all Australian capitals, as well as Los Angeles, San Francisco, Vancouver (Nov.–Mar. only), from throughout the South Pacific,

Tokyo, Osaka, Shanghai, Hong Kong, and London. You can also fly from east coast Australian cities to Wellington, Christchurch, and Queenstown.

Air New Zealand is part of the **Star Alliance** (www.staralliance.com), which also includes United, U.S. Airways, Air Canada, and Lufthansa. This allows for seamless bookings and transfers from throughout the world, but if you can book one of Air New Zealand's discounted fares, the prices are hard to beat. To source these fares, use the Worldwide Sites link at www.airnewzealand.com.

Other Airlines

The short flight across the Tasman Sea from Australia takes about 3.5 hours and crosses two time zones. Check with Air New Zealand (www.airnewzealand.com.au) for the best fares, and then contact Australia's national carrier, **Qantas** (13-13-13, www.qantas.com.au), with flights between all major cities in both countries. **Freedom Air** (0800/600-500, www.freedomair.co.nz) has flights from major Australian cities to its hub at Hamilton, as well as to Auckland, Palmerston North, Wellington, Christchurch, and Dunedin.

From North America, you can book through **United** (www.ual.com) or **Air Canada,** but you'll be flying south on an Air New Zealand plane. The good thing about booking through Air New Zealand is that options may include free stopovers in the South Pacific, or onward flights to Australia for a little more than the base fare.

From other points in the Pacific, **Air Niugini** (09/977-2230, www.airniugini.com), **Air Pacific** (09/379-2404, www.airpacific.com), **Air Vanuatu** (09/367-2324, www.airvanuatu .com), and **Garuda** (09/366-1862, www .garuda-indonesia.com) offer the most flights.

From Asia, the following airlines have flights to Auckland: **Asiana Airlines** (09/256-6681, http://us.flyasiana.com), **Cathay Pacific** (09/379-0861, www.cathaypacific.com), **EVA Airways** (09/358-8300, www.evaairways.com), **Garuda** (09/366-1862, www.garuda-indonesia .com), **Korean Air** (09/914-2000, www.korean air.com), **Malaysia Airlines** (09/373-2741, www.malaysiaairlines.com), **Singapore Airlines** (09/303-2129, www.singaporeair.com), and **Thai Airways** (09/377-3886, www.thaiair.com).

British Airways (09/356-8690, www.british airways.com) is the only European airline that flies to New Zealand. From mainland Europe, the airlines of many countries have code-sharing agreements with Air New Zealand or Asian airlines. Contact your local national carrier for details.

From South America, **Aerolineas Argentinas** (09/379-3675, www.aerolineas .com) and **Lan Chile** (09/309/8673, www .lanchile.com) provide links to Auckland from their respective hubs.

Getting Around

New Zealand is one of the easiest countries in the world to get around by public transportation, and for self-drive holidays you will find a huge number of rental cars and campervan companies offering vehicles at reasonable prices. The only downside to road travel in New Zealand is the roads themselves. Outside of Auckland, there are no freeways, and very few divided highways. The highway between Auckland and Wellington, the two largest North Island cities, is just 650 km (400 mi), yet you should allow at least nine hours non-stop. Roads on the South Island take even more time to negotiate. For example, after getting off the ferry in Picton, it's just 100 km (62 mi) to Nelson, yet you should allow at least two hours for this narrow, winding route.

Visitor centers across the country serve as travel agents for trains, buses, and ferries.

PUBLIC TRANSPORTATION
Air
The major domestic airline is **Air New Zealand** (09/366-2400 or 0800/737-000, www.airnew zealand.com), with scheduled flights between all major cities, resorts, and large provincial towns. When booking an international flight to New Zealand, it is best to book onward domestic flights at the same time. Not only will you save money, but baggage restrictions do not apply to connecting domestic flights. Other domestic airlines include **Great Barrier Airlines** (09/256-6500 or 0800/900-600, www.greatbarrierairlines.co.nz) between Auckland and Great Barrier Island; **Soundsair** (04/801-0111 or 0800/505-005, www.sounds air.com) flies between Wellington and northern South Island centers; and **Stewart Island Flights** (03/218-9129 or 0800/843-475, www.stewartislandflights.co.nz) links

Invercargill with Stewart Island. Looking for a real adventure? Then contact **Air Chathams** (03/305-0209, www.airchathams.com) for flights to these remote islands from Auckland, Wellington, and Christchurch.

Rail

TranzScenic (04/495-0775 or 0800/872-467, www.tranzscenic.co.nz) operates long-distance passenger trains in New Zealand. On the North Island, the **Overlander** runs between Auckland and Wellington. On the South Island, the **TranzCoastal** follows the east coast from Picton to Christchurch. From Christchurch, the fabulously scenic **TranzAlpine** train crosses the Southern Alps to terminate at Greymouth on the west coast. The cost of rail travel is slightly higher than by bus, but a variety of discounts are available by traveling at certain times of day and by reservation. For example, the 12-hour Auckland–Wellington trip costs $80–210 depending on the time of travel, class of travel, and advance booking.

Bus

The main long-distance bus company is **Intercity Coachlines** (09/623-1503, www .intercitycoach.co.nz), with a complex network of bus routes on both islands. Intercity **Travelpasses** (www.travelpass.co.nz) allow great flexibility along 17 popular routes over a three-month period; the $588 pass allows travel between Auckland and Christchurch via Rotorua, Wellington, Queenstown, and Milford Sound. Options range from five days of travel for $387 to 15 days for $845. All passes are valid for 12 months. Another Intercity option is a **Flexipass** (www.backpackerbus .co.nz), which is sold in blocks of five hours' travel. For example, a 60-hour pass will get you around both islands for $585.

Shuttle buses run on scheduled routes and on-demand throughout the country. They range from a full-size bus to a car run by the local cab company, but most often are small minivans. The service is efficient and cheaper than the major bus companies, and you'll often get a colorful commentary thrown

© ANDREW HEMPSTEAD

Rail lines and roadways often follow the same route.

in for free. Shuttle bus service usually links up with Intercity's schedules, so when you arrive at a bus depot, these local companies will be waiting. Although we have listed the shuttle buses in the *Getting There and Around* sections of the travel chapters, the best way to find out local routes and schedules is at any information center.

Backpacker buses offer another way to get around the country cheaply. Some are simply an inexpensive bus service, while others are more like a "Green Tortoise" experience. The largest bus company catering exclusively to the backpacker market is **Kiwi Experience** (09/366-9830, www.kiwiexperience.com). It allows time for activities along the way, overnights at backpacker lodges, and stops at supermarkets for food. Attracting the young "party" crowd, it offers 20 itineraries, with ticketing sold for each route or for a set period of time (the Full Monty is $1,850). We've heard many good things about **Magic Travellers Network** (09/358-5600, www.magicbus.co.nz), which operates very modern coaches along a network encompassing both islands. The "Magic Bus" offers a lot more flexibility than Kiwi Experience; travelers can get on and off as with regular scheduled buses and use whatever facilities they desire. The company also makes activity and food stops, as well as books accommodations and guarantees seats. The new kid on the block is **Stray Travel** (09/309-8772, www.straytravel.co.nz), with services throughout both islands. This company has an advantage for travelers looking to explore more remote regions, plus their passes—including the Max Pass ($1,200) which covers the entire network—are valid for unlimited travel for 12 months.

Ferry

The least expensive and most enjoyable way to travel between the North and South Islands is by ferry. Two companies ply this route year-round: **Interislander** (04/498-3302 or 0800/802-802, www.interislander.co.nz) and **Bluebridge** (04/471-6188 or 0800/844-844, www.bluebridge.co.nz). Fares are similar (adult

$49–65, vehicle and driver $169–225), but you get the least expensive fares by booking as far in advance from within New Zealand with Interislander. Visitor centers throughout the country act as booking agents.

Considering the amount of traffic these services handle, the operations are remarkably efficient and reliable. If you've left you're rental vehicle in Wellington, picking up another is a simple affair in Picton, but you should let your rental car company know your arrival time.

Other scheduled ferries are operated by **Fullers** (09/367-9111, www.fullers.co.nz) from Auckland to islands through the Hauraki Gulf, **SeaLink** (09/300-5900 or 0800/732-546, www.sealink.co.nz) between Auckland and Great Barrier Island, and **Stewart Island Experience** (03/212-7660 or 0800/000-511, www.stewartislandexperience.co.nz) linking Bluff to Stewart Island in the far south.

DRIVING

The most important thing to remember is *you drive on the left-hand side of the road in New Zealand* (as in the U.K. and Australia). Try to get the rules of the road before you drive, especially if you're used to driving on the right side of the road (and look up the rules of "roundabouts").

The **New Zealand Automobile Association** (www.aa.co.nz) is invaluable if you're a member. With proof of any overseas AA membership, you can pick up its excellent maps covering every area of New Zealand in detail, accommodation guides covering everything from tent sites to first-class hotels, and touring information. Offices are located in all major cities and most towns. If you join the AA ($110 for six months), you get assistance with emergency breakdowns—simple problems are fixed on the spot or your vehicle is towed to the nearest service station.

Petrol is about $1.40 per liter throughout the country.

Car Rental

To rent a car you must be at least 21 years old, have a current international driver's license

© ANDREW HEMPSTEAD

One-way bridges are just some of the many local driving hazards.

(or a domestic permit from Australia, Austria, Canada, Fiji, Germany, Namibia, The Netherlands, South Africa, Switzerland, the U.K., or the U.S.), and have comprehensive automobile insurance (arranged by the rental agencies).

All major international car rental agencies usually offer both car and camper-van rentals, as do many other small rental outfits throughout the country. Most agencies include unlimited mileage in the daily rate, but check before signing up. In summer, the major agencies charge from $60 a day for a compact vehicle, discounted up to 50 percent in the off-season. Four-wheel drives and minivans (known locally as people-movers) generally start at $120 per day. These agencies, along with their Auckland telephone numbers and international websites, include: **Avis** (09/379-2650, www.avis.com), **Budget** (09/976-2270, www .budget.com), **Hertz** (09/367-6350, www .hertz.com), **National** (09/309-3336, www .nationalcar.com), and **Thrifty** (09/309-0111, www.thrifty.com). Each of these agencies has offices in all cities, most towns, at the ferry

terminals in Wellington and Picton, and at most airports.

The smaller, local car rental agencies offer small economy cars such as Toyotas, Hondas, Mitsubishis, and Nissans, typically one or two years old, starting at about $40 per day for unlimited mileage or $30 per day plus about 15 cents per km. Some fly-by-night agencies have been known to rent unreliable cars and are reluctant to return your money even when you've been stranded; ask for recommendations from fellow travelers. **Scotties** (09/303-3912, www .scotties.co.nz), a local agency based in Auckland, maintains a large fleet of vehicles with reasonable rates. Other agencies may offer cheaper deals, but for reliability (vehicles are all only a couple of years old and covered by the maximum insurance available), this agency is best. Scotties also has an outlet in Christchurch, the perfect opportunity for a one-way trip through the country. Other local companies with outlets throughout the country include **Europcar** (09/379-5080, www.europcar .co.nz), **Letz** (09/257-2734, www.letz.co.nz),

Omega (09/377-5573, www.omegarentalcars
.com), and **New Zealand Rent-a-car** (09/275-
2422, www.nzrentalacar.co.nz).

Camper-Van Rental

Cruising around New Zealand in a rented
camper-van is an extremely popular way to
see the country. There are plenty of inexpensive and excellent camping facilities, so it's
only the initial rental cost that can be steep.
Many companies offer camper-vans and fully
equipped motor homes, usually on an unlim-
ited-kilometer rate only and for a minimum
number of days. Most have low-season rates
May–September, but in summer, you must
reserve well in advance. **Maui** (09/275-3013
or 0800/651-080, www.maui-rentals.com) is
a large operation based near the airport, with
transfers from throughout the city to the depot
and hundreds of vehicles of many configura-
tions. Other agencies specializing in camper-
van rentals include: **Adventure Deluxe Motor
Homes** (09/256-0255, www.nzmotorhomes
.co.nz), **Backpacker Camper-vans** (09/255-
0620 or 0800/422-267), **Britz** (09/275-9090
or 0800/831-900, www.britz.com), and **Kea
Campers** (09/441-7833 or 0800/520-052,
www.keacampers.com). For singles and cou-
ples, **Spaceships** (09/309-8777, www.space
ships.tv) make for a good deal. Basically converted minivans painted bright orange, the rear
door lifts around a tent, while inside is storage
including a water tank and cooler, as well as a
DVD system. Standard summer rates are $150
per day, which includes a portable barbecue
and all cooking utensils.

Buying a Vehicle

If you plan to be in New Zealand for several
months, one of the cheapest ways to travel is
to buy a used car as soon as you arrive, then
sell it when you leave. Used-car dealers are required by law to provide a warrant of fitness
(WoF) less than 28 days old and valid for six
months on all cars sold. This allows you to
buy something fairly cheaply that must run for
at least six months. However, expect to pay at
least $1,000–3,000 for a used car that still has

some life in it. You hear stories of those who
have bought a good used car from a dealer,
traveled around New Zealand for almost six
months, and then re-sold it for more than they
originally paid.

You can buy registration for six months
(about $200) or one year (about $400). Note:
You'll be heavily fined for a vehicle without
current warrant of fitness and registration papers. Insurance is also recommended—an insurance company can arrange third party, fire,
and theft or full coverage. For the best deal,
call the companies advertising in the Yellow
Pages of the telephone directory and ask for
a quote.

If you belong to an automobile association,
you can have the car inspected before you buy
at the **Vehicle Inspection Service Centre** in
Auckland (Papakura Ami Building, East St.,
09/296-1837)—a very wise idea. Reservations
are necessary. Or look in the Yellow Pages
under "vehicle inspection service" and call for
a pre-purchase check quote—usually about
$130. The AA also operates **Lemon Check**
(www.lemoncheck.co.nz), an online service
that for $25 gives out a complete history of
vehicles using their VIN.

Before you arrive, use the Internet, not so
much to find the actual vehicle you intend to
buy, but to get an idea of prices. The website
www.carselect.co.nz is a good starting point.
The Wednesday and Saturday editions of the
Auckland *Herald* and the *Saturday Star* newspapers advertise a large selection of used cars.
Also check out notice boards at backpacker
lodges and in the Auckland Visitor Centre.
While you're at the visitor center, ask for the
handout on buying or selling your own car—
it even lists and explains newspaper abbrevia-
tions such as warrant of fitness, registration,
and insurance.

At weekend "car fairs" owners sell their
own vehicles. These are held throughout the
country, including in Auckland at **Ellerslie
Racecourse** (Hwy. 1, Greenlane Interchange,
09/529-2233, www.carfair.co.nz) each Sunday 9 A.M.–noon. Also in Auckland, check
out **Backpackers Car Market** (20 East St.,

09/377-7761, www.backpackerscarmarket .co.nz), where travelers sell vehicles to each other. Naturally, the best-value cars are sold early in the day at both places, but often sellers drop their prices as the day wears on. Although some buyers pay on the spot, generally a deposit secures a car and final transactions are made early in the workweek.

Visas and Officialdom

Rules and regulations come and go. The best way to find out exactly what you need is to visit a reputable travel agent; you can also visit the nearest New Zealand Embassy or New Zealand Consulate General—these are listed online at the **Immigration New Zealand** website (www.immigration.govt.nz).

ENTERING NEW ZEALAND
The basic entry requirements for visitors staying up to six months on nonworking visas are a fully paid onward or round-trip ticket, sufficient funds ($1,000 per month, or at least $400 per month if you're staying with a New Zealand citizen or have prepaid accommodation), and a passport (valid for at least three months beyond the date of departure from New Zealand). Australian passport holders and Australian residents with current resident return visas do not need a permit or another visa.

New Zealand has a **visa waiver agreement** with many countries. For residents of these countries, this means you do not need to apply for a visa before arriving. Upon arrival in New Zealand—and after meeting the above requirements—you will be issued a **Visitors Permit** for tourist visits of up to six months by British citizens, provided they hold passports that give them the right of permanent residence in the U.K.; for visits up to three months by citizens of Austria, Belgium, Canada, Denmark, Finland, France (if normally resident in continental France), Germany, Greece, Iceland, Indonesia, Ireland, Italy, Japan, Kiribati, Liechtenstein, Luxembourg, Malaysia, Malta, Monaco, Nauru, The Netherlands, Norway, Portugal, Singapore, Spain, Sweden, Switzerland, Thailand, Tuvalu, and the United States (not applicable to American Samoans or any other U.S. nationals); for visits up to 30 days by citizens of France (normally resident in Tahiti or New Caledonia).

If you wish to stay longer than the above entry permits allow (Australian citizens and citizens of Commonwealth countries and Ireland who live in Australia are exempt), you must get prior permission in the form of a visa. It is illegal to work, make financial gains, study, overstay the period indicated on your entry permit, or settle in New Zealand without permission before entering the country.

Visas: Citizens of all countries other than those listed above require visas to enter New Zealand. Travel agents usually arrange all necessary visas and other documentation—but allow plenty of time (at least several weeks), especially if you haven't a passport. Another source of information on vacation and work visas is your nearest New Zealand embassy or consulate; find these and all current immigration regulations at www.immigration.govt.nz.

CUSTOMS
The **New Zealand Customs Service** website (www.customs.govt.nz) is a clearinghouse of information pertaining to what you can and can't bring into the country. If you're over 17 years old, in addition to personal effects, you can bring duty-free items into New Zealand worth up to NZ$700, plus 200 cigarettes or 50 cigars or 250 grams of tobacco, 4.5 liters of wine or beer (six 750-milliliter bottles), and 1,125 milliliters of spirits (hard liquor). Contact your own country's customs office to find out what you may bring back duty-free.

New Zealand is understandably strict on agricultural requirements. Before landing in New Zealand you're required to fill in a declaration form stating whether you have been on a farm within the last 30 days, and what foods, plants, or animal products you are carrying. The *New Zealand—A Growing Land—Passenger Arrival Information* brochure is available from any New Zealand embassy or consulate. If you've been on a farm, your boots or shoes may be examined for dirt. Bicycles and camping equipment, such as tents and sleeping bags, may also be checked for soil particles, insects, and other pests. Attempting to bring in drugs (other than prescription) is asking for big trouble, as is a dishonest declaration on any official documents—don't risk it.

Recreation

A multitude of exciting activities awaits you in the great New Zealand outdoors. Spectacular scenery lies around every bend, and action-packed adventures are more than likely to lure you off the beaten track into some of the most beautiful countryside you're ever likely to see. Whether you want to run wild white-water rapids, ski the slopes of a smoldering volcano, skim the shallows in a high-speed jetboat, cast a fly rod in an icy stream, settle back to watch cricket or lawn bowls, or have a bet on "the trots," New Zealand offers it all.

TRAMPING

Also known as hiking, trekking, and backpacking, tramping is one of the favorite outdoor pursuits of New Zealanders and visitors alike. The small population, vast areas of wilderness (some still unexplored), diverse landscapes, and wide variety of terrain guarantee a good walking experience. Tramping is most popular November–April when the weather is best.

A great way to really see New Zealand is through the use of the National Walkway Network. The idea of a national walkway was passed as an Act of Parliament in 1975, with the aim of providing a network of tracks eventually linking the farthest point north to the farthest point south; this plan has been abandoned, however. More than 150 walkways have been created, passing through public and private property to points of scenic, historic, or cultural interest. The DOC classifies each hike as one of four types:

Easy Access Tracks—well-formed track suitable for families or those in wheelchairs

Short Walks—well-defined track suitable for people of average physical fitness

Great Walk/Easy Tramping Track—a formed track with overnight accommodations

Tramping Track—a less well-defined trail with often steep gradients

Route—lightly marked route for use only by well-equipped, experienced trampers.

Details on individual walks appear in each travel chapter, in brochures available at DOC offices, and on their website: www.doc.govt.nz. **Federated Mountain Clubs of New Zealand** (04/233-8244, www.fmc.org.nz) is a national association of over 100 tramping and mountaineering clubs.

Great Walks

"Great Walks" is a designation given to nine of New Zealand's premier hiking trails. Each is famous for its own unique and outstanding scenery. They all require backcountry experience and at least one overnight camping or in trailside huts.

On the North Island, the **Lake Waikaremoana Track** wanders around Lake Waikaremoana in Te Urewera National Park; the **Tongariro Northern Circuit** in Tongariro National Park traverses a barren volcanic landscape. The **Heaphy Track** in Kahurangi National Park and the **Abel Tasman Coast Track** meander across the northern tip of the South Island; the **Hollyford Track, Kepler Track,** and **Milford Track** traverse rugged alpine landscapes around Queenstown and in Fiordland National Park; and the **Rakiura Track** crosses the untouched wilderness of Stewart Island. The final track isn't a track at all; the **Whanganui Journey** is a river trip through Whanganui National Park.

ENVIRONMENTAL CARE CODE

1. Protect plants and animals – they're unique, and often rare.

2. Remove rubbish – carry out what you carry in.

3. Bury toilet waste well away from waterways, tracks, campsites, and huts.

4. Keep streams and lakes clean – drain used water well away from the water source into the soil to allow it to be filtered, and boil drinking water for 10 minutes or chemically treat it.

5. Take care with fires – portable stoves are less harmful and more efficient, but if you make a fire, use only dead wood, douse it with water afterward, and check the ashes before leaving.

6. Camp carefully – leave no trace of your visit.

7. Keep to the track – avoid damaging fragile plants.

8. Consider others.

9. Respect the cultural heritage.

10. Enjoy your visit.

tuatara, a lizard-like reptile

© ANDREW HEMPSTEAD

All tracks are extremely popular during the summer; huts are spaced at regular intervals (approximately a six-hour walk between each) but in peak periods, especially January, they can become overcrowded and you need to carry your own tent and stove (huts range $10–45 per person). The Milford Track is the most well known, and because of its popularity, booking (up to one year ahead) is required by the DOC (for independent walkers); you can also hike it as part of a guided group November–March. Get all the facts and options (most can be done independently or with a guiding company) well in advance to avoid disappointment (find more details in the appropriate travel chapters).

Commercial Operators

Many commercially operated trekking tours cover both North and South Islands. You can book these through travel agencies, New Zealand Tourism Board offices, and Visitor Information Network offices. They offer straight hiking trips, or hiking combined with moun-tain climbing, canoeing, jetboating, or river rafting. Overnight or several-day trips generally include a combination of activities, camping gear or cabin accommodations, all meals, equipment, and transportation. Most are offered only during the summer; at least one experienced guide takes each tour.

MOUNTAINEERING

Of many first-class climbing areas, the main ones are **Mount Taranaki** (2,517 meters/8,258 ft) and **Mount Ruapehu** (2,796 meters/9,173 ft) on the North Island, and a multitude of climbs in the skyscraper peaks of the **Southern Alps** on the South Island. Eight out of the 13 national parks are mountainous, providing reasonably good access and well-equipped huts. All park visitor centers have climbing and tramping information and weather forecasts. **Mount Cook** (3,744 meters/12,280 ft), **Mount Tasman** (3,497 meters/11,473 ft), **La Perouse** (3,078 meters/10,098 ft), and **Mount Sefton** (3,157 meters/10,358 ft) in Aoraki/Mount

Cook and Westland National Parks are very popular with experienced climbers—but only when weather conditions are just right. Many routes are long and difficult, demanding experience and appropriate equipment, and most of the mountains have glaciers, demanding ice- and rock-climbing ability. You'll find few solid-rock climbs in New Zealand—the best is on the firm granite of the **Darran Mountains** in Fiordland National Park.

The climbing season is November–April, but mountaineers attempt more and more winter climbing each year and are always discovering new routes. Several guiding companies offer climbs, walks, and various levels of instruction. Bring your own equipment to New Zealand because it's expensive to buy; however, the latest equipment is available should you need it. The Department of Survey and Lands publishes excellent topographical maps of most areas; buy them at any of its offices in all major cities, or in the larger bookshops. For more information on climbing and mountaineering, contact the New Zealand Alpine Club, headquartered in Christchurch (03/377-7595, www.alpineclub.org.nz), or the **Federated Mountain Clubs of New Zealand** (www.fmc.org.nz).

WHITE-WATER RAFTING

If you seek the adrenaline high fueled by apprehension, panic, and sheer fear, look no further. Whether you're a professional rafter or a total beginner looking for instant thrills, New Zealand has a river to suit. Both islands are crisscrossed with rivers that offer the rafter everything from the peaceful pleasure of drifting with the current through spectacular scenery to wild, churning, white-water rapids where you cling on with all your strength and pray—between icy-cold dunkings. Soaking wet, feet like blocks of ice, heart pounding, poised at the top of a fearsome rapid, you may wonder for a moment why you're doing this—but when it's all over, you know you'll be back for more.

The Rivers

The **Wairoa**, a rapids-filled river meandering

down from the Kaimai Range to meet the ocean near Tauranga, provides both quiet water and short bursts of raging Class III to Class V rapids. The highlights are aptly named "Waterfall" and "Roller Coaster." The nearby **Rangitaiki River** (not as wild) comes down from the Ahimanawa Range to meet the ocean just north of Whakatane. The **Motu River** provides quiet-water stretches through breathtaking scenery and several exciting rapids as it winds through the Raukumara Range (East Cape) to come out at Haupoto. Hydro-development has tamed much of the **Tongariro River,** but a few sections still offer exciting rafting action. The **Mohaka** (near Gisborne), **Ngaruroro** (between Napier and Hastings), and **Rangitikei** (south of Wanganui) offer combinations of quiet water and rugged scenery and wild, heart-stopping rapids that can raise the hair on the neck of even the experienced rafter. On the South Island, the most popular rafting is on the **Kawarau** and **Shotover Rivers** near Queenstown (a large choice of companies offers Class III to Class V rapids), the **Rakaia River** near Christchurch, and the wild **Landsborough River.** Generally the best months for rafting are October–January, though most operators run the rivers till April, depending on water levels and weather conditions. The high-water levels on all rivers are usually in October–December and sometimes January. The low-water levels are in February and March.

Commercial Operators

Many commercial river-rafting companies operate on both the North and South Islands (more in the south), and more spring up each rafting season. Trips generally go between October and April, dependent on water levels and weather; most companies include full- or part-length wet suits and provide the mandatory life jackets. Choose a good and safe operator—avoid trips that have a reputation for fooling around, falling into the rapids for fun, etc.—they usually employ the least-experienced guides. Ask around about safety records; check with the local information center; and make sure the company is a member of the **New Zealand**

Rafting Association (03/696-3849, www .nz-rafting.co.nz). In addition to member listings, this website has lots of handy rafting information and an online booking form. On the **North Island** tours operate out of Rotorua rafting the Rangitaiki River, out of Taupo and Turangi rafting the Tongariro, Mohaka, and Rangitikei Rivers, and out of Tauranga rafting the Wairoa. On the **South Island** tours operate out of Christchurch rafting the Waimakariri River, out of Westport rafting the Buller, Karamea, and Mohikinui Rivers, and out of Queenstown (lots of companies) rafting the Shotover, Dart, Waiatoto, and Kawarau Rivers.

Life jackets are mandatory, and on some trips, crash hats are also provided. Keep in mind that it's always possible to find yourself unexpectedly bodysurfing the rapids. Before you start out, you're taught basic paddling skills, how to stay afloat and ride the rapids if you're ejected, and how to get back to the raft or shore. A minimum age is often set depending on the difficulty of the river.

Wear a bathing suit, shirt, shorts, wool sweater, waterproof jacket, thick wool socks, and tennis shoes or sneakers (essential)—take a change of clothes for later. Leave your camera behind unless you're doing a float trip or one of the mildest grade rivers (or have a waterproof camera that you can firmly attach to yourself)—you generally don't have much time between rapids to take photos.

CANOEING AND KAYAKING

Several tour companies offer canoe or kayak trips; you can also rent canoes without guides for a few hours or for an entire river camping trip. On the North Island, canoe tours operate out of Wanganui using the **Whanganui River.** On the South Island, you can canoe the **Kawarau River;** tours operate out of Queenstown. Because of the nature of the rivers, life jackets, crash helmets, and wet suits are essential; most equipment can be rented. For more remote areas, helicopter services are available to fly you in to the rivers. For more information, contact the **New Zealand Recreational Canoeing Association** (04/560-3590, www.rivers.org.nz).

FISHING

Often called an angler's paradise, New Zealand fishing is world famous. Some of the friendliest New Zealanders are found congregating around rivermouths and lakeshores, fishing rods in hand, hats covered in assorted flies and lures. Originally, brown trout ova from the U.K. via Tasmania (Australia) and rainbow trout ova from the Russian River in California were introduced to New Zealand waters in the late 1860s. Streams and rivers providing both fast- and slow-flowing water, crystal-clear lakes, and an abundant supply of food all helped the fish thrive in their new environment, and modern hatcheries and good conservation methods ensure that New Zealand's good fishing continues.

Lake and River Fishing

In general the north is known for large rainbow trout, the south for large brown trout, and quinnat salmon run in many of the rivers of the North Island's lower west coast and the South Island's east coast.

North Island: Most lakes, particularly **Lake Taupo** (New Zealand's largest) and **Lake Tarawera,** are stocked with rainbow trout, but the rivers seem to attract the larger rainbows and browns. The finest fishing is naturally found at off-the-beaten-track locations; boats are often necessary to get to the best stream mouths. Fly-fishing is at its best in rivers and streams that flow into lakes April–June when the fish swim upstream to spawn, and November–December when they return to the lake. Use a wet lure fly and fast-sinking line downstream, and a weighted nymph on floating line upstream.

South Island: Most lakes are stocked with brown trout, some with rainbow trout and landlocked salmon. The fishing is good, at times similar to prime times on the North Island lakes, but anglers use a dry fly and floating line. Spinning is popular from the shore, as is trolling with weighted lines from a boat. Dry flies (or lures) mainly snag brown trout in the rivers, and in some eastern rivers, Pacific salmon. In South Westland, brown trout come in from the sea in late summer and are caught on both wet and dry fly and spinners.

The rivers of the east coast are great for salmon fishing. Try the Ashburton, Rakaia, Rangitata, Waimakariri, and Waitaki Rivers October–April (Jan.–Mar. are the best months).

For fishing information, pick up a copy of the *New Zealand Fishing News* (which has the largest circulation of any New Zealand sports magazine) or *New Zealand Fishing World*. Find links to both magazines at www.fishing.net.nz.

Equipment

Bringing your own fishing gear into New Zealand is permitted but it may be fumigated. Thigh waders are suggested for South Island fishing, chest waders for North Island. For all types of trout fishing, the experts suggest you have one reel with five replaceable spools and the following lines: a floating line of 5–7 weight, A.H.D. fast-sink line of 8–10, a shooting head line (preferably number 10), a floating line with sink tip for nymphing, and a medium sinking line of 8–9. Dry flies and nymphs such as the Red Tipped Governor, Royal Wulff, Adams, Blue Dun, Hare, and Copper all work well in New Zealand. Streamer or lure flies representing smelt are best bought locally.

Regulations

Most anglers flyfish or troll. Spinning or lure fishing is fairly uncommon—most of the best fishing areas are designated for fly-fishing only. Each of the 12 local regions has its own fishing rules, and fishing seasons vary area by area. **Fish and Game New Zealand** (04/499-4767, www.fishandgame.org.nz) is the government department responsible for managing the country's freshwater fisheries. Copies of all the regulations are available from DOC offices throughout the country and on the department website.

Licenses: One license is valid in 11 of the 12 regions. The cost is $18.50 per 24 hours or $92 for the season. Children pay $4 and $18.50 respectively. To fish in Lake Taupo and its watersheds requires a separate license, which is available at the local DOC office and at local sporting stores. It costs adult $19.50, child $4.50 for 24 hours, and adult $75.50, child

$11.50 for a season pass. Regulations through the country allow a 20-meter public right-of-way along the banks of fishing rivers and lakeshores; however, permission is required from the owner if you need to cross private land to reach the water.

Big-Game Fishing

Also known as deep-sea fishing, this is a popular (and expensive) sport concentrated along 500 km (310 mil) of the northern east coast of the North Island. The season is generally January–April, attracting flocks of overseas visitors eager to haul in a trophy from the sea. A fishing license is not required. Broadbill, striped, black, and blue marlin; hammerhead, mako, and thresher shark; and yellowtail, kingfish, and tuna are the main game-fish species. The most prolific fighting big-game fish is the striped marlin—the most successful months are December–June; catch sharks November–May and tuna December–March. Big-game fishing clubs abound from Whangarei to the Bay of Islands, and international tournaments are held each year. To try your luck, head up to the Bay of Islands via the coastal route, comparing charter prices at the deep-sea fishing resorts as you head north. If you join the prestigious **Bay of Islands Swordfish Club** (www .swordfish.co.nz) in Russell and catch something worthwhile, the fish is officially weighed in, you're issued a certificate, and you become eligible for most club trophies. Charter boats (gear provided) and experienced crews are always available, but cost from $800 per day, so unless you have a large budget you'll need to find several other people willing to share costs.

SCUBA DIVING

Coral reefs, caves, multicolored sponges, various large brown kelps, friendly fish, and a large number of shipwrecks lure the scuba diver and underwater photographer to New Zealand shores. When the weather is suitable, underwater visibility is about 9–12 meters (30–40 ft) along the coast, but around the offshore islands it's usually 18–24 meters (60–79 ft) and on good days exceeds 45 meters (148 ft). The **Bay of Islands, Hauraki Gulf, Coromandel**

Peninsula, Cook Strait, and **Milford Sound** all offer good diving. **The Poor Knights Islands,** a small island group off the northeast coast of the North Island, are "a diver's dream," offering century-old sunken ships as an added feature. Water temperatures vary 14–22°C (57–72°F), lower in the far south; locals recommend wet suits. Summer usually provides the calmest weather; diving conditions are at their best January–April. Some years a plankton bloom occurs in spring and early summer, clouding the coastal waters. No underwater flora or fauna are dangerous to divers apart from sharks—and they're rarely seen. Gear can be rented with at least a PADI Diver's Certificate or equivalent. **Dive HQ** has 20 affiliated stores around the country, each with equipment sales, rentals, and charter information. The Auckland store is at 136 Greenlane Rd., Greenlane (09/520-7300, www.divehq.co.nz).

SAILING

New Zealanders are water people—if they're not *in* the water, they're on it. Auckland is a good place to get a taste of sailing. Here, **Pride of Auckland** (09/373-4557, www.prideof auckland.com) offers short harbor trips aboard 45-foot yachts, or you can have the thrilling opportunity to sail an America's Cup yacht with **Sail NZ** (Viaduct Harbour, 09/359-5987 or 0800/724-569, www.sailnewzealand.co.nz). Another sailing option is the **Søren Larsen** (09/817-8799, www.sorenlarsen.co.nz), a square-rigged tall ship that dominates the harbor during the November–March sailing season. Weekdays are spent on overnight journeys through the Hauraki Gulf and to the Bay of Islands and Bay of Plenty (around $250 per person per night), then she returns to Auckland for the weekend, departing each Saturday and Sunday for three- and five-hour trips around the harbor. The rest of the year, the *Søren Larsen* takes adventurers on two-week journeys through the South Pacific.

Bareboat charters are popular November–May (the yachting season), and you have the choice of hiring a crew or sailing it yourself (previous sailing experience is necessary). Some companies also offer crews that give instruction; most supply all the necessary equipment minus bedding and food. Premier sailing locations are liberally dotted around the country's coastline; the major operators on the North Island are found in the **Bay of Islands, Hauraki Gulf** (Auckland), and **Marlborough Sounds.** Prices are not cheap, about $100–350 per day (the more expensive sleep up to six people), but special rates are offered for longer hire periods.

SURFING

You can find surf throughout the year around the entire coastline. The best-known surfing area is around **Raglan** west of Hamilton. Considered New Zealand's premier point break, with three left-breaking points in a row, it's rarely flat and has powerful and often large waves typical of the North Island's rugged west coast. Other popular North Island areas are **New Plymouth, Bay of Plenty,** and **Gisborne.** The beach at Mount Maunganui has one of the world's only artificial surfing reefs. On the South Island, surfing beaches are most accessible on the **east coast.** A large variety of beach breaks, river bars, and reef points lie along the coastline; however, quality surf over three meters is rare. Wet suits are necessary from autumn through spring, year-round on the South Island.

CYCLING

New Zealand is an ideal place for a bicycling vacation if you're reasonably fit. Temperate climate, excellent roads, low traffic density, and a wide variety of terrain and scenery appeal to those with enough time to see the country at a slower pace. However, a beginner cyclist may find the terrain too steep and demanding to be pleasurable, particularly on the mountainous South Island, and the traffic rather frightening on narrow roads. Talk to experienced cyclists before you commit yourself to a cycling tour of the country. One way of dealing with carrying your gear is to pack up everything you don't need for a few days in cardboard boxes, then mail them to your next destination a few days down the road. This way you always have clean clothes and other basic necessities to look forward to as a reward at the end of a few days' hard work.

If you haven't cycled before, a reasonably priced tour is a good way to start. If you're taking your own bicycle over to New Zealand, buy a bike box and wash the tires well—New Zealand is strict on pest control and your entire bike will be washed if there's a speck of foreign dirt on the tires (same goes for tents and hiking boots). When in New Zealand, be sure to pick up **Pedallers' Paradise** (www .paradise-press.co.nz), comprising one lightweight book for each island. **Bike NZ** (www .bikenz.org.nz) represents biking organizations across the country.

Rentals and Commercial Touring

You'll find bike rentals in every tourist town across the country. For long-distance touring, **Adventure Cycles** (1 Laurie Ave., Parnell, Auckland, 09/309-5566 or 0800/335-566, www.adventure-auckland.co.nz) is a good first stop. This company rents bikes by the day or week, with daily rentals $30–40, weekly rentals for $90–150, or pay an extra $40 to be outfitted with panniers. Adventure Cycles also sells a variety of touring gear, including maps.

Auckland-based **Pedaltours** (09/585-1338 or 0800/302-096, www.pedaltours.co.nz) offers a variety of bicycle adventure tours ranging from an overnight ride through the Canterbury vineyards ($750 pp) to a 15-day Northern Highlights adventure ($5,390). Accommodations in small country inns or farmstays and all meals are included. **Flying Kiwi Wilderness Expeditions** (03/573-8126 or 0800/693-296, www.flyingkiwi.com) combines bus and bike travel, allowing cyclists to ride as much or as little as they wish each day. The tours, which run 4–28 days, are well priced.

ADRENALINE SPORTS

New Zealand has a well-deserved reputation for extreme sports. Some of these, such as mountaineering and white-water rafting, are practiced around the world while others were either developed in New Zealand or are still unique to the country. Even mainstream adventure sports usually have a Kiwi twist—white-water rafting companies at Rotorua, for example, run the world's highest commercially rafted waterfall. At Waitomo, black-water rafting is a local term for floating down underground rivers, while at Rotorua, a local entrepreneur brings zorbing to a world audience. But it is Queenstown, on the South Island, that draws the most thrill seekers.

Note: If you plan to try any adventure sport—whether it be scuba diving or bungy jumping—read your travel insurance policy very carefully, as many exclude these type of "dangerous" activities. Some policies offer optional "extreme sports" riders for an additional fee.

Bungy Jumping

This is one of the most popular ways to get an adrenaline rush in New Zealand. Imagine standing on a high bridge spanning a river-filled canyon, your ankles securely tied together with a towel and bungy cord, the river far below. And then, in front of a large audience who enthusiastically does a "countdown," you dive off for a long, long free fall. At the end of the fall, just before you hit the water or after you are momentarily submerged to your waist (you choose between a wet or dry fall), the elastic rope rebounds and you're flying upward toward the bridge again. This continues until you run out of momentum, and then you're rescued by boat and taken to shore. To experience this you have to cough up at least $100, but those who have taken the plunge proudly swagger around the countryside in a specially designed bungy-jumping T-shirt—and you have to *do* it to get the shirt. If this sounds like something you'd like to try, head for Queenstown, where the operators are the most experienced in the country—they started it all.

Jetboating

The world-famous Hamilton jetboats were invented in New Zealand and are very popular. Commercial jetboat companies operate tours throughout both islands, providing trips of varying lengths through spectacular scenery. Jetboating is particularly popular on the Shotover

River in the Queenstown area. Experienced boat pilots operate the jetboats and provide thrilling rides ranging from a short ride skimming the shallows to combination trips including jetboating, white-water rafting, and a helicopter ride. Jetboating tends to be expensive, but if you like whizzing across rapids only centimeters deep, twisting and churning to just miss overhanging branches and the occasional bridge pylon, whirling 180 degrees on the spot at high speed, this activity is a must. The scenery is always spectacular—on the Shotover River you see abandoned gold mines and equipment along the way. Expect to get wet, particularly if you're selected to sit in the back seat. Take your camera in a waterproof container and firmly attach it to yourself. Mandatory life jackets are supplied, and some operators also provide light waterproof jackets.

SKIING AND SNOWBOARDING

New Zealand ski fields, as they are delightfully known, provide some of the most spectacular skiing and boarding in the world. Winter sports enthusiasts are lured from the Northern Hemisphere for excellent skiing and boarding on uncrowded treeless slopes June–October. Good weather, magnificent scenery, and reasonable costs (by international standards) complete the picture. In addition to 17 commercial resorts, New Zealand is home to around a dozen **club fields.** Often facilities are fairly basic—simple rope tows with no grooming—but accommodation is provided and you will be welcomed with open arms.

Apart from numerous conventional ski fields, you can fly up to the mountaintops for an ex-

hilarating heli-skiing, glacier skiing (ski-plane), or ski-touring adventure in virgin powder. Heli-skiing is particularly good in the Harris Mountains near Wanaka (South Island), offering more than 60 different runs (600–1,200 vertical meters/1,969–3,937 ft) on 35 mountains.

Although New Zealand slopes never seem to get crowded, the best time to ski is still midweek; most New Zealanders are weekend skiers, but August is usually busy all month when families with school-age children take their skiing vacations.

The Ski Fields

Of the 28 recognized skiing areas in the country, most are in the Southern Alps—many are club ski fields with a friendly atmosphere making up for limited facilities. On the North Island the two major commercial ski fields, **Whakapapa** and **Turoa,** are both situated on the volcanic slopes of Mount Ruapehu in Tongariro National Park. Other fields are operated by ski clubs in both Tongariro and Egmont National Parks. On the South Island the major commercial ski fields are **Mount Hutt** at Methven, **Coronet Peak** and **The Remarkables** near Queenstown, and **Treble Cone** and **Cardrona** near Wanaka. Smaller commercial ski fields, with a variety of lifts, cafeterias, and ski equipment rental, but limited adjacent accommodations, are found at **Rainbow Valley** near St. Arnaud; **Porter Heights** near Christchurch; **Erewhon, Mount Dobson,** and **Fox Peak** in central South Island; and **Lake Ohau** near Aoraki/Mount Cook National Park. Larger fields offer varying ski packages.

Accommodations and Camping

A great thing about traveling through New Zealand is the wide range of accommodations available to suit all budgets. Free campsites, inexpensive holiday parks, budget dorm beds for backpackers, cozy bed-and-breakfasts, farmstays, holiday homes, first-class motels, hotels, and luxury lodges—New

Zealand has it all. Don't be afraid to try something new while traveling through the country—traditional hostels have private rooms, campgrounds have motel rooms, and some of the fanciest hotels have rooms set aside for budget travelers.

In addition to the information provided

below and individual accommodations detailed through this book, the **Automobile Association** produces the annual *Accommodation Guide* listing all hotels and motels. It can be purchased at AA offices throughout the country, or check www.aatravel.co.nz. Another source of pre-trip planning is www.jasons.com, the website of a company that produces a free accommodation guide.

BACKPACKER LODGES

In no part of the world is this form of accommodation more popular, and as a consequence, budget travelers are spoiled by both choice and standard. These lodges, primarily catering to those traveling on a budget, appeal to everyone, with the choice of bunk-bed dorms, and single and double rooms; shared bathroom, kitchen, and laundry; a common room; and a laid-back atmosphere where it's usually a breeze to make new friends. Often extras are provided, such as bicycles for guest use, swimming pools, transportation, and more. Expect

© ANDREW HEMPSTEAD

Backpacker lodges are located in towns and cities across the country.

to pay $15–35 for a single bed in a dormitory that may have anywhere from three to twelve beds, $20–50 per person in a double or twin room with shared bath.

While the YHA has traditionally dominated the backpacker market, New Zealand is blessed with hundreds of privately operated lodges. For example, Nelson, on the South Island, is a mid-sized town, yet has over 20 private backpacker lodges.

Pick up the latest "blue book" (officially *BBH Backpacker Accommodation*) at visitor centers, backpacker lodges, or go online to www .bbh.co.nz; it lists over 360 of the best lodges, rated by guests and given a percentage that is generally accurate and a great help in choosing a place to spend the night. The guide is produced by **Budget Backpacker Hostels New Zealand,** which also offers the **BBH Club Card.** At a price of $40, this card generates an automatic discount at all listed lodges, includes $20 worth of phone calls, and is good for a variety of other discounts—all in all an excellent investment that pays for itself quickly.

YHA New Zealand

Scattered through the country are 57 properties affiliated with YHA New Zealand (03/379-9970 or 0800/278-299, www.yha.co.nz). Many of the hostels, ranging from cozy little farmhouses to wonders of modern architecture, are in prime locations—often not far from the center of local attractions. Sleeping in bunk beds in single-sex dorms (most YHA properties now also have double rooms), guests share communal bathroom, kitchen, living room, and laundry. You often need to supply linen or a sleeping bag, or rent it for a small nightly fee.

You don't have to be a member of YHA New Zealand/Hostelling International to stay in affiliated properties, but members save $3 per night. Other benefits come with membership—discounts on car rental, bus and ferry travel, attraction admissions, and some commercial activities.

In New Zealand, the joining fee is $10, then $30 annually for membership, or pay a $3 per night surcharge for 15 nights to gain membership.

Memberships are valid internationally. If you plan to travel extensively using hostels, join Hostelling International before you leave home. YHA New Zealand is a member of the **International Youth Hostel Federation,** a worldwide organization that represents 4,500 hostels in 60 countries. Joining the affiliate association in your home country entitles you to reciprocal rights in New Zealand. Local contact addresses include **HI-USA** (301/495-1240, www.hiayh.org), **HI-Canada** (613/237-7884, www.hihostels.ca), **YHA England and Wales** (0870/770-8868, www.yha.org.uk), and **YHA Australia** (02/9261-1111, www.yha.com). For other countries, click through the links provided at www.hihostels.com.

HOTELS

Hotels come in all shapes and sizes, and have just one thing in common—they are licensed to serve alcohol. This means that a "hotel" can be an old pub with a few basic rooms upstairs or, at the other end of the scale, a luxurious, upscale chain hotel such as a Hyatt or Hilton.

In the old pub hotels, rooms cost from $30 s, $40 d; they often (but not always) share bathrooms and have a communal lounge area. Generally rooms lack a television or telephone. Some old hotels have been restored, offering old-style luxury from $80 s, $100 d. These establishments often are called "boutique hotels."

New Zealand has plenty of first-class hotels, including widely recognized international hotel chains. Found in all major cities and tourist areas, they cost from $180 s or d. The Tourist Hotel Corporation of New Zealand (THC) once operated a string of first-class hotels throughout the country, but all have been sold. Most of the buildings have retained their former glory and are in the most beautiful areas, have the best views, and are often the center of activities in remote areas. Even if you're camping down the road, you'll probably visit one during your trip—to buy tour tickets, eat (some have reasonable cafés as well as first-class restaurants), be entertained, or just admire the architecture (e.g., the Grand Chateau in Tongariro National Park).

MOTELS

For the most part, New Zealand motels are different from the usual motels of other countries. Each room is a complete apartment—great value for the price. For about $70–140 s or d, you get a living room with TV; a fully equipped kitchen including utensils, pots and pans, and toaster (occasionally even a blender); a bathroom with shower; and sometimes even your own washer and dryer. A "studio" is a one-room unit; one-, two-, and three-bedroom units have separate sleeping areas. Motels often also provide a swimming pool, spa, playground, and/or other facilities. "Motor lodges" and "motor inns" are generally larger properties, with only some rooms having a kitchen, but with a restaurant on-site. Fresh milk is usually left in the fridge and continental breakfast can be delivered to your door for a small charge. Single travelers usually pay $10–20 less than the price for a double, while children bring a minimal extra charge. The standard check-in time is 2 P.M. and check-out is 10 A.M.

Most motels belong to a chain, but are independently owned and operated. These include **Best Western** (www.bestwestern.co.nz), **Budget Motel Chain** (www.budgetmotelchain.co.nz), **Golden Chain** (www.goldenchain.co.nz), and **Host Accommodation** (www.hostaccommodation.co.nz). Other chains, such as **Accor** (www.accorhotels.com.au) and **Choice Hotels** (www.choicehotels.co.nz), manage a wide range of properties under a variety of brand names. Before you leave home, check these websites for discounted Internet rates. Another good source of pre-trip planning information is the **Motel Association of New Zealand** website (www.nzmotels.co.nz).

BED-AND-BREAKFASTS

Bed-and-breakfasts, most of which are very comfortable and full of character, range in price, starting at $45 s, $55 d and going up to well over $500. The breakfasts usually are hearty enough to last until dinner. They're a great way to meet New Zealanders and are very popular, especially in the larger cities. If you have some idea of what area you want to stay in and if you'll be there during a vacation period, it's wise to book a room ahead of time.

The New Zealand Bed and Breakfast Book, updated annually by Moonshine Press (www.bnb .co.nz), is invaluable for those visitors who enjoy the personal feel of staying in private homes.

Farmstays

Farmstays are simply farm-based bed-and-breakfasts. Guests can either join in farm activities or just stay there and do their own thing. Many offer extras such as pool, tennis court, horseback riding, golf, hunting, and fishing. Some accommodations are in family homes with shared facilities; some may be in separate houses. A stay can range from one night with breakfast to several weeks' full board, and prices vary accordingly at about $70–200 d per night, depending on the activities offered.

HOLIDAY HOMES

Many holiday homes, or "baches," throughout New Zealand are available for rent when the owners are not occupying them. The best way to find out what's available and where is to buy a copy of *Baches and Holiday Homes to Rent* by Mark and Elizabeth Greening. Available at bookstores or online at www.holidayhomes .co.nz, the 2007 edition lists 900 properties and retails for $19.95.

CAMPGROUNDS AND HOLIDAY PARKS
Free, or Almost Free

If you enjoy camping out and have a tent and stove, New Zealand is a camper's paradise. You can put up a tent pretty much anywhere off the beaten track—but avoid camping close to tramping tracks and areas designated as "reserves." No Camping signs are only too obvious in areas where you're not permitted to camp—those who camp there anyway may be asked to move on or be fined. In remote but popular areas (such as along the road to Milford Sound), campsites with limited facilities and a source of drinking water have been provided at minimal charge ($4–10 per person per night). Serviced DOC campgrounds

(flush toilets, hot showers, kitchen, laundry) are $8–12 per person.

Holiday Parks

Holiday parks (also called motor camps) are one of New Zealand's best accommodation values, and great places to meet fellow travelers—particularly vacationing New Zealanders. They provide accommodation options

---

HOLIDAY PARK TERMINOLOGY

With so many accommodation options at holiday parks, it can be confusing trying to work out exactly what means what. The following descriptions and accompanying price ranges should help:

Campsite: a camping site with no services ($8-18 per person)

Caravan site: a site with power and other services ($10-18 per person)

On-site caravan: a caravan (trailer) with cooking facilities. Generally bathroom facilities are shared and no linen is supplied but can be rented ($35-55 s or d)

Cabins: the most basic cabins have bunk or single beds with no linen. Cooking and bathroom facilities are shared ($35-60)

En suite cabin: a cabin with its own bathroom, but shared cooking facilities ($45-70)

Tourist cabin: a cabin with cooking facilities and hot and cold water, with a shared communal bathroom ($40-80)

Tourist flat: contains both a kitchen and bathroom. Frequently has a separate bedroom and television ($50-100)

Motel unit: bedding and towels provided in a self-contained room with a kitchen and bathroom serviced daily ($80-150)

Backpacker lodge: many holiday parks have a self-contained building with dormitory beds, shared bathrooms, and a communal kitchen ($15-24 per person)

Holiday parks, such as this one at Mount Maunganui, often enjoy prime seaside settings.

ranging from tent sites to motel units (see the sidebar "Holiday Park Terminology" for detailed descriptions). Facilities vary greatly, but generally, each park has a large communal kitchen with full cooking facilities (provide your own crockery, utensils, pots and pans), a fridge, microwave, and dining area; a coin-operated laundry; and separate male and female bathrooms. Bed linen and blankets can be rented at most holiday parks, but it'll work out cheaper to hit a large department store and purchase your own before hitting the road. Additional facilities may include a TV and/or game room, tour booking service, bike rentals, basic groceries, public telephones, public Internet access, an outdoor swimming pool, a barbecue area, a sauna, and a playground for the kids.

Food

New Zealand is a land of plenty. Rich, creamy dairy products; lamb "fed on lush meadow grass and mother's milk"; and the brown, furry kiwifruit (brought over from central China almost a century ago, it was called a Chinese gooseberry and renamed for export) are just a few of the many delicious items New Zealand produces. Most of the food should be familiar to visitors; New Zealand boasts French, Greek, Chinese, Mexican, Japanese, Thai, Italian, East Indian, North American, Vietnamese, and vegetarian, as well as traditional New Zealand and Polynesian restaurants. A Maori *hangi* (feast), featuring Maori specialties steamed to perfection in an underground oven, is an eating experience that shouldn't be missed.

WHAT TO EAT
Meats
Lamb is naturally one of the most popular traditional dishes. Often cooked as a juicy roast with garlic and rosemary and served slightly pink with a tangy mint sauce, lamb is generally on the menu of almost every restaurant in the country. Hogget, or one-year-old lamb, is stronger tasting than younger lamb but not

as strong as mutton. Beef is excellent and reasonably priced in restaurants—and nothing beats sizzling, thick juicy steaks and sausages, crisp salads, chilled wine or beer, good company, and cicadas singing from the trees at a traditional New Zealand "barby." Chicken or "chook" is another favorite. Sausages or "bangers" come in all shapes and sizes and are most frequently served at barbecues. New Zealanders are also partial to farm-raised or "homegrown" venison (expensive unless bought patty-form in a venison burger), veal, duck and pheasant (some of the sporting-lodge restaurants specialize in game), and wild pork. If you like experimenting with different tastes, try muttonbird—it's a Maori delicacy that tastes like fish-flavored chicken.

Hot meat pies loaded with lamb or beef and gravy enclosed in flaky pastry, commonly served over the counter at bakeries or pub-style with mashed potatoes, peas, and gravy, are virtually a national dish. If you're a pie fancier, try the many kinds of savory pies—egg and bacon, pork, and mincemeat; they make a quick and filling inexpensive lunch. When you're in the mood for potato chips, try salt-and-vinegar flavor.

Seafood

New Zealand's bountiful variety of shellfish includes *tuatua, pipi, paua* (abalone), mussels, oysters (several varieties), scallops (great in Marlborough, season Aug.–Feb.), and crayfish (actually spiny rock lobster, but crayfish sounds more appealing). Other seafood, such as tuna, marlin, blue nose cod, flounder, *hapuku*, kingfish, John Dory, snapper, squid, and *tarakihi*, are all good tasting and widely available. Bluff oysters (try them fresh during the winter in the south of the South Island) and marinated

HOKI OR HAKE

New Zealand is a wonderful place to indulge in seafood, but there's more to that chalkboard of freshly caught delicacies than you might imagine. Like red wines made from different grapes, each fish species has its own distinct taste – but figuring out exactly which is which can be difficult.

Renaming foods to make them more appealing and user-friendly is a recent trend, epitomized in New Zealand by the once-obscure Chinese gooseberry, which is now successfully marketed around the world as kiwifruit. For the most part, though, when we buy fruit or vegetables or meat, we all know exactly what it is and where it came from. Seafood, especially fish, is a different matter and its true origin can be very confusing, especially when it's been battered and deep-fried at a corner fish-and-chip shop.

Hoki is the most important species to the New Zealand commercial fishing industry, but you'll rarely see it sold under this name. It's the standard at fish-and-chip shops (and the fish portion of your Filet-O-Fish at McDonalds),

but it's usually sold as **blue hake,** or **whiptail,** or even as **whiting,** which is a completely different species. Australia, the biggest importer of *hoki,* sells this same fish as **blue grenadier.**

The **hapuku** (or *hapuka*) you see on the menu will more often than not actually be a fillet of the unimaginatively named **blue nose cod.** The more expensive **sea bass** may also be blue nose cod, or it may in fact be hapuku. **Snapper** is arguably the best-tasting saltwater fish caught in New Zealand waters. It's also among the most expensive, which leads to **sea perch** being sold as **small snapper.** Occasionally a restaurant will go to extremes, "Europeanizing" the species by calling it **schnapper** to give an exotic air to what is already a wonderfully tasting fish.

The worst-kept secret among New Zealand's fish-loving public is the way **shark** is marketed. With a reputation as man-eaters, you'd think we'd be eager to get our own back, but no, shark is generally sold as **flake** and the unattractively named **dogfish shark** is marketed as **lemonfish.**

mussels are very popular with connoisseurs—if you can't get fresh, look for them canned in the supermarket. Freshwater-fish lovers can easily find salmon (fresh and smoked), whitebait (tiny transparent fish fried in batter or cooked in fritters—another New Zealand delicacy), and eels. To sample a rainbow or brown trout fresh from a crystal-clear stream is a real treat—both are superb. Trout are not sold commercially, but if you catch one yourself (it's not too difficult!), most restaurants will prepare it for you on request. Fish-and-chips, wrapped in paper and newspaper from the local takeaway or fish-and-chips shop, are one of the best and least expensive ways to sample a wide variety of New Zealand seafood.

Fruit and Veggies

Fresh fruit and vegetables are abundant throughout the year. Try some of the more exotic ones if you have the chance. A few you may not recognize are aubergines (eggplants), beetroot (red beets), bilberries (blueberries), courgettes (small zucchinis), feijoas (an exotic-tasting fruit available Apr. and May), Chinese gooseberries or kiwifruit (high in vitamin C, best May–Dec.), *kumara* (a root vegetable similar to a sweet potato), rock melon (cantaloupe), and tamarillos or tree tomatoes (red, jellylike fruit found May–Dec.). Strawberries, raspberries, boysenberries, and loganberries are best in January and February, melons and avocados after Christmas, passion fruit in March and April, and asparagus in September.

Dairy Foods

New Zealand's rich dairy foods are lethal to the waistline but oh-so-good. Ice cream, especially the fruit-flavored ice creams loaded with chunks of real fruit, takes top place for any sweet tooth. Creamy milk is still delivered in glass bottles (New Zealanders generally prefer glass to cartons, though both are available), and a wide variety of tasty cheeses, including local camembert, feta, gouda, romano, gruyère, New Zealand blue vein, brie, and cheddar, are readily available.

Desserts

Every tearoom in the country offers a variety of cakes filled with fresh cream, custard- or fruit-filled tarts, and cream buns. The famous and traditional dessert, pavlova, is made of meringue, crunchy on the outside and gooey inside, filled with whipped cream and fresh fruit—traditionally strawberries and kiwifruit, dribbled with passion fruit. Both New Zealand and Australia take pride in the invention of this dessert (natives of each argue over where it was created) in honor of dancer Anna Pavlova, who visited New Zealand in the 1920s.

MEALS
Breakfast

One of the things New Zealand lacks is chain-type restaurants serving cheap breakfasts at breakfast time and all hours. The best breakfasts are undoubtedly provided by bed-and-breakfasts, usually either continental—orange juice, rolls or croissants, and coffee—or cooked breakfasts ("a grill")—eggs, bacon or sausages, grilled tomatoes, toast, and marmalade. Usually at least one local café or hotel in each town is open for breakfast. Vegemite and Marmite, salty spreads made from yeast extract, are usually provided for serious toast spreading, as well as jam or jelly—New Zealander, Australian, and British children grow up on Vegemite or Marmite sandwiches and seem to experience withdrawals if deprived for some length of time. An alternative is to have a reasonably priced brunch (from about 10 A.M.) in one of the many tearooms scattered across the land.

Lunch

The least expensive and most delicious way to have lunch is to stop at a deli and buy a loaf of bread, butter, and a variety of cheeses, fresh fruit, and other goodies. Hot meat pies are also tasty and cheap, and numerous takeaways sell fish-and-chips, sausages, pies, battered and deep-fried goods, and of course hamburgers. Another alternative is the tearoom. You'll find tearooms in just about every town in New Zealand. They start with morning tea at about 10–11 A.M., progress to lunch, and follow it with afternoon tea—but eating in a tearoom can often end up costing you more because you can't resist trying something new. They sell all sorts of hot pies, sandwiches, and filled rolls (typically meat and salad, just salad, or egg salad and cheese), and other intriguing morsels such as baked beans and melted cheese on toast, and fat sausages filled with mashed potato and cheese. All sorts of desserts are available.

Dinner

Dinner is often called "tea" by New Zealanders. Cooking your own dinner is the least-expensive method, but reasonably priced takeaways are everywhere—Chinese is one of the most popular. Pubs offer good deals on dinners, and some chain restaurants (such as Cobb & Co., attached to pubs) offer substantial meals at fairly reasonable prices. Many restaurants have a special BYO (bring your own) license that lets you carry your own beer and wine in. This means they don't need a liquor or wine license so the food is generally less expensive. Some of the fanciest restaurants have a strict dress code requiring men to wear jackets and ties (almost phased out) and women to be "smartly dressed"; all restaurants require decent attire and you may not enter without a shirt and shoes. If you think you want to splurge on a meal or entertainment sometime during your stay, take a good jacket, dressy dress, and appropriate shoes, just in case—old battered tennis shoes and jeans are somewhat frowned upon. Tipping is neither required nor expected, but is appreciated if extra-good service is given.

DRINKS

New Zealand has excellent public water supplies, and tap (faucet) water is safe to drink throughout the country. All the usual fruit juices, mineral waters, and soft drinks are available—try Lemon and Paeroa, lemon-flavored mineral water from Paeroa in the North Island. A wide range of beer and wine, both local and imported, is available from licensed hotels or pubs, bottle shops (often attached to the hotel), or discount bottle stores. For the best deals and choices, pick out something at the discount bottle store, and then take it to a BYO restaurant; a small corkage fee is generally charged for opening the bottle.

Tips for Travelers

EMPLOYMENT AND STUDY

It is estimated that at any one time there are around 60,000 Australians living and working in New Zealand. Exact figures are difficult to come by as the informal **Trans-Tasman Travel Arrangement** allows citizens from the two countries to travel and work in either country without needing formal work visas. All other international visitors wishing to work or study in New Zealand must obtain authorization *before* entering the country. You will need an offer of employment to receive a work visa, and then upon arrival in New Zealand, a work permit (valid for three years) will be granted. Fees range from $150–300 for processing the original application.

For young travelers looking for casual work, the New Zealand government offers the **Working Holiday Scheme** to those aged 30 and under who are residents of the United States, Canada, the United Kingdom, Ireland, France, Germany, Scandinavian countries, and Japan. To apply for this type of working visa, you should apply from your home country, be able to show an onward ticket, and evidence of NZ$4,200 in accessible funds. Costs range from free to a nonrefundable processing fee of NZ$150, depending on your country of residence. When granted, this visa allows the holder to work in casual employment, such as fruit picking, waiting tables, or at ski fields, for up to

23 months. Aside from job boards at backpacker lodges and ads in local papers, handy websites include www.seasonalwork.co.nz, www.picknz .co.nz, and www.nzjs.co.nz.

For information on the above visas, as well as general information on immigrating to New Zealand, log on to the **Immigration New Zealand** website (www.immigration.govt.nz).

TRAVELERS WITH DISABILITIES

A lack of mobility should not deter you from traveling to New Zealand, but you should definitely do some research before leaving home.

If you haven't traveled extensively, start by doing some research at the website of the **Access-Able Travel Source** (www.access-able.com), where you will find databases of specialist travel agencies and lodgings in New Zealand that cater to travelers with disabilities. **Flying Wheels Travel** (507/451-5005, www.flyingwheelstravel.com) caters solely to the needs of travelers with disabilities. The **Society for Accessible Travel and Hospitality** (212/447-7284, www.sath.org) supplies information on tour operators, vehicle rentals, specific destinations, and companion services. For frequent travelers, the annual membership fee (adult US$45, senior US$30) is well worthwhile. **Emerging Horizons** (www.emerginghorizons.com) is a U.S. quarterly magazine dedicated to travelers with special needs. **Rest New Zealand Tours** (09/486-0636, www.restnztours.co.nz) is an Auckland-based travel agency with a number of guided and self-drive tours designed for travelers in wheelchairs. If you are traveling to New Zealand in winter, **Disabled Snowsports New Zealand** (03/443-4085, www.disabledsnow sports.org.nz) is an excellent resource. Their website details each resort and their respective facilities, or you can just call and find out the best place to rent equipment.

Enable New Zealand (06/353-5800, www .enable.co.nz) is an information and referral service for people with disabilities. The organization provides a wide range of information and services, with the offshoot website www

.weka.net.nz providing information for visitors with disabilities, including support services and rental outlets. The **Royal New Zealand Foundation of the Blind** (09/355-6900, www .rnzfb.org.nz) offers a wide range of services from offices in all major cities.

TRAVELING WITH CHILDREN

The natural wonders of New Zealand make it a marvelous place to bring children on a vacation, and luckily for you many of the best things to do—walking, watching wildlife, and more—don't cost a cent.

Admission and tour prices for children are included throughout the travel chapters of this book. As a general rule, these reduced prices are for children aged 4–17 years. For two adults and two or more children, always ask about family tickets. Children under four nearly always get in free. Most hotels and motels will happily accommodate children, but always try to reserve your room in advance and let the reservations desk know the ages of your kids. Often, children stay free in hotels and motels, while holiday parks have reduced fees for children. Generally, bed-and-breakfasts aren't suitable for children and in some cases don't accept kids at all; ask ahead.

As a general rule when it comes to traveling with children, let them help you plan the trip, looking at websites and reading up on New Zealand together. To make your vacation more enjoyable if you'll be spending a lot of time on the road, rent a larger vehicle. Don't forget to bring along favorite toys and games from home—whatever you think will keep your kids entertained when the joys of sightseeing wear off.

A handy source of information is **Kidspot New Zealand** (www.kidspot.co.nz), a fantastic website filled with kid-friendly activities, events, and destinations, as well as a message board and a page of deals and specials. **Kids Friendly New Zealand** (www.kidsfriendlynz .com) is an e-zine filled with helpful hints for traveling families. Another useful online tool is the website **Travel with Your Kids** (www .travelwithyourkids.com).

Health and Safety

New Zealand is a healthy country. Vaccinations are not required to enter. There are no dangerous wild animals or poisonous snakes to worry about; the only poisonous spider is the *katipo*, but it's rarely seen.

Water

The drinking water is good tasting and safe to drink from the tap throughout the country. However, **Giardia,** an intestinal parasite, is present in many New Zealand lakes, rivers, and streams (even in very cold water). It is spread by fecal contamination and can be passed to humans as a result of poor personal hygiene, unhygienic food handling, or contaminated drinking water. To avoid contamination, *always* treat drinking water from outdoor sources (lakes, streams, rivers) by boiling it for 10 minutes, by chemical purification with iodine solutions (available at chemist shops/pharmacies), or by filtration through *Giardia*-rated filters (pore size five micrometers or less). If you enjoy soaking in natural hot springs or thermal pools (public or private), keep your head above water at all times and don't let the water enter your nose or ears—there's always the possibility of getting amoebic meningitis (inflammation of the brain) in hot pools.

Medical Needs

Public and private hospitals and medical treatments are of high standards, but it's wise to have health insurance, as medical and hospital treatments due to illness are not free.

Accident compensation (covering personal injuries occurring while in New Zealand) is free and kicks in automatically if you're in an accident; it includes compensation for medical and hospital expenses or permanent incapacity directly due to the accident, no matter whose fault it is. (The insurance does not cover a loss of earning ability.)

If you take a prescription drug of any kind, take adequate supplies with you, and the prescription in case you run out. Chemists (pharmacies) are open normal shopping hours, and they usually have after-hours chemists listed on the door. Also, if you wear eyeglasses or contact lenses, take your prescription or a spare pair.

If you should need an ambulance, dial 111 in major centers; the telephone number is also listed inside public telephone booths and in the front section of all telephone directories.

Tips to Prevent Jet Lag

A long-distance flight causes your body's natural clock to go haywire, and air-conditioning causes dehydration. Try to get plenty of sleep the night before flying; wear loose, comfortable clothing and footwear during the flight; walk around the plane regularly (about once an hour) to reduce swollen feet and ankles; and drink plenty of water, fruit juices, or soft drinks (and no alcohol) throughout the flight. If you still arrive tired and grumpy with swollen feet, check into a hotel the first night and sleep as long as you can—then your vacation will get off on the right foot.

Information and Services

MONEY

New Zealand has been on the decimal currency system based on dollars and cents since 1966: 5-, 10-, 20-, 50- and 100-dollar notes, and 10-, 20-, 50-cent, $1, and $2 coins are used. All prices quoted in this book are in New Zealand dollars unless noted.

Trading banks are open Monday–Friday 9:30 A.M.–4:30 P.M., closed weekends and public holidays; however, automatic teller machines (ATMs) are widely available, and bank offices at airport terminals provide foreign exchange services for all international arrivals and departures (occasionally closed for late-night departures).

Foreign currency can be exchanged at most banks, airport money-changing facilities, and foreign exchange brokers in major cities and tourist towns like Queenstown. Travelers checks are the safest way to carry money, but a fee is often charged to cash them if they're in a currency other than New Zealand dollars. All major credit and charge cards are honored at banks, gas stations, and most commercial establishments. Before assuming your card of choice will be accepted, ask ahead of time at accommodations such as bed-and-breakfasts and at many small-town businesses. This advice is especially apt for those traveling with American Express cards. ATMs can be found in almost every town, but check with your bank at home regarding overseas availability of your account.

Cash and Credit Cards

For those planning on spending a month or more in New Zealand, a good way to have access to money is to open a bank account on arrival in New Zealand and have your bank at home wire money over. Of course the exchange rate will be nonfluctuating (often an advantage), but you'll be making interest while you travel.

When you first enter New Zealand, you may be asked to prove that you have enough money with you to cover your intended length of stay—$1,000 per month, or at least $400 per month if you have a guarantee of accommodation from a New Zealand resident, or evidence of pre-paid accommodation, or an American Express, Bankcard, Diners Club, MasterCard, or Visa credit card. This seems to happen with regularity to those expecting to stay in the country for at least a couple of months without a work visa (you must obtain permission to work and a work visa before entry).

Tipping, Taxes, and Surcharges

Tipping is neither required nor expected, although is becoming a common practice in better city and tourist town restaurants.

New Zealand imposes a 12.5 percent **goods and services tax (GST)** on all consumer purchases. By law, this tax must be included in the advertised price, so when you see a hotel room advertised for $200, that is exactly what you will pay.

CURRENCY EXCHANGE

The New Zealand dollar has remained fairly steady against other currencies over the last decade. Current exchange rates (into NZ$) for major currencies are:

AUS$1	=	$1.12
CDN$1	=	$1.22
€1	=	$1.74
HK$10	=	$1.80
UK£1	=	$2.60
US$1	=	$1.30
¥100	=	$1.20

Online, the Bank of New Zealand (www .bnz.co.nz) has a handy currency converter, or go to www.xe.com/ucc.

On weekends and public holidays, most restaurants add a 15 to 20 percent surcharge to your bill. This is to offset the cost of paying staff double or more their usual wage at these times.

MAPS AND TOURIST INFORMATION
Maps
Bookstore chains such as **Whitcouls** stock a wide selection of maps, but better still are specialty shops such as the **Auckland Map Centre** (corner of Queen and Wyndham Sts., 09/309-7725, www.aucklandmapcentre.co.nz), which sell maps designed specifically for hiking (topographical maps), camping (road/access maps), and fishing, as well as historic maps and atlas. **Hema Maps** (www.hemamaps.com) and **Wises** (www.wises.co.nz) both produce reliable maps and atlas throughout the country. Look for them in bookstores, petrol stations, and outdoor retailers. The **New Zealand Automobile Association** (www.www.aatravel.co.nz) provides basic driving maps free to AA members from around the world.

Tourist Information
Before you go, get on the Internet and spend some worthwhile time at the official website of **Tourism New Zealand** (www.newzealand.com). You'll first be directed to websites specific to your home country or region, from where you can access information on accommodations, sights, activities, transportation, general travel hints, an Air New Zealand booking engine, and funky online Travel Planners.

Once you've arrived in New Zealand, head to one of the more than 80 **i-SITE Visitor Centres** scattered throughout the country and at major airports. They are the place to learn about local attractions, make accommodation bookings, and plan and book onward bus and ferry travel. Many also have public Internet access.

COMMUNICATIONS
Postal Services
All **mail** posted in New Zealand must have New Zealand postage stamps attached. Letters

HOLIDAYS

On nationwide holidays a newcomer can quickly feel stranded as New Zealand appears to close down. Try not to travel to a new place on a holiday, don't count on restaurants being open, and stock up on necessities the day before. Also, many regions, individual cities, and towns celebrate their anniversary days by taking a day off work. If the holiday falls Tuesday-Thursday, it's celebrated on the previous Monday. If it falls Friday-Sunday, it's celebrated on the following Monday.

NATIONAL
- New Year's Day: January 1
- Waitangi Day: February 6
- Good Friday and Easter Monday: late March/early April
- Anzac Day: April 25
- Queen's Birthday: first Monday of June
- Labour Day: fourth Monday of October
- Christmas Day: December 25
- Boxing Day: December 26

LOCAL
- Wellington Day: January 22
- Auckland Day: January 29
- Northland Day: January 29
- Nelson Day: February 1
- Taranaki Day: March 8
- Otago Day: March 23
- Southland Day: March 23
- Hawke's Bay Day: October 17
- Marlborough Day: November 1
- Canterbury Day: November 16
- Westland Day: December 1

are $0.45 to destinations within New Zealand, letters and postcards to Australia are $1.50, and $2 to all other destinations. **PostShops** are located in every town across New Zealand. Many offer more than just stamps, with books and magazines for sale, ATMs, and foreign exchange counters. Each is open Monday–Friday and those in larger centers are also open Saturday morning. The website of **New Zealand Post** is www.nzpost.co.nz.

Telephone

Local calls from a public telephone box (or booth) are generally made using a plastic phone card—buy a $5, $10, $20, or $50 card at a dairy, service station, or Telecom Centre. You can place trunk or long-distance calls through the long-distance operator, and costs are based on the duration of the call. National and international toll calls can be dialed directly or placed through the operator (more expensive). International calls made using a phone card can be remarkably inexpensive if you pick the right card. Staff at visitor centers are usually the best source of information regarding phone cards.

Vodafone Rent (09/275-8154, www.voda rent.co.nz) is a handy service with desks at the airports in Auckland, Wellington, and Christchurch. To rent a cell phone costs $25 per week or $80 per month. Calling charges are around $1 per minute for domestic calls. Like every other New Zealander with a cell phone, incoming calls do not incur any charges, even for incoming international calls. Prepaid dual-band SIM cards can be purchased in New Zealand.

Internet

The Internet is well entrenched in the New Zealand way of life and you can expect the same level of service as in other parts of the world. Internet terminals are located at most visitor centers, all libraries, and at many cafés. All but the most remote backpacker lodges provide computers and Internet access, as do major city hotels. Wireless Internet is offered at many accommodations, some cafés, and at major airports.

If you can't access your email account away from your home or work computer, open an email account with **Hotmail** (www.hotmail .com) or **Yahoo!** (www.yahoo.com). Although there are restrictions to the size and number of emails you can store and junk mail can be a problem, these services are handy for traveling and, best of all, free.

WEIGHTS AND MEASURES
The Metric System

New Zealand officially adopted the metric system in 1976, though you still hear people talking about their height in feet and inches, golfers talking in yards, and seamen talking in nautical miles. Metric is the primary unit used in this book, but we've added imperial conversions for readers from the United States, Liberia, and Myanmar, the only three countries that have not adopted the metric system. You can also refer to the metric conversion chart in the back of this book. Also helping out visitors from these three countries are rental car companies, who usually mark their speedometers in both kilometers and miles per hour.

Time

New Zealand is the first country west of the international dateline and therefore the first to see the sun rise each day. It's 12 hours ahead of Greenwich Mean Time, making it three hours ahead of Japan, nine ahead of Moscow, 17 before Washington, D.C., and 20 hours ahead of California. Like much of the rest of the world, it does practice daylight saving time, which could throw these calculations off at certain times of year.

Electricity

New Zealand runs on 230 volts AC, 50 hertz, and most power sockets accept only three-pin flat plugs. If you're taking an electric appliance, such as a razor or hair dryer, buy a voltage transformer and suitable plug adapter from a hardware store in New Zealand, or an appliance that can switch to the appropriate voltage.

RESOURCES

Glossary

COMMON NEW ZEALAND WORDS AND PHRASES

abseiling rappelling

Aussie an Australian

bach holiday home

barbie barbecue

bastard usually an endearment, but sometimes used as an insult

bathroom literally the room with bath and basin – the toilet is usually separate

beaut beautiful

Beehive the main government building in Wellington

big smoke city

bike or motorbike motorcycle

biscuits cookies (scones resemble American biscuits)

bloke a guy or man

bludger someone who "borrows" something but does not necessarily give it back; e.g., "May I bludge a cigarette?" Also, someone who is lazy

bonkers a bit crazy

bonnet the hood of a vehicle

boot the trunk of a vehicle, or footwear

Boxing Day 26 December – a national holiday

brolly umbrella

bush the wild, untouched areas of native forest and woodland

BYO restaurants are either "licensed" or BYO – bring your own beer or wine

caravan a small, mobile house-trailer generally used for vacations

carpark parking lot

cheesed off mad at something or someone

chemist pharmacy

choppers teeth; e.g., "Sink your choppers into this, mate!"

ciggies cigarettes

clothes pegs clothespins

coach long-distance bus

"Come again!" "Repeat what you just said, please."

cordial a bottle of concentrated fruit-flavored juice, which is reconstituted into a drink by adding water

crook ill, not feeling well

cuppa usually refers to a cup of hot tea

dairy small shop selling basic groceries, snack foods, and newspapers; often open when everything else in the area is closed

deli delicatessen, a more expensive version of a dairy

dole unemployment benefits

domain a well-tended public park with lots of flowers and trees

dressing gown bathrobe

dustbin garbage can

dustmen garbage collectors (they also call themselves "garbologists!")

eiderdown a warm quilt, most often filled with feathers

entrée an appetizer, eaten before the main course of a meal

"Fair dinkum" "Honestly, it's true," or, if asked in a questioning tone, "Is that true?"

"Fair go" "Give me a chance."

flat apartment

flicks the movies or cinema

footie/football rugby league; American football is called "gridiron"

footpath sidewalk

fortnight two weeks

fridge refrigerator

gallon The New Zealand imperial gallon is bigger than an American gallon.

"G'day" a greeting meaning good day, or hi! The Australian version sounds more like "geday."

go for a burn go for a fast ride in a car

"Good on yer, mate" "Good for you, pal."

greengrocer fruit and vegetable (veggie) shop

greenstone jade

ground floor first floor (street level)

gumboots everyone has a pair of these rubber boots for rainy days

hire rent

hotel any accommodation licensed to serve alcohol

jumper/jersey sweater

kiwi a flightless bird; the national symbol of New Zealand; many New Zealanders also like to call themselves "Kiwis"

laundrette laundromat or laundry

left luggage an area in a railway station, airport, etc., where you can safely leave your baggage, usually for a small fee

letter box mailbox

licensed as in a restaurant licensed to serve alcohol

lift elevator

loo toilet, usually in a room of its own

mate friendly way of addressing someone, be they friend or stranger; e.g., "G'day mate, how ya goin'?"

metal surface the road surface is gravel, not paved

milk bar a shop selling dairy products, hot snack foods, some canned food, sweets, and candy bars; open longer hours than most shops and on weekends

motor camp a safe, clean place to stay inexpensively, with tent and caravan sites, cabins and tourist flats, and communal bathroom, kitchen, and laundry

motorway freeway/highway/autobahn

mozzies mosquitoes (their bite is not as bad as that of sandflies)

muckin' around/muckin' about fooling around

nappies diapers

ocker a derogatory way of describing a person from Australia

paddock a field

pavement sidewalk

peckish a bit hungry

petrol fuel/gas

petrol station gas station

piss beer (don't be offended if a Kiwi invites you to "come over and drink some piss")

postman/postie mailman

prang car or bike accident

pushbike bicycle

return ticket a round-trip ticket, to destination and back

rubber an eraser

rubbish garbage

rubbish bins garbage cans

sandfly a tiny biting insect (the bite leaves an itchy welt that when persistently scratched leaves a small scar) that can drive you bonkers unless you're armed with strong insect repellent

sandshoes tennis shoes/gym shoes/sneakers

school primary and secondary school, or junior and senior high; does not apply to college or university education

sealed road paved road

serviette napkin

"She'll be right" everything will be okay (heard often)

ski field alpine resort, regardless of its size

stirrer a troublemaker or person who likes to joke around

takeaway food to go, to take out

tea has various meanings – can be a cup of tea, a light evening meal, or dinner, depending on the context (it's always best to confirm the exact meaning before you show up at someone's place!)

telly television

toll call a long-distance telephone call

torch flashlight

tramp/tramper/tramping hike/hiker/hiking

trundler shopping cart

tucker food

varsity university

wee small (or early, as in "wee hours")

whinge whine; e.g., "He's a bit of a whinger."

woolies usually means long underwear or outer winter wear

Yank an American

Yank tank slang for a large American-made car

COMMON MAORI WORDS AND PHRASES

ao cloud
aotearoa Land of the Long White Cloud (one of several translations)
atua god
awa river, valley
haere mai welcome
haera ra farewell
haka a war dance and chants performed by the men
hangi a Maori feast where the food is cooked/steamed in an earth oven
hau wind
Hawaiiki legendary homeland of the Maori
kia ora good luck
kumara sweet potato
makomako bellbird
mana prestige
manu bird
maunga mountain
moana sea or lake
moko tattoo
motu island, or anything that is isolated
pa fortified village
pakeha foreigner, white person, European
po night

puna spring of water
rangi sky
roto lake
rua two; e.g., Rotorua: two lakes
tapu sacred
utu retribution
wai water
whanga bay, stretch of water, inlet
whare house
whenua land

SOME COMMON MISUNDERSTANDINGS

French fries are called hot chips and potato chips are just called chips. If you like ketchup with your fries, ask for tomato sauce (ketchup also exists but it's completely different from American-style ketchup).

A cultural note on cuisine: Beetroot (red beets) is slapped in almost everything, including all hamburgers. If you don't want it, be sure to specify "no beetroot."

A note on dates: In New Zealand, the day comes before the month, followed by the year; e.g., June 11, 1956, is written 11/06/56.

In New Zealand (and Britain and Australia), the **letter z** is pronounced **"zed."**

Suggested Reading

All the books listed below can mainly be found at bookstores throughout New Zealand or in major libraries throughout the country, unless otherwise noted.

NATURAL HISTORY

Chambers, Stuart. *Birds of New Zealand Locality Guide.* Auckland: Arun Books, 2000. Listings of all of New Zealand's native birds along with their favored habitats and locations.

Crowe, Andrew. *Which New Zealand Bird?* Auckland: Penguin Group, 2002. An easy-to-read field guide suitable for bird-watchers of all persuasions.

Hutching, Gerard. *The Penguin Natural World of New Zealand.* Auckland: Penguin Group, 2004. The ultimate reference to New Zealand's natural history; subjects in this large tome are arranged alphabetically.

Jacobs, Warren (photographer). *A Portrait of New Zealand.* Auckland: New Holland Publishers. First published in 1982 and reprinted annually, this is the most popular showcase of New Zealand scenery.

Ombler, Kathy. *A Visitor's Guide to New Zealand's National Parks.* Auckland: New Holland Publishers, 2005. Another good souvenir book on New Zealand's national parks loaded with recreational information and color photographs.

Parkinson, Brian. *The Reed Field Guide to Alpine Flora and Fauna.* Auckland: Reed Publishing, 2001. Descriptions of over 170 plants and animals, with stunning color photos to make identification easy.

Thornton, Jocelyn. *The Reed Field Guide to New Zealand Geology.* Auckland: Reed Publishing, 2003. A comprehensive, illustrated layperson's guide to the geology of New Zealand. Includes fossils.

Turbott, E. G. *Buller's Birds of New Zealand.* New Zealand: Whitcoulls Publishers, 1967. New Zealand's native birds in color. This book is out for print, but widely available at local secondhand bookstores.

HUMAN HISTORY

Begg, George. *Burt Munro Indian Legend of Speed.* Self-published, 2003. The story of an eccentric South Island inventor who still holds a land-speed motorbike record, as told by one of his best friends. Another Munro story is *One Good Run* (by Tim Hanna), which was released in 2006 to coincide with the release of the movie *The World's Fastest Indian.*

Best, Elsdon. *Polynesian Voyagers.* Dominion Museum Monograph No. 5. New Zealand: A.R. Shearer, Government Printer, 1975. A compact history of the Polynesian deep-sea navigators, explorers, and colonizers—the Maori voyage from their ancient homeland, Hawaiiki, to Aotearoa, New Zealand.

Buck, Sir Peter. *The Coming of the Maori.* New Zealand: Whitcoulls Publishers, 1950. Maori ethnology; the exciting adventures of early Polynesian Pacific navigators. Look for it at used bookstores.

Gentry, Kynan. *Raising the Capital.* Auckland: Reed Publishing, 2006. Tells the story of Wellington's history, with special focus on specific companies and the role of government.

Rogers, Anna. *Illustrated History of the West Coast.* Auckland: Reed Publishing, 2005. From Maori searching out jade through colorful gold rushes to modern day tourism, this well-presented book tells the story of the South Island's west coast.

RECREATION

Becht, Richard. *The Team New Zealand Story 1995–2003.* Auckland: Saint Publishing, 2003. Tells the story of New Zealand's unlikely rise to yachting supremacy from winning the America's Cup in 1995 to the country's subsequent defenses.

DuFresne, Jim. *Tramping in New Zealand.* Australia: Lonely Planet, 2006. An easy-to-read backpacking guide to all the major hiking tracks in the country.

Kent, John and Patti Magnano Madsen. *New Zealand's Top Trout Fishing Waters.* Auckland: Reed Publishing, 2004. Find out how, when, and where to catch New Zealand's fighting trout. Includes guiding contacts and tackle shops.

Gould, Peter. *The Complete Taupo Fishing Guide.* Auckland: William Collins Publishers Ltd., 1983. There are more recent books dedicated to fishing in Lake Taupo, but this is the classic, with advice on tackle, weather, fishing etiquette, and entertaining fishing yarns.

Gould, Rex. *New Zealand Skiing and Snowboarding Guide.* Auckland: Reed Publishing, 2006. A guide to most of New Zealand's commercial and club ski fields, with terrain and run descriptions, facilities, suitability for beginner or pro, how to get to each field, and brief accommodation, food, and entertainment information.

Gould, Rex. *Top New Zealand Golf Courses.* Auckland: Reed Publishing, 2005. Beginning each chapter with general sightseeing information and continuing with the statistics and descriptions of 59 golf courses, this book is a must-have for those planning a golfing holiday in New Zealand.

Hackett, A. J. *Jump Start.* A. J. Hackett International, 2006. The autobiography of the adventurous New Zealander who started the bungy jumping craze and, as a result, put New Zealand on the map as one of the world's premier adventure destinations.

Howe, Kerry. *Coastal Sea Kayaking in New Zealand.* Auckland: New Holland Publishers, 2005. Touted as a "practical touring manual," this book combines information about specific destinations with general kayaking tips and hints.

Leland Jr., Louis S. *A Personal Kiwi-Yankee Dictionary.* Gretna, Louisiana, U.S.A.: Pelican Publishing Company, 1990. An entertaining pocket-sized guide to the English language and colloquial New Zealandisms written specifically for Americans.

Moore, Colin. *Outdoors in New Zealand.* Auckland: New Holland Publishers, 2002. Locals know Moore as a columnist for the *New Zealand Herald.* This book is a compilation of his stories encouraging readers to take advantage of the country's many recreational opportunities.

Moore, Colin. *Weekends for Trout Fishing in New Zealand.* Auckland: New Holland Publishers, 2003. Outdoor writer Moore divides the country into 13 regions, and then goes on to describe the best fishing spots in each.

Robertson, Glenys. *Exploring North Island Volcanoes.* Auckland: New Holland Publishers, 2006. This themed recreation guide is like no other—the focus is on walks to, around, and over volcanoes throughout New Zealand.

Rushton, Nigel. *Pedallers' Paradise.* Christchurch: Paradise Press, 2006. Two in-depth volumes (one to each island) to major highway routes, alternative routes, connecting roads, and scenic routes of tourist interest, plus terrain, distances, gradients, surface,

road conditions, and location of accommodations along each route.

Sefton, Alan. *Sir Peter Blake: An Amazing Life.* Dobb's Ferry, New York: Sheridan House, 2005. New Zealander Blake was the preeminent yachtsman of his time, winning every major yacht race in the world before being murdered by pirates in 2001.

Thomson, Joelle. *Celebrating New Zealand Wine.* Auckland: New Holland Publishers, 2004. A great souvenir for wine-lovers, this big and beautiful coffee-table book describes the history, the future, and the styles of New Zealand wine.

GUIDEBOOKS AND MAPS

Budget Backpacker Hostels. *BBH Backpacker Accommodation Guide.* Updated twice annually with input from more than 200 backpacker lodges as well as travelers, this small booklet is invaluable for backpackers. It lists prices, facilities, and a unique "rating" system to help ease accommodation choices. It's available from all lodges listed, visitor centers, and online at www.bbh.co.nz.

Greening, Mark and Elizabeth Greening. *Baches and Holiday Homes to Rent.* Nelson, N.Z.: Mark and Elizabeth Greening, 2007. An excellent guide to New Zealand homes and retreats available for rent, with descriptions and tariffs.

Hema Maps. *New Zealand Touring Atlas.* This company's top-quality maps and atlas are available at bookstores, grocery stores, and petrol stations throughout New Zealand.

Jason Publishing Co., Ltd. *Jasons Motels, Apartments & Motor Lodges.* Updated annually, an advertising-driven guide to accommodations throughout the country. Available free at visitor centers. Website: www.jasons.com.

Lay, Graeme. *Globetrotter New Zealand Travel Map.* Auckland: New Holland Publishers, 2005. This more-than-a-map highlights scenic routes, sightseeing highlights, has city maps, and climate and distance charts.

New Zealand Automobile Association. *AA Accommodation Guide.* Updated annually, this guide to New Zealand's hotels, motels, and holiday parks is worth its weight in gold. It is available from all AA offices and many bookstores.

New Zealand Automobile Association. *New Zealand Classic Road Atlas.* (Classic Edition). This invaluable companion for those driving around New Zealand divides the country into 15 double-page maps, with city maps making up the back pages. The AA also produces other maps and atlas. Go to www.aatravel.co.nz for a catalogue.

Saker, Nicola. *Blue Sky Kitchen.* Auckland: New Holland Publishers, 2004. Although many of the recipes in this book could be cooked up anywhere, the focus is on out-door cooking in New Zealand—perfect for a camping trip.

Taber, Andrew. *The Great New Zealand Pie Guide.* Auckland: Renaissance Publishing, 2006. Details the best meat pies and the bakeries that produce them.

Thomas, James. *The New Zealand Bed and Breakfast Book.* Wellington: Moonshine Press, 2005. A comprehensive guide to bed-and-breakfasts, homestays, and farmstays throughout the country, including a short description of each one, what to expect from the hosts, and rates that are updated annually.

YHA New Zealand. *YHA NZ Backpacker Map.* This free pocket-sized fold-out map tells you the locations of all the YHA hostels throughout New Zealand, local sights, outdoor recreational information, and services and discounts available to members.

Internet Resources

TRAVEL PLANNING

The Edge
www.theedge.co.nz
Get a taste for youth culture in New Zealand by tuning in online to this New Zealand radio station.

New Zealand Mountain Safety Council
www.mountainsafety.org.nz
A fantastic resource for those planning on spending time in the New Zealand outdoors.

Tourism Industry Association of New Zealand
www.tianz.org.nz
Represents tourism-related companies.

Tourism New Zealand
www.newzealand.com
This website should be the starting point for planning your trip; includes an order form for brochures.

GOVERNMENT

Department of Conservation
www.doc.govt.nz
This government department oversees management of national parks and scenic reserves throughout New Zealand. The website details facilities, natural history, and up-to-date park information.

Fish and Game New Zealand
www.fishandgame.org.nz
Use this website to learn about fishing and hunting regulations, and to read up on information about the various fish species and their habitat.

Immigration New Zealand
www.immigration.govt.nz
Check this government website for anything related to entry into New Zealand.

MetService
www.metservice.co.nz
Log on to the government's official weather service site to view conditions throughout the country and for five days in advance.

New Zealand Government
www.govt.nz
The official website of the New Zealand government.

New Zealand Historic Places Trust
www.historic.org.nz
A nonprofit organization whose charter is to manage historic sites.

ACCOMMODATIONS AND CAMPING

Budget Backpacker Hostels New Zealand
www.bbh.co.nz
Brings together backpacker lodges across the country with a useful rating system that is regularly updated and available online.

New Zealand Bed and Breakfast Book
www.bnb.co.nz
The online version of a popular bed-and-breakfast book.

Top 10 Holiday Parks
www.top10.co.nz
An online directory of 50 of New Zealand's best holiday parks.

YHA New Zealand
www.yha.co.nz
New Zealand arm of Hostelling International.

GETTING THERE AND AROUND

Air New Zealand
www.airnewzealand.com
New Zealand's national airline.

Fullers
www.fullers.co.nz
Plan your touring around Auckland and Northland using this website.

InterCity Coachlines
www.intercitycoach.co.nz
National passenger bus service to over 600 towns and communities.

Interislander
www.interislander.co.nz
Use this website to make ferry reservations between the South and North Islands.

Real Journeys
www.realjourneys.co.nz
A large tour provider in Queenstown and Fiordland National Park.

TranzScenic
www.tranzscenic.co.nz
Passenger rail service across New Zealand.

PUBLISHERS AND BOOKSTORES

AA Travel
www.aatravel.co.nz
Use this website to order and view Automobile Association maps and guidebooks.

Craig Potton Publishing
www.craigpotton.co.nz
Prolific publisher of New Zealand nonfiction, especially nature-oriented coffee-table books.

Hema Maps
www.hemamaps.com
A large selection of top-quality maps and atlas, with sample layouts on the website.

Jasons
www.jasons.com

This publisher produces a wide range of free maps and accommodation guides, with much of the same information presented on their website.

New Holland Publishers
www.newhollandpublishers.co.nz

Dynamic and creative New Holland is a relatively young publishing company with a great selection of books.

New Zealand Books Abroad
www.nzbooksabroad.com

Major New Zealand publishers have their books for sale outside the country at websites such as Amazon.com, but this company specializes in selling local titles to a worldwide audience.

Reed Publishing
www.reed.co.nz

Publisher of a wide range of New Zealand fiction and nonfiction, including field guides.

Whitcoulls
www.whitcoulls.co.nz

This New Zealand bookstore chain is represented in most towns and cities across the country, but they also ship online orders worldwide.

Index

www.moon.com

For helpful advice on planning a trip, visit www.moon.com for the **TRAVEL PLANNER** and get access to useful travel strategies and valuable information about great places to visit. When you travel with Moon, expect an experience that is uncommon and truly unique.

HANDBOOKS | METRO | OUTDOORS | LIVING ABROAD

MAP SYMBOLS

═══ Expressway	**(** Highlight	✗ Airfield	↓ Golf Course
─── Primary Road	○ City/Town	✈ Airport	**P** Parking Area
─── Secondary Road	⊙ State Capital	▲ Mountain	▲ Archaeological Site
▪ ▪ ▪ Unpaved Road	⊛ National Capital	✛ Unique Natural Feature	▲ Church
------ Trail	★ Point of Interest		🗎 Gas Station
·········· Ferry	• Accommodation	◥ Waterfall	Glacier
┼─┼─┼ Railroad	▼ Restaurant/Bar	▲ Park	Mangrove
═══ Pedestrian Walkway	▪ Other Location	🚩 Trailhead	Reef
▥▥▥ Stairs	⋀ Campground	✗ Skiing Area	Swamp

CONVERSION TABLES

°C = (°F - 32) / 1.8
°F = (°C x 1.8) + 32
1 inch = 2.54 centimeters (cm)
1 foot = 0.304 meters (m)
1 yard = 0.914 meters
1 mile = 1.6093 kilometers (km)
1 km = 0.6214 miles
1 fathom = 1.8288 m
1 chain = 20.1168 m
1 furlong = 201.168 m
1 acre = 0.4047 hectares
1 sq km = 100 hectares
1 sq mile = 2.59 square km
1 ounce = 28.35 grams
1 pound = 0.4536 kilograms
1 short ton = 0.90718 metric ton
1 short ton = 2,000 pounds
1 long ton = 1.016 metric tons
1 long ton = 2,240 pounds
1 metric ton = 1,000 kilograms
1 quart = 0.94635 liters
1 US gallon = 3.7854 liters
1 Imperial gallon = 4.5459 liters
1 nautical mile = 1.852 km

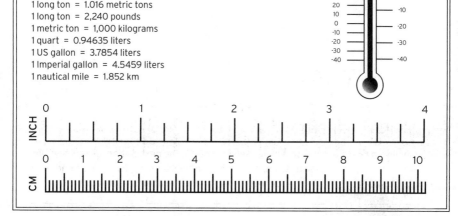

MOON NEW ZEALAND

Avalon Travel Publishing
a member of the Perseus Books Group

1400 65th Street, Suite 250
Emeryville, CA 94608, USA
www.moon.com

Editor: Erin Raber
Series Manager: Kathryn Ettinger
Copy Editor: Amy Scott
Graphics and Production Coordinator:
 Elizabeth Jang
Cover Designer: Elizabeth Jang
Map Editor: Albert Angulo
Cartographers: Suzanne Service, Kat Bennett,
 Chris Markiewicz, Aaron Lui
Cartography Director: Mike Morgenfeld
Indexer: Judy Hunt

ISBN-10: 1-56691-716-6
ISBN-13: 978-1-56691-716-2
ISSN: 1544-4287

Printing History
1st Edition – 1987
7th Edition – October 2007
5 4 3 2 1

Text © 2007 by Andrew Hempstead.
Maps © 2007 by Avalon Travel Publishing, Inc.
All rights reserved.
Some photos and illustrations are used by permission
and are the property of the original copyright
owners.

Front cover photo: Archway Islands at
Wharariki Beach near Farewell Spit, Tasman District
© Rob Suisted, www.naturespic.com
Title page photo: © Andrew Hempstead
Photos on pages 4–8 © Andrew Hempstead

Printed in the United States of America by Malloy.

Moon Handbooks and the Moon logo are the property
of Avalon Travel Publishing. All other marks and
logos depicted are the property of the original
owners. All rights reserved. No part of this book may
be translated or reproduced in any form, except brief
extracts by a reviewer for the purpose of a review,
without written permission of the copyright owner.

Although every effort was made to ensure that
the information was correct at the time of going
to press, the author and publisher do not assume
and hereby disclaim any liability to any party for any
loss or damage caused by errors, omissions, or any
potential travel disruption due to labor or financial
difficulty, whether such errors or omissions result
from negligence, accident, or any other cause.

KEEPING CURRENT

If you have a favorite gem you'd like to see included in the next edition, or see anything
that needs updating, clarification, or correction, please drop us a line. Send your
comments via email to feedback@moon.com, or use the address above.